ASKING THE RIGHT QUESTIONS:
A STUDENT STUDY GUIDE

BUSINESS LAW

SECOND EDITION

THE LEGAL, ETHICAL, AND INTERNATIONAL ENVIRONMENT

ASKING THE RIGHT QUESTIONS:
A STUDENT STUDY GUIDE

EDWARD J. GAC
RHONDA CARLSON

BUSINESS LAW
SECOND EDITION
THE LEGAL, ETHICAL,
AND INTERNATIONAL ENVIRONMENT

HENRY R. CHEESEMAN

PRENTICE HALL, ENGLEWOOD CLIFFS, NJ 07632

Project manager: Amy Hinton
Acquisitions editor: Donald Hull
Editorial assistant: John Larkin
Manufacturing buyer: Ken Clinton

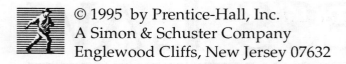
Printed in the United States of America

10   9   8   7   6   5   4   3   2

ISBN   0-13-309774-9

Prentice-Hall International (UK) Limited, *London*
Prentice-Hall of Australia Pty. Limited, *Sydney*
Prentice-Hall Canada Inc., *Toronto*
Prentice-Hall Hispanoamericana, S.A., *Mexico*
Prentice-Hall of India Private Limited, *New Delhi*
Prentice-Hall of Japan, Inc., *Tokyo*
Simon & Schuster Asia Pte. Ltd., *Singapore*
Editora Prentice-Hall do Brasil, Ltda., *Rio de Janeiro*

DEDICATION

To our fathers:

Oliver Carlson
Paul Gac

In youth we learn: in age we understand.
Marie Ebner von Eschenbach

CONTENTS

PREFACE

This is the third undertaking we have embarked upon in collaboration with Professor Henry R. Cheeseman of the University of Southern California. The first was the publication of *Asking the Right Questions: A Study Guide and CPA Review*, which was written to accompany Professor Cheeseman's excellent text, *Business Law: The Legal, Ethical, and International Environment.* At that time, we were concerned that the marketplace was already overcrowded with too many entries. But broad-based peer acceptance has proven that concern to be unfounded. Professor Cheeseman's first text is well on its way to becoming a classic in the field of legal studies in business and is being adopted by more and more institutions of higher learning every year. It is thorough without being tedious. It is clear in its use of legal language without being condescending to either the teacher or student. It is precise, fluent, and written with an economy of words which must be an editor's dream. In short, we are delighted to be associated with such an excellent text, and we welcome the opportunity to work with Professor Cheeseman again.

This text is a follow-up to that earlier work and is intended to be a companion publication to *Business Law 2E: the Legal, Ethical, and International Environment* by Professor Cheeseman. The basic philosophy for this text is to improve on those attributes of the first book which worked so well and to build on the feedback we have acquired in the interim. It all starts with the question: what is the basic role of a study guide? For lack of a better term, the key ingredient of a study guide is that it should *add value* for the student. By adding value, we mean that the student's learning experience should be enriched, not burdened, by the use of this supplemental material. This enrichment should include more than just opportunities to memorize information bytes for the inevitable mid-term and final exams. The unfortunate consequence of this test bank mentality is that it all too often fosters what we call bath tub learning. Students absorb a lot of material for a computer-graded exam and then flush it afterwards. No thought is given to why the answer was right or wrong. *The only thing that is worse than a wrong answer on an exam is a right answer for the wrong reason.*

It is the development of the underlying right reasoning process that the student should be learning from the study guide. The study guide should give the student guidance first and foremost, on where to start to study these materials. *What are the right questions which students should be asking themselves so as to gain some insights into how law works and how the public policies behind those laws developed?*

In examining a number of student study guides, we have found that they generally fall into two main categories. The first is the memorization aid already mentioned. The hallmark of this type is a mere test bank of the usual true/false, multiple choice, and identification questions. Usually no essay questions are included. At the other extreme, some of the newer study guides attempt to do too much. It is one thing to supplement the text, it is entirely another matter to replicate it by the overuse of cases. The text should be the primary source of cases. The study guide should provide students with opportunities to test themselves on their comprehension of the key elements of the law found in those cases, as opposed to being sent down yet another road of trying to decipher one more jurist's logic.

In addition, most study guides fail to give the student a *systematic key* to learning the material at hand. The study of law is essentially the study of a special type of logic. Thinking like a lawyer is not just a mystical antidote used by law professors to make their students wonder how their minds work. It is rather a real set of logical and progressively insightful inquiries which will lead the student to a defensible conclusion. That conclusion, hopefully, will have taken into account the best elements of both sides of the controversy as well as the general welfare of the society within which and under whose auspices the controversy takes place.

Once that process has begun, the study guide should provide opportunities for *meaningful self-testing*. That is to say, the testing process should provide an opportunity for the student to interpolate the key issues into an integrated way of thinking about the materials in the chapter. The usual testing methods of true/false, multiple choice, and identification should certainly be used. They are efficient and reflect the most likely way a student will be actually tested. But even if the testing is to be limited to this format, the answers to these questions should be provided as they are in this volume to give some insight into the issues being tested. *All of the answers to the objective questions are explained in a narrative format rather than just the correct letter, true/false answer, or page reference to the text.*

To gain added value, the self-testing process should include multi-issue essay questions which will give the student an opportunity to see how issues fit into the big picture of the law. Very few issues studied in modern business law today can readily stand alone. A real appreciation of the integration of those issues means just that: the problem at hand most likely has consequences in a number of related areas. For example, in the area of consumer law, if a person is injured by a product, we recommend that students ask a series of sequential and related questions:

1. What were the basic terms of the contract between the buyer and the seller?
2. Did this contract contain any express or implied promises of warranty?
3. Were there any attempts to impose limitations on those warranties? If so, do these limitations meet the requirements of both substantive and procedural due process?
4. What are the possible noncontractual avenues which may be available to the consumer? These would include the remedies afforded by traditional tort law and/or the more recent remedies found in the law of strict or products liability?
5. In addition to any contract and/or tort law remedies, are there any relevant statutory protections available to the consumer at either the local or national level?
6. Finally, what is your (the student's) overall view of the proper equities in this case? Remember, first and foremost, the duty of the law and its agents is to reach an equitable result whenever possible rather than just a technically correct one.

These are the objectives for which we wrote the student study guide, a philosophy which attempts to balance between having neither too little nor too much material, but rather the right materials which will give students a sense of guidance and direction towards seeing the big picture. It is not intended to be a substitute for proper advice from a licensed legal professional, but rather to give students a greater overall appreciation of how the law works. An analogy which we raise in our Business Law course outline goes along these lines--we study music appreciation, not to play the instruments but rather to appreciate the value of the harmony they create. So it is with law. As business students, we study law not necessarily to practice law, but to appreciate its importance in every business and personal decision we make.

With that extended introduction to the general objectives of the book, the individual components of the text are outlined on the next few pages:

I. The Overview:

The overview is designed to introduce the student to the big picture of what is going on in this area of the law. Wherever possible, we tried to interject any historical, economic, political, or policy references which might help the student bring this big picture into focus. For example, Professor Cheeseman properly points out that the word tort is derived from the French word for wrong. We might add that the French word's Greco-Roman origins, in turn, are derived from the word *torquere* meaning to be twisted. When you think of what has happened to you if you are at the receiving end of the tort, you have been twisted in one way or another! These overviews are intended to be a running essay of personalized commentary on various legal issues of the day which will help students bring into focus the public policy undercurrents behind the laws reviewed in each chapter.

II. Hypothetical Multi-Issue Essay Questions and
VI. Key Question Checklist Answers to Essay Questions:

As mentioned earlier in this preface, we confess to having a very strong prejudice in favor of essay questions. we personally believe that higher education generally, and business law particularly, have been allowed to go too far down the road of exclusive use of objective testing. Such forms of testing do have their place in the universe of teaching, but you will not get by in Real World 101 with a Number Two pencil!

We need to give students many more opportunities to practice, develop, and hone their writing skills. This is particularly true of the law teaching profession. We have a long and distinguished history of education based on effective communication skills coupled with the substantive knowledge of law. To forego the use of those precious skills is to waste one of the key patrimonies of our profession.

The questions are purposely designed to be multi-issue, fairly complex, and challenging. Yet they are not so oblique or obfuscated as to cause the student to despair in frustration. They are meant to be an integrative exercise which brings together the key objectives of the materials covered in each chapter. In addition, they are purposely designed to provide a sense of levity and humor to the entire process. Many of them are patterned after real-life cases or situations, although all the names have been changed. Any coincidental use of real persons, living or dead, is strictly unintentional.

The key question checklist answer is designed to do two things. The first is to answer the essay question in a recommended format, not a required one. As students seek to develop their own critical thinking skills, these answers should provide models which can help students find their unique path to the resolution of the case. The second objective is to integrate the essay into the key question checklist. This shows the student not only where the issues are in the question but also how the answer can fit into the integrated multi-issue logic of the particular area of law.

III. Key Question Checklist:

Based on the views discussed earlier in the preface, we believe that the student should be developing a sense of asking the right questions throughout his or her study of law. As illustrated by the consumer law example, most law problems do not fit neatly into a yes or no answer. They present, instead, a myriad of issues which need to be examined. The questions are designed to provide the student with a logical and sequential approach to the materials listed in the chapter. The objective is that the questioning process will take hold early in the course and continue to develop in sophistication and scope as the course moves into the more technical subjects such as the UCC or antitrust laws. Learning to use these checklists will prove to be an invaluable aid to the wide variety of possible issues posed by the substantive materials in each chapter. They are also designed to assure that key concepts are not overlooked in the examination and review of the materials from the text. They are, in effect, intended to be a logic-based road map. Conversely, this road map can also be used by the instructors in order to assure that both sides of the podium are "singing from the same sheet music."

IV. Objective Questions and
V. Answers to Objective Questions:

There are thirty objective questions for every chapter in the book: ten are key term identification questions, ten are true/false, and ten are multiple choice. We use narrative descriptions of the underlying reasoning and logic used for the particular answers is given for all the questions. These materials are designed to help you study the law in a new and innovative way by going beyond the official answer. They are designed to help students prepare for the sort of testing which is widely used in college classes and on professional qualification exams such as the AICPA paralegal examinations.

Finally, the single most constant source of satisfaction for us personally in writing this text continues to be the encouragement of our students. As teachers, we must remind ourselves that we are most fortunate to hold such a position of trust and service. Writing a text such as this is one way to express our personal gratitude for being in such a fortunate position. We hope you find this book of value both as a student and as a matter of personal edification.

Edward J. Gac, J.D.
Associate Professor of Business Law and Taxation
University of Colorado at Boulder

Rhonda Carlson, J.D., M.L.S.
Legal Writer

ACKNOWLEDGMENTS

A work of this scope is not the product of any one person's efforts. Many people have had an indispensable hand in helping this book become a reality.

First and foremost, we are grateful to Professor Henry R. Cheeseman for his ongoing faith and encouragement of our work. His excellent text is the constant guidepost and inspiration for this entire project.

In addition, we would like to acknowledge the writing efforts of two teaching assistants from Business Law 3000 at the University of Colorado: Gregory Piel and Emily Keiming. Both contributed to the preparation of the objective questions and answers for this text, and we are most grateful to them.

We would also like to acknowledge and thank the members of the Faculty Services Office of the University of Colorado College of Business, headed by Winnie Bartley. She, along with Debbie Hess and Kathleen Exman, have spent countless hours of work on various revisions of this manuscript. Their kindness, cheerfulness, and patience throughout this project is most appreciated.

Finally, we would like to thank the members of the Editorial Staff at Prentice Hall--Don Hull, our editor, Andrea Cuperman, editorial assistant to Don Hull, and Kristin Dackow, project manager, for their kindness, support, and encouragement throughout this entire project. Our thanks to all.

As with any such work, there may be points of disagreement or error in the text. In spite of all the efforts listed above, any such errors are ours alone.

ASKING THE RIGHT QUESTIONS:
A STUDENT STUDY GUIDE

BUSINESS LAW

SECOND EDITION

THE LEGAL, ETHICAL,
AND INTERNATIONAL ENVIRONMENT

CHAPTER 1

THE NATURE OF AMERICAN AND INTERNATIONAL LAW

Never doubt that a small group of thoughtful committed citizens can change the world. Indeed it's the only thing that ever has.

Margaret Mead

I. Overview:

One of the first objectives of this opening chapter centers around illustrating attempts by great thinkers to answer the unanswerable. How law and ethics are defined by any one individual is ultimately related to his or her personal view of the larger global issues including morality, religion, and philosophy as well as the social sciences. When painting the picture entitled "What is law?," the broadest brush possible must be used. The interweaving of all these disciplines into one area of study, generically called jurisprudence, is what makes law study so formidable, complex, and perplexing. By the same token, those difficulties are what make it so challenging and stimulating. The study of law must start with open channels for new ideas not only from the mind, but also from the heart. Law and its various mechanisms is not just a set of rules of conduct but rather the end product of how society has decided to help or hurt its members. It is no wonder that the fascination with law and law studies is at its zenith today. Students have come to appreciate that law represents the embodiment of the social environment we all live and work in. By analogy, compare the legal environment

to the water in which the life of the sea takes place. Big fish may eat little fish and so forth, but if the water itself is contaminated, all its inhabitants suffer. So too must the law be constantly examined for its societal safety. Law must be clean based on solid moral underpinnings and proper ethics. Where it fails, the legal environment may become polluted.

The categorization of schools of jurisprudence starts with a comparison of the old and the new. The traditional schools of thought find their roots in ancient history. The Natural School of jurisprudence is not only a school of thought vis-a-vis law but also finds proponents throughout many religions of the world. It is still considered one of the foundations of legal thinking today and is espoused by many, including Justice Clarence Thomas. The Historical School of jurisprudence was founded in large part by Friedrich Karl von Savigny who felt law was a product of a nation's history. Advocates of a more proactive role for law may find comfort in the Sociological School of jurisprudence. Members of that school see law as a tool to be used in social engineering. Compare that philosophy with the views proffered by members of the Command School of jurisprudence. Advocates of this school are usually members of the ruling class or royalty. Absolute monarchies are an anathema to participatory democracy because such forms of government are really only dictatorships-by-birth.

In spite of the divergent views espoused by the traditional schools of jurisprudence, the schools have a common denominator. They are all rooted on some sort of morality-based foundation. The modern schools of jurisprudence have stepped away from this commonality by finding justification for their points of view in economics, political science, or sociological agendas. The efficacy of these newer theories is untested by the litmus test of time and continues to be a source of spirited and sometimes raucous debate.

One interesting aspect of all schools of jurisprudence is that their proponents try to establish norms of ethical behavior. Ethics is derived from the Latin word *ethicus*, meaning moral. In that sense all these systems represent ways of finding moral foundations upon which a system of law can be built. These moral systems have, in turn, been sought to be identified by a number of notable scholars ranging from Karl Marx, John Stuart Mill, and Immanuel Kant to John Locke. In all these systems, a methodology is set forth by establishing guideposts for behavior. If these guideposts are universally accepted, the odds are very high that they will no longer be "advisory" but rather "required by law." The process by which moral-based ethical behavior is first *desired*, then *expected*, and finally *mandated* is really the evolution of law. Hopefully with each new generation, the law will evolve in a positive sense, which will best balance the legitimate interests of all parties concerned, both public and private.

Your role as a student of law is to try to develop a sensitivity to how complicated the administration of law is in our society today. This course is not designed to act as a substitute for professional law school training. It is designed to help you appreciate the value and importance of law and ethics in both your personal and business behavior. The law is too complex and perplexing, but imagine a world without it. Imagine a world of Cimmerian darkness-a world described by Homer in the 8th Century B.C. as a region of perpetual gloom.

II. Hypothetical Multi-Issue Essay Question:

Ms. Jane Doe was one of the first executives hired by the Mega-Widgets Corporation. She is a recent graduate of the I.O.U. College of Business and has a degree in Artificial Accounting Intelligence. Her relationship with her supervisor, Mr. Leer started on good terms, but it soon became clear that Mr. Leer sought some kind of personal relationship with her. He began bombarding her with unwelcome invitations for drinks, lunch, dinner, breakfasts, and trysts. Ms. Doe made it clear she was not interested in any personal relationship with her married supervisor.

When Ms. Doe reject Mr. Leer's advances, he became belligerent and decide to "get even" by downgrading Ms. Doe's job performance ratings and holding her up to scorn and obloquy in front of her coworkers. Ms. Doe suffered emotional and physical setbacks and took prolonged sick leave. She finally quit.

During the period of Ms. Doe's employment, Mega-Widgets had a published anti-sexual harassment policy. It called for a reporting of all incidents directly to one's immediate supervisor. Ms. Doe did not follow the steps out in the policy, and Mega-Widget got wind of all the problems only after she quit. Should Mega-Widgets now be held liable for the actions of Mr. Leer?

III. Key Question Checklist:

A. What is the definition of social behavior that would apply to the issue at hand?
  1. Is this a social form of control?
  2. Is this expectation a form of control?
     a. Is this control formalized?
     b. Religious standards?
     c. Peer group pressure?
     d. Ethical standards?
     e. A legislative enactment?
     f. Public policy?
  3. Does a combination of any of the above apply?

2

B. Once you have identified what kind of societal expectation of behavior is at issue, what standard of behavior is most appropriate?
   1. Is the standard codified by law?
   2. Is the standard supported by one or more schools of ethical behavior?
   3. Is the standard supported by one or more schools of jurisprudence?

C. How would you personally respond to this issue if you were placed in the position of having to pass judgment in this case?
   1. That would you see as the critical issue?
   2. What body of law and/or ethical standards would you use?
   3. How would you apply these standards to the facts at hand?
   4. Are there any overriding equity concerns which you might raise in the resolution of this case?

IV.   Objective Questions

Terms:

1. That which must be obeyed and followed by citizens subject to its sanction or legal consequences; a body of rules of action or conduct prescribed by controlling authority, and having binding legal force is called _____.

2. A follower of the Sociological School of jurisprudence who believes that the purpose of law is to shape social behavior is known as a(n) _____.

3. The Natural School of Law adheres to the position that law should be based on what is correct. This is also referred to as a _____ _____ of law.

4. "Battered woman's syndrome," and the "reasonable woman standard" are two legal doctrines which are evolving out of a new school jurisprudential thought known as _____ _____ _____.

5. The famous case of *Brown v. Board of Education*, overturned the old _____ _____ _____ doctrine that condoned separate school facilities based on race.

6. The school of jurisprudential thought which believes that promoting market efficiency should be the central concern of legal decision making is known as the _____ _____ _____ school.

7. Because there were many unfair results due to the limited remedies allowed in the early English Law Courts, a second set of courts called the _____ _____, were established in England.

8. The highest source of law found in the U.S. is found in the _____.

9. Under the U.S. Constitution, with the consent of the Senate, the President may enter into _____ with other nations.

10. Adherence to precedent (a rule of law established in court decisions) is known by the Latin term _____ _____, meaning to stand by the decision.

3

True/False:

1. _____ The Law and Economics school professes that market efficiency should be the ultimate goal of legal decision making.

2. _____ The Court of Chancery provided for only limited law remedies in the early English court system.

3. _____ The Critical Legal Studies movement is widely accepted and very influential.

4. _____ The law includes constitutions, statutes, court decisions, and administrative regulations.

5. _____ One of the functions of the law is to limit individual freedoms.

6. _____ Under our jury system, the same results will occur in the interpretation of the same criminal statute.

7. _____ The Analytical School of Jurisprudence maintains that the law is an aggregate of social traditions and customs that have developed over the centuries.

8. _____ The rules of the Law Merchant were based on common trade practices and usage.

9. _____ Treaties are classified as having a higher standing in our system of laws than federal, state, or local enactments.

10. _____ Presidential executive orders are expressly provided for in the U.S. Constitution.

Multiple Choice:

1. Which of the following is not a function of law?
   A. Facilitating planning.
   B. Maintaining the status quo.
   C. Shaping moral standards.
   D. All of the above are functions of law.

2. Which of the following is not a goal or belief of the Critical Legal Studies movement?
   A. Legal rules are used by the powerful to maintain the status quo.
   B. Subjective decision-making by judges should be permitted.
   C. Conservative, not liberal, legal theorists are responsible for the unfairness of the legal system.
   D. All of the above are goals or beliefs of the Critical Legal Studies movement.

3. The famous U.S. Supreme Court decision of *Roe v. Wade* gave women the constitutional right to:
   A. Engage in military combat.
   B. Use the defense of battered woman syndrome in criminal uses.
   C. An abortion.
   D. Job security for pregnant women.

4. Documents such as the U.S. Constitution, the Magna Carta, and the United Nations Charter all reflect, at least in part, the theories espoused by proponents of the:
   A. The Historical School of jurisprudence.
   B. The Law and Economic School of jurisprudence.
   C. The Command School of jurisprudence.
   D. The Natural Law School of jurisprudence.

5. Judge Richard Posner is the unofficial head of the following school of jurisprudential thought:
   A. Critical Legal Studies School.
   B. The Law and Economics School.
   C. The Command School.
   D. The Analytical School.

6. Tilly Target was constantly beaten by her drunken "significant other" until she could no longer tolerate it. Last week, she proceeded to remove a key part of her boyfriend's anatomy which enables him to sing in a boys choir. Ms. Target's best defense would be found in which of the following schools of jurisprudential thought:
   A. The Command School.
   B. The Law and Economics School.
   C. The Feminist Legal Theory School.
   D. The Sociological School.

7. The Merchant Court was first established as a separate set of courts in:
   A. England.
   B. U.S.A.
   C. New York City.
   D. San Francisco.

8. The Hindu Law called *dharmasastra* in San Skrit, has evolved in the Anglo-Hindu system now used in:
   A. North Yemen.
   B. North Korea.
   C. Indochina.
   D. India.

9. Islamic law, also known as *Sharia*, is the only law of:
   A. Sub-Saharan Africa.
   B. Spain.
   C. Turkey.
   D. Saudi Arabia.

10. Which of the following was not a branch of the early English system of courts:
    A. Small Claims Court.
    B. Law Courts.
    C. Chancery Courts.
    D. Merchant Courts.

V. Answers to Objective Questions:

Terms:

1. *Law.* This is the end product of an evolutionary process which ultimately reflects how a society decides to both help and punish its members.

2. *Realist.* This school of jurisprudence advocates the use of law as an instrument for change and often uses social engineering. Affirmative action principles are reflective of this sort of thinking.

3. *Moral theory.* This is still one of the most important schools of jurisprudence and was espoused by Justice Clarence Thomas in his confirmation hearings to the U.S. Supreme Court.

4. *Feminist Legal Theory.* This school of thought advocates a woman's perspective on a number of key legal issues.

5. *Separate but equal.* This case illustrates the need to have the law be flexible based on changes in our nations cultural, technological, social, and economic environment. In this case, the U.S. Supreme Court held that "separate but equal" is inherently discriminatory and unconstitutional.

5

6. *Law and Economics*. This school of thought was founded at the University of Chicago and has gained many high profile advocates from both the law profession, such as Judge Richard Posner, and the economics profession, such as Milton Friedman.

7. *Chancery Courts*. These were the first equity-based courts and were headed by the Lord Chancellor. The early appointees to this position were invariably clerics who were to represent the "King's conscience."

8. *Constitution*. This is the supreme law of the land and any federal, state, or local law which is found to be in conflict with it is unconstitutional and therefore unenforceable.

9. *Treaties*. Once ratified, treaties become part of the supreme law of the land. Only the federal government may enter into treaties with other nations.

10. *Stare decisis*. This is the first of many Latin terms you will be exposed to in your study of law.

True/False:

1. True. Judge Posner is considered the unofficial head of this school of jurisprudence.

2. False. It was the limitation on remedies in the law court which led to the creation of the equity-based Court of Chancery.

3. False. The Critical Legal Studies movement has not been widely adopted. Although some law schools teach and study this theory, it is not nearly as widely

recognized as the Law and Economics school.

4. True. All of these are sources of law, although much debate revolves around the notion of judge-made law.

5. False. Maximizing individual freedom within the bounds of the needs of the larger society is one of the hallmarks of the U.S. Constitution.

6. False. As illustrated in the text accompanying the case of *Standefer v. United States*, different juries may reach different results under any criminal statute.

7. False. This definition applies to the Historical School of jurisprudence.

8. True. These rules developed during the Middle Ages among merchants who traveled about England and Europe.

9. True. Once ratified, treaties become part of the supreme law of the land.

10. False. These powers are derived express delegations from the legislative branch and otherwise implied from the U.S. Constitution.

Multiple Choice:

1. D. The law is designed to foster all of these functions.

2. D. Advocates of the Critical Studies movement believe that both conservative and liberal thinkers are responsible for the unfair and inequitable state of the legal system.

3. C. *Roe v. Wade* gave women a constitutional right to an abortion. This issue remains one of the most inflammatory controversies in the land.

4. D. Elements of most of these schools could arguably be found in all these documents, but the Natural Law School has long been held as the most important contributor to the underlying philosophies of these key historical documents.

5. B. The Law and Economics School was founded at the University of Chicago where Judge Posner taught before being appointed to the Federal Court of Appeals.

6. C. Although Ms. Target may have taken "command" of the situation and may now get rich on the book and movie rights to her story, the most likely source of sympathy for her defense will be found in the Feminist Legal Theory of the "battered woman syndrome."

7. A. The rules of the Law Merchant were first administered as a separate court in England. That court was absorbed in the regular law court system in England in the early 1900's.

8. D. Most of the world's population of Hindus live in India, a country with a population of over 900 million people. Anglo-Hindu law is a combination of Hindu law and English common law.

9. D. In the most Islamic countries, the *Sharia* forms the basis of family law but coexists with other laws, except for Saudi Arabia where it is the only law.

10. A. Small claims courts are a more modern development designed to afford quick inexpensive access to the courts where the issues in dispute are relatively small in value.

VI. Key Question Checklist Answers to Essay Question:

A. *What is the definition that would apply to the issue at hand?*

There has always been a social norm both in and out of the work place that personal relationships should be just that--a matter of personal choice. Where there is any sort of coercion, duress, or physical or emotional abuse in the process of cultivating a personal relationship, many social norms are violated. Personal relationships are not barred *per se* in the workplace. To do so would create constitutional problem with regard to freedom of association. However, where the relationship sought is in violation of the norms discussed above, there is a possible violation of a combination of religious, peer group, ethical, public policy, and legislative prohibitions.

B. *Once you have identified what kind of societal expectation of behavior is at issue, what standard of behavior is most appropriate?*

In this case, it appears that a *prima facie* harassment case on the basis of sex can be brought against Mr. Leer. Under Title 29 of the Code of Federal Regulations, Section 1604.11, Harassment on the basis of sex is a violation of sec. 703 of Title VII. Unwelcome sexual advances, and requests of a sexual nature constitute sexual harassment when:

(1) Submission to such a conduct is made either explicitly or implicitly a term or condition of an individual's employment.

(2) Submission to or rejection of such conduct by an individual is used as basis for employment decisions affecting such individuals.

(3) Such conduct has the purpose or effect of unreasonably interfering with an individual's work performance or intimidating, hostile or offensive working environment.

C. *How would you personally respond to this issue if you were placed in the position of having to pass judgment in this case?*

All of the schools of ethics and jurisprudence would condemn this sort of behavior to one degree or another. The Natural Law School has traditionally been less protective of women's rights, but even there, no one can really defend this sort of obnoxious attitude toward women. Unfortunately, in the evolution of law, this is still a very large issue. In 1987, 42 percent of all women (and 14 percent of all men) surveyed by the U.S. Merit System Protection Board reported that they experienced some sort of uninvited and unwanted sexual attention on the job.

The critical issue here is that where there is a showing of an illegal act of sexual harassment by an employee, should the employer be held accountable in addition to the individual? Title 29 of the Code of Federal Regulations, Section 1604.11(c) goes on to say:

> Applying general Title IV principles, employers, (and) employment agents, ...are responsible for (their) acts and those of (their) agents and supervisory employees with respect to sexual harassment...

Given this standard, it does appear that Mega-Widgets Corporation may not have done enough to protect Ms. Doe. Their reporting system assumed that the immediate supervisor is not a harasser. The policy gives the supervisor the opportunity not only to cut off any complaints but also to aggravate the situation. For an employer to be shielded from the wrongful acts of its employees, it must show that its anti-sexual harassment policy was *effective*. Here it was not, and it would be equitable and proper to hold Mega-Widgets liable. The recent court decision against the nation's largest law firm, Baker and McKenzie, illustrates this shift in our society's attitude toward sexual harassment in the workplace.

CHAPTER 2

JUDICIAL AND ALTERNATIVE DISPUTE RESOLUTION

He that wrestles with us strengthens our nerves and sharpens our skill. Our antagonist is our helper.

Edmund Burke

I. Overview:

One of the most prevalent myths in the folklore of law and lawyers is found in the dramatization of trials. In the world of pop culture, no one knows until the end who really did it until a surprise witness shows up to "finger" the bad guy. In more modern versions, the attorney first has an illicit affair with the client and then proceeds to get her acquitted. Regardless of the outcome, the process is always full of glamour and intrigue.

Welcome to Real World 101! A trial rarely resembles the goings on found in the entertainment media. Trials are long, tedious, emotionally and financially draining processes for all parties concerned. In many ways a trial represents a failure by the parties to reach some sort of satisfactory solution of the issue beforehand. Rarely do the parties actually want to go through the machinations of being led through a labyrinth of pleadings, motions, and the like, feeling all the while totally dependent on the sometimes questionable competence of their attorneys. Unlike the make-believe world of entertainment, the job of an attorney is to keep his or her client out of court. The attorney's professional advice should anticipate and resolve potential legal problems before, rather than after, the fact.

Assume a dispute does arise which cannot be avoided. The first step taken may not be at the courthouse door. Because of all the frustrations associated with the trial process, one of the fastest growing arenas of law-related activities is found in alternative dispute resolution mechanisms. The more traditional methods are arbitration and mediation. In both cases, a disinterested third party is called in to assist the disputing parties. With arbitration, the parties agree to be bound by the arbitrator. In mediation, the third party acts to bring the parties together but cannot bind them to an agreement. Newer mechanisms are exemplified by judicial referees, fact-finders, and ombudsmen. In addition, most governmental agencies have internal administrative remedies available for resolution of problems persons may be having with the agency.

If none of the these out-of-court methods are feasible, the court trial process comes to the fore. The steps used in the trial process are itemized in the key question checklist.

II. Hypothetical Multi-issue Essay Question:

Mr. Cav E. At-Emptor is fed up. He has suffered through the ownership of a model XXX Luxmobile auto for the past nine miserable months since he bought it new from Loud and Obnoxious Motors. The car has spent more time in the repair shop than on the road and is now out of warranty. Mr. At-Emptor still owes over four years worth of payments on the car and has decided he is tired of paying for the car twice--once to buy it and once again to repair it. His sales contract has a clause allowing for arbitration of disputes on a voluntary basis through an automobile industry funded panel. Mr. At-Emptor decides not to take advantage of this procedure. He cites the "lemon law" and seeks a full refund instead. Assuming this law requires the consumer to use all noncourt measures first, what can Mr. At-Emptor do?

III. Key Question Checklist:

A. Does the dispute or controversy in question lend itself to out-of-court resolution?
   1. Is private and informal settlement possible?
   2. Are there any formal alternative dispute resolution mechanisms available?
      (a) Arbitration?
      (b) Mediation and conciliation?
      (c) Administrative remedies?
      (d) Minitrials?
      (e) Ombudsmen?
      (f) Independent fact-finding?

B. If the dispute or controversy needs to be resolved in a court of law, which court has jurisdiction?
   1. Is there subject matter jurisdiction?
   2. Is there jurisdiction over the person (*in personam*)?
      (a) Was proper service of process made on this person?
      (b) Does a long arm statute apply?
   3. Is there jurisdiction over the property of the lawsuit?
      (a) Is there jurisdiction over the thing (*in rem*)?
      (b) Is the subject matter within the geographical limits of the court (jurisdiction *quasi in rem*)?
   4. What would be the proper location (venue) for this lawsuit?

C. Once jurisdiction is established, was the proper sequence of pretrial steps taken?
   1. Complaint filed by the plaintiff?
   2. Summons issued by the court?
   3. Answer filed by the defendant?
      (a) Any affirmative defenses?
      (b) Any cross-complaints?
   4. Discovery process?

5. Any pretrial motions or judgments applicable?
   (a) Judgment on the pleadings?
   (b) Summary judgment?
6. Any other pretrial steps applicable?
   (a) Pretrial hearing?
   (b) Settlement conference?

D. Was the trial sequence properly followed?
   1. Jury selection (*voir dire*)?
   2. Opening statements by both plaintiff and defendant?
   3. Plaintiff presents his or her case?
   4. Defendant presents his or her case?
   5. Rebuttal and rejoinder by plaintiff?
   6. Closing arguments by both sides?
   7. Judge instructs jury?
   8. Jury deliberation and return of verdict?
   9. Entry of judgment?
      (a) Acceptance of the jury's decision by the court?
      (b) Judgment notwithstanding the jury's decision or verdict (N.O.V.)?

E. After the trial is completed, are any appeals from the decision applicable?
   1. In a civil case, either party may appeal?
   2. In a criminal case, only the defendant can appeal?

IV. Objective Questions:

Terms:

1. The process of bringing, maintaining, and defending a lawsuit is called _____.

2. An arrangement in which the lawyer receives a percentage of the amount recovered from the client upon winning or settling the case is called a _____ _____ _____.

3. A plaintiff must have some stake in the outcome of the lawsuit to have _____ _____ _____.

4. The authority of a court to hear a case is called _____.

5. A summons served within the territorial boundaries of a state is called _____ _____ _____.

6. A statute that extends a state's jurisdiction to nonresidents who were not served a summons within the state is called a _____ _____ _____.

7. The party accusing the defendant of a legal wrong is called the _____.

8. In addition to a defendant's answer, a defendant may cite why her action was justified or that the statute of limitations has run. This additional statement is called an _____ _____.

9. The act of other parties taking an interest and becoming involved in a lawsuit is called _____.

10. A pretrial motion that asserts that there are no factual disputes to be decided by the jury and that the judge should apply the relevant law to the undisputed facts to decide the case is called a _____ _____.

True/False:

1. ____ A corporation is only subject to personal jurisdiction in the state in which it is incorporated.

2. ____ State long arm statutes require that a nonresident have at least minimum contact with the state.

3. ____ Courts will freely grant requests for change of venue if one of the parties makes such a request.

4. ____ An answer is a defendant's response to a plaintiff's complaint.

5. ____ A major purpose for pretrial hearings is to promote settlement by the parties.

6. ____ To be granted a jury trial, both parties must agree to and request a jury trial.

7. ____ In a criminal case, only the defendant, and not the prosecutor, can appeal a case after the trial court's final judgment.

8. ____ Generally, courts are inclined to uphold arbitration decisions rather than overturn them.

9. ____ In mediation and conciliation, the third party renders a decision.

10. ____ Whether an issue is subject to arbitration is a matter for the arbitrator to decide.

Multiple Choice:

1. John and Jane have a car accident with Harry. Harry is a friend of John and Jane and decides not to sue. However Harry's girlfriend, Helga, wants to sue John and Jane. Helga cannot sue because she does not have:
   A. Standing to sue.
   B. Personal jurisdiction.
   C. Venue.
   D. Subject matter jurisdiction.

2. A plaintiff, by filing a law suit, automatically becomes subject to this. However, the defendant must be served a summons to become subject to:
   A. Standing.
   B. Personal jurisdiction.
   C. Venue.
   D. Subject matter jurisdiction.

3. State Zeon wishes to extend its jurisdiction over Defendant Darin through us of its long arm statute. Under what circumstances may Zeon do this?
   A. If Darin committed a tort in Zeon.
   B. If Darin made a contract in Zeon and then breached it.
   C. If Darin transacted business in Zeon that caused injury to another person.
   D. All of the above.

4. Plaintiff Pam obtains a judgment in state Zeon against Defendant Debbie, who lives in state Yalut. Pam tries to collect the judgment by attaching Debbie's property in Yalut. This is known as:
   A. *In rem* jurisdiction.
   B. A long arm statute.
   C. *Quasi in rem* jurisdiction.
   D. None of the above.

5. Plaintiff Paul decides to sue Defendant Dan. The suit involves a car accident between Paul and Dan. Paul must:
   A. File a reply.
   B. File an answer.
   C. File a complaint.
   D. None of the above.

6. Assume the same facts as in question 5. Once Paul initiates the suit by filing the first document, Dan must:
   A. File a reply.
   B. File an answer.
   C. File a complaint.
   D. None of the above.

7. Assume the same facts as in question 5. Dan now decides the car accident was really Paul's fault. Paul has already initiated his lawsuit. What must Dan do to assert his claim against Paul?
   A. File a reply.
   B. File a cross-complaint.
   C. File an answer.
   D. None of the above.

8. Assume the same facts as in question 7. After Dan asserts his claim against Paul, what must Paul do?
   A. File a reply.
   B. File a cross-complaint.
   C. File an answer.
   D. None of the above.

9. Assume the same facts as in question 8. Paul believes Dan's claims are ridiculous. Paul enters a motion stating that there are no factual disputes, but only a disagreement over the relevant traffic laws. Therefore, Paul asks that the judge apply the law and decide the case. Paul's motion is a motion for:
   A. Discovery.
   B. Intervention.
   C. Summary judgment.
   D. None of the above.

10. Assume the same facts as in question 9. Now assume that before Paul initiates the suit in court, the two decide to resolve their dispute outside of court since litigation is so costly. Paul and Dan agree to have a neutral third party decide the dispute and render a decision. Paul and Dan have elected to resolve the dispute by:
    A. Mediation.
    B. Minitrial.
    C. Judicial referee.
    D. Arbitration.

V. Answers to Objective Questions:

Terms:

1. *Litigation.* Most disputes are, in fact, resolved by nonlitigation processes.
2. *Contingency fee arrangement.* There continues to be much controversy over this form of fee arrangement.
3. *Standing to sue.* An interest in a lawsuit must be more than just secondary or tangential; standing to sue requires a legally recognized stake in the outcome.
4. *Jurisdiction.* Jurisdiction can be established in a number of ways--by statute, case law, and the like.
5. *Service of process.* Process servers have a high risk job due to the emotionally charged nature of many court proceedings.
6. *Long arm statute.* Without such statutes, state boundaries could be used as moats to avoid legal proceedings.
7. *Plaintiff.* This party carries the initial burden of proving the alleged wrong.
8. *Affirmative defense.* An affirmative defense will, in effect, add an additional burden of proof to the opposing party's case.
9. *Intervention.* Intervention allows public interest groups to take part in court cases which have socio-economic implications for society as a whole.
10. *Motion for summary judgment.* This motion has also been disparagingly referred to as "being laughed out of court."

True/False:

1. False. A corporation may be subject to personal jurisdiction in the state where it is incorporated, in the state where it has its principal office, and in the state where it is doing business.
2. True. Minimum contacts usually includes doing business in the state.
3. False. Courts will usually grant requests for a change of venue if such a change is necessary to avoid prejudice resulting from publicity or some other influence. Courts will not grant a change of venue if the parties are merely forum shopping.
4. True. Without an answer, the defendant may lose by default.
5. True. Settlement is encouraged at all stages of the trial process.
6. False. Only one party must request a jury trial.
7. True. In a civil case, either party may appeal the trial court's decision.
8. True. Generally courts show great deference to arbitration decisions in order to promote alternative dispute resolution.
9. False. In mediation and conciliation, the third party acts as a communication channel but does not render a decision. The parties must come to settlement on their own.
10. False. Whether an issue is subject to arbitration is a matter for the courts, not the arbitrator, to decide.

Multiple Choice:

1. A. Helga cannot sue. To have standing, a party must have a stake in the outcome of a suit. Since Helga was not involved in the accident, she does not have a stake in the suit and cannot sue on behalf of Harry. B, C, and D are incorrect because these are elements that the court of the state or region must satisfy. The plaintiff must bring the suit in a court which satisfies these elements, but they are not requirements that the plaintiff herself must personally satisfy.

2. B. A defendant must be served a summons to be personally subject to the jurisdiction of a court. A is incorrect because standing is an issue involving a plaintiff's potential stake in the outcome of a suit. C and D are incorrect because, although they are both required to properly bring a suit, they are not established by the defendant being served a summons.

3. D. A, B, and C are all circumstances where a state may extend its jurisdiction through use of a long arm statute.

4. C. *Quasi in rem* jurisdiction is a means by which a prevailing party in a law suit may try to satisfy a judgment. A is incorrect because *in rem* jurisdiction is jurisdiction to hear a case because of jurisdiction over the property of the lawsuit. B is incorrect because a long arm statute is a statute that extends a state's jurisdiction to nonresidents who were not served a summons within the state.

5. C. A complaint is a document filed by the plaintiff that defines the problem. A is incorrect because a reply is an answer in a cross-complaint situation which the original plaintiff files to the cross-complainant. B is incorrect because an answer is a document filed by the defendant in response the plaintiff's complaint.

6. B. Once Paul files the complaint, Dan must file an answer, which is a response to Paul's complaint that must be filed with the court and served on Paul. A is incorrect because a reply is an answer in a cross-complaint situation which the original plaintiff files to the cross-complainant. C is incorrect because a complaint is the document filed by Paul that defines the problem.

7. B. A cross-complaint is an addition to Dan's answer that says Dan was injured by Paul, not vice-versa. A is incorrect because a reply is an answer in a cross-complaint situation which the original plaintiff files to the cross-complainant. Here, Paul would file a reply. C is incorrect because an answer is a response to the plaintiff's complaint which must be filed with the court. Although a cross-complaint is an addition to Dan's answer, B is the correct answer since it more specifically answers the question.

8. A. A reply is an answer in a cross-complaint situation which the original plaintiff (Paul) files to the cross-complainant (Dan). B is incorrect because a cross-complaint is the addition to Dan's answer that said Dan was injured by Paul, not vice-versa. C is incorrect because an answer is Dan's response to Paul's complaint.

9. C. A motion for summary judgment is a pretrial motion that asserts that there are no factual disputes to be decided by the jury and that the judge should apply the relevant law to the undisputed facts to decide the case. A is incorrect because discovery is a process during which both parties engage in various activities to discover facts of the case from the other party and witnesses prior to trial. B is incorrect because intervention is the act of other parties taking an interest and becoming involved in a lawsuit.

10. D. Arbitration is a form of alternative dispute resolution in which the parties choose an impartial third party to hear and decide the dispute. A is incorrect because in mediation, the third party does not render a decision, but rather helps the parties come to a resolution themselves. B is incorrect because a minitrial is a short session in which the lawyers for

each side present their cases to representatives of each party who have the authority to settle the dispute. C is incorrect because a judicial referee is a court appointee who conducts a private trial and renders a judgment.

VI. Key Question Checklist Answers to Essay Question:

A. *Does the dispute in question lend itself to out-of-court resolution?*

The vast majority of consumer complaints are resolved outside the court system. It is in the best interests of business goodwill to cultivate the loyalty of happy customers. It is never too late in the dispute process to reach some sort of private settlement. Unfortunately, the more time and money that is spent on the issue, the greater the likelihood of both sides hardening their positions. There is an optional arbitration provision available to Mr. At-Emptor. He may not trust this mechanism based on his negative experience with his car and the dealer. Although contractually optional, he may have to use the arbitration procedure as a precondition to being able to file a complaint in court under the state lemon law. Connecticut and California have recently incorporated such provisions in their versions of lemon laws.

B. *If the dispute needs to be resolved in a court of law, which court has jurisdiction?*

If the out-of-court methods do not provide an adequate resolution of the problem, Mr. At-Emptor must initiate a lawsuit in a court having a proper basis for jurisdiction. Here a state court will most likely have jurisdiction over both the subject matter and the parties. Assuming proper service of process is made on the defendants, the lawsuit will have begun.

C. *Once jurisdiction is established, was the proper sequence of pre-trial steps taken?*

Once the actual pretrial process has begun, both parties will have their day in court. The defendants may choose to counterclaim based on the contract amounts still due or make pretrial motions to dismiss.

D. *Was the trial sequence properly followed?*

The actual trial will allow both parties to present their sides of the case to the jury in accordance with proper procedures as supervised by the judge. In civil cases, a judge retains the ultimate power to enter the final judgment jury verdict notwithstanding if he or she feels that the jury decision was somehow based on biased, emotional, or inflamed factors.

E. *After the trial is completed, are any appeals from the decision applicable?*

Because this is a civil case, either party can appeal the judgment rendered by the trial court.

CHAPTER 3

CONSTITUTIONAL AUTHORITY TO REGULATE BUSINESS

The United States Constitution has proven itself the most elastic compilation of rules of government ever written.

Franklin D. Roosevelt

I. Overview:

The scales of justice have long been one of the key symbols of our judicial system. They represent the systems' effort to show evenhandedness and give fair weight to the evidence presented by competing parties. This symbol can also be used to illustrate the key learning objective of this chapter. Our founding fathers struggled long and hard to create a balance of power between the three branches of government in much the same way as the justice system attempts to weigh the evidence. This process of balancing between the competing sovereignties of federal, state, and local governments is a process of constant evolution and, like the scale, will constantly shift with the addition and deletion of new political, social, and demographic weights.

What makes this constitutional balancing both fascinating and yet sometimes traumatic is that business people and their entities, represented by all sorts of firms from the smallest sole proprietorship to the largest multinational corporation, are caught in the middle of these sovereign "turf wars." In today's legal environment, there is little doubt about the power of the government to create, regulate, control, and even ban business activities. The real question appears to be which flag to salute--the federal government, the state, the local government, or some combination of all of the above? Where the rules of the game seem to shift almost daily between competing referees, it becomes most difficult for businesses to play the game.

The basic ground rules for business are set out in the U.S. constitutional provisions directly addressed to business, such as the Commerce Clause, and in larger protections accorded to all persons in the Bill of Rights and other key amendments. Many business entities are classified as *juristic* persons (law created entities which are given a limited and controlled legal existence) such as corporations or trusts. Subsequent chapters will go into more detail on how and when these forms of doing business may be used. In the context of constitutional allocation of control over business activity, the most important provision is the Supremacy Clause. Under this clause, the national sovereign can preempt control over any particular form of business it chooses to. This clause, combined with very broad judicial interpretation of the Commerce Clause, has been a part of the process which attempts to create an even playing field for business, i.e., the federal sovereign has long believed that a states power to control commerce under its constitutional police power should be harnessed if it encumbers the national flow of commerce or if it somehow unduly favors local business at the cost of competing political entities such as other cities, states, on even regional interests. The balancing of the scale continues.

What makes this process of setting out the business playing rules even more difficult is that many of our basic rights, set out in the Bill of Rights such as freedom of speech, press, religion, and assembly, have been held by our courts to apply in varying degrees to business enterprises. How, when, where, and to what extent these rights should apply to business continues to be both a source for constant academic debate and a regulatory dilemma for both government and business alike. Law works best where all the players involved have a "bright line" or clear signal to use as a guidepost for their actions. When that line is blurred, all are disserved.

II. Multi-issue Essay Question:

Brew Ha Ha Brewery is located in New Salem, California and is engaged in the business of producing specialized low alcohol products for specifically identified niche markets. It produces diet beers for the overweight crowd, young malts for the young at heart, and aged malts for the over-the-hill yuppie couch potatoes.

Brew Ha Ha's newest product seeks to cash in on the latest craze, a revival of witchcraft! Their new product is named "The Devil Made Me Do It!" The "Devil" beer has the same low alcohol content as all its other products but is designed to look like a steamy caldron of some witch's brew which will conjure up images of the rich and diverse history of occult practices throughout the world.

The Texas State Liquor Control Board took umbrage at this product's motives and felt that it would foster and encourage the practice of witchery in its fair state. It thus decided to ban the sale of "The Devil Made Me Do It!" within the state on the grounds that this product would undermine the morals of its citizens through the practice of witchcraft. The Board claims its actions are allowable under both the U.S. and local constitutions. Brew Ha Ha, in turn, claims its constitutional rights are being violated. What result?

III. Key Question Checklist:

A. Is this business activity issue one which is specifically addressed in the U.S. Constitution?
   1. If the activity is specifically addressed, which branch of government is charged with the responsibility of enforcement over that activity?
   2. Can an allocation of control over the activity be derived from one of the general business control clauses such as the Commerce Clause or State Power Clause?

B. Once you have decided which general direction of control may be taken by a governmental entity, you then must inquire as to:
   1. Any checks and balances which may be in place?
      (a) Is there a sharing of power over this issue with any other governmental entity?
      (b) If there is any sharing of power, who is the "first among equals" to act on this issue?

C. What are the business's courses of action if it chooses to resist the governmental action taken against it?
   1. Can it raise higher constitutional rights and protections which may be put in jeopardy by this governmental action?
   2. Which court should ultimately resolve competing constitutional protections in which a business may be caught in the middle?

IV. Objective Questions:

Terms:

1. Under the U.S. Constitution, the states delegated certain powers to the federal government. These powers are known as _____ powers.

2. Under the U.S. Constitution, the three branches of government are given different powers. This is known as the doctrine of _____ _____ _____.

3. When a state law conflicts with a federal law, the federal law will take precedent. This concept is known as the _____ _____.

4. The constitutional provision which addresses the issues of a national market and free trade among the states is known as the _____ _____.

5. The power the states retained to regulate private and business activity within their borders is the _____ _____.

6. Dangerous speech, defamatory language, and obscene speech are examples of _____ _____.

7. Examples of speech which are not prohibited under the 1st Amendment, but may be restricted are _____ speech and _____ speech..

8. The 1st Amendment contains two religion clauses. The _____ _____ prevents a state from establishing or promoting a state religion. The _____ _____ _____ prohibits the government from prohibiting or inhibiting people from participating in their religion.

9. Although the freedom is not absolute, the _____ is the only business given explicit constitutional protection.

10. The 14th Amendment's Due Process Clause has two categories of due process; _____ due process and _____ due process.

True/False:

1. ____ The Bill of Rights was part of the U.S. Constitution as originally adopted in 1787.

2. ____ The federal government has the exclusive right to regulate foreign commerce.

3. ____ If a states law is in its best interest, it can preempt any relevant federal law.

4. ____ All provisions of the Bill of Rights are applicable only to the federal government.

5. ____ The Freedom of Speech Clause extends to protect both speech and conduct.

6. ____ Offensive speech, like obscene speech, can be forbidden under the 1st Amendment.

7. ____ Commercial speech can never be restricted under the 1st Amendment.

8. ____ Government action that "impacts" on religion, but does not "promote" it is valid.

9. ____ The requirements of the Due Process Clause apply to both state and federal government, but never to private individuals.

10. ____ The U.S. Supreme Court uses different standards when reviewing equal protection cases, depending on the classification affected.

Multiple Choice:

1. The federal government is given the power to set international trade policies in the U.S. Constitution under which doctrine or clause?
    A. Doctrine of Separation of Powers.
    B. Commerce Clause.
    C. Preemption Doctrine.
    D. Supremacy Clause.

2. Under the *Miller v. California* standard for determining whether speech is obscene, there is a three-part test which is analyzed from the viewpoint of:
    A. An objective standard.
    B. The person who produced the allegedly obscene speech.
    C. The person who is offended by the obscene material.
    D. Contemporary community standards.

3. If the government believes certain offensive language is inappropriate to air on a television program, the government:
    A. Can do nothing; even though it is offensive, it is completely protected by the 1st Amendment.
    B. Can completely ban the speech since offensive language is like obscene language and can be entirely forbidden.
    C. Can regulate the language, restricting it to certain times the language can be aired.
    D. Can use its discretion to do any of the above.

4. If the government believes certain commercial speech should be regulated, the government must:

    A. Prove a substantial interest in restricting the speech.
    B. Prove the restriction advances the government's interest.
    C. Prove the restrictions are not more extensive than necessary.
    D. All of the above.

5. Ian Informant calls Janet Journalism at the Daily Reporter to tip her off about a scandalous politician. Janet meets with Ian and writes a very controversial story on the politician. Assume a law suit arises under a state law and this state has a "shield law."
    A. Janet and the Daily Reporter are not protected by the 1st Amendment because a journalist can never write detrimental articles about politicians.
    B. Janet and the Daily Reporter are protected by the 1st Amendment and cannot be forced to reveal that Ian was the source because of the shield law.
    C. Janet and the Daily Reporter are protected by the 1st Amendment but can be forced to reveal that Ian was the source.
    D. None of the above.

6. Assume the same facts as in question 5 except that the suit is brought under a law allowing federal prosecution.
    A. Janet and the Daily Reporter are not protected by the 1st Amendment because a journalist can never write detrimental articles about politicians.
    B. Janet and the Daily Reporter are protected by the 1st Amendment and cannot be forced to reveal that Ian was the source because of the shield law.
    C. Janet and the Daily Reporter are protected by the 1st Amendment but can be forced to reveal that Ian was the source.
    D. None of the above.

7. State X passes a law requiring all Caucasian citizens to pay an additional fee of $20 when applying for a driver's license. In examining the constitutionality of this requirement, the Supreme Court is likely to use which standard?
   A. Strict scrutiny.
   B. Intermediate scrutiny.
   C. Rational basis.
   D. Any of the above.

8. State X passes a law requiring that all lifeguards hired for public swimming pools must be men. In examining the constitutionality of this law, the Supreme Court is likely to use which standard?
   A. Strict scrutiny.
   B. Intermediate scrutiny.
   C. Rational basis.
   D. Any of the above.

9. Patron Paul is thrown is jail by the police for thirty days without a hearing for allegedly punching Customer Carl at the Big Bear Bar. Have the police violated any constitutional provisions?
   A. No, because Carl told the police what happened, so the procedural due process requirement has been met.
   B. No, because a reasonable person could understand it is illegal to injure someone else, so the substantive due process requirement has been met.
   C. Yes, because procedural due process requires a notice and a hearing.
   D. Yes, because a law against punching someone in a bar violates substantive due process.

10. Competitive Car Company lobbies several Congress members to pass a law giving U.S. car companies a tax break. Is this action protected under the Constitution?

A. Yes, it is protected by the freedom to petition.
B. No, the freedom to petition only protects individuals, not companies.
C. No, this issue is governed by the individual states.
D. None of the above.

V. Answers to Objective Questions:

Terms:

1. *Enumerated.* These powers are expressly named or granted to the federal government by the Constitution.
2. *Separation of powers.* Under this doctrine, one branch is not permitted to encroach upon the domains of the other two branches.
3. *Preemption doctrine.* If certain matters are considered of national importance and the federal government has addressed the issue, states may not pass laws which are inconsistent with federal law. Federal law takes precedence over state law.
4. *Commerce Clause.* This provision is found in Article I, Section 8, Clause 3 of the U.S. Constitution and is the cornerstone of an enormous amount of exclusive legislative and regulatory power over interstate commerce by the federal government.
5. *Police power.* Based on the 10th Amendment to the U.S. Constitution, the authority to secure the general health, safety, welfare and morals within their boundaries is conferred upon the states.
6. *Unprotected speech.* These are all forms of expression which have been found in varying degrees to be unprotected by the freedom of speech rights guaranteed by the 1st Amendment to the U.S. Constitution.

7. *Offensive, commercial.* Both of these forms of speech enjoy limited protection under the 1st Amendment. As such, they may not be totally barred, but are subject to restrictions on a case by case basis.

8. *Establishment Clause, Free Exercise Clause.* While not seeking to establish an "official" state religion, our system seeks to strongly protect the individual's right to practice his or her own religious beliefs.

9. *Press.* Our founders appreciated the necessity for a free and open press. The press is sometimes called the "Fourth Estate."

10. *Substantive, procedural.* Substantive goes to content, and procedural goes to application. In both cases, constitutional guarantees are sought to be meaningful in both context and application. They are based on the 5th and 14th Amendments.

True/False:

1. False. The Bill of Rights was not part of the original Constitution and was not adopted until 1791.

2. True. The Commerce Clause of the U.S. Constitution grants the federal government the exclusive right to regulate commerce with foreign countries.

3. False. Under the Supremacy Clause of the U.S. Constitution, federal laws, treaties, and regulations are the supreme laws and may preempt any conflicting state laws.

4. False. Through the incorporation doctrine, the Supreme Court has held that most provisions of the Bill of Rights apply to the states as well as the federal government.

5. False. The Freedom of Speech Clause protects oral, written, and symbolic speech, but not conduct.

6. False. Offensive speech can be restricted by the government, but cannot be completely forbidden.

7. False. Commercial speech, like offensive speech, can be subject to certain time, place, and manner restrictions.

8. True. Under the Establishment Clause, the government can impact on religion with laws that have a secular, as opposed to a religious, purpose.

9. True. The Due Process Clause imposes no duty on private individuals.

10. True. Depending on the classification which a given law may impact, the Court may apply a strict scrutiny, intermediate scrutiny, or rational basis test.

Multiple Choice:

1. B. The Commerce Clause gives the federal government the exclusive power to establish and regulate international trade.

2. D. The Court in *Miller* set out a three-part test which requires application of "contemporary community standards" in determining whether certain speech appeals to prurient interest, is patently offensive, or has any social value.

3. C. Offensive speech has limited protection under the 1st Amendment. The government cannot forbid such speech, but can restrict it in certain ways.

4. D. For the government to be allowed to restrict commercial speech, it must prove A, B and C. This is because commercial speech has limited protection under the 1st Amendment. Therefore, the government bears some burden in showing restriction of such speech is justified.

5. B. The press is the only business granted express protection under the 1st Amendment. Therefore, as long as Janet and the Daily Reporter act within the law, this speech is protected. The state's shield law protects Janet from having to divulge that Ian was the informant. However, this protection is not derived from the 1st Amendment. A is incorrect because the 1st Amendment does protect such speech provided it does not violate another law. C is incorrect because the shield law protects Janet's informants.

6. C. State shield laws only protect the press under state law. If a suit is brought under a federal law, the 1st Amendment protects the speech, but not Ian's identity. A is incorrect because the 1st Amendment does generally protect such speech. B is incorrect because the shield law is not effective in a federal court.

7. A. This law classifies persons based on race, which is a suspect class. Therefore, strict scrutiny would be the appropriate test. B is incorrect because intermediate scrutiny is used for other protected classes such as sex, age, or national heritage. C is incorrect because rational basis applies when the classification is neither suspect or protected.

8. B. Because this classification is based on gender, the appropriate test is intermediate scrutiny. A is incorrect because strict scrutiny is generally used for the suspect class of race. C is incorrect because rational basis applies when the classification is neither suspect or protected.

9. C. Regardless of the facts of this punching incident, Paul is entitled to notice and a hearing before he is jailed. A is incorrect because Carl's recitation of the facts does not satisfy the procedural due process requirement of a notice and hearing. B is incorrect because even if substantive due process is satisfied, this alone is not enough to put Paul in jail. D is incorrect because such a law does not violate substantive due process. However, procedural due process must also be satisfied.

10. A. The freedom to petition applies to both individuals and businesses. C is incorrect because the states must provide their citizens this freedom under the 1st Amendment.

VI. Key Question Checklist Answers to Essay Question:

A. *Is this business activity addressed in the U.S. Constitution?*

The issue of the regulation and control of the sale of alcoholic products has had a long and controversial history in the U.S. In 1919, Congress passed the 18th Amendment to the U.S. Constitution which banned the manufacture, sale, or transportation of intoxicating liquors in the U.S. After years of futile efforts to enforce this ban, the 18th Amendment was repealed in 1933 by the 21st Amendment to the U.S. Constitution.

B. *Which government entity has jurisdiction over the issue?*

As part of the repeal of the 18th Amendment, Section 2 of the 21st Amendment allowed state and local jurisdictions the option to regulate the transportation, importation, or possession of intoxicating liquors within their jurisdictions Because the 21st Amendment specifically gave states local options over the control and regulation of the sale of intoxicating liquors, it appears that the Texas Liquor Board does have the presumptive power to act on this issue. In addition, traditional police powers to protect the health, safety, and morals of its citizens are also entrusted to state and local authorities.

States have very broad powers regarding the control of intoxicating products, as was seen in the *Capital Cities Cable Case* discussed in the text, but this power is not absolute. There is an expectation by the federal government that any exercise of the local option power of liquor control will be suspect and preempted by the national goals of free commerce required by the Commerce Clause. Thus, even though the state may be the first to act in these types of cases, it may not always have the last word in these matters.

C. *How can Brew Ha Ha resist the government action taken against it?*

In addition to concerns over power-sharing between national and state governments in cases involving the sale of intoxicating commercial products, we have a possible "larger" issue--that of free speech. Any attempt to limit free speech, albeit by a commercial entity rather than a private person, is always subject to great scrutiny by the courts.

This question was based on a real incident which occurred in Texas in 1991. The Dixie Brewing Co. of New Orleans sought to market a beer in Texas called "Blackened Voodoo Lager." The Texas liquor authorities sought to ban the product because it believed the lager would promote occult practices. It later rescinded the proposed ban for fear of legal challenges.

Those challenges would most likely have been made on the grounds of commercial free speech and interference with the free flow of goods in interstate commerce. At a minimum, the state of Texas would have the burden of proof in showing that the sale of this product would damage the health, safety, morals, and

welfare of its citizens as required under the use of its state police powers.

CHAPTER 4

THE INTERNATIONAL LEGAL ENVIRONMENT

The world must be made safe for democracy.

Woodrow Wilson

I. Overview:

The word oxymoron is defined as a combination of contradictory or incongruous words or phrases. To many, the term international law represents one such example. At best, defining international law along the traditional domestic lines of a body of rules of behavior and mechanisms designed to enforce those rules cannot work as well when the protagonists are sovereign nations. By definition sovereignty incorporates the notion of freedom from external controls and supreme power over one's own affairs. Perhaps that might be a starting point to resolve this oxymoronic dilemma. A nation does need to have control over its internal affairs, but its national interests and the welfare of its citizens do not end at its borders. Nations, just like individuals, can only find protection for their own rights when they are willing to honor the rights of others. Law eventually works its way through to a system of cooperative behavior for the larger mutual good. All law calls for some sacrifice of individual freedoms for the betterment of the corporate body. This is the fundamental reality upon which all law is ultimately based. Consequences of failures to honor that reality at the global level are readily apparent to all of us. If the role of law is to act as a mechanism for civilization which makes violence the last resort, then international law is a goal worth striving for by all nations.

The second interesting aspect of any comparison between international law of nations and international commerce is the sheer breadth and scope of commerce. International trade has become the lifeblood of nations, and international business entities are its circulatory system. In quite blunt terms, the scale and power attained by many large multinational banks, manufacturers, and diversified business organizations has simply surpassed the ability of any one country to control them. That is not to say that these are renegade free agents with no accountability. It is to say, however, that the world-wide staging area of economic competition is such that these players are big enough and strong enough to have the rules written for in their favor. Witness the world-wide and sometimes fawning competition by countries for new plants and financial investments created by these entities.

This chapter seeks to outline some of the basic terminology used in international law. It also describes some of the key players on that stage. Like any good play, this stage is filled with intrigue, pathos, and sometimes epic Greek tragedy. The failures of whole nations only magnify our own fallibilities, because international law is the most fragile of all legal systems. Yet in an age of possible nuclear self-destruction, do we have any choice? Like it or not, as William James said: "The things we cherish most are at the mercy of the things we cherish least."

II. Hypothetical Multi-issue Essay Question:

Mario LaFast is a U.S. resident who has finally made it to the top of the auto racing world. He just signed a three year contract to drive for Enzo Frank and his Formula One Supercharged Turbo Racing Team in Italy. Mario's retainer is over $10 million annually plus a percentage of the winning purse if he finishes third or higher. The Formula One race calendar starts in South America in late spring and finishes in late fall in Australia. The races are held in a total of sixteen different countries.

All of the host countries have their own tax systems, and they all seek to tax, as income, winnings from auto races. In addition, many of these tax laws measure income on a world wide basis. Thus income earned in a race in Italy may be reportable on Mario's tax returns filed in New York. If all the possible taxes are independently and fully imposed by every nation in which Mario won, his tax bill would exceed his income because of "double-taxation" on the same income by more than one taxing entity. What can Mario do?

III. Key Question Checklist:

This outline is designed to help students identify which issues fall into the realm of international law and which sources of law may be applicable. In addition, students will be introduced to some of the key players and concepts used for resolution of disputes in the international arena.

A. The first question which must be examined in international law issues is: who has the authority to act?
  1. Constitutional powers?
    (a) Federal government's authority to act?
      (1) Article I, Section 8, Clause 3 vests Congress with power to regulate commerce with foreign nations?

      (2) Article II, Section 2, Clause 2, gives the President authority to make treaties with advice and consent of the Senate?
      (3) Supremacy clause acts as preemption of federal power over states in case of conflict?
  2. State power?
    (a) Shared with federal government but subject to preemption?
    (b) Actions of states measured by impact on interstate commerce?

B. Sources of international law?
  1. Treaties?
    (a) Limited to federal government?
      (1) Bilateral--treaty between two nations?
      (2) Multilateral--treaty between more than two nations?
      (3) Convention--treaty sponsored by an international organization?
  2. Custom?
    (a) Established practices followed by two or more nations when dealing with each other?
      (1) Consistent and recurring?
      (2) Recognized as binding legal obligation by the parties involved?
    (b) Often customs are a precursor to treaty codification?
  3. General principles of law?
    (a) Recognition of established domestic principles of law for resolution of international issues?
  4. Judicial decisions and teachings?
    (a) Not binding as *stare decisis*?
  5. Comity?
    (a) Deference by one nation to the laws and decisions of other nations?
    (b) Not required, only a courtesy?

C. What are the main international organizations which may be used to help resolve international disputes between nations?
 1. The United Nations?
   (a) Largest and most comprehensive international organization?
   (b) Divided into many subdivisions based on functional areas of:
     (1) Security?
     (2) Economic and social functions?
     (3) International Court of Justice?
       (aa) Jurisdiction limited to nations who voluntarily agree to submit to its jurisdiction?
       (bb) Nations are not bound by its decisions?
 2. Other major international communities?
   (a) Andean Economic Community?
   (b) Associates of Southwest Asian Nations?
   (c) Caribbean Common Market?
   (d) Central American Common Market?
   (e) Economic Community of West Africa?
   (f) European Free Trade Agreement?
   (g) European Community (Common Market)?
   (h) Latin American Integration Association?
   (i) Organization of Petroleum Exporting Countries?
   (j) North American Free Trade Agreement?

D. What are some of the legal principles used to help resolve international disputes?
 1. Voluntary acts of the parties?
   (a) Choice of forum agreed upon?
   (b) Choice of law agree upon?

 2. Courts limited by:
   (a) Act of State Doctrine?
     (1) Limits ability of a court to question internal acts of states?
     (2) Based on separation of powers?
   (b) Doctrine of Sovereign Immunity?
     (1) Countries, as defendants, are granted immunity from suits in other countries?
     (2) U.S. has codified the rules in U.S. with the enactment of the Foreign Sovereign Immunities Act of 1976?
       (aa) Allows foreign government to waive immunity?
       (bb) Allows jurisdiction over certain commercial activities carried on by foreign governments in the U.S.?
   (c) Extradition treaties?
 3. Noncourt mechanisms?
   (a) International arbitration?
     (1) Voluntary contractual agreement?
     (2) Enforced by enabling statutes in U.S.?
       (aa) United Nations Convention on recognition and enforcement of foreign arbitration awards adopted by U.S. in 1970?
       (bb) Amended by Federal Arbitration Act?

IV. Objective Questions:

Terms:

1. Canada, Mexico, and the United States entered into an international trade agreement that created the largest free trade area in the world. This treaty is called the _____ _____ _____ _____ _____.

26

2. The most important of all international organizations is the _____ _____.

3. The power of Congress to regulate commerce with foreign nations is granted by the _____ _____.

4. An agreement or contract between two or more nations that is formally signed by an authorized representative and ratified by the supreme power of each nation is called a _____.

5. The largest and most important economic community of nations in Africa is the _____ _____ _____ _____.

6. The influence of this economic group is inexorably tied to the world wide supply and price of oil. It is the _____ _____ _____ _____ _____.

7. The extension of courtesies to other countries that are not obligations of law, but rather based on respect, good will, and civility is called _____.

8. This international court is located in the Hague, the Netherlands, and is the judicial branch of the United Nations. It is called the _____ _____ _____ _____ or the _____ _____.

9. The doctrine which provides that judges of one country cannot question the validity of an act committed by another country within that other country's own borders is known as the _____ _____ _____.

10. A nonjudicial method of dispute resolution whereby a neutral third party decides the case is called _____.

True/False:

1. ____ Under the Treaty Clause of the U.S. Constitution, states may enter into treaties with foreign nations.

2. ____ The President is the agent of the United States in dealing with foreign nations.

3. ____ International courts are not bound by the doctrine of *stare decisis*.

4. ____ The United Nations was created by a multilateral treaty on October 24, 1945.

5. ____ Individuals or businesses may have cases decided by the International Court of Justice.

6. ____ The European Court of Justice is a lower court branch of the World Court.

7. ____ The United States grants absolute immunity to foreign governments from suit in U.S. courts.

8. ____ An action based on a commercial activity carried on in the United States will not make a foreign nation immune from suit in U.S. courts.

9. ____ The U.S. is a signatory to the United Nations Convention on Recognition and Enforcement of Foreign Arbitral Awards.

10. ____ A nation has the authority to criminally prosecute its citizens that commit crimes in other countries.

Multiple Choice:

1. Which of the following statements is true of international law?
   A. There is no single source of international law.
   B. No single world court is responsible for interpreting international law.
   C. There is no world executive branch that can enforce international law.
   D. All of the above.

2. Which of the following is not a source of international law?
   A. Custom.
   B. State law.
   C. Treaties.
   D. Comity.

3. To establish that a practice has become a custom, you must show:
   A. Consistent and recurring action by two or more nations over a considerable period of time.
   B. Recognition that the custom is binding.
   C. A and B.
   D. Neither A nor B.

4. Which of the following is not a significant international organization?
   A. Supreme Court of the United States.
   B. United Nations.
   C. International Court of Justice.
   D. International Monetary Fund.

5. Which of the following is not a branch of the United Nations?
   A. Security Council.
   B. General Assembly.
   C. Secretariat.
   D. Common Market.

6. Which of the following are regional development banks?
   A. Inter-American Development Bank.
   B. Asian Development Bank.
   C. Caribbean Development Bank.
   D. All of the above.

7. Which of the following is not an Africa-based economic organization?
   A. CARICOM.
   B. EFTA.
   C. LAIA.
   D. All of the above.

8. The North American Free Trade Agreement:
   A. Created the world's largest free trade area.
   B. Eliminates all tariffs on nonagricultural trade by 1995.
   C. Establishes tariffs for many agricultural products.
   D. B and C.

9. Organizations which conduct international arbitration include:
   A. American Arbitration Association.
   B. International Chamber of Commerce.
   C. United Nations Commission on International Trade Law.
   D. All of the above.

10. To avoid the problems of judicial resolution of international disputes, the parties to an international transaction should include the following in their contracts:
    A. Choice of law clause.
    B. Exclusionary clause.
    C. Choice of forum clause.
    D. A and C, but not B.

V. Answers to Objective Questions:

Terms:

1. *North American Free Trade Agreement.* This treaty creates the largest free trade area in the world. It was ratified after much heated debate over jobs, environmental issues, and immigration issues.
2. *United Nations.* This organization, created after World War II, is the spiritual successor to the League of Nations, which was dissolved in April 1946.
3. *Commerce Clause.* Only the federal government may enter into treaties with other nations, and these treaties become part of the law of the land.
4. *Treaty.* Treaties can be classified as bilateral, multilateral, and/or conventions.
5. *Organization of African Unity.* This is a relatively new organization formed in 1991, but because of its large membership and wide ranging treaty provisions, its importance is expected to grow dramatically.
6. *Organization of Petroleum Exporting Countries.* The influence of this group will never be insignificant, but it has been reduced by the discovery of oil in areas like the North Sea and Alaska.
7. *Comity.* This term is sometimes referred to as "comity of nations" in the international setting.
8. *International Court of Justice or World Court.* Remember the decisions of this court are only binding if a nation agrees to be bound.
9. *Act of State Doctrine.* The underlying reasoning for this doctrine is restraint on the part of the judiciary which permits the executive branch to arrange affairs with foreign governments.

10. *Arbitration.* Arbitration is almost always faster, cheaper, and more efficient than going to a judicial tribunal.

True/False:

1. False. Only the federal government can enter into treaties.
2. True. Treaty negotiations are often long and tortuous processes where much goes on behind the scenes. Witness the hard-fought give and take between the U.S. and Mexico on issues relating to employment and environmental law enforcement mechanisms relating to the NAFTA treaty.
3. True. As a matter of practicality, they do follow their own past decisions for guidance in making decisions, even though they are not bound by them.
4. True. This organization has grown dramatically over the past half century, yet many analysts say it has still fallen short of achieving its original goals.
5. False. Only nations can have cases decided by the International Court of Justice, but nations may bring a case on behalf of an individual or business.
6. True. This court, located in Luxembourg, represents the judicial branch of the European Community or Common Market.
7. False. The U.S. grants qualified or restricted immunity to foreign governments, as outlined in the Foreign Sovereign Immunities Act of 1976.
8. True. One of the exceptions to absolute foreign immunity provided by the Foreign Sovereign Immunities Act of 1979 provides for a suit to be brought on the basis of commercial activity.
9. True. The U.S. signed this convention in 1970 and amended the preexisting Federal Arbitration Act to reflect this international law.

29

10. True. Enforcement of these criminal laws is carried out with the help of extradition treaties. Unfortunately, these treaties are not fully in place throughout the world, and many safe havens are available to rich miscreants fleeing from justice.

Multiple Choice:

1. D. This loose knit structure of international law is what has led some critics to call international law an oxymoron.
2. B. State laws are generally not considered a source of international law although state statutes can be applied to international entities doing business in those states. If, however, state laws are in conflict with a treaty, the Preemption Clause of the Constitution renders the conflicting state or local law void.
3. C. Custom may be found in any number of sources such as government policy statements, diplomatic correspondence, and speeches by the nation's leaders.
4. A. Even though the impact of the court's decisions may have an impact around the world, it is not technically classified as an international organization in the same sense that the International Court of Justice is.
5. D. The organization of the Common Market is separate from the United Nations even though both organizations have member nations which belong to both groups.
6. D. The main objective of these organizations is to assist in the economic development of its member nations.
7. D. All of the above represent regional organizations based outside of Africa. The Organization of African Unity, made up of 51 African countries, represents the largest organization of countries from the African continent.

8. A. The NAFTA free trade area encompasses not only the world's largest geographic trade area, it also is the richest with a $6.5 trillion market.
9. D. All of these organizations provide arbitration services to international clients. More and more international business contracts have arbitration clauses included at the outset.
10. D. The use of these clauses is a practical, if not legal, necessity in today's international legal environment.

VI. Key Question Checklist Answers to Essay Question:

A. *Who has the authority to act with regard to this international law issue?*

Mario certainly has a mixed blessing in having made it to the top of the racing world. On the plus side, he is a world celebrity who really does live out the fantasy of "life in the fast lane!" The down side of all this is that life has gotten far more complicated from the days when he was drag racing behind the high school parking lot.

Under our taxing structure, income taxes can be imposed by both the federal and state governments. Some taxes paid to the states can be taken as either a business expense above the line for arriving at adjusted gross income or as a personal itemized deduction after having arrived at adjusted gross income. This would all be well and good if Mario racing activities were limited to the confines of the U.S.

But his income source will not only be the U.S. Because our tax laws seek to impose a tax on world-based income, Mario must seek ways of avoiding double taxation. The federal government will be the source of any protection which may be afforded to him on this issue in the U.S. He must look at the national governments of other nations seeking to impose their taxes. Those national policies will preempt any state laws which may be in conflict with national the policies enumerated in the tax laws.

B. *What source of international law would best address this issue?*

The best source of protection available to Mario will be tax treaties. These are either bilateral or multilateral agreements entered into by various nations which are designed to allow each other to tax a "fair share" of Mario's overall world-wide income without creating confiscatory double taxation. Under these treaties, each nation decides how to defer taxation to other nations where that income is already earned and taxed in the other nation. By use of certain agreed upon parameters of exclusions from income or credits for taxes paid to other countries, the net intended effect is to allow taxation of the same income only once in each country where it is earned.

All this is easier said than done. The world of international taxation is one of the most difficult areas of law, accounting, and business practice. It takes years just to learn the ropes and is extremely technical in nature. Mario should seek advice and counsel from professionals trained in these matters.

C&D. *What organization would become involved in this issue, and what international law principles would it use to resolve the problem?*

In case two or more of the countries seeking to tax Mario reach an impasse on how his income should be taxed, they may choose to voluntarily submit their disagreement to the one of the international tribunals such as the U.N. International Court of Justice. In the alternative, the countries may choose to seek a voluntary form of arbitration. If arbitration is chosen, enforcement will still be an issue if they are not signatories to an arbitration enforcement convention.

In any event, Mario's best route on this issue is to have his contract set out, at the beginning, a choice of law and choice of jurisdiction. Even there, remember, each country as a sovereign can still ultimately control the taxation of income earned within its own borders.

Mario has decided to move to Monaco because of the favorable tax laws there. Even if he is still taxed elsewhere, he will do just fine, thank you, at the casinos in Monte Carlo.

CHAPTER 5

INTENTIONAL TORTS, NEGLIGENCE, AND STRICT LIABILITY

We are all servants of the laws to the end that it may be possible for us to be free.

Cicero

I. Overview:

The word tort is not readily familiar to students who have not yet studied law. Like so many words of art found in the law, it has a special meaning derived from an essentially simple principle. The word is literally derived from the French word for wrong. That French term, in turn, is derived from the Latin phrase *torguere* meaning to twist, or *tortus* meaning to be twisted or wrested aside. When we consider that the odds are high that sooner or later we may be twisted by an auto accident, job-related injury, or some similar event, the term starts to make sense. Injuries of all sorts are an unfortunate fact of life. What makes those injuries actionable., i.e., where a court will recognize legal grounds for bringing a lawsuit, is when someone may have committed a noncontractual wrong for which a court, after appropriate proceedings, may grant a remedy. In other words, sometimes when we get twisted, the law provides an opportunity to correct the situation if the twist is found to be wrongful.

Tort law structure is divided into three main classifications:

1. Intentional torts.
2. Unintentional torts (negligence).
3. Strict liability.

Of these three, the first category, intentional torts, are the most readily identifiable because they are very often concurrently classified as crimes. A crime is generally defined as an act in violation of a local or national penal statute. The remedy for crimes is sought by governmental authorities on behalf of the victim for all of us because the act is classified as an act against the common welfare of society. The civil remedy for the same act is an action for intentional tort. This lawsuit is brought by the victim directly against the perpetrator of the intentional tort. Damages are paid directly to the victim after proper proceedings are held. The major classifications of intentional torts are acts against the person, and acts against property. Acts against persons include assault, battery, false imprisonment, defamation of character, invasion of privacy, slander, libel, and abuse of the legal process. One recent example of the abuse of legal process was found in Colorado where a group of tax protesters filed liens on the personal assets of government employees as a way to object to government tax collection procedures. An example of an act against property would be intentional trespass upon someone else's land.

The second category, unintentional or negligence torts, is both far more prevalent and more difficult to clearly identify. The first thing to remember is that responsibility can be imposed regardless of intent. This is a consequence-oriented result in the law as compared to the intent-oriented result discussed in the law of intentional torts.

The second major point is that the term negligence is in fact a legal conclusion arrived at only when a special set of sequential circumstances have taken place. These circumstances are generally called elements. Just as the make up of all physical substances can be broken down into key components, so may many legal doctrines. The doctrine of negligent tort is made up of five key elements. These elements are:

1. A showing of a duty of care owed by the defendant to the plaintiff.
2. A showing of a breach of that duty.
3. A showing of injury to the plaintiff.
4. A showing of causal nexus or connection between the breach of duty and the injury (actual cause).
5. A tying of that actual cause to the legal responsibility for the consequences of the act or omission. This connection between actual and legal cause is referred to as proximate cause.

If all five circumstances are found, and there are no recognized defenses, excuses, or statutory immunities, a legal conclusion of negligence can be reached. An immunity is an exception from liability recognized in the law, usually based on an overriding public policy. Thus the key to the study of negligent torts is the proper identification and use of the elements of negligence. Think of the use of elements as essential building blocks in the construction of a foundation on which a conclusion of negligence can be built. If any of the blocks are missing, the building will not stand.

The third major area of tort law is found in what has generally come to be classified as strict liability torts, i.e., liability without fault. This is not to say that it is automatic liability, but rather that a different set of elements have evolved in certain cases involving special kinds of activities which are considered ultra-hazardous and with regard to the use of certain products. This doctrine is fully discussed in Chapter 21 of this text. At this juncture, it is important to remember that this doctrine may represent one of the options available to an injured tort victim.

Under all three classifications of tort, the burden of proof remains with the plaintiff to show that he or she has been wronged and that he or she is entitled to some sort of court-ordered remedy from the defendant. The steps used to arrive at that outcome are set out in the Key Question Checklist.

II. Hypothetical Multi-issue Essay Question:

One day while Gabby and Crabby were driving through the intersection of College and 28th in Boulder, their car was struck by Mario. Mario ran the light at high speed but said, in his defense, that he thought he had the green light. In fact, Mario is color blind, but relied on the expectation that the green light was at the bottom of the signal. The Boulder City light repair crew had just reversed them in order to make more drivers think twice before going for the yellow. Thus, the red was at the bottom.

In the meantime, Gabby was unconscious with grave head injuries and was rushed to a nearby hospital. Crabby, uninjured but somewhat hysterical, accompanied him to the hospital. When they arrived, the only surgeon on duty was an exhausted Dr. Franklin Pierce. He had just completed a complicated lobotomy on a former Hell's Angel, now an outstanding business consultant. Dr. Pierce told Crabby that her husband Gabby needed brain surgery but that he was too worn out to undertake it.

Crabby, quite frantic, seized Dr. Pierce by the shoulders and said intensely: "Doctor, you must! Money means nothing to me when my dear Gabby's life is concerned. I will see that you are paid $50,000. Oh, doctor, I promise!" Dr. Pierce agreed to do the operation and completed it in a professional manner. Gabby died four days later, and Crabby now refuses to pay.

Discuss the legal consequences of this case to all parties involved.

III. Key Question Checklist:

A. Classification: Is this act or omission a(n):
1. Intentional tort?
2. Unintentional (negligence) tort?
3. Strict liability tort?

B. If it is intentional, how would you classify the alleged tort?
1. What are the key elements you would identify? For example: In assault,
    (a) Is there the threat of immediate harm or offensive contact?
    (b) Would this action arouse apprehension of imminent harm in the eyes of a reasonable person?
    (c) Is it actionable?
2. Are there any appropriate defenses possible?
    (a) Assumption of risk?
    (b) Last clear chance?
    (c) Contributory negligence?
    (d) Comparative negligence?
3. Any immunities applicable here?
    (a) Intrafamily immunity (which, by statute, limits opportunities of family members to sue one another based on public policy designed to protect the family unit)?
    (b) Charitable immunity (which, by statute, limits lawsuits against charitable entities in order to keep those entities solvent for the larger public good)?
    (c) Government immunity (where the sovereign, by statute, can limit where, how, and to what extent it will allow itself to be sued)?
4. What, if any, are the secondary consequences of this act?
    (a) Any criminal charges possible here?
    (b) Any agency-based consequences to third parties?

C. If it is unintentional or (negligence based), are the elements in place?
1. What is the basic duty that was owed by the defendant to the plaintiff in this case? (Remember, the duty is not necessarily defined by statute but rather by how a reasonable person would be expected to act under these circumstances).
2. Did the defendant act below the standard set out above, i.e., would that act or omission constitute a breach of duty?
3. Was there an injury suffered by the plaintiff such that it would allow him or her to bring an action before the court?
4. Was the injury the physical or causal result of the defendant's act or omission?
5. If it was the result of the defendant's act or omission, would it be equitable to hold the defendant liable for the harm, i.e., was the act or omission the proximate cause and legal cause of the injury?
6. Would you excuse the defendant based on any of the recognized defenses such as:
    (a) Assumption of risk?
    (b) Last clear chance?
    (c) Contributory negligence?
    (d) Comparative negligence?
7. Even if responsibility may be forthcoming, is it cut off by the imposition of any public policy-based immunity?
    (a) Government immunity?
    (b) Intrafamily immunity?
    (c) Charitable immunity?

D. If it is a case of strict liability-based tort law, which classification of strict liability law would be most appropriate?

1. Abnormally dangerous or ultrahazardous activity?
2. Product liability issue? (See Chapter 21)

IV. Objective Questions:

Terms:

1. A tort is a civil wrong where an injured individual sues an offending party seeking _____ or monetary compensation.

2. An unintentional tort where the offending party commits an act or omission that a reasonable man would not commit is categorized as a _____ tort.

3. The intentional tort of _____ requires only a reasonable apprehension of immediate harm, whereas the tort of _____ involves harmful or offensive contact with another person.

4. A false statement about a person, which is subsequently intentionally or accidentally published to a third person, is called the tort of _____ _____ _____.

5. A false statement which is spoken to a third person is _____; the name for a false statement which is written in a letter, newspaper, book, etc., or broadcast via movie, video, television show, or radio is _____.

6. If a defendant acts with _____ _____, he makes a false statement knowingly or with reckless disregard of its falsity.

7. The law against _____ _____ _____ protects a person's right to live without unwarranted or undesired publicity.

8. Proving causation for an unintentional tort case requires two elements. The act of the person charged must be both the actual cause or _____ _____ _____, as well as the legal or _____ cause.

9. Under the _____ _____ doctrine, damages are computed according to the fault of the plaintiff as well as the fault of the defendant so that the defendant only pays for the percentage of damage that he caused.

10. The obligation not to cause anyone harm or risk of harm is known as the _____ _____ _____ element in the law of negligence torts.

True/False:

1. _____ All torts are also crimes.

2. _____ To be liable for an intentional tort, the perpetrator must have intended the result of his act as well as the act itself.

3. _____ A person is liable for false imprisonment if he restrains a person with threats of immediate or future physical harm.

4. _____ "Publication" to a third party in defamation of character means that a statement must appear in written form in a newspaper, book, magazine, etc.

5. _____ Public figures and officials have the same degree of protection under defamation laws as common citizens do.

6. ____In the tort of invasion of privacy, unlike defamation of character, truth is not a defense, because a statement need not be false to be a violation.

7. ____In determining a person's duty of care under negligence, whether the person acted within the reasonable person standard is determined by that person's subjective intent at the time.

8. ____Usually, if certain harm was a foreseeable result of a person's negligent act, the act is said to be the proximate cause of the damages.

9. ____Under *res ipsa loquitur*, there is an inference that the defendant was negligent and must therefore bear the burden to prove he was not negligent.

10. ____ Under the traditional common law doctrine of contributory negligence, a plaintiff cannot recover damages from a defendant even if the plaintiff was only at fault for a very small part of his own injury.

Multiple Choice:

1. Mr. Temper, a 5-foot, 4-inch, 100 pound hot head, tells Mr. Big, a professional wrestler, that he is going to "make him regret he set foot in this bar." At the same time, Temper clenches and raises he fists. Big looks at Temper from head to toe and responds, "Yeah, right."
   A. Big can sue Temper only for assault.
   B. Big can sue Temper for assault and battery.
   C. Big can sue Temper for intentional infliction of emotional distress.
   D. Big has no cause of action.

2. Thug approaches Joe, who is standing in line to buy a movie ticket, from behind. Thug plans to hit Joe over the head with a baseball ball. Completely unaware, Joe bends over to tie his shoe just as Thug swings. Consequently, Thug strikes Ann who was standing in front of Joe, fracturing her skull.
   A. Joe can sue Thug for assault; Ann can sue Thug for battery.
   B. Joe has no cause of action against Thug; Ann can sue only for battery.
   C. Ann can sue Joe for negligence; Joe can sue Thug for contributory negligence.
   D. Joe has no cause of action against Thug; Ann can sue for both assault and battery.

3. To be liable for false imprisonment, the perpetrator may intentionally confine a person with:
   A. Physical force or barriers.
   B. Threats of physical harm.
   C. False arrest.
   D. All of the above.

4. Mr. Gossip tells Ms. Nosy that, "Flashy is a drug dealer. That's how she can afford to drive that Ferrari." Is Gossip liable for defamation of character against Flashy?
   A. Yes, because it is a false statement which was told to a third party.
   B. Yes, because all that is necessary is that the statement be false.
   C. No, because telling only Nosy does not really hurt Flashy.
   D. No, because Gossip only said this, but did not write it.

5. Speedy approaches an intersection in his car as the light turns yellow. Instead of slowing down, Speedy speeds up and runs a red light. Mr. Walker, a pedestrian waiting to cross the street, yells and waves his fist at Speedy as he drives by. Unfortunately, Walker startles Ms. Precious who is also waiting to cross, and Precious drops the $500 vase she just bought. Is Speedy liable for the damage to the vase?
   A. No, because Speedy had no duty to drive carefully.
   B. No, because running the light is not a breach of the duty.
   C. No, because Speedy's running of the light was not the proximate cause of the broken vase.
   D. Yes, because the plaintiff, Precious, suffered injuries.

6. Assume the same facts as in question 5 except that Precious does not notice Walker. After the walk signal illuminates, Precious looks both ways, does not see Speedy, and begins to cross the street. Speedy, however, hits Precious, breaking her leg, as he runs the red light.
   A. Speedy is liable for negligence, and Precious can recover damages.
   B. Speedy is liable for an intentional tort, and Precious can recover damages.
   C. Speedy is not liable for negligence because his acts were not the proximate cause of Precious' injuries.
   D. Speedy is not liable for an intentional tort because intentional torts are wrongs against property only.

7. Ms. Rich's house is broken into about once a month when she leaves town. Usually, the burglar steals jewelry, watches, and other personal items from her house. One time when going out of town, Rich rigged a gun to go off when her bedroom door was opened. Slimy subsequently broke into her house and was shot. Rich's state distinguishes between types of visitors.
   A. Rich is liable because she owes Slimy and all other visitors a duty of ordinary care.
   B. Rich was perfectly justified in doing this since she knew someone would break in; she is not liable for protecting her property like this.
   C. Rich is not liable because she was not at the house when this happened.
   D. Rich is liable because she cannot willfully, or wantonly, injure Slimy.

8. Assume the same facts as in question 8 except that Rich does not set the rigged gun. Slimy enters the house through a window in the kitchen. The pipes under the kitchen sink have a leak. Slimy steps down onto the floor, slipping in a puddle of water, falling and breaking his tailbone.
   A. Slimy has a good case against Rich since having leaky pipes is clearly negligent and therefore a breach of the duty of ordinary care owed Slimy.
   B. Slimy has a good case against Rich because she assumed the risk of a break-in when she left town.
   C. Slimy has no case against Rich because stepping in the puddle of water was an intervening event.
   D. Slimy has no case against Rich because Rich does not owe him a duty of ordinary care.

9. Couch Potato decides shoveling his walk after a huge snowstorm is just too much work. Three days later his walk is a sheet of ice. Social Visit, on the way to see her friend Couch Potato, notices the ice but proceeds up the walk anyway. Social Visit slips and cracks her knee cap. Assume Couch Potato was 60 percent at fault and Social Visit was 40 percent at fault.
   A. If this is a contributory negligence state, Social Visit can recover 60 percent of the damages.
   B. If this is a partial comparative negligence state, Social Visit can get no recovery.
   C. If this is a pure comparative negligence state, Social Visit can recover 60 percent of the damages.
   D. If this is a contributory negligence state, Social Visit can recover 40 percent of the damages.

10. Assume the same facts as in question 9 except the Couch Potato is only 40 percent responsible and Social Visit is 60 percent responsible.
   A. If this is a traditional common law contributory negligence state, Social Visit can get no recovery.
   B. If this is a partial comparative negligence state, Social visit can get no recovery.
   C. If this is a pure comparative negligence state, Social Visit can recover 40 percent of the damages.
   D. All of the above.

V. Answers to Objective Questions:

Terms:

1. *Damages.* The tort must fit into one of the three recognized categories.

2. *Negligence.* This is the second of the three categories of tort law.
3. *Assault, battery.* These acts are also often classified as crimes.
4. *Defamation of character.* Note that publication to a third person is required.
5. *Slander, libel.* Oral and written statements are separately classified.
6. *Actual malice.* Malice is very difficult to prove.
7. *Invasion of privacy.* Privacy is not specifically mentioned in the U.S. Constitution, but has been recognized as a limited right by the courts.
8. *Causation in fact, proximate.* Both elements are required.
9. *Comparative negligence.* This is a relatively new method as opposed to the old common law rule of contributory negligence.
10. *Duty of care.* This is the first element of unintentional (negligence) tort law.

True/False:

1. False. Torts are causes of action founded in common law. In torts, one private party sues another. Crimes are statutory wrongs which are prosecuted by the government. While some torts are also crimes, not all torts fall in this category. For example, negligently denting another car's bumper is a tort, but not a crime, in most jurisdictions.
2. False. The perpetrator need only have intended his original act, not its result, to be liable.
3. False. A threat of immediate harm may be considered false imprisonment. However, a threat of future harm is not.
4. False. Publication in this context means that a third person heard or saw the untrue statement, not that it was written in a formal publication.

5. False. Public figures and officials can only recover for defamation if they prove the defendant made a false statement knowingly, or with reckless disregard for its falsity, i.e., actual malice.

6. True. The tort of invasion of privacy protects one's right to live without unwarranted or undesired publicity. Whether a fact is private is the relevant issue, not whether it is truthful.

7. False. Under a reasonable person standard, courts determine how an objective, careful person would have acted in a certain situation. The defendant's subjective thoughts or intentions are not considered.

8. True. In determining proximate cause, if a certain event was a foreseeable result of a negligent act, that will generally satisfy this part of the causation requirement.

9. True. Because the defendant has superior knowledge and because the evidence suggests there was a negligent act, *res ipsa loquitur* shifts the burden from the plaintiff to the defendant.

10. True. Under contributory negligence, if the plaintiff contributed in any way to his own injuries, he cannot recover from the defendant under the traditional common law. The more modern view is to use comparative negligence doctrines.

Multiple Choice:

1. D. Since Big is obviously not frightened by this threat, he cannot sue for assault. Because Temper never hit Big, there is not harmful or offensive touching, and therefore, no battery. C is incorrect since Big does not suffer any emotional damage from this threat.

2. B. Since Joe was never in apprehension of harm, nor actually harmed by Thug's actions, he has no cause of action. Ann can sue for battery since she was harmed, but not for assault since she was not in apprehension of harm. A is incorrect since Joe has no cause of action. C is incorrect because Ann cannot make a case that Joe was negligent for tying his shoe. Also, there is no contributory negligence here at all. D is incorrect because Ann cannot sue for assault.

3. D. All three of these types of restraint are considered false imprisonment.

4. A. The elements of defamation of character require both (1) a false statement and (2) the telling or writing of the statement to a third party. B is incorrect because the second element is missing. C is incorrect because while the degree of harm may affect the amount of damages, the elements do not require a certain level of harm. D is incorrect because defamation of character may be in either slander or libel form.

5. C. While Speedy's act was certainly negligent, the chain of events from speeding through the light to breaking the vase is very long and unforeseeable. Consequently, since foreseeability is generally the test for proximate cause, Speedy is not liable for the vase. A and B are incorrect because Speedy did have a duty and subsequently breached that duty. Therefore, even though Speedy is not liable for the vase, these are not the correct reasons. D is incorrect because although Precious suffered damages, that alone is not enough to recover damages.

6. A. Since Speedy owed Precious a duty of care, breached that duty, and caused Precious injury, he was negligent and is liable. B is incorrect because nothing suggests Speedy intended to hit Precious. C is incorrect because hitting a person in a crosswalk is certainly a foreseeable result of running a red light. Therefore,

there is proximate cause. D is incorrect because this is not an intentional tort. Also, intentional torts are wrongs against both persons and property.

7. E. Although Slimy is a trespasser, Rich cannot willfully or wantonly injure him. A, B, and C are all incorrect because a trespasser is owed a certain, lower duty by a property owner.

8. D. Rich owes Slimy a duty not to willfully or wantonly injure him. However, she does not owe a duty of ordinary care. A and B are incorrect because although having the puddle may be negligent, Rich does not owe Slimy a duty higher than the willful or wanton standard. C is incorrect because the theory of intervening events is irrelevant here.

9. C. In a pure comparative negligence state, Social Visit can recover the amount Couch Potato is responsible for, regardless of whether she is more than 50 percent responsible. A is incorrect because, in a contributory negligence state, Social Visit could not get anything if she is responsible for even a minor part of her injuries. B is incorrect because, even in a partial comparative negligence state, Social Visit could recover since she is less than 50 percent responsible. D is incorrect because, in a contributory negligence state, Social Visit would get no recovery.

10. D. A is correct because under traditional common law contributory negligence, Social Visit cannot recover because she is partially responsible. B is correct because, under partial comparative negligence, Social Visit cannot recover because she is more than 50 percent at fault for the injury. C is correct because, under pure comparative negligence, Social Visit can recover any amount for which Couch Potato is responsible.

VI. Key Question Checklist Answers to Essay Question:

A. *Is this act or omission a tort?*

We have two basic sets of possible contract-tort based actions against Mario and the City of Boulder, and a contract-based dispute between the Estate of Gabby and Franklin Pierce and/or his employer, the hospital. For purposes of this chapter, we will focus on the tort issues.

B. *Should this be classified as a negligent tort?*

In both cases, neither Mario nor the City of Boulder employees intended any harm, so an intentional tort was not likely here. Nor is there any particularly ultrahazardous activity or dangerous defect in any product apparent in the facts as presented. Thus, strict liability does not seem likely here. There is a distinct possibility of negligence on the part of both Mario and/or the City of Boulder. The following set of key questions might be appropriate for the student to use in answering the tort law aspects of the problem:
  1. Classification of the tort:
     (a) Was Mario's act a(n):
        (1) Intentional tort?
        (2) Unintentional or negligent tort?
        (3) Strict liability tort?
     (b) Was the City of Boulder's act a(n):
        (1) Intentional tort?
        (2) Unintentional or negligent tort?
        (3) Strict liability tort?

C. *Assuming you decide that both acts being examined are classified as negligent torts:*

  1. What was the basic duty owed by Mario to his fellow users of the road?

Would this duty be in any way modified by his physical condition, i.e., his colorblindness? Mario's basic duty was to operate his car in a safe manner as expected of a reasonable person under all the circumstances. This duty may, in fact, be modified by his physical limitation of colorblindness because he must be even more careful than the average driver not to rely solely on the position of the lights to see if it is safe to enter the crossing. In other words, he may have to compensate for his physical limitations by taking extra precautions.

2. What was the basic duty owed by the City of Boulder to the users of the road? As for the City, it too had a duty to make sure that the signals could be relied on by all drivers. Were either of these two duties not lived up to by either Mario and/or the City of Boulder? If so, would you classify these acts and/or omissions a breech of the duties owed? In both cases, it appears that both parties acted below the standard of care and were in breach of that duty.

3. Assuming you decided that both Mario and the City of Boulder did act below the standard of care set out in the duty of care, was there an injury suffered by the plaintiff such that it would allow him or her to bring a tort action before the court? Was the injury the physical or causal result of the defendant's act or omission? Was it the proximate and legal cause of the harm? The injuries to the plaintiffs were a direct result of Mario's presence in the intersection at the wrong time. His presence could, at least in part, be attributed to Mario's reliance on switched signals.

4. If you assumed that Gabby and Crabby were harmed by Mario's and the City of Boulder's acts, how would you allocate the percentage of harm among the defendant(s)? In spite of Mario's attempt to shift a portion of the responsibility to the City, the primary responsibility for the accident will rest with him as the driver who had the opportunity to avoid the accident in the first place.

D. *Would you excuse either Mario and/or the City of Boulder based on:*

1. Any of the recognized defenses such as assumption of risk, or last clear chance, or contributory negligence, or comparative negligence? From the facts as given, it appears that none of the defenses would apply vis-à-vis Mario.

2. Do any of the recognized immunities apply in this case such as governmental/immunity, or intrafamily immunity, or charitable immunity? As for immunities, governmental immunity may be applicable to the City of Boulder.

CHAPTER 6

BUSINESS TORTS AND INTELLECTUAL PROPERTY RIGHTS

There is no surer way to misread any document than to read it literally.

Learned Hand

I. Overview:

One of the great debates currently being waged in the halls of the U.S. Congress and state legislatures is to what extent should a government entity act as a partner in the promotion of new business opportunities. As a matter of public policy and related tax policy, there is no question that government sanctioned jump starts to business can bring long term benefits to the larger community by way of jobs and additional tax revenues. This chapter focuses on several areas of well accepted legal partnerships, i.e., areas of law with long established rules which provide innovative, creative, and new methods of special business legal protections in the name of the larger public good. These protected areas revolve around the law of patents, copyrights, and trademarks. They are designed not only to reward original effort but also to foster and encourage continued new contributions to the common good by creating an economically protected relationship between the writer, inventor, et. al. and the government.

The areas of patent, copyright, and trademark law are all individually complex and call for use of highly specialized law practitioners. They have a common denominator in that each of these areas provides a legally protected mechanism for rewarding the creator of work in the economic

marketplace. This reward system revolves around two basic principles:

1. Exclusive use of the economic benefits which result from the protected activity.
2. Legal recourse against those who somehow infringe upon this exclusive economic protection.

Where proper statutory procedures are used, the benefits can be great. For example, once a patent is granted, the inventor can reap the exclusive economic benefits for fourteen or seventeen years depending on the type of patent issued. The protection provided under copyright laws is even longer. Since 1976, U.S. copyright laws have extended protections for authors and other creative persons for their lives plus fifty years. The protection can be even longer for copyrights registered by business entities. In the area of trademarks and related marks, the continued use of the registered mark, coupled with renewals can extend the protections of law indefinitely. The most important caveat in trademark law is: "Use it or lose it." Failure to maintain legal protection of trademarks, service marks, or related marks can lead to a loss of protection for them. If the mark is allowed to become a common term for a product, it may be deemed generic and no longer entitled to protections which come with exclusive use of the term. One example of such a generic term is found in the word aspirin. Because the original marketers of the product did not protect the name vigorously enough, the name aspirin has fallen into the generic pool of language used to describe products with those chemical properties found in that product, i.e., aspirin.

The best way for a student to approach these areas of the law is to recognize that each of these legally recognized areas of protection carries with it a benefit/burden dichotomy--the benefits of the protective statute will pass to those who know how to use the statute. Proper use of the statute calls for all the individual elements required under the statute to be complied with. Once that burden has been met, the benefits will follow. Students should, therefore, familiarize themselves with respective steps required to obtain patent, copyright, or trademark exclusive use protection as described in the chapter. The multi-issue essay question will illustrate the process and how it is used to protect intellectual property rights.

II. Hypothetical Multi-issue Essay Question:

Ted Huie, Fred Dewie, and Ned Louie are all recent graduates of the prestigious law school, I OWE U, located in scenic Backwater, Massazona. Having all recently passed the tough Massazona State Bar Examination, they decided to forego the riches of Wall Street and start their own law practice in Backyard which is just down the road from Backwater. Their chosen area of specialization in law practice is patents, copyrights, and trademarks. They want to use their proper surnames in advertising their new law firm but are concerned that the use of the law firm name Huie, Dewie, and Louie may raise a few concerns at Walt Disney Studios, Inc. Walt Disney Studios has long held the copyright to the cartoon duck characters named Hewey, Dewey, and Louie, and our newly-admitted law practitioners don't want to start their law careers by running "afowl" of the law! What advice would you give them on this issue?

III. Key Question Checklist:

A. Is the area of endeavor qualified for some particular form of legal protection?
1. Is it a patent law issue?
2. Is it a copyright law issue?
3. Is it a trademark or related mark issue?
4. Can this activity qualify for more than one sort of legal protection?

B. Once you have decided which area of the law this issue falls under, you must then decide which of the respective steps apply. For example, if the issue relates to copyright:
1. Is this material copyrightable?
2. That are the possible methods available to you in gaining copyright protection?
3. Have copyright notice procedures must be complied with?
4. Once a proper copyright has been obtained, what protections are accorded to the owner of the copyright?
   a. What is the protection period accorded to an individual?
   b. What is the protection period accorded to a business entity?
5. In case of copyright infringement, what are the remedies available to a successful plaintiff?
   a. Damages?
   b. Injunctive or equitable relief?
   c. A combination of 1 and 2?

IV. Objective Questions:

Terms:

1. A type of unfair competition that occurs when a small company tries to pass one of its products as those of a larger rival is

   _____ _____ .

2. A product formula, pattern, design, compilation of data, customer list, or other business secret is a _____ _____.

3. False statements about a competitor's products in comparative advertising are called _____ _____ .

4. The tort of _____ is an attempt by another person to appropriate a living person's name or identity for commercial purposes.

5. Objects such as inventions, writings, trademarks, etc. which are often a business's most valuable asset include _____ property.

6. A patent may not be granted if the invention was used by the public for more than one year prior to the filing of the patent application. This is known as the _____ _____ doctrine.

7. Writings that are capable of visual perception are _____ _____ .

8. A requirement for a mark to be under federal protection when an ordinary term has become a brand name is a _____ _____ .

9. A distinctive mark, symbol, name, word, motto, or device that identifies the goods of a particular business and distinguishes the business and products of the holder from those of its competitors are all ways of identifying a _____ .

10. State laws that allow persons and companies to register trademarks and service marks are _____ statutes.

True/False:

1. ____ If the owner of a trade secret does not take all reasonable precautions to protect a trade secret, the secret will no longer be protected under unfair competition laws.

2. ____ A disparaging statement is any statement, true or false, which is made by one party about the products, services, property, or reputation of another business.

3. ____ When a plaintiff proves disparagement, he can recover both actual and general damages.

4. ____ Suits brought under the Federal Patent Statute of 1952, Copyright Revision Act of 1976, and the Lanham Trademark Act are properly brought in federal court, not state court.

5. ____ Design patents are valid for fourteen years and can be renewed at the end of that time.

6. ____ Corporations and businesses are given copyright protection for either seventy five or 100 years while individuals are protected for the life of the author plus fifty years.

7. ____ A trademark registration is valid for ten years and can be renewed at the end of that time.

8. ____ The registration of a trademark is given nationwide effect as notice that the mark is the registrant's property.

9. ____ If the registrant of a trademark does not use the registered trademark symbol, the registrant will lose all protection and have no remedy against infringements.

10. ____ Only the party to whom a trademark was originally registered can seek cancellation of the trademark.

Multiple Choice:

1. All of the following are necessary to prove the tort of palming off except:
   A. The defendant used the plaintiff's logo, symbol, mark, etc.
   B. There is a likelihood of confusion as to the source of the product.
   C. At least one consumer purchased the product under the mistaken belief that the product was that of the well established company.
   D. All of the above are necessary to prove the tort of palming off.

2. If a defendant is liable for the tort of palming off, the plaintiff can:
   A. Recover the profits made by the defendant from use of the trade secret.
   B. Recover damages suffered.
   C. Either A or B, but not both.
   D. Both A and B.

3. Individual Ivan, an amateur scientist, discovers the trademarked trade secret of TechniCorp. Which of the following is correct?
   A. Ivan is liable for misappropriation of a trade secret regardless of how he discovered it.
   B. Ivan is liable for misappropriation of a trade secret only if he used unlawful means to obtain it.
   C. Ivan is not liable for misappropriation of a trade secret because only corporate competitors are liable for this tort.
   D. None of the above.

4. Entrepreneur Ellen develops a line of hair products and markets the products as the "Michael Jackson Line." Assume Michael Jackson did not authorize Ellen to develop and market this line, but that she did so on her own. Which of the following is correct?
   A. Ellen has committed the tort of appropriation.
   B. Ellen has committed the tort of palming off.
   C. Ellen has committed the tort of disparagement.
   D. None of the above.

5. Inventor Elizabeth invented a new process for making sunglasses that are 100 percent scratch resistant. Inventor Elizabeth patented the process under the Federal Patent and Trademark Office in Washington, D.C. Which of the following is correct?
   A. The design is protected under both federal and state law.
   B. The patent is good for seventeen years.
   C. The patent can be renewed at the end of the patent period.
   D. All of the above are true.

6. Author Allen and Author Ann worked as coauthors on a book. Both agreed that the book is a masterpiece and should be copyrighted. Which of the following is correct?
   A. Allen and Ann must agree to copyright the book under either one of their names, but not both.
   B. Allen and Ann can each copyright their own work.
   C. Allen and Ann are protected under copyright law for 75 years.
   D. Allen and Ann cannot copyright the book.

7. Assume now that Allen and Ann are journalists. They work together for several weeks writing news briefs and stories on an upcoming presidential election. Which of the following is correct?
   A. Allen and Ann must agree to copyright the news under either one of their names, but not both.
   B. Allen and Ann can each copyright their own work.
   C. Allen and Ann are protected under copyright law for 75 years.
   D. Allen and Ann cannot copyright the news.

8. Sneaky Sam tries to copy the copyrighted work of Famous Fran. Which of the following is correct?
   A. Sam is not liable unless he copies the entire document.
   B. Sam is not liable unless the portion he copies is word for word.
   C. Sam is liable even if he copies only part of the document and it is not word for word.
   D. Sam is liable even if he only copies a brief quotation for comment in a book review.

9. To register a mark, which of the following must be met?
   A. The mark has actually been used in commerce.
   B. The applicant verifies an intention to use the mark in commerce and actually does so within six months of registering.
   C. Either A or B.
   D. None of the above.

10. Trader Tom is involved in the commerce of his state, Nelow. However, Tom is never involved in commerce outside Nelow or with other states. Which of the following is correct?
    A. Tom can only register his mark under state law.
    B. Tom can register his mark under either state or federal law.
    C. Tom can only register his mark under federal law as there are no state trademark laws.
    D. None of the above.

V. Answers to Objective Questions:

Terms:

1. *Palming off.* These torts are particularly aimed at luxury goods manufacturers.
2. *Trade secret.* Determine the efforts taken by the company to keep it secret.
3. *Product disparagement.* Comparative advertisements are OK if they are truthful.
4. *Appropriation.* We are all entitled to reap the benefits of our personal identity.
5. *Intellectual.* Patents, copyrights, etc. qualify as intellectual property.
6. *Public use.* The rule seeks to impose a duty on the inventor to act in a timely manner.
7. *Tangible writings.* As hi-tech evolves, expect this definition to be expanded.
8. *Secondary meaning.* This meaning often has tremendous value; consider the value of terms like Coke and Pepsi.
9. *Trademark.* In many ways, these have become a new international language of business.

10. *Antidilution*. The burden is placed on the person seeking the benefit of the law's protection.

True/False:

1. True. Remember the "Use or lose" maxim.
2. False. A disparaging statement is a false, not a true, statement. True statements, although they may be damaging, are not disparaging statements.
3. False. When a plaintiff proves disparagement, he or she can recover only actual damages.
4. True. These are federally protected intellectual property enactments.
5. False. Although design patents are valid for fourteen years, they cannot be renewed.
6. True. See the Copyright Revision Act of 1976.
7. True. With proper protection, renewals can last to infinity.
8. True. The protection is provided under federal statutes.
9. False. Use of the symbol is not mandatory. However, certain remedies may be lost if the symbol is not used.
10. False. A third party is free to seek cancellation of a previously registered trademark.

Multiple Choice:

1. C. Only A and B must be proven to prove the tort of palming off. Actual consumer confusion does not have to be shown.
2. D. The plaintiff can recover both profits and damages suffered and is not limited to choosing either one or the other.

3. B. To be liable, Ivan must have obtained the trade secret through some unlawful means. A is incorrect because if Ivan used lawful means, he is not liable. C is incorrect because individuals as well as corporations can be liable for trademark infringement.
4. A. Unauthorized commercial use of another person's name constitutes the tort of appropriation. B is incorrect because palming off involves one merchant trying to sell his goods or services as those of a well-known competitor. Here, there was exploitation of a famous person's name. C is incorrect because disparagement involves making false statements about a competitors product or services.
5. B. The process patent is protected for seventeen years. A is incorrect because the design is protected under only federal, not state, law. C is incorrect because the patent cannot be renewed at all.
6. B. Allen and Ann can each copyright his or her own work since they are the original authors of the work. A is incorrect because each can copyright his or her own work. C is incorrect because Allen and Ann are protected for their lives plus fifty years under copyright law. D is incorrect because such original works can be copyrighted.
7. D. News cannot be copyrighted.
8. C. If Sam copies a substantial and material part of Fran's work, he is liable for copyright infringement even if it is not word for word. A is incorrect because Sam need only copy a substantial and material part of the work to be liable. B is incorrect because the work need not be copied word for word for Sam to be liable. D is incorrect because using a brief quotation for comment in a book review falls under the fair use doctrine and is permissible.

9. C. Either A or B can be shown to register a mark.
10. A. Since Tom's business is purely intrastate, he can only register his mark under state law. B is incorrect because federal law requires that the commerce be interstate to be federally protected. C is incorrect because Tom must register under state law, not federal law.

VI. Key Question Checklist Answers to Essay Questions:

A&B. *Once you have decided which area of the law the issue fits under, which protective steps must be taken?*

The use of a company name may be subject to scrutiny under any number of protected areas of the law including patents, copyrights, and/or trademarks or related marks. The most likely areas of concern center around copyright and trademarks. There is already a legally recognized copyright protection accorded to Walt Disney Studios, Inc. for the creative cartoon characters known as Hewey, Dewey, and Louie. They have long been very popular with children and adults alike and have been vigorously protected by the owners of the copyright. In addition, trademark law may come into play where the owner of a cartoon character has marketed cartoon-related products using the likeness of the three ducks in question.

Is a surname copyrightable or subject to trademark protection? Normally a surname, standing alone, with no creative work attached thereto or without any secondary distinctive meaning, may not be protected. Here both elements--creative work and secondary distinctive meaning--can be found in the names associated with the cartoon character. Thus Walt Disney Studios, Inc. would have proper grounds for seeking protection for the continued exclusive use of these names as used for the cartoon characters in the public media and in trade.

C. *Once this protection is found to be in place, what is the extent of the protection provided?*

Does it accord protection in all situations or can legitimate distinctions be made where there is no dilution of the rights and protections provided for under the statute? Consider *Mead Data Central, Inc. v. Toyota Motor Sales, U.S.A., Inc.,* 875 F.2d 1026 (2nd. Cir 1989). In addition, is it fair use to list one's own surname as a business entity which coincidentally sounds and looks the same as another person's protected intellectual property? The need for specialized professional counsel is readily apparent.

D. *Assuming that our new law partners violated Walt Disney Studio, Inc.'s copyright and trademark protections, what remedies may be available to the owners of these protections?*

They may well be able to collect money damages for harm caused to the plaintiff's business and reputation. But, what they may really want is injunctive relief which would prevent the defendants from using these "ducky" names!

CHAPTER 7

BUSINESS AND COMPUTER CRIMES

The history of the great events of the world is scarcely more than the history of crimes.
                                                      Voltaire

I. Overview:

One of the most frequently asked questions of members of the legal profession is: "How can you defend someone you know is guilty of a crime?" The answer lies in a simple truth: we are not only defending the accused but also the criminal justice system itself. Because of this dual role, no other area of law is more ripe with controversy than criminal law and criminal procedure.

The American system of criminal law has been at the center of constant debate since the inception of the republic. On one side, there is a clear duty on the part of the sovereign to protect its populace from the ravages of miscreants whose behavior simply cannot be tolerated. On the other hand, the easier it is for the sovereign to punish, incarcerate, or even condemn its members to death, the less free the entire society is in the end. One of the badges of a totalitarian government is the ease with which it may act against its citizens. Consider the plight of the victims of the Holocaust in the Nazi era whose leaders did not worry about due process.

Our criminal justice system is designed to afford maximum protection for its members. It is the government's burden of proof to show guilt beyond a reasonable doubt under the law of criminal procedure. The accused is entitled to an entire set of legal protections generically called due process. That phrase is derived from two provisions in the U.S. Constitution: one in the 5th Amendment pertaining to actions by the federal government and one in the 14th Amendment pertaining to actions by state governments. Under these provisions and the numerous federal, state, and local criminal codes, our system tells the sovereign we are presumed innocent until properly proven guilty according to the rules of the game. What upsets so many people in our society today is a concern that the rules may have been bent too far in favor of the accused.

As students of the legal system and as potential leaders in business, your job is to know what those rules of the game are and to learn how to comply with them as responsible members of society. Failure to do so is not only bad for business; it is bad for everyone.

II. Hypothetical Multi-issue Essay Question:

Mergatroyd T. Wheeler has really come on to something. He has found a way in which his newly patented automobile engine could run on alternative energy. That alternative source of energy is found in a secret process which can turn cow pies into horsepower. His tests showed he could get twenty miles per pie (mpp) behind the wheel of his prototype named B.S. Bukaroo.

Mergatroyd took his idea to a large and prestigious investment banking firm, Wee, Cheatum, and Howe, to promote and sell shares in his new company named Go Pies. The financial records of the company were certified by I, Know, and Nothing CPAs. Shares in the new company were publicly sold to investors from all fifty states.

The company failed because the engine would only run on extremely odiferous pies, and now a number of disgruntled investors are pressing to bring RICO actions, at both the criminal and civil levels, against all parties involved.

III. Key Question Checklist:

A. All crimes must be specifically defined by statute.
   1. Is this statute:
     (a) Federal?
     (b) State?
     (c) Local?
   2. Does the statute clearly set out the elements of the crime?
     (a) The definition of the prohibited act (*actus reus*)?
     (b) The type of intent (*mens rea*) used?
       (1) Specific intent?
       (2) General intent?
       (3) Absolute liability without a requirement of any *mens rea*?

B. Once you have identified the statute to be applied, look at the facts of the case to see if this behavior would fall under the purview of the statute.
   1. Is this behavior specifically prohibited by the statute?
   2. Is this behavior required by the statute?
   3. Does this behavior clearly fall into the intent of the statutory scheme? Substantive due process calls for a proper match between the definition of the crime and the application of that definition to the behavior in question.

C. Once you have decided that substantive due process has been met, you must then decide whether the procedural due process aspects of the case have been complied with?
   1. Procedural due process requires that the rules of the game be complied with by the accuser when seeking the enforcement of sanctions imposed by a criminal statute. Examples of procedural due process steps would include:
     (a) Proper arrest procedures?
     (b) Proper "Miranda" warnings?
     (c) Proper use of warrants for searches and seizures?

D. If there is a problem with either the substantive or procedural due process as used in this case, what are the consequences to the accused and the accuser?
   1. If the steps used by the government were somehow improper, has its burden of proof been met?
   2. Can some of the evidence be excluded?
   3. What effect will this exclusion have on related aspects of the case, such as civil liabilities for the behavior in question?

E. As a matter of public policy, is this statute working for the good of the larger society?
   1. Is it creating more problems than solutions?
   2. Or is it too weak a solution to a much larger problem?

IV. Objective Questions:

Terms:

1. In a criminal context, the _____ _____ refers to the guilty act, while the _____ _____ refers to the accused's guilty intent.

2. Crimes can be divided into three separate classifications: _____, _____, and _____.

3. To be found guilty of a crime, the accused must be found to have had the required state of mind. Where the accused purposely commits an act, this is _____ intent. Where the accused acts recklessly, this is _____ intent.

4. To arrest someone, the police must usually obtain a warrant. The warrant must be based on a showing of _____ _____.

5. When a person is formally charged with a crime, he or she is issued either a _____ from a grand jury or an _____ from a magistrate.

6. At a criminal trial, the government's burden of proof requires that it prove _____ _____ _____ _____ that the accused is guilty.

7. Assault, battery, and murder are examples of crimes against the _____ while robbery, burglary, and theft are examples of crimes against _____.

8. Criminal conspiracy, attempt to commit a crime, and aiding and abetting are all examples of _____ crimes.

9. The Supreme Court created the _____ _____ _____ to allow use of otherwise illegal evidence from a search if the police reasonably believed they were acting lawfully.

10. The 5th Amendment's privilege _____ _____ provides that no person will be forced to be a witness against himself.

True/False:

1. ____ In a criminal action, the parties are the victim and the defendant.

2. ____ If a statute imposes absolute liability for a crime, *mens rea* does not have to be proven.

3. ____ Even today, corporations are never held criminally liable because it is impossible for a corporation to have a criminal mind.

4. ____ If police do not have time to get an arrest warrant against a fleeing person, they can arrest the person without probable cause.

5. ____ A grand jury determines a person's guilt in serious crimes such as murder.

6. ____ If the accused enters a plea of *nolo contendere*, the government has the option of accepting the plea or requiring the defendant to plead either guilty or innocent.

7. ____ In a criminal trial, all jurors must unanimously find the accused guilty beyond a reasonable doubt for a conviction.

8. ____ Under RICO, to prove a pattern of racketeering, no less than two predicate acts must be committed within a ten-year period.

9. ____ To be liable for criminal conspiracy, the accused must have actually committed a crime.

10. ____ The exclusionary rule prevents illegally obtained evidence from being used against the person searched.

Multiple Choice:

1. Vice President Vance works for Capital Corp. Vance forged several official documents to get money from Bigtown Bank. The bank ultimately loaned money to Capital Corp. for various business operations.
   A. Only Vance can be liable for these actions since an employee of a corporation is always liable for his illegal action, and the corporation can never be held liable because it cannot form *mens rea*.
   B. Only the corporation can be liable for these actions because the forgeries benefited the corporation. Vance is not liable because he did not personally benefit.
   C. Neither the corporation nor Vance can be liable because the forgeries benefited only the corporation. Since the corporation cannot form *mens rea*, it cannot be guilty of a crime.
   D. Both Vance and the corporation can be liable. Vance is liable for forgery regardless of whether he or the corporation benefits. The corporation may be liable for the crimes of its employees.

2. Accused Adam is tried by a jury. Only one of the jurors is not convinced beyond a reasonable doubt that Adam is guilty. All other jurors are sure Adam is guilty.
   A. Adam is convicted because a majority of the jurors believe he is guilty.
   B. Adam is acquitted because in a criminal trial, the jury must be unanimous to convict.
   C. Adam is convicted because although one juror is not convinced beyond a reasonable doubt, the government only has to prove Adam's guilt by a preponderance of the evidence.
   D. None of the above.

3. Andy Accountant manages the financial accounts of Multimill Co. Andy decides Multimill will not notice a $10,000 withdrawal from a few of its accounts. Ultimately, Andy takes about $100,000 from Multimill Co. Andy has committed:
   A. Theft.
   B. Extortion.
   C. Embezzlement.
   D. Larceny.

4. Hardcore Cop enters a house with a valid search warrant which states he can search for and seize any firearms such as guns, pistols, etc. However, Hardcore sees a large bag of cocaine laying on the coffee table and seizes that as well.
   A. Hardcore legally seized the cocaine because it was sitting out in plain view.
   B. Hardcore legally seized the cocaine because, once he had a valid search warrant, he could take anything he thought was suspicious.
   C. Hardcore illegally seized the cocaine because, if it is not listed on the warrant, it can never be seized.
   D. None of the above.

5. Hardcore Cop arrests Running Randy for alleged bank robbery. Before he says anything else, Hardcore says, "You might as well admit it now and save us both a lot of time." Randy looks at him and replies, "All right, all right, I did it--Are you happy?"
   A. Randy's confession is admissible evidence since Hardcore not did coerce him.
   B. Randy's confession is inadmissible because an accused person must have a lawyer for a confession to be used as evidence.
   C. Randy's confession is inadmissible because Hardcore did not inform him of his Miranda rights.
   D. None of the above.

6. Defendant Dan is acquitted on murder charges. Under such circumstances, the government can:
   A. Conduct a new trial.
   B. Appeal the decision to a higher court.
   C. Do nothing, this decision stands.
   D. None of the above.

7. Defendant Dan is convicted on murder charges. Under such circumstances, Dan can:
   A. Conduct a new trial.
   B. Appeal the decision to a higher court.
   C. Do nothing, this decision stands.
   D. None of the above.

8. Convicted Chris is found guilty of criminal RICO violations. Chris had bought several expensive cars and stock in a well known, legitimate computer company with money from his racketeering activity. What is the appropriate punishment for this crime under these circumstances?
   A. Imprisonment.
   B. Forfeiture of the car.
   C. Forfeiture of the stock.
   D. All of the above.

9. Shady Sharon and Shifty Sherman agree they are going to rob Wealthy Wendy. Sharon and Sherman drive to Wendy's house. At this point, Sharon and Sherman would be liable for:
   A. Criminal conspiracy.
   B. Attempt to commit a crime.
   C. Aiding and abetting the commission of a crime.
   D. None of the above.

10. Assume the same facts as in question 9 except that Sharon and Sherman have only agreed to do this, but are not yet in the car. At this point, Sharon and Sherman would be liable for:
    A. Criminal conspiracy.
    B. Attempt to commit a crime.
    C. Aiding and abetting the commission of a crime.
    D. None of the above.

V. Answers to Objective Questions:

Terms:

1. *Actus reus, mens, rea.* Both elements are necessary to the definition of a crime.
2. *Felonies, misdemeanors, violations.* These classifications are set out in statutes.
3. *Specific, general.* The statutes describe the type of intent required.
4. *Probable cause.* Case law interpretation of this standard is controversial.
5. *Indictment, information.* Each state has its own detailed rules of criminal procedure.
6. *Beyond a reasonable doubt.* This does not mean absolute certainty.
7. *Person, property.* These classifications are similar to those used in the law of intentional torts.
8. *Inchoate.* This means partial, unfinished, or incomplete.
9. *Good faith exception.* This is a very controversial issue and is subject to ongoing revision by the U.S. Supreme Court.
10. *Against self-incrimination.* This is one of our basic projections against governmental abuse of power.

True/False:

1. False. In a criminal trial, the parties are the government and the defendant. The victim does not bring criminal charges, but may have a separate civil action.
2. True. A statute imposes absolute liability on a specific type of crime where proof of *mens rea* is not a necessary element.
3. False. Corporations can be held criminally liable even though the corporation itself does not have *mens rea*. The corporation is liable for the criminal acts of it managers, agents, and employees.
4. False. Even if police do not have time to get an arrest warrant, any arrest must be based on probable cause.
5. False. A grand jury does not determine guilt or innocence. The grand jury decides if there is sufficient evidence to hold the accused for a trial.
6. True. The government can choose to accept this plea or require the accused to plead either guilty or innocent.
7. True. All jurors must unanimously agree that the government has convinced them beyond a reasonable doubt that the accused is guilty. If even one juror is not so convinced, the jury is considered a hung jury.
8. True. Under RICO, a pattern of racketeering activity can be established by any two predicate acts committed within a ten-year period.
9. False. To be liable for criminal conspiracy, the accused must only have overtly acted to further the crime. Actual commission of the crime is not required.

10. True. Where the search is unreasonable, evidence obtained will not be admissible against the person searched.

Multiple Choice:

1. D. A corporate officer or director is always individually liable for the crimes he/she commits whether to benefit himself/herself or the corporation. In addition, the corporation is liable for the criminal acts of its officers or directors. A is incorrect because the corporation can be held liable even though it does not have *mens rea*. B is incorrect because Vance is liable for this illegal act even if he did not personally benefit. C is incorrect for reasons explained above.
2. B. In a criminal trial, all jurors must unanimously agree beyond a reasonable doubt that the accused is guilty. A is incorrect because a majority is not sufficient for conviction. C is incorrect because the preponderance of evidence standard only applies to civil trials, not criminal trials.
3. C. Because Andy has stolen money which his employer entrusted to him, this is embezzlement. A and D are incorrect because Andy was entrusted with the money. B is incorrect because extortion is a threat to expose something about another person.
4. A. Under the plain view doctrine, Hardcore can seize evidence which is in plain view. This evidence is admissible even though it is beyond the specific scope of the warrant. B is incorrect because a warrant does not generally allow seizure of items not on the warrant unless they fit into some exception. C is incorrect because certain exceptions do allow such seizures.
5. C. A confession which is obtained before a person is advised of his Miranda rights, is generally not admissible as evidence. A is incorrect because although police coercion is illegal, the critical issue

54

in this question is whether Randy was advised of his rights. B is incorrect because Randy need only be aware of his rights before a confession can be used. The presence of a lawyer is an option for Randy, but not required if he wishes to confess.

6.   C.   Once a defendant is acquitted, the government cannot appeal, ask for a new trial, etc. Such actions would violate the double jeopardy clause of the 5th Amendment.

7.   B.   If Dan is convicted, he can appeal this decision to a higher court.

8.   D.   Under criminal RICO, the guilty defendant can be imprisoned or fined. In addition, forfeiture of any other property gained through RICO violations is permitted.

9.   A.   Since Sharon and Sherman actually drove to Wendy's house, this would be considered an overt act. An overt act is all that is required to prove criminal conspiracy. Actual commission of the crime is not necessary. B is incorrect because they have not actually tried to commit the crime yet. C is incorrect because the crime has not yet been committed.

10. D.   Until Sharon and Sherman make an overt act, they are not liable for anything. There must be something beyond a mere agreement.

VI. Key Question Checklist Answers to Essay Question:

A.   *Under which statute is the activity classified as a crime?*

The RICO (Racketeer Influenced and Corrupt Organization) statute is a federal statute designed to go after white collar criminals associated with racketeering activities. Even though it can preempt state and local laws covering similar activities, it can be prosecuted in tandem with those statutes. We will assume only the federal law applies here. The elements called for under the statute are:

(1) A prohibited pattern of acts, which in this case may involve securities and or mail fraud.

(2) The specific intent to defraud investors.

B.   *Does this behavior fall under the purview of the statute?*

If it can be shown that the accused parties made fraudulent misrepresentations about the performance capabilities of the "cow pie" engine to investors, then this behavior may come under the purview of the RICO statute. There is great controversy over the proper fit between the acts defined in the RICO statute as opposed to the normal business risks that come with investing in new ventures. Many commentators have argued that RICO should not be used as a wedge to recover losses from simple bad judgment.

C.   *Have the procedural due process steps been complied with?*

Assuming that the inventor, the investment bankers, and the CPA firm were all properly warned of their rights and all business records were properly searched, it appears likely that they may be criminally liable for securities fraud.

D.   *What are the consequences of failure to comply with due process?*

If any of the procedures were not used properly, the criminal case against the accused would most likely fail based on the exclusionary rule. That rule would keep out tainted evidence. It is interesting to note, however, that even though the criminal case may fail, civil damages may still be imposed in a separate trial. The lower burden of proof coupled with the possibility of nonexclusion of the tainted evidence in that forum only exacerbates the problem for the accused under this broad reaching statute.

E. *What are the public policy implications of this case?*

As a matter of public policy, government does need statutes like RICO to go after white collar crime and racketeering-related activities. As mentioned, the concern of many critics of the law is that it is casting too large a net and dragging in innocent legitimate business entities. When a law becomes too big a club, can a beating be far behind?

CHAPTER 8

ETHICS AND SOCIAL RESPONSIBILITY OF BUSINESS

There are no shortcuts to any place worth going.

Beverly Sills

I. Overview:

The novel *Spartacus* was written by the French author Bernard Joseph Saurin in 1760. The novel was named after the Thracian slave who died in 71 B.C. after leading a revolt against the Roman authorities. In this novel, Saurin wrote: "The law often permits what honor forbids." That quote truly encapsulates what the study of ethics vis-à-vis law is all about. While it may have been legal to trade in human misery and subjugation, could it ever be morally acceptable under any of the systems of ethics discussed in this chapter?

The study of ethics revolves around the examination of rules, conduct, and character through a morally-tinted microscope. That law should be grounded in some sort of morality-based foundation is self-evident. Yet painful history has shown us over and over the prices paid when there is an abyss between law and ethics. Sometimes these gaps can only be closed by conflagrations and wars so costly that we are reminded of an old anonymous proverb: "Adam ate the apple, and our teeth still ache."

The goals of all the ethical schools of thought are to seek some sort of morally-based rationale for human behavior. This rationale may be found in outside sources as seen in schools of ethical fundamentalism or in the rule that provides the greatest good to society as illustrated by utilitarianism. Others such as Kant and Rawls have sought to devise formulas of behavior based on universal rules or social contract respectively. In all these systems, a morally-based methodology is sought as a guidepost for behavior. If these guideposts are universally accepted, the odds are very high that they will no longer be advisory, but rather required by law. The process by which morally-based ethical behavior is first desired, then expected, and finally mandated is really the evolution of law. Note that law is the last stage in this often painful process.

Because so much of our legal and economic activities are conducted in the corporate format, juristic (law-made) business entities cannot ignore this constant and dynamic tug and pull between ethics and law. This dynamic is well illustrated by the differences between the thinking of the court in *Dodge v. Ford Motor Company* in 1919 and today's social audits of corporate citizenship. We have either come a long way or become hopelessly bogged down in political correctness depending on your personal point of view. The bottom line in the study of ethics is ultimately personal. Imagine a world without a concern for law and ethics. As French author Stephanie Félicité Genlis said in 1793, "The man whose probity consists in merely obeying laws cannot be truly virtuous or estimable; for he will find many opportunities of doing contemptible and even dishonest acts, which laws cannot punish."

II. Hypothetical Multi-Issue Essay Question:

Taxes are a necessary evil most of us have to live with as a cost of not only doing business but also as an expense of living in a free society. As Justice Oliver Wendell Holmes said in 1927, "Taxes are what we pay for civilized society." But must we pay even in death? The federal government has a long established set of wealth transfer taxes designed to pay back the government for the protection it provided to a decedent during his or her accumulation of wealth. One such tax is the federal estate tax which is imposed on decedents whose estates are valued at over $600,000 at the time of death.

You are a newly graduated associate of the Ras, Ma, and Tas law firm which represents the estate of Dealing Don, the late, great Aspen rental real estate mogul. The fair market value of his rental real estate holdings is over $6 million. Your senior partner finds an Internal Revenue Code section which allows a "use" value for family owned businesses. This use value is intended to preserve family farm ownership. Should you convert these city rental units to agricultural "use" in order to reduce their reported value to under $600,000?

III. Key Question Checklist:

This checklist is designed to help illustrate the evolution of jurisprudential thinking from an *expectation,* to a *norm* of behavior, to an eventual *mandate* of society at large upon its members. Consider which schools of ethics you would personally find most appropriate to apply to both the personal and corporate behaviors raised in the essay question.

A. What definition of behavior would apply to the issue at hand?
   1. Is this a social norm?
   2. Is this exception a form of control?
      (a) Is this control formalized?
      (b) Religious standards?
      (c) Peer group pressure?
      (d) Ethical standards?
      (e) A legislative enactment?
      (f) Public policy?
   3. Does a combination of any of the above apply?

B. Once you have identified what kind of societal expectation of behavior is at issue, what standard of behavior is most appropriate?
   1. Is the standard codified by law?
   2. Is the standard supported by one or more of schools of ethical behavior?
      (a) Ethical fundamentalism?
      (b) Utilitarianism?
      (c) Kantian or deontology ethics?
      (d) Rawls' social justice theory?
      (e) Ethical relativism?

C. What standard of ethical responsibility should be applied to the business entity?
   1. Maximizing profits?
   2. Moral minimum?
   3. Stakeholders interests?
   4. Corporate citizenship?

D. How should the corporate entity have sought to prevent this issue?
   1. Code of ethics?
   2. Corporate social audit?

E. How would you personally respond to this issue if you were placed in a position of judgment?
   1. What do you see as the critical issue?
   2. What body of law and/or ethical standards would you use?
   3. How would you apply these standards to the facts at hand?
   4. Are there any overriding equity concerns which you might raise in the resolution of this case?

IV. Objective Questions:

Terms:

1. A theory that says law should be based on morality and ethics is called _____ _____ _____ _____.

58

2. When a person looks to an outside source for ethical rules or commands, he or she might be categorized as a _____ _____.

3. A moral theory which dictates that people must choose the action or follow the rule that provides the greatest good to society is called _____ _____.

4. A moral theory which says that people owe moral duties that are based on universal rules is called _____ _____.

5. Basing one's behavior on the adage: "Do unto others as you would have them do unto you" is called the _____ _____.

6. A moral theory that says each person is presumed to have entered into a social contract with all others in society to obey moral rules that are necessary for people to live in peace and harmony is called a _____ _____.

7. A theory of social responsibility that says a corporation must consider the effects its actions have on persons other than its stockholders is called _____ _____.

8. A theory of social responsibility that says a business has a responsibility to do good is called _____ _____.

9. Under the traditional business judgment rule, directors of a corporation owe a _____ _____ to act on an informed basis, with reasonable care, and in good faith.

10. This act generally makes it a crime for U.S. companies to bribe a foreign official for purposes of conducting business. It is called the _____ _____ _____ Act of 1977.

True/False:

1. ____ Under Kantian ethics, morality is judged by a person's act or motives.

2. ____ Moral Minimum is a theory of social responsibility which says that business is responsible for helping to solve social problems that it did little if anything to cause.

3. ____ Law and ethical standards never conflict with one another. If something is a law, it is, by definition, ethical.

4. ____ Company codes of ethics are a form of Ethical Fundamentalism.

5. ____ Under Ethical Fundamentalism, a person looks solely within himself or herself for ethical codes or commands.

6. ____ Immanuel Kant would support the Golden Rule.

7. ____ John Locke and Jean Jacques Rousseau would support the Social Contract theory of morality.

8. ____ Ethical Relativism has been widely adopted as a moral theory because of its strict guidelines.

9. ____ A corporation which moves jobs overseas to take advantage of lower pay scales is adhering to the Stakeholder Interest school of corporate ethics.

10. ____ Social audits are now the norm in the corporate arena.

Multiple Choice:

1. Literal Larry believes that all ethical standards and rules are set out in a book called *Ethics For All* which was written by a prominent ethical theorist. Larry refers to this book for guidance and rules by which to lead his life. Which of the following moral theories most accurately describes Larry's conduct?
   A. Kantian Ethics.
   B. Utilitarianism.
   C. Ethical Relativism.
   D. Ethical Fundamentalism.

2. Societal Sarah believes people should take actions which benefit society as a whole the most. Which of the following moral theories most accurately describes Sarah's beliefs?
   A. Kantian Ethics.
   B. Utilitarianism.
   C. Rawl's Social Justice.
   D. Ethical Fundamentalism.

3. Individual Ingrid firmly believes that each person must look at her own feelings of what is right and wrong to decide what is ethical. Which of the following moral theories most accurately describes Ingrid's beliefs?
   A. Utilitarianism.
   B. Ethical Fundamentalism.
   C. Rawl's Social Justice.
   D. Ethical Relativism.

4. Dutiful Daisy always considers how she would feel in another person's place before she takes any action. Then, Daisy only acts in accord with how she would want others to behave in the same circumstances. Which of the following moral theories most accurately describes Daisy's conduct?
   A. Kantian Ethics.
   B. Ethical Relativism.
   C. Ethical Fundamentalism.
   D. Utilitarianism.

5. Fair Fran believes that fairness is the essence of justice. In addition, Fran believes all people in a society have a contract with one another to obey moral rules. Which of the following moral theories most accurately describes Fran's beliefs?
   A. Utilitarianism.
   B. Ethical Fundamentalism.
   C. Rawl's Social Justice.
   D. Ethical Relativism.

6. C.E.O. Ceo believes her corporation must consider what effects it may have on its employees, suppliers, customers, etc. Which of the following social responsibility theories does Ceo most likely subscribe to?
   A. Corporate Citizenship.
   B. Stakeholder Interest.
   C. Moral Minimum.
   D. Maximizing Profits.

7. C.E.O. Crusader believes his corporation can be influential and should be responsible for helping solve many social problems. Crusader believes his corporation should address problems above and beyond those actually caused by the corporation. Which of the following social responsibility theories does Crusader most likely subscribe to?
   A. Corporate Citizenship.
   B. Stakeholder Interest.
   C. Moral Minimum.
   D. Maximizing Profits.

8. Advocate Andrew believes corporations should not only be held accountable for their financial states, but also for some level of social responsibility. Andrew's beliefs would most likely be defined as:
   A. A code of ethics.
   B. A social contract.
   C. A corporate social audit.
   D. A distributive justice theory.

9. Corporate codes of ethics can be derived from principles educated by:
   A. Ethical Fundamentalism.
   B. Utilitarianism.
   C. The Categorical Imperative.
   D. All of the above.

10. Nobel Prize winner Professor Emeritus Milton Friedman would favor a corporate code of conduct which would:
    A. Maximize profits at all costs.
    B. Maximize profits based on open and free competition.
    C. Maximize profits as long as the corporation plays within the rules without fraud or deception.
    D. B and C only.

V. Answers to Objective Questions:

Terms:

1. *Moral theory of law*. Without it, law has no foundation.
2. *Ethical fundamentalism*. The Natural Law School of jurisprudence is considered to be one of the oldest, and it is still quite important in the study of law and ethics.
3. *Utilitarianism*. Many people have difficulty with this theory because of its lack of absolute or bottom line standards.
4. *Duty ethics*. This is traceable to religious doctrines.

5. *Categorical imperative*. The key advocate was Kant.
6. *Social contract*. Many of the newer schools of jurisprudence are variations on this basic theme.
7. *Stakeholder interest*. The difficulty lies in defining who is a stakeholder.
8. *Corporate citizenship*. This debate has gone on since the inception of the corporate form.
9. *Fiduciary duty*. It is the highest standard of duty implied by law.
10. *Foreign corrupt practices*. Note, the payment may be legal if it was lawful under local written laws of the foreign country where the payment was made.

True/False:

1. True. The test is based on the categorical imperative.
2. False. Moral Minimum is a theory of social responsibility which says that corporate social responsibility is to make a profit while avoiding harm to others. Corporate Citizenship is a theory of social responsibility that says business is responsible for helping to solve social problems that it did little if anything to cause.
3. False. The law may be contrary to a person's ethical standards.
4. True. The real question is whether they are being enforced or whether this is just the latest form of public relations.
5. False. Just the opposite is true. Under ethical fundamentalism, one looks to an outside source. This source may be from religious or political teachings and the like.
6. True. The Golden Rule is generally accepted as being based on the categorical imperative preferred by Kant.

7. True. Under this theory, there is an implied contract which states: "I will follow the rules if everyone else does."
8. False. Even though ethics remain an extremely personal decision, few people deny that some universal ethical rules should apply to everyone.
9. False. Most proponents of this school of thought would argue that such a move is based on the shareholder's interest alone.
10. False. In spite of the enlightened self-interest which can arise from checking for safety and environmental and consumer protections, social audits are still the exception, not the rule, on the corporate scene.

Multiple Choice:

1. D. One of the key criticisms of any form of fundamentalism is that it tends to be too simplistic by trying to answer all questions at all times which is easier said than done.
2. B. This approach tends to balance various interests involved and weigh in favor of the most benefit possible for the least social cost or harm.
3. D. Many people have difficulty with this theory because of the lack of outside controls on Ingrid's decisions.
4. A. This theory is also often referred to as the Golden Rule.
5. C. This theory represents one of the newer schools of jurisprudence.
6. B. The debate goes on as to how big the stakeholder class should be.
7. A. Most corporations have only bought into this theory on a limited basis.
8. C. A corporate social audit, in theory, would hold a corporation accountable for its social responsibility as well as its financial status.

9. D. All of these theories can and do provide rational bases for guidelines which can be used in a corporate code of ethics.
10. D. Professor Friedman holds the traditional view that the social responsibility of business is to serve its shareholder first through profits lawfully gained.

VI. Key Question Checklist Answers to Essay Question:

A. *What definition of behavior would apply to the issue at hand?*

A tax law practitioner has a duty to represent his or her client in an ethical manner as prescribed by the professional canons of ethics. For example, candidates for admission to the bar swear to "not counsel or maintain any suit or proceeding which shall appear to be unjust, nor any defense except ... to be honestly debatable under the law of the land."

B. *What standard of behavior would be most appropriate to apply?*

The behavior expected here would be to use all *legal* arguments to favor your client's position. This would include any reasonable interpretations of Internal Revenue Code sections which may be applicable in the case at hand.

C. *Which standard of ethical responsibility should be applied to the law firm?*

The law firm should affirm maximum advocacy for its client, but guard against unethical behavior which would pervert the true intention of this code section, i.e., it cannot make white black or vice versa only to save taxes. If there is no plausible way these parcels could be used as agricultural properties, you and the firm should ethically advise your client against using such a IRC code section in this case.

D. *How should the firm have sought to prevent this problem?*

Perhaps, some earlier estate planning should have been done to prevent this problem. In any event, the present tax problem must be ethically dealt with by legitimately arguable positions regarding the code sections involved.

E. *How would you respond to this situation if you were placed in a position of judgment?*

As mentioned in the overview, the bottom line rests within ourselves. We all have a duty to pay taxes. These taxes can be avoided legally and ethically. They cannot, however, be evaded by specious claims not based in any sort of reality. A line has been crossed, and in the end, we must develop our best personal instinct on how not only to draw that line, but also how to do so ethically.

CHAPTER 9

NATURE AND CLASSIFICATION OF CONTRACTS

We have too many high-sounding words, and too few actions that correspond with them.
Abigail Adams

I. Overview:

A contract is an agreement between two or more parties which provides not only for performance of duties called for under the agreement, but also for legal remedies in case of breach. Because of the possibility of having to ask a court of law for a remedy, think of a contract as a private arrangement on the surface. But like an iceberg, the bulk of its real existence is found below the surface. The difference between an agreement at the surface and a contract below the surface is the law's recognition that certain requirements, called elements, are in place. If these elements are properly arrived at between private parties, the larger society, represented by its courts, will enter the fray and enforce the rights and duties called for under the contract.

This chapter introduces students to the four basic elements of contract and some of the terminology that they will be using throughout the remainder of the course. The elements of contract are analogous to the legs on a chair or table. They not only provide support but are also its essence, i.e., a table will not only fall if a leg is missing, it is not even really a table. An agreement with all four elements is elevated in the eyes of the law to the status of contract. Without these legs, the agreement fails legally and will not stand. Thus, even though all contracts are agreements, not all agreements are contracts. To be a contract the agreement must show:

1. Mutual assent.
2. Consideration.
3. Capacity.
4. Legality.

The second major objective of this chapter is to introduce students to key terms and phrases used in the study of contract law. One of the hallmarks of the hi-tech information explosion is techno-babble. Walk into a room of specialists from any given area of endeavor and you will hear them talking in code, using language which is often unintelligible to the layperson. Yet that specialized language provides the key to the body of knowledge. The study of law is no different than any other academic specialty in that sense. Lawyers have been referred to as "word merchants," and the profession's use of words of art has long predated the hi-tech world of today, in spite of the movement to use clearer and more straightforward language in legal documentation. However the need to know some basic terms remains essential.

The key terms used here tend to be dichotomous, and you can use that dichotomy as a learning tool. Take for example, the number of parties to a contract. At least two parties are required in all contracts. One of those two parties has to initiate the contract formation process. The person starting the mutual assent process with a promise is the *offeror*, the other person is the *offeree*. Next, look at the dichotomy of the promises being used: is it a promise for a promise (*bilateral*) or is it a promise for an act (*unilateral*)? Have these promises been *expressly* made or can they somehow be *implied* from the circumstances? Does the form which this agreement is taking require certain *formalities* (such as a negotiable instrument), or can it be in any manner chosen by the parties (*informal*) as long as the elements of contract are met?

Once an agreement has been formed by the parties, are the performance obligations already fully met (*executed*), or are there still remaining performance obligations on the part of one or more of the parties (*executory*)? In addition, you may have to examine issues of enforceability. If all the elements are in place, the agreement is now considered a *valid contract*. If one or more of the essential elements is missing, the agreement is not raised to the status of contract and may be legally *void*. There are also certain situations where a contract is created but yet will not be enforced. If a legal defense is found to be in place, such as a writing requirement, the contract may be an *unenforceable contract*. Sometimes, certain persons are given a legally recognized power to avoid the contract after it has been entered into. These contracts are *voidable*, and examples of this sort of situation will be found in cases involving young people with limited mental capacity. All these concepts will be more fully explored in subsequent chapters and in their respective key question checklists.

II. Hypothetical   Multi-issue   Essay Question:

T. Bear is a champion pure-bred American Cocker Spaniel. He is big and strong and has a heart of gold. T. Bear's only bad habit is that he loves to explore and has a tendency to run off if not kept on a leash. Last week his owner made the mistake of letting T. Bear run loose near Boulder Creek. T. Bear ran off into the woods and got lost. He has been missing for a week and his frantic owner has posted signs all over Boulder and in the newspapers as follows:

"Reward of $1,000.00 to anyone who finds and returns my dog, T. Bear."

Signed, Owner

Last night, after reading the poster, Ms. Margaux d'Vin goes into the woods in search of T. Bear. She finds him sleeping with wolves in the woods. Ms. d'Vin picks up T. Bear and proceeds to take him towards the owners home. Half way back, T. Bear recognizes the neighborhood, jumps out of Ms. d'Vin's arms, and runs home to his happy owner. Ms. d'Vin becomes less than ecstatic when the owner decides not to pay the reward, claiming that T. Bear came home on his own. Does Ms. D'Vin have any contract rights against the owner?

III. Key Question Checklist:

This checklist is designed to introduce the student to the use of contract elements in the "building" process of constructing a contract.

A. Which body of contract law will control the formation, rights, duties, and remedies of this agreement?
   1. The common law of contracts?
      (a) Historically derived from English common law.
      (b) Found almost entirely in state court decisions and statutes.
   2. The Uniform Commercial Code (UCC)?
      (a) Historically also derived from English law but also heavily influenced by the "Law Merchant" which is traceable back to international trade during the Middle Ages. As such, the influence of Roman civil law can also be found in the roots of the UCC.

65

(b) The UCC is a set of state laws and has been adopted, at least in part, in all fifty states. Where it has been adopted, it preempts common law. If applicable, which subsection of the UCC applies?

B. Assuming the agreement is covered by the common law of contracts, are the four elements of contract in place? (Note: the UCC also requires the four elements but allows many variations as to how those four elements are arrived at and interpreted.)

1. Mutual assent?
   (a) Who is the offeror?
   (b) Who is the offeree?
   (c) What are the terms of the offer?
      (1) Does the offer call for a promise in return (bilateral)?
      (2) Does the offer call for an act in return (unilateral)?
      (3) Does the offer provide for a time, place, and manner in which the promise or act can be provided as an acceptance?
   (d) Was there an acceptance?
      (1) Who is the offeree? Did the return promise or act by the offeree comply with the terms provided for in the offer?
      (2) If the acceptance did comply with the terms of the offer, do we have mutual assent?
      (3) If the acceptance did not comply, what is the nature of the noncompliance?
         (aa) Is it a rejection?
         (bb) Is it a counter-offer?
         (cc) Is it only dickering which may keep the offer open?
      (4) Are there any implied in fact or quasi-contract factors in place?

2. Consideration?
   (a) Is there a legally recognized value or detriment at issue in this agreement?
   (b) Was this value bargained for in this contract?

3. Capacity?
   (a) Was there any recognized limitation on either of the parties to contract?
      (1) Based on age?
      (2) Based on mental capacity?
      (3) Based on punishment?
      (4) Based on statutory limitations?
   (b) Is this contract void or voidable?

4. Legality?
   (a) Is there any aspect of this agreement which is illegal on its face?
   (b) Even if the agreement appears legal on its face, is the underlying intent of the agreement to violate the law or any public policy?
   (c) Is this contract void or voidable?

C. Once the four elements of contract are found to be in place, check for important dichotomous definitions as to the nature of this contract.
   1. Is it formal or informal?
   2. Is it executed or executory?
   3. Even if the contract is formed, are there any defenses in place which may make it unenforceable?

IV. **Objective Questions:**

Terms:

1. A contract entered into by way of exchange of promises of the parties, a "promise for a promise," is called a

_____ _____.

2. A contract that has been fully performed on both sides, a completed contract, is called a _____ _____.

3. An agreement that is expressed in written or oral words is defined as a _____ _____.

4. A contract that requires a special form or method of creation is called a _____ _____.

5. A contract where agreement between parties has been inferred because of their conduct is a(n) _____ _____.

6. A contract that is not formal, yet is fully enforceable and may be sued upon if breached is a _____ _____.

7. An agreement by the issuer of the letter to pay a sum of money upon the receipt of an invoice and bill of lading is a _____ _____ _____.

8. The theory that says the intent to contract is judged by the reasonable person standard is known as the _____ _____ _____ _____.

9. A contract that has no legal effect because one of the essential elements of a contract is missing is called a _____ contract.

10. A contract where a party has the option to avoid his contractual obligations, and if a contract is avoided, both parties are released from their contractual obligations is called a _____ contract.

True/False:

1. ____ When parties voluntarily enter into a contract, the terms of the contract become private law between the parties.

2. ____ Form contracts, which offer goods on a take-it-or-leave-it basis, are the common type of contracts today.

3. ____ The Restatement of the Law of Contracts is binding law.

4. ____ For an agreement to be formed, there must first be an offer and acceptance.

5. ____ Under contract law, the subjective intent of the parties is important.

6. ____ Under a bilateral contract, there is no contract until the offeree performs the requested act.

7. ____ If a contract contains ambiguous language as to whether it is unilateral or bilateral, it is assumed to be unilateral.

8. ____ If an offeree in a unilateral contract has already partially completed performance, the offer cannot be revoked.

9. ____ Actual contracts are always express contracts, and never implied-in-fact contracts.

10. ____ Parties to a contract may voluntarily perform a contract that is unenforceable.

Multiple Choice:

1. Joe is a house painter who offers to paint Jennifer's house for $2000 by May 1. Jennifer promises to pay Joe $2000 for the paint job if he completes it by May 1. This is a:
   A. Bilateral contract.
   B. Unilateral contract.
   C. Voidable contract.
   D. Executed contract.

2. Hellen wants to order a cup of cafe lattè, but she cannot decide on a single or a double. She is thinking about a single, but holds two fingers up to the clerk when she orders without actually stating which strength she wants. The clerk prepares a double, and Hellen now refuses it, saying she only wanted a single. In deciding the terms of Hellen's order, a court will look at:
   A. The objective intent of the offeree.
   B. The subjective intent of the offeree.
   C. The objective intent of the offeror.
   D. The subjective intent of the offeror.

3. Which of the following is not a source of law or guidance in contract law?
   A. The common law of contracts.
   B. The Uniform Commercial Code.
   C. The Restatement of the Law of Contracts.
   D. All of the above are sources of contract law.

4. Regarding contract law, which of the following is incorrect?
   A. The offeror is the party who makes an offer.
   B. The offeree is the party to whom the offer is made.

C. The parties to a contract can form an enforceable contract for any goods or services they choose.
D. All of the above are correct.

5. On September 1, Max makes an offer to sell his car to Nelson. Nelson tells Max he "needs a few days." On September 5, Nelson tells Max he will buy the car. Which of the following is correct?
   A. Max is an offeree.
   B. A contract was formed on September 5.
   C. A contract was formed on September 1.
   D. Nelson may void the contract once it is formed since he accepted the offer and therefore may subsequently reject it.

6. Which of the following is not a basic element needed to form a contract?
   A. The contract must be written.
   B. There must be an agreement.
   C. Consideration must be given for performance.
   D. All of the above are necessary elements to form a contract.

7. Homeowner Helen tells Neighborhood Kid, "If you mow my lawn, I'll pay you $5." Which of the following is correct?
   A. Helen and Kid have a bilateral contract.
   B. Helen and Kid have a formal contract.
   C. Helen and Kid have a unilateral contract.
   D. Helen and Kid have a quasi-contract.

8. Assume the same facts as in question 7. Also assume Kid begins mowing the lawn and has only part of it left when Helen tells him, "I've decided to revoke my offer. I don't want my lawn mowed, and I'm not going to pay you." Which of the following is correct?

A. Helen cannot revoke the offer since Kid has substantially performed.
B. Helen can revoke the offer any time prior to the completion of mowing the lawn.
C. Kid can recover payment for the portion of the lawn he has mowed, but not the whole $5.
D. None of the above.

9. Which of the following is not required to establish an implied-in-fact contract?

A. The plaintiff provided property or services to the defendant.
B. The plaintiff expected to be paid and did not provide the property or services gratuitously.
C. The contract was voidable, but not void.
D. The defendant was given an opportunity to reject the property or services, but failed to do so.

10. On November 12, Debbie offers to sell her china cabinet to Ester for $500. Ester accepts the offer and pays Debbie $500 on November 13. However, Debbie is very busy and unable to deliver the china cabinet to Ester until November 19. Which of the following is correct?

A. On November 13, the contract was executory.
B. On November 20, the contract is executed.
C. This contract is an informal contract.
D. All of the above are correct.

V. Answers to Objective Questions:

Terms:

1. *Bilateral contract.* Most contracts are bilateral rather than unilateral.
2. *Executed contract.* Full performance discharges the parties from any further obligations.
3. *Express contract.* Express terms are always the first step used in interpretation of a contract.
4. *Formal contract.* In spite of appearances to the contrary, most contracts are informal.
5. *Implied-in-fact contract.* Often courts are asked to write in the terms based on the behavior of the parties.
6. *Informal contract.* The contract may be extensive, yet still informal, so long as the elements are still in place.
7. *Letter of credit.* This is a good example of a formal contract which calls for specific terminology, etc.
8. *Objective theory of contracts.* This theory is designed to give courts a measure by which to ascertain the intent of the parties.
9. *Void contract.* No contract is created in the first place.
10. *Voidable contract.* A contract is created but may be avoided by one or both of the parties.

True/False:

1. True. But, that agreement is subject to court review.
2. True. This is sometimes known as the "battle of the forms."
3. False. The Restatement of the Law of Contracts is a compilation of law principles as agreed upon by the drafters. However, it is not law.

4. True. This is the first of the four elements of a contract.

5. False. Contract law is governed by the objective theory of contracts which states that the parties' objective intentions are controlling, not their subjective intentions.

6. False. A bilateral contract is formed upon the exchange of promises. No act of performance is necessary to create a bilateral contract. However, under a unilateral contract, no contract is formed until the offeree performs the requested act.

7. False. If a contract contains ambiguous language as to whether it is unilateral or bilateral, it is assumed to be bilateral, not unilateral.

8. True. Equity calls for giving the offeree a fair opportunity to complete the act.

9. False. Actual contracts may be express contracts or implied-in-fact contracts.

10. True. Courts look favorably upon such actions if they are based on good ethics and moral obligations.

Multiple Choice:

1. A This is a bilateral contract because both parties have engaged in making a promise in exchange for the other's promise. It is not unilateral because a unilateral contract calls for one party's promise in exchange for the other party's act. It is not voidable, under the facts as given, because there is no showing of any problem with legality, capacity, and the like. At this stage, the contract is executory rather than executed because there are still existing duties of performance by both parties.

2. C. The objective intent of the offeror, as reasonably interpreted by the offeree, will prevail. A court will take into account the words, conduct, and surrounding circumstances involved. Hellen's silence, coupled with her two finger signal, show her objective intent to order a double strength cafe lattè.

3. D. A, B, and C are all sources of contract law.

4. C. The parties to a contract cannot form an enforceable contract for any illegal purpose or result. A is a correct statement because an offeror is the party who makes an offer. B is a correct statement because the offeree is the party to whom the offer is made. D is incorrect because C is an incorrect statement.

5. B. A contract is formed when an offeree accepts the offeror's offer. When Nelson agreed to buy the car, there was an agreement. A is incorrect because Max is an offeror. C is incorrect because a contract was not formed until September 5, when Nelson accepted Max's offer. D is incorrect because, once Nelson accepts the offer, there is an agreement and an enforceable contract. Nelson cannot revoke his acceptance once he has entered the agreement.

6. A. An enforceable contract may be written or oral. B and C are necessary elements to form a contract. D is incorrect because A is not a necessary element to form a contract.

7. C. Helen has made a promise which is contingent on Kid's performing the act of mowing her lawn. Because the contract does not involve a return promise from Kid, but rather his performance, this is a unilateral contract. A is incorrect for the reason discussed above. B is incorrect because a formal contract requires a special form. Such a form was neither necessary nor used in this case. D is incorrect because here a quasi-contract gave Helen an express promise to pay Kid

if he performed the act of mowing her lawn. A quasi-contract is an equitable remedy for situations where no contract existed.

8. A. Once Kid has substantially performed the act of mowing the lawn, Helen cannot revoke her offer. B is incorrect because Helen is prohibited from revoking her offer as soon as Kid begins performance or completes substantial performance of the act of mowing the lawn. C is incorrect because Kid can recover the entire $5.

9. C. The plaintiff need not prove the contract was voidable or void to prove an implied-in-fact contract. A, B, and D are all necessary elements to prove implied-in-fact contracts.

10. D. A is correct because on November 13, only Ester has performed her half of the contract. Debbie has not delivered the china cabinet and therefore her half of the contract. Because only one party has performed the contract, it is still executory. B is correct because on November 20, both parties have performed the contract. Therefore, the contract is executed. C is correct because an informal contract is any contract which does not require a special form or method of creation.

VI. Key Question Checklist Answers to Essay Question:

A. *Which body of law will control this agreement?*

If there is any contract in existence in this case, it would be covered by the common law of contracts. The UCC would apply only if the subject matter of the contract is specifically covered by one its subsections such as sales of goods or negotiable instruments. Here the subject matter of the alleged contract is the providing of a service by Ms. d'Vin to T. Bear's owner. Such services are not generally covered by the UCC unless they are somehow connected to a sale or lease of goods or the use of negotiable instruments.

B. *Assuming the agreement is covered by the common law of contracts, are the four elements of contract in place?*

The offeror here is T. Bear's owner, and the offeree is anyone who finds and returns T. Bear. The offer is unilateral in nature because it makes a promise (to pay $1,000) in return for an act (finding and returning T. Bear). The contract is not formed until the act is initiated and/or completed. Had the owner asked for a promise to find his dog, the contract would be bilateral and mutual assent would be arrived at upon acceptance of his promise with a second promise by the offeree. Because the promise called for an act, once the act is initiated, equity would dictate that the owners promise should not now be withdrawn. The underlying theory is that the offeree must be given a fair opportunity to complete the act he has begun at the behest of the offeror. This is the implied in fact aspect of this contract.

There appears to be an affirmative detriment undertaken by Ms. d'Vin here. She did something she did not have to do (go searching in the woods for T. Bear) in reliance on the owners promise of a reward. Although this was not bargained for the traditional bilateral promise setting, the consideration requirement would still be met because the bargain aspect of the consideration element is met in performing the act called for as acceptance.

There is no evidence of any lack of capacity here in the legal sense. T. Bear's owner was not so bright in letting T. Bear run loose knowing that he had a tendency to run off. He may be stupid, but stupidity alone is not a legal defense to lack of capacity.

There is no illegality on the face or in the underlying intent of the contract. Rewards are legal if they call for a legal act. Conversely, if T. Bear's owner offered a reward for finding dogs for illegal dog fights, than the legality element would not be met.

C.   *What is the nature of this contract?*

This contract was informal in that no specific formality was required as long as the basic elements were in place. The contract is executory in that all the performance duties have not yet been completed. T. Bear's owner should pay the reward. T. Bear may have run up to the house, but he was found by Ms. d'Vin who acted in good faith and should be paid. The owner cannot use T. Bear's actions as a defense to his duty to pay.

CHAPTER 10

AGREEMENT

A lean agreement is better than a fat judgment.

Proverb

I. Overview:

The first element of contract is a finding of mutual assent between the contracting parties. Mutual assent is defined as a reciprocal agreement based on a meeting of minds of all the parties to a contract. The steps leading to mutual assent start with the offer and acceptance process. These steps can be broken down into subparts, and a familiarization of those subparts is essential to the study of contract law.

By analogy, think of the game of chess. The offer is the first move made by a player in a chess game. How, when, and where that opening gambit (the offer) is made will control how, when, and where the other player responds by way of acceptance. The response must be made in a timely and effective manner in order to qualify as an acceptance. Thus one of the first questions to be asked by students is: whose move is it? Second, what moves can be made? Third, what are the legal consequences of having made or not made certain moves? Remember, in spite of all the civility involved in the contract negotiating process, it is still an adverse or gamelike relationship where each side is acting in its own self-interest.

The offer is broken down into three main subcomponents: intent, certainty, and communication. As an alternate memorization device, students may consider using an anagram called the QQC test. The first Q represents quality of the offer. In the eyes of the offeree, does this offer sincerely represent an objective intent to be bound? The second Q stands for quantity of the offer. If necessary, can a court, looking at this offer, find a basis upon which it could be measured, i.e., is the quantity of the offer readily determinable? The C represents communication. The offer must be communicated to the offeree in order to be effective.

Once a good offer is made, the other player must make his or her opening response. Remember, that response is dictated in many ways by the terms of the offer. Under the traditional common law *mirror image rule*, the acceptance must reflect the terms of offer. If it fails to do so, it may be deemed to be a rejection of the offer. And if it brings new terms to the table, it may be deemed a counteroffer. A counteroffer is, in fact, a new offer and sets the whole cycle of play into motion again from the reverse angle. The original offeror is now the new offeree.

Once we have a good offer, coupled with a good acceptance, the first element of contract, agreement or mutual assent, is arrived at. There are many variations on this basic theme as illustrated by the common law rules on advertising, auctions, and implied contracts based on the actions of the parties. They all have one common denominator; sooner or later some sort of basis for mutual assent must be found before a court will go forward with enforcement of the agreement.

II. Hypothetical Multi-Issue Essay Question:

Ed and Bob were long time friends, having known each other since high school. Over all these years, Ed was known as a car nut. His most prized possession is a 1923 Model P2 Alfa Romeo last raced in the 1925 Grand Prix of France by the legendary race driver, Antonio Ascari. This car is considered a classic from the golden era of sports car racing.

Unfortunately, Ed's wife, Rosanne, didn't look at his car the same way. She was always complaining to Ed how he would spend money on the car rather than on more mundane matters such as food, clothing, and shelter for their children, Enzo, Mario, and the Duetto twins, Guiseppe and Emilio.

One late Friday afternoon, after a round of golf, Ed and his friend Bob are comparing notes on their respective domestic situations over a beer at Putter's Tap. Ed says to Bob, "You know, I'm really tired of Rosanne being on my case over the Alfa. For $5,000 I would sell it to you just to shut her up!" Bob did not respond at the time. But on the following Monday, Bob showed up at Ed's office with a certified check for $5,000 and said "Sold!" Ed does not want to see his precious Alfa go, and both parties are now before your court. What result?

III. Key Question Checklist:

This checklist is designed to introduce students to the process of identifying and using the first of the four elements of contract formation--agreement.

A. Whose move is it? Who has the power to make the opening move called an offer?

B. If a statement or promise is made, does it constitute a good offer? Are the elements in place using the QQC test?
    (1) Was there evidence of an objective intent to be bound (quality)?
    (2) Was there evidence of definite or reasonably certain terms (quantity)?
    (3) Was the offer effectively communicated to the offeree (communication)?

C. If you find that a good offer was made to a clearly identified offeree, the next move must be made by the offeree.
    (1) What if the offeree does not respond?
    (2) What if the offeree responds in an untimely manner?

D. Assuming the offeree does attempt to respond with an acceptance, you must then examine the proposed acceptance.
    (1) Does it reflect the terms of the offer per the mirror image rule?
    (2) If it does not reflect those terms, is it seeking further clarification or negotiation, or is it a rejection of the offer?
    (3) If it is a rejection of the offer, does it constitute a new offer (counteroffer)?

IV. Objective Questions:

Terms:

1. Under contract law, the person who makes the offer is called the _____ while the person to whom the offer is made is called the _____.

2. Auctions that are merely invitations to make an offer where the seller may refuse the highest bid are called _____ _____ _____.

3. Generally, for an acceptance to create a contract, the acceptance must be _____, i.e., without any conditions.

4. An offer may be terminated by the parties in three ways: _____ by the offeror, _____ by the offeree, or _____ by the offeree.

74

5. Under the _____ _____, acceptance of a bilateral contract occurs when the offeree dispatches the acceptance by an authorized means of communication.

6. If a certain term is not expressly included in the contract, courts may supply the term based on a reasonable standard. Such terms are called _____ _____.

7. When the parties enter into an agreement but stipulate that essential terms will be supplied later, an _____ _____ _____ occurs.

8. When one party pays consideration to the other to keep the offer open for a certain period of time, this is called an _____ _____.

9. An equitable doctrine adopted by the courts to protect an offeree who has changed his position in justifiable reliance on the offer is called _____ _____.

10. If the object of the offer is made illegal before acceptance, the offer is terminated by operation of law. Such a termination is called a _____ _____.

True/False:

1. _____ To be legally bound to a contract, the parties must have had subjective intent to be bound when the contract was made.

2. _____ Advertisements are generally considered offers and are binding on a company if subsequently accepted.

3. _____ Although silence is not usually considered acceptance, an offeree may indicate that silence means acceptance.

4. _____ If an offeree inquires into the offer regarding certain terms or information, this is considered rejection of the offer.

5. _____ Death of either party terminates an offer only if the other party is given notice.

6. _____ Under the modern law of contracts, if a contract term is missing, the courts will hold that no contract has been made.

7. _____ An offer can only be accepted by a party or party's representative if it was first communicated to him or her by the offeror.

8. _____ Agreements to agree where the price term is left open are never enforceable.

9. _____ Once an offeree accepts an offer, the offer terminates as to all other offerees.

10. _____ In most states, revocation of an offer is not considered effective until it is actually received.

Multiple Choice:

1. Fast Food Inc. mailed a letter to Ambitious Allen on May 1, 1993, offering to sell a fast food franchise. The offer stated it would not be withdrawn prior to June 5, 1993. Which of the following is correct?
   A. The offer cannot be assigned to another party by Allen if Allen chooses not to accept.
   B. A letter of acceptance from Allen to Fast Food sent on June 5, 1993, and which is received by Fast Food on June 6, 1993 does not create a valid contract.
   C. The offer is an irrevocable option which can be withdrawn prior to June 5, 1993.
   D. The Statute of Frauds does not apply to the proposed contract.

2. Owner Owen offered to sell a parcel of land to Purchasing Paul for $90,000. The offer was made by Owen in a signed writing and provided that it would not be revoked for five months if Paul promised to pay Mix $250 within two days. Paul agreed to do so. Which of the following is correct?
   A. Paul's agreement to pay Mix $250 is insufficient consideration to form an option contract.
   B. Owen may withdraw the offer any time prior to Paul's payment of the $250.
   C. An option contract is formed.
   D. Although an option contract is formed, the duration of such a contract is limited to three months.

3. SuperStore published advertisements containing price quotes and a description of products which it would like to sell. Customer Chris demands the right to purchase one of the products at the quoted price. Which of the following statements is correct under general contract law?
   A. SuperStore must sell the product which Chris demands at the quoted price.
   B. Chris has accepted SuperStore's firm offer to sell.
   C. SuperStore has made an offer.
   D. Chris has made an offer.

4. One morning, Helpful Harry reads in the local newspaper that Mrs. Widow is advertising a $100 reward for her lost poodle. While walking to the grocery that afternoon, Harry sees a small white poodle. As he gets closer, he realizes it is Mrs. Widow's poodle. He picks up the dog and returns it to Mrs. Widow. Which of the following is correct?
   A. Harry is entitled to the reward because he knew about it and performed the act.
   B. Harry is entitled to the reward regardless of whether he knew about it before or not.
   C. Harry is not entitled to the reward because he would have done the act anyway.
   D. Harry is not entitled to the reward because he has not met the necessary requirements to form a unilateral contract.

5. Assume the same facts as in question 4 except Harry read nothing in the paper about the reward. Which of the following is correct?
    A. Harry is entitled to the reward because he knew about it and performed the act.
    B. Harry is entitled to the reward regardless of whether he knew about it before or not.
    C. Harry is not entitled to the reward because he would have done the act anyway.
    D. Harry is not entitled to the reward because he has not met the necessary requirements to form a unilateral contract.

6. Restaurant Randy talks to Supplier Sam on Monday about getting a food shipment. Randy is not sure whether he will need the shipment or not. However, Randy tells Sam, "I think I'll probably need the stuff by Friday. So, if you don't hear from me by Wednesday, bring me the stuff on Friday." Sam delivers on Friday. Which of the following is correct?
    A. A contract was formed on Monday when this exchange occurred.
    B. A contract was formed by Randy's silence.
    C. A contract was never formed because silence can never be acceptance.
    D. None of the above.

7. Artist Annie works and displays her paintings in a local gallery. Millionaire Marty sees her work and is particularly interested in a seascape painting. Annie says she will sell it for $50,000. Marty tells her he really likes the painting.

However, he will only buy it if the price is $45,000. Which of the following is correct?
    A. Marty's counteroffer terminates Annie's offer of $50,000.
    B. If Annie agrees to Marty's offer, she will be bound by a contract to sell the painting for $45,000.
    C. If Annie rejects the offer, Marty cannot then agree to the $50,000 price and bind Annie.
    D. All of the above.

8. Assume the same facts as in question 7 except Annie does not offer a price of $50,000. Instead, Annie tells Marty to "Make me an offer." Marty leaves, saying he'll be in touch with Annie later. A few days later, on June 3, Marty sends Annie a letter offering her $40,000. Annie receives the letter on June 5. Annie writes back on June 6, saying $40,000 is a bit low and proposes a sale price of $45,000. Marty receives this letter on June 8. Marty thinks it over and decides $45,000 is a fair price. Marty sends a letter on June 10 accepting the $45,000 price. Meanwhile, Annie decides she really deserves $50,000 for the painting. Annie calls Marty on June 11 to tell him the offer of $45,000 is revoked and she is now setting the price at $50,000. Annie receives Marty's acceptance letter on June 12.
    A. Annie's letter to Harry on June 6 becomes effective as an offer when she mails it on June 6.
    B. Annie's letter to Harry on June 6 becomes effective as an offer when Harry receives it on June 8.
    C. Annie's letter to Harry on June 6 becomes effective as an acceptance when she mails it on June 6.
    D. Annie's letter to Harry on June 6 becomes effective as an acceptance when Harry receives it on June 8.

9. Assume the same facts as in question 8. Which of the following is correct?
   A. Harry's letter to Annie on June 10 becomes effective as an acceptance when Harry mails it on June 10.
   B. Harry's letter to Annie on June 10 becomes effective as an acceptance when Annie receives it on June 12.
   C. Harry's letter on June 10 never becomes effective as an acceptance because Annie revokes the offer before she receives it.
   D. None of the above.

10. Assume the same facts as in question 8. Which of the following is correct?
   A. Annie's phone call on June 11 is a counteroffer.
   B. Annie's phone call on June 11 is a revocation of the offer.
   C. Annie's phone call on June 11 is immaterial because there was already a valid contract at that point.
   D. None of the above.

V. Answers to Objective Questions:

Terms:

1. *Offeror, offeree.* You must learn to readily identify the key players in the study of contract law.
2. *Auction with reserve.* With a reserve, the proposed seller keeps the back door open in case he or she considers bids to be too low. Eventually, market realities are forced upon such sellers if they want to sell their goods.
3. *Unequivocal.* If conditions are attached, it may be a rejection coupled with a counteroffer. Note the UCC has modified this rule somewhat in sales between merchants.
4. *Revocation, rejection, counteroffer.* All three of these methods may be used to kill an offer.
5. *The mailbox rule.* Remember this rule applies only to acceptances. In spite of the complications created by the rule, it has many practical benefits. Consider for example what happens every April 15th vis-à-vis constructive delivery of tax returns to Uncle Sam.
6. *Implied terms.* The UCC has allowed for a greatly expanded use of implied terms in commercial contracts.
7. *Agreement to agree.* The basic underlying agreement is in place, and the parties have agreed to fill in the blanks at a later time.
8. *Option contract.* Under Section 25 of the Restatement Second of Contracts, an option contract is a promise which meets the requirements for the formation of a contract and limits the promisor's power to revoke an offer.
9. *Promissory estoppel.* Under Section 90 of the Restatement Second of Contracts, the elements of promissory estoppel are a promise clear and unambiguous in its terms; reliance by the party to whom the promise is made, with the reliance being both reasonable and foreseeable; and injury to the party asserting the estoppel as a result of his reliance.
10. *Supervening illegality.* Legality is one of the four elements of contract and must be in place at the time of the formation of the contract.

True/False:

1. False. Only objective intent is required. Subjective intent is immaterial.
2. False. Advertisements are generally considered invitations to make an offer.

3. True. The offeree may determine that his own silence will mean assent. However, the offeror is generally not allowed to do this.

4. False. Mere inquiries or questions about the offer do not amount to a counteroffer.

5. False. Notice is not necessary. Death or incompetence of either party terminates the offer even without notice.

6. False. Generally, if a term is missing the courts will imply a term based on a reasonable standard.

7. True. An offer cannot be accepted by a third party who was not intended to be the offeree.

8. False. Agreements to agree that leave the price term open are enforceable if the price is determined by an appraiser or on an exchange at a future date.

9. True. Assuming a single offer was open to more than one offeree, acceptance by one of the offerees terminates that offer vis-a-vis the other offerees.

10. True. The so-called mail box rule operates as to constructive receipt of acceptances, not as to revocation of offers.

Multiple Choice:

1. A. An offer cannot be assigned to another party. A valid acceptance may only come from the person to whom the offer was directed. B is incorrect because the letter of acceptance, mailed on June 5, creates a valid contract. C is incorrect because the offer is not an irrevocable option because there was no consideration given. D is incorrect because the Statute of Frauds applies to contracts which cannot be performed within one year of entering into the agreement.

2. C. An option contract is an irrevocable offer that is actually a contract if supported by sufficient consideration. Here, Owen's offer was an offer to form an option contract. Therefore, A is incorrect. B is incorrect because the formation of an option contract results in an irrevocable offer to enter into another contract for the term agreed upon. D is incorrect because an option contract may be formed for any agreed upon period.

3. D. Published price quotes and descriptions of products are merely invitations for interested parties to make an offer. Chris's demand to purchase one of the products at the quoted price is an offer by Chris to buy the product from Kraft. A is incorrect because SuperStore has the option to either accept or reject Rice's offer. B and C are incorrect because Chris does not have an offer to accept.

4. A. To be entitled to receive the award, Harry must have known about the reward and performed the required act. B is incorrect because Harry must know about the reward. C is incorrect because Harry is entitled to the reward under these facts. D is incorrect because Harry has met the requirements.

5. D. Since Harry did not know about the reward, he is not entitled to receive it.

6. B. Silence can serve as a means of acceptance if it is determined to be so by the offeree. A is incorrect because, on Monday, Randy still had not accepted the offer of food shipment. C is incorrect because silence can serve as acceptance in certain circumstances.

7. D. The original offer was killed by the counteroffer and now Marty is the offeror, i.e., the original roles are reversed.

8. B. Annie's letter on June 6 is a counteroffer, rejecting Harry's offer of $40,000 and proposing a price of $45,000. A counteroffer is effective when it is received by the offeror.
9. A. Harry's letter to Annie on June 10 is an acceptance of her counteroffer of $45,000. An acceptance becomes effective when it is sent.
10. C. Since Harry's letter on June 10 is an acceptance and effective when he sent it, there was already an enforceable contract when Annie called on June 11. Annie cannot revoke her offer after Harry has already accepted it.

VI. Key Question Checklist Answers to Essay Question:

A. *Whose move is it?*

The first move here would be Ed's. If he was really interested in selling the car, he would either make an offer or solicit offers for the car.

B. *Are the elements of the QQC test in place?*

In order for the statement made by Ed to be construed as an offer, the three elements of a good offer would have to be found. The quantity and communication elements are readily in place. The quantity of $5,000 is stated and the statement was directly made to Bob. The real issue is the quality of the offer. Can this statement be seen through the eyes of the offeree as evidence of an objective intent to enter into an agreement? As will be seen in subsequent chapters, the value exchange does not always have to be *quid pro quo* as long as the legal requirements of consideration are met. Sometimes people sell off valuables at less than fair market value for personal

reasons. The question still remains, could Bob seriously see this as a real offer knowing as much as he does about Ed's personal situation?

C. *If a good offer was made, what can the offeree now do?*

Assume that Ed's statement was an offer to Bob, did Bob respond in a timely manner? It appears that timing of his response would be considered reasonable in that he acted on the next regular business day.

D. *Was the response here qualified as an acceptance?*

The attempted acceptance complied with the mirror image rule in that there were no material changes to the offer as presented by Ed. In addition, this response was directly communicated to Ed.

CHAPTER 11

CONSIDERATION

The greatest of all gifts is the power to estimate things at their true worth.

La Rochefoucauld

I. Overview:

Consideration is the second of the four elements of contract. Spotting consideration in a contractual setting sounds easier than it really is, and when consideration is missing, the result is not necessarily an absence of contract. It is one of those elements of contract law which seems unduly complex. Perhaps a historical footnote on the issue may be of value.

Consideration is that element of a contract which is designed to show the underlying inducement to enter into the contract. It is meant to place value on the contract in order to assure evidence of a bond between the parties. In the Middle Ages, contracts between members of the privileged classes did not require consideration because a man's word was his bond. That bond was evidenced by his family seal. The seal was affixed to the contract by way of pressing the *signatorius annulus* (signet ring) against melted wax onto the contract. Not everyone was a member of nobility, but all wanted their contracts to be binding. Thus the concept of looking to bargained-for value in place of the seal evolved into the modern day law of contracts. Today only a few states still accept seals as a substitute for consideration. Waxed seals have become an anachronism best used for love letters, and the only common modern use of seals is the embossed seal of a notary public, whose job it is to act as a legal witness to an administration of an oath.

Consideration today is made up of two subcomponents: detriment and bargain theory. Detriment represents the value of the contract, i.e., the glue that brought the parties to the table in the first place. It is actually a very practical requirement. Without value being put at issue, a court looking at the situation may simply say the matter is moot (nothing in controversy). Detriment is usually divided into two main categories: affirmative detriment where a person promises to do something he or she has no obligation to do but for the contract and negative detriment where a person abstains from doing something he or she has a legal right to do but for the contract.

The second subcomponent of consideration is found in bargain theory. Bargain theory is designed to isolate and identify the value used as consideration. Think again of a contract a table supported by four legs, those legs being the four elements of contract. Just as a table can only stand on its own legs, so each contract needs to identify its own consideration element. Consideration bargained for in one contract cannot be used to support another.

What if you have examined an agreement for consideration and found it lacking? You may still have a contractual result based on either the equitable doctrine of promissory estoppel or on specific statutory grounds which allow for a consideration waiver or substitute. Promissory estoppel literally means that a promise made, even though not supported by consideration, will not be allowed to be withdrawn. It is estoppel prevented by one's own act because of the harm which would befall the other party if it were allowed to be withdrawn.

The second major category of consideration exceptions from contracts is found in statutory provisions based on public policy. For example, the U.S. Bankruptcy

Code allows for court-approved reaffirmation of debts which have already been discharged. Another example is found in many state statutes which provide protection to eleemosynary (charitable) organizations making pledges as enforceable contracts even though the donors may not be getting any consideration in return for their gifts.

II. Hypothetical Multi-Issue Essay Question:

Cannon Phlake is rich and famous after having patented the world's first "phart phree phlakes" multigrain breakfast cereal sold under the brandname "Morning Mucusx." Mr. Phlake does have one major problem; his wife Tammy is no longer sexually interested in him. She constantly referred to him as "just a flake." So Mr. Phlake started using the illegal services of Ms. Misty Blue, a famous prostitute. Because he is rich, Ms. Blue waived her usual pay-as-go policy and let Mr. Phlake run up a tab for her services. The tab currently stands at $5,000. Mr. Phlake signed a credit charge to Ms. Blue in the amount of $5,000. He marked the credit card form as payment for "champagne". The credit card company paid Ms. Blue $5,000, and now Mr. Phlake is refusing to pay his credit card bill. He is alleging a lack of consideration due to illegality. How would you decide?

III. Key Question Checklist:

This checklist is designed to introduce students to the process of identifying and using the second of the four elements of contract formation-- consideration.

A. The first step in any consideration issue is to recognize its necessity as one of the four basic elements of contract. You must therefore ask yourself where the consideration is in this purported contract?

B. Once you have identified the existence of consideration, then proper subclassification of its elements must be made.
   (1) Is there affirmative determinant?
   (2) Is there negative detriment?
   (3) Is there a combination of both 1 and 2?
   (4) Was this determinant bargained for in the contract?

C. If you found that consideration was missing in your original examination of the issue, can you still arrive at a contractual result by way of a recognized substitute for consideration?
   (1) Does promissory estoppel apply?
      (a) Was a promise made lacking consideration?
      (b) Was the promise made with a reasonable expectation of reliance on the part of the promisee?
      (c) Did the promisee actually rely on the promise in a reasonable manner?
      (d) Would an injustice result if the promise is now allowed to be withdrawn?
   (2) Does a statutory substitute to the consideration requirement apply as an exception to the general rule?

D. Is there a contract?

IV. Objective Questions:

Terms:

1. Consideration has two elements. There must be both _____ _____ and a _____ _____ _____.

2. A contract where one or both parties can choose not to perform their obligations and therefore lacks consideration is called an _____ contract.

3. A contract in which a person promises to do something which he is already obligated to do is unenforceable because the person has a _____ _____.

4. If a party believes a contract arrangement was insufficient, she may attempt to reach a compromise with the other party. Such a compromise is called a(n) _____ when it is agreed to and _____ when it is performed.

5. If a debtor agrees to pay a debt which has already been discharged by bankruptcy, this is called a _____ _____.

6. Several types of promises are enforceable without consideration. These exceptions to the general rule are usually based on _____ _____.

7. In examining the adequacy of consideration, the courts use the _____ _____ _____ standard to determine whether the consideration is legally sufficient.

8. A contract where a buyer agrees to purchase all requirements of an item from one seller is called a(n) _____ _____.

9. A contract where a seller agrees to sell all production of an item to one buyer is called a(n) _____ _____.

10. If a party with a valid legal claim agrees not to sue the wrongdoer in exchange for a payment of consideration, this is called a _____ _____.

True/False:

1. ____A completed gift promise can be rescinded since there is no consideration in such promises.

2. ____Generally, if a contract only has nominal consideration, courts will find this legally sufficient.

3. ____Promises based on a person's prior act or performance, i.e., past consideration, are not enforceable even though the other party received a benefit.

4. ____Option to cancel clauses make a contract unenforceable even if supported by consideration since the parties may cancel the contract.

5. ____Liquidated debts can be compromised without consideration since such debts are not fixed or determinable.

6. ____Option to cancel clauses render a contract illusory in all cases.

7. ____Most states hold that moral obligation is treated as legal consideration.

8. ____Generally, if an existing contract is modified, new consideration must be given to avoid the preexisting duty rule.

9. ____If the parties to an existing contract rescind the contract and form a new contract, no new consideration is required.

10. ____The doctrine of promissory estoppel is also sometimes referred to as the equitable doctrine of detrimental reliance.

Multiple Choice:

1. Sneaky Sam is trying to avoid performing a promise to pay Promised Peter $500. Sam is attempting to show that lack of consideration on Peter's part justifies avoiding payment of the $500. Sam will prevail if he can establish that:
   A. Peter's only claim of consideration was relinquishment of a legal right.
   B. Prior to Sam's promise, Peter had already performed the requested act.
   C. The contract is executory.
   D. Sam's asserted consideration is worth only $250.

2. Texas Textiles contracted with Southern Oil in January to provide its regular supply of fuel oil from April 1 through September 31. The contract required Texas Textiles to take all of its oil requirements from Southern Oil at a fixed price subject to an additional amount not to exceed 10 percent of the contract and only if the market price increases during the term of the contract. By the time performance was due on the contract, the market price had already risen 20 percent. Southern Oil seeks to avoid performance.

   Which of the following will be Southern Oil's best argument?
   A. There is not a contract since Texas Textile was not required to take any oil.
   B. The contract fails because of lack of definiteness and certainty.
   C. The contract is unconscionable.
   D. Texas Textiles has ordered amounts of oil unreasonably disproportionate to its normal requirements.

3. Which of the following is *not* an element of promissory estoppel?
   A. The promisor made a promise that lacks consideration.
   B. The promisor should have reasonably expected to induce the promisee to rely on the promise.
   C. The promisee does not actually rely on the promise.
   D. Injustice would be caused if the promise is not enforced.

4. Betsy and Charlie enter into a contract where Charlie agrees to pay Betsy $1,000 per month and Betsy agrees to love and cherish Charlie forever. Which of the following is correct?
   A. The contract is enforceable in most states since each party has given consideration for the agreement.
   B. The contract is enforceable in most states since moral obligation is a sufficient substitute for legal consideration.
   C. The contract is unenforceable in most states since consideration must always be in the form of money payments.
   D. None of the above.

5. Edward Employee has organized birthday parties for all the other employees in his office for 10 years. One day, Brenda Boss tells Edward he has done such a great job, she is going to pay him an extra $200 this month. However, when Edward gets his check, it is the same amount it has always been. Which of the following is correct?
   A. Brenda's promise is unenforceable because it is based on past consideration.
   B. Brenda's promise is unenforceable because it is based on an illusory promise.
   C. Brenda's promise is enforceable because Edward performed a service for the company and deserves to be paid.
   D. None of the above.

6. Computer Corp. contracts with Nuts-N-Bolts to buy all the screws Computer Corp. needs to assemble its computers. Which of the following is correct?
   A. The contract is unenforceable because it is so vague it is an illusory promise.
   B. The contract is unenforceable because it does not involve a bargained for exchange.
   C. The contract is enforceable as a requirements contract.
   D. The contract is enforceable as an output contract.

7. Luxury Hotel contracts with Lush Lawn to have Lush Lawn mow the grass and keep up the gardens on the Hotel grounds for 10 years. However, there is a clause in the contract that states that if the hotel chooses, the contract may be terminated provided Luxury Hotel pays Lush Lawn a sum of $2,000 on termination. Which of the following is correct?
   A. The contract is unenforceable because an option to cancel clause makes the contract an illusory promise.
   B. The contract is unenforceable because the $2,000 payment is past consideration.
   C. The contract is enforceable because only one party has the option to cancel.
   D. The contract is enforceable because the option to cancel clause is supported by consideration.

8. Certain promises are enforceable without consideration. Which of the following is such an exception?
   A. Promises to pay debts barred by the Statute of Limitations.
   B. Promises to pay debts barred by discharge in bankruptcy.
   C. Promissory estoppel.
   D. All of the above.

9. Super-Chain Store agrees to purchase all its film needs from Photo-Perfect and no other film suppliers. There is nothing in the contract regarding "best efforts." Which of the following is correct?
   A. This is an exclusive dealing contract and will most likely be found illusory and unenforceable.
   B. This is an exclusive dealing contract and will most likely be found enforceable after the best efforts duty is implied.
   C. This is not an exclusive dealing contract and will most likely be found illusory and unenforceable.
   D. This is not an exclusive dealing contract and will most likely be found enforceable even without the best efforts duty implied.

10. Sunshine Orange Juice contracts with Manny's Market to deliver orange juice three times per week on Mondays, Wednesdays, and Fridays. Sunshine soon realizes this is a big commitment since Manny's is a little ways out of town. After a couple of weeks, Sunshine delivers only on Monday and Wednesday. Manny calls Sunshine when the Friday shipment does not come. Sunshine says Manny will have to pay an extra $50 per week for Friday deliveries. Manny agrees because he has to have an orange juice shipment for the weekend. Which of the following is correct?
   A. The contract is unenforceable because Sunshine had a preexisting duty.
   B. The contract is unenforceable because Sunshine rescinded the old contract.
   C. The contract is enforceable because Manny agreed to it regardless of a preexisting duty.
   D. The contract is unenforceable because there was new consideration given.

V. Answers to Objective Questions:

Terms:

1. *Legal value, bargained-for-exchange.* Remember, elements are the building blocks of a contract, and they must all be in place before an agreement is elevated to the status of contract.
2. *Illusory.* Courts do not want to be concerned with agreements which are not taken seriously by the protagonists themselves.
3. *Preexisting duty.* The element of consideration must be separately found for each new contract. Unless it falls into one of the exceptions, consideration from a prior contract may not be recycled into a new contract.
4. *Accord, satisfaction.* This method is used to replace the consideration originally bargained for with new consideration.
5. *Reaffirmation agreement.* Even though the debt may have been legally discharged, by not having been paid, it remains a moral obligation. Reaffirmation provides an opportunity for the law to be in better harmony with ethics.
6. *Public policy.* Public policy exceptions to general rules are usually equity-based doctrines which have evolved out of these laws and/or legislative enactments.
7. *Shock the conscience.* Normally, courts do not become involved with second-guessing the fair market value of an exchange unless the amount of consideration is so grossly inadequate that it "shocks the conscience."
8. *Requirements contract.* These terms are very commonly used in commercial UCC contracts between merchants.
9. *Output contract.* The UCC allows for far more after-contract latitude in the interpretation of these contracts.
10. *Release agreement.* The giving up of a legal right to a cause of action is considered a form of valid consideration in the eyes of the law.

True/False:

1. False. One such a promise is executed, it cannot be rescinded. It can be rescinded if it is executory.
2. False. Nominal consideration is not generally considered sufficient.
3. True. Past performance is not legally sufficient consideration.
4. False. If supported by consideration, option to cancel clauses do not render a contract unenforceable.
5. False. Liquidated debts are fixed and cannot be compromised without consideration.
6. False. These clauses do not render a contract illusory if a party to the contract has given legal consideration for the right to cancel.
7. False. Only a minority of states hold that moral obligations are enforceable.
8. True. This new consideration may consist of doing something new, making payment at an earlier time than originally required, or accepting consideration different from that required in the contract.
9. True. No new consideration is needed if the entire contract is new. For this exception to the general rule to apply, the parties must voluntarily agree to the changes in contract terms.
10. True. The doctrine of promissory estoppel is based on the premise of justifiable good faith reliance and the enforcement of promises which gave rise to that reliance.

Multiple Choice:

1. **B.** If Sam's promise was made in exchange for past consideration, which is not valid consideration, Sam will prevail. A is incorrect because relinquishing a legal right is sufficient to act as consideration. C is incorrect because an executory contract does not allow a party to avoid performance of the agreement. D is incorrect because a court will not consider the value of the consideration.

2. **D.** This is a requirements contract. Therefore, Texas Textile's ordering of unreasonably disproportionate amounts of oil would be a breach. A, B, and C are incorrect because a requirements contract is valid and enforceable.

3. **C.** The third element of promissory estoppel requires that the promisee actually relied on the promise.

4. **C.** Moral obligations are not usually treated as legal consideration.

5. **A.** Past performance is not considered valid consideration. B is incorrect because illusory promises are contracts where one party can choose not to perform. C is incorrect because although Edward performed a service, this was done without a promise from Brenda.

6. **C.** A is incorrect because requirements contracts are not too vague to be enforced. B is incorrect because this was bargained for.

7. **D.** The $2,000 to be paid on termination is consideration for the right to cancel. A is incorrect because if supported by consideration, such clauses do not make the contract illusory. B is incorrect because this is not past consideration. C is incorrect because either or both parties may have the option to cancel.

8. **D.** A, B, and C are all examples of public policy-based exceptions to the general rule.

9. **B.** If the contract does not address the best efforts rule, the court will likely imply such a term. When such a term is implied, the contract is not illusory. A is incorrect because exclusive dealing contracts are not automatically illusory and unenforceable. C is incorrect because this is an exclusive dealing contract. D is incorrect because with the best efforts rule implied, it will be enforceable.

10. **A.** B is incorrect because the old contract was not rescinded and doing so would not render the new contract unenforceable. C is incorrect because the preexisting duty rule applies in such situations. D is incorrect because there was no new consideration given.

VI. Key Question Checklist Answers to Essay Question:

A. *What is the consideration in this purported contract?*

There is no question that Mr. Phlake and Ms. Blue have engaged in an illegal fraud on the credit card company by reason of the misrepresentation make on the credit card form. As a victim of the fraud, the credit card company may bring both civil and criminal complaints against both parties. The credit card company did give legal consideration in payment of the charge, but the alleged consideration listed by Mr. Phlake and Ms. Blue was based on illegal acts and is therefore not valid.

B. *What elements of consideration are present?*

The credit card company gave affirmative detriment in that it paid Ms. Blue money it would not otherwise be required to pay. Mr. Phlake and Ms. Blue did not give valid consideration because of the underlying illegality of the transaction for which the credit card charge was made. Thus, there was no legal consideration validly bargained for.

C. *Is there a substitute for consideration?*

There is an alternative theory for the credit card company but not Mr. Phlake or Ms. Blue. The credit card company can argue promissory estoppel in that it paid the credit card voucher based on a reasonable expectation that the charges were legally incurred. A denial of reimbursement would create a harmful result.

D. *Is there a contract?*

The legal result is that even though there is no legal consideration here, equity (and the criminal law) would dictate that Mr. Phlake and Ms. Blue be liable to the credit card company for full reimbursement for payments made by the company.

CHAPTER 12

CAPACITY AND LEGALITY

He who derives the advantage ought to sustain the burden.

Legal Maxim

I. Overview:

Contracts are important. Personal and business success is measured in large part by how well a person can provide for his or her own best interests in contracts. A disadvantageous contract can lead to personal and business disasters such as bankruptcies, loss of credit worthiness, and criminal violations. Because of the possible severe consequences, the fabric of contract law is thoroughly interwoven with a concern that parties entering into these agreements are doing so with free will, full knowledge of all the material circumstances, and a recognized capacity to contract. Capacity is the legal qualification, competency, and fitness to enter into contracts. It is the third of the four essential ingredients to a contract. As with the other three elements, if the capacity element is missing, a contract cannot result from the agreement in question. Capacity to contract is presumed between adults. It is protected legally in both the federal and all state constitutions. Before this legally sanctioned right is limited, such limitations must be justified on the basis of sound public policy.

An important area of concern in the law of contract capacity limitation is found in the public policies which seek to protect certain individuals from the sometimes harsh results of contracts. Even though protection can sometimes be seen as a euphemism for punishment on the part of the protected party, the simple reality is that sometimes people do need to be protected from themselves and others.

The first category of persons needing protection is the young, i.e., the legal minor. All states have established certain minimum age requirements as a threshold which must be crossed before a person is allowed to contract on his own (now age 18 in most jurisdictions). Prior to that threshold age, attempts to contract by such young persons may have limited success. In the area of necessities and certain statutorily recognized situations such as insurance and military enlistment, these contracts may be enforceable against a minor. But as a matter of public policy, the general rule is that the minor is allowed, for his or her own protection, to legally avoid the consequences of contractual entanglement. This avoidance is not always a free ride. If there is misrepresentation by the minor or equity concerns for an adult who dealt with the minor in good faith, some reimbursement may be due from the minor.

The second major area of public policy-based protection from contract capacity is found in the area of persons with varying degrees of limited mental capacity. Just as we do not want very young people signing mortgages, we do not want documents enforced against persons who had no real ability to comprehend the material elements of those documents. This is not a matter of excusing someone from the binding effects of a contract based on simple ignorance. If that were the case, courts would surely be even more inundated than they already are. What this area of the law is concerned about is a real lack of capacity to protect oneself. Because contract results can be harmful, a lack of a mental ability to protect one's self-interest is considered fatal to the contracting process.

A person who has been judged incompetent simply has lost the power to contract for himself or herself and needs to have someone else act in his best interest in a fiduciary (trust) role. Attempts to contract with persons legally declared incompetent are void. Persons who are not legally declared incompetent can seek to avoid contracts based on some sort of lesser capacity. Be it based on mental limitations, drunkenness, drug use, or other affliction, they must prove to a court that at the time they entered into the disputed agreement, they lacked the cognitive ability to understand the material elements of the transaction. The burden of proof is on the person raising the issue of limited capacity, and courts will look at those issues on a case by case basis. Simple ignorance, emotional weakness, or a predilection for doing stupid things are not sufficient grounds for avoidance of a contract. As with minors, contracts with persons of limited capacity can later be ratified. If the contract is disaffirmed, restoration or restitution may be appropriate depending on the individual circumstances of each case.

The second objective of this chapter is to introduce you to the element of legality and its role in the formation and enforcement of contracts. Most people think of a contract as a two party situation: A contracts with B, each legally capable of providing recognized legal value. Note how the phrase legal keeps cropping up through the language of contracts. That is because a contract is not only a two party situation. All contracts have a hidden third party which is the larger society represented by the courts. If A and B have a dispute about what the contract terms really provided, where must they ultimately turn to get an answer? Courts are that third party, C, whose job it is to provide a resolution of the problem between A and B.

In the process of resolving a contract problem, can anyone realistically expect courts to use any other ground rules other than their own? The legality element of contract simply refers to those ground rules. If A and B want their agreement honored in a court of law as a valid and binding contract, that agreement must be recognized first and foremost as a legal agreement. To do otherwise would be asking a court to become a party to an agreement which contravenes the basis for its existence, its *raison d'etre*.

When a court examines an agreement for its legality component, there are three key questions which it asks:

1. Is this agreement illegal *per se*?
2. If this agreement is legal on its face, may it have an intent or consequence which is against public policy?
3. If there is an element of illegality or violation of public policy, is it a material aspect of this contract, or is the problem incidental or collateral to the agreement?

The first question is really the easiest to answer. If the agreement calls for an illegal act on its face, the agreement is void and cannot be raised to the status of a legal contract. Thus, a contract for a murder by an underworld figure cannot and will not be enforced by a court of law. The real world result might be otherwise, but that result is certainly not within the purview of legality.

The second question is much more difficult to answer in that public policy is a moving target. Courts look at the reality of these agreements, even if they appear legal on their faces. For example, a simple buy/sell agreement looks perfectly legal. But what if the agreement is designed to act as a restraint of trade by discriminating as to who can sell to whom at fixed prices? Or what if we are looking at a prenuptial agreement which looks fair on its face but gives all the property to the party against whom a divorce action is brought? Is this really just a liquidation of property or an illegal punitive measure against a party who is exercising a legal prerogative? What about an exculpatory clause which goes too far?

The third area of concern goes to the issue of enforceability once the problem area is identified. Not all illegalities are fatal to the entire contract. If a court finds that the illegality or public policy concern is not at the heart of the contract, it may still enforce the agreement, because the legality is considered collateral or incidental.

II. Hypothetical Multi-Issue Essay Question:

Bunco Bullhead (age 45) has a multitude of problems. He has long been addicted to alcohol, gambling, and questionable personal habits. These proclivities are all readily available to him at his favorite watering hole, Joe's Bar and Gambol, in his home town, Tim Buck II. Bunco particularly enjoys Joe's place because Joe provides free drinks as long as players continue to gamble. In addition, Bunco's credit limit on his Happy Card was extended to $5,000. Happy Card's motto is "Why Worry About Paying--We Don't!"

Last night Bunco got drunk and lost his newly credited $5,000 at Joe's poker table. In addition, Bunco signed a note to Joe for an additional $5,000 which he also lost. Bunco now refuses to pay both his credit card bill and his note to Joe alleging a lack of capacity and legality at the time. How do you decide?

III. Key Question Checklist:

A. Under what public policy is there a possible limitation of capacity to contract?
   1. Punishment?
   2. Protection?
   3. Statutory limitation such as a trust or corporate form?

B. Assume the limitation is imposed as a matter of protection?
   1. Is this protection based on a question of age?
      (a) Is a general limitation imposed by statute (usually age 18)?
      (b) Are there any specific exceptions to the general limitation applicable in this case?
         (1) Military enlistment contracts?
         (2) Health related contracts?
         (3) Insurance contracts?
         (4) Other special types of contracts?
      (c) Are there any common law exceptions to the general limitation applicable in this case?
         (1) Contracts for necessaries?
         (2) Contracts for marriage?
   2. Is this protection based on an issue of mental competency?
      (a) Has this person been declared legally incompetent?
      (b) If not legally incompetent, on what basis is the person claiming protection from this contract consequence?
         (1) Diminished mental capacity?
         (2) Drunkenness or drug use?
         (3) Undue influence?
         (4) Fraud?
   3. If the person is allowed to get protection from the consequence of the contract, how will that protection be granted?
      (a) Will the person be able to have the contract declared void (as in the case of a legally incompetent person)?

91

(b) Will the person be able to avoid the contract?
  (1) If so, what are the consequences to the other party?
  (2) Are they entitled to restitution?
  (3) Are they entitled to any compensation based on implied contract?

C. Is there illegality on the face of the contract?
  1. Does the contract call for any acts which are in violation of any national, state, or local statutory provision?
  2. If so, does the illegality involved go directly to the material heart of the contract, or is it incidental?
  3. Can the contract be somehow divided so as to partially enforce the legal portion without enforcing the tainted portions of the contract?

D. If the contract appears legal on its face, does it have intent or consequences which may be deemed to be in violation of a recognized public policy?
  1. Does it attempt to limit or restrict free trade?
  2. Does it contravene the laws of family relationships?
  3. Does it offend the legal process in any way?
  4. Does it seek to impose an unconscionable limitation on the rights and remedies of the other party in case of disagreements?

E. Was this agreement arrived at in good conscience?
  1. What were the relative bargaining positions of the parties?
  2. Were there reasonable alternatives available to the parties?

3. Are there any oppressive words of art or terms which deny remedies without recourse?
4. Does the value of the exchange disturb the conscience of the court?
5. If there is an objectionable provision, is it a material element of this contract, or is it incidental?
6. Can the contract be partially enforced?

IV. Objective Questions:

Terms:

1. Generally, in determining contractual capacity, the party asserting _____ of the person in question bears the burden of proof.

2. Minors are allowed to disaffirm contracts they have entered into with adults under the _____ _____.

3. A minor who enters into a contract and subsequently reaches the age of majority may _____ the contract, and in so doing, become bound by the contract.

4. When a minor chooses to leave home and live apart from her parents, this is known as _____.

5. If a person has been adjudged insane, any contract entered into by that person is _____.

6. Illegal contracts are contracts contrary to _____ or _____.

7. Licensing statutes enacted to protect the public from unlicensed persons trying to recover payment are called _____ statutes.

8. In an effort to protect goodwill, the seller of a business may enter into an agreement with the buyer not to engage in a similar business in a certain area for a certain time. Such contract provisions are

_____ _____

_____ _____.

9. A contractual provision which relieves one or both parties from tort liability for ordinary negligence is called a(n)

_____ _____.

10. To prevent enforcement of oppressive, unfair, or unjust contracts, courts developed an equitable doctrine called the

_____ _____

_____.

True/False:

1. ____A minor may disaffirm one part of the contract and enforce another part, binding the competent part.

2. ____The infancy doctrine is a subjective standard, allowing courts to examine the minor's maturity, experience, knowledge, etc.

3. ____If a minor ratifies a contract before reaching the age of majority, she is bound by the contract and can no longer disaffirm it.

4. ____Parents are never liable for any contracts entered into by their children.

5. ____Contracts by persons who are alcoholics or drug addicts are automatically voidable.

6. ____Banks and financial institutions may never be exempted from usury laws.

7. ____An exculpatory clause can relieve the parties from tort liability arising from willful conduct, recklessness, and gross negligence as well as ordinary negligence.

8. ____A person who is protected by a regulatory statute but enters into a contract that violates the statute may enforce the contract against the other party.

9. ____A contract can never be divided into legal and enforceable parts and illegal and unenforceable parts. That is, the contract must be enforced or rejected in whole.

10. ____The definition of unconscionability is an objective, standard definition which is applied uniformly in all cases.

Multiple Choice:

1. Drinker Doug entered into a written agreement to sell a parcel of land to Sober Shawn for $50,000. At the time the agreement was executed, Doug had consumed a large amount of alcoholic beverages which significantly impaired his ability to understand the nature and terms of the contracts. Shawn knew Doug was very intoxicated and that the land was valued at $125,000. Doug, now completely sober, wishes to avoid the contract. The contract is:
   A. Void.
   B. Legally binding on both parties in the absence of fraud or undue influence.
   C. Voidable at Doug's option.
   D. Voidable at Doug's option only if the intoxication was involuntary.

2. On May 1, 1993, Mint, a 16-year-old, purchased a sail boat from Sly Boats. Mint used the boat for six months at which time he advertised it for sale. Which of the following statements is correct?
   A. The sale of the boat to Mint was void, thereby requiring Mint to return the boat and Sly to return the money received.
   B. The sale of the boat to Mint may be voided by Sly at his option.
   C. Mint's use of the boat for six months after the sale on May 1 constituted a ratification of that contract.
   D. Mint may disaffirm the May 1 contract at any time prior to reaching majority.

3. Minor Matt, a 16-year-old, contracts with City Cycles to buy an $8,000 motorcycle. Which of the following is correct?
   A. The contract is voidable by Matt.
   B. The contract is void as soon as it is made.
   C. The contract is voidable by City Cycles.
   D. The contract is voidable by either Matt or City Cycles.

4. Assume the same facts as in question 3 except that it is two years later and Matt has reached the age of majority. Matt has not disaffirmed the contract and has made payments on the motorcycle while he has been 18. Which of the following is correct?
   A. The contract is void and Matt has no obligation to pay.
   B. The contract is now voidable by City Cycles.

C. Matt has ratified the contract and is now bound by it.
D. Matt has ratified the contract but is not responsible for payments from when he was a minor.

5. Insane Ida has been adjudged insane. Ida enters a contract to sell her large family estate to Swindler Sandy for $500. Which of the following is correct?
   A. The contract is voidable by Ida.
   B. The contract is voidable by Ida's legal guardian.
   C. The contract is not voidable and can be enforced.
   D. The contract is void.

6. Assume the same facts as in question 5 except Ida has not been adjudged insane, but has an impairment which makes her legally insane. Which of the following is correct?
   A. The contract is voidable by Ida.
   B. The contract is voidable by Sandy.
   C. The contract is not voidable and can be enforced.
   D. The contract is void.

7. Cleanhands Cathy hires Hitman Harry to get rid of her wealthy brother, Millionaire Mike, so that she can inherit his estate. Cathy pays Harry $5,000. Which of the following is correct?
   A. The contract is void as contrary to statute.
   B. The contract is void as contrary to public policy.
   C. The contract is voidable if Cathy disaffirms it.
   D. None of the above.

8. WallStreet Walter is being prosecuted for a white collar crime. During jury recess one day, Walter approaches one of the jurors and offers her $50,000 if she will vote for his acquittal. Which of the following is correct?
   A. The contract is void as contrary to statute.
   B. The contract is void as contrary to public policy.
   C. The contract is voidable if the juror disaffirms it.
   D. None of the above.

9. Oppressive Orville owns several commercial buildings in a large city. Startup Sam wants to open a business making handmade yo-yo's. Sam has been looking all over town but cannot find a space to rent. Orville knows rental spaces are tight right now and agrees to rent to Sam. However, Orville includes an exculpatory clause that releases him from liability resulting from his own negligence in maintaining the plumbing or wiring. Which of the following is correct?
   A. The exculpatory clause is enforceable since courts generally favor exculpatory clauses.
   B. The exculpatory clause is enforceable since renting property is an essential service.
   C. The exculpatory clause is unenforceable since there was obviously unequal bargaining power.
   D. The exculpatory clause is unenforceable since courts never enforce exculpatory clauses.

10. Wilma Widow is destroyed and heartbroken when her husband of forty-five years dies. Shyster Sherman convinces Wilma that she should employ him so that she is sure to inherit all her husband's property. Anxious and worried about the horrible possibilities Sherman described, Wilma agrees to hire him for $10,000. Which of the following is correct?
    A. Wilma can sue to recover any amount paid since this contract is void as contrary to a statute.
    B. Wilma can sue to recover any amount paid since she was ignorant of the facts.
    C. Wilma can sue to recover any amount paid since she was induced to enter the contract under duress and undue influence.
    D. None of the above.

V. Answers to Objective Questions:

Terms:

1. *Incapacity.* Note that this burden of proof can vary in difficulty depending on the basis for the claimed incapacity. Diminished capacity tends to be relative and circumstantial. Thus it is often the most difficult to prove.
2. *Infancy doctrine.* The basic theory behind the doctrine is to protect the young from contract abuses of adults.
3. *Ratify.* Ratification relates back to the inception of the contract and can be evidenced by words, acts, or even silence.
4. *Emancipation.* Even though the person may still be technically a legal minor, his or her lifestyle may show otherwise. Many young persons live on their own, get married, and even have children.

5. *Void*. Remember, there is a critical difference between void and voidable. In a void situation, no contract ever came into being in the first place. In a voidable situation, someone has a back door which allows him to get out from under the obligations of an otherwise enforceable contract.

6. *Statutes, public policy*. Both of these are sources for possible declarations of illegality in contract law.

7. *Regulatory*. Most professions are covered by such statutes ranging from lawyers and doctors to most tradespeople.

8. *Covenants not to compete*. Courts impose definite time and space limitations regarding where these covenants are allowed. Remember, these provisions are an exception to the general rule which makes anticompetition clauses illegal.

9. *Exculpatory clause*. There are limitations on when and where these clauses can be used based on equity and the court's views on procedural due process.

10. *Doctrine of unconscionability*. Even though there is no one single definition of this doctrine, look to the overall fairness of the contract process, i.e., would it be equitable to both parties to enforce the contract? The statement quoted from Chief Justice Fuller at the beginning of this chapter provides an excellent capsulation of this concept.

True/False:

1. False. A minor must disaffirm the whole contract, or none of the contract, but cannot pick and choose certain portions.

2. False. The infancy doctrine is based on an objective standard. The standard is determined by the minor's age alone.

3. False. A person is only bound by a ratified contract if she ratifies the contract after she reaches the age of majority.

4. False. Parents are liable for their children's contracts for necessaries of life that they have not adequately provided and surety contracts they sign on behalf of their children.

5. False. A person's degree of intoxication at the time a contract is made is the relevant issue. Also, if the person's mental capacity is permanently impaired, that person may be considered legally insane.

6. False. Banks and financial institutions are sometimes allowed exceptions to usury laws for loans above a certain dollar amount.

7. False. Exculpatory clauses only release the party from the liability arising from ordinary negligence.

8. True. This is an exception to the general rule of unenforcability of illegal contracts.

9. False. A court may divide the contract and enforce part while not enforcing another part.

10. False. The definition of unconscionability is flexible and varies from case to case.

Multiple Choice:

1. C. Doug lacked legal capacity when the contract was made and therefore has the power to void the contract. A is incorrect because the contract is voidable, not void. B is incorrect because Doug is not bound by the contract since he did not have legal capacity. D is incorrect because the intoxicated person may void the contract even if intoxication was voluntary.

2. D. Tom may disaffirm the contract at any time prior to reaching the age of majority. A is incorrect because the contract is voidable, not void. B is

incorrect because the adult cannot void the contract, only the minor can void it. C is incorrect because a minor cannot ratify the contract until reaching the age of majority.

3. A.   Matt may void the contract if he chooses. He may also perform the contract. City Cycles is bound by Matt's decision. B is incorrect because the contract is voidable, not void. C is incorrect because City Cycles does not have any options here. D is incorrect for the same reason as C.

4. C.   Matt can ratify the contact by his conduct. Since he did not disaffirm the contract and has continued to pay, he has ratified and is now bound by the contract. A is incorrect because the contract is not void. B is incorrect because once ratified, the contract is not voidable. D is incorrect because ratification relates back to the date of the contract.

5. D.   Once a person is judged insane, any contracts entered into are void. A through C are incorrect because the contract is void, not voidable.

6. A If a person is legally insane, but not adjudged insane, contracts entered into by that person are voidable, but not void.

7. A.   This is a contract to commit a crime which is void as against a criminal statute. B is incorrect because, although this is against public policy, the specific issue is the statute. C is incorrect because the contract is already void regardless of what Cathy does.

8. B.   Contracts that obstruct the legal process are void as against public policy. A is incorrect because this is a public policy issue, not a statutory issue. C is incorrect because the contract is void regardless of what the juror does.

9. C.   Exculpatory clauses that result from unequal bargaining power are generally unlawful. A is incorrect because the clause will not be enforced, and courts do not generally favor exculpatory clauses. B is incorrect because it is not applicable in this situation. D is incorrect because courts do, sometimes, enforce exculpatory clauses.

10. C.   Wilma entered into this contract when she was under extreme duress from her husband's death and Sherman's pressure. Such contracts are illegal. A is incorrect because this is not a statutory issue. B is incorrect because she was not ignorant of the facts.

VI.   Key Question Checklist Answers to the Essay Question:

A&B.   *Under what public policy is there a possible limitation, and assuming the limitation is imposed as a matter of protection, should that protection be accorded in this case?*

The public policy under which Bunco is seeking exemption from the consequences of his agreements with Joe and Happy Card is protection based on diminished capacity. Even though Bunco may be a certified member of both Alcoholics and Gamblers Anonymous, that fact alone will not give him a basis for avoiding contract. Because he has not been declared legally incompetent, the presumption of legal competency will stand until he can prove diminished capacity. If he can show that Joe knew Bunco had these weaknesses and took advantage of him by weakening his resistance with more alcohol, he may be able to show undue influence.

If Bunco was able to convince a court that his capacity was, in fact, lost due to undue influence, he would be able to avoid the legal consequences of his note with Joe. He would probably still have to pay Happy Card because it did not exert any undue influence over him. Bunco does have an uphill battle here. His intoxication was voluntarily induced, and if Bunco was snookered in more ways than one, he really has no one to blame but himself.

C. *Is there any evidence of illegality on the face of the contract?*

Assuming that Joe's Bar and Gambol is duly licensed to do business as a gaming and drinking establishment, there appears to be no illegality on its face.

D. *Does the contract have an illegal intent or consequence?*

It does not appear to violate public policy as presented in this case.

E. *Was this agreement arrived at in good conscience?*

On this issue it can be argued by Mr. Bullhead that unconscionable methods were used to reduce his mental capacities, and that behavior should now render the contracts unenforceable. As was mentioned earlier in this answer, this argument will most likely fail because his intoxication was voluntarily induced. In addition, he was fully aware of the practice before he even set foot in good old Joe's. As the old saying goes: "It comes with it!"

CHAPTER 13

GENUINENESS OF ASSENT

He is not deemed to give consent who is under a mistake.

Latin legal phrase

I. Overview:

The first set of defenses to the enforcement of contracts in this chapter revolves around the issue of free will. Where free will is compromised, mutual assent is also compromised, and the agreement may not stand as a contract. What makes this area of the law difficult it that courts and juries are asked to exercise 20/20 hindsight when looking back on how the parties were thinking as they were embarking on the road to contract formation. The subjectivity of measuring intent has always been a troublesome puzzle to unravel; yet without it, the objective facts placed before a court may not show the reality of consent. Because of the potential harshness of a bad contract, courts want to be very sure that the assent element of contracts is just that--free and real consent to the agreement.

Factors which mitigate or diminish the genuineness of assent can be tracked on a scale of incremental culpability. At the bottom of the scale is an innocent mistake which an be either unilateral of bilateral. In a contract mistake, one or both of the parties is acting under an erroneous belief about some aspect of the contract. Normally, if only one (unilateral) of the parties is mistaken, there will be no grounds for rescission unless that mistake is coupled with some sort of bad faith or abuse on the part of the nonmistaken party, i.e., one step further up the culpability ladder.

Where the mistake is mutual (bilateral), either party may seek rescission if the mistake is considered material, i.e., so important that no real meeting of the minds ever occurred.

The next increment up the slope of culpability is found in the area of misrepresentation or concealment. The shade of gray turns darker when a person is actively seeking to mark the cards or pass them under the table. Here we can see that freedom of assent is even further compromised than in mistake alone. Now the element of *scienter* (guilty mind) enters the picture, and the grounds for rescission are greatly increased. If the misrepresentation is material, known to be so by the maker, made with the intent to deceive, and is justifiably relied upon by an innocent and injured party, then the elements of fraud are in place. With a finding of fraud, the injured party may seek rescission and/or civil damages. In addition, the state may choose to prosecute the wrongdoer under the penal code. Contract fraud not only sits at the top of the culpability scale but can also be found at the top of the charts on the most popular white collar criminal list. Its many permutations can be found in virtually all aspects of commercial activity, and as with so many areas of criminal behavior, the consumer pays the ultimate cost of these crimes through passed on costs for insurance, credit, and any number of other services undermined by these sorts of activities.

Another highly sensitive area of mutual assent is found in the law of undue influence. Undue influence involves taking away a person's free will through any manner of physical, emotional, or psychological manipulation. It can happen in any relationship, and where it is alleged, the person claiming to be the victim of undue influence has the burden of proof in showing the alleged duress. One important exception to this general rules involves persons who act in a fiduciary role. Fiduciary is a term derived from the Latin word *fides* meaning faith, honesty, confidence, or trust. A person in a fiduciary role is entrusted with acting for the benefit of another. Most professionals in law, accounting, the healing arts, and business find themselves in fiduciary rules to one degree or another. As for the fiduciary, the burden of proof is now reversed. In dealing with their respective clients, patients, or beneficiaries, a contract is presumed to be under undue influence, and the burden of proof is on the fiduciary to show that the transaction is as arm's length, i.e., fairly arrived at. Most all of the so-called "learned professions" have codes of conduct and canons of ethics designed to address issues of this sort.

II. Hypothetical Multi-Issue Essay Question:

Refer back to the essay question in Chapter 5. In that question our protagonists were Gabby and Crabby. Gabby was injured in an auto accident involving Mario and the City of Boulder. Remember also what happened to poor Gabby. He died after having been successfully operated on by a very tired Dr. Franklin Pierce. The issues involving possible tort liabilities were reviewed in Chapter 5. We now revisit the problem to review the genuineness of assent issue in the agreement made between Crabby and Dr. Pierce.

Remember the circumstances under which the agreement was entered into. Crabby implored and exhausted Dr. Pierce to perform the operation in spite of his weariness. She promised him $50,000 to perform the operation. Her state of mind at the time of the promise was one of extreme panic and fear for her husband's life. Dr. Pierce professionally completed the operation and seeks the agreed-upon compensation for services rendered. Crabby now claims her assent was not genuine. How do you decide?

III. Key Question Checklist:

A. Was the agreement entered into on the basis of any mistaken fact?
1. Was the mistake unilateral?
   a. If so, did the other party know of the mistake and seek to take advantage of it?
   b. Was the advantage taken conscionable?
   c. Is rescission allowable?
2. Was the mistake bilateral?
   a. If so, was it a mistake of material fact?
   b. Do one or both of the parties want rescission of the agreement?

B. Was there any misrepresentation or concealment in this transaction?
1. Was the misrepresentation or concealment of a material fact?
2. Was it intentional or unintentional?
3. Was it justifiably relied upon to the detriment of the other party?
4. What are the consequences?
   a. Are there grounds for rescission?
   b. Are there additional civil remedies available?
   c. Are there any criminal law consequences to the wrongdoer?

C. Can undue influence be used as a basis for a lack of genuineness of assent?
1. Is this a nonfiduciary relationship? If so, has the burden of proof been met by the person alleging undue influence?
2. Is this a fiduciary relationship? If so, has the fiduciary met his burden of proof to show a lack of undue influence, i.e., has the presumption of undue influence been overcome?

IV. Objective Questions:

Terms:

1. When only one party is mistaken about some aspect of a contract, this is called _____ _____. However, the mistaken party is not usually allowed to rescind the contract.

2. A fact that is important to the subject matter of a contract is known as a _____ fact.

3. When one party consciously decides to induce another party to rely and act on a misrepresentation, this is called _____.

4. If a party makes a misrepresentation with knowledge that it is false or without sufficient knowledge of the truth, this is called _____.

5. When one party threatens to do some wrongful act unless the other party enters a contract, this is called _____.

6. An action to undo the contract is called _____.

7. When a person is deceived as to the nature of his or her act and does not know what he or she is signing, this is mostly like to be _____ _____ _____.

8. If both parties know the object of the contract, but are mistaken about its value, this is called a _____ _____ _____ _____.

9. When a person is deceived as to what he is signing, this is _____ _____ _____ _____; while _____ _____ _____ _____ occurs when a party has been fraudulently induced to enter a contract.

10. Where one person takes advantage of another's weakness and unduly persuades that person to enter into a contract, this is called _____ _____.

True/False:

1. ____Either party may rescind the contract if there is a mutual mistake in value.

2. ____Where a party has been fraudulently induced to enter a contract, the innocent party can either rescind the contract or enforce the contract and sue for damages.

3. ____To be actionable, a fraudulent misrepresentation must be in spoken or written words.

4. ____Where there is fraud in the inception, the contract is voidable by the innocent party.

5. ____Fraud by concealment occurs when one party fails to disclose a fact.

6. ____If the nonmistaken party knew (or should have known) of the other party's mistake, the nonmistaken party cannot enforce the contract.

7. ____An ambiguity in a contract may constitute a mutual mistake of material fact and therefore make the contract rescindable by either party.

8. ___Justifiable reliance is generally found unless the innocent party knew the misrepresentation was false or so extravagant as to be obviously false.

9. ___Where one party makes an innocent misrepresentation, the aggrieved party may rescind the contract, but not sue for damages.

10. ___If a confidential relationship is found, a contract that benefits the dominant party is presumed to be entered into under undue influence.

Multiple Choice:

1. Ted enticed Fred to enter into a sales contract by intentionally telling Fred certain material facts which Ted knew were untrue. Assume no other relevant facts. On what legal basis can the contract be avoided?
   A. Voidable because of undue influence, which created no real assent.
   B. Voidable because of fraud, where no real assent took place.
   C. Voidable because of duress, which prevented real assent.
   D. Voidable because of mistake, which did not allow real assent to take place.

2. Ed is an auditor for the IRS, became emotionally involved with Rhonda. At the urging of Rhonda, and fearing that she would sever their relationship, Ed reluctantly waived a tax audit settlement which was grossly unfair to the IRS, Ed's employer's best chance for rescinding this outcome is to show that Ed acted under:
   A. A lack of express authority.
   B. Duress.
   C. Undue influence.
   D. There was no consideration.

3. On June 1, Farmer Brown contracted to sell a red barn to Rancher Ron. However, unknown to either party, the barn had burned down on May 20. If Ron sues Brown for breach of contract, Brown's best defense is:
   A. Fraud.
   B. Economic duress.
   C. Mutual mistake of fact.
   D. Misrepresentation.

4. Investor Ivan contracted to buy a large area of land for housing development from Owner Ellen. Before signing the contract, Ivan asked Ellen if she knew of any reason why houses could not be built on the land. Though Ellen knew there was a difficult to discover the soil condition which would make building impossible, she said nothing. Which of the following is correct?
   A. Ellen has committed fraud by concealment.
   B. Ellen has committed an innocent misrepresentation.
   C. Ellen has committed a misrepresentation of law.
   D. Ellen has committed silence as misrepresentation.

5. Assume the facts as in question 4. Which of the following is correct?
   A. Ivan may sue for damages or rescind the contract.
   B. The contract is void.
   C. The contract is enforceable by either Ivan or Ellen.
   D. None of the above.

6. Landlord Larry threatens to evict Tenant Theresa if she does not agree to pay $600 per month in rent. However, Theresa's lease is still in effect and only requires her to pay $500 per month. Theresa is afraid she will not be able to find another place to live so she agrees to pay the extra $100 per month. Which of the following is correct?
   A. The new contract is enforceable by Larry.
   B. The new contract is void.
   C. The new contract is voidable by Theresa.
   D. None of the above.

7. Assume the same facts as in question 6 except instead of eviction, Larry threatens to beat Theresa up if she does not agree to pay $600 per month.
   A. The new contract is enforceable by Larry.
   B. The new contract is void.
   C. The new contract is voidable by Theresa.
   D. None of the above.

8. Andy Agent entered into an insurance contract which contained a substantial arithmetical mistake in favor of the insured. Agent asserts mistake as a defense of his nonperformance. Agent will prevail:
   A. Only if the mistake is found to be mutual.
   B. Only if the error was not caused by his negligence.
   C. If the error was unilateral and the other party knew of it or should have known of it.
   D. If the contract was drafted by the other party.

9. In which of the following types of misrepresentation may the innocent party *not* usually rescind the contract?
   A. Fraud in the inception.
   B. Fraud in the inducement.
   C. Silences as a misrepresentation.
   D. Misrepresentation of law.

10. Mary contracts to sell an old ring she found in her basement to Jane for $15. Unknown to either Mary or Jane, the ring is a rare stone which is worth $7,000. Jane has the ring appraised and tells Mary the ring's true value. Which of the following is correct?
    A. Mary may rescind the contract.
    B. Jane may enforce the contract.
    C. The contract is void.
    D. None of the above.

V. Answers to Objective Questions:

1. *Unilateral mistake.* Rescission is allowed only under limited circumstances where the unilateral mistake is tied in with other parties' actual or constructive knowledge of the mistake, where there are clerical or mathematical errors, or where enforcement would lead to an unconscionable result.

2. *Material.* Look at the essential purpose of the contract when trying to identify material facts, i.e., but for this element, would the parties be in this contract at all?

3. *Fraud.* The elements of fraud are intentional false misrepresentation by the wrongdoers coupled with justifiable reliance by the injured innocent party.

103

4. *Scienter*. This term is derived from the Latin work meaning "to know." In addition to contracts, this term is often used in the definition of numerous crimes.

5. *Duress*. In identifying this element, look for situations where wrongful acts or threats are used to take away another's free will to act or make a contract.

6. *Rescission*. This amounts to an "unmaking" of the contract, i.e., relieving the parties of any obligations under the contract.

7. *Fraud in the inception*. Such contracts are void rather than just voidable.

8. *Mutual mistake in value*. The contract remains enforceable by either party because the subject matter of the contract is not at issue.

9. *Fraud in the inception; fraud in the inducement*. As compared to a void agreement in the use of fraud in the inception, fraud in the inducement allows the innocent party to avoid the contract if she chooses, because she knew what she was signing but was fraudulently induced at the time to sign.

10. *Undue influence*. This may occur in any relationship and calls for the person alleging undue influence to show the burden of proof. The burden is reversed if a fiduciary or confidential relationship is involved.

True/False:

1. False. Generally, the contract remains enforceable by either party because the identity of the subject matter of the contract is not at issue.

2. True. The innocent party in such a situation has an option of doing either of these things.

3. False. A misrepresentation may occur by the party's conduct.

4. False. Contracts where there has been fraud in the inception are void rather than just voidable.

5. False. Fraud by concealment occurs when one party takes specific action to conceal a material fact. This goes beyond mere failure to disclose.

6. True. The law does not want to allow the nonmistaken party to unfairly take advantage of the other party's mistake.

7. True. Remember, the mistake must be material.

8. True. The law is not designed to protect the terminally stupid in all cases.

9. True. This is an attempt not to "punish" an innocent mistake.

10. True. This rule applies to fiduciaries and persons in confidential relationships.

Multiple Choice:

1. B. Ted made a false misrepresentation of a material fact with an intent to deceive. Fred detrimentally relied on this representation. Therefore, the elements of fraud are in place. A is incorrect because undue influence is the use of some sort of control which makes the decision involuntary. C is incorrect because duress is a threat which is associated with fear. D is incorrect because only mutual mistakes would make this contract voidable, and there was no showing from the facts given that a mutual mistake took place.

2. C. Here, the emotional involvement was so overwhelming that the decision was not voluntary and was the product of undue influence. A is incorrect because Ed probably had express authority to waive the audit. B is incorrect because duress is a threat which induces fear. D is

incorrect because there was probably consideration involved in the audit settlement.

3. C. Both parties were unaware of a material fact. A is incorrect because Brown did not fraudulently misrepresent the fact to Ron. B is incorrect because there was no duress.

4. D. By saying nothing when Ivan asked a direct question, Ellen has committed silence as misrepresentation. A is incorrect because fraud by concealment requires specific action to conceal something, not just failure to disclose. B is incorrect because Ellen did not make a statement of fact that she reasonably believed. C is incorrect because the soil condition is not a matter of law.

5. A. Ivan has the option of either suing for damages or rescinding the contract. B is incorrect because Ivan may enforce the contract if he chooses, so it is not void. C is incorrect; Ellen may not enforce the contract.

6. C. Because Theresa entered into this contract under duress, she may void the contract. A is incorrect because Larry may not enforce a contract when he used duress to induce Theresa to enter into it. B is incorrect because the contract is voidable, not void.

7. B. Where there is physical duress, the contract is void, not just voidable.

8. C. Here the contract may be rescinded if the mistake is material and the other party knew of it or should have known of it. A is incorrect because mutual mistake is not the only possible defense. B is incorrect because Agent might win even if the error was caused by his negligence. D is incorrect because this does not automatically create a defense if there is still harm created by the mistake.

9. D. Usually misrepresentation of law does not provide a basis for rescission of contract. All the other forms of misrepresentation do allow the innocent party to seek and get rescission of the contract.

10. B. Here, there was a mutual mistake of value. In such a situation, the contract remains enforceable by either party because the party because the identity of the subject matter of the contract is not at issue. A is incorrect because Mary cannot rescind the contract for mutual mistake of value. C in incorrect because the contract is enforceable, not void.

VI. Key Question Checklist Answers to the Essay Question:

A. *Was the agreement entered into on the basis of any mistaken fact?*

There appears to be no material mistake of fact in this problem on the part of either party. Crabby knew Dr. Pierce was tired and did not really want to operate. He, in turn, did operate in a professional manner in spite of his weariness. The fact that Gabby died anyway was not attributable in any way to how the operation was performed. As was discussed earlier in Chapter 5, the tort issues are to be resolved between Crabby and/or both Mario and the City of Boulder.

B. *Was there misrepresentation or concealment?*

There appear to be no indices of misrepresentation, concealment or fraud in this problem. Both parties entered into the agreement with "all cards on the table."

C.   *Was there undue influence?*

The doctor-patient relationship is clearly classified as a fiduciary relationship. As such Dr. Pierce has the burden of proof to show that any transaction entered into between him and his patient entered into without any undue influence.   Because undue influence is presumed, Dr. Pierce must show that the contract was entered with free and genuine consent on the part of Crabby who was acting as Gabby's agent due to Gabby's physical condition at the time.   What makes this a difficult problem for Dr. Pierce is that the price offered for the operation by Crabby ($50,000) may be higher than the normal fee charged for a comparable operation. Perhaps Dr. Pierce should have realized that Crabby was in a state of extreme agitation and told her the offer was above and beyond fair market value. It may be argued by Crabby that the excessive fee was a form of economic duress coupled with an abuse of fiduciary position.

Dr. Pierce, in turn, has a legitimate claim to some sort of fair compensation for his services. These services were delivered in a competent manner and it would be inequitable for him not to be paid, notwithstanding the fiduciary relationship. Therefore, Dr. Pierce will likely be paid for his services. The only real issue is whether he will be paid what was originally offered or only the fair market value of comparable services. The probable result lies in the latter based on equity coupled with the concern of courts about contracts which may be overly advantageous to the fiduciary.

CHAPTER 14

WRITING AND CONTRACT FORM

After all is said and done, more is said than done.

Anonymous

I. Overview:

The origins of the writing requirement for certain contracts are found in two roots: one historical and one practical. The historical root goes back to early English common law as developed under William the Conqueror and his successors. Status in that society was almost entirely measured by how much land one had control over. Being Lord of the Manor meant privilege, power, and rank. Thus contracts involving the transfer of land ownership were of utmost importance because of the bearing they had on social status. These important contracts were evidenced by highly ritualized written processes of titled transfers to land. The original title to the land was often traceable to a knight's *fief* or fee for services provided to the sovereign. From this phrase, the highest recognized ownership in land today is still called fee simple absolute.

The second root of the writing requirement is found on a more mundane level, having less to do with knights in shining armor and more with practicality. A writing is considered the best and most neutral evidence of the parties' intent at the time the agreement was entered into. The writing does not lose its memory; it does not take sides. Thus when English lawmakers wrote the Statute of Frauds, they decided the statute would serve them with the best of both worlds--impose a writing requirement on the most important contracts to act as the best evidence in a court of law.

The English version of the Statute of Frauds has been carried over to our legal system virtually intact for over three hundred years with land contracts still being the most important. All U.S. states have adopted their own versions of the statute, and they are virtually uniform in that they require contracts involving interests in land, consideration of marriage, one year plus, third party guarantees, and others to be in writing. The most significant addition to this list came with the adoption of the Uniform Commercial Code. Under the provisions of the UCC, contracts for the sale of goods for more than $500 need to be in writing. Thus, the first question which needs to be answered is: does the statute cover this contract or not?

Once you have decided the contract is covered, what are the effects of having failed to use a writing? Several possibilities may occur at this juncture. The parties may proceed to voluntarily perform the contract. But if one or both decide to assert the statute, its teeth are found in it being used as a defense to enforcement, i.e., if the party against whom contract enforcement is sought has not signed, it may not be enforced against him or her. There are equity-based exceptions to this general rule based on partial performance and promissory estoppel.

Once the contract is finally reduced to writing, the next element of the Statute of Frauds takes hold: the parol evidence rule and the exceptions to it. Think of it the parol evidence rule as being similar to Janus, the figure from Roman mythology, who was guardian of portals and patron of beginnings and endings. He faced both ways at once symbolizing his power to let in or keep out the muses. So too does the parol evidence rule acts as a guardian of the gate of contract. The exclusion face of the rule states that the writing is intended to express the final intent of the parties. All prior or contemporaneous statements must ultimately have been reflected in writing and will remain barred from the interpretation of the instrument. This provision is designed to prevent a fraudulent rewrite of the document after the fact with new evidence.

The converse is found in the exceptions to the parol evidence rule. Long ago, an anonymous legal scholar first said: "The Statute of Frauds should not be used to perpetrate frauds." The exceptions to the parol evidence rule are designed to let in additional information not shown on the original writing in certain limited circumstances. These special circumstances are grounded in public policy and simple practical necessity. Public policy provides an overriding basis in cases involving fraud, misrepresentation, deceit, bad faith, power to avoid based on age or mental capacity, duress, undue influence, and mistake. All these elements are considered in the best interest of public policy and will be allowed into evidence, notwithstanding the statute if the facts warrant it.

The second area of exception to the parol evidence rule involves the explanation of ambiguities. If the contract, as written, contains ambiguous language, parol evidence is allowable to clear the ambiguity as long as it is consistent with the original terms. The nature of the evidence allowable under this rule can range from oral statements made by the parties on up to entire standards of usage and trade used by a particular industry. This exception is particularly important to contracts covered by the UCC. Again the underlying theory is prevention of fraud. Just like Janus, fraud can be prevented by either keeping evidence in or out depending on the individual equities knocking at the contract door.

II. Hypothetical Multi-issue Essay Question:

Last week Luckie Hoyle really did get lucky. He won the Florida State Lottery and just picked up his first of fifty annual installments of $1 million. He couldn't wait to go cruising up and down the streets of West Palm Beach to show all those "old money" people that he was now on Easy Street, too. He wanted to flaunt the flashiest car he could so he went down to Palm Beach Zoomo Motors. He discussed a number of options for the new twelve cylinder Super-Zoomo he ordered. The options included a fax, full bar, and a "blow it out your ears" boombox in the trunk. These options were all listed on the order form which both he and Zoomo Motors signed. The price of the car was $300,000, and it was to be delivered in thirty days. The color of the car was listed on the form as "Look At Me Red!"

When the car arrived, Luckie was aghast. The car was a loud and obnoxious shade of pink similar the color used on houses of ill repute along Really Easy Street. Zoomo says this color is designed to call attention to the driver, and it is a shade in the red spectrum. Luckie refuses to accept delivery and Zoomo seeks enforcement of the contract. Luckie says he and the salesperson were talking about a shade similar to Italian Racing Red when they wrote the contract. Does Luckie have any defenses to the enforcement of this contract?

III. Key Question Checklist:

This checklist is designed to help students identify those factors which may indicate the existence of a possible defense to the enforcement of a contract. One of these factors is the writing requirements associated with certain contracts.

A. Does this contract come under the writing requirements of the Statute of Frauds?
   1. Does it involve an interest in land?
   2. Can the contract be performed in a one year or less?
   3. Does the main purpose of this contract promise to answer for the debt or duty of another?
   4. Is this a contract made in consideration of marriage?
   5. Is this a promise to make at will?
   6. Is this a reaffirmation of a barred debt?
   7. Is this an agent's contract for which the underlying contract would require a writing?
   8. Is this contract for the sale of goods for more than $500?

B. Even if there was a writing requirement, can one of the exceptions to that requirement be used here?
   1. Has there been some partial performance of the contract already completed?
   2. Are the elements of promissory estoppel applicable here?
      (a) Did the promise induce action or forbearance by another?
      (b) Was there reasonable and foreseeable reliance?
      (c) Would injustice result without enforcement of the promise?

C. Once you have determined that a writing is required and in place, is the writing sufficient?
   1. Have the proper formalities been met?
   2. Has the party against whom contract enforcement is sought signed?
   3. Is there any integration of any other written material involved?

D. How, when, and where should you use the parol evidence rule in this case?
   1. What evidence is now excluded under the rule?
      (a) All prior, contemporaneous, contradictory, or inconsistent evidence leading up to the contract is excluded.
   2. What evidence can now still be allowed as an exception to the parol evidence rule?
      (a) Public policy based exceptions:
         (1) Fraudulent inducements.
         (2) Misrepresentations.
         (3) Duress.
         (4) Undue influence.
         (5) Mistake.
         (6) Deceit.
         (7) Bad faith.
         (8) Proof of age or mental capacity power of avoidance.
      (b) Allowable consistent evidence which clears up ambiguities on the face of the contract:
         (1) Prior statements or writings made by the parties.
         (2) Usage or trade in the industry.
      (c) Are there any limitations on exceptions to the parol evidence rule imposed in this contract by a merger or integration clause?

IV. Objective Questions:

Terms:

1. A given or required right to use someone's land without owning or leasing it is called an _____.

2. The doctrine that allows the court to order an oral contract for the sale of land to be specifically performed if performance is necessary to avoid injustice is called the _____ _____ doctrine.

3. A promise where one person agrees to guaranty the debts or duties of another is called a _____ contract.

4. A rule that says that if a written contract is a complete and final statement of the parties' agreement, any prior or contemporaneous oral or written statements that alter, contradict, or are in addition to the terms of the written contract are inadmissible in court regarding a dispute over the contract is called the _____ _____ rule.

5. The clause in a contract that stipulates that it is a complete integration and the exclusive expression of the agreement and that parol evidence may not be introduced to explain, alter, contradict, or add to the terms of the contract is called a _____ clause.

6. Land as well as buildings, trees, soil, minerals, timber, and other things permanently affixed to the land is called _____ property.

7. An interest in land for a person's lifetime which is transferred to another party on that person's death is a _____ _____.

8. Where the main purpose of a transaction and an oral collateral contract is to provide pecuniary benefit to the promisor or guarantor, and the collateral contract is treated like an original contract and does not have to be in writing to be enforced, this is called the _____ _____ _____.

9. The rule that requires that all agent's contracts to sell property must be in writing to be enforceable is called _____ _____ _____.

10. When a contract contains some but not all of the terms of the parties' agreement, this is called _____ _____.

True/False:

1. ____ If an oral contract that should have been in writing under the Statute of Frauds is already executed, either party can rescind the contract.

2. ____ The doctrine of past performance applies to both partially performed and executory contracts.

3. ____ The one year period of the Statute of Frauds begins to run on the day one of the parties begins performance of the contract.

4. ____ The Statute of Frauds requires a written contract be signed by the party against whom enforcement is sought.

5. ____ Parol evidence is permitted to show a contract is void or voidable, to explain ambiguities, and to correct obvious clerical or typographical errors.

6. ____ Contracts to construct buildings or insure buildings do not have to be in writing under the Statute of Frauds because no ownership interest in the real property is being transferred.

7. ____ Both implied and express easements have to be in writing under the Statute of Frauds.

8. ____ To be an enforceable contract, the entire writing must be in one document.

9. ____ The parties to a written contract may stipulate that their contract is a complete integration and that parol evidence may not be introduced at all.

10. ____ To be legally binding, a written contract does not have to be drafted by a lawyer or formally typed.

Multiple Choice:

1. Many unwritten contracts which fall outside the Statute of Frauds are enforceable. Which of the following is an example of such a contract?
   A. A unilateral contract because such an agreement is formed and executed at the same time.
   B. A C.O.D. contract.
   C. A lease of office space for seven years with an option for three more.
   D. A school principal's agreement entered into on June 1 with a lunchroom supervisor for employment to begin August 31 and end on May 31.

2. Portia Purson is trying to introduce oral evidence in court to explain or modify a written contract she had with Bonnie Banks. Bonnie has pleaded the parol evidence rule. In which of the following circumstances will Purson not be able to introduce the oral evidence?
   A. The alleged modification was made several days after the written contract was executed.

   B. There was a mutual mistake of fact and also a unilateral mistake by Purson that is known by Bonnie.
   C. The oral evidence is introduced to clarify the meaning of a term used in the written contract.
   D. The contract indicates that it was intended as the entire contract between the parties, and Purson's point is covered in detail.

3. USA Lumber Co. contracts to buy all the timber on a large area of land. Which of the following is correct?
   A. The contract must be in writing only if the contract will take more than one year.
   B. The contract must be in writing because timber attached to the land is real property.
   C. The contract need not be in writing since timber is merely a fixture.
   D. None of the above.

4. Hardware Co. verbally contract to buy $2,000 worth of hammers from Heavy Duty Co. Heavy Duty delivers $300 worth of the hammers and sends a bill for $300. Hardware Co. seeks to avoid the contract, alleging that it is unenforceable under the Statute of Frauds. Which of the following is correct?
   A. Under the doctrine of promissory estoppel, the court may order Hardware to complete the contract.
   B. Under the doctrine of part performance, the court may order Hardware to complete the contract.
   C. Under the equal dignity rule, Hardware must pay $300.
   D. None of the above.

111

5. Ann makes a written contract with Betty to sell her car for $5,000. Two days later, Betty asks if Ann will throw in the bike rack with the car. Ann agrees. Which of the following is correct?
   A. The sale of the bike rack is enforceable if the contract has a merger clause.
   B. The sale of the bike rack is enforceable if the contract is a form contract.
   C. The sale of the bike rack is unenforceable under the parol evidence rule.
   D. The sale of the bike rack is unenforceable under the equal dignity rule.

6. A written agreement was signed by both parties which was intended to be their entire agreement. The parol evidence rule will prevent the admission of evidence which is offered to:
   A. Explain the meaning of an ambiguity in the written contract.
   B. Establish that fraud had been committed in the formation of the contract.
   C. Prove the existence of a contemporaneous oral agreement which modifies the contract.
   D. Prove the existence of a subsequent oral agreement which modifies the contract.

7. Employee Edgar received a verbal offer of employment from Competitive Co. for a year and a half. However, after a few months, Competitive laid off Edgar for economic reasons. Edgar is suing Competitive Co. for lost wages. Which of the following is true?
   A. Edgar will lose because such a contract must be signed by both parties to be enforceable.
   B. Edgar will win because contracts for employment are not covered by the Statute of Frauds.
   C. Edgar will win because Edgar's partial performance is a substitute for a written agreement.
   D. Edgar will lose because the contract needed to be in writing.

8. Homeowner Henry contracts with Broker Bob to have Bob sell his house. Which of the following is correct?
   A. The contract must be in writing only if Bob will be employed for more than one year.
   B. Under the equal dignity rule, the contract must be in writing.
   C. Under promissory estoppel, the contract must be in writing.
   D. The contract must be in writing only if Bob's commission will be greater than $500.

9. Supportive Sam phoned Lender Lena and told her that, if she would loan money to Needy Nel, he would pay Lena back if Nel could not. Which of the following is correct?
   A. Sam made a secondary promise.
   B. Sam made a primary promise.
   C. Sam made a joint promise.
   D. None of the above.

10. Under a contract for the sale of land, the Statute of Frauds:
   A. Requires that the entire agreement be in one single document.
   B. Requires the purchase price be fair.
   C. Does not apply if the land's value is less than $500.
   D. Does no require the agreement be signed by all parties.

112

V. Answers to Objective Questions:

Terms:

1. *Easement.* Easements are considered to be interests in real estate for purposes of the writing requirements imposed by the Statute of Frauds.
2. *Part performance.* When examining these cases, look for elements of good faith material reliance on the part of the person seeking to use this exception to the writing requirements of the Statute of Frauds.
3. *Collateral (or guaranty).* The most common example of this sort of contract is found in promises made by a parent to back up agreements entered into by their children with third parties.
4. *Parol evidence (rule).* The parol evidence rule keeps evidence out unless the evidence qualifies under one of its exceptions based on public policies or clarification of ambiguities.
5. *Merger.* In spite of the wide spread use of these clauses, they cannot be used to keep out public policy exceptions to the parol evidence rule.
6. *Real property.* This classification is based on traditional case law combined with statutory definitions. These issues will be further detailed in the chapters on real and personal property.
7. *Life estate.* Upon the death of the life tenant, the property passes to the holder of the remainder interest or back to the grantor by reversion. Life estates are a commonly used planning devise.
8. *Leading object exception.* This exception to the writing requirement is used in contracts involving promises for the debt of another. It is also known as the "main purpose" rule.
9. *Equal dignity rule.* This is an umbrella-type provision which extends the coverage of the Statute of Frauds requirement to contracts closely related to agreements which are already covered by the statute.
10. *Partial integration.* Parol evidence may be allowed to fill in the gaps if the parties have not fully integrated their agreement in the original document.

True/False:

1. False. If such a contract has already been executed, neither party can rescind the contract on the ground of noncompliance with the Statute of Frauds.
2. False. The doctrine of past performance applies only to partially performed contracts.
3. False. This period begins to run the day after the contract is made, regardless of when performance begins.
4. True. Ordinarily, both parties will sign the contract.
5. True. Those are all exceptions to the parol evidence rule.
6. True. These contracts do not fall under the equal dignity rule requirement, but as a practical matter, they too should be in writing.
7. False. Only express easements must be in writing.
8. False. Several writings may be integrated to form a single written contract.
9. True. Such an agreement is called a merger or integration clause.
10. True. Generally the law only requires that there be a written memorandum containing the essential terms of the parties agreement. These writings can be, and often are, quite informal.

113

Multiple Choice:

1. D. Contracts which may be performed within one year, beginning the day after and ending on the anniversary of the day the contract was entered into are not covered by the Statute of Frauds and need to be in writing. Here, the contract could be performed within one year. A is incorrect because unilateral contracts are not necessarily formed and executed at the same time. B is incorrect because C.O.D. is a shipping term. C is incorrect because such a lease is an interest in real property. Therefore, such a contract must be in writing.

2. D. The parol evidence rule protects written contracts, intended to be complete, from the substitution of a new and different agreement. A is incorrect because the rule allows oral evidence of a subsequent agreement. B is incorrect because the rule allows oral evidence to show the existence of a mutual mistake regarding the contract or a unilateral mistake by one party that is known by the other. C is incorrect because the rule allows oral evidence to explain the meaning of terms used in the contract.

3. B. Timber, attached to the land, is real property. A is incorrect because the Statute of Frauds applies here regardless of how long the contract will take. C is incorrect because timber is real property, not a fixture.

4. A. Under promissory estoppel, a court may order partial or complete performance of the contract to avoid an unjust result against Heavy Duty. B is incorrect because the doctrine of part performance applies to contracts for real property. C is incorrect because the equal dignity rule applies to agents who sell real property.

5. C. The written contract for the sale of the car is the final statement of the parties' agreement. Verbal testimony will not be allowed to alter such a contract except in special circumstances. A is incorrect because a merger clause explicitly disallows any parol evidence. B is incorrect because whether this is a form contract is irrelevant in this case. D is incorrect because the equal dignity rule applies to agents for the sale of real property.

6. C. If the contract was intended to be their entire agreement, the rule will not allow evidence to show a contemporaneous oral agreement which modifies the contract. A is incorrect because the rule allows evidence to explain the meaning of ambiguous words or phrases. B is incorrect because the rule allows evidence to prove fraud. D is incorrect because subsequent oral agreements may be proven under the rule.

7. D. The employment contract was for more than one year and must therefore be in writing to be enforceable. A is incorrect because the Statute of Frauds does not require that both parties sign the contract. B is incorrect because employment contracts for greater than one year are covered by the Statute of Frauds. C is incorrect because the doctrine of partial performance is not applicable to employment contracts.

8. B. Agents who sell real property must have a written contract with the other party. A is incorrect because here, the length of Bob's employment is irrelevant. C is incorrect because promissory estoppel does not require writing and is not applicable here. D is incorrect because the amount of the commission is irrelevant when the contract is for such an agent.

114

9. **A.** Such a promise to pay the debts of another if that person fails to perform is called a collateral or secondary promise.

10. **D.** The Statute of Frauds requires contracts for the sale of land to be in writing and to be signed by the party against whom enforcement is sought, not necessarily all parties. A is incorrect because there may be several integrated writings. B is incorrect because the purchase price is not addressed by the Statute of Frauds. C is incorrect because contracts for the sale of land must be in writing regardless of the amount paid.

VI. Key Question Checklist Answers to the Essay Question:

A&B. *Does the contract come under the writing requirements of the Statute of Frauds?*

This contract appears to be one of the types of contracts specifically covered by the modern version of the Statute of Frauds. The UCC has specifically added a writing requirement for contracts involved in the sale of personal property valued at $500 or more. The auto is classified as personal property, and the sales price of $300,000 more then adequately covers the $500 minimum amount.

C. *Once you have determined that a writing is required and in place, is the writing sufficient?*

The instrument involved in this contract appears to meet the basic requirements of the statute. The proper formalities have been met, and it has been signed by both parties to the contract. Thus, neither party can claim as a basis for nonenforcement a failure to sign by the party to be charged. There appears to be no attempted integration of any other writings into this contract.

D. *How and when should you use the parol evidence rule in this case?*

The parol evidence rule would keep out any prior or contemporaneous evidence not found in the writing. For example if Luckie should now allege that what he really wanted all along was a car painted Midnight Black, that evidence would be excluded outright because of its inconsistency. There appear to be no public policy grounds upon which Luckie can claim allowance of additional terms here. He was not victimized by fraud, duress, or bad faith. If he was, then public policy would allow those factors into evidence. Luckie's best hope would be to show that he is trying to admit consistent evidence to clear up an ambiguity on the face of the contract. He can argue that he is not trying to change the color from red to black, but rather only to clarify what shade of red was really intended in this transaction. He might want to want to use standard industry color charts to show these cars usually use race-inspired shades of deep Italian Red (racing colors of Italy), rather than cosmetics-based shades of pink. In addition, there appears to be no merger or integration clause which would bar him from introducing such evidence.

If Luckie should get lucky twice and get another car in Real Italian Racing Red he should then remember the first rule of Italian driving: "What's behind you is behind you!," and drive off into the West Palm Beach sunset laughing all the way to the bank.

CHAPTER 15

THIRD PARTY RIGHTS AND DISCHARGE OF CONTRACTS

There are only two mistakes one can make along the road to truth: (1) not going all the way, and (2) not starting.

Buddha

I. Overview:

Previous chapters on the law of contracts dealt with the establishment of the respective rights and duties of two persons entering into the contracting process. As the old saying goes: "It takes two to tango." Now we are looking at the possibility of a new dance partner cutting in. As at the high school prom, this new participant may not always be a welcome sight! Yet the rules of contract, like dance floor etiquette, require that third parties be allowed to join the dance where proper circumstances are in place. This chapter reviews those situations which allow a new dancer onto the floor and describes what legal tune plays for him.

Third parties can become involved in a contract *ab initio* (from its inception) or after the fact. Contracts with third party involvement from the beginning are generically labeled intended beneficiary contracts. These contracts are broken down to into two subcategories: donee and creditor. The donee beneficiary contract is probably the one most students will be familiar with and most likely to be a participant in. Consider what happens when records of new born infants are filed with local authorities. The insurance industry has long used this source of public information to notify the new parents that the party's over. They must now act like responsible citizens and provide for their young in case any unforeseen calamity befalls them. Thus, insurance is taken out for young Junior as beneficiary of his parent's insurance policy even though Junior has not paid for the policy, does not yet have the personal capacity to enter into contracts, and is really only concerned with staying dry and his next meal. He is now a third party intended (donee) contract beneficiary. And if his rights have vested under the contract, the contract cannot be altered, canceled, or rescinded without his consent. Other examples of third party donee beneficiaries can be found in trusts and contracts to make a will.

The second category of intended third party beneficiaries is found in the law of creditors rights. When there is a preexisting debtor/creditor relationship, that relationship may act as the basis for a second contract where the named creditor beneficiary may be protected as an intended beneficiary. For example, suppose A borrows money from B to buy a car, and the car is used as collateral for the loan. B can now be named as a loss-payee (a person named in the policy to be paid in case of loss) up to the amount owed, even though B has not paid for or been a signatory to the insurance policy between A and his or her insurance company.

The third category, incidental beneficiaries, are not really intended beneficiaries at all but rather wallflowers in the contract dance. The law is very straightforward on this point: if you do not qualify as an intended beneficiary based on donee or creditor grounds, you are classified as an incidental beneficiary and will not have any legally recognized standing to sue for protection under the contract. There is one minor exception to this rule in certain government contracts. Ordinarily, a taxpayer who objects to these contracts is classified as an incidental beneficiary, with no standing to sue, unless he or she can show that they belong to a class for whose primary and immediate benefit the government contract was made. For example, a taxpayer who is charged a special assessment for a sidewalk repair in front of his house may have standing to sue if the sidewalk repair was defective.

The second major category of third party involvement in contracts is the introduction of a third party after the contract has already been formed. This third party joins the dance by way of assignment or novation. In assignment, one of the original parties transfers rights or duties to a new third party participant. Compare this with a novation, derived from the Latin *nova*, meaning new. In a novation, the original contract with A and B is ended when a new contract is entered into between one of the original parties and a new party, C. The most common example is found in the assumption of mortgage obligations. In these forms of after-formation involvement of third parties, the law of assignment is far more important. Public policy in the law of contracts favors the transferability of contract rights and duties. There are, however, situations where this general rule does not apply and consent of the other parties is required for a valid transfer. These include situations involving personal services, creditworthiness, trust, and/or fiduciary relationships. In addition, such transfers may barred or limited by the agreement itself or by statute. In any event, if there is a material change of risk in the obligations covered by the agreement, limitations are likely to apply vis-a-vis the transferability of rights and duties under the contract. Consider the world of finance, commodities, and the like. All of these commercially critical practices are facilitated by the transfer of contract rights from one person or business entity to another.

The second objective of this chapter is to examine the basic rules with regard to the discharge of contracts. The rules of performance and breach of contract are rooted in common sense. Most contracts are completed legally when the parties have lived up to their reciprocal obligations under that contract. Conversely, a breach is found when a failure of performance is not somehow excused by law. We are expected to live up to our performance obligations and no more. If those obligations are not met, breach of contract is the result.

The evaluation process of contract performance issues is best broken down into time sequence subparts: precontract, during the contract, and postcontract. In precontract issues, what are the covenants entered into before performance is to be initiated? Were there any conditions which may affect the rights and duties of the parties to contract? Conditions are certain events which have a triggering effect on the obligations of contract. The timing of conditions can be superimposed upon the contract. A precondition or condition precedent calls for the event to take place before the contract goes into effect. For example: "I will buy this car if my mechanic signs off on the engine inspection." A concurrent condition calls for two or more events to coincide in time. Consider an escrow where a third party is used as a holder of property and is instructed to act vis-à-vis that property only upon satisfaction of mutually dependent acts of third parties. This is a common form of property transfer used in the sale of real estate. The escrow holds the deed to the property from the seller until the buyer has delivered the purchase price in a form acceptable to both parties. A condition subsequent is found where performance may be excused by a certain event after the contract was entered into. For example, a parolee is

117

allowed to stay out of prison as long as the conditions of the parole release are met.

There are certain circumstances which will act to excuse nonperformance. These circumstances are also based in common sense. Can it really be reasonable to expect personal service contracts to be enforced after death or disability? Or does it make sense to accept performance after destruction of a unique subject matter of the contract? For example, if you bid millions of dollars for a Van Gogh's "Irises" at an auction, and it was destroyed by lightning, is it reasonable to expect the seller to come up with an exact duplicate? A third form of excuse is found in subsequent illegality. If a contract was legal at time it was formed, but subsequent events have made its enforcement illegal, courts will no longer enforce its performance covenants based the new illegality.

In addition to excused nonperformance, there are a number of possible circumstances which may result in a discharge from any further contractual performance. These fall into two main categories: discharge by acts of the parties or by operation of law. Discharge by acts of the parties are voluntary postcontract formation events such as mutual recission, reformation, accord and satisfaction, a substituted contract, or novation. In all these scenarios, the parties have, in effect, reentered the bargaining and created a new deal.

In an operation of law discharge, something has happened where the court steps in and declares this contract performance obligation can no longer be enforced. Examples of such legal impediments to enforcement would include the running of a statute of limitation or bankruptcy. In both cases, any further performance under the contract has been legally ended. If, however, the contract duty has not been discharged, excused, or performed, and the absolute duty to perform has been breached, one must examine what remedies are available to the nonbreaching party.

II. Hypothetical Multi-issue Essay Question:

Mr. Daro Cepheus was a star in the world of high finance and was in line for a big promotion at Bailout Bank when he found out he was passed over by Ms. Mydras Volans. Her star shone even brighter, and Daro decided not to get mad, but get even. Daro devised an intricate method of selling the same corporate bond all over the world to multiple investors.

He would make multiple sales by having the original certificates held at the bank and send out facsimiles and tell investors the reasons for the delay in sending the originals was due to the postal service. In the meantime, investors from Chad, Mongolia, Japan, France, and Hong Kong, in that order, all sent him $1 million each, for the same bond. Daro is now watching sunsets in Rio while the investor in Hong Kong was the first to smell a rat and contact Bailout Bank. Assuming Daro cannot be found, what are the legal consequences to the remaining parties involved?

III. Key Question Checklist:

This checklist is designed to help students classify which form of third party contract is being examined and to help students ascertain the respective rights and duties of each party in the contract.

A. Does this contract create third party beneficiary rights at the time of its formation?
1. Does this third party qualify as an intended beneficiary?
   (a) Is this person a donee beneficiary?
   (b) Is this person a creditor beneficiary?
   (c) Have this person's rights vested under this contract?
      (1) If the rights of the intended beneficiary have vested, what are the legal consequences to the original parties to the contracts?
2. Is this person not qualified as an intended beneficiary?
   (a) If the person is deemed to be an incidental or unintended beneficiary, can he still be protected by an exception to the general rule?
   (b) What are the legal consequences to the original parties if this person is found to be an incidental beneficiary?

B. Is this contract subject to involvement of third parties after the time of its formation?
1. Is this contract subject matter limited vis-à-vis assignability?
   (a) Is it a personal service contract?
   (b) Is it an assignment of future rights?
   (c) Would an assignment alter the risks agreed upon in the original contract?
   (d) Is this an assignment of a legal action?
   (e) Is there an antiassignment clause?
      (1) Does an exception apply?
2. If assignment is allowable here, have the proper steps been taken?
   (a) Is there a writing requirement? Has this requirement been complied with?
   (b) Is notice required to be given to all interested parties?
      (1) What are the consequences of failure of required notice?
      (2) If the procedures of assignment have been complied with, what are the new rights and duties of:
         (aa) The original obligor?
         (bb) The original obligee?
         (cc) The new third party?
   (c) Any defenses against the original assignor which can now be carried over to the new assignee?
      (1) Fraud?
      (2) Duress?
      (3) Undue influence?
      (4) Age or mental capacity issues?
      (5) Illegality?
3. What if there were an improper multiple assignment?
   (a) Does the American Rule apply?
   (b) Does the British Rule apply?
   (c) Does the Massachusetts Rule apply?
   (d) Is there a tangible token involved?
   (e) Is this a secured transaction under the UCC?

C. Is there a novation taking place rather than an assignment?
1. Is there a new third party?
2. Does new party assume all the duties originally undertaken by the first obligee?
3. Is the first obligor absolved from any further obligations?

D. What are the basic performance covenants under this contract?

E. Are these covenants subject to any conditions?
   1. Are there any conditions precedent?
   2. Are there any concurrent conditions?
   3. Are there any conditions subsequent?
   4. Are there any excuses from enforcement of the condition?

F. Assuming no conditions are in effect, are there any excuses from enforcement of this contract?
   1. Is there objective impossibility of performance?
   2. Is there a death or disability in connection with a personal service contract?
   3. Has there been destruction of the subject matter of the contract?
   4. Is there now a supervening illegality involved in this contract?

G. Have the parties changed their performance obligations by?
   1. Mutual recission?
   2. Accord and satisfaction?
   3. Substitution?
   4. Novation?
   5. Substantial performance?
   6. Partial performance?

H. Is there an operation of law change to performance obligations under this contract?
   1. Has a statute of limitations run on enforcement?
   2. Is there any other legal impediment to enforcement?

IV. **Objective Questions:**

Terms:

1. The termination of an enforceable contract by full performance of the duties is called _____.

2. A contract entered into with the intent to confer a benefit or gift on to intended third party is called a _____.

3. A third party who is benefits unintentionally when the contract is performed is called a(n) _____ beneficiary.

4. The transfer of contractual rights is called an _____, while the transfer of contractual duties is called a _____.

5. The party owed a right under the contract is called the _____, while the party who owes a duty of performance is called the _____.

6. A clause that prohibits the assignment of rights under the contract is known as a _____ clause.

7. A clause which permits the assignment of the contract only upon receipt of an obligator's approval called a _____ clause.

8. A statement that is a constructive notice to all later assignees of the filling assignee's rights in the contract is known as a _____ statement.

9. An agreement that substitutes a third party for one of the original contracting parties and makes the new party obligated to perform the contract is called a(n) _____.

10. If the delegatee has not assumed the duties under a contract and is not legally liable to the obligee for nonperformance, this is called _____ _____ _____.

True/False:

1. ____ An intended third party beneficiary can enforce the contract against the party who promised to render performance.

2. ____ Generally, any member of the public can sue as an incidental beneficiary on contracts entered into by the government.

3. ____ If a third party intended beneficiary tries to enforce his rights under a contract, the promisor can assert only personal defenses he has against the third party beneficiary.

4. ____ The rights of an intended third party beneficiary must be vested before the beneficiary can enforce the contract against the promisor.

5. ____ Generally, if a contract is conditional upon meeting a third party's satisfaction, the courts will apply a personal satisfaction test.

6. ____ Legal actions involving both personal rights and contract rights are assignable.

7. ____ An assignor cannot partially assign his contract rights. Either the entire contract is assigned, or none of it is.

8. ____ Any successive assignee who does not obtain the assigned contractual right can sue the assignor for damages.

9. ____ A firm can delegate duties to any of its qualified employees even if the obligee places special trust in the obligor.

10. ____ A temporary impossibility excuses a party from performance if he withdraws during the time the contract performance is suspended.

Multiple Choice:

1. Ted Harley sold his moped factory to Fred Davidson. As part of the contract, Fred assumed the existing mortgage on the property held by Brewer Bank. Regarding the rights and duties of the parties, which of the following is correct?
   A. The promise by Fred need not be in writing to be enforceable by Brewer.
   B. Brewer is a creditor beneficiary of Fred's promise and may recover against him personally in the event of default.
   C. Brewer is not in privity of contract since it was not a party to the assignment.
   D. Ted has no further liability to Brewer and can not ride off into the sunset worry free.

2. Which of the following is *not* true of donee beneficiary contracts?
   A. The donee beneficiary must be identified under the contract to be conferred with a gift or benefit.
   B. The promisee is the contracting party who directs the benefit.
   C. The promisor agrees to confer performance for the benefit of the donee beneficiary.
   D. The donee beneficiary must have the capacity to enter into contracts.

3. Public policy disfavors the assignment of certain contract rights. Generally, which of the following is freely assignable?
   A. Personal services contracts.
   B. Assignment of nonexistent future rights.
   C. Assignment of existing future contract rights.
   D. Assignment of legal actions.

4. Parent owned an insurance policy on her life, on which she paid all the premiums. Daughter was named the beneficiary. Parent died and the insurance company refused to pay the insurance proceeds to Daughter. An action by Daughter against the insurance company for the insurance proceeds will be:
   A. Successful because Daughter is a third party donee beneficiary.
   B. Successful because Daughter is a proper assignee of Parent's rights under the insurance policy.
   C. Unsuccessful because Daughter was not the owner of the policy.
   D. Unsuccessful because Daughter did not pay any of the premiums.

5. Nagel and Fields entered into a contract in which Nagel was obligated to deliver certain goods to Fields by September 10. On September 3, Nagel told Fields that Nagel had no intention of delivering the goods required by the contract. Prior to September 10, Fields may successfully sue Nagel under the doctrine of:
   A. Promissory estoppel.
   B. Accord and satisfaction.
   C. Anticipatory repudiation.
   D. Substantial performance.

6. Andy and Bertha make a contract where Charles is the intended beneficiary. Charles sues Bertha to enforce his rights under the contract. Which of the following is correct?
   A. Bertha can assert any defenses she has against Andy.
   B. Bertha can assert any defenses she has against Charles.
   C. Both of the above.
   D. None of the above.

7. Assume the same facts as is question 6. Which of the following is correct?
   A. Charles' interest in the contract vested when he learned of and consented to the contract.
   B. Charles' interest in the contract vested as soon as Andy and Bertha formed the contract, before he knew of it.
   C. For Charles' interest to vest, Charles must change his position in reliance on the contract.
   D. None of the above.

122

8. Employee Ellen contracts with Calloway Co. to perform certain services for three years. However, within six months, Ellen sells her house and must move away. Which of the following is correct?
   A. Ellen is excused from performance of the contract because of the objective impossibility of performance.
   B. Ellen is excused from performance of the contract because of frustration of purpose.
   C. Ellen is not excused from the contract and is liable for damages.
   D. None of the above.

9. Developer Dan contracts with Arnie Architect to have Arnie draw up plans for a new golf course club house for $40,000. Which of the following is correct?
   A. This is a personal services contract and is therefor never assignable.
   B. Arnie can assign his right to the $40,000.
   C. Dan can prevent Arnie from assigning Arnie's right to the $40,000 as this is a personal services contract.
   D. Arnie can assign the contract since it is a future right.

10. Ellen and Fred have a contract where Ellen is to bake 100 pies for Fred's restaurant for payment of $500. Ellen bakes and delivers the 100 pies. Ellen then assigns her right to the $500 payment to Grant. Which of the following is correct?
    A. In assigning this right, Ellen can no longer sue Fred for nonperformance.
    B. Ellen and Grant can now both sue for nonperformance.
    C. Fred can sue Ellen for assigning this right.
    D. None of the above.

V. Answers to Objective Questions:

Terms:

1. *Discharge.* A discharge cancels any further obligation under a contract.
2. *Donee beneficiary.* Look for the lack of consideration.
3. *Incidental.* Most people who do not qualify as a donee or creditor beneficiary fall into this third category.
4. *Assignment, delegation.* These and the answers to question 5 are dichotomous terms which can be used as a learning tool.
5. *Obligee, obligor.* Proper identification of the terms is essential to the study of third party rights.
6. *Antiassignment.* Courts generally interpret these clauses narrowly.
7. *Approval.* Courts limit the use of such clauses.
8. *Financing.* These are provided for under the UCC.
9. *Novation.* This term is derived from the Latin term meaning "new."
10. *Declaration of duties.* Note the requirement of notice to the obligee.

True/False:

1. True. The intended beneficiary has standing to sue.
2. False. Usually, members of the public cannot sue on contracts entered into by the government since incidental beneficiaries cannot sue as third party beneficiaries.
3. False. The promisor can assert rights he has against the promisee as well as the third party beneficiary.
4. True. Sometimes the donor can change his or her mind vis-à-vis the benefits given under the contract.

5. False. If a contract is conditioned upon meeting a third party's satisfaction, courts will generally apply the objective, reasonable person test.
6. False. Legal actions involving personal rights are not assignable.
7. False. An assignor can partially assign his contract rights to one or more people.
8. True. The assignee steps into the legal shoes of the assignor and is entitled to the transfer of benefits formerly owned by the assignor.
9. True. The rule is subject to the limitations imposed by the rules of fiduciaries and personal service contracts.
10. False. A temporary impossibility excuses a party from performance only during that time. Once this circumstance is no longer exists, the party must perform.

Multiple Choice:

1. B. When a purchaser assumes an existing mortgage, the purchaser's promise to pay the mortgage creates a creditor-beneficiary relationship. A is incorrect because a mortgage is within the Statute of Frauds. C is incorrect because an intended beneficiary of a contract may sue to enforce the contract. D is incorrect because Ted is still liable to Brewer after the assignment in which there was no novation.

2. D. Often, donee beneficiaries are too young or incompetent to enter into contracts for themselves. Legal capacity is not one of the requirements of becoming a donee beneficiary.

3. C. Assignment of future rights in existing contracts are generally assignable, subject to any statutory restrictions such as laws relating to garnishment. The others are all generally limited by public policy from assignment.

4. A. Daughter was the intended third party donee beneficiary *ab initio*. There was no assignment here which makes B incorrect. C and D are incorrect because the donee beneficiary does not have to pay for or own the policy created for her benefit.

5. C. The doctrine of anticipatory repudiation is in effect because Nagel told Fields that Nagel had no intention of delivering the goods prior to the date of performance. A is incorrect because promissory estoppel acts as a substitute for consideration and is not relevant here. B is incorrect because accord and satisfaction is an agreement where a party with an existing duty of performance under a contract promises to do something other than perform the duty originally promised in the contract. D is incorrect because the doctrine of substantial performance would allow for a contract obligation to be discharged even though the performance tendered was not in complete conformity with the terms of the agreement. Here Fields is suing Nagel for breach of contract.

6. C. A is correct because Bertha can raise any defenses she has against the original party to the contract. B is correct because Bertha can raise any defenses she has against the third party beneficiary when he sues to enforce the contract.

7. A. Charles' interest can vest when he learns and consents to the contract, when he changes his position in reliance on the contract, or when he sues on the contract. B is incorrect because at this point Charles knows nothing and cannot have a vested interest. C is incorrect because changing his position in reliance on the contract is only one way for his interest to vest, not the only way.

8. C. Ellen has breached the contract and is liable for damages. A is incorrect because Ellen's inability to complete the contract is subjective, not objective. B is incorrect because the doctrine of frustration of purpose is not applicable here.

9. B. If payment of the $40,000 is all that is left to complete the contract, Arnie is free to assign this to whomever he chooses. A is incorrect because personal services contracts can be assigned if payment is all that is required or both parties agree. C is incorrect because Dan cannot control who Arnie assigns payment to. D is incorrect because this is not a future right.

10. A. Once Ellen assigns this right, Grant stands in her shoes, and she gives up the right to sue Fred. B is incorrect because Ellen cannot sue Fred. C is incorrect because Fred cannot sue Ellen for assigning the right to payment.

VI. Key Question Checklist Answers to Essay Question:

A. *Does this contract create third party beneficiary rights at the time of its formation?*

This contract did not identify any intended third party beneficiaries at the time of its creation. It did, however, anticipate that third parties would eventually become involved. The market for corporate bond obligations is such that it can be readily expected that these notes will be transferred a number of times before they have fully matured. Thus, third party involvement will come after the original bond is sold to the first buyer by way of assignment.

B. *Is this contract subject to involvement of third parties after the time of its formation?*

This sort of contract is freely assignable as a financial obligation, and any attempts to limit its transferability would be narrowly construed by the courts. The technical procedures for a required writing were complied with, but there was obvious fraud because of multiple sales of the same asset by Mr. Cepheus.

Because we have a multiple assignment here, a number of options are available to the court depending on which rule is being used in its jurisdiction. Under the American Rule, the investor from Chad would be first in line for relief. Under the British rule, the investor from Hong Kong would prevail because of his notice being given first to Bailout Bank. In addition, he can argue that the investor from Chad failed to but should have demanded physical delivery of the tangle token, the bond itself. In all likelihood, the investor from Hong Kong would therefore win. The other investors may want to consider going after Bailout Bank under an agency theory of liability for the fraud committed by its former employee.

D-H. *What are the basic performance obligations under the contract?*

The basic performance obligation was to sell only what was owned. Here, there was no act of a party or operation of law excuse for the actions taken by Mr. Cepheus.

CHAPTER 16

CONTRACT REMEDIES AND TORTS ASSOCIATED WITH CONTRACTS

The common law is nothing else but statutes worn out by time.

Sir John Eardley Wilmot

I. Overview:

As was noted in the prior chapter, we are expected to live up to our performance obligations. If these obligations are not met or somehow excused, a breach of contract is the result in the eyes of the law. There are a number of possible circumstances which may result in a discharge from any further contractual performance. These fall into two main categories: discharge by acts of the parties or by operation of law. Discharge by acts of the parties are voluntary postcontract formation events such as mutual recission, reformation, accord and satisfaction, a substituted contract, or novation. In all these scenarios, the parties have, in effect, reentered the bargaining and created a new deal.

In addition, the contract obligation may have been met and breached with less than full performance. In substantial performance, one hundred percent of the performance was not provided. If the breach was not material nor intentional, the nonbreaching party may sue for damages but not recission. For example, if a $100,000 house has the wrong door knob on it, and replacement would cost $100, the original contract can still be enforced less the price of the correct door knob. Compare this

with a house with no doors. The failure to provide doors may be construed as only partial performance of a house building contract because of lack of security. The nonbreaching party may then sue for recission or recover damages.

The first objective of this chapter is to introduce students to remedies in contract after a breach has taken place. An overview of the remedies available to the nonbreaching party in contract can be compared to the various directions posted on a map when your car has broken down. Because your trip has been brought to an abrupt halt, you must decide which options make the most sense to you. Do you try to go back where you started? Can the car be fixed where you are, or do you need a tow to your original destination? By analogy, contracts can also be brought back (recission), fixed (damages or reformation), or taken forward to their original destination (specific performance). The majority of remedies provided by the courts for contract breach fall into the category of a repair by way of monetary damages. In this repair process, there is an attempt to provide the innocent party with a financial replacement for the benefits which he or she had under the original contract.

Think of monetary damages as an ascending staircase, starting at the bottom with token or nominal damages and going all the way to punitive damages. Nominal damages are applicable where there is little real economic consequence arising from the breach. These damages are sometimes called a Pyrrhic victory, named after the victory of Pyrrhus, King of Epirus, over the Romans at Asculum in 279 B.C. The victory was so costly that the war was ultimately lost. In a nominal damage award, the winner wins in principle but not in significant economic terms.

The next step is found in compensatory or actual damages. These damages seek to restore the benefit of the bargain by providing a monetary substitute for what was lost due to the breach. For example, if Mario had a deal with Zoomo Motors for a new car priced at $20,000 and had to buy a comparable model from Zamay Motors for $30,000 due to Zoomo's breach, the actual measure of compensatory damages would be $10,000. If Mario had a resale contract for the car to A.J. for $40,000 and Zoomo knew of this second contract, Zoomo may also be liable for an additional $10,000 in consequential damages to Mario. In addition, had Zoomo's breach been related to a bad faith tort within the contract setting, punitive damages may also be granted by the court. Punitive damages are a form of court imposed civil punishment. Normally, punitive damages are not granted for a contract breach alone, but if the bad faith involved shocks the conscience of the court, tort damages may be applicable. One other damage measure possibility lies in the area of liquidated or agreed upon damages set by the parties. A court will examine these damages to make sure that they are not a disguised penalty.

The other two paths available to the nonbreaching party are going backwards or going forward with the contract. In going backwards, a court is asked to return the parties to their precontract position by way of recission or restitution, i.e., undo the contract. A common example of recission is found in return of deposit clauses in purchase contracts or in consumer protection statutes which provide for a three day cooling off period after the contract is signed. These statutes generally allow for a unilateral right of recission within the three day period.

The last category of remedies involves going forward with the original terms of the agreement. These remedies are classified as equitable remedies because the breach cannot be adequately compensated by normal economic damage measures. The underlying theory is that the contract must somehow be enforced as a matter of equity and fair play rather than substituted by money alone. Equitable remedies are traceable to the English legal history of the Court of Chancery and are found in modern day versions of specific performance, quasi-contract, and injunctive relief.

The second objective of this chapter is to look at those situations where a civil wrong, defined as a tort, is somehow associated with the contract setting in question. Ordinarily, recovery for breach of contract alone is limited to damages. However, with the addition of a contract-related tort to the equation, tort damages may also be added by courts. The major areas of concern in the contract setting are:
1. Intentional interference with contract relations.
2. Breach of implied covenants of good faith and dealing.

If the elements of these torts are found, courts may impose punitive damages far in excess of actual contract damages. Be sure to examine the *Pennzoil v. Texaco* case for a graphic illustration of this principle.

II. Hypothetical Multi-issue Essay Question:

Ms. Dee Minimis entered into a contract with Mr. Lex Loci to sell her roller skate instruction business, Derbytown Rollerball, Inc., on January 1, 1994 for $10,000. Roller skating was on the wane, and Dee wanted to get out while the getting was good. Under the terms of the contract, Dee agreed not to compete with Lex for a reasonable period of one year within a five mile radius of Derbytown's business location. In addition, the contract had a liquidated damages clause of $5000 in case the noncompetition clause was breached by Ms. Minimis. Dee took the proceeds of the sale and lost it all on the Derbytown lottery. She also realized that she made a big mistake in selling the business because of the advent of the in-line skate. She decided to establish Derbytown Superskate next door to her former place of business. She is not worried about the liquidated damages clause because of her insolvency. Lex Loci wants to sue Ms. Dee Minimis for breach of performance and asks the court for all possible remedies provided by law. What result?

III. Key Question Checklist:

A. What are the basic performance covenants under this contract?

B. Are these covenants subject to any conditions?
   1. Are there any conditions precedent?
   2. Are there any concurrent conditions?
   3. Are there any conditions subsequent?
   4. Are there any excuses from enforcement of the condition?

C. Assuming no conditions are in effect, are there any excuses from enforcement of this contract?
   1. Is there objective impossibility of performance?
   2. Is there a death or disability in connection with a personal service contract?
   3. Has there been destruction of the subject matter of the contract?
   4. Is there now a supervening illegality involved in this contract?

D. Have the parties changed their performance obligations by?

1. Mutual recission?
2. Accord and satisfaction?
3. Substitution?
4. Novation?
5. Substantial performance?
6. Partial performance?

E. Is there an operation of law change to performance obligations under this contract?
   1. Has a statute of limitations run on enforcement?
   2. Is there any other legal impediment to enforcement?

F. Has a breach of contract taken place?
   1. What was the specific performance obligation in question?
   2. Was this obligation excused or discharged?
      (a) By acts of the parties?
      (b) By operation of law?

G. Is there any agreement within the contract itself as to how any breach may be resolved?
   1. Is there any voluntary recission and/or restitution allowed?
   2. Is there any liquidated damages clause?
      (a) Is this clause fair on its face?
      (b) Was this clause fairly arrived at the bargaining process?

H. Is there any statutory provision, such as a consumer law, which would allow recission?

I. What are the possible law or monetary measures applicable in this case if liquidated damages do not apply?
   1. Nominal damages?
   2. Actual damages?
   3. Consequential damages?

4. Any punitive damages?
    (a) Was there a tort involved?
        (1) Intentional interference with contract relations?
        (2) Breach of covenant of good faith and fair dealing?
        (3) Any other tort such as deceit or fraud?

J. Do any equitable remedies apply?
    1. Specific performance?
        (a) Is this contract subject to specific performance enforcement?
            (1) Personal services contracts cannot be specifically enforced in the affirmative sense. They can be the subject of injunctive relief.
        (b) Is the remedy at law adequate?
            (1) Is the benefit of this contract unique?
        (c) Would undue hardship be created on the breaching party if the contract were to be specifically enforced?
    2. Reformation?
        (a) Should the court rewrite the contract in order to have it reflect the true intent of the parties?
    3. Quasi-contract?
        (a) Do the facts create a contract result even though an actual contract may not be in place?
        (b) What would be the appropriate measure of damages in quasi-contract?

K. Are there any contract-related torts at issue in this case?

IV. Objective Questions:

Terms:

1. Damages based on contract-related torts are generally stated as _____ damages.

2. This covenant is implied in certain types of contracts when determining the objective of the contract. It is called the covenant of _____ _____ _____ _____ _____.

3. When a party to a contract renders performance exactly as required by the contract, thereby discharging the contract, it is called _____ _____.

4. When one contracting party informs the other that he will not perform his contractual duties when due, it is known as _____ _____.

5. The nonbreaching party may recover _____ _____ compensation for injuries in the form of money.

6. When a remedy is based on the concept of fairness and includes specific performance, reformation, quasi-contract, and injunction, it is referred to as an _____ remedy.

7. This remedy compensates the nonbreaching party for foreseeable damages. The nonbreaching party must know or have reason to know that the breach will cause special damages. This remedy is called _____ _____.

8. This remedy provides that the parties may agree in advance. However, the actual damages must be difficult to determine, and the amount must be a reasonable estimate of the harm that would result from a breach. It is called _____ _____.

9. The avoidance or reduction of damages caused by a breach of contract is called _____.

10. The process of undoing a contract is called _____.

True/False:

1. _____ Punitive damages are generally rewardable for breach of contract.

2. _____ Concurrent conditions arise when there is both a condition precedent and a condition subsequent.

3. _____ Injunctions are used by courts to order the affirmative performance of certain acts.

4. _____ An accord is a completed contract to settle a contract dispute which discharges the original contract.

5. _____ The nonbreaching party may only recover monetary damages from the breaching party if the breach was material.

6. _____ Generally, only equitable remedies are available for breach of contract.

7. _____ To be liable for special damages, the breaching party must know or have reason to know that the breach will cause special damages to the other party.

8. _____ In certain circumstances, a liquidated damages clause may be considered a penalty and therefore not be enforceable.

9. _____ The nonbreaching party is under no obligation to avoid damages after a contract breach.

10. _____ If a party breaches the implied covenant of good faith and fair dealing, the nonbreaching party may be able to recover punitive, as well as other, damages.

Multiple Choice:

1. Which of the following is *not* an element of the tort of intentional interference with contract relations?
   A. A valid enforceable contract between contracting parties.
   B. Money damages must also be awarded.
   C. Third-party knowledge of the contract.
   D. Third-party inducement to breach the contract.

2. Which of the following is *not* classified as an equitable remedy?
   A. Mitigation of damages.
   B. Injunction.
   C. Specific performance.
   D. Reformation.

3. Feuding Fran and Fighting Fred have a dispute over a contract. Eventually, Fran and Fred agree that Fran will pay a reduced amount for Fred's performance of reduced duties. Which of the following is correct?

A. Fran and Fred have resolved the dispute by reaching accord and satisfaction.

B. Fran and Fred have resolved the dispute by reaching only an accord.

C. Fran and Fred have not resolved the dispute, and either party can rescind the contract.

D. Fran and Fred have not resolved the dispute, and both parties must fully perform the contract.

4. Competent Construction Co. (CCC) contracts to build a house for Yuppie Muppie. Yuppie requests that a specific type of tile be installed in the floor of the entry way. However, CCC mistakenly uses the wrong tile. Which of the following is correct?

A. CCC has committed a minor breach of the contract.

B. Yuppie can deduct the cost of installing the right tile from the contract price.

C. Yuppie can sue CCC to recover the cost to install the right tile if Yuppie has already paid CCC.

D. All of the above.

5. Builder Boris contracts to construct a large office building for Dr. Dan at a contract price of $1 million. The contract provides that all trim and doors will be made of top quality oak. However, Boris cannot tell the difference and mistakenly uses a lower quality oak. Which of the following is correct?

A. Dan can do nothing since this is only a minor breach.

B. Dan can get monetary damages even though this is a minor breach.

C. Dan can get an equitable remedy even though this is a minor breach.

D. None of the above.

6. Assume the same facts in question 5 except that before Boris begins any work, Dan rescinds the contract. Also, assume Boris's cost to complete the contract would have been $750,000. Which of the following is correct?

A. Boris can recover nothing since there has been no performance, and therefore, Boris has lost nothing.

B. Boris can recover $250,000.

C. Boris can recover $1 million.

D. Boris can only recover what he has already spent on materials.

7. Restaurateur Ralph contracts to have Custom Construction build a restaurant. The contract states that the restaurant will be completed by June 1 and has a liquidated damages clause in case the deadline is not met. However, Custom Construction falls further behind schedule, and the restaurant is not completed until September 10. Which of the following is correct?

A. The liquidated damages clause will be enforced regardless of the amount, since actual damages would be extremely difficult to determine.

B. The liquidated damages clause will not be enforced if actual damages are determined later.

C. The liquidated damages clause will not be enforced because courts almost never enforce such clauses since they are considered penalties.

D. None of the above.

8. Max contracts with Ned to sell 300 kites to Ned's Kite Shop for $1000. At the last minute, Max calls Ned and rescinds the contract. Luckily, after much searching, Ned is able to find Orville who also sells kites. Orville agrees to sell 300 kites for $1000. If Ned sues Max, which of the following is correct?
    A. Ned will be awarded consequential damages.
    B. Ned will be awarded compensatory damages.
    C. Ned will be awarded liquidated damages.
    D. Ned will be awarded nominal damages.

9. George's Garage contracts to buy $5000 worth of car parts from Susan Supplier. However, Carl's Car Shop hears of the contract and calls Susan. Carl offers Susan $6000 if she will breach the contract with George. Which of the following is correct?
    A. Carl is liable for intentional interference with contractual relations.
    B. Carl is liable for a breach of the covenant of good faith and fair dealing.
    C. Carl is not liable for any torts, but is liable for contract damages.
    D. None of the above.

10. Specific performance is used as a remedy when:
    A. The nonbreaching party cannot specifically request it.
    B. The breaching party requests it in lieu of money damages.
    C. Money damages will not suffice.
    D. None of the above.

V. Answers to Objective Questions:

Terms:

1. *Punitive.* These damages are a form of civil punishment and are used in tort law to deter the defendant from engaging in similar conduct in the future.
2. *Good faith and fair dealing.* Breach of this implied covenant results in a contract-related tort.
3. *Strict performance (or complete performance).* This performance is what is called for under the contract.
4. *Anticipatory breach.* This type of material breach triggers rights in the other party to stop his own performance and seek remedies. It is designed to mitigate harm to the nonbreaching party.
5. *Monetary damages.* This is the most common of the remedies provided in contract cases. They are designed to give the nonbreaching party the economic benefit of the bargain.
6. *Equitable.* Remedies in equity are historically traceable to the English Court of Chancery and were originally based on appeals to the King's conscience.
7. *Consequential damages.* To be liable, the breaching party must know or have reason to know that the breach would cause these damages to the other party.
8. *Liquidated damages.* Courts want to be sure that these damages are fairly arrived at and do not act as a penalty against the breaching party.
9. *Mitigation.* This doctrine applies to all measures of damages.
10. *Recission.* This remedy tries to put the parties back into the position they were in before the contracting process began.

True/False:

1. False. In the absence of a contract-related tort, such as intentional interference with contract relations, punitive damages are not generally awarded for contract breach.
2. False. Concurrent conditions arise when parties to a contract must render performance simultaneously.
3. False. Injunctions are court orders which prohibit a person from doing a certain act.
4. False. An accord is only an agreement of how to resolve a contract dispute. It is not a completed contract.
5. False. The nonbreaching party may recover damages even if the breach is only minor.
6. False. Generally, only monetary damages are available for breach of contract. Equitable remedies are only used if monetary damages are insufficient.
7. True. The key element is foreseeability.
8. True. If the actual damages are determinable or the liquidated damages clause provides for a large recovery, the clause may not be enforced.
9. False. The nonbreaching party is under an obligation to avoid or reduce any further damages after the breach. This is called mitigation.
10. True. Such a breach is also a tort. Therefore, tort damages, such as punitive damages, may be awarded.

Multiple Choice:

1. B. Money damages are not a required element of this contract-related tort. A, C, and D are required elements.
2. A. Mitigation is used in damage awards, and requires the nonbreaching party to take reasonable steps to reduce damages. B, C, and D are all equitable remedies.
3. B. Where there is only an agreement, but not completion of the agreement, this is accord, but not satisfaction. A is incorrect for the reason above. C is incorrect because this is a resolution and neither party can rescind the contract without being held liable. D is incorrect because if an alternative agreement has been reached, the parties do not have to fully perform the original contract.
4. D. A is correct because though this is a breach, it is minor. B and C are correct because these are the remedies that Yuppie has.
5. B. Monetary damages are available even if the breach is minor. A is incorrect since Dan does have some recourse. C is incorrect because an equitable remedy is probably not available since monetary damages would suffice.
6. B. Boris can recover the amount of profit he would have had on the contract. A is incorrect because Boris has lost his expected profit and can recover this amount. C is incorrect because Boris cannot recover the whole contract price, but only his expected profit. D is incorrect because Boris can still recover his expected profit even if he has spent money on materials.
7. A. In such a situation, damages are difficult to calculate. If the amount of liquidated damages is reasonable, the clause will be enforced. Be is incorrect because if the liquidated damages clause is enforceable, actual damages will not be awarded. C is incorrect because if certain requirements are met, such clauses will be enforced.
8. D. Although Max breached this contract, Ned was able to completely mitigate damages and cannot recover any significant amount of money. Therefore, Ned did not suffer any monetary damage.

However, if Ned wants to sue Max on principle, he will be awarded nominal damages.

9. A. Since Carl knew of this contract and intentionally induced Susan to breach it, he is liable for intentional interference with contractual relations. B is incorrect because since Carl was not a party to the contract, he did not have a duty of good faith and fair dealing. C is incorrect because since Carl was not a party to the contract, he could not breach it.

10. C. This is the only element of specific performance which applies. It is sought where money will not suffice.

VI. Key Question Checklist Answers to Essay Question:

A&B. *Are there any performance covenants under this contract?*

Ms. Dee Minimis had a number of performance obligations under the terms of her contract with Mr. Lex Loci. The most obvious, of course, was to pay the agreed upon price for the business. The most important performance obligation covenant was the condition subsequent involving her duty not to compete for a period of one year within a five mile radius of Derbytown Rollerball.

C,D,&E. *Were there any excuses from performance or changes in the law?*

Ms. Dee Minimis does not appear to qualify for any of the excuses from her performance obligations, such as accord and satisfaction or novation, based either on the actions of the parties or on legal excuses such as a statute of limitation.

F. *Has a breach taken place?*

Ms. Dee Minimis had a definite duty to honor the noncompetition covenant in her contract with Mr. Lex Loci. The clause appears to be a reasonable provision connected with the sale of a business and does not create an undue limitation on competition. In addition, this obligation is not excused or discharged by reason of her teaching in-line skating, rather than roller-skating, instruction. The nature of both enterprises is essentially the same.

G. *If there any agreement within the contract as to how any breach may be resolved?*

There is a specific provision in this contract for liquidated damages. Normally, where such a provision provides a true alternative performance and is not a penalty, courts will honor the provision. Here the liquidated damages clause appears fair on its face and was openly bargained for by both parties. The problem is that even if Ms. Minimis were willing to pay the $5000, she is not in a financial position to do so because of her lottery habit. Her insolvency is a product of voluntary acts.

I. *What are the possible law or monetary measures applicable if liquidated damages do not apply?*

Because the liquidated damages clause is rendered ineffective due to Ms. Minimis' insolvency, the imposition of any money damages would not provide Mr. Loci with any effective law-based remedy in this case. Equitable remedies must therefore be examined.

J. *Do any equitable remedies apply?*

Because personal services are involved in this contract, affirmative enforcement cannot be granted. This bar to enforcement of personal services contracts is rooted in the 13th Amendment to the U.S. Constitution which prohibits forced or coerced labor. Thus, Ms. Minimis cannot be forced to teach in-line skating. She can, however, be subjected to a negative injunction from providing those services in violation of the noncompetition clause. Because the money damages in this case, liquidated or otherwise, are illusory, the injunctive remedy can be granted as a remedy for breach of the noncompetition clause.

K. *Are there any contract-related torts at issue in this case?*

Ms. Dee Minimis may have engaged in both intentional interference with the contract between Mr. Lex Loci and his new clients as well as in bad faith and dealing with Mr. Loci at the outset. If the elements of these torts are found, punitive damages may be imposed by the court.

Chapter 17

FORMATION OF SALES AND LEASE CONTRACTS

Any intelligent fool can make things bigger, more complex, and more violent. It takes a touch of genius-and a lot of courage-to move in the opposite direction.

E.F. Schumacher

I. Overview:

The residents of the Hawaiian Islands were recently witness to one of nature's most interesting phenomenons: a total solar eclipse. As obscured as the sun's light may have been, there still shone around the shadow of the moon a ring of light called a *penumbra*. When you begin to examine the Uniform Commercial Code (UCC) as a specialized body of contract law, it appears to have eclipsed the common law of contracts, although the light of the common law still shines on. The UCC is intended to cover a number of areas of contract formerly resolved by common law, but the basic elements for both are the same. The four elements of contract are still in place just as the light continues to surround the moon's shadow. What is vastly different is the implementation of how those elements are arrived at in light of commercial realities.

Early on, the Law Merchant of England set up special rules for commercial contracts with the realization that the law should be written to foster and encourage commerce rather than encumber it. The early *faire* courts were established by and for merchants. They were designed to have law reflect the needs of commerce. Some of the principles which evolved included:

1. Holding merchants to a higher standard established by their peers.
2. Providing for a uniformity of interpretation for commercial contracts.
3. Providing for a uniformity flexibility in the formation, modification, and termination of commercial contracts so as to allow for the realities of the marketplace.
4. Retaining the common law essential ingredients of equity, fair play, good faith, and conscionability in commercial dealings.

The UCC is both the literal and spiritual descendent of the Law Merchant. Its predecessor, the 1906 Uniform Sales Act, was ultimately adopted by 30-seven states. It was, in turn, eclipsed by the UCC beginning in 1952. One of the key authors of the UCC was Professor Karl Llewellyn whose hallmark was legal realism. The law should reflect the realities of commerce which are already working rather than impose unnecessary obstacles or impediments to business. The UCC has been adopted, at least in part, in all fifty states. It continues to be one of the single most important legislative enactments in American legal history. It is updated and revised in order to keep up with the changing realities of the marketplace. The steps involved the formation, modification, and interpretation of a UCC contract are set out in the key question checklist.

II. Hypothetical Multi-Issue Essay Question:

Benny, a bakery owner, entered into an oral contract with Alfa, a "natural" farmer, to buy five tons of whole grain unprocessed wheatgerm to be used in Benny's famous "Wowee" brand muffins. The contract price was $17,500 per ton and the wheatgerm was to be shipped on Lionel Lines, Inc. The contract was for one year.

After two tons had already been shipped, Alfa informed Benny that he may not be able to deliver more because he fears the threat of the greenhouse effect on his crops. This notice took place on June 3, 1990, when the market price for comparable wheatgerm was $19,000 per ton.

Benny went to Alfa's competitor, Romeo, on December 1, 1990 and purchased the remaining three tons of wheatgerm for $20,500 per ton. Benny now sues Alfa for the difference between the contract amount and the price he paid Romeo for the wheatgerm. What result?

III. Key Question Checklist:

A. Is this contract covered by one or more of the provisions of Article 2 or 2A of the Uniform Commercial Code?
  1. What is the main purpose of this transaction?
    a. A sale (Article 2)?
    b. A lease (Article 2A)?
    c. A service (may not be covered)?
  2. What is the main subject matter of this contract?
    a. Does it qualify as a good per the UCC?
    b. What classification of good is applicable here?

B. What is the status of the parties entering into this agreement?
  1. Are either one or both classified as a merchant?
  2. Are either one or both classified as a nonmerchant?

C. Once you have established the coverage of this transaction by the UCC and the status of the parties involved, are the proper elements of formation of a contract in place?
  1. Has the mutual assent process been met per UCC?
    a. How was the offer made?
      (1) Does the firm offer rule apply?
    b. How was the acceptance made?
      (1) Was there an acceptance by an act?
  2. Has the consideration requirement been met?
  3. Do both parties have the legal capacity to enter into a contract?
  4. Is there any problem with illegality on the face of or in the underlying intent of this agreement?
  5. Does the UCC Statute of Frauds apply here?
    a. What was the written documentation?
    b. Any exceptions applicable?

D. Having established the formation of the UCC contract, what rules of interpretation would you use in case of any dispute?
  1. Express terms of the contract?
  2. Course of performance--undertaken by the parties since the contract was formed?
  3. Course of dealing--prior to and leading up to the contract?
  4. Usage of trade--what is par for the industry on this issue?

E. Any contract modifications allowable here?
  1. Any new consideration necessary here?
  2. Any new writing requirements?
  3. Principles of equity and good faith commercial reasonableness requirements met?

IV. Objective Questions:

Terms:

1. The doctrine which states that courts have the power to determine whether an entire contract or a contract clause is unfair or inequitable is called the _____ doctrine.

2. Tangible things that are moveable at the time of their identification in the contract are called _____.

3. A person who deals in goods of the kind involved in the transaction, or by his occupation holds himself out as having knowledge or skill peculiar to the goods involved in the transaction, is called a _____ under the UCC.

4. The rule that says if a merchant offers to buy or sell goods and gives a written and signed assurance on a separate form that the offer will be held open, he cannot revoke the offer for the time stated or if not time is stated, for a reasonable time is called the _____ _____ rule.

5. The rule that says a yet to be determined term can be read into a contract is called the _____ _____ rule.

6. Goods that by nature or usage of trade are equivalent to any like unit goods of the same grade and quality are called _____.

7. A person who in good faith and without knowledge that the sale violates the ownership or security interests of a third party buys the goods in the ordinary course of business from a person in the business of selling goods of that kind is called a _____ _____ _____ _____ _____.

8. A sale that involves the provision of both a service and a good in the same transaction is called a _____ _____.

9. A shipment that is offered to the buyer as a replacement for their original shipment, when the original shipment cannot be filled is known as an _____ _____.

10. The rule that says an open term can be "read into" a UCC contract is generally known as the _____ _____.

True/False:

1. ____Disparity of bargaining power alone may make a contract unconscionable.

2. ____Article 2 applies to all mixed sales which include a good and a service.

3. ____If a confirmation contains additional or different terms than those in the offer, it extinguishes the offer and acts as a counteroffer under the UCC.

4. ____Under the UCC, as in common law, an agreement modifying a sales contract must be supported by consideration to be binding.

5. ____Under the UCC, output contracts and requirements contracts cannot have an open quantity term since the quantity of goods that the parties intend to buy or sell cannot be implied.

6. ____Nonmerchants are held to a subjective standard of honesty in contracting while merchants are held to an objective standard of fair dealing in the trade.

7. ____Growing crops, timber, and other things are considered "goods" under the UCC, Article 2 even if they are not severed from the realty.

8. ____Rules established for sales contracts by Article 2 of the UCC take precedent over the common law of contracts.

9. ____If a seller ships nonconforming goods in response to a buyer's offer, this constitutes both an acceptance of the offer and a breach of the sales contract.

10. ____Under the UCC, as in common law, an agreement modifying a sales contract must be supported by consideration to be binding.

Multiple Choice:

1. Mega Wigets Supply offered to sell to Racing Widgets Corporation 20 units of widget subassemblies at $1,000 per unit under specified delivery terms. Racing Widgets accepted the offer as follows: "We accept your offer for 20 units at $1,000 per unit per inspection by USAC." Which of the following is correct?
   A. A contract was formed on Mega Wigets' terms.
   B. Racing Widgets' reply constitutes a conditional acceptance, not a counteroffer.
   C. Racing Widgets' reply constitutes a counteroffer, and no contract was formed.
   D. A contract was formed on Racing Widgets' terms.

2. With regard to a contract by the UCC Sales Article, which one of the following statements is correct?
   A. Merchants and nonmerchants are treated alike.
   B. The contract may involve the sale of any type of personal property.
   C. The obligations of the parties to the contract must be performed in good faith.
   D. The contract must involve the sale of goods for a price of more than $500.

3. Office Wholesalers writes a letter offering to sell 20 desks to Fantastic Furniture for $300 each. Fantastic Furniture writes back, "We accept your offer for 20 desks, but we would really like 30 desks. Please ship 10 more desks at the same price." Which of the following is correct?
   A. Fantastic Furniture made a counteroffer, so no contract has been formed.
   B. Fantastic Furniture's acceptance was effective and established new terms for the contract.
   C. This contract is void because it does not meet the requirements of the Statute of Frauds.
   D. Fantastic Furniture accepted Office Wholesalers' offer, and there is a contract for at least 20 desks.

4. Fine Jewelry orders 30 pairs of earrings from Artist Anita. Anita accepts and agrees to supply the earrings. However, no mention is made of price. Which of the following is correct?
   A. Fine Jewelry must pay Anita a reasonable (probably market) price.
   B. The contract fails for indefiniteness since the parties never agreed.
   C. Either party can void the contract before performance without being liable for damages.
   D. None of the above.

5. Merchant Marty and Nonmerchant Nancy negotiate a contract for the sale of goods which is covered by Article 2 of the UCC. Which of the following is correct?
   A. Merchant Marty and Nonmerchant Nancy are both held to the same standard of good faith since the contract is governed by the UCC.
   B. Merchant Marty and Nonmerchant Nancy are both held to an objective standard since a standard applies if one party is a merchant.
   C. Merchant Marty is held to an objective standard of good faith while Nonmerchant Nancy is held to a subjective standard of good faith.
   D. None of the above.

6. Article 2 of the UCC governs only sales for goods, not real estate. Which of the following is not covered by Article 2?
   A. Minerals, oil, or gas which are removed by either the buyer of the seller.
   B. Growing crops or timber which are removed by either the buyer or the seller.
   C. Structures or materials which are removed by the seller.
   D. All of the above are covered by Article 2.

7. Under the UCC Sales Article, a firm offer is created only if the:
   A. Offeree is a merchant.
   B. Offeree gives some form of consideration.
   C. Offer states the time period during which it will remain open.
   D. Offer is made by a merchant in a signed writing.

8. Merchant Mike and Merchant Mary negotiate a sales contract by exchanging preprinted forms. If the acceptance contains additional terms, those terms will not become part of the sales contract if:
   A. The offer expressly limits the acceptance to the terms of the offer.
   B. The additional terms materially alter the terms of the original contract.
   C. The offeror notifies the offeree that he objects to the additional terms within a reasonable time.
   D. None of the above will become part of the sales contract.

9. Which of the following is *not* an exception to the writing requirements of the UCC Statute of Frauds?
   A. Contracts for the sale of goods over $500.
   B. Contracts for specially manufactured goods.
   C. Admissions in pleadings or in court.
   D. Part payment and acceptance.

10. Which of the following states has excluded Article 2 of the UCC in its legislative enactments:
    A. Colorado.
    B. New Mexico.
    C. Louisiana.
    D. New York.

V. Answers to Objective Questions:

Terms:

1. *Unconscionability.* Section 2-302 of the UCC allows courts to refuse enforcement of a sales contract if it finds either all or part of the contract to be unconscionable.

2. *Goods*. Because of the broad application of this definition, the UCC specifically seeks to avoid listing all the possible items which may be classified as goods. Rather, it seeks to specifically exclude certain items such as money, stocks, bonds, and patents.

3. *Merchant*. Even though this provision has been broadly interpreted so as to include all sorts of part time or hobby sellers as merchants, courts have disagreed about whether farmers are merchants within the UCC definition.

4. *Firm offer*. The net effect of this rule is to create a common law option contract result without having to provide the consideration required by the common law. The maximum period allowed under this rule is three months.

5. *Open terms*. The UCC seeks to recognize commercial realities by allowing the parties to leave major terms of the contract open at the time of its formation. Under the common law rule of indefiniteness, many of these open terms would not be allowed.

6. *Fungible*. This term is derived from the old English term "fundas," meaning common land. In the UCC, it is not land, but rather goods, that are identical with others and can be replaced by similar weight, measure, and number.

7. *Good faith purchaser for value*. A good faith purchaser for value is a person to whom good title can be transferred from a person with a voidable title. The real owner cannot reclaim goods from a good faith purchaser for value.

8. *Mixed sale*. Look at the main objective of the transaction to see if it is covered by the UCC or the common law of contracts.

9. *Accommodation shipment*. The accommodation is a counteroffer from the seller to the buyer. The buyer is free to either accept or reject the counteroffer.

10. *Gap-filling rule*. The UCC is much more tolerant of open terms than the common law. These provisions reflect the "legal realism" of the UCC in recognizing the realities of the marketplace.

True/False:

1. False. Gross disparity in bargaining power may make a contract unconscionable. However, some disparity alone is not usually enough to declare a contract unconscionable.

2. False. Mixed sales may or may not be governed by Article 2. This determination is made on a case by case basis.

3. False. Except under specific circumstances, confirmations with additional or different terms do not extinguish the offer. The UCC is more liberal in this respect than the common law.

4. False. New consideration is not required to support a contract modification under the UCC.

5. False. Under the UCC, output contracts and requirements contracts are the only types of contracts where the quantity term can be left open.

6. True. These standards are set out Section 2-103(1)(b) of the UCC. This standard is designed to reflect the so-called "higher" standards on merchants who are expected to know the rules of the business they are in.

7. True. This rule is set out in Section 2-107(2) of the UCC. These items are goods if they can be severed from the realty without causing material harm to it.

8. True. This reflects the "eclipse" factor discussed in the overview.
9. True. See Section 2-206(1)(b) of the UCC.
10. False. Consideration is not required to support a modification under the UCC. See Section 2-209(1).

Multiple Choice:

1. D. A definite expression of acceptance sent within a reasonable time operates as an acceptance even though it states additional or different terms. Between merchants, such terms become part of the contract unless the offer expressly limits acceptance to its terms, they materially alter it, or notification of objection is given within a reasonable time. A is incorrect because the offer did not limit acceptance to its terms, and Mega Wigets made no objection to the additional terms. B is incorrect because the reply with additional terms was not conditioned upon acceptance of those terms. C is incorrect because the reply was not a counteroffer. It was a definite expression of acceptance which formed a contract.

2. C. Both parties, whether merchants or nonmerchants must perform the contract in good faith. A is incorrect because merchants and nonmerchants are treated differently in different circumstances. B is incorrect because certain types of personal property are not covered by the UCC. D is incorrect because the contract may be for any price if the other requirements are met.

3. D. Fantastic Furniture's acceptance of the offer for 20 desks was definite and unconditional. Fantastic Furniture did, however, request an additional 10 desks. Whether the extra 10 desks will be sold is a separate issue. A is incorrect because the acceptance for 20 desks was definite and unconditional. B is incorrect because the 10 extra desks is not a new term of the original contract. The 20 desks will be sold. However, the extra 10 desks are separate. C is incorrect because the contract is written in the form of letters exchanged between the parties.

4. A. A contract with an open price term is enforceable under the UCC. When no price is specified, the buyer pays a reasonable price. B and C are incorrect because such a contract is valid and enforceable.

5. C. Since Merchant Marty is a merchant, he is held to a higher, objective standard of good faith. Nonmerchant Nancy is not a merchant and is therefore held to a lower, subjective standard of good faith. A is incorrect because merchants and nonmerchants are held to different standards under the UCC. B is incorrect for the same reason.

6. A. Minerals, oil, or gas which is removed by the buyer is not considered a good. However, if such resources are first removed from the land by the seller, they are considered goods. B and C are incorrect because both are considered goods under the UCC.

7. D. Both these elements need to be in place in order to constitute a firm offer, which makes A incorrect. B is incorrect because no consideration is required and C is incorrect because if no time period is stated, the UCC allows for a statutory limit of three months for the offer to be kept open.

8. D. A, B and C are all excluded from becoming additional terms if they are part of the acceptance.

9. A. B, C and D are all specifically provided for in UCC as exceptions to the writing requirements of the UCC State of Frauds.

10. **C.** Because of the French-based civil law tradition historically used in Louisiana, only parts of the UCC have been adopted by that state. Article 2, 6 and 9 have been excluded from its adoption of the UCC.

VI. Key Question Checklist Answer to Essay Question:

A. *Is this contract covered by one or more of the provisions of Article 2 or 2A of the UCC?*

The main purpose of this transaction was the sale of goods. A sale consists of passing title from seller, Alfa, to buyer, Benny for a price, $17,500 per ton of wheatgerm. Alfa may have provided some services by way of harvesting the grain, but those services were only incidental to the main purpose of the contract. Growing crops are classified as goods under the UCC regardless of whether the buyer or the seller severs the crop from the realty. Both the subject matter and purpose of the contract bring it under the purview of the UCC.

B. *What is the status of the parties entering into this agreement?*

Benny would definitely be classified as a merchant in that a baker is expected to have knowledge and skills related to ingredients used in making bread products. The courts are divided as to whether farmers are merchants within the UCC definition. Your assumption on the merchant status of Alfa should be made clear at this point because it may impact the remainder of your answer. For purposes of resolving the problem, assume here that Alfa is a merchant based on his knowledge of grains.

C. *Are the proper elements of the formation of a UCC sales contract in place?*

This contract does not raise any issues of capacity, legality, or consideration. The real problem lies in the formation of mutual assent and failure to put it into writing. The UCC is much more open-ended than the common law in its requirements for formation of contract. A contract for sale of goods may be made in any manner sufficient to show an intent to be bound, including conduct. Here there was oral offer to buy and an acceptance by shipment of conforming goods.

The contract was for more than $500 and should have been in writing. There are three exceptions to the writing requirements of the UCC Statute of Frauds:
1. Specially manufactured goods.
2. Admissions in pleading in courts.
3. Party payment or acceptance.

Here we have partial acceptance based on the first two tons shipped. There was no refusal to accept those goods, so the contract is enforceable to that extent. The remainder of the contract may not be enforceable by Benny because he failed to get a writing. Had there been a written confirmation sent by Alfa, the writing requirement would have been met if no objection was made to the terms within 10 days after the date of receipt. Had the writing requirement been met this way, Alfa would be in breach of his duty to deliver the remaining three tons.

D. *Having established the formation of a UCC contract, what rules of interpretation would you use in case of any dispute?*

Because there was no writing, the best method available for interpretation is course of performance since the contract was entered into. If it is decided that the writing

143

requirement was met by way of a written confirmation, that writing would act as the express terms of the contract.

E. *Are there any modifications allowable here?*

Alfa seeks a modification mid-term in the contract. It appears that an unsubstantiated fear of the greenhouse effect would not be a commercially reasonable basis upon which to seek excuse from continued performance. Benny, in turn, may have waited too long to buy the goods elsewhere. The market price at the time of the alleged breach was $19,000 and his actual damages may be limited to the difference between his contract price of $17,500 and $19,000 for each of the remaining three tons. This assumes that Alfa was bound by the contract. If the Statute of Frauds defense applied, Alfa would be discharged from any further obligations. The most likely result here, however, will be that the Statute of Fraud defense will not prevail due to the part payment or part performance exception to that rule. As such, Alfa will most likely be bound by the contract and have to pay for his alleged breach.

CHAPTER 18

TITLE, RISK, AND INSURABLE INTEREST

When everything has to be right, something isn't.

Stanislaw J. Lee

I. Overview:

Under the common law of contracts, ownership title has always played a critical role. It has been the linchpin which holds together the benefit/burden dynamics of rights and duties towards property interest. The UCC has greatly modified these rights and duties in contracts covered by it. By placing less emphasis on title alone, it has allowed controversies involving title, risk of loss, and insurable interest to be more independently resolved from each other. The underlying purpose behind allowing this sort of "separate path" resolution of each of these issues is found in the gaps created by the common law emphasis on title alone. For example, under the common law, title was generally required to obtain an insurable interest on property. Assume A was selling to B. Only A could insure the property until such time as B took title. But what about B's nontitle economic interests in A's property? If B already had a contract of resale for the property, should not the economic benefits anticipated from that resale contract also be insurable? The UCC recognized that in order to protect and foster commerce, the traditional rules based on title were simple inadequate to protect the realistic needs of commerce.

Passage of title under the UCC begins with the process of identification of the goods.

Once the goods are identified as being part of the proper subject matter of a UCC contract, determine what the parties have expressly stated vis-a-vis that issue. The UCC is similar to many other areas of the law in that it tries to balance freedom of contract with a need for clearly ascertainable ground rules. Title can pass from seller to buyer in any legal manner expressly agreed upon by the parties. However, if the parties are silent or ambiguous on this issue, the UCC will impose its own title-transfer rules upon the parties. What makes these rules particularly problematic is the possible intervention of third party rights. In its efforts to protect reliance on the enforceability of commercial contracts, the UCC has given innocent third parties much more protection than was provided under the common law of contracts. That protection has often been provided at the expense of prior title holders. These modified rules will be outlines in the key question checklist.

The common law risk of loss rules have also been substantially amended by the UCC. Under the traditional rules of common law, the risk of loss stayed with the title. Here too, the UCC allows the parties to address the issues explicitly, and if they fail to do so, the statute will impose its own set of risk-shifting rules. Once the goods are identified, the UCC will allocate the risk of loss based on the overall nature of the contract. Note that this identification of contract, be it conditional, shipment, delivery, or consignment, is what determines the risk of loss, not who has title. Students must first, therefore, be able to identify the essence of the contract in order to be able to ascertain which rights and duties the UCC attributes to the respective parties arising from that designation. As in the case of the UCC title rules, the possible infusion of third party rights always looms overhead when risk of loss is attributed.

Compare all three issues: title, risk of loss, and insurability to the lines indicated on a medical monitoring device. Each line is independently giving the reader critical information yet they are components of a larger issue--the overall health of the patient. In UCC contract resolution, each of these issues is independently answered as part of the process of resolving the overall rights and duties under the contract. They are all separate issues but yet are mutually-dependent as part of one legal being.

II. Hypothetical Multi-Issue Essay Question:

Lancelot Loefric and his wife Mercia were shopping around for a new luxury car. They test drove a number of machines and were concerned with finding the right combination of style, luxury, snob appeal, and safety. Price was no object because Lancelot made millions selling scripts to TV soaps. He was constantly thinking of brilliant new ways to revive dead characters through the use of dream sequences and shower scenes.

Last week Lancelot and Mercia signed a sales contract with Hot Air Autos, Inc. to buy, on approval, a new model Zoroastermobile number 1234567. It is equipped with all the latest features including airbags for all occupants of the car. Under the terms of the sale, Lancelot and Mercia could return the car anytime up to a week after the contract was signed. One day before the week expired, Lancelot hit a pothole and six airbags blew up at once inside the car. He lost control, and the car was wrecked. Lancelot tows the wrecked car back to Hot Air, and they refuse to take it back. What result?

III. Key Question Checklist:

A. Have the goods been identified? (And what is the general nature of this contract as reviewed in the prior chapter?)
   1. Are the goods already in existence?
      a. Have they been designated?
      b. If not yet designated, have the parties agreed upon designation?
      c. Are the goods fungible?
   2. Are the goods "futures"?
      a. Have the parties identified the time of designation?
      b. If the parties have not identified the time of designation, what UCC rule will apply?
         (1) Crops?
         (2) Unborn young animals?
         (3) Other future goods?

B. Once you have identified the goods, the passage of title to those goods must be ascertained.
   1. Have the parties explicitly agreed upon the passage of title?
   2. If the parties have failed to agree on passage of title, what UCC title rule applies?
      a. Destination contract?
         (1) Has the seller delivered the goods?
         (2) Has the seller tendered delivery?
      b. Shipment contract?
         (1) Has the seller made proper shipping arrangements with a common carrier?
         (2) Has the seller delivered the goods into the carrier's hands?
      c. Nonshipment transfer of title?
         (1) Is a document of title required?

(2) If no document of title is required, have the goods have been identified at the time of contracting?

C. Assuming you have identified the passage of title from seller to buyer, the rights of third parties must then be ascertained.
1. Is there any third party involvement in this contract?
2. Was the title in the hands of the second party void or voidable?
   a. If void, the third party cannot get any greater rights of title than those held by the second party?
   b. If voidable, it may be possible for the third party to obtain greater rights of title than were held by the second party if he or she qualifies as a:
      (1) Good faith purchaser for value?
      (2) Buyer in the ordinary course of business?
   c. Rights of original owner?
      (1) If the title was void in the hands of the second party, the original owner may still claim title.
      (2) If the title of the second party was voidable, the original owner may not recoup title vis-a-vis a good faith purchaser for value of a buyer in the ordinary course of business.
      (3) Original owner may have reimbursement rights for lost title against the second party.
   d. Rights of creditor's under a security interest?
      (1) If third party qualifies as a buyer in the ordinary course of business, that third party will take title free of the creditor's security interest.

(2) Creditor may be able to seek reimbursement against the second party who sold to the buyer in the ordinary course of business.

D. Assuming title to the goods has now been ascertained, who bears the risk of loss on those goods?
1. Have the parties explicitly agreed as risk of loss?
2. If there is not a specific agreement, how will the UCC allocate the risk of loss?
   a. Shipment contract?
   b. Destination contract?
   c. Goods held by seller?
   d. Any conditional sale provisions?

E. What are the respective insurable interests of the parties?
1. Is there an insurable interest based on title?
2. Is there an insurable interest based on a security interest?
3. Is there an insurable interest based on any other economic interest in this contract?

IV. Objective Questions:

Terms:

1. The principle of distinguishing the goods named in the contract from the seller's other goods is called _____ _____ _____.

2. When a merchant allows a customer to take goods for a specified time in order to see if the goods fit their needs, this is called a _____ _____ _____.

3. A contract that requires the seller to ship the goods to the buyer via a common carrier is a _____ _____.

4. The right to be able to reclaim goods sold with an imperfect title from the purchasers is called _____ _____ while a _____ _____ is a title that a purchaser has if the goods were obtained by fraud or some other misrepresentation.

5. A person who in good faith and without knowledge that the sale violates the ownership or security interests of a third party buys the goods in the ordinary course of business from a person in the business of selling goods of that kind is a _____ _____ _____ _____ _____ _____.

6. A delivery term that requires the seller to arrange to ship the goods and put the goods in the carrier's possession is _____ _____ _____ _____ _____ _____. The seller bears the expense and risk of loss until this is done.

7. A delivery term that requires the seller to deliver and tender the goods alongside the named vessel or on the dock designated and provided by the buyer is _____ _____ _____ _____. The seller bears the expense and risk of loss until this is done.

8. A sales contract that requires the seller to deliver conforming goods to a specific destination is a _____ contract.

9. A delivery term that requires the seller to bear the expense and risk of loss until the goods are unloaded from the ship at its port of destination is called _____.

10. A contract that requires the seller to bear the expense and risk of loss of the goods during transportation is a _____ _____, _____ _____ contract. The seller is under no duty to deliver replacement goods to the buyer since there is no contractual stipulation that the goods will arrive at the appointed destination.

True/False:

1. ____The seller retains title and risk of loss of both existing and future goods until she identifies them to a sales contract.

2. ____Under a destination contract, title passes to the buyer as soon as the goods are identified in the contract.

3. ____If a buyer rejects or refuses to receive goods, or justifiably revokes acceptance of the goods, title to the goods revests in the seller.

4. ____If a person with a voidable title to goods transfers title to a good faith purchaser for value, the real owner cannot reclaim goods from such a purchaser.

5. ____In entrusting cases, the buyer of the goods bears the risk of loss even though he is an innocent party. The purpose of this principle is to promote confidence in commercial transactions.

6. ____Under shipment contracts, the risk of loss passes to the buyer when the seller delivers the goods to the carrier. Therefore, the buyer bears the risk of loss during transportation.

7. ____In a sale on approval, the sale is effective as soon as the buyer takes possession of the goods.

8. ____Goods sold pursuant to a sale or return contract are subject to the claims of the seller's creditors while the buyer possesses them since the title to the goods still belongs to the seller.

9. ____The buyer may obtain an insurable interest in goods before the title or risk of loss passes to him.

10. ____The buyer and seller may never have an insurable interest in the same goods at the same time.

Multiple Choice:

1. Which of the following is *not* classified by the UCC as a conditional sale:
   A. Sale on approval.
   B. Sale with open terms.
   C. Sale or return.
   D. Sale on consignment.

2. Which of the following is false?
   A. "F.O.B." means the seller is responsible for delivering the goods to the carrier. The seller bears the risk of loss to this point.
   B. "F.A.S." means the seller must deliver the goods alongside a vessel or dock. In addition, the seller bears the risk of loss until the buyer has possession.
   C. "C.I.F." means the seller is responsible for certain costs,

including cost of insurance and freight. The seller bears the risk of loss until the goods are on the carrier.
   D. "No arrival, no sale" means the seller bears the risk of loss during transportation.

3. In July, Santa's Station agreed to buy 5,000 bushels of pears from Holiday Pear Growers. The pears were to be delivered weekly beginning in late November. Which of the following is correct?
   A. The pears are future goods when the contract is made, but the contract is still enforceable.
   B. The pears are future goods when the contract is made, and therefore the contract is unenforceable.
   C. The pears are not identified until Holiday Pear Growers ships them.
   D. None of the above.

4. Assume the same facts as in question 3. Also, assume Holiday Pear Growers and Santa's Station agree this will be a destination contract. Which of the following is correct?
   A. Holiday Pear Growers must deliver the pears to Santa's Station or some other designated place, and Holiday Pear Growers bears the risk of loss in transportation.
   B. Holiday Pear Growers must ship the pears via a common carrier, and Santa's Station bears the risk of loss in transportation.
   C. Holiday Pear Growers must deliver the pears to Santa's Station or some other designated place and Santa's Station bears the risk of loss in transportation.
   D. Holiday Pear Growers bears the risk of loss until Santa's Station takes possession of the pears.

149

5. Lucrative Larry contracts to buy a new Porsche at Pam's Dealership. Larry agrees to pay $70,000 for the new car. Pam's dealership deals extensively and exclusively in Porsches. However, Pam bought the car from another dealer, Paul, before selling it to Larry. In addition, Pam wrote a check for the car which later bounced. Which of the following is correct?
   A. Paul can reclaim the car from Larry.
   B. Larry was a good faith purchaser for value and can keep the car.
   C. Paul entrusted the car to Pam so he bears the risk of loss.
   D. Pam possessed good title at the time she sold the car.

6. Assume the same facts as in question 5 except instead of $70,000, assume Larry paid $700 for the new car.
   A. Paul can reclaim the car from Larry.
   B. Larry was a good faith purchaser for value and can keep the car.
   C. Paul entrusted the car to Pam so he bears the risk of loss.
   D. Pam possessed good title at the time she sold the car.

7. On May 1, Home Designs contracts to buy fifty sofas from Furniture Manufacturer for $200 per sofa for a total contract price of $10,000. Home Designs and Furniture Manufacturer agree that Home Designs will bear the risk of loss beginning on May 1 even though the sofas are still in Furniture Manufacturer's warehouse. Which of the following is correct?
   A. The risk of loss agreement is unenforceable since Furniture Manufacturer must bear the risk while the goods are in its possession.
   B. The risk of loss agreement is unenforceable since who bears the loss is governed by the UCC, not the parties.
   C. The risk of loss agreement is enforceable since the parties agreed to it and the goods exist and have been identified to the contract.
   D. None of the above.

8. Assume the same facts as in question 7 except there is no risk of loss agreement. In addition, assume Furniture Manufacturers breaches the contract by tendering nonconforming goods and Home Designs revokes acceptance when the goods are received. Before the sofas are returned, they are destroyed by a fire. Which of the following is correct?
   A. Furniture Manufacturers is liable for damage beyond the amount that Home Design's insurance will cover.
   B. Furniture Manufacturers is liable for the total contract price of $10,000.
   C. Home Designs must bear the entire loss of $10,000.
   D. Home Designs must bear the loss from damage beyond the amount which Furniture Manufacturers' insurance will cover.

9. Vacuum Valerie Co. allows Bachelor Bob to take home and use a SuperDuper Vacuum for two weeks to see if he likes the vacuum without buying it. If, at the end of two weeks, Bob wants to buy the vacuum, Valerie will sell it to him for "a great price." Which of the following is correct?
   A. This is a sale on consignment.
   B. This is a sale or return.
   C. This is a sale on approval.
   D. None of the above.

10. Assume the same facts as in question 9. Also, assume at the end of the first week, Bob's house burns down, through no fault of his own, destroying the vacuum. Which of the following is correct?
    A. Bob bears the risk of loss and is liable to Vacuum Valerie Co. for the cost of the vacuum.
    B. Vacuum Valerie Co. bears the risk of loss and cannot recover from Bob.
    C. Vacuum Valerie Co. and Bob must split the cost of the vacuum.
    D. None of the above.

V. Answers to Objective Questions:

Terms:

1. *Identification of goods.* This process is used for a number of reasons throughout the UCC, including allocating title, risk and insurable interest.
2. *Sale on approval.* This is one of several types of conditional sale transactions recognized by the UCC.
3. *Shipment contract.* See Section 2-401(2)(a) of the UCC. Under this section the seller is required to make proper shipping arrangements and deliver the goods into the carrier's hands.
4. *Void title, voidable title.* These doctrines are designed to protect the reliance factor of good faith purchasers in the stream of commerce.
5. *Buyer in the ordinary course of business.* See Section 1-201(a) of the UCC. If a person qualifies under this section, he takes the goods free of any third-party security interests in the goods.
6. *Free on board point of shipment.* See Section 2-319(1)(a) of the UCC.

7. *Free alongside point of shipment.* See Section 2-319(2)(a) of the UCC.
8. *Destination.* Such contracts require the seller to bear the risk of loss of the goods during their transportation.
9. *Ex-ship.* See Sections 2-322(1) and (2)(b). This term requires the seller to bear the expense and risk of loss until the goods are unloaded from the ship at its point of destination.
10. *No-arrival, no-sale.* See Section 2-324(a) and (b) of the UCC.

True/False:

1. True. Identification is the first step in the allocation of risk of loss process.
2. False. Under a destination contract, title passes to the buyer when the seller tenders delivery of the goods to the specified location.
3. True. See Section 2-401(4) of the UCC.
4. True. This rule is designed to assist the innocent third party.
5. False. In entrusting cases, the entrusting party bears the risk of loss even though both she and the buyer are both innocent parties.
6. True. Generally, see Section 2-319 for this set of rules in shipment contracts.
7. False. In a sale on approval, the sale is effective when the buyer accepts the goods. Acceptance of the goods requires acts beyond merely taking possession.
8. False. Goods sold pursuant to a sale or return contract are only subject to the claims of the buyer's creditors while the buyer possesses them. In addition, while the buyer has possession of the goods, he also has title to the goods.
9. True. This is one of the changes the UCC made from the common law of contracts which relied on title.

10. False. A buyer and seller may have an insurable interest in the same goods at the same time.

Multiple Choice:

1. B. Open terms are allowed under the UCC in certain contracts and are not classified as conditional sales. A, C, and D are all classified as conditional sales under the UCC.
2. B. While the seller must deliver the goods alongside a vessel or dock, the seller only bears the risk of loss until the goods are delivered, not until the buyer takes possession. A is correct. C is correct. D is correct.
3. A. Since the pears are not grown yet, they are future goods. However, the pears are identified in the contract, and the contract is enforceable. B is incorrect because the contract is enforceable. C is incorrect because the pears are identified in the contract since the pear trees are growing crops.
4. A. A destination contract requires the seller to deliver the goods to the buyers place of business or some other designated place. B is incorrect because the seller is not required to ship the goods via common carrier under a destination contract. C is incorrect because the buyer does not bear the risk of loss while the seller is delivering the goods. D is incorrect because the seller only bears the risk of loss until the goods are delivered to the designated place.
5. B. Since Larry acted honestly in this contract and paid value of $70,000 for the car, he is a good faith purchaser for value. Under such circumstances, Paul cannot reclaim the car. A is incorrect for the reason discussed above. C is incorrect because Paul did not entrust the car to Pam, but thought he was selling it to her. D is incorrect because Pam had a voidable title at the time she sold the car.

6. A. Here, Larry did not pay "value" or sufficient consideration for the car and he is not a good faith purchaser for value. Therefore, Paul can reclaim the car. B is incorrect for the reason discussed above. C is incorrect for the reason discussed in question 5. D is incorrect for the reason discussed in question 5.
7. C. The parties may agree about who will bear the risk of loss if the goods under the contract are damaged as long as the goods exist and are identified and the obligation of good faith is met. A and B are incorrect for the reason discussed above.
8. A. B is incorrect because the breaching seller is only liable for the amount the buyer's insurance does not cover. C is incorrect because the buyer can recover the amount not covered by insurance from the breaching seller. D is incorrect for the reason discussed in answer A.
9. C. A is in incorrect because a sale on consignment is usually between two merchants for retail sale of the seller's goods. B is incorrect because a sale or return is usually between two merchants for retail sale of the seller's goods. However, the goods may be returned to the seller if they are not resold by the buyer.
10. B. Under a sale on approval, the seller bears the risk of loss until the buyer accepts the goods. Here, Bob had not yet accepted the vacuum but was still using it on a trial basis. A and C are incorrect for the reason discussed above.

VI. Key Question Checklist Answers to Essay Question:

A. *Have the goods been identified?*

The main purpose of this transaction was the sale of goods. Hot Air Autos may have provided some services by way of maintenance and repair of the auto for purposes of preparation for sale or after the fact by way of warranty.

Those services, however, would be considered only incidental to the main purpose of the contract. Automobiles are classified as goods under the UCC. Thus both the subject matter and the main purpose of the contract fall under the purview of the UCC.

Hot Air Autos is definitely classified as a merchant and is expected to have the knowledge and skills associated with the business of preparing autos for retail sales. Lancelot and Mercia, in turn, would be classified as consumers. It does not appear from the facts presented that they had any intent to engage in resale of the auto. Their main purpose was to purchase the car for personal use.

This contract does not raise any issues or capacity, legality, or consideration. The real issue revolves around the formation of mutual assent and the interpretation of the terms of the contract. Under the UCC, a contract for the sale of goods may be made in any manner sufficient to show an intent to be bound, including conduct. The four elements of contract appear to be in place here.

Where there are express written terms, those will be examined first as a source of interpretation. If there were no express written terms, a court could move to course of performance, course of dealing, and usage of trade in the particular industry involved.

The goods involved in this contract are covered by the UCC. An automobile is a personal good, and it is standard practice to identify autos in sales contracts by the manufacturer's serial number affixed to the body of the car. The serial number was used in this contract.

B. *Once the goods have been identified, has passage of title taken place?*

The parties here have explicitly agreed to certain conditions as part of their contract. Those express conditions are tied to a sale on approval to be finalized within one week after the contract was signed. The buyers had the right to return the automobile at any time prior to the expiration of that one week period.

C. *Are any rights of third parties involved?*

There is no third party involvement in this case except for the possibility of an insurance company paying one of the parties for their loss and then stepping into their legal shoes by subrogation. There was no evidence of any third party involvement as a good faith purchaser for value or buyer in the ordinary course of business. Had Lancelot and Mercia sold the car to their neighbor Figaro three days after the contract, then Figaro may have taken better title to the car than Lancelot and Mercia had at the time.

D. *Who had the risk of loss?*

Because the parties did not explicitly agree on who assumed the risk of loss in this contract, the UCC general rules with regard to conditional sales must be examined. Under the UCC, the risk of loss remains with the seller on approval contracts until the buyer accepts. There is an exception to this rule if harm to the goods was caused by the buyer's negligence. Here it appears that Lancelot's loss of control was due to a defect in the product, not his own negligence. Thus the loss falls on the seller.

E. *What are the respective insurable interests of the parties?*

Both parties had an insurable interest in the car based on their respective economic contract interests as recognized by the UCC regardless of title.

CHAPTER 19

REMEDIES FOR BREACH OF SALES AND LEASE CONTRACTS

The law obliges us to do what is proper, not simply what is just.

DeJure ac Pacis

I. Overview:

"If it's OK, don't fix it." This old maxim holds as true for UCC sales contracts as well any other sphere of endeavor. The UCC even provides multiple mechanisms for midterm corrections and adjustments to avoid breakdowns down the contract road. Sometimes breakdowns can and do occur, both intentional and unintentional. These lapses in performance are breaches of contract. A breach is defined by *Black's Law Dictionary* as: "a failure by a party to a contract to carry out a term, promise, or condition of the contract." The key objectives of this chapter center around illustrating the consequences of a breach in a UCC sales contract.

The best way to consider these issues is to divide your studies into A and B columns: breach by buyer on one side compared to breach by seller on the other. In addition, each column should be further divided into two main categories: out-of-court remedies and in-court remedies. Whenever possible, out-of-court remedies should be pursued first before resorting to the use of our already overburdened judicial system.

The seller's remedies for buyer's breach start with the out-of-court anticipatory remedies of further or adequate assurances reviewed in the prior chapter. The seller, for example, demands cash payments if the buyer is insolvent. In addition the seller may withhold delivery by retaining possession or stopping goods already placed in transit. The seller may also cancel any further obligations under the breached contract and proceed to resell the goods still in his possession. The seller may also lay claim to all or a portion of the buyer's advance payment depending on the existence of a liquidated damages clause.

If the seller does need to use the litigation process, he or she may first seek to recover goods already in possession of the buyer by way of an action for replevin (recovery). Note that the seller may not use self-help to retrieve the property. If the seller resells the goods for scrap or salvage value, the difference between the price realized and purchase price can be recovered. In addition, incidental, consequential, and/or lost profit damages may also be applicable.

If the seller is in breach, the buyer also has both in and out-of-court options available. The anticipatory remedy of adequate assurance is reciprocal for both parties. The buyer may accept defective goods and deduct the cost from the unpaid amount. In addition, the buyer may cover his needs by purchasing substitute goods elsewhere. If the parties have agreed upon liquidated damages, that provision may be utilized if it is not punitive.

If the buyer chooses to use the litigation process, a number of options are available. The goods themselves may be sought by way of specific performance, replevin, or recovery from an insolvent buyer. In addition, the buyer may obtain substitute goods from another party and sue for the difference in price.

There are two other factors to keep in mind which apply to all parties involved. The first is the doctrine of mitigation and conscionability. Whoever is seeking assistance from the courts must show that he or she is acting in good faith and trying to minimize damages after the injury has been inflicted by the breach. The nonbreaching party is expected to exercise ordinary care and reasonable diligence to avoid any further claims against the breaching party. Second, the person seeking remedies in-court under the UCC must not be "legally lazy." She must bring her court action within the time provided by the UCC Statute of Limitations. That statute provides for a four year period after the breach to bring a lawsuit.

II. Hypothetical Multi-Issue Essay Question:

Felicity and Dudley Shoebottom own and operate Shoebottom Championship English Bulldog Kennels. Their motto is: "Our dogs have a lot of sole!" They specialize in the breeding and sale of show dogs with big feet. In an auction held on January 1, 1994, they bid $5000 in writing for a litter of six two-week old bulldogs being sold by SpenSir Farms. Because the puppies were too young at the time to be taken from their mother, Phoebe, they were to be picked up and paid for on March 1, 1994.

Felicity and Dudley visited the dogs on February 1, 1994. They named them Humphrey, Beaufort, Bangor, Arundel, Cuthbert, and Tatton. They also raised some concerns about their feet being too small for Shoebottom standards. They decided to wait for the agreed-upon delivery date.

On March 1, 1994, they refused to pay for and accept the dogs. The puppies are healthy in every respect. What result?

III. Key Question Checklist:

A. Who is in breach of the UCC contract?
   1. Buyer?
   2. Seller?
   3. Both?

B. Assuming the buyer is in breach, what out-of-court remedies does the seller have?
   1. Have the parties explicitly provided for contractual remedies?
   2. Can the seller use any of the anticipatory remedies provided for in the UCC?
      a. Anticipatory assurance?
      b. Anticipatory repudiation by the buyer?
   3. Can the seller use any other out-of-court remedy?
      a. Withhold delivery?
      b. Retain some or all of buyer's advance payment?
      c. Stop goods in transit?
      d. Resell goods?
      e. Cancel the contract?

C. Assuming the out-of-court remedies are exhausted or not applicable, what in-court remedies does the seller have?
   1. Sue for damages?
      a. Actual damages?
      b. Incidental damages?
      c. Consequential damages?
   2. Sue for repossession of the goods through replevin?

D. Assuming the seller is in breach, what out-of-court remedies does the buyer have?
   1. Have the parties explicitly provided for contractual remedies?
   2. Can the buyer use any of the anticipatory remedies provided for in the UCC?
      a. Anticipatory assurance?
      b. Anticipatory repudiation by the seller?
   3. Can the buyer use any other out-of-court remedy?
      a. Reject nonconforming goods?

155

b. Deduct damages from unpaid purchase price?
c. Cancel the contract?

E. Assuming the out-of-court remedies are exhausted or not applicable, what in-court remedies does the buyer have?
1. Sue for damages?
a. Actual damages?
b. Incidental damages?
c. Consequential damages?
2. Sue for possession of the goods?
a. Specific performance?
b. Replevy the goods?
c. Recover goods in possession of an insolvent seller?

F. Any other factors to be taken into account?
1. Mitigation by party seeking remedies?
2. Statute of Limitations complied with?

IV. Objective Questions:

1. A remedy that is agreed upon before legal action takes place is a _____ _____.

2. A reward to the injured party in a breach-of-contract situation which places that party in as good a position as if the breaching party's contractual obligations were fully performed is a _____.

3. The act of the seller purposely failing to deliver goods to the buyer, if the seller feels the buyer has wrongful breached the sales contract is called a _____ _____.

4. When goods are resold, _____ _____ are reasonable expenses incurred in stopping delivery, transportation charges, storage charges, sales commissions, etc.

5. When the breaching party in a sales contract is forced to perform her half of the contract anyway, _____ _____ occurs. This usually occurs when the goods in question are unique, such as art or antiques.

6. A remedy in which the buyer gets the goods back from the seller if the buyer makes partial or full payment for the goods before they are received and the seller becomes insolvent within ten days after receiving the first payment is called _____.

7. A remedy in which only conforming goods that are identified in the contract may be recovered is called _____.

8. A buyer may _____ if the seller fails to make delivery of the goods or repudiates the sales contract or the buyer rightfully rejects the goods or justifiably revokes their acceptance.

9. Damages that include any foreseeable loss caused to the buyer because of the seller's breach and injury to a person or property resulting from such a breach are called _____ damages.

10. Damages that will be paid upon a breach of contract that are establish in advance are called _____ damages.

True/False:

1. ____ If part of the goods under an installment contract have been delivered and the buyer materially breaches the contract, the seller may withhold delivery of the remainder of the goods.

156

2. ____If a buyer makes advance payment on the price of a contract and then breaches the contract and the seller justifiably withholds delivery of the goods, the buyer is not entitled to restitution since he breached the contract.

3. ____If the buyer is solvent, the seller cannot stop small deliveries in transit.

4. ____The seller's right to reclaim goods is not subject to any third party rights since the buyer never paid for the goods.

5. ____If a buyer breaches or repudiates a contract while the seller is still in possession of the goods, the seller is under a duty to choose an alternate that will minimize loss.

6. ____When a seller rightfully cancels a contract because of a buyer's breach, both the seller and the buyer are discharged from any further obligation under the contract.

7. ____If the seller breaches the contract and the buyer is a merchant, the buyer may be required to resell the goods for the breaching seller.

8. ____Replevin actions, like the right to cover, are available to a buyer even if the goods are not identified to the contract.

9. ____If a liquidated damages clause is declared void as a penalty, actual damages may still be recovered.

10. ____The parties to a contract may agree to reduce or extend the time limitation set by UCC Statute of Limitations.

Multiple Choice:

1. Joe Dokes manufactures "Dokey Bikes" for off-road use. He gets an order from Bolder Bikers for 100 units priced at $1000 per unit. Halfway through the manufacturing process, Bolder Bikers breached their contract with Joe by repudiating the contract. Joe may now choose to:
   A. Complete the manufacture of the bikes and sell them to another buyer.
   B. Cease manufacturing and resell the partially completed bikes for scrap or salvage value.
   C. Beat Bolder Bikers president, Mr. Rock, back into the Stone Age.
   D. Proceed in any other reasonable manner.

2. Dedley Hardware Co. received an order for $1,200 of assorted hardware from Petty. The shipping terms were F.O.B. Master Freight Line, seller's place of business, 2/10, not/30. While the goods were in transit to Petty, Dedley learned that Petty was insolvent. Dedley gave Master instructions to stop shipment of the goods. Master complied with these instructions. Regarding the rights, duties, and liabilities of the parties, which of the following is correct?
   A. Dedley's stoppage in transit was improper if Petty's assets exceeded its liabilities.
   B. Petty is entitled to the hardware if it pays cash.
   C. Once Dedley correctly learned of Petty's insolvency, it had no further duty or obligation to Petty.
   D. That Petty became insolvent in no way affects the rights, duties, and obligations of the parties.

157

3. Which of the following is not a seller remedy for a buyer's breach?
   A. The right to withhold delivery of goods.
   B. The right to stop goods in transit.
   C. The right to resell goods.
   D. The right to cover.

4. Buyer Ben and Seller Sandy contract for the sale of goods. Sandy may withhold delivery of the goods if:
   A. Ben rejects or revokes acceptance of the goods.
   B. Sandy finds another buyer willing to pay more.
   C. The goods are unfinished at the agreed time of delivery.
   D. Sandy may withhold delivery of goods under any of the above conditions.

5. Assume the same facts as in question 4 except that Sandy does not decide to stop delivery of the goods until they are in transit. Which of the following is correct?
   A. Sandy must always notify the carrier in writing that the goods should not be delivered.
   B. Sandy is responsible for the carrier's costs in stopping the delivery.
   C. Sandy can stop delivery of any size shipment even if Ben is solvent.
   D. None of the above.

6. Buyer Biff and Seller Sissy contract for the sale of goods. After the goods have been delivered to Biff, Sissy can reclaim them if:
   A. Biff was insolvent when the goods were received.
   B. Biff's check for the goods bounces.
   C. Both of the above.

D. None of the above. Sissy can only reclaim the goods if Biff revokes his acceptance.

7. Buyer Billings breaches his contract for the sale of goods with Seller Sanford. Sanford still has possession of the goods at the time of the breach. Which of the following is correct?
   A. Sanford can resell the goods and sue Billings for the total contract price.
   B. Sanford can either resell the goods or sue Billings, but not both.
   C. Sanford can resell the goods and sue Billings for any loss on the sale and incidental damages.
   D. Sanford can resell the goods and sue Billings only for incidental damages.

8. Novel Nick contracts to buy a $10,000 antique table from Antiques Unlimited. However, Antiques Unlimited breaches the contract and refuses to deliver the table. In a suit under this contract, Nick's best option would be to:
   A. Sue to replevy the table.
   B. Sue for money damages.
   C. Sue to cover.
   D. Sue for specific performance.

9. Buyer Barbara contracts to buy $10,000 in goods from Seller Samantha. However, when Barbara receives the goods, they are nonconforming, causing Barbara damages of $1,000. Which of the following?
   A. Barbara may deduct $1,000 from the unpaid purchase price.
   B. Barbara must reject the whole delivery to recover anything.
   C. Barbara cannot deduct any amount from the purchase price but must sue to recover the $1,000 in damages.
   D. None of the above.

10. Assume the same facts as in question 9 except Barbara and Samantha included a clause in the contract limiting each party's remedies. Which of the following is correct?
    A. Such clauses are unconscionable and unenforceable.
    B. The remedies agreed on are in addition to those provided for under the UCC.
    C. Consequential damages can be limited even for personal injuries if the contract is for consumer goods.
    D. None of the above.

V. Answers to Objective Questions:

Terms:

1. *Prelitigation remedy.* This is a remedy that is agreed upon by the parties prior to actual litigation. Oftentimes these settlements are arrived at, virtually on the courthouse steps.

2. *Remedy.* Remedies are designed to give the parties the "benefit of the contract," i.e., they are intended to give the fruit of the labor through a similar or like kind substitute for what was lost by way of the breach.

3. *Withholding.* This remedy is available to the seller if the buyer wrongfully rejects or revokes acceptance of the goods, fails to make a payment when due on or before delivery, or repudiates the contract in whole or in part.

4. *Incidental damages.* These damages usually include delivery or transportation charges, storage charges, sales commissions, and the like. They do not include attorney's fees unless specifically agreed upon in the contract.

5. *Specific performance.* The UCC version of the specific performance remedy expands the coverage given under the common law of contract to include situations where the goods are "commercially unique" and thus may include terms and conditions relating to price and other marketplace factors apart from the uniqueness of the goods themselves.

6. *Recovery.* This remedy is provided for under Section 2-502 of the UCC and is juxtaposed with federal bankruptcy laws. Any buyer seeking to use this remedy would be well-advised to consult with his legal counsel first.

7. *Capture.* This remedy is provided for under Section 2-502(2) and is part and parcel of this set of buyers remedies from an insolvent seller. Note, the buyer may not resort to self-help methods in these situations.

8. *Cover.* This allows the buyer to purchase substitute goods if the conditions listed in Section 2-712(3) are met. The buyer's cover must be made in good faith and without unreasonable delay.

9. *Consequential.* These damages include all sorts of "fall out" or "domino effect" kinds of harm which arose out of the initial breach. They are often much higher than the actual damages. In all cases, be sure to look for the element of foreseeability in situations involving these damages.

10. *Liquidated.* Many students confuse this term with executed. These damages still have to be paid and thus may be executory. They are, however, agreed upon in advance and thus can save litigation cost and effort. They may not be so severe as to be considered a penalty.

True/False:

1. True. This remedy is provided for under Section 2-703 of the UCC.
2. False. In this situation, the buyer is entitled to restitution which is determined either in part by the liquidation damages clause or by the process set out in the UCC.
3. True. This would be considered a breach by the seller.
4. False. The seller's right to reclaim goods is subject to third party rights of good faith third party buyers.
5. True. This is also sometimes referred to as mitigation.
6. False When a seller rightfully cancels a contract because of a buyer's breach, only the seller is discharged from any further obligations under the contract.
7. True. This is provided for by Section 2-603 of the UCC.
8. False. Replevin actions are only available if the goods are identified to the contract and the buyer can show that he made a reasonable effort to buy the goods elsewhere or that such an effort will be futile.
9. True. See Section 2-718(1) for this remedy.
10. False. The parties to a contract may agree to reduce the Statute of Limitations. However, they may not agree to extend this time period.

Multiple Choice:

1. C. Section 2-704(2) allows for A, B and D as options to be used by a seller not in breach. As tempting as it may be, Joe is not allowed to pummel Mr. Rock into a pebble.
2. B. An unpaid seller who has delivered the goods to a carrier for shipment and who learns of the buyer's insolvency may stop the goods in transit. Whenever a buyer is insolvent, the seller has the right to refuse to deliver the goods unless the buyer tenders cash for the goods and pays for all goods previously delivered. A is incorrect because the right to stop goods in transit does not depend upon the balance sheet test, but upon insolvency in the equity sense. C is incorrect because Dedley still had the duty to deliver the goods per the contract provided that Petty paid cash for those and any other goods previously delivered on credit. D is incorrect because Petty's insolvency affects the rights, duties, and obligations of the parties as described above.
3. D. The right to cover is a buyer's remedy in case of a breach by the seller.
4. A. B is incorrect because Sandy is bound by the contract even if she finds a buyer to pay more. C is incorrect because Sandy has a duty to comply with the contract requirements and would be responsible for any resulting damages due to late delivery of the goods. D is incorrect because B and C are incorrect.
5. B. A is incorrect because notification may be made orally under some circumstances. C is incorrect because unless Ben is insolvent, Sandy cannot stop delivery of goods in transit if the shipment is very small.
6. C. D is incorrect because Sissy can reclaim the goods even if Biff does not revoke his acceptance but instead meets one of the conditions in A or B.
7. C. Sanford can both resell the goods and sue for damages. A is incorrect because if Sanford resells the goods, he can only sue Billings for the loss on the sale, not the total contract price. B is incorrect because Sanford has both these remedies and will not be required to choose one or

the other. D is incorrect because Sanford can sue for the loss on the sale as well as incidental damages.

8. D. Where the goods under the contract are unique, such as antiques, the buyer may obtain specific performance. A in incorrect because replevy does not apply specifically to unique goods. Specific performance is a better option. B is incorrect because money damages are really insufficient when the contract is for such a unique item. C is incorrect because the right to cover is the purchasing of substitute goods. Such a remedy would be insufficient in this situation.

9. A. If Barbara accepts the nonconforming goods, she may deduct the amount of damages from the unpaid purchase price. B is incorrect because she may accept the delivery and still recover damages if the goods are nonconforming. C is incorrect because Barbara may deduct damages from the unpaid purchase price.

10. B. If the parties agree to certain remedies, these are in addition to those provided under the UCC unless the parties specify that the agreed upon remedies will be the exclusive remedies. A is incorrect because such clauses are generally honored. C is incorrect because such a limitation is prima facie unconscionable.

VI. Key Question Checklist Answers to Essay Question:

A. *Who breached the contract?*

It appears from the facts given in this case that the buyer may be in breach of contract. The condition of the puppies is certified as healthy, and the size of their feet was not made a material precondition to acceptance at the time of the agreed-upon delivery. The goods therefore appear to be conforming and the seller has tendered delivery of those goods per the explicit terms of the contract.

B. *What out-of-court remedies does the seller have?*

The parties did not specifically provide for any remedies, such as liquidated damages, under the terms of the contract. There was some evidence of anticipatory repudiation on February 1, 1994, but it was not specific enough to warrant a call for anticipatory further assurances by SpenSir Farms at that time. At this point, the seller may cancel the contract and resell the dogs. There was no advance payment made by the buyer which could be retained.

C. *What in-court remedies does the seller have?*

After SpenSir Farms has resold the puppies (they all found goods homes in Fatman, California), the buyer can be sued for the difference in market price at the time and place of tender and the unpaid contract price. In addition, they may ask for any incidental damages, less expenses saved as a consequence of Shoebottom's breach. If these measures are inadequate because SpenSir got $5,000 for the dogs on resale, they can argue for lost profit losses by showing a capacity to supply more dogs and the possibility of making two sales instead of one.

SpenSir must show that the measure of damages asked for were arrived at in good faith and that every attempt was made to mitigate them whenever possible. In addition, the litigation must have been initiated within the time frame allowed by the UCC Statute of Limitations, which is four years from the time of the breach.

CHAPTER 20

SALES AND LEASE WARRANTIES

Ignorance is not bliss - it's oblivion.
                                    Philip Wylie

I. Overview:

Buyer beware! Throughout the history of common law, the law's expectations of buyer protection started and ended with the buyers themselves. A person entering the marketplace was expected to personally know the seller and to resolve any differences directly with him or her. The role of government and its courts as a source of buyer protection was expected to be minimal. That all worked well enough in the preindustrial age populated by small communities with direct dealings between the buyer and seller. What are the realistic chances today of an aggrieved buyer working out a problem directly with a scion of Mr. Ford or Mr. Honda? The postindustrial global marketplace has become too complex to expect a buyer to resolve these issues directly with the seller. The law has stepped in with numerous remedial measures to help alleviate the shortcomings created by *caveat emptor*.

The UCC rules of warranty are one such statutory set of buyer protections. How to recognize and use these warranty protections is outlined in the key question checklist. Before going to the checklist, remember that there are five common denominators applicable to all warranties. First, determine whether any sort of warranty may be in existence either by acts of the parties or by imposition of law. Examine the scope and nature of the promises or assurances made under the alleged warranty. Second, decide if there has been any nonconformance with the terms of the warranty in the time frame covered by the transaction. This time frame may be limited to just the initial sale, or the period of performance may have been extended by way of postsale promises. Third, if there has been a breach of warranty by reason of nonconformity to the promises made, has this breach caused an injury of any sort? Fourth, ascertain the measure of the alleged injury. Finally, are there any defenses, contractual or otherwise, applicable in this case? Remember, warranties represent only one path to rectification of harm. Other avenues may include tort law including the various permutations of product liability reviewed in the next chapter, consumer protection statutes, and equitable remedies.

II. Hypothetical Multi-Issue Essay Question:

"Et Yet?" is a famous landmark in Backwater. Their motto is: "What you see is what you get!" It provides a unique combination restaurant, motorcycle repair, and tattoo parlor for the travel weary road warrior. The proprietor, Ima Easy, serves a wonderful *plat d'jour* called "Mystery Meat." Any customer who can correctly guess what kind of road kill is used in this dish gets it free. Sometimes the lines are a block long just to get into this popular spot.

Last week, Big Mike the Bike ate at Et Yet? He ordered the daily special, but couldn't stay long enough to get a tattoo. He had to get back to his job as Vice-President for Finance at Leveraged Corporate Junk Buyouts Incorporated. Two days later, Mike noticed a new tattoo was appearing on his cheeks. It seems the *sous chef* mistakenly mixed some tattoo ingredients into his secret mystery meat sauce on the day Mike ate at Et Yet? What result?

III. Key Question Checklist:

This checklist is designed to help students review one of the main possible avenues of protection which the law provides to a consumer injured by a product--warranty theory.

A. Does this contract come under the purview of the UCC?
   1. Is it a sale of a good covered by Article 2?
   2. Is it a lease of personal property covered by Article 2A?

B. Assuming the contract is covered by the UCC, first determine the explicit agreements entered into by the parties with regard to warranties.
   1. Have the parties agreed upon any express warranties?
      a. Are there any affirmations of fact or promises made with regard to the conformance of the goods?
      b. Are there any specific descriptions of the goods?
      c. Were any models or samples used?
   2. Was the express warranty (or warranties) made a material element or basis for the bargain?
   3. Were there any agreed-upon disclaimers of warranties by the parties?
      a. Was the language used specific enough?
      b. Was the disclaimer conscionable?

C. After you have reviewed the transaction for express warranties, decide which title warranties may be imposed (implied) by the UCC?
   1. Warranty of good title?
      a. Did the seller have valid title to the goods?
      b. Was the transfer of title rightful?

   2. Warranty of no security interests?
      a. Are there any third party security interests in the goods?
      b. If there are third party security interests, is the buyer aware of them?
   3. Any other title warranties applicable?
      a. Lessor's warranty against interference?
      b. Warranties of no infringements to third parties' rights in patents, trademarks, or copyrights?

D. Determine what implied warranties of quality may be imposed by the UCC?
   1. Implied warranty of merchantability?
      a. Is the seller or lessor a merchant?
      b. Are the goods fit for the ordinary purpose for which they are used?
      c. Are the goods adequately contained, packaged, and labeled?
      d. Do they conform to the promises or affirmations made on the container or label?
      e. Are all the units of even kind, quality, and quantity?
      f. Are the goods passable to the trade?
      g. If fungible, are they of fair or middle quality?
      h. Implied warranty of fitness for human consumption?
   2. Implied warranty of fitness for a particular purpose (applies to all sellers)?
      a. Has the buyer or lessee expressed a particular need?
      b. Does the seller or lessor have reason to know (actual knowledge is not required) of buyer's or lessee's particular need?
      c. Are statements by the seller or lessor made to serve this particular need?

d. Is there reasonable reliance by the buyer or lessee on the statements made by the seller or lessor?

3. Implied warranty arising from a course of dealing or usage of trade?
   a. Are the parties to the contract knowledgeable members of the industry?
   b. What element of the warranty is at issue?
      (1) Prior dealings?
      (2) Usage of trade?

E. Issues of priority if more than one warranty applies?
   1. Intent of the parties?
      a. Express warranties over implied except for implied warranties of fitness for a particular purpose?
      b. Exact language and samples from bulk over general language of description?
   2. Inconsistent intent based on conflicting warranties?
      a. First priority to warranties of fitness for a particular purpose?
      b. Express warranties?
      c. Implied warranties of custom or usage of trade?
      d. Implied warranties of merchantability?

F. Breach of warranty?
   1. Any disclaimers applicable?
   2. Damages?
      a. Contract damages?
      b. Personal damage?
      c. Any third party damages?
         (1) Which UCC option applies?
      d. Any limitations or damages applicable?
         (1) By contract?
         (2) By statute?

G. Consider any noncontract remedies which may be available such as common law torts or the more modern elements of product liability law?

IV. Objective Questions:

Terms:

1. The UCC warranty that guarantees that the seller of goods has valid title to the goods he is selling and that the transfer of title is rightful is called _____ _____ _____ _____.

2. A warranty made by a seller of lessor who is a merchant who regularly deals in goods of the kind sold or leased automatically warrants that the goods are delivered free of any third party patent, trademark, or copyright claim is called a warranty of _____ _____.

3. A warranty that is created when a seller or lessor makes an affirmation that the goods he is selling or leasing meet certain standards of quality, description, performance, or condition is called an _____ warranty.

4. A test to determine merchantability based on what the average consumer can expect to find in food products is known as the _____ _____ test.

5. A warranty that arises where a seller or lessor warrants that the goods will meet the buyer's or lessee's expressed needs is known as the warranty of _____ _____ _____ _____.

6. Under a warranty against _____, the lessor warrants that no person holds a claim or interest in the goods that arose from an act or omission of the lessor that will interfere with the lessee's enjoyment of his leasehold interest.

7. Under the theory of _____ _____ _____ _____, buyers and lessees can recover for breach of an express warranty if the warranty was a contributing factor that induced the buyer to purchase the product or the lessee to lease the product.

8. A test to determine merchantability based on what the average consumer can expect *not* to find in food products is the _____ _____ test.

9. A warranty that governs the actions of a seller or lessor with whom the customer has never dealt is a(n) _____ _____ _____ _____ _____ _____ _____.

10. A warranty that governs the actions of a seller or lessor based on previous dealings with the same seller or lessor is a(n) _____ _____ _____ _____ _____ _____ _____ _____.

True/False:

1. _____If a buyer is aware of a third party creditor's interest in the goods the buyer is contracting to buy, the buyer may recover from the seller for breach of the warranty of no security interests if the creditor legally repossesses the goods.

2. _____A seller's statement of opinion and statement of value can create an express warranty.

3. _____The implied warranty of fitness for a particular purpose applies to merchant sellers and lessors, but not nonmerchant sellers and lessors.

4. _____As long as the goods are fit for their ordinary purpose, a seller can never be held liable for breaching a fitness warranty.

5. _____Under the Magnuson-Moss Warranty Act, sellers or lessors who make express written warranties may not disclaim implied warranties of merchantability and fitness for a particular use.

6. _____A buyer who furnishes specifications for goods to a seller can hold the seller liable if a third party claim arises out of compliance with the specifications. This is because the seller gives a warranty of no infringement.

7. _____Express warranties may be written, oral, or inferred from the seller's conduct.

8. _____Manufacturers are not liable for express warranties made by wholesalers and retailers unless the manufacturer authorizes or ratifies the warranty.

9. _____In effect, to impose liability for a breach of the implied warranty of merchantability, a plaintiff must show that an appreciable number of people may be injured by the product.

10. _____In establishing a breach of the implied warranty of fitness for a particular purpose, the seller or lessor must have actual knowledge of the buyer's or lessee's particular purpose and rely on this knowledge.

Multiple Choice:

1. If there are inconsistencies in warranties given by the seller, which of the following is *not* used by the UCC in determining intent:
   A. A sample from an existing blank displaces inconsistent general language of description.
   B. All warranties are equal in interpretation under the UCC.
   C. Exact or technical specifications displace inconsistent models or general language of description.
   D. Express warranties displace inconsistent implied warranties other than implied warranties of fitness.

2. Innocent Ira bought a used car from Larry's Lemon Cars (LLC). LLC told Ira that the car was fully guaranteed for sixty days after the sale. In addition, LLC told Ira any defect which might show up in the sixty day time period would be repaired for free. However, the contract that Ira and LLC signed said: "LLC makes no warranties with respect to this car." Ten days later, the car broke down, and LLC refused to make any repairs. Which of the following is correct?
   A. LLC has breached its express warranty.
   B. Ira can still prove a breach of the warranty of fitness for a particular purpose.
   C. The disclaimer is effective because written disclaimers always override verbal warranties.
   D. None of the above.

3. Merchant Melinda, a merchant who regularly sells stereo equipment to the public, sells a Sonic stereo to Customer Cathy. Which of the following is correct?

   A. Melinda automatically warrants that she has a valid title to the stereo.
   B. Melinda automatically warrants that there are no third party interests in the stereo.
   C. Melinda automatically warrants that there are not third party patent, trademark, or copyright claims.
   D. All of the above.

4. Assume the same facts as in question 3 except that Melinda tells Cathy that "This stereo is worth twice what you are paying for it." Which of the following is correct?
   A. Melinda has created an express warranty as to the value of the stereo.
   B. Melinda has created an implied warranty as to the value of the stereo.
   C. Melinda has not created an express warranty because statements of value do not create such warranties.
   D. Melinda has not created an express warranty because express warranties must be written, not oral.

5. Assume the same facts as in question 3 except that Melinda states that this stereo will serve Cathy's needs because "This stereo is guaranteed to last ten years." However, Sonic only guarantees the stereo will last for five years. Which of the following is correct?
   A. Sonic may be held liable for Melinda's express warranty.
   B. Sonic may only be held liable for Melinda's express warranty if it ratifies the warranty.
   C. Sonic can never be held liable for a warranty made by a retailer.
   D. None of the above.

6. Assume the same facts as in question 5. Which of the following is correct?
   A. If the stereo breaks down in three years, both the warranties of merchantability and fitness have been breached.
   B. If the stereo breaks down in six years, the warranty of fitness has been breached, but the warranty of merchantability has not.
   C. Both of the above.
   D. None of the above. The warranties of merchantability and fitness are only breached if thestereo breaks down before the ten years has expired.

7. Which of the following is not required to prove a breach of the implied warranty of merchantability?
   A. The product was not merchantable at the time of the sale.
   B. The product proximately caused the plaintiff's injury.
   C. The seller-merchant gave an express warranty of merchantability at the time of sale.
   D. All of the above are required to prove a breach.

8. Restaurateur Rudolf owns a large chain of restaurants. For ten years, Rudolf has purchased new restaurant dishwashers from Dealer Dan. Although it is not customary in his business, Dan has always assembled the internal parts of the dishwasher before delivering it to Rudolf. However, on his last sale to Rudolf, Dan did not assemble the internal parts and when Rudolf turned on the dishwasher, extensive damage was done. Which of the following is correct?
   A. Dan has breached the implied warranty arising from usage of trade.
   B. Dan has breached the implied warranty arising from a course of dealing.
   C. Both of the above.

   D. None of the above. Dan was not required to assemble the internal parts and therefore cannot be held liable for his failure to do so.

9. Which of the following is not necessary to show an implied warranty of fitness for a particular purpose?
   A. The seller was a merchant.
   B. The seller has reason to know the particular purpose for which the buyer is purchasing the goods.
   C. The seller states that the goods will serve the buyer's purpose.
   D. The buyer relies on the seller's skill and judgment and purchases the goods.

10. Merchant Mary sells a used car to Customer Carl. The contract states that Carl purchases the car "as is." Which of the following is correct?
    A. Such a disclaimer is unconscionable and will not be enforced.
    B. Such a disclaimer is only effective if Carl has examined the car.
    C. Such a disclaimer is an expression which makes clear that there are no implied warranties.
    D. Such a disclaimer is only effective if this is the usual course of dealing in the trade.

V. Answers to Objective Questions

Terms:

1. *Warranty of good title.* This warranty is provided under Section 2-312(1)(a) of the UCC. This warranty is imposed on sellers unless properly disclaimed.
2. *No infringements.* This warranty is provided under Sections 2-312(3) and 2A-211(2) of the UCC and is imposed unless otherwise agreed.

167

3. *Express.* This is still the most important source for finding warranties in UCC contracts of sale or lease. They can be either written, oral, or even inferred from the conduct of the seller or lessor.

4. *Consumer expectation.* This is the more modern view adopted by the majority of courts when looking at the merchantability of food products.

5. *Fitness for a particular purpose.* Three elements must be in place at the time of contracting for this warranty to be in place: (1) the seller or lessor has reason to know of a particular purpose for which the product is being contracted, (2) statements are made by the seller or lessor that this good will serve that purpose, and (3) there is reliance on the part of the buyer or lessor on the skill and judgment of the seller or lessor.

6. *Interference.* See Section 2A-211(1). This provision is similar to the warranty of no infringements and is implied by the UCC.

7. *Basis of the bargain.* Look for a fact pattern wherein the express warranty was a contributing factor (not necessary the only factor) in inducing the sale. These factors can include statements made before, during and/or even after the bargain was entered into (in cases modifying an existing contract).

8. *Foreign substance.* This test has been adopted by a few states and makes it easier to adjudicate warranty claims involving food products. Some consumer groups are opposed to this test because they argue that it gives too much protection to the seller in cases where the substance is not foreign yet still defective.

9. *Implied warranty arising from usage of trade.* This warranty is looks at what is "par for the course." It is designed to assure that persons entering into a trade or business are held to the prevailing standards imposed by that trade or business.

10. *Implied warranty arising from a course of dealing.* This warranty looks at the established practice between the parties as a base-line expectation level of performance, i.e., the course of dealing may have established a precedent in setting a standard for later dealings between the same parties.

True/False:

1. False. If the buyer is aware of such third party creditor interests at the same time of sale, he cannot recover damages from the seller for breach of the warranty of no security interests.

2. False. Statements of opinion and statements of value do not create express warranties.

3. False. The implied warranty of fitness for a particular purpose applies to both merchants and nonmerchants.

4. False. A seller may be held liable for breaching a fitness warranty even if the goods are fit for their ordinary purpose.

5. True. This is a crucial consumer protection aspect of the Act.

6. False. If a buyer furnishes specifications for certain goods, the seller cannot be held liable if compliance results in a third party claim.

7. True. Sections 2-312(1) and 2A-210(1) are not limited just to written affirmations.

8. True. This concept comes from the law of agency.

9. True. This rule is intended to protect the seller from being liable for a users unique idiosyncrasies where the harm can be shown to have been caused solely by that idiosyncrasy.

10. True. These are all elements of this warranty as set out in Section 2-315 and 2A-213 of the UCC.

Multiple Choice:

1. B. All warranties are not equal and these rules of interpretation are designed to establish priorities. A is provided for under Sections 2-317(b) and 2A-215(b). C is provided for under 2-317(a) and 2A-215(a). D is provided for under 2-317(c) and 2A-215(c).

2. A. The words "LLC makes no warranties with respect to this car" do not disclaim the express warranty that LLC made to Ira as a basis of the bargain. In addition, under these circumstances, the disclaimer is inoperable since such a construction is unreasonable. B is incorrect because there is no mention of Ira's expressed needs in buying the car or LLC's assurance that the car would satisfy these needs. C is incorrect because the disclaimer will not override such an express warranty where such construction is unreasonable.

3. D. A and B are correct because sellers of goods automatically warrant that they have valid title to the goods they sell and that the goods are delivered free from any third party security interests. C is correct because Melinda regularly deals in stereos and therefore warrants that the goods are delivered free of any third party patent, trademark, or copyright claims.

4. C. Under the UCC, statements of value and opinion do not create express warranties. A is incorrect because this does not create an express warranty. B is

incorrect because such statements do not create any type of implied warranty. D is incorrect because express warranties may be oral or written. However, the statement made here is not an express warranty because it is a statement of value.

5. B. A manufacturer is not liable for the express warranties made by the wholesaler or retailer unless he ratifies or adopts the statement. A is incorrect because Sonic cannot be held liable for this unless it ratifies the statement. C is incorrect because Sonic can be liable for such statements under certain circumstances.

6. C. A is correct because if the stereo breaks down in three years, this is less than the warranty of merchantability of five years and less than the warranty of fitness of ten years. Therefore, both warranties are breached. B is correct because the warranty of fitness is breached because the stereo broke down in less than ten years. However, the warranty of merchantability was only for five years and therefore was not breached. D is incorrect because the warranty of merchantability is not breached if the stereo breaks down after five years.

7. C. Implied warranty of merchantability is implied at the time of sale. The merchant does not have to make any express statements for this warranty to be implied. A and B are both required in order to prove a breach of the implied warranty of merchantability. D is incorrect because C is not needed to show a breach of the implied warranty of merchantability.

8. B. Since Dan has assembled the internal parts of the dishwasher for Rudolf for the last ten years, he has established a course of dealing. Therefore, Dan's failure to assemble the parts on the last sale is a

breach of the implied warranty arising from a course of dealing. A is incorrect because assembling the parts is not a common usage in the trade since the problem states it was not customary in his business to do this. Therefore, Dan did not breach the implied warranty arising from usage of trade. C is incorrect because A is incorrect. D is incorrect because even though Dan was not required to assemble the parts, he has been doing so for ten years and established a course of dealing.

9. A. Both merchant and nonmerchant sellers may imply a warranty of fitness for a particular purpose. Both B and C are required to imply a warranty of fitness for a particular purpose.

10. C. Such a statement, barring other conflicting warranties, is enforceable as a disclaimer because it is a clear expression that the buyer should be aware that there are not implied warranties. A is incorrect because such disclaimers are enforced unless the specific circumstances suggest they are unconscionable. B is incorrect because the statement is effective alone. Therefore, Carl does not have to inspect the car if the statement is made. However, if Carl does inspect the car, this is another way for Mary to disclaim any warranties. D is incorrect because the statement is effective alone. However, if this is the usual course of dealing in the trade, this another way for Mary to disclaim any warranties.

VI. Key Question Checklist Answers to Essay Question:

A. *Does the contract come under the purview of the UCC?*

Sales of food products are now covered under the UCC as a sale of a good. In the past, the sale of food by a restaurant was considered incidental to the providing of a service.

B. *Assuming the contract is covered by the UCC, first determine the explicit agreements entered into by the parties with regard to warranties?*

There appear to be no express warranties or disclaimer of warranties applicable to this case. "What you see is what you get!" does not specifically address any one of the products or services provided by Et Yet? The vagueness of the motto makes it difficult to attribute any specific promise to it. Conversely, that same ambiguity would make it difficult for Et Yet? to label the motto a disclaimer.

C. *Which title warranties may be imposed (implied) by the UCC?*

Title to the goods in question is not at issue here. It appears that Et Yet? had lawful title to the goods and the transfer was rightful.

D. *What implied warranties of quality may be imposed by the UCC?*

Within the implied warranty of merchantability, the UCC incorporates the implied warranty of fitness for human consumption. The basic rules of sale by a merchant and fitness of ordinary purpose apply. In addition the majority of states have added the consumer expectation test when examining the merchantability of food products. Even though patrons of Et Yet? may expect to eat all sorts of exotic foods, no one really expects to get a tattoo as part of the deal. The consumer expectation here is breached by the introduction of foreign matter (tattoo ingredients) in the mystery meat sauce. The UCC implied warranty of merchantability has likely been breached in this case.

It does not appear that an implied warranty of fitness for a particular purpose would apply in this case. The buyer expressed no particular need upon which specific statements of assurance could have been made by the seller.

E. *Are there issues of priority if more than one warranty applies?*

It appears that only one warranty will be applied here, and that is the implied warranty of merchantability.

F. *Is there a breach of warranty?*

Because the motto has been deemed not to be an express warranty nor a disclaimer, the warranty breach here is based on the implied warranty of merchantability as it applied to food products. The food product was unfit for human consumption. The damages for the breach of warranty would be both in contract and in tort. The contract damages would be based on actual, incidental, and consequential damages arising out of the unwanted tattoo. The tort damages would be measured in the same way with the possible addition of punitive damages.

Mike must bring his case to court within the time frame set out in the UCC Statute of Limitations, four years after the breach.

G. *Are there any nonwarranty remedies here?*

Make has definite possibilities both under tort law and consumer protection statutes.

CHAPTER 21

PRODUCT LIABILITY

Security is mostly a superstition. It does not exist in nature ... Life is either a daring adventure or nothing.

Helen Keller

I. Overview:

Traditional negligence doctrines have failed to adequately protect consumers hurt by defective products. Courts led the way to newer avenues of recourse by way of the doctrine of strict liability. A sampling of arguments from the two sides of the public policy debate surrounding this doctrine are set out below. The actual mechanics of the doctrine are found in the Restatement (Second) of Torts at Section 402A and in the key question checklist.

On the side of product users, the following points are worth considering:

1. Traditional tort law doctrines based on fault and defenses related thereto have not always adequately served the injured person. The evolution of strict liability doctrines are a logical consequence of having this deficiency in the law.

2. Contract law, both common and UCC, has also failed to provide adequate assurance to the victims of product harm. Consumers traditionally have had less real bargaining power in contracting when it comes to attaching responsibility for harm created by a product.

3. Various legislative enactments at both local and national levels designed to protect consumers tend to be reactive rather than proactive. Bans on products are enacted only after so many injuries have occurred that the products continued existence in the marketplace can no longer be tolerated. For example, consider how long it took to get three-wheel all-terrain vehicles and lawn darts off the market. Or do semiautomatic "street sweepers" really serve any legitimate societal purpose?

4. As a practical matter, the protections against defects in products are best provided by the manufacturers of those products. Compared to the consumer, they have the resources to research, develop, and test against harm. Can you as a buyer of an automobile really test the airbag before you buy the car?

5. The sanctions imposed by law for defective products should act as a deterrent to further introduction of faulty products into the marketplace. If the sellers of goods know this, they will try harder to make products safer in the first place.

6. Manufacturers and other members of the chain of distribution have traditionally had the "deep pockets" to fight off the "little guy" by using so-called "hard ball" tactics in fighting all claims regardless of the equities of the individual claims.

7. There is an extreme inconsistency among the states in the rules of evidence and the like which make or otherwise legitimate claim a "crap shoot" when going after nationally-based business organizations who can seek out the more "business friendly" forum.

As persuasive as some of these arguments may be, the other side of the coin has its own convincing points. Some key arguments for the seller against the current products liability are as follows:

1. The cost of the present system has simply run amok and is a model of inefficiency. For every dollar that is spent on paying for the cost of the harm done by defective products,

nearly fifty percent is spent on the transfer cost without reaching the victim.

2. Technology never has been and cannot be expected to be one hundred percent precise. The potential harm created by products is dependent on the state of the art at the time, and to require more is to impose 20/20 retroactive hindsight.

3. The present day procedural rules have allowed a deep pocket mentality to set in. Rules like joint and several liability of cotortfeasors allow an entity with only a small percentage of responsibility to be liable out of proportion to that level of responsibility based only on its financial resources.

4. Many socially beneficial products are kept out of the U.S. marketplace because of fears raised by our product liability system in the eyes of potential importers. Conversely, the enhanced costs of U.S. products based on built-in liability insurance costs makes U.S. products less competitive overseas. This diminished participation in the worldwide marketplace hurts all of us. The rules of product liability in the U.S. compared to those of Japan illustrate this point.

5. There is a prevailing lottery mentality as a result of large damage awards from product liability cases. The harm done may be minimal, but the pain and suffering losses coupled with potential punitive damages have inspired too many consumers (and their attorneys) to go down the treasure hunt path in the courts.

6. Some products, by definition, are involved in high risk and must be assured of some legal protections in order to be financially viable in the marketplace. Consider, for example, such hi-tech medicinal devices like heart pace makers and the like. Recent testimony before Congress by the manufactures of such devices indicated the distinct possibility that lawsuits may eventually drive such products off the market entirely.

This creates a "lose-lose" scenario for all concerned.

The steps used in attaching liability for harm done by products are set out in the key question checklist. One unfortunate aspect of having all these protections has been the creation of a false comfort. That mind-set says: "If there is harm, the blame falls on everyone but me!" The law is there to be used by the innocent, good faith victim of harm. If, however, a person harmed suffers from legal myopia, a tendency to see only what he wants to see, he should not be surprised if the law does not protect him in all events. Just as it was wrong to expect the buyer to find his own way in *caveat emptor*, it is also wrong to expect the UCC, the government, and its courts to cover buyers in all instances. Buyer beware may be outdated in the legal sense, but it makes just as much sense as ever in the reality that all product liability claims can somehow be expected to be a sure bet. Yet when you consider real cases like the one used in the essay, you can see why the law must act to restrain reckless and callous design, manufacturer, and sale of truly harmful products.

II. Hypothetical Multi-Issue Essay Question:

Clint Wayne and his fiancee, Molly Oakley, of Boulder, were as infatuated with their guns as they were with each other. They collected all sorts of new and antique weaponry and were NRA certified expert marksmen. One of Clint's prized possessions is his 1953 Big Bang Long Barrel (a.k.a. the tumescent tool that won the West!). This model was a deliberate copy of the 1873 Colt Peacemaker. The Long Barrel was manufactured by the Big Bang Company from 1953 to 1973, when it was replaced by its current snub-nosed model, the Saturday Night

Bobbitt. Current gross sales are better than ever at over $90 million per year with a net profit of $22 million for 1993. The owner of the Big Bang Company is Mr. I.M.A. Big-Bang IV.

One of the reasons for the replacement of the original Long Barrel model in 1973 was a pesky little problem of the gun going off when it was accidentally bumped. When the gun was fully loaded, and uncocked, the hammer rested against the end of the firing pin, which in turn, was in contact with the bullet. Thus, even a slight contact with the hammer could set off a chain reaction which fired the gun. To avoid this possibility, the Big Bang Company instruction manual specifically advised owners to keep the chamber under the hammer by loading only five bullets. The company has refused, however, to formally recall the gun and could not be forced to do so under current gun control laws.

On a fateful day last month, Clint was picking up Molly to go to the shooting range. He has his Big Bang Long Barrel on the front seat of his pickup truck and pushed it aside to clear the seat for Molly. The gun fell to the floor, discharged, and killed Molly instantly.

Assume your court has jurisdiction over all the parties and issues presented in this controversy. What are consequences of this accident to Clint, Molly's estate, the Big Bang Company, and Mr. I.M.A. Big-Bang IV.

III. Key Question Checklist:

A. Does this case come under the purview of products liability law?
1. Is this case involved in the sale of a product or service related to a product?
2. Was the product or related service provided by a:
   a. Manufacturer?
   b. Wholesaler?
   c. Distributor?
   d. Retailer?
3. Was the user of the product or related service a:
   a. Buyer?
   b. User?
   c. Bystander?

B. Are there any traditional tort theories of liability applicable?
1. Did the defendant owe a duty of care to the plaintiff?
2. Did the defendant fail to exercise this duty of care?
3. Was the plaintiff injured?
4. Was the injury proximately caused by the defendant's failure to exercise this duty of care?
5. Any defenses or immunities applicable?
6. Is this an abnormally dangerous activity?

C. Can the tort theory of strict liability be applied here per the Restatement (Second) of Torts, Section 402A?
1. Was the alleged product defective based on:
   a. Manufacturer?
   b. Design?
   c. Packaging?
   d. Instructions?
   e. Inadequate testing or inspection?
   f. Inadequate selection of component parts or materials?
   g. Improper safety certification?
2. Does this defect render the product unreasonably dangerous to the user?

D. Any defenses to product liability applicable?
1. Supervening event?
2. Assumption of risk?
3. Generally known danger or unavoidably dangerous product?

174

4. Government contract defense?
5. State of the art defense?
6. Misuse of the product?
7. Statute of Limitations?

E. Any other related consumer protection statutes applicable?
1. Magnuson-Moss Warranty Act?
2. Other federal consumer statutes?
3. State consumer protection statutes?

F. If product liability is found, what measure of liability should be used?
1. Actual damages?
2. Punitive damages?
3. Offset due to:
   a. Contributory negligence?
   b. Comparative negligence?
4. Market share liability?

IV. Objective Questions:

Terms:

1. A statute that limits the sellers' liability to a certain number of years from the date when the products was first sold is a statute of _____.

2. A defect that occurs when a manufacturer does not place a warning on the packaging of products that could cause injury if unknown is called a _____ _____ _____ defect.

3. The defense to a product liability action in which the defendant must prove that (1) the plaintiff knew and appreciated the risk, (2) the plaintiff voluntarily assumed the risk, and (3) the plaintiff's undertaking of the risk was unreasonable is known as the _____ _____ _____ defense.

4. The liability defense that says the plaintiff abused the product that in ordinary amounts would not be dangerous is called _____ _____.

5. A legal theory that says all manufacturers of fungible products who have been sued by a plaintiff using those products must be able to prove their innocence or be assessed damages based on the number of units produced at the time that the plaintiff purchased the product is called _____ _____ _____.

6. The doctrine of _____ _____ applies to sellers and lessors of products who are engaged in the business of selling and leasing products.

7. When a manufacturer fails to properly assemble, test, or check the quality of its product, this is mostly to be defined as a _____ _____ _____.

8. A defense to a product liability action that says that some necessary products are unavoidably dangerous but serve a valuable social function is called the _____ _____ defense.

9. A liability defense that is not allowed because of the ability of manufacturers to corrupt design and safety standards that are usages of trade is called the _____ _____ _____ _____ defense.

10. Products that are made from the same chemical base or are otherwise identical but sold under different brand names by different manufacturers are called _____ products.

True/False:

1. ____Compliance with federal or state safety standards for product design automatically absolves a defendant from product liability.

2. ____In the case of a supervening event, only the party who caused the defendant harm and all sellers after him are liable, but prior sellers are absolved from strict liability.

3. ____Manufacturers are liable for damages caused by both foreseeable and unforeseeable misuse of products.

4. ____Generally, to receive punitive damages, the plaintiff must prove the defendant intentionally injured him or acted with reckless disregard.

5. ____Strict liability, like negligence, requires the injured person to prove the defendant breached a duty of care.

6. ____Only persons who are injured because they *relied* on a misrepresentation may recover against a seller for the tort of intentional misrepresentation.

7. ____Negligence per se automatically establishes that (1) the defendant breached his duty of care, (2) there was an injury to the plaintiff, and (3) there was causation.

8. ____The doctrine of strict liability applies only to sellers who are engaged in the business of selling products.

9. ____In a suit under market share liability, each defendant must prove that he did not produce the product which caused the plaintiff's injury.

10. ____All parties in the chain of distribution of a defective product are strictly liable for injuries caused by that product even though they did not personally cause the defect.

Multiple Choice:

1. Pharmaceutical Company of America (PCA) produces and packages aspirin for sale to stores including Smith's Corner Store. Patsy Prepared buys a bottle of PCA aspirin at Smith's. Two weeks later Patsy's friend, Sarah Sickly takes two aspirin for a headache while she is at Patsy's house. Within minutes, Sarah is deathly ill and is rushed to the hospital. Sarah suffered extensive injuries from a toxic substance in the aspirin. Which of the following is correct?
   A. Sarah cannot sue PCA or Smith's because she did not buy the aspirin and is therefore not in privity with PCA.
   B. Sarah cannot sue PCA or Smith's because they are protected by the defense of unavoidably dangerous products.
   C. Sarah cannot sue PCA or Smith's because she assumed the risk of taking the aspirin.
   D. Sarah can sue PCA or Smith's even though she did not buy the aspirin and is not in privity.

2. Neighbor Nel sells her lawn mower to Homebody Homer because she is moving away. Homer is injured by a defective part in the lawn mower. Which of the following is correct?
   A. Nel is strictly liable for the defect in the mower since she was in the chain of distribution.
   B. Nel is strictly liable for failing to provide adequate instructions.
   C. Nel is strictly liable because she is not a merchant and this was a casual sale.
   D. Nel is not strictly liable because only manufacturers can be held liable.

3. Pedestrian Pat is injured while standing on the corner of an intersection when Biker Becky's new motorcycle speeds out of control because of a defective part. Which of the following is correct?
   A. In most jurisdictions, Pat can sue the motorcycle manufacturer even though he was only a bystander.
   B. In most jurisdictions, Pat cannot sue the motorcycle manufacturer since he was only a bystander.
   C. Biker Becky is strictly liable for the defect.
   D. None of the above.

4. Wilfred takes a medication for his heart condition. The medication is produced by seven different pharmaceutical companies. Unfortunately, Wilfred experiences seriously damaging side effects about which he was not warned by any of the pharmaceutical companies. Wilfred wants to sue the medication manufacturer. However, the medication is fungible, and Wilfred cannot identify the pharmaceutical company responsible for the drug he took. Assume Wilfred is in a state that allows suits based on market share liability. Which of the following is correct?
   A. Each of the seven defendant pharmaceutical companies must prove they did not make the medication Wilfred took.
   B. Wilfred must sue each company based on the number of units of the medication they produce.
   C. Wilfred cannot sue unless he identifies the pharmaceutical company most likely to have made the medication he took.
   D. None of the above.

5. Which of the following is correct? To recover for strict liability, the injured party must show:
   A. That the product was defective.
   B. That the product was the cause of the injury.
   C. Who caused the product to become defective.
   D. All of the above must be shown to recover for strict liability.

6. The crashworthiness doctrine is a duty imposed on automobile manufacturers to:
   A. Design cars to reduce the possibility of accidents. This includes such things as high quality brakes and bumpers.
   B. Design cars to take into account the possibility of people's bodies striking something in their own car.
   C. Give specific instructions as to how a car is to be operated.
   D. Post conspicuous signs on the car.

7. Snack Foods Inc. (SFI) is a manufacturer of snack foods which sells its products to several stores including Shore Stop Stores (SSS). Because of defective packaging by SFI, Consumer Chris is injured when he eats a bag of popcorn he bought at SSS. Which of the following is correct?
   A. Chris can sue SFI for defective packaging, but not SSS, since only the manufacturer can be held strictly liable for defective packaging.
   B. Chris can sue SFI for fraud, but not SSS.
   C. Chris can sue both SFI and SSS since SFI produced the defective packaging and SSS is in the chain of distribution.
   D. None of the above.

8. Which of the following is incorrect? To establish a defense of assumption of risk, the defendant must prove:
   A. The plaintiff knew and appreciated the risk.
   B. The plaintiff voluntarily assumed the risk.
   C. The plaintiff's undertaking of the risk was unreasonable.
   D. All of the above must be shown to establish a defense of assumption of risk.

9. Drug Manufacturer Inc. (DMI) produces a very effective but strong drug, XIT. Unfortunately, XIT has several side effects. DMI takes every measure to warn users of the possible side effects. However, Patient Paul takes XIT and suffers the side effects of hair loss, weight gain, and irritability--all warned against side effects. Which of the following is correct?

   A. DMI is strictly liable for the defect in design.
   B. DMI is strictly liable for the failure to warn.
   C. DMI is strictly liable because this was a generally known danger.
   D. DMI is not strictly liable because the drug is an unavoidably dangerous product.

10. Gardener Glen buys a lawn mower from Hank's Hardware Supplies. Glen in injured when he tries to trim his hedges with the lawn mower. If Glen sues HHS under a theory of strict liability, what is HHS's best defense?
    A. Supervening event.
    B. Misuse of a product.
    C. Unavoidably dangerous product.
    D. Generally known dangers.

V. Answers to Objective Questions

Terms:

1. *Repose.* These statutes remain controversial because the harm done by certain products may be a long time in coming as illustrated by some cancer-causing toxins found in the food chain.
2. *Failure to warn.* Because certain products are inherently dangerous, manufacturers and sellers of such products have a duty to warn users about those dangers. Failure to warn about these inherent dangers can support a product liability action.
3. *Assumption of risk.* We all assume numerous risks in every day activities which cannot always be avoided such as driving. This defense works best where the seller or lessor can show that the plaintiff's undertaking of the

risk was unreasonable under all the circumstances involved in the particular case.

4. *Abnormal misuse.* Some commentators have criticized this defense for being too narrow. Note that it only protects the seller or lessor against abnormal misuse. Normal misuse is expected to be guarded against. Critics would argue that any misuse is improper and should be allowed as a defense.

5. *Market share liability.* This theory is also sometimes called enterprise liability or horizontal liability. Because of the social engineering aspects of this theory, it remains controversial in public policy debates on products liability.

6. *Strict liability.* This doctrine evolved out of the frustrations raised by traditional tort law defenses used in product liability cases.

7. *Defect in manufacturer.* This is one of several categories of defect defined in Section 402A of the Restatement 2d of Torts. Others include design, packaging, warnings, instructions, testing, component selection, and safety certifications.

8. *Unavoidably dangerous.* This is a reality-based concept which holds that the law can only go so far in protecting against certain risks and that the social benefits derived from these products outweigh the risks. Note, fair warnings are still required.

9. *Common usage of trade.* This rule is designed to prevent tort liability collusion among manufacturers who might want to argue that certain harms simply "come with" the activity.

10. *Fungible.* This concept is usually used in cases involving market share or enterprise liability doctrine cases.

True/False:

1. False. While noncompliance with federal or state safety standards for product design is *prima facie* evidence of a defect in design, compliance alone does not necessarily absolve a defendant from product liability.

2. True. The supervening event breaks the chain of liability tracing.

3. False. Manufacturers are liable for damages caused by foreseeable misuse of a product, but not unforeseeable misuse.

4. True. Note these damages are commonly used in product liability cases in order to send a signal to the manufacturer.

5. False. Under strict liability, the injured person does not have to prove the defendant breached the duty of care.

6. True. This tort is also commonly known as fraud and it may incur criminal liability to the perpetrator as well.

7. False. Negligence per se automatically established that the defendant breached his duty of care. However, the plaintiff must still prove that he suffered and that the defendant's product was the cause of injury.

8. True. If a hybrid transaction is involved, look at the dominant element of the transaction to see if the doctrine applies.

9. True. This rule tends to reverse the normal burdens of proof and thus remains controversial.

10. True. This is another controversial element of strict liability doctrine. The assumption is that this rule will force the parties to get good insurance.

Multiple Choice:

1. D. Sarah does not have to be in privity with the manufacturer or retailer of the aspirin since strict liability is a tort

doctrine. Under strict liability, sellers are liable to the ultimate user or consumer. A is incorrect because Sarah does not have to be in privity. B is incorrect because aspirin is not an unavoidably dangerous product. C is incorrect because taking aspirin is not generally considered an unreasonable risk.

2. C. Nonmerchants who are involved in casual sales cannot be held strictly liable. A is incorrect because this was a casual sale, and Nel is not a merchant regularly involved in the sale of lawn mowers. B is incorrect because this was a casual sale, and she was not responsible for giving instructions on the use of the lawn mower. D is incorrect because wholesalers and retailers in the line of distribution can also be held strictly liable.

3. A. Most jurisdictions provide protection for people who are injured even if they are only bystanders. B is incorrect for the reason stated above. C is incorrect because Becky is a consumer and not strictly liable for a defect which is the fault of the manufacturer.

4. A. In a suit based on market share liability, the plaintiff sues all manufacturers and they, in turn, must prove they did not produce the product which caused injury. B is incorrect because Wilfred must sue all seven manufacturers. Whether and how much each manufacturer is liable is dependent on whether they can prove they did not produce the medication. C is incorrect because under market share liability, Wilfred need not first identify the pharmaceutical company most likely to have produced the medication he took.

5. C. Under strict liability, the injured party does not have to prove who caused the product to become defective. However, that party must show that the product was defective and that the product was the cause of injury. A is required. B is required. D is incorrect because the injured party does not have to show who caused the defect.

6. B. It is unrealistic to expect cars not to crash, and when they do, it is scientifically provable that secondary crashes will take place inside the car. Thus, the crashworthiness doctrine forces the manufacturers to take that reality into account when they are designing a car.

7. C. The manufacturer and all other merchants in the chain of distribution can be held liable for defective packaging. A is incorrect because SSS, as a retailer, is also strictly liable for defective packaging. B is incorrect because there is not evidence of fraud here.

8. D. A, B, and C are all elements of the traditional doctrine of assumption of risk. In practice, the defense is narrowly applied by the courts.

9. D. Although this drug is unsafe in certain ways, it apparently serves a valuable social function. In addition, DMI adequately warned all of the side effects Paul experienced. Therefore, under the principle of unavoidably dangerous products, DMI is not liable. B is incorrect because DMI did warn of all the side effects. C is incorrect because such a drug would not be classified as a generally known danger, but an avoidably dangerous product.

10. B. Trimming hedges is an obvious misuse of the lawnmower. In addition, this is arguably an unforeseeable misuse. Therefore, HHI would not be liable. A is incorrect because there was not supervening event which caused a defect in the lawn mower. C is incorrect because lawnmowers are a frequently used product and not considered

unavoidably dangerous. D is incorrect because under the circumstances, misuse of the product is a more applicable defense.

VI. Key Question Checklist Answers to Essay Question:

A. *Does this case come under the purview of products liability law?*

Yes, this case involves the sale of a product which is classified as a good under the UCC. Some services may be incidentally involved by way of repairs and the like, but the dominant purpose of the transaction is the sale of a good. The user of the product here was the buyer-owner, Mr. Clint Wayne, and the injured party was a user-bystander, Ms. Molly Oakley.

B. *Are there any traditional tort theories of liability applicable?*

Of the possible theories listed under the traditional law of tort, abnormally dangerous activities is most likely to be raised and will most likely fail. As dangerous as guns are, their use is far from unusual in our society. There are over 200 million weapons in the U.S., most of them legally owned. The harm created by these weapons is well-documented on the news every night. Thus the harm done by them is a "normal" element of every day life in the U.S., like it or not.

C. *Can the theory of strict liability be applied?*

There is no question, but that a theory of strict liability can be applied based on defects in design, manufacture, instruction, inadequate selection of component parts, and more under Section 402A of the Restatement 2d of Torts. It can be reasonably assumed that any weapon should have built into it reasonable safety mechanisms to guard against unintended misfires from a mere incidental contact with the gun. Guns can and do bump against other objects or fall and should not go off like a loaded hand grenade when they do. To design a gun with a hammer resting against the firing pin creates a definite danger to both the user and the bystanders. To assume that the user will keep the gun only partially loaded is myopic at best and callous to the reality of how guns are actually used. Giving warnings or instructions to only partially load is akin to telling drivers not to go over a unreasonably slow speed limit because the car my not be able to stop.

D. *Are there any defenses to product liability here?*

The defendants may argue that the gun falling off the seat was an intervening event and that there is an assumption of risk in using a generally known dangerous product like a gun. In addition, our current gun laws exempt this product from the Consumer Product Safety Commission's power to recall. These defenses should not be allowed to bar recovery. Other gun manufacturers made comparable products to adequate safety mechanisms at the same time as this one, so the state of the art defense should not be allowed. As for risk assumption, the risks associated here are with gun safety, not hand grenade-like attributes of a gun. There was no apparent willful misuse of the product by Mr. Wayne. In related cases, over 40 people have been killed by this product including baggage handlers who were handling bags containing these same weapons. As for the statute of limitations, guns have a unusually long life span of use because they do not wear out.

181

Witness the large trade in antique and collectable firearms in this country.

E. *Are any other related consumer protection statutes applicable?*

There has been some recent activity on the part of Congress to stem some of the harm done by all these weapons. Consider the Brady Bill and the ban on certain assault weapons. But as a practical matter, annual gun deaths of all sorts will soon outnumber the death toll of auto-related deaths in this country and for those people (as well as Ms. Oakley), it is all too little too late.

F. *If product liability is found, what measure of liability should be used?*

Because this product is not fungible but unique to the Big Bang Company, only those persons and entities in the chain of distribution should be held liable. As for damages, throwing the "book" at them with the full complement of actual and punitive damages would not be nearly enough. Maybe they should be forced to toss the loaded guns back and forth to each other to see how many times they go off without harm. Guns bring out a certain fanaticism in this country for which there seems to be no cure. As Sir Winston Churchill once said: "A fanatic is one who can't change his mind and won't change the subject."

CHAPTER 22

CREATION OF NEGOTIABLE INSTRUMENTS

To an imagination of any scope, the most far-reaching form of power is not money, it is the command of ideals.

Oliver Wendell Holmes

I. Overview:

The law and language of commercial paper contains some of the most befuddling terminology within a profession already beset with too much prattle. Many students find it to be the nadir of their legal studies, and generally place it on a par with a root canal or some sort of highly invasive medical procedure. A colleague once described the practice of law as an attempt by the attorney to lead his or her client through a minefield without either of them being blown up in the process. The law of negotiable instruments is one such minefield. It is tricky, dangerous, and full of unpleasant surprises. Yet the importance of negotiable instruments as a tool of commerce cannot be denied, and the minefield must be crossed.

Because this area of the law is so complex, the study of commercial paper is best begun with an introduction to key terms, the players who use those terms, and the mechanics of the negotiation process. Remember, that a special set of formalized contracts are being used as a substitute for money, extension of credit, and recordkeeping. Like so many areas of specialized human endeavor, this techno-babble may sound strange and unreasonably complex at first blush. But as you develop an appreciation for the actual scope of commercial transactions carried on with negotiable instruments, it is hoped that you will see that there is a rhyme and reason to it.

One of the main objectives of this chapter centers around how to identify the key elements of a negotiable instrument. There are six components or elements in all UCC negotiable instruments. The compliance formalities are strict. If these elements are found to be in place, a substitute medium for money has been created. This substitute is not just a matter of convenience, but rather a virtual necessity which has evolved as the next stage past money. Currency was first devised as method of providing an alternative method of exchange to barter. Even though barter is still used by many in the underground economy, the vast majority of commercial dealings provide for sale of goods or services in exchange for legal tender or a money substitute.

Out of this process, one can readily see that use of cash as a form of payment is not always practical or wise. An entire financial services industry, the traveler's check, is premised on the risks inherent in the use of large amounts of cash for travel. Those same concerns apply to the commercial marketplace. Money simply does not work as well as negotiable instruments for purposes of convenience, safety, recordkeeping, and extension of credit. Negotiable instruments are important money substitutes, and as such, it is critical that the elements of negotiability be identified and in place before these documents are passed to third parties.

Another problematic misconception held by first-time students of negotiable instruments is the difference between negotiability and legality. Many students proceed to duly memorize the elements of negotiability and learn how to identify them in an instrument. Having done that, they proceed to declare an instrument that lacks a missing critical element of negotiability as legally null and void. Nonnegotiability does not *ipso facto* preclude legality. Even though an instrument may fail to meet the requirements proscribed by the UCC for negotiability, that fact does not render it illegal. Nor is it necessarily barred from being enforced as a contract.

II. Hypothetical Multi-issue Essay Question:

Farmer Jake Gothic is fed up. After severe drops in farm commodity prices combined with bad weather, he was almost broke. His only consolation was that he qualified for the simplified income tax form, the 1040SI. The form has only two lines: (1) How much did you make? (2) Send it in!

Unfortunately Jake's problems were not over. After he claimed a medical deduction for his hot tub and a home office use for his privy, he was audited by the IRS. His revised tax bill was $6,000, due and payable by high noon on April 16th. Failure to do so would have him suffer the same fate that befell Al the Taxdodger Capone.

Jake is so angry at the results of the audit that he decided to pay his tax bill in a unique way. He shaved the side of his cow, Bessie, and wrote the following on her in permanent ink:

April 16, 1994

To:	Bailout Bank
	Farmland, U.S.A.
Pay to the order of:	The IRS $6,000
Signed:	Angry Farmer Jake Gothic
For:	To the Infernal Revenue Sewer for taxation without representation!

Jake walked Bessie into the IRS office where the cow proceeded to leave a natural deposit. What result?

III. Key Question Checklist:

This checklist is designed to help the student meet two objectives with regard to negotiable instruments. The first is to introduce the overall role of a money substitute that negotiable instruments play in the flow of commerce. Second, the questions are designed to help identify the elements which go into the creation of a negotiable instrument under the UCC.

A. Which body of law is to be applied to this instrument?
  1. Do nonnegotiable rules of common law contract apply?
  2. Do negotiable rules of the UCC apply?

B. If the document is to be negotiated, how will it be classified under the UCC?
  1. Draft?
    (a) Three parties to the transaction?
    (b) 1st party (drawer) provides an unconditional order to pay?
    (c) 2nd party (drawee) receives the order to pay from 1st party?
    (d) 3rd party (payee) is to receive the money rendered to be paid?
    (e) Did 2nd party (drawee) agree or accept the order from the 1st party (drawer)?
    (f) Is the time of payment agreed upon?
      (1) Time and sight draft?
      (2) Trade acceptance?
      (3) If no contract terms, UCC imposed time?
  2. Check?
    (a) Three parties to the transaction: drawer, drawee, and payee?
    (b) Is the drawee a bank?
    (c) Is the time of payment agreed upon?
      (1) Contract terms?
      (2) If no contract, UCC imposed time?

3. Promissory note?
   (a) Two parties to the transaction?
   (b) Is there a debt relationship between these two parties?
      (1) Extension of credit?
      (2) Is there a promise made by maker to pay the payee?
      (3) Is the time of payment agreed upon?
         (aa) Contract terms?
         (bb) If no contract, UCC imposed time?
      (4) Any collateral?
4. Certificate of deposit?
   (1) Two parties to the transaction?
      (a) Depositor (payee)?
      (b) Bank (maker)?
   (2) Is there a promise to pay by the maker in exchange for a deposit?
   (3) Is the time of payment agreed upon per the contract?
5. Other forms of negotiable instruments?
   (1) Documents of title?
   (2) Letter of credit?

C. After you have identified the type of instrument you will be working with, you must determine whether the elements of a negotiable instrument are in place as required by the UCC. The first element of a UCC negotiable instrument is that the instrument be in writing. Is this writing?
1. Handwritten?
2. Printed?
3. Combination of 1 and 2?
4. Permanent?
5. Portable?

D. The second element calls for signature by the maker or drawer. Is this signature:
1. By use of personal name?
2. By use of a trade or assumed name?
3. By use of an informal name, nickname, or initials?

4. By use of any other symbol or device?
5. Is the signature located somewhere on the instrument?
6. Was the signature provided by an authorized representative of the maker?

E. The third element calls for an unconditional promise or order to pay. Is this:
1. A promise to pay (note or CD)?
2. An order to pay (draft or check)?
3. Is the promise or order conditioned in any way?
   (a) If so, does the condition destroy negotiability, or does it fall into the list of allowable conditions?

F. The fourth element calls for payment to be made of a sum certain in money. Does the payment require:
1. A sum certain?
2. Payable exclusively in money?
   (a) U.S. funds?
   (b) Foreign funds?

G. The fifth element requires that the instrument be payable on demand or at a definite time. Is the payment called for?
1. A demand instrument?
   (a) On demand?
   (b) On sight?
   (c) On presentment?
   (d) Silent as to when payment is due?
2. A time instrument?
   (a) A definite time stated on the face of the instrument?
   (b) On or before stated date?
   (c) At a fixed period after a stated date?
   (d) A fixed period after date?
3. Is there an acceleration clause?
4. Is there an extension clause?

H. Does the instrument have the magic words (indispensable requirement) as the sixth element?
   1. Is it payable *to order*?
      (a) A specific person?
      (b) A specific entity?
      (c) Assigns of a specific person or entity?
      (d) Is the payee nonascertainable (destroys negotiability)?
   2. Is it payable *to bearer*?
      (a) Payable to anyone in physical possession of the instrument?
      (b) Is it indorsed in blank?
      (c) Is it not made out to a specific payee?

IV. Objective Questions:

Terms:

1. It is used as a substitute for cash, a credit device, and a recordkeeping device used to conduct various business and personal functions. It is called a _____ _____.

2. Drafts and checks are considered _____ _____ _____ because the drawer orders the drawee to pay the payee.

3. Commercial paper payable on demand, on sight, on presentation, or at no specifically stated time is called a _____ instrument.

4. The requirement of negotiable instruments that says they must be able to be easily transported between areas is called the _____ _____.

5. A clause in a negotiable instrument that gives the maker the right to pay the amount due prior to the maturity date of the note is called a _____ _____.

6. The transfer of assets from an assignor to an assignee in a trade acceptance is known as _____.

7. A negotiable instrument payable at some date in the future is known as a _____ _____.

8. A note secured by personal property is generally known as _____ _____.

9. A note secured by real property is generally known as a _____.

10. A negotiable instrument developed to represent the interest of the different parties in a transaction that uses storage or transportation between the parties is generally known as a _____ _____.

True/False:

1. ____A holder in due course takes an instrument subject to any defenses that could be asserted against the payee.

2. ____Once a drawee accepts a draft and the draft is returned to the drawer, the drawer can no longer transfer the draft as a negotiable instrument.

3. ____A promissory note is an order to pay and can be freely transferred.

4. ____ To satisfy the writing requirement of negotiability, the writing must be on a preprinted form. Typewritten or handwritten writings are not acceptable.

5. ____ To satisfy the permanency requirement, a writing must be on paper. No other objects are acceptable.

6. ____ An agent is never personally liable on a negotiable instrument which he signs.

7. ____ A conditional promise to pay that does not qualify as a negotiable instrument is unenforceable and void.

8. ____ An instrument which refers to consideration paid is conditional and therefore nonnegotiable.

9. ____ If the value of a negotiable instrument is affected by inflation or deflation, this does not affect its negotiability.

10. ____ The negotiability of an instrument is not affected if the instrument is undated, postdated, or antedated.

Multiple Choice:

1. Generally speaking, the laws of commercial paper and negotiable instruments in effect in the U.S. today are found in:
   A. The Uniform Negotiable Instruments Law.
   B. Bells of Exchange and the Law Merchant.
   C. Article 3 of the Uniform Commercial Code.
   D. Article 10 of the Uniform Commercial Code.

2. On July 1, 1994, Hector agrees to sell Rhonda a cast iron replica of a carnival riding horse for $1000. Hector delivers the horse. Rhonda gives Hector $500 in cash and a written instrument, signed by Rhonda, in which she promises to pay the balance by the end of the Month. The instrument property identifies the riding horse. Under the UCC, Rhonda has given Hector a:
   A. Promissory note.
   B. Negotiable draft.
   C. Trade acceptance.
   D. Negotiable time draft.

3. Shady Sharon received a check from Trusting Tim for goods Tim purchased. Sharon knew the goods were defective and unusable. However, by the time Tim discovered this fact, Sharon had negotiated Tim's check to Builder Bob for a new patio Bob was building for Sharon. Which of the following is correct?
   A. Bob is not a holder in due course because Tim has a claim against Sharon.
   B. Bob is not a holder in due course because he is not the payee.
   C. Bob is a holder in due course.
   D. Sharon is a holder in due course.

4. Which of the following is incorrect?
   A. A negotiable instrument may contain an acceleration clause.
   B. A negotiable instrument may allow the maker to satisfy a note by performance of services or payment of the money.
   C. A negotiable instrument may have an extension clause.
   D. A negotiable may be lacking a specified due date.

5. Budgeting Bill writes a check on June 1 to Craftsman Cameron for goods Bill bought from Cameron. However, Bill postdates the check for June 10. Which of the following is correct?
   A. The check is payable on June 1.
   B. The check is payable on or after June 10.
   C. The check is payable as soon as Cameron has possession of it.
   D. The check is nonnegotiable since it is postdated.

6. Ann writes a check but does not make it payable to a specific payee. Which of the following is correct?
   A. Ann has created a promise to pay.
   B. Ann's check is void because it is ambiguous.
   C. Ann's check is void because it is conditional.
   D. Ann has created a bearer instrument.

7. Handyman Hank drafts an instrument in which he promises to supply certain services in exchange for goods he received from Jolly Joe. Which of the following is incorrect?
   A. The instrument is nonnegotiable.
   B. The instrument is unenforceable.
   C. The instrument is not governed by UCC Article 3.
   D. All of the above are incorrect.

8. Agent Al works for SuperCorp and frequently signs negotiable instruments on behalf of SuperCorp. All signs the instruments as follows: Agent Al, agent for SuperCorp. Which of the following is correct?
   A. Both Al and SuperCorp are liable on the instrument.
   B. Only Al is liable on the instrument since he signed it.

C. Only SuperCorp is liable on the instrument.
D. Al is liable on the instrument if SuperCorp is unable to pay.

9. Which of the following renders an instrument nonnegotiable?
   A. The instrument states that it is drawn on a letter of credit.
   B. The instrument is subject to implied or constructive conditions.
   C. The instrument is subject to the condition of another promise.
   D. All of the above render an instrument nonnegotiable.

10. Which of the following qualifies as a sum certain?
   A. A sum with a stated interest rate.
   B. A sum with stated different rates of interest before and after default.
   C. A sum with costs of collection or attorney's fees or both upon default.
   D. All of the above qualify as a sum certain.

V. **Answers to Objective Questions:**

Terms:

1. *Negotiable instrument.* This term was adopted in the revision of Article 3 of the UCC. The term formerly used as a generic description of negotiable instruments was commercial paper.
2. *Orders to pay.* These are distinguished from promissory notes and certificates of deposit which are classified under the UCC as promises to pay. Remember, because the bank is holding your money in your checking account, you have the power to decide how that money is to be disbursed.

3. *Demand.* These instruments are payable at any time after they are issued. This term can be used as part of a draft, check, or promissory note. It is not usually found on a certificate of deposit because of an agreed upon period of time which must expire before payment is made with interest.

4. *Portability requirement.* This rule is designed to ensure free transfer of the instrument. Even though unusual methods may be used as illustrated by the essay question, as a practical matter the best practice is to use traditional paper so that the instrument will be readily accepted.

5. *Prepayment clause.* The use of prepayment, acceleration, or extension clauses in a negotiable instrument does not affect its negotiability. Such clauses are commonly found in promissory notes.

6. *Factoring.* This is the transfer of accounts receivable from an assignor to an assignee by use of the trade acceptance form of negotiable instrument.

7. *Time instrument.* These instruments are payable at a designated future date, as compared to a sight or demand instrument which is payable "on demand" or "on sight."

8. *Collateral note.* Collateral is the security against repayment sometimes required by lenders as compared to a signature note which requires the debtor's promise to repay.

9. *Mortgage.* Almost all real estate financing is facilitated through some sort of mortgage arrangement. This body of law will be covered in more detail in subsequent chapters.

10. *Document of title.* These include warehouse receipts, bills of lading, and the like,

True/False:

1. False. A holder in due course who takes an instrument has many defenses that could be asserted against the payee.

2. False. The drawer can freely transfer the draft as a negotiable instrument.

3. False. A promissory note, while it can be freely transferred, is a promise to pay, not an order to pay.

4. False. A writing may be in preprinted, typewritten, or handwritten form and will thus satisfy the writing requirement for negotiability.

5. False. A writing must be on some type of permanent object. However, it does not have to be on paper, and several other objects have been found to satisfy the requirement.

6. False. An agent is personally liable on a negotiable instrument which he signs if he does not disclose his identity and identify the maker or drawer.

7. False. A conditional promise to pay that does not qualify as a negotiable instrument is enforceable under normal contract law.

8. False. If consideration paid is referred to on the instrument, this does not destroy its negotiability.

9. True. Inflation or deflation does not affect negotiability.

10. True. Postdating, antedating, or not dating an instrument does not affect its negotiability.

Multiple Choice:

1. C. Article 3 of the UCC provides the main body of law used in the U.S. today with regard to commercial paper and negotiable instruments. A and B were precursors to the UCC, and D is incorrect because the UCC has only 9 main articles

2. A. A promissory note is a two party instrument in which the maker promises to pay the payee a specified sum of money. Rhonda is the maker, and Hector is the payee. A promissory note may make reference to the underlying transaction, such as the sale of the horse, without destroying negotiability. Answers B and D are incorrect because a draft, whether negotiable or not, is a three party instrument. A draft is an instrument in which one party orders a second party to pay a third party a sum of money. C is incorrect because a trade acceptance is a type of draft which contains an order by a seller of goods directing the buyer to pay the seller of the goods.

3. C. Bob is a holder in due course since he negotiated the instrument without notice that Sharon had fraudulently induced Tim to pay for the goods. A is incorrect because Bob is a holder in due course even though Tim has a claim against Sharon. B is incorrect because Bob can be a holder in due course without being a payee. D is incorrect because Sharon no longer holds the instrument.

4. B. An instrument which may be satisfied by the performance of services does not meet the sum certain requirement and is therefore nonnegotiable. A, C, and D are all permissible clauses in negotiable instruments.

5. B. A postdated check is payable on or after the date on the check. A and C are incorrect because the check is not payable before June 10. D is incorrect because a postdate does not render a check nonnegotiable.

6. D. A check which is not payable to a certain person is a bearer instrument. A is incorrect because a check is an order to pay. B is incorrect because such an omission does not render the check void for ambiguousness. C is incorrect because such an omission does not make the check conditional.

7. B. Although such an instrument is nonnegotiable, it is enforceable under normal contract law. A and C are true statements about the instrument. Since the instrument provides for payment in services, it is nonnegotiable and therefore not governed by UCC Article 3.

8. C. If Al notes that he is only an agent and that SuperCorp is, in fact, the maker of the instrument, he cannot be held liable on the instrument. A, B, and D are incorrect because as long as Al fulfills the above requirements, he is not liable on the instrument.

9. C. An instrument which is subject to the condition of another promise is nonnegotiable. A and B are permissible and do not affect the negotiability of an instrument.

10. D. A, B, and C all qualify as a sum certain under Sec. 3-106(1) of the UCC.

VI. Key Question Checklist Answers to Essay Question:

A. *Which body of law is to be applied to this instrument?*

Farmer Jake is involved with a processing of a payment for an amount owed to the IRS arising out of the audit. In spite of the entire body of federal law generated by the Internal Revenue Code and its various regulations, the main focus of this question will center around the UCC rules as they apply to this instrument used by Farmer Jake to pay his tax deficiency.

B. *If the document is to be negotiable, how will it be classified under the UCC?*

This instrument is purported to be a check as defined by the UCC. The drawer is Farmer Jake. The drawee is Bailout Bank of Farmland, U.S.A., and the payee is the IRS.

C-H. *Are the six elements of a negotiable instrument as required by the UCC in place on this instrument being offered as a check to the IRS?*

In order to qualify as a negotiable instrument under the UCC, the document must incorporate the six essential ingredients. These six elements are a writing, signature, unconditional promise or order to pay in a certain sum of money on demand or at a definite time. The document must incorporate the magic words to order or bearer as required by the UCC.

First, the writing used here is handwriting on the side of the cow. Jake used permanent ink and the instrument is portable. The IRS can walk Bessie down the street to the Federal Reserve Bank or to Jake's bank to process the draft. Second, Jake may use any form of informal name or nickname he chooses as long as his identity is clearly identified. Third, he is also allowed to add informational items on the check if he chooses. Usually these negotiations are found in the lower left-hand corner and have no effect on negotiability. The order to pay written on the side of Bessie is not conditioned in any way. Fourth, the amount stated is a sum certain, six thousand U.S. dollars, and is not commingled with any other sort of tender of payment. Fifth, because there is not language written on Bessie which attempts to set any time frame for payment, the instrument can be considered to be a demand instrument. Finally, this instrument has the one of the required forms of magic words: "Pay to the Order of." Just because Jake has no love lost for the IRS and adds colorful descriptors, those items will not render the instrument nonnegotiable. In any event, the IRS is not coy about how it is paid as long as it is paid. It regularly cashes shirts written in blood and the like. Jake should just make sure he gets a better tax adviser next year so he won't have to give the IRS his bull too.

CHAPTER 23

TRANSFER OF NEGOTIABLE INSTRUMENTS

If one wants to know the real value of money, he needs but to borrow some from his friends.
Confucius

I. Overview:

As seen in the prior chapter, the UCC's technical requirements for the creation of a negotiable instrument are quite detailed. Some cynics have argued that these technicalities were written in order to assure continued employment for lawyers and bankers. Their real underlying motivation is to prepare the document for transfer to, and acceptance by, third parties as a substitute for money. The document is literally put in circulation, and that path of circulation may sometimes circumvent the globe before it comes home to its place of origin. Throughout this entire journey it will be passed on from one party to another under the same basic ground rules--the UCC rules of transfer and negotiability. The key objectives of this chapter center around outlining those ground rules as set out in Article 3 of the UCC.

The two basic methods of third party acquisition of instruments are by assignment and negotiation. The common law of contracts generally covers assignment issues. A negotiable instrument can be assigned as well as negotiated but not vice-versa. An instrument that does not meet the formalities set out in the prior chapter cannot be negotiated. Thus you must first examine the document itself for the elements of a negotiable instrument. If the instrument fails on that score, look to the law of assignment to resolve the issue. If the elements of negotiability are in place, then look to the last element listed: "payable to order or bearer." These are the two methods of negotiable transfer allowed by Article 3. These words provide your first roadsigns to which direction this instrument may take on its travels through the hands of third parties. Remember it is only a clue to the first step. Subsequent steps in the negotiation process may convert the instrument from one method of transfer to the other. Think of them as the two rails of a railroad track. They are connected and run parallel to each other yet never really meet. The instrument must ride on one or the other, but not both at the same time, in order to stay on its path of negotiation.

The first path of transfer is by physical possession of the instrument if the document is designated as bearer paper. Bearer paper is negotiated by delivery of the document. Think of it as analogous to money. You do not have to sign it, indorse it, or in any way change the "paper" itself to change ownership. It only takes a legal physical transfer. Because this method is so open-ended, substantial risks inure with its use. Witness the use of travelers checks as testimony for the dangers of using bearer-types of exchange. The same dangers apply to bearer negotiable instruments.

The second method allowed by Article 3 involves order paper. This document has been made payable to a specific payee or indorsed to a specific indorsee. As such, further negotiable transfer to a third party calls for not only delivery as required for bearer paper, but also indorsements. All indorsements have three subissues and should be examined in light of these three subcomponents: name, qualification, and restriction. In addition, the collateral issues of agency and special situations will be further detailed in the key question checklist.

II. Hypothetical Multi-Issue Essay Question:

Pollie and Esther Sarg have been in the "rag" trade for many years, specializing in one-piece lounging outfits suitable for the lifestyles of the rich and infamous. They have been having many difficulties collecting from some of their more notorious customers whose checks kept bouncing due to insufficient funds. To make matters worse, Pollie and Esther's largest trade creditor, Synthetics R US is threatening to cut off their supply of raw materials unless they are paid more quickly. Pollie, Esther, and Synthetics entered into an agreement wherein all checks received from retail customers would be directly signed over and delivered to Synthetics at the end of each business day. The stamp used by Pollie and Esther on back of these checks reads as follows:

"Pay to Synthetics R US as a condition of our agreement to speed up payment without recourse, signed
Pollie and Esther Sarg"

Last week, six customer checks bounced when they were deposited by Synthetics R US. What result?

III. Key Question Checklist:

A. Does the document in question qualify as a negotiable instrument under the UCC?
   1. Are the six elements of negotiability in place?
      (a) If so, which method of transfer is allowed per the original terms of the instrument?
         (1) Order?
         (2) Bearer?
   2. If the document does not qualify as a negotiable instrument, what methods of transfer may still be used?
      (a) Assignment?
      (b) Novation?

B. Assuming the document qualifies as a *bearer* instrument:
   1. How was it created?
      (a) A signature with naming of a specific payee or indorsee?
      (b) Was the instrument made payable to cash?
      (c) Does it otherwise fail to specify a payee?
   2. How was it negotiated to a third party?
      (a) Voluntary delivery of the instrument?
      (b) Was this delivery legal?
         (1) Is there an innocent third party involved?
   3. Was there any crossover?
      (a) From bearer to order?
      (b) From order to bearer?

C. Assuming the document qualifies as an *order* instrument:
   1. How was it created?
      (a) Is it payable to a specific payee?
      (b) Is it indorsed to a specific indorsee?
   2. How was the instrument negotiated to a third party?
      (a) Was there an indorsement?
      (b) Was there delivery of the instrument?
   3. Was there any crossover?
      (a) From order to bearer?
      (b) From bearer to order?

D. Assuming an indorsement was used, what were the subcomponents of indorsement?
   1. Was it a blank indorsement?

(a) Blank does not specify a particular indorser?

(b) Blank indorsement creates a crossover to bearer paper?

2. Was it a special indorsement?
   (a) Specifies a specific payee?
   (b) Creates or keeps the paper on order instrument?

3. Was it an unqualified indorsement?
   (a) Does not disclaim or limit liability?
   (b) Indorser liable on instrument if not paid by maker or drawer?

4. Was it a qualified indorsement?
   (a) Does it disclaim or limit liability of indorsee?
      (1) Blank qualified: using the term "without recourse"?
      (2) Special qualified: payable to specific person or entity with the term "without recourse?"

5. Was it a nonrestrictive indorsement?
   (a) No conditions attached to the payment of the funds?
   (b) No instructions attached to the payment of the funds?

6. Was it a restrictive indorsement?
   (a) Condition attached to the payment of the funds?
   (b) Prohibition against further indorsement?
   (c) Restricted to deposit or collection only?
   (d) Indorsement in trust?

E. Any collateral issues related to this negotiation?
   1. Misspelled or extraneous language on the indorsement?
   2. Multiple payees or indorsees?
   3. Any missing indorsements?
      (a) Depository bank rule?
      (b) Interbank rule?
   4. Agency issues?

(a) Unauthorized indorsements (forgery)?

(b) General rule applies: inoperative as to named person unless one of the following exceptions apply:
   (1) Ratification by person whose signature was forged?
   (2) Preclusion from denial of forged signature against person whose signature was forged?
   (3) Instrument was paid or taken for value in good faith?

5. Who pays for the forgery or unauthorized signature?
   (a) General rule: loss falls on the party who first takes the forged instrument after the forgery unless one of the following two exceptions apply:
      (1) The impostor ruler?
      (2) The fictitious payee rule?

IV. Objective Questions:

Terms:

1. When (1) a nonnegotiable instrument is transferred and (2) the transfer fails to qualify as a negotiation, an _____ occurs. This transfers the rights of the transferor to the transferee.

2. A separate piece of paper attached to the instrument on which the indorsement is written if there is no room on the instrument itself is an _____.

3. An indorsement that does not specify a particular indorsee is a _____ _____.

4. An indorsement that contains the signature of the indorser and specifies the person to whom the indorser intends the instrument to be payable is a _____ _____.

5. An indorsement that is treated as a promise to pay the holder or any subsequent indorser the amount of the instrument if the maker or drawer defaults on it is a _____ _____.

6. An indorsement that disclaims or limits liability on the instrument is an _____ _____.

7. An indorsement that contains some sort of instruction from the indorser is a _____ _____.

8. An instrument is _____ _____ when it is payable to two or more people with "and" between their names and requires both of their indorsements to negotiate the instrument.

9. An instrument is _____ _____ _____ _____ when it is payable to two or more people with "or" between their names and requires only one of the named persons to indorse the instrument.

10. A rule that says if an impostor forges the indorsement of the named payee, the drawee or maker is liable on the instrument and bears the loss is called the _____ _____.

True/False:

1. ____ For order paper to be negotiated, there must be both indorsement and delivery.

2. ____ Bearer paper can be converted to order paper, but order paper cannot be converted to bearer paper.

3. ____ Order paper that is indorsed in blank is automatically converted to bearer paper.

4. ____ A qualified indorsement protects the indorser who wrote it and all subsequent indorsers from liability.

5. ____ A conditional indorsement destroys the negotiability of an instrument since it is dependent on a specified event.

6. ____ A restrictive indorsement, though it purports to prohibit further negotiation, is ineffective to destroy the negotiability of the instrument.

7. ____ If there is a proper indorsement in trust, the indorser is personally liable to the clients or heirs of the fiduciary to whom it was indorsed.

8. ____ If an indorsee does not comply with the instructions of a restrictive indorsement, he is liable to the indorser for losses which result from such noncompliance.

9. ____ If the name of the payee is misspelled on an instrument, the payee cannot indorse the instrument, and it is therefor nonnegotiable.

10. ____ When an instrument contains additional language, words of negotiation take precedence over words of assignment.

Multiple Choice:

1. The following indorsements appear on the back of a negotiable promissory note made payable "to bearer." The note is in the possession of Ernie Mark.

   > Pay to Elizabeth McCaully
   > (signed) Kathleen Schultz
   > (signed) Sabrina de Chien
   > without recourse

   Which one of the following statements is correct?
   A. Ernie Mark is not a holder because Jacobs' qualified indorsement makes the note nonnegotiable.
   B. Ernie Mark can negotiate the note by delivery alone.
   C. The unqualified indorsement of Ernie Mark is required in order to further negotiate the note.
   D. In order for Ernie Mark to negotiate the note, Ernie Mark must have given value for it.

2. Mr. Torte is in possession of a negotiable promissory note made payable "to bearer." Mr. Torte acquired the note from Sonia de Pup for value. The maker of the note was Lord Byron. The following indorsements appear on the back of the note:

   > (signed)T. Bear
   > Pay Mr. Torte
   > (signed) Sonia de Pup
   > (signed) Mr. Torte
   > without recourse

   Mr. Torte presented the note to Lord Byron, who refused to pay it because he was financially unable to do so. Which of the following statements is correct?

   A. T. Bear is not secondarily liable on the note because his indorsement was unnecessary for negotiation.
   B. T. Bear is not secondarily liable to Mr. Torte.
   C. Sonia de Pup will probably not be liable to Mr. Torte unless Mr. Torte gives notice to Sonia de Pup of Lord Byron's refusal to pay within a reasonable time.
   D. Mr. Torte would have had secondary liability to T. Bear and Sonia de Pup if he had not qualified his indorsement.

3. Original Orville writes a check "payable to cash" for $100. Orville gives the check to Careless Carl. Carl looses the check at the grocery store. Shopper Sherman finds the check and subsequently gives it to Neighbor Nel as payment for a patio set Sherman received from Nel. Which of the following is correct?
   A. The check was negotiated from Carl to Sherman.
   B. The check is order paper.
   C. The check was negotiated from Sherman to Nel.
   D. All of the above are correct.

4. Assume the same facts as in question 3. Which of the following is incorrect?
   A. Nel has full rights in the check.
   B. Carl has recourse against Nel since Carl did not voluntarily deliver the check to Sherman.
   C. Carl has recourse against Sherman since the check was not voluntarily delivered to Sherman.
   D. All of the above are incorrect.

5. Amy Allen writes a check payable to Ben Baker for $50. Ben indorses the back of the check as follows:

(signed) Ben Baker

Ben then delivers the check to Cathy Carter. Which of the following is incorrect?
A. Amy's check to Ben was order paper.
B. Ben's indorsement of the check was a special indorsement.
C. When Ben signed the check, it was converted into bearer paper.
D. Cathy can negotiate the check.

6. Assume the same facts as in question 5 except Ben indorses the check as follows:

Pay Dan Davis
(signed) Ben Baker

Ben then delivers the check to Dan. Which of the following is correct?
A. When Ben signed the check, it was converted to bearer paper.
B. Ben's indorsement of the check was a special indorsement.
C. Amy does not have to pay Dan since she only negotiated the check to Ben.
D. All of the above are correct.

7. Assume the same facts as in question 6. Which of the following is correct?
A. Ben is liable to Dan if Amy defaults on payment of the check.
B. Ben's indorsement was an unqualified indorsement.
C. Amy is liable for nonpayment even after it is negotiated from Ben to Dan.
D. All of the above are correct.

8. Image Insurance Co. makes a check payable to Attorney Ann. The check is for a claim settlement with Ann's client, Client Courtney. Ann indorses the check as follows:.

(signed) Attorney Ann
without recourse

Ann then delivers the check to Courtney. Which of the following is correct?
A. This indorsement guarantees payment of the check.
B. This is an unqualified indorsement.
C. This is a blank qualified indorsement.
D. This is a special qualified indorsement.

9. Assume the same facts as in question 8. Also assume that after Courtney receives the check, she indorses it as follows:

Pay to Furniture Fred
(signed) Client Courtney.

Courtney then delivers the check to Fred in exchange for new furniture. Which of the following is correct?
A. Courtney is not liable if the insurance company does not pay the check.
B. Fred has no recourse if the insurance company does not pay the check.
C. Ann is liable if the insurance company does not pay the check.
D. Courtney is liable if the insurance company does not pay the check.

10. Which of the following is not a type of restrictive indorsement?
A. A qualified indorsement.
B. A conditional indorsement.
C. An indorsement in trust.
D. An indorsement for deposit.

V. Answers to Objective Questions:

Terms:

1. *Assignment.* The rules of the common law of contracts will apply.
2. *Allonge.* This paper must be firmly affixed to the instrument as required by Sec. 3-202(2) of the UCC.
3. *Blank indorsement.* This indorsement is allowed by Sec. 3-204(2) of the UCC, and it may consist of a mere signature.
4. *Special indorsement.* Under Sec. 3-204(1), this indorsement consists of the signature of the indorser and specifies the indorser.
5. *Unqualified indorsement.* Most indorsements are unqualified.
6. *Qualified indorsement.* Look for the term "without recourse" to identify this kind of indorsement. It does not stop further negotiation.
7. *Restrictive indorsement.* Four types of restrictive indorsements are allowed under Sec. 3-205 of the UCC.
8. *Payable jointly.* This is allowed under Sec. 3-116 of the UCC.
9. *Payable in the alternative.* As compared to "payable jointly," under this sort of instrument, either party can indorse and negotiate the instrument.
10. *Impostor rule.* The reason behind this rule is to make sure that the drawer and maker know their indorsee when he or she further negotiates the instrument.

True/False:

1. True. See Sec. 3-201(1) of the UCC.
2. False. Both bearer and order paper can be converted from one to the other and back again.
3. True. See Sec. 3-204 of the UCC.
4. False. A qualified indorsement protects only the indorser who wrote the qualified indorsement. Subsequent indorsers are not protected by the first indorser's qualified indorsement.
5. False. A conditional indorsement does not destroy the negotiability of an instrument even though it is dependent on a specified event.
6. True. Under Sec 3-206(1), it is treated as a special indorsement.
7. False. A proper indorsement in trust releases the indorser from personal liability to clients or heirs of the fiduciary.
8. True. Restrictive indorsements are effective against all holders except intermediary banks in the collection process.
9. False. If the name of the payee is misspelled on an instrument, the payee can indorse the instrument with the misspelled name, her correct name, or both. The negotiability of the instrument is not destroyed.
10. True. See Sec. 3-204(4) of the UCC. Extra words with an indorsement do not affect the indorsement.

Multiple Choice:

1. B. Since the last indorsement did not name a specific indorsee, Ernie Mark, who has possession of the negotiable note, may negotiate it by delivery alone. A is incorrect because qualified indorsements may be used to disclaim contract liability if the instrument is dishonored, but do not destroy its negotiability. C is incorrect because Ernie Mark need not indorse the note since the last indorsement did not name a specific indorsee. This bearer paper may be negotiated by mere delivery of the

instrument. D is incorrect because value is not required for negotiation.

2. C. Indorsers of a note or draft have secondary liability in that the holder can hold them liable if the primary parties fail to pay. The holder, however, must give the indorsers timely notice of dishonor to hold them secondarily libel. Thus Mr. Torte must give Sonia de Pup, a previous indorser, timely notice of dishonor in order to hold her secondarily libel. A is incorrect because an indorsement causes liability whether the indorsement was required or not. B is incorrect because if there are multiple indorsers, each is liable to subsequent indorser or holders. D is incorrect because the liability is from previous indorser to subsequent indorser, not the reverse.

3. C. Although the check was not negotiated to Sherman since Carl did not voluntarily deliver it to him, Sherman negotiated the check to Nel. Nel was a third party who took the check in good faith and without notice that the check had not been negotiated to Sherman. Since the check was "payable to cash," it was a bearer instrument and Nel is a holder in due course. A is incorrect because Carl did not voluntarily deliver the check to Sherman. Therefore, the check was not negotiated. B is incorrect because an instrument made "payable to cash" or payable to no specific payee, is a bearer instrument, not an order instrument.

4. B. Carl does not have recourse against Nel because Nel is a holder in due course. Carl's only recourse is against Sherman. A is a correct statement because Nel, as a holder in due course, has full rights in the check. C is a correct statement because Carl has recourse against Sherman since the check was not negotiated to Sherman.

D is incorrect because A and C are correct statements.

5. B. Ben's indorsement was not a special indorsement because it did not specify the person to whom the check was payable. Instead, Ben only signed his name. A is a correct statement because Amy's check to Ben was payable specifically to Ben Baker. Therefore, the check was order paper, not bearer paper. C is a correct statement because Ben did not name a specific indorsee when he indorsed the check and it is therefore converted to bearer paper. D is incorrect because A and C are correct statement.

6. B. Since Ben indorsed the check payable to Dan Davis, the check had a special indorsement, not a blank indorsement. A is incorrect because a special indorsement makes the check order paper, not bearer paper. C is incorrect because Amy must pay the holder of the check. Ben was free to negotiate the paper to Dan or anyone else he chose.

7. D. A is correct because indorsers are liable to indorsees. The fact that Amy wrote the check originally does not release Ben from liability. In fact, Ben's indorsement of the check is a guarantee of payment. B is correct because Ben's indorsement was unqualified since he did not sign it "without recourse." C is correct because Amy is ultimately liable for payment on the check. Even if Amy defaults on payment of the check and Dan receives payment from Ben, Ben can then recover from Amy.

8. C. This indorsement is blank because Ann did not make the check payable to a specific indorsee. A is incorrect because Ann indorsed the check "without recourse." Therefore, Ann does not guarantee payment of the check. B is incorrect because an indorsement without

recourse is a qualified indorsement. D is incorrect because a special indorsement names a specific indorsee.

9. D. Courtney is liable if the insurance company does not pay the check since her indorsement was unqualified. The fact that Ann's indorsement to Courtney was qualified does not protect Courtney from liability on the check. To be protected from liability, Courtney would have had to make her own qualified indorsement on the check. A is incorrect because Courtney is liable for the reasons discussed above. B is incorrect because Fred has recourse against both the insurance company and Courtney. C is incorrect because Ann's qualified indorsement protects her from liability if the insurance company does not pay the check.

10. A. A qualified indorsement protects the indorser from liability but is not a type of restrictive indorsement. B, C and D are all types of restrictive indorsements.

VI. Key Question Checklist Answers to Essay Question:

A. *Does the document in question qualify as a negotiable instrument?*

The documents in question qualify as negotiable instruments under the UCC. A proper check is a writing, signed by a drawer. It has a conditional order to pay a sum certain on demand or at a definite time, and it must have the "magic" words payable "to order" or payable "to bearer" on the face of the instrument.

B. *Is it a bearer instrument?*

It is possible that Pollie and Esther may have originally taken some of these checks as bearer paper. However, in the process of further negotiation, they have converted the documents to order paper by reason of the type of indorsement used in transferring the checks to Synthetics R Us.

C. *Is it an order instrument?*

In all probability, most checks written to any commercial entity start out as order paper and stay in that mode throughout the entire negotiation process.

D& E. *What are the subcomponents of the indorsement used, and are there any collateral issues?*

All indorsements must be examined for their three subcomponents: name, qualification, and restrictions. The indorsement language used by Pollie and Esther can be classified as a special, qualified, and nonrestrictive indorsement. It is special as opposed to blank, because, it names a specific indorsee, Synthetics R Us. Thus, if it were bearer paper beforehand, it has now been converted to order paper. If it were order paper in the hands of Pollie and Esther, it now continues to remain order paper in the hands of Synthetics R Us.

The use of the language "without recourse" renders this indorsement qualified. As a qualified indorsement, several legal consequences befall the third party taker of the instrument. This qualification language is allowed by the UCC, and it tells future parties that the indorser has sought to limit or disclaim her liability on this instrument. There is no guarantee by the indorser that the money will be collected from the person or entity ultimately responsible for payment on the instrument.

The indorsement appears restrictive but is not. It only makes reference to the agreement entered into between the parties and does attempt to impose any preconditions to indorsement or subsequent negotiation. Nor does it provide any specific instructions as to how or where the instrument may be further negotiated. Attempts to bar further negotiation outright by use of restrictive indorsement will not be honored by the courts.

Based on the special, qualified, and nonrestrictive indorsement, Synthetic must seed collection on the bounced checks either from the original drawers or indorsers prior to Pollie and Esther.

CHAPTER 24

HOLDER IN DUE COURSE, LIABILITY, AND DEFENSES

The ways by which you may get money almost without exception lead downward.

Henry David Thoreau

I. Overview:

This chapter has two main objectives: first, to introduce the student to the unique UCC concept of holder in due course (HDC) and second, to illustrate the basic liabilities (and defenses thereto) which arise out of the use of negotiable instruments. The focus of these two objectives, therefore, now turns to the third party who becomes involved with a negotiable instrument. How, when, and where will the UCC protect that third party and when will it not? Because any discussion of negotiable instruments is interwoven with their role as a substitute for money, a comparison with money may be useful. If someone hands you a dollar which is clearly a photocopy of currency, should you accept it in lieu of currency? Or should you be put on notice that there is a problem and act accordingly? The doctrine of holder in due course is designed to protect good faith third party takers of money substitutes. It is designed to create justifiable reliance on instruments where the elements of HDC are in place. It is not designed to protect those who think play money is real and do not bother to learn the rules. Like so many protections afforded by the law, it is really only a matter of degree, not absolute immunity from one's own ignorance.

The degrees of protection afforded to third party takers of instruments begin with a comparison between the common law of contracts and the UCC. Under the common law, an assignee steps into the shoes of the assignor. Generally, he or she undertakes the assignor's obligations and benefits from his rights. The problem with this "what you see is what you get" philosophy is that it may not provide enough protection for third parties who may not be aware of the history behind the document. As a buyer of commercial paper, you want to buy only what you see and not get ambushed by potential lawsuits lurking in the bushes. The law of assignment simply does not cut off enough history and often allows third party takers of documents to be stuck with legal entanglements which were not of their making.

The HDC concept allows for a fundamental shift in the law in that, where its elements are in place, the taker will be free of all claims and most of the defenses which could otherwise be asserted by other parties having contact with the instrument. These elements are set out in the key question checklist. Remember, as radical as this shift is from the common law of contract assignment, the metamorphosis is not complete. The HDC still takes the instrument subject to a number of defenses called real defenses. In addition, past abuses of HDC principles have led to some statutory overlay on the part of Congress through its delegation of regulatory authority to the Federal Trade Commission (FTC). In the area of consumer credit transactions, the FTC has stepped in by preempting the HDC rule. The law of contract under this rule subjects the HDC of consumer credit paper to all the defenses and claims of the consumer. Various states have also promulgated similar rules as outlined in the Uniform Consumer Credit Code or by case law.

The second objective of this chapter is to review the liability, defense, and discharge aspects of negotiable instruments. No contract is forever. It may last a long time, but it will end. Negotiable instruments are a highly formalized and technically complex set of contracts used primarily as a money substitute. Paper money eventually wears out and needs to be taken out of circulation. So too must a negotiable instrument ultimately run its course. That course may be just a matter of days in the case of a check, or many years as seen in long term notes.

There are two main theories for attaching liability in negotiable instruments. The first is found in the rights and duties arising out of the signatures of parties to the instrument. These rights and duties are essentially derived from contract law as modified by the UCC. The second source of liability is found in a set of warranties imposed by the UCC. Warranties are promises imposed by the statute upon those who want to be players in this game. These promises are not always actually expressed by the party against whom the warranties are imposed, but the responsibility to live up to them is there none the less. Think of them as duties which arise out of using the road of negotiation: if you go down this road, you must follow the rules of the road.

In addition, remember that by their very nature, negotiable instruments are meant to be handled by many people. The adjudication of the rights and duties of numerous takers of these instruments vis-à-vis each other is of critical importance through the entire spectrum of UCC studies. How those respective rights and duties finally fall into place at the point of discharge of a negotiable instrument is the second major objective of this chapter. In the end, the law must provide some form of resolution. A judge cannot sit on the bench and just mutter: "Comme ci, comme sa?" The UCC rules on discharge help make the judge's job a little easier.

II. Hypothetical Multi-Issue Essay Question:

Tippee Tonic was a store manager for Acme Pig-Pens, the world's largest supplier of sanitary hog housing. Their bilevel Calistoga model, equipped with a state of the art mud bath, is a runaway best seller. As the manager of Acme's anchor store, Tippee was authorized by his employer to indorse and deposit all checks payable to Acme into the corporation's accounts at Hogsbreath Bank.

Tippee went hog crazy over Blossom Foxfire, who never seemed to have enough money. Blossom wanted to be swept away on a romantic interlude and said she didn't care if they went to "Myorca or Youroca as long as we get out of Hogsbreath." Tippee couldn't resist the offer. He indorsed several checks made out to Acme's order and deposited them in his own account at Hogsbreath Bank. The checks totaled $20,000, and now Tippee and Blossom are nowhere to be found.

Acme demands that Hogsbreath Bank credit its account and the bank defends by stating that Tippee had the power to indorse. What result?

III. Key Question Checklist:

A. Was the transfer of this instrument in compliance with the UCC rules of negotiation?
1. Is this a transfer of a nonnegotiable instrument?
   (a) If so, is it an assignment?
      (1) Assignee acquires assignor's rights?
      (2) Assignee becomes subject to defenses and claims assertable against assignor?
2. Is this an improper negotiation of a negotiable instrument?
   (a) If so, is it an assignment?

(1) Transferee takes subject to claims and defenses assertable against the transferor?

3. Does the third party taker of this instrument qualify as a holder in due course (HDC). (The four elements of the HDC are a holder, who takes for value, in good faith, and without notice.)
   (a) Any evidence of forgery, alteration, or irregularity?
   (b) Are the elements individually in place per questions B-F?

B. Is this taker a holder?
1. Is this person in possession of the instrument?
2. Was the instrument:
   (a) Indorsed in his or her order?
   (b) Indorsed to a bearer?
   (c) Indorsed in blank?
3. Is there a forgery?
   (a) Any person who takes after a forged indorsement cannot be a holder?

C. Was there a taking for value?
1. Was there performance for agreed upon consideration?
2. Did the taker acquire a security interest in lieu of the instrument?
3. Did the taker acquire the instrument in payment of or as security for an antecedent claim?
4. Did the taker give a negotiable instrument or irrevocable commitment as payment for the instrument?
5. Do any of the limitations on this element apply?
   (a) Limited HDC based on value purchased?
   (b) Involuntary HDC status by collecting bank?

(c) Was the instrument acquired at a judicial sale or under legal process?
(d) Was it part of an estate liquidation?
(e) Was it part of a bulk transfer not in the ordinary course of business?

D. Was the instrument taken in good faith (subjective test)?
1. Honesty in fact?
2. Based on actual belief based on the circumstances present?

E. Was the instrument taken without notice of a defect (objective test)?
1. Possible defects in the instrument:
   (a) Is it overdue per a definite time of payment?
   (b) Has it been dishonored by payment refusal after presentation?
   (c) Is there notice to the taker of any claim against or defense to the instrument?
      (1) Is the instrument incomplete?
      (2) Is the instrument irregular?
      (3) Is the instrument voidable?
      (4) Is there notice of discharge?
      (5) Is there a claim to it by another person?

F. Did the instrument bear any evidence of forgery, alterations, or irregularity?

G. Does the shelter principle exception apply?
1. The present holder does not qualify as a HDC?
2. The present holder acquired the instrument from an HDC?
3. Limitations to shelter principle applicable?
   (a) Was the present holder a party to fraud or illegality with regard to this instrument?

(b) Was this person a prior holder who had notice of a claim or defense?

H. If the present holder qualifies as an HDC, he takes the instrument free of personal defenses but still subject to real defenses. Are there any real defenses in place (derived from principles of contract)?
1. The contract defense of age minority?
2. The contract defense of adjudicated mental incapacity?
3. The contract defense of extreme duress (usually associated with force or violence)?
4. The contract defense of illegality?
5. Was there fraud in the inception?
6. Has the instrument been discharged in bankruptcy court?
7. Was there a forgery?
8. Was there a material alteration of the instrument (only a partial defense to the extent of the alteration)?

I. Personal defenses which cannot be raised by a taker who qualifies as an HDC?
1. Breach of contract?
2. Fraud in the inducement?

J. Any preemption of UCC rules of HDC applicable in this case?
1. FTC consumer credit law?
2. State legislation?

K. What is the origin of liability sought to be imposed for payment under this instrument? (Remember a party to an instrument can be held liable under one or more of these theories; they are not mutually exclusive.)
1. Signature liability under law of contract?
2. Warranty liability under the UCC?
3. Negligence or conversion liability under tort (detailed in chapters covering torts)?

L. Assume signature liability is sought. The following set of elements should be examined:
1. Is there a signature in place on the instrument in question?
   (a) Written signature?
   (b) Alternative to a written signature?
      (1) Name?
      (2) Word?
      (3) Mark?
      (4) Any other symbol?
2. How was the signature affixed to the instrument?
   (a) Handwritten?
   (b) Typed?
   (c) Printed?
   (d) Stamped?
   (e) Any other manner?
3. Has this signature been exercised or adopted to authenticate the instrument?
   (a) Trade name?
   (b) Assumed name?
   (c) Any other names used?
4. Primary liability is based on what capacity the signer acted in with regard to this instrument. Is the signer a:
   (a) Maker of promissory note?
   (b) Maker of a certificate?
   (c) Acceptor of a draft?
   (d) Acceptor of a check?
5. Secondary liability arises when two elements are in place: presentment coupled with dishonor and having a secondarily liable party.
   (a) Has there been:
      (1) A proper presentment for payment of the instrument?
      (2) Was the instrument dishonored upon presentment?
      (3) Was notice of dishonor timely given to the person secondarily liable on the instrument?
   (b) Is there a person who is classified as having secondary liability upon

default or failure to pay by a primary liable party? Is there a:

(1) Drawer of a check?

(2) Drawer of a draft?

(3) Indorser of a negotiable instrument?

M. Assume warranty liability is sought. The following elements should be examined:

1. The following warranties are imposed (implied) by the UCC with regard to the transfer of a negotiable instrument:

    (a) Does the transferor have good title, or is it authorized to act for someone who does have title?

    (b) Are all the signatures genuine or duly authorized?

    (c) Have there been any material alterations to the instrument?

    (d) Are there any defenses of any party good as against the transfer?

    (e) Did the transferor have any knowledge of any insolvency proceedings against the maker, acceptor, or owner of an unaccepted instrument?

2. In addition to the imposed or implied transfer warranties, the UCC also imposes warranties at the time the instrument is presented for payment. These are called presentment warranties:

    (a) Does the presenter have good title, or is he authorized to present by a person who has good title?

    (b) Does the presenter have any knowledge of any unauthorized signatures by the maker or drawer?

    (c) Does the presenter know of any material alterations to the instrument?

N. Once you have established theories of liability, you must determine liability based on the facts at hand.

1. Maker of the instrument?

    (a) Liability based on a promise to pay?

2. Drawee of an instrument?

    (a) Has primary liability been accepted based on the face of the instrument?

3. Drawer of an instrument?

    (a) Has secondary liability if drawee fails to pay upon presentation?

4. Indorser of an instrument?

    (a) Unqualified indorsement creates secondary liability if the instrument is dishonored as to a holder or subsequent indorser.

    (b) Qualified indorsers do not have a secondary contract-based signatory liability for a dishonored instrument. They do remain liable for the warranty liabilities imposed by the UCC.

5. Accommodation party (one who acts as a guarantor)?

    (a) Accommodation party?

        (1) Has primary liability on the instrument?

    (b) Accommodation indorser?

        (1) Has secondary liability after the instrument has been dishonored as to payee or holder?

O. Are there any agency issues involved in this case?

1. Was there a principal/agent relationship established?

2. Was there an authorized agency here?

    (a) Principal is liable?

    (b) Agent may also be liable unless the instrument clearly identified agency capacity?

(c) If principal/agency capacity was not disclosed, agent may be liable solely?

(d) Both principal and agent liable if agent signs both names on the instrument?

3. Was the agency unauthorized?

(a) Purported agent's signature does not act as principal's signature?

(b) Agent is liable?

(c) Principal can become liable if purported agent's signature is ratified by the principal?

P. Discharge from liability?

1. Payment?

(a) By person primarily liable?

(b) Good faith payment by drawer on unaccepted draft or check?

2. Cancellation?

(a) On face of instrument in any manner apparent?

(b) Destruction or mutilation of the instrument with intent to discharge the obligation?

(c) Intentional striking out of signature of indorser?

3. Reacquisition?

(a) Intervening indorsers discharged?

(b) Subsequent nonHDC holders discharged?

4. Discharge by impairment of recourse on collateral?

(a) Release of obligor from liability?

(b) Surrender of collateral?

IV. Objective Questions:

Terms:

1. When this occurs in two situations: (1) value is given if the holder pays money for a negotiable instrument; and (2) value is given if the holder performs an agreed upon act in return for a negotiable instrument, it is called _____ _____ _____ _____.

2. A person who has purchased a limited interest in a negotiable instrument who is a holder in due course only to the extent of the interest purchased is called a _____ _____ _____ _____ _____.

3. The doctrine that says a holder cannot qualify as an HDC if she has notice that there is any adverse claim against or defense to its payment is called the _____ _____ doctrine.

4. The rule that says a holder who does not qualify as a holder in due course in his own right becomes a holder in due course if he acquires the instrument through a holder in due course is called the _____ _____.

5. A defense that can be raised against both holders and holders in due course is called a _____ _____.

6. A defense that can be raised against enforcement of a negotiable instrument by an ordinary holder is called a _____ _____.

7. A type of liability that can apply to both signers and nonsigners who are transferors is called _____ _____.

8. The type of liability that (1) makers of promissory notes and certificates of deposit and (2) acceptors of drafts and checks have is called _____ _____.

10. To be _____ is to be relieved from liability on negotiable instruments; this can be accomplished by (1) payment, cancellation, or reacquisition of an instrument, (2) impairment or recourse of collateral, or (3) alteration of the instrument.

True/False:

1. _____ A holder in due course can never acquire better rights then the transferor had.

2. _____ A holder does not necessarily have to own the instrument to transfer it, negotiate it, enforce payment of it in his own name, or discharge it.

3. _____ The UCC concept of value and the contract concept of consideration are the same and can be used interchangeably.

4. _____The defense of fraud in the inducement is a real defense and can be raised against a holder in due course.

5. _____Implied warranties are made when a negotiable instrument is originally issued.

6. _____Transfer warranties are not made when an instrument is transferred for no value.

7. _____Notice of presentment and notice of dishonor are effective when sent, not when received.

8. _____Both an authorized agent and her principal are liable if the agent signs a negotiable instrument indicating that she is an agent, but failing to specifically identify her principal.

9. _____When a party other than the indorser pays a negotiable instrument, that party is discharged from liability but none of the subsequent parties are discharged.

10. _____The Federal Consumer Product Safety Commission has eliminated the HDC status for the sale of certain consumer goods.

Multiple Choice:

1. To the extent that a holder of a negotiable promissory note is a holder in due course, the holder takes the note free from which of the following defenses?
   A. Nonperformance of a condition precedent.
   B. Discharge of the maker in bankruptcy.
   C. Minority of the maker where it is a defense to enforcement of a contract.
   D. Forgery of the maker's signature.

2. Wealthy William gives Busy Betsy a check for $100,000 as payment for Betsy's business. Betsy indorses the check and negotiates it to Contractor Cathy who has just built a house for Betsy. Which of the following is correct?
   A. Cathy is a holder in due course because building the house satisfies the contract concept of consideration, and that is all that is needed under the UCC.
   B. Cathy is a holder in due course because she performed the agreed upon consideration which satisfies the UCC concept of value.
   C. Cathy is not a holder in due course because she has not satisfied the UCC concept of value.
   D. None of the above.

3. Borrowing Bob borrows $500 from Loaner Linda. Bob signs a promissory note promising to repay Linda the $500 plus interest at the end of the year. Linda sells the note to Holder Henry for $300 in cash and $200 due in 30 days. Henry is:
   A. A limited holder in due course to the amount of $300.
   B. A limited holder in due course to the amount of $200.
   C. A holder in due course to the amount of $500.
   D. None of the above.

4. Assume the same facts as in question 3 except Linda sells the note to Henry at a discount. Henry pays only $250 for the $500 note. Henry is:
   A. A limited holder in due course to the amount of $250.
   B. A holder in due course to the amount of $250.
   C. A holder in due course to the amount of $500.
   D. Not a holder in due course or a limited holder in due course since he did not pay the full $500.

5. Naive Nancy acquires an instrument from Dealing Diedre. The instrument has a face value of $1,000. However, Nancy, who has never dealt with such negotiable instruments before, is ecstatic because she believes she got a great deal since she paid only $250. Which of the following is correct?
   A. Nancy did not take the instrument in good faith since under an objective test for honesty no reasonable person could have believed this was a legitimate negotiation.
   B. Nancy may be a holder in due course if, under the subjective test, she believed the negotiation was legitimate.
   C. Nancy did not take the instrument in good faith unless Diedre actually believed the negotiation was legitimate.
   D. Nancy did not take the instrument in good faith since she purchased it at a deep discount.

6. Trusting Tina writes a check to Sneaky Sam for $50. Sam alters the check by adding a zero and rewriting the amount to read $500. Sam then negotiates the check to Creditor Carol as payment for a debt he owed. Which of the following is correct?
   A. Tina must pay Carol $500 since Carol took the check free of any defenses.
   B. Tina must pay Carol $500 since material alteration is a personal defense which Tina cannot assert.
   C. Tina does not have to pay $500 since material alteration is a real defense which she may assert.
   D. None of the above.

7. Blare bought a house and provided the required funds in the form of a certified check from a bank. Which of the following statements correctly describes the legal liability of Blare and the bank?
   A. The bank has accepted; therefore, Blare is without liability.
   B. The bank has not accepted; therefore, Blare has primary liability.
   C. The bank has accepted, but Blare has secondary liability.
   D. The bank has not accepted, but Blare has secondary liability.

8. Edward writes a check to Fred for $500. Fred indorses the check "without recourse" and negotiates the check to Grace. Which of the following is correct?
   A. Fred has disclaimed the transfer warranty that no defenses of any party are good against the transferor.
   B. Fred has disclaimed the transfer warranty that all signatures are genuine or authorized.
   C. Fred has disclaimed any presentment warranties.
   D. None of the above. Fred cannot disclaim any implied warranties.

9. Amy delivers bearer paper to Brian. Brian then negotiates the check to Carmen. Which of the following is correct?
   A. Amy is liable to both Brian and Carmen for transfer warranties.
   B. Carmen can recover on transfer warranties from both Amy and Brian.
   C. Carmen can recover on transfer warranties from only Brian.
   D. There are no transfer warranties on bearer paper.

10. Unstable Edwin writes a check to Middle Mildred for $300. Mildred endorses the check and negotiates it to Suspicious Susan. Susan believes Edwin's checking account is overdrawn and the check may bounce. Which of the following is correct?
   A. Susan can hold Mildred liable since she is afraid Edwin's checking account is overdrawn.
   B. Susan can hold Edwin liable since she is afraid Edwin's checking account is overdrawn.
   C. Susan cannot hold anyone liable until the check is actually dishonored.
   D. None of the above.

V. Answers to Objective Questions:

Terms:

1. *Performance of agreed upon consideration.* The second basic building block in the construction of HDC status is to show that the holder has given value for the negotiable instrument. Under Section 3-303 of the UCC, both scenarios listed in the question qualify as giving value for purposes of this section.
2. *Limited holder in due course.* HDC status will be extended to this person only to the extent of his or her interest purchased in the instrument.
3. *Red light.* This doctrine says that a holder cannot qualify as an HDC if he or she has notice of unauthorized signatures or alternations to the instrument, or of any adverse claim against it, or of any defenses to its payment.
4. *Shelter principle.* This rule applies to anyone in the chain of title who can trace his or her title back to a holder in due course. In order to prevent laundering of negotiable instruments, this rule cannot be used for the benefit of persons who were parties to fraud or illegalities affecting the instrument. It also applies to prior holders who had notice of a defense or claim against the instrument.
5. *Real defense.* These defenses are considered too important as a matter of public policy to be cut off in favor of HDCs. They include minority, mental incompetence, extreme duress, fraud in the inception, bankruptcy, forgeries, and material alterations (only to the extent of the alteration).

6. *Personal defense.* These defenses ordinarily arise out of the initial contract relationship which gave rise to the instrument, such as breach of contract or fraud in the inducement. Because of possible abuses of having these defenses cut off by the HDC status, the Federal Trade Commission rules on credit transactions have modified these defense cut-offs vis-à-vis certain transactions involving consumer goods.

7. *Warranty liability.* The law implies certain warranties on transferors of negotiable instruments. These warranties not only apply to signers but also to transferors. The theory behind these warranties is to shift the risk of loss to the party who was in the best position to prevent the loss, i.e., the person who dealt face to face with the wrongdoer.

8. *Primary liability.* This is an absolute liability to pay a negotiable instrument, subject only to certain real defenses. Secondary liability is similar to that of a guarantor of a simple contract. It arises when the party primarily liable on the instrument defaults and fails to pay the instrument when due.

9. *Accommodation maker.* A person who signs an instrument guaranteeing payment is primarily liable on the instrument. That is, the other party can seek payment on the instrument from the accommodation maker without first seeking payment from the maker.

10. *Discharged.* Discharge is defined as an action or event that relieves certain parties from liability on negotiable instruments. All the items listed in this question qualify as a basis for discharge from liability on a negotiable instrument under the UCC.

True/False:

1. False. A holder in due course, by definition, can acquire better rights than the transferor had. A holder in due course takes the instrument free from all claims and all personal defenses that can be asserted against the transferor.

2. True. A holder need not necessarily own the instrument to negotiate it.

3. False. Certain things may constitute consideration but not meet the UCC definition of value.

4. False. The defense of fraud in the inducement is a personal defense and, therefore, cannot be raised against a holder in due course.

5. False. Implied warranties are only made when the instrument is transferred, not when it is originally issued.

6. True. An instrument must be transferred for value to have transfer warranties.

7. False. Notice of presentment is effective when it is received. Notice of dishonor is effective when it is sent.

8. False. If an agent signs a negotiable instrument indicating that she is an agent but does not identify her principal, only the agent is liable. The principal is not liable on such an instrument. However, the agent can recover from the principal if she is made to pay.

9. False. When a party other than the indorser pays a negotiable instrument, that party and all subsequent parties are discharged from liability.

10. False. The HDC rules with regard to certain consumer credit transactions have been eliminated by the Federal Trade Commission.

Multiple Choice:

1. C. A holder in due course takes an instrument free of personal defenses but is subject to real defenses. Breach of contract or nonperformance of a condition precedent describes a personal defense. B is incorrect because bankruptcy is a real defense. C is incorrect because when a minor disaffirms a contract, it is treated as a real defense. D is incorrect because a forgery of a maker's or drawer's signature is a real defense.

2. B. Performance of the agreed upon consideration satisfies the UCC concept of value. A is incorrect because the holder must satisfy the UCC concept of value, not the contract concept of consideration. Though here they are similar, what qualifies as consideration may not necessarily qualify as value. C is incorrect because Cathy has satisfied the UCC concept of value.

3. A. Henry is a limited holder in due course to the amount for which he has paid--$300. In 30 days, when Henry pays the remaining $200, he will be a holder in due course to the full amount of $500. B is incorrect because Henry is a holder in due course to the amount which he has paid, not the amount he has not paid. C is incorrect because Henry is not a holder in due course to the full amount of $500 until he pays the remaining $200 due in 30 days.

4. C. Although Henry bought the note at a $250 discount, he is a holder in due course to the full amount of the note-- $500. A is incorrect because Henry is not a limited holder in due course, but a holder in due course to the full amount of the face value of the note. B is incorrect because Henry is a holder in due course to the full amount of $500, not merely the discounted price he paid for the note-- $250. D is incorrect because buying a negotiable instrument at a discount does not destroy a holder's ability to be a holder in due course. In fact, if all other requirements are met, the holder is a holder in due course to the full amount of the face value of the instrument.

5. B. In determining good faith, courts use a subjective test in deciding the honesty of the holder. Here, the circumstances suggest that Nancy was acting in good faith since she was inexperienced in such transactions. A is incorrect because the test for honesty is not an objective, but a subjective, test. The test is based on the person in question, not the reasonable person. C is incorrect because the subjective test is applied only to the holder, not to the transferor. D is incorrect because purchasing an instrument at a deep discount does not necessarily destroy the holder's good faith.

6. C. Material alteration is a real defense and may be raised against Carol in this situation. Carol's only recourse is against Sam. A is incorrect because Carol takes the instrument free from any personal defenses, but not real defenses. Material alteration is a real defense and can be raised in this situation. B is incorrect because material alteration is a real defense, not a personal defense. Therefore, it can be raised in this situation.

7. C. A certified check is a check in which the payer bank has accepted the check and has agreed in advance to pay. Thus, the bank is primarily liable. The drawer, Blare, has secondary liability on the check. A is incorrect because the drawer retains secondary liability. B is incorrect because the bank accepts the check when it certifies it by accepting the check. The

bank has primary liability, and the drawer has secondary liability. D is incorrect because although Blare has secondary liability, the bank has accepted.

8. A. Generally, transfer warranties cannot be disclaimed. However, here Fred indorsed the check "without recourse" which is a disclaimer to the transfer warranty that no defenses of any party are good against the transferor. Such an indorsement warrants that the transferor has no knowledge of defenses. B is incorrect because the transfer warranty that all signatures are genuine or authorized cannot generally be disclaimed. C is incorrect because such an indorsement does not affect presentment warranties. D is incorrect because Fred can disclaim at least one implied transfer warranty.

9. C. When bearer paper is delivered, the transfer warranties are made by the transferor only to the immediate transferee. Therefore, here, Carmen can only recover against Brian, but not Amy. Amy does have transfer warranty liability to Brian. A is incorrect because Amy is not liable to Carmen for transfer warranties. B is incorrect because Carmen cannot recover for transfer warranties from Amy. D is incorrect because there are transfer warranties on bearer paper although they are somewhat limited.

10. C. Both Edwin and Mildred are secondarily liable on the check. However, such liability does not come into effect until (1) the instrument is properly presented for payment, (2) the instrument is dishonored and (3) notice of the dishonor is timely given to the person to be held secondarily liable on the instrument. Here, Susan only suspects Edward's checking account is overdrawn, but the check has not been dishonored

yet. Susan cannot hold anyone liable until the check is actually dishonored. A and B are incorrect because Susan cannot hold anyone liable until the check has been dishonored.

VI. Key Question Checklist Answers to Essay Question:

A-F. *Were checks to Acme Pig-Pen Company transferred in compliance with the UCC rules of negotiation, and did Acme qualify as a holder in due course?*

It appears that the UCC rules of negotiation were complied with up to the point of Acme having acquired these checks from third parties. These checks were payable to Acme, and Acme qualified as a holder by way of having physical possession of the checks. It may also be assumed that the checks were obtained by Acme in exchange for value by way of the company having provided goods or services for them. In addition, prior to Tippee's involvement with the check indorsement process, there was no evidence of any bad faith on the part of Acme, nor of any notice, actual or constructive, of any problems, including forgeries alterations or irregularities. Thus, Acme qualifies as an HDC on these checks.

G-J. *If Acme qualifies as an HDC on these checks prior to the acts of Tippee with regard to the indorsements, what defenses, if any, may Acme use vis-à-vis prior makers or indorsers of these negotiable instruments?*

Because Acme is an HDC, that status will allow it to take these checks free of personal defenses which may have arisen in the negotiation process prior to Acme getting the checks. This HDC status will not protect

213

Acme vis-à-vis any real defenses which may have arisen such as minority, adjudicated mental incapacity, extreme duress, illegality, fraud in the inception, or bankruptcy discharge. In addition, if the checks were related to the sale of consumer goods, then the personal defenses may not have been cut off due to the preemption of UCC rules by the FTC consumer credit laws. In this case, it appears that the products in question were most likely to be used by the buyers as farm equipment, in spite of a trend of having pot-bellied pigs as personal pets.

K&L. *Can Acme now hold Hogsbreath Bank liable for having honored the checks presented to it by Tippee? Would it be under signature liability?*

The Hogsbreath Bank may be liable under a theory of conversion. The bank can successfully argue that no forgery occurred. Had there been an out and out forgery, the bank would be liable for improper payment of the checks on presentation for not knowing its indorser or for failing to handle the document in the proper manner.

The signatures on the checks by the original drawer and subsequent indorsers prior to the checks arriving at Acme are not in dispute here. Primary liability on the checks remains with the acceptor of the check. The checks themselves were not dishonored at the point of presentment, so no secondary liability is at issue.

M. *Could any warranty liabilities be asserted against Hogsbreath Bank?*

In addition, the transfer and presentment warranties were lived up to by the original parties. The real problem here was the breach of warranties by the indorser, Tippee, acting in violation of his employment contract. Tippee was engaged in forgery when he proceeded to deposit the checks made to Acme's order into his own personal account at Hogsbreath Bank.

N. *Based on the above-mentioned theories of liability, what are the respective responsibilities of the parties under these instruments?*

The respective liabilities of the various parties to these instruments are as follows:
1. The drawees of the original instruments upon presentment are discharged from any further liability.
2. The original drawers of the instrument, the people who wrote the checks, are also discharged because of the payments made by the drawer.

O. *What are the effects of agency law in this case?*

Here there was a principal/agency relationship established between Acme and Tippee Tonic. The scope of the agency was limited, and that limitation was duly communicated to Hogsbreath Bank. Because the acts of Tippee constituted forgery, they were beyond the scope of authority granted to Tippee by Acme. Hogsbreath Bank should be charged with that knowledge. Tippee was authorized to indorse Acme's checks for purposes of deposit, not into his personal account. The bank is therefore liable to Acme by reason of allowing forged and unauthorized indorsements to go through the negotiation process. The bank must now credit Acme's account based on its mistakes and seek reimbursement from Tippee if he can be found. They should try either Myorca or Yourorca.

CHAPTER 25

CHECKS, ELECTRONIC FUND TRANSFERS, AND THE BANKING SYSTEM

There is time for work and time for love. That leaves no other time.

Coco Chanel

I. Overview:

As a target of derision, the banking profession has always kept pace with the members of the bar. When the Bank of America world headquarters building was dedicated in San Francisco, a large amorphous stone sculpture was placed near the portico. It was quickly nicknamed the "Bankers Heart" by local pundits. This resentment may be based on some of the same sources of contempt for any number of professions. The larger society resents its dependence on them. It objects to code language used by the members of these groups and wishes life would go back to a simpler time when one did not need to formally contract for everything or make a federal case out of every dispute. Would that it were so! The realities of the today's financial services marketplace simply have put paid that sort of wishful longing. We live in an age of Spaceship Earth which is quickly rendering the use of paper money obsolete. The transfer of money substitutes is more complicated than ever because it is, at least in part, more efficient than ever. Money sitting in Tokyo can be transferred to New York City in seconds. As with any fast moving train, a few people get left at the station and resent it. In the meantime, welcome aboard for the ride.

The rules of rights and duties involving checks are really not all that new to the layperson. Most students have a ongoing contractual relationship with a bank and are already familiar with the basic rules involving negotiable instruments. The best way to approach issues involving checks is to first examine the underlying contractual obligations between the respective parties. Then determine what public policy based limitations are imposed on the parties by the UCC and the courts. The duties imposed on banks can be very strict and difficult to avoid. Finally, look to see if the transaction falls into the sphere of hi-tech transfers of money substitutes.

Many futurists predict that the year 2000 A.D. will herald the age of the paperless society. Given the proclivity of law to sometimes inadequately protect those of us in an unequal bargaining position, equity and good conscience should dictate the rules of the electronic road as well as the paper road. Recent revisions to the UCC vis-à-vis wire transfers and the like reflect attempts by both scholars and practitioners of banking to have the code better reflect this inexorable move into the next millennium. In all events, the law of checks, wire transfers, and money substitute transfer systems cannot afford to disserve its constituents by being a lager.

II. Hypothetical Multi-issue Essay Question:

Patric Vanman worked long and hard at Bailout Bank as a paper-pushing, computer-punching bankocrat. He needed a vacation. He bought a brand new sports car and decided to drive it across Canada from Vancouver to Nova Scotia on scenic Highway One. He was to leave on the 15th of the month and come back four weeks later. Because he was to be paid in the interim, he filled out a direct deposit form asking Bailout to credit his paycheck directly to his personal account while he was gone. Bailout sent his check to his house instead, and Patric bounced checks all across Canada without knowing it. The Royal Canadian Mounted Police were just about to catch him as he crossed the border. What result?

III. Key Question Checklist:

A. What is the basic contractual relationship between the parties with regard to the negotiable instrument at issue?
1. Maker/payee?
2. Drawer/drawee?
3. Drafter/draftee?
4. Nonbank institution/customer?
5. Payee/depository bank?
6. Depository bank/intermediary bank?
7. Intermediary bank/payor bank?

B. You must then identify the particular negotiable instrument at issue. Is it:
1. A normal check?
2. A certified check?
3. A traveler's check?
4. A cashier's check?

C. Once you have established which relationship or relationships are in play, you must identify the point or points of the negotiation cycle at which the issue arises. Did the problem occur at:
1. The point of creation of the negotiable instrument?
2. The point of initial introduction of the negotiable instrument into the negotiation cycle?
   (a) Delivery?
   (b) Indorsement?
   (c) New third party involvement?
3. The point of initial processing for payment?
   (a) Deposit by payee?
   (b) Presentment directly by payee?

4. The point of intermediary transfer between banks?
   (a) Was the instrument presented directly by the depository bank to the payor bank?
   (b) Did the depository bank use the services of an intermediary collecting bank?
5. The point of presentment for payment at payor bank?
   (a) Provisional credit?
   (b) Deferred posting?
   (c) Deadlines met?

D. Based on your identification of the instrument, respective parties to the transaction, and the time frame in which the issue arose, you must decide what the respective duties and rights of the parties are based on both contract law and the UCC.
1. Did the bank live up to its basic duties to its customers?
   (a) Honor checks written against his or her account?
   (b) Accept deposits into customer's account?
   (c) Collect checks deposited into customer's account on other banks and make payable to or indorsed to the customer?
2. Did the customer live up to his or her basic duties to his or her bank?
   (a) Supply sufficient funds to pay any checks written against their account?
   (b) Inspect bank statements and canceled checks?
   (c) Notify the bank of any problems in a timely manner?

3. Did the financial institutions live up to their basic duties vis-à-vis each other?
   (a) Did the depository bank put the instrument into the collection process in a timely manner?
   (b) Did the intermediary bank process the instrument in a proper and timely manner?
   (c) Did the payor bank accept or reject the instrument for payment?

E. Are there any special or unusual factors which will affect the rights and duties of the various parties involved?
   1. Death of a customer?
   2. Stop payment order?
   3. Stale, postdated, or antedated checks?
   4. Incomplete checks?
   5. Forged or altered instrument?
      (a) Bank's responsibilities?
      (b) Customer's responsibilities?
      (c) Forger's liabilities?
   6. Any setoff?
   7. Any legal action affecting the account?

F. Any electronic fund transfer mechanism being used?
   1. Automated teller machine?
   2. Point of sale terminal?
   3. Telephone or personal computer based transfer?
   4. Automated clearinghouse?
   5. Application of the Electronic Funds Transfer Act?
      (a) Unsolicited card?
      (b) Lost or stolen card?
      (c) Collection error?
      (d) Statements supplied?
      (e) Prearranged transfer?

IV. Objective Questions:

Terms:

1. A certified check, cashier's check, or traveler's check, the payment for which the bank is solely or primarily liable for are all examples of a _____ _____.

2. When there are sufficient funds in a customer's account to pay a check, but the bank does not do so, this is a _____ _____.

3. The rules for bank deposits and collections for checking accounts offered by commercial banks, NOW accounts, and other checklike accounts are set out in _____ _____ of the UCC.

4. A bank in the collection process, which is not the depository or payor bank, is called a _____ _____.

5. The term for crediting a payee's account against the drawer's check prior to actual clearance is known as a _____ _____.

6. The rule that allows banks to fix an afternoon hour of 2:00pm or later as a cutoff hour for the purpose of processing items is called the _____ _____.

7. A check that is presented for payment by the payee or holder where the depository bank is also the payor bank is known as an _____ _____ _____.

8. A check presented for payment by the payee or holder where the depository bank and the payor bank are not the same bank is called a _____ _____ _____.

9. There are four notices or actions that affect the payment of a check that has been presented for collection and is in the process of being posted. These are called the _____ _____.

10. An order by a drawer of a check to the payor not to pay or certify a check is called a _____ _____ _____.

True/False:

1. ____ There are three parties to an ordinary check: the drawer, the drawee, and the payee.

2. ____ Certified checks become stale six months after they are issued.

3. ____ If the holder of a check requests certification on the check, the drawer and any party who indorsed the check before certification are discharged from liability.

4. ____ A drawer can stop payment on a certified check just as he can on an ordinary check.

5. ____ A traveler's check must be signed twice to be considered a negotiable instrument.

6. ____ Most states have legislation that a bank is liable if it pays a stale check unless it received the customer's permission to do so.

7. ____ Under the UCC, if the drawer of a check omits certain information, the risk of loss on such a check is on the bank if the incorrect amount is charged to the customer's account.

8. ____ Drawers, payees, holders, and indorsers can all stop payment on a check.

9. ____ Generally, loss on a forged signature check falls on the bank, not on the customer's account since the forger has usually disappeared.

10. ____ Under the right to setoff, a bank can apply funds from a customer's account to pay any overdue loans the customer may have.

Multiple Choice:

1. Customer Chris opens a checking account at Busy Bank. Chris writes a check to Landlord Len for rent. Chris receives a paycheck from Boss Beatrice and takes it to the bank for deposit. Which of the following is correct?
   A. Busy Bank must accept the check from Beatrice as a deposit.
   B. Busy Bank must collect on the check from Beatrice.
   C. Busy Bank must honor the check written to Len.
   D. All of the above.

2. Assume the same facts as in question 1. Which of the following is correct regarding Chris' various transactions?
   A. A creditor/debtor relationship has been formed.
   B. A principal/agent relationship has been formed.
   C. Both of the above.
   D. None of the above. There is no special relationship between a customer and his bank.

3. Customer Cassandra has a checking account with Bakerville Bank. Cassandra presents a check for certification by Bakerville Bank. The Bank certifies the check. Cassandra then gives the check to Dealer Dan as down payment on a new car she bought. Dan indorses the check and delivers it to Boater Bob for a new boat Dan bought. Which of the following is correct?
   A. Cassandra is secondarily liable in the check.
   B. The check is payable only for six months, but not beyond that since it will be stale.
   C. Bakerville Bank can revoke certification of the check at its option.
   D. All of the above are correct.

4. Assume the same facts as in question 3 except that Dan, not Cassandra, has the check certified before delivering it to Bob. Which of the following is correct?
   A. Cassandra is secondarily liable on the check.

B. The check is payable only for six months, but not beyond that since it will be stale.
   C. Bob cannot hold Cassandra liable on the check.
   D. All of the above are correct.

5. Traveler Tina has planned a world tour and decides to get traveler's checks from her bank. Which of the following is incorrect regarding Tina's traveler's checks?
   A. The traveler's checks are issued without a named payee.
   B. The traveler's checks are three-party instruments.
   C. Tina can stop payment on the traveler's checks if they are lost or stolen, but not negotiated.
   D. All of the above are correct regarding Tina's traveler's checks.

6. Bumbling Betsy never balances her check book and is never quite sure how much money she has. Unfortunately, Betsy only has $100 in her account when she writes a $200 check to Kitchen Komfort for a new set of dishes. Kitchen Komfort seeks payment on the check. Which of the following is correct?
   A. Betsy's bank can dishonor the check.
   B. Betsy's bank can pay the check for Betsy although she has insufficient funds, but is not required to do so.
   C. Both of the above.
   D. None of the above. Betsy's bank must pay the check since dishonoring the check would be unfair to Kitchen Komfort.

7. Assume the same facts as in question 6 except Betsy has $500 in her account when she writes the check. Also, assume Betsy's bank wrongfully dishonors the check to Kitchen Komfort. Which of the following is correct?
    A. The bank is liable to Betsy for wrongfully dishonoring the check.
    B. Kitchen Komfort can sue the bank for wrongfully dishonoring the check.
    C. Kitchen Komfort has no recourse and must bear the loss.
    D. Betsy has no recourse and must bear the loss.

8. Juggling John knows his checking account is low, and he would be unable to pay a check at present. However, in a week, John will have more money in his account. John writes a check to Understanding Ulga, his landlord, on June 1 and postdates the check for June 10. Ulga forgets to hold the check and takes it to the bank on June 2. Which of the following is correct?
    A. If John's bank pays the check, it is liable for any actual damages suffered by John.
    B. Ulga is liable for any actual damages suffered by John since she did not hold the check.
    C. The postdated check is not negotiable.
    D. John must bear the cost of any actual damages suffered since he should not have postdated the check.

9. Preoccupied Patty owes Shady Sherman $50. Patty writes a check to Sherman, but in her haste, does not fill in the amount. Patty tells Sherman to fill in $50 and gives him the signed check. Sherman, though, fills in the amount for $1,000. Sherman then takes the check to the bank for payment. Which of the following is correct?
    A. If the bank pays the check, it is liable for $950.
    B. If the bank pays the check, it is liable for $1,000.
    C. If the bank pays the check, it is not liable at all since Patty bears the risk of loss in this situation.
    D. None of the above.

10. Which of the following is not one of the four legals?
    A. Receipt of a stop payment order from the drawer.
    B. The payor's bank's exercise of its rights of setoff against the customer's account.
    C. Receipt of service of a court order or legal process that "freezes" the customer's account, such as a writ of garnishment.
    D. All of the above are one of the four legals.

V. Answers to Objective Questions:

Terms:

1. *Bank check.* These checks are often used when a payee is concerned that a drawer's normal check may not be honored by the drawee due to insufficient funds. With these checks, the payee has more comfort because they are considered much closer to a cash equivalent.

2. *Wrongful dishonor.* When a customer opens a checking account at a bank, the customer is expected to keep sufficient funds in the account to pay any checks written against it. Thus, when the drawer bank receives a

properly drawn and payable check, the bank is under a duty per Section 4-401(a) of the UCC to honor the check and change the drawer's account in the amount of the check.

3. *Article 4*. Article 4 controls if Article 3 and 4 conflict per UCC 4-102(a). In addition, Article 4 was substantially amended in 1990 to better incorporate the hi-tech changes that have taken place in the banking industry.

4. *Intermediary bank*. This bank is used to help facilitate the collection process on negotiable instruments. This bank, by definition, is not the depository or payor bank.

5. *Provisional credit*. Under Section 4-201(a) a bank may provisionally credit the customer's account for a deposit of a check into his or her account. Even though the depository bank does not have to pay the customer the amount of the check until final settlement, this section allows payment in the meantime. If the check is dishonored by the payor bank, the provisional credit is reversed.

6. *Deferred posting rule*. This rule is set out under Section 4-108 and applies to all banks in the collection process. Any check or deposit of money received after the 2:00p.m. cutoff hour is treated as received on the next banking day.

7. *On us item*. If both the drawer and payee or holder have accounts of the same bank, the depository bank is also the payor bank. The check is then called an "on us" item when it is presented for payment by the payee or holder.

8. *On them item*. If the drawer and the payee or holder have accounts at different banks, the payor and depository bank are not the same bank.

A depositor has the option of physically presenting the check for payment at the payer bank if he or she so chooses.

9. *Four legals*. These notices or actions can prevent the payment of a check if they are received by the payor bank before it has finished its process of posting the check for payment.

10. *Stop payment order*. An oral stop-payment order is binding on the bank for fourteen days; a written stop-payment order is binding for six months and may be renewed for additional six month periods.

True/False:

1. True. There is a debtor/creditor relationship between the bank and its customer. When a check is drawn on a checking account, the drawer (creditor) is ordering the drawee (bank) to transfer his or her money to a third party, the payee.

2. False. Certified checks do not become stale after six months. They are payable even six months after they are issued.

3. True. The bank has assumed primarily liability for the negotiable instrument.

4. False. A drawer cannot stop payment on a certified check. In addition, the certifying bank can only revoke its certification under certain circumstances.

5. True. A traveler's check must have the second signature to be considered a negotiable instrument.

6. True. Remember, the UCC is not a federal statute but rather a uniform act which the individual states can adopt either in part or entirely. Most states have adopted this provision of the UCC.

7. False. Under the UCC, if the drawer of a check omits certain information, the risk of loss on such a check is on the drawer,

not the bank if the incorrect amount is charged to the customer's account.

8. False. Only drawers can stop payment on a check since only they have a contractual arrangement with the bank.

9. True. Although the bank could try to recover on a forgery from the forger, the forger is usually not available or is judgment proof. Therefore, the bank bears the loss.

10. True. The banker's right of setoff is derived from common law principles which were in place prior to the enactment of the UCC. It is considered one of the "four legals" which can prevent the payment of a check if received by the payor bank before it has finished its process of posting.

Multiple Choice:

1. D. A, B, and C are all examples of Busy Bank's duties in servicing its customer, Chris.

2. C. A is correct because a creditor/debtor relationship is formed when Chris deposits money in the account. B is correct because a principal/agent relationship is formed when Chris deposits his paycheck and when he writes a check to Len. D is incorrect because these special relationships are formed.

3. A. Cassandra, as the drawer of the check, remains secondarily liable on the check although it has been certified. B is incorrect because a certified check does not become stale after six months. C is incorrect because the bank is not permitted to revoke certification of the check at its option.

4. C. Once Dan has certified the check, Cassandra, as the drawer of the original check, is released from liability. Therefore, Bob cannot hold Cassandra

liable on the check. A is incorrect because Cassandra is released from liability on the check as discussed above. B is incorrect because a certified check does not become stale after six months.

5. B. Traveler's checks are two-party checks because the bank acts as both the drawer and the drawee. A is a true statement. C is a true statement.

6. C. A is correct because the bank can dishonor a check if the customer's account has insufficient funds. B is correct because the bank can pay the check and charge Betsy's account for the overdraft later. D is incorrect because the bank is not required to honor a check if the customer's account has insufficient funds.

7. A. If the bank wrongfully dishonors the check, it is liable to its customer, Betsy. B is incorrect because the bank is not liable to Kitchen Komfort since Kitchen Komfort is not its customer and therefore has no contractual relationship with the bank. C is incorrect because Kitchen Komfort has recourse against Betsy. D is incorrect because Betsy can hold the bank liable and therefore, need not bear the loss.

8. A. If the bank pays the postdated check before the date on the check (June 10), the bank is liable for any actual damages suffered by John. B is incorrect because Ulga is not liable. The bank is responsible for honoring the postdate. C is incorrect because a postdated check is a negotiable instrument. D is incorrect because John is permitted to postdate a check. In addition, the bank must honor the postdate.

9. C. If Patty, the drawer, leaves part of the check blank, the bank may pay the check as it is filled out by the payee (Sherman) in good faith. Patty, not the bank, bears

the risk of loss in such a situation. A and B are incorrect because the bank is not liable if it paid the check in good faith. Patty must bear this loss.

10. D. A, B, and C are each one of the four legals. In addition, the fourth is receipt of a notice affecting the account, such as a notice of the customer's death, judgment of incompetence, or bankruptcy.

VI. Key Question Checklist Answers to Essay Question:

A. *What is the basic contractual relationship between Patric and Bailout Bank with regard to the negotiable instruments in question?*

Poor Patric is lucky not to be in jail, and his travels certainly did not help foster better U.S.-Canadian relations. The basic relationship which needs to be examined first is the one between Patric and Bailout Bank. Even though Patric may be an employee of the bank, and for some purposes, an agent, his key role here is customer. Because he has a personal account at the bank, a creditor/debtor contract relationship has been established between him and the bank. When he writes checks on his account, he is the drawer and the bank is the drawee. A debtor/creditor relationship has been created. The bank is the debtor, and Patric is the creditor.

B. *What is the definition of the particular negotiable instrument used in this case?*

The checks involved here would be considered normal drafts on Patric's personal checking account at Bailout Bank. There is no evidence of the bank having undertaken any extra or special duties related to certification or cashiers checks. Maybe Patric should have used travelers checks. They would have

provided him with protection in case of theft. But even more important, the payees would have also been better protected than they were in accepting Patric's personal checks.

C. *After having established the definition of the relationship between Patric and Bailout Bank vis-à-vis these negotiable instruments, at what point or points of the negotiation process did a problem arise?*

The point of negotiation in question is dishonor of Patric's checks at presentation for payment. The dishonor was proper because of insufficient funds in Patric's account at the time. The payor bank may accept and process a deposit per instructions it had agreed upon with Patric before he left for his trip. Patric can argue, that even though there were insufficient funds in the account, that insufficiently was created by Bailout's failure to live up to its contractual obligations. That failure created a wrongful dishonor of Patric's checks when they were presented for payment. Because of their negligence, Patric can now claim damages proximately caused by the wrongful dishonor. In addition, he should be compensated for any consequential damages or liabilities caused by criminal prosecution. At the bare minimum, Bailout should now honor the checks, pay any bounce fees, and write letters of apology to all parties involved in the negotiation of Patric's checks. Patric loved his trip and doesn't want to be *persona non-grata* in Canada.

E&F. *Are there any other unusual factors or electronic fund transfer issues in this case?*

There are none other than the fact that the bank dropped the ball here, and Patric is now looking for a job elsewhere. He is afraid his paychecks may also bounce.

CHAPTER 26
CREDIT, SURETYSHIP, AND LENDER LIABILITY

A trifling debt makes a man your debtor, a large one makes him your enemy.

Seneca

I. Overview:

Credit is really a shibboleth for risk. Inherent in our business enterprise system is the principle that risk will be rewarded if well placed and punished if not. The riches of wise credit extension are the stuff of financial dynasties, and it is no accident that most economic measures of a nation's growth are tied to the success of its financial institutions. Conversely, failure to wisely administer and manage these key elements in our society leads to costly debacles such as the current savings and loan bailout. The law has long reflected this win/lose dichotomy of the credit marketplace. Many of the protections and remedies accorded to creditors have long historical tracings in the common law. In today's highly codified scheme of things, most of the rights and duties of the both debtor and creditor are found in the statutes, but the principles hearken back to an earlier age of debtor's prisons and the like. The possibilities for fraud, chevisance, and conspiracy by charlatans in this area of the law have provided both the challenge and opportunity to seek a balance between the competing rights and duties of debtors and creditors. If the law takes an uneven hand to either side, the long term interests of the entire economic system is disserved.

In your examination of credit relationships, remember that most disputes have more than one level of controversy. On the surface, the most apparent problem revolves around resolution of the differences between the debtor and creditor. At the sub strata, a second dispute is often found: that of competing creditors fighting over priority rights to the debtor's property. A proper examination of any credit case answers both aspects.

There are three basic relationships which you must establish before going into the details set out in the key question checklist. How was the debtor/creditor relationship established? Which body of case law, statute, or combination thereof is to be used in defining the respective rights and duties of the debtor and creditor? What about the rights and duties of third parties as they relate to this issue?

II. Hypothetical Multi-Issue Essay Question:

Ms. Zoie Zonna lived and commuted for many years in Los Angeles working as a zygostates for the L.A. Mint. Her job was golden, but she hated putting up with the tailgaters who were always nearly running into her. She invented and patented the "Z.Z. Tail-Gator." This device was attached to an auto tailpipe and emitted an odious methane-based flatulence when someone got too close for comfort. Zoie was on her way to making a fortune because so many drivers saw her invention as a dream come true.

Based on her expected high income, Zoie moved to Colorado and bought the famous "How's Your Aspen? Ranch." The financing was arranged with $2 million down, a first mortgage deed of trust payable to Snow Bank for $10 million and a second mortgage deed of trust payable to Downhill Bank for $2 million. Snow Bank's loan officer was high on the Rockies and failed to record the mortgage before the Downhill Bank's recordation.

Unfortunately for Zoie, both the California Air Resources Board and the EPA have now banned her product for being in violation of tailpipe emissions standards. She is nearly broke and doesn't want to go back to her old lifestyle. What result?

III. Key Question Checklist:

A. What is the nature of the transaction at issue?
1. Are there a set of reciprocal promises in place?
   (a) A promise to provide a service or good by the creditor?
   (b) In exchange for a promise to pay for the same by the debtor?
2. How is the transaction evidenced between the parties?
   (a) By a writing?
   (b) By an oral agreement?
   (c) A combination of 1 and 2?
3. To which of the debtor's properties was the service or accession provided?
   (a) Personal?
   (b) Real property?
   (c) Both?

B. Once the transaction has been identified, you must then examine its elements or components. The first component is security, or lack of it, in the initial promise. Did the debtor provide any security to protect his or her promise to pay the debt?
1. If there was security provided, move on to subsequent checklist questions. If not, what was the expectation of the parties?
   (a) Was there a promise to repay by a certain time and place?
   (b) Was there a promise to reward the creditor with interest or other consideration for having extended the credit?
   (c) Was there any agreement as to consequences of default such as liquidated damages?

C. Assuming the security for the protection of repayment is based on *personal property* and not explicitly provided for in the agreement between the parties, do any lien theories apply?
1. Common law liens based on continued possession by creditor?
   (a) Artisan?
   (b) Laborer?
   (c) Innkeeper?
   (d) Common carrier?
   (e) Other service provider?
2. Statutory liens?
   (a) Under UCC?
   (b) Under state laws other than UCC?
   (c) Federally enacted statutes such as the Internal Revenue Code or the like?

D. Assuming the security for the protection of repayment is based on *real property*, how was it created?
1. By mortgage?
2. By deed of trust?
3. By land contract?
4. By mechanics lien?

E. If a mortgage was used, are the elements of mortgage in place?
1. Owner of real property borrows from creditor?
2. Creditor uses owner's interest in real property as collateral to secure repayment of the debt?
3. Were the proper recording procedures complied with?

F. If a note and deed of trust were used, are the elements of the same in place?
1. Owner/trustor of real property borrows from a creditor?

2. Is this debt secured by the owner/trustor's interest in real property?
3. Is this debt evidenced by a note and deed of trust in favor of the creditor?
4. Is the deed of trust placed in the hands of a trustee until the amount borrowed is paid?
5. During the period of payment, is the owner/trustor allowed to retain legal possession of the property and be responsible for taxes and the like?
6. Were the proper recording procedures complied with?

G. If a land contract was used, are the elements in place?
1. Owner agrees to sell his or her interest in real property?
2. Owner retains title until fully paid?
3. Buyer entitled to legal possession and use during payment period?
4. Buyer responsible for taxes and alike?
5. Any recording requirements complied with?

H. If a mechanics and/or materialman's lien is used, are the elements in place?
1. Was a good or service provided as an accession (added value) to debtor's real property?
2. Was the proper statutory procedure used to create a lien by the person providing the accession?
   (a) Filed notice?
   (b) Notice stated all material terms?
   (c) Notice filed in a timely manner?
   (d) Notice given to the owner of the real property?
3. Was there any contractual modification of normal lien rights?

I. In case of default by the debtor, what are the enforcement options available to the creditor for repayment of the amount owed?
1. Strict foreclosure?
   (a) Reversion of title back to creditor?
   (b) Creditor's full satisfaction limited to the value of property, i.e., no deficiency allowed?
   (c) No rights to surplus value by debtor?
2. Power of sale?
   (a) Agreed upon in contract or allowed by statute?
   (b) Sale of property by creditor in good faith?
   (c) Net proceeds used toward debt reduction?
   (d) May or may not have deficiency based on statute?
   (e) Surplus payable to debtor?
   (f) Any statutory or contractual redemption rights?
3. Foreclosure sale (most common method)?
   (a) Allowed by contract or statute?
   (b) Does the party seeking the sale have a recognized interest in the property (includes lienholders)?
   (c) Was the property sold in good faith at a judicially supervised sale?
   (d) Were the net proceeds used toward reduction of the debt?
   (e) May or may not have deficiency based on statute?
   (f) Surplus payable to debtor?
   (g) Any statutory or contractual redemption rights?

J. Any third party involvement in this transaction?
1. Surety?
   (a) Did the third party make a promise to be liable for payment of the debtor's debt?
   (b) Was this promise made in exchange for:
      (1) Legal consideration (compensated)?
      (2) Gratuitously (accommodation)?
   (c) Were there any preconditions to being primarily liable when the debt was due?
   (d) Any defenses available to the surety?
2. Guarantor?
   (a) Did the third party make a promise to be liable for payment of the debtor's debt?
   (b) Was this promise made in compliance with the Statute of Frauds?
      (1) Excepted from the statute if the benefit of the debt was principally for the benefit of guarantor.
3. Upon payment of the debt by the surety or guarantor after default by debtor, what remedies may be available to the surety and/or the guarantor?
   (a) Right of subrogation?
   (b) Right of reimbursement?
   (c) Right of contribution from other cosureties or coguarantors?
4. Rights of any other creditors affected by this transaction?
   (a) Other secured creditor?
   (b) Other unsecured creditors?

K. Any other judicial or statutory factors which must be taken into account?
1. Prejudgment remedies of creditors?
   (a) Attachment?

2. Postjudgment remedies of creditors?
   (a) Execution?
   (b) Garnishment?
   (c) Bankruptcy laws?
3. Any limitations based on statute or public policy?
   (a) Consumer protection statutes?
   (b) State homestead laws?
   (c) Federal limitations on garnishment?

IV. Objective Questions:

Terms:

1. An arrangement by which a property owner borrows money from a creditor and uses a deed as collateral for repayment of the loan is called a _____.

2. A situation in which a third party purchases real property that secures a debt in the form of a mortgage or deed of trust and agrees to make future payments on the related debt is known as _____.

3. A party who acts as a surety in a transaction without receiving compensation for acting in that capacity is an _____ _____.

4. A postjudgment remedy directed against the property of a debtor in the possession of a third party is known as _____.

5. The security interest of a creditor in property of a debtor that minimizes the creditor's risk of extending unsecured credit is called _____.

6. A prejudgment remedy by which a creditor seizes property belonging to a debtor to aid in collection of a debt upon resolution of a pending lawsuit between the debtor and the creditor with respect to that debt is _____.

227

7. In a legal proceeding brought by a creditor against a debtor with respect to a past-due debt, the _____ is the court decision rendered against the debtor.

8. The rights acquired by a surety or guarantor from a creditor against a debtor after the surety or guarantor pays a debt owed to the creditor by the debtor are known as _____ _____.

9. The party extending credit in a credit transaction is known as a _____.

10. The owner/debtor in a mortgage transaction is the _____.

True/False:

1. ____ In a transaction involving unsecured credit, the creditor may look to collateral pledged by the debtor to satisfy the debt obligation in the event the debtor fails to make payment when due.

2. ____ A creditor (lienholder) can have the sheriff seize property subject to a lien and sell it at a judicial sale immediately after the debtor fails to make a payment when due.

3. ____ Failure to record a mortgage or deed of trust in accordance with the applicable recording statute renders the instrument invalid and legally unenforceable between the parties to the instrument.

4. ____ If a mortgagor defaults on a mortgage, the mortgagee can declare the entire debt due and payable immediately.

5. ____ To exercise the right of redemption with respect to real property, a mortgagor is required to pay only those amounts then in default.

6. ____ Under a surety contract, the surety is a codebtor who is primarily liable to pay the debt when it is due.

7. ____ Those creditors who do not assent to a composition agreement may proceed to collect their claims only after the claims of those creditors involved in composition agreements have been satisfied.

8. ____ Generally, guaranty contracts, but not surety contracts, must be in writing to be enforceable.

9. ____ Under the Uniform Fraudulent Transfer Act (UFTA), only those transfers made with intent to hinder, delay, or defraud creditors may be set aside as fraudulent transfers.

10. ____ Under the foreclosure sale method of foreclosure, the mortgagee is not permitted to bring a legal action to recover any deficiency.

Multiple Choice:

1. Ike Investor sells 200 acres of prime farm land to Frank Farmer. Ike and Frank enter into a five year land sale contract pursuant to which Frank agrees to pay Ike principal and interest in five equal annual installments. Which of the following is correct?
   A. If Frank defaults in his payment obligation, Ike must wait until the end of the five year cure period before he may declare a forfeiture and retake possession of the property.
   B. Ike retains title to the land until Frank has satisfied all of his payment obligations.
   C. During the five year contract period, Frank has the right to possession and use of the property.
   D. B and C above.

2. Charlie Creditrisk borrowed $10,000 from Aloof Bank. In investigating Charlie's financial status after Charlie defaulted on his loan payments, the Bank discovered that Charlie owns a speed boat worth $15,000, a stereo and other entertainment equipment worth $7,500, and miscellaneous sporting equipment worth $6,000. Charlie supports himself on the $2,000 his parents give him each month. The Bank can obtain:
   A. A writ of garnishment immediately for a portion of the $2,000 Charlie's parents give him each month.
   B. A lien on Charlie's stereo equipment by recording its lien and notifying Charlie.
   C. A writ of execution for the seizure of Charlie's speed boat after obtaining a judgment against Charlie.
   D. A writ of execution for the immediate seizure of the speed boat.

3. Assume the same facts as in question 2. If the Bank obtains a judgment and a court order:
   A. Upon the seizure and sale of Charlie's property, a certain amount must be set aside so that Charlie can provide shelter for himself and his family.
   B. The Bank will be unsuccessful in recovering anything from Charlie's assets because of statutory exemptions.
   C. The gifts of money received from Charlie's parents cannot be reached through garnishment.
   D. The Bank will have liens on Charlie's property which may then be foreclosed.

4. The lien granted to contractors and laborers who make improvements to real property is known as a(n):
   A. General lien.
   B. Mechanic's lien.
   C. Artisans lien.
   D. Chattel lien.

5. Danny Digithead borrowed $15,000 from George Generous to provide startup capital for his new accounting firm. George required that Danny find a cosignor and that he pledge certain corporate securities as collateral. Fran Friend agreed to cosign. When unrest in Eastern Europe caused Danny to fear a drop in the stock market, George allowed him to sell the corporate securities. As a result of the sale of the securities, Fran:
   A. Remains liable in the event that Danny defaults.
   B. Is completely discharged by the sale of the collateral.
   C. Is partially discharged to the extent of the value of the collateral sold.
   D. None of the above.

6. Fred borrowed $2,500 from Barney and promised to repay the loan by the end of the year. On December 1, Gilligan promised to pay the $2,500 if Fred failed to pay Barney. On December 31, Fred defaulted on his payment obligation to Barney.
   A. Gilligan is a surety and is therefore primarily liable to Barney.
   B. Gilligan is a guarantor and is therefore primarily liable to Barney.
   C. Gilligan is a surety and is therefore secondarily liable to Barney.
   D. Gilligan is a guarantor and is therefore secondarily liable to Barney.

7. Arlyn Athlete purchases a $2,700 racing bike from Bob Bicycle who agrees to give Arlyn until November 1 to pay for the bike. On September 1, Richie Rich calls Bob and promises to pay the $2,700 if Arlyn fails to pay on November 1. Arlyn fails to pay on November 1, and Bob demands that Richie pay the $2,700. Richie refuses saying that his promise is not legally enforceable. Which of the following statements is most correct?
   A. Richie is a surety and, therefore, Bob need not seek payment from Arlyn before demanding payment from Richie.
   B. Richie is a guarantor and, therefore, Bob need not seek payment from Arlyn before demanding payment from Richie.
   C. Richie's promise to act as guarantor is unenforceable because it is not in writing.
   D. Richie's promise to act as surety is enforceable even though it is not in writing.

8. Pete, a professional carpenter, decides to surprise his neighbor Judy by putting a much needed new roof on her house while she is away on vacation. To protect his financial interests, Pete takes all the steps required by state law to perfect his mechanic's lien. Judy refuses to pay Pete. Which of the following is correct?
   A. Pete may foreclose on his lien, sell the property, and satisfy his debt out of the proceeds of the sale.
   B. Pete must seek and obtain a judgment prior to foreclosing on his lien.
   C. Pete did not obtain a perfected lien because Judy did not agree to hire Pete to perform the work.

   D. Pete did not obtain a perfected lien because Judy did not agree to the filing of the lien.

9. Assume the same facts as in question 8 except that Judy hired Pete to perform the roofing work while she was away on vacation. Which of the following is correct?
   A. Pete may foreclose on his lien, sell the property, and satisfy his debt plus interest and costs out of the proceeds of the sale.
   B. Judy has the right of redemption prior to foreclosure.
   C. If Judy's house is sold to satisfy the mechanic's lien, any surplus must be paid to Judy.
   D. All of the above.

10. Abe borrows money from City Bank. His friends Betty, Chuck, and Denise cosign. Abe defaults, and Denise steps forward and repays the debt. Denise is entitled to:
    A. Be subrogated to the rights of City Bank against Abe.
    B. Be reimbursed for all expenses incurred as a result of the arrangement.
    C. Contribution from Betty and Chuck for their proportionate share of the debt.
    D. All of the above.

VI. Answers to Objective Questions:

Terms:

1. *Mortgage.* The vast majority of real estate in this country, and throughout the world for that matter, is purchased through the use of this or some similar sort of collateralized credit arrangement.

2. *Assumption.* This sort of provision has become less commonly used in the past twenty years with the advent of large interest rate swings in the 1970's. Most financial institutions now insist on a "fresh start" with each new buyer and therefore limit the use of these sort of provisions.

3. *Accommodation surety.* Most people who take on this role are either family members or close friends of the principal debtors.

4. *Garnishment.* This action is usually directed at wages due the debtor, banks in possession of funds belonging to the debtor or against third parsons in possession of the property of the debtor.

5. *Collateral.* The two main sources of law with regard to the rights and duties of the parties to collateral are common law vis-a-vis real property and Article 9 of the UCC vis-a-vis personal property.

6. *Attachment.* In securing a writ of attachment, most state statutes require that the creditor must show that the debtor is in default, that a statutory ground for attachment is applicable, and that the debtor is trying to transfer the property.

7. *Judgment.* This is a finding by a court that the debtor owes a past due debt to the creditor who brought the action in court. This finding provides the basis under which post judgment collection remedies may be sought.

8. *Subrogation rights.* This term literally means that the surety or guarantor has now stepped into the legal shoes of the debtor.

9. *Creditor.* This is the lender in the transaction. Most of us, sooner or later, will act as a creditor. Most people limit their creditor capacity to family and friends. As debtors, most of us deal with commercial credit entities.

10. *Mortgagor.* It is interesting to note how the law of real estate allows a debtor to be an owner. One common saying in real estate circles is that we never really own the land, we only pay rent to the state. If you do not believe that, just skip your real estate taxes and see what happens!

True/False:

1. False. Unsecured credit does not require any security (collateral) to protect the payment of the debt.

2. False. If no statutory procedure exists, the creditor must bring a lawsuit and obtain a judgment against the debtor. Once a judgment has been obtained, the sheriff can seize the property and sell it at a judicial sale.

3. False. Failure to record a mortgage or deed of trust does not affect either the legality of the instrument or the rights and obligations of the parties to the instrument. Failure to record may affect the priority of the holder's rights vis-a-vis others who have recorded.

4. True. This is a standard provision found in most mortgage instruments subject to state law limitations.

5. False. To exercise the right of redemption with respect to real property, a mortgagor must pay the full amount of the debt including principal, interest, and other costs incurred by the mortgagee because of the mortgagor's default.

6. True. This added means of payment is why creditors seek surety comfort wherever possible.

7. False. Creditors not assenting to a composition agreement may proceed to collect their claims in their own way without regard to the timing specified in composition agreements.

8. True. These contracts are covered by the Statute of Frauds unless they fall into the "main purpose" exceptions.

9. False. The UFTA lists several types of transfers that may be set aside as fraudulent.

10. False. The mortgagee may bring a legal action to recover any deficiency subject, however, to any limitations on deficiency judgments.

Multiple Choice:

1. D. Answers B and C are both correct. Answer A is incorrect because under a land sale contract, Ike may declare a forfeiture and retake possession of the property at the point in time that Frank defaults in his payment obligation.

2. C. Execution is a postjudgment remedy that may only be given effect after a judgment has been obtained.

3. C. Garnishment is directed against property of the debtor in the possession of another. These gifts are not Charlie's property until made, and therefore garnishment is not available with respect to these gifts. Answer A is incorrect because the homestead exemption relates to real property, not those items of personal property listed. Answer B is incorrect because most states do not provide an exemption for the items of personal property listed. Answer D is incorrect because a lien does not arise merely as a result of obtaining a judgment. Some further action such as attachment or execution is required.

4. B. These titles vary from state to state depending on local statutes.

5. B. A surety is completely discharged from liability if the creditor enters into an agreement with the principal debtor to alter the debtor's obligation without the consent of the surety.

6. D. A guarantor is one who is liable to pay the debt of another only after the original debtor defaults in his or her repayment obligation, and therefore the guarantor is secondarily liable.

7. C. Guaranty contracts generally must be in writing to be enforceable, unless the "main purpose" of the guarantee is to benefit the guarantor, which is not evident from the facts of the question.

8. C. Pete has no contractual rights to enforce because there was no mutual assent to the formation of a contract.

9. D. The difference now is that Judy consented to the work by Pete.

10. D. A, B, and C are all remedies allowed under the law of suretyship.

VI. Key Question Checklist Answers to Essay Question:

A. *What is the nature of this transaction?*

The nature of these transactions centers around a series of bilateral contracts entered into between Ms. Zonna and two creditors. In both cases, credit was extended by the banks in exchange for a promise to repay. The transactions called for a writing because contracts involving interest in real estate are covered by the Statute of Frauds. The creditors provided a service to the debtor which benefited her ability to acquire her interest in real property.

B-E. *Did the debtor provide any security for her debt? How was the security created? Are the elements of a mortgage in place?*

From the facts as presented, Ms. Zonna signed two mortgaged deeds of trust to Snow and Downhill banks respectively. In both cases, she borrowed the money and used it towards the purchase price of the ranch. Also, in both cases, the creditors secured the debt owed to them by having a mortgage note signed to their favor by Ms. Zonna. In addition, under the deed of trust method of financing the purchase of real property, the legal title to the property is handed over to a trustee during the payment period covered by the note. In the interim period, Ms. Zonna is allowed to retain legal possession of the property as owner/trustor. In addition, she will also be responsible for taxes and the like relating to the property. It appears that not all the proper filing procedures were followed in that the first bank to issue credit (Snow Bank) failed to file its mortgage in a timely manner. This will not relieve Ms. Zonna of any liability on her note to Snow Bank, but it may affect the priority of Snow Bank's claim on the property in case of foreclosure.

I. *What enforcement options are available to the creditors upon default?*

The most likely method of enforcement of a debt secured by real property is foreclosure and sale. The parties may have modified this likelihood by contract but such contract provisions are narrowly construed and may not be as valid against public policy. In this case, both the banks and Ms. Zonna have an interest in the ranch. She has made a substantial down payment plus any equity value based on appreciation in value since the time of the purchase. The banks, in turn, have their respective security interests per the unpaid balances of the mortgage notes owed to them

by Ms. Zonna. If Ms. Zonna finds herself in default because of her inability to pay, the banks may seek foreclosure on the ranch, subject to any redemption rights provided by statute. They may them seek to have the court conduct a judicially supervised sale. Most states, including Colorado, will allow a deficiency judgment against the debtor if the sale does not raise enough revenue to pay the debt. If the state of Colorado had an antideficiency statute similar to the one enacted in California, Ms. Zonna could not be held liable for more than the value of the property at the time of the court-ordered sale. In case the property has appreciated in value, Ms. Zonna would be entitled to the net surplus from the proceeds of the sale.

J&K. *Is there any third party involvement? Are there any other judicial or statutory factors?*

There was no involvement of any surety or guarantor in this transaction. There was, however, the aforementioned failure by Snow Bank to file its mortgage note in a timely manner. Even though that delay does not directly affect the amount owed to them by Ms. Zonna, it may have an adverse effect on their ability to collect. If the ranch had depreciated in value, and Ms. Zonna was judgment proof, Snow Bank's rights to proceeds from the judicial sale would be subrogated to the rights of Downhill Bank. For example, if the ranch were worth $5 million, Downhill would get its $2 million first. Snow Bank would get the remaining $3 million but would probably lose out on the remaining $7 million owed to it due to Ms. Zonna's insolvency. Snow Bank's loan officer will probably have to find a new high.

It's too bad that the California Air Resources Board and the EPA did what they did. The world really needs a good "Z.Z. Tail-Gator," and Ms. Zonna could be enjoying the fruits of her labor on the ranch.

CHAPTER 27

SECURED TRANSACTIONS

Creditors have better memories than debtors.
Benjamin Franklin

I. Overview:

Earlier chapters of this book compared the relationship of the UCC to the common law of contracts as being akin to an eclipse. The UCC may cover a segment of the law heretofore resolved by contract, but the penumbra of common law still shines on underneath. Article 9 of the UCC is a particularly good example of this interaction between the old and new. The original sources of the law of secured transactions involving personal property can be found in a combination of common law contracts, real property law, debtor and creditor law, and the law of liens. The UCC has sought to interpolate the best elements of all these areas into a cogent and organized structured system of facilitating secured credit transactions for the sale of personal property.

This system is premised on the legal realism that merchants doing business with each other are expected to live up to a higher standard of both knowledge and behavior of the law. In addition, that same realism attempts to protect the innocent third parties' good faith reliance on the legitimacy of the marketplace whenever possible. These ends are mainly sought through the use of the recordation principles long established in real property law transactions. These recordation rules are designed to give creditors notice not only of the debtor's obligation, but even more important, to give notice to other creditors that this security-based transaction has taken place which will establish an order of priority or pecking order among the creditors.

Several practical factors make the law of secured transactions in personal property particular troublesome. First, compared to real estate, personal property is portable. In many legal systems the distinction between real and personal property is described as *portables* versus *nonportables*. The same is true for many multilateral tax and trade treaties. Being more moveable, the role of making sure that the security interest attaches and stays with portable goods is of critical importance. Second, in a society based on credit, there is a strong likelihood that most large personal goods, such as automobiles and the like, may have more than one creditor looking to that good for security. This reliance on that good may come from either the original acquisition of the good or from subsequent transactions after the good is acquired. The ordering of priorities between multiple creditors having claims to the same goods becomes a critical issue.

Finally, just as there are likely to be multiple creditors, so are there likely to be multiple users. The vertical chain of distribution starts with supplies of raw materials to manufacturers, distributors, and retailers. On the horizontal level, the users start with the consumer, his or her family, and go on to third party users or acquirers. With each shift, there lies the probability of having to recognize new duties and obligations vis-à-vis all parties having a legal relationship to those goods. All in all, it can very quickly become a tangled web, but the UCC and the common law rules with regard to liens, surety, guaranty, and collection provide some very good rules for both debtor and creditor.

II. Hypothetical Multi-Issue Essay Question:

Arnold Dweek owned and operated Ex Post Facto Motors, specializing in exotic autos having twelve or more cylinders. Unfortunately for Arnold, most of his cars only ran on a fraction of the cylinders sitting under the hood. Arnold took out a floor loan with Bailout Bank in order to finance an average inventory of twenty cars on his lot. The loan, in the amount of $1 million, covered all present and after-acquired cars on the lot. A financing statement was filed by Bailout Bank at the County Recorder's Office. Arnold normally had a turnover in his inventory of two cars per week selling at an average price of $65,000 per unit. Since he was intent on maintaining his exotic image, he never retained any trade-ins having less than twelve cylinders. Those cars were resold to a wholesaler.

Because the economy has slowed Arnold's sales to a trickle, he has decided not to use the proceeds from the wholesale resales of trade-ins to repay Bailout Bank. Instead he wired the money to his account in Rio. As a matter of fact, Arnold is now working on his tanning program on the beach in Rio, and Bailout Bank is seeking repossession of twenty trade-in cars sold to Wholesale Motors by Ex Post Facto Motors. Another ten were resold directly to retail customers by Arnold personally. What result?

III. Key Question Checklist:

A. Is this property covered by Article 9 of the UCC? Is it:
  1. A good?
    (a) A consumer good to be bought or used for personal, family, or household purposes?
    (b) An item of equipment bought or used primarily for business purposes?
    (c) Farm products (including crops, livestock, and supplies) to be used or produced for farming purposes?
    (d) Inventory held for sale or lease, including materials and partially completed works in progress?
    (e) Fixtures which were originally personal property but are affixed so as to become a part of the real property?
  2. An instrument?
    (a) Check?
    (b) Note?
    (c) Stock?
    (d) Bond?
    (e) Other investment security?
  3. Chattel paper which is a contract representing both a monetary obligation and a security interest?
  4. A document of title?
    (a) Bill of lading?
    (b) Warehouse receipt?
    (c) Any other documentation of ownership?
  5. Accounts or rights to payment not otherwise evidenced by an instrument?

B. Once you have decided to the subject matter comes within the scope of Article 9, then look at the nature of the agreement. Is it:
  1. A two party contract?
    (a) Buyer or debtor?
      (1) Buys the goods, etc. on credit?
      (2) Gives a secured interest to the seller or lender in the goods?
    (b) Seller or lender?
      (1) Sells the goods, etc. on credit?
      (2) Is given security in those goods?

2. A three party contract?
   (a) A seller who sells the goods to buyer without use of credit?
   (b) A buyer:
      (1) Who bought from the seller without use of credit vis-à-vis the seller?
      (2) Who obtained credit from a lender in order to finance the purchase from the seller?
      (3) Who exchanged a security interest in the goods to the lender in return for the lender's extension of credit?
   (c) A lender:
      (1) Who extended credit in order to facilitate the purchase?
      (2) Who took back a security interest in the purchased goods in exchange for extending the credit?

C. Does the agreement have the basic elements of a security agreement as called for under Article 9 of the UCC (attachment)?
   1. Is it in writing, or is there possession of the collateral by the creditor?
   2. Is it between the debtor and the secured party?
   3. Does it clearly describe the collateral?
   4. Does it clearly describe all the material terms relating to the promise to repay the creditor?
   5. Does it set forth the creditor's rights in case of default by the debtor?
   6. Did the creditor give value to the debtor?
   7. Does the debtor have rights in the collateral?

D. Once you have established that the agreement is covered by Article 9 of the UCC and that a security interest has been created and attached to the collateral, you must examine the perfection of that security interest. Perfection establishes the rights of the creditor vis-à-vis other creditors. Three methods of perfection are possible. Is it:
   1. By use of a filing statement?
      (a) A written statement containing:
         (1) Debtors name and mailing address?
         (2) Name and address of secured party?
         (3) Description of the collateral?
      (b) Filed in a public place per local requirements of state law?
   2. By creditor's possession of the collateral during the period of repayment of the debt?
   3. By a purchase money security agreement in consumer goods?
      (a) Consumer goods?
      (b) Credit extended to enable purchase?
      (c) Security interest obtained by creditor at time of purchase?

E. Once the security interest has been created, attached, and perfected, determine what priorities are now in place vis-à-vis multiple parties claiming rights to the collateral. Is it:
   1. Secured vs. nonsecured party?
      (a) Secured party has priority.
   2. Two secured parties in either of whom has perfected?
      (a) First attach wins.
   3. Two secured parties and only one has perfected their interest?
      (a) Perfected party wins.

4. Two secured parties, both perfected?
   (a) First to perfect wins:
       (1) By filing first, or
       (2) Having physical possession first.
5. If the property become commingled with other goods, the security interests are rated in proportion to the cost of goods?
6. If it is inventory, a perfected purchase money security interest will prevail over a perfected earlier nonpurchase money security interest if notice is given to the first secured party before the debtor receives possession of the inventory?
7. If it is noninventory, a perfected purchase money security interest will prevail if the perfection was made within ten days after the debtor received possession of the collateral without any requirement of notice to the prior creditor?
8. Buyers in the ordinary course of business from a merchant take free of any perfected or unperfected security interest in merchant's inventory?
9. Buyers of secondhand goods take free of security interests if:
   (a) They do not have actual or constructive knowledge of the security interest?
   (b) Give value?
   (c) Purchased the goods for personal, family, or household purposes?
10. Mechanics and artisans liens are given priority over all other security interests if:
    (a) Given in ordinary course of business?
    (b) Security is given in the goods to secure payment for the services?

F. In case of debtor's default on payment of the debt, the creditor may:
   1. Take possession of the collateral and:
      (a) Sell it, with proper notice?
      (b) Lease it, with proper notice?
      (c) Otherwise dispose of it?
      (d) Provide proper accounting of proceeds?
   2. Relinquish the security interest and proceed to judgment on the underlying debt?
      (a) May have possible deficiency judgment?
   3. Debtor may have right of redemption if:
      (a) Collateral not yet disposed of?
      (b) Proper payments made by debtor?

G. Termination of the security interest?
   1. By debtors performance discharge?
   2. Filing a termination statement?

IV. Objective Questions:

Terms:

1. Items of tangible and movable personal property purchased or used primarily for personal, family or household purposes are known as _____ _____.

2. The security interest in after-acquired property, future advances, or sale proceeds is known as a _____ _____.

3. As a secured creditor, one must _____ his security interest to establish his rights against other creditors who claim an interest in the same collateral.

4. One who wishes to extend a financing statement must file a _____ _____ up to six months prior to the expiration of the financing statements term.

5. The type of security interest that arises when one extends credit to a debtor for the purchase of consumer goods is known as a _____ _____ _____ _____.

6. In a secured transaction, the debtor and the secured party enter into a _____ _____ to create or provide for a security interest.

7. Those items of tangible personal property that have been affixed to real estate so as to become a part thereof are called _____.

8. A writing that evidences both a monetary obligation and a security interest is known as _____ _____.

9. The order in which competing claims may be satisfied from the same collateral is known as _____.

10. Money lent to the same debtor by the same creditor secured by the same collateral is known as a _____ _____.

True/False:

1. ____ Perfection of a security interest in commercial paper can only be accomplished by filing a financing statement.

2. ____ If collateral subject to a perfected security interest is sold, the security interest will attach to the proceeds resulting from the sale of the collateral.

3. ____ A buyer in the ordinary course of business takes the goods free of any security interest previously created by his seller even if the buyer knows of the existence of the security interest.

4. ____ A secured party may repossess collateral securing an obligation by any means available, including trickery or stealth, so long as the repossession does not result in a breach of the peace.

5. ____ In all circumstances in which the secured party seeks to dispose of collateral in her possession, she must notify the debtor in writing about the time and place of such intended disposition.

6. ____ To perfect a security interest in fixtures, the secured party must file a financing statement in the office where mortgages on real estate are filed or recorded.

7. ____ Typically, the lender or seller in a secured transaction grants a security interest to the borrower or buyer.

8. ____ When collateral is disposed of by a secured party, the disposition discharges the security interest under which it is made, but does not discharge any subordinate security interests or liens.

9. ____ If collateral subject to a perfected security interest increases in value, the secured party may hold the increased value or profits as collateral.

10. ____Repossession tactics allow for some breach of the peace as a price for protecting creditors from errant debtors.

Multiple Choice:

1. Tipsy Bank loaned $5,000 to Wilbur's Winery for working capital purposes. Wilbur's Winery granted a security interest in all of its inventory of wine. The Bank filed a valid financing statement. The Winery sold $10,000 worth of wine to a local distributor shortly before defaulting on its obligation to the Bank. Which of the following is most correct?
   A. The distributor is entitled to keep the wine if it can prove it was a buyer in the ordinary course of business.
   B. The distributor may keep the wine only if it lacked all knowledge of the Bank's security interest.
   C. The Bank is entitled to regain possession of the wine because it had filed a financing statement.
   D. None of the above.

2. Emily borrowed $2,400 from Zach to finance her Mediterranean cruise. Emily signed an agreement in which she agreed to give Zach a security interest in her personal paintings and to repay the loan in one year. Before leaving on her cruise a month later, Emily sold the paintings to Daniel. When Emily showed no sign of returning after nearly two years, Zach sought to repossess the paintings from Daniel in satisfaction of his loan. Which of the following is correct?
   A. Zach is entitled to repossess the paintings because he had a perfected purchase money security interest in them.

B. Zach is not entitled to repossess the paintings because he failed to file a financing statement within ten days of attaining his purchase money security interest.
   C. Zach did not attain a perfected purchase money security interest because paintings do not constitute consumer goods.
   D. None of the above.

3. Amber borrowed $10,000 from Ruby. To secure the debt, Amber gave Ruby possession of her valuable crystal collection. In addition, Amber signed a valid security agreement specifically describing the crystal collection. Ruby never filed the security agreement. Before the repayment date, Diamond Doug, who had won a large damage award in a lawsuit against Amber sought to satisfy his damage claim by forcing the sale of Amber's crystal collection. Which of the following is correct?
   A. Doug may validly force the sale of the crystal because legal damages have priority over secured transactions.
   B. Doug has the right to force the sale of the crystal in satisfaction of his claim because his attachment occurred before Ruby filed a financing statement.
   C. Doug is not entitled to force the sale of the crystal because Ruby perfected her security interest through possession of the crystal.
   D. Doug and Ruby will share proportionately in the proceeds from the sale of the crystal because his attachment occurred before Ruby filed a financing statement.

239

4. Assume the same facts as in question 3. Which of the following is correct?
   A. If Ruby fails to return the crystal after the debt has been repaid, Amber may use self-help to repossess the crystal.
   B. If the value of the crystal increases dramatically while in Ruby's possession, she must return a proportionate amount of the crystal to Amber.
   C. While the crystal is in her possession, Ruby is a bailee and must act in good faith and exercise extreme care to preserve the crystal.
   D. None of the above.

5. McGuckins' Lawn Supplies sold a riding lawn mower to Ed on credit for use in his large yard. McGuckins took a purchase money security interest in the lawn mower to secure payment but did not file a financing statement. Ed promised not to dispose of the lawn mower without McGuckins' consent. Ed subsequently defaulted on the payments and sold the lawn mower to his neighbor Karl for $500 without disclosing McGuckins' interest and without McGuckins consent. Under the circumstances:
   A. McGuckins' security interest is not perfected against other creditors of Ed or against Karl since McGuckins did not file a financing statement.
   B. Karl would take the lawn mower free of McGuckins' security interest even if McGuckins had filed.
   C. McGuckins has priority against anyone because the transfer was invalid without McGuckins' consent.
   D. Karl takes the lawn mower free of any security interest.

6. Huge Company owned a series of variety stores across the country. Huge

Company borrowed $30,000 from Giant Company and gave Giant Company bonds to hold as security for repayment of the loan. Which of the following is correct?
   A. Giant Company may only perfect its security interest by properly filing a financing statement.
   B. This arrangement would not be classified as a secured transaction under the UCC because it is not possible to grant a security interest in bonds.
   C. Giant Company has a perfected security interest with respect to the bonds.
   D. If the proceeds of the bonds were originally used to build a warehouse, Giant Company would need to file a financing statement in the real estate records to perfect its security interest.

7. Lynnette borrowed $5,000 from Jeannette and signed a written agreement. The agreement stated that Lynnette agreed to repay the loan on January 15 and that Jeannette could have possession of an antique automobile she was to inherit from her elderly Aunt Annette if Lynnette failed to repay the loan. Which of the following is correct?
   A. Jeannette is the secured party and has a security interest in the automobile.
   B. There was no security interest created because Jeannette did not sign the writing.
   C. There was no security interest created because Lynnette has no possessory or ownership interest in the automobile.
   D. A security interest was created only if the proceeds of the loan were used to purchase the automobile.

8. Mary purchased new furniture in the amount of $10,000 from Joe's Furniture in Sacramento, California and agreed to make payments at $100 per month for 100 months. In addition to its purchase money security interest, Joe's Furniture filed a valid financing statement to protect its security interest (assume that financing statements are valid for 5 years in California). After 4 years, Mary moved to New York and took the furniture with her. Which of the following is correct?

   A. A secured creditor in New York who files a valid financing statement with respect to the furniture will have priority over Joe's Furniture in any event.

   B. Joe's Furniture has four months to perfect its security interest by filing a new financing statement in New York.

   C. Joe's Furniture has one year to perfect its security interest by filing a new financing statement in New York.

   D. None of the above.

9. Under Sec. 90504 of the UCC, where a creditor chooses not to retain collateral, but rather to dispose of it, he or she must first apply the proceeds to:

   A. His or her personal bank account.

   B. Satisfy subordinate security interests.

   C. Pay reasonable expenses related to the disposition costs.

   D. The creditor may keep all proceeds in any event.

10. GI-GO (Garbage In/ Garbage Out) is a high-technology oriented firm that develops computer hardware. It has secured a patent for its latest hardware system. To finance the marketing for this system, GI-GO took out a loan from Easy Money Finance Company and gave its rights under the patent and chattel paper as security. If GI-GO defaults:

   A. Easy Money is entitled to whatever it can collect from the collateral after proper notification to the debtors and obligors.

   B. Easy Money has no recourse against GI-GO beyond the collateral.

   C. GI-GO is entitled to any surplus of collections made by Easy Money after deduction of expenses.

   D. Easy Money has no collection rights with respect to licensing of the patent since patents are not subject to the UCC.

V. Answers to Objective Questions:

Terms:

1. *Consumer goods.* Note the same goods may fall into a number of possible categories depending on the intended use of the goods.

2. *Floating lien.* These security interests are most commonly used vis-à-vis inventory where the collateral changes in character, classification, or location over a period of time.

3. *Perfect.* The perfection of the security interest establishes the right of a secured creditor against other creditors who claim an interest in the collateral.

4. *Continuation agreement.* The extension provided by this agreement can last up to six months per Sections 9-403(2) and (3) of the UCC.

5. *Purchase money security interest.* This interest can be taken or retained by the seller of an item to secure its price, or it can be taken by one who advances funds to enable one to acquire rights in the collateral.

6. *Security agreement.* Under Sec. 9-105(1), this can be any agreement between the debtor and the secured party that secures payment on performance of an obligation.

7. *Fixtures.* These personal properties can become part of real property by way of attachment, weight, or most important, by reason of the intent of the parties.

8. *Chattel paper.* This is defined by UCC Sec. 9-105(1)(b) and, in most cases, consists of a negotiable instrument coupled with a security agreement.

9. *Priority.* As much of the law of Article 9 is directed at establishing rights between competing creditors as it is towards defining creditors versus debtors rights.

10. *Future advance.* These are used in conjunction with revolving lines of credit and the like where certain personal property of the debtor is designated as collateral for future loans.

True/False:

1. False. Generally, a security interest in money and most negotiable instruments (including commercial paper) can only be perfected by taking possession of the collateral.

2. True. Unless otherwise stated in the security agreement, the secured party automatically has the right to receive the proceeds of the sale.

3. True. This rule is designed to protect buyer's expectations in the marketplace.

4. False. The UCC prohibits repossession through fraud, trickery, artifice, or stealth, nor may the creditor use force or threats of violence.

5. False. Notice of sale or disposition is not required if the collateral is perishable or threatens to decline steadily in value or is of a type customarily sold on a recognized market.

6. True. A financing statement must be filed by the secured party.

7. False. In the typical secured transaction, the borrower or buyer grants a security interest in his property to the seller or lender.

8. False. The disposition discharges the security interest under which it is made as well as any subordinate security interests or liens.

9. True. However, if the collateral is money, any increases or profits must either be remitted to the debtor or applied to reduce the balance of the secured debt.

10. False. Under Sec. 9-503, the creditor may not create a breach of the peace to repossess collateral upon a debtor's default. Breach of the peace is defined locally by each state and not by the UCC.

Multiple Choice:

1. A. A buyer in the ordinary course of business who purchases goods from a merchant takes the goods free and clear of any perfected or unperfected security interest in the merchant's inventory, even if the buyer knows of the existence of the security interest.

2. D. Zach did not have a purchase money security interest in this situation because Emily did not use the money to purchase the paintings. To protect his security interest, Zach should have filed a financing statement. Because he failed to file a financing statement, Zach's security interest is unperfected against third parties.

3. C. It is not necessary to file a financing statement to perfect a security interest if one has possession of the collateral.

4. D. Answer A is incorrect because the right of self-help relates to the right of the secured party to repossess collateral. Amber would have to bring a replevin action to regain possession of the crystal. Answer B is incorrect because the secured party is entitled to retain the collateral, even if it increases in value. Answer C is incorrect because the secured party is only required to act with reasonable care with respect to the collateral, unless agreed otherwise.

5. D. The lawn mower was a consumer good because it was to be used by Ed for personal purposes. McGuckins purchase money security interest was perfected without filing. Karl took free of the security interest because he bought without knowledge of the security interest, for value, and presumably for personal purposes. Answer A is incorrect because a purchase money security interest is perfected without filing and given priority over other perfected creditors of the debtor. Answer B is incorrect because Karl would have taken subject to the security interest if McGuckins had filed a financing statement. Answer C is incorrect because the prohibition against transfer is not effective against innocent third parties who give value.

6. C. Generally, possession is the only method available to perfect a security interest in investment securities such as bonds.

7. C. To create a valid security interest, the debtor must have rights in the collateral. Here, it is merely speculation that Lynnette will ultimately inherit the automobile, and thus no security interest

was created. Answer B is incorrect because it is not necessary that the secured party sign the security agreement to create a valid security interest. Answer D is incorrect because there are other types of security interests than purchase money security interests.

8. B. Joe's Furniture has the shorter of four months or the period of time remaining under the original California perfection (here, one year) to file in New York. Answer A is an incorrect statement because the original perfection continues if the proper steps are taken to perfect in the new state. Answer C is incorrect because the secured party must file the new financing statement in the shorter of the two periods discussed above.

9. C. Under Sec. 9-504(1)(a), reasonable expenses of retaking, holding, and preparing the collateral for sale, lease, or other disposition are paid first.

10. C. The secured party must account to the debtor for any surplus from collection, less reasonable expenses incurred. Answer A is incorrect because Easy Money is liable for any surplus to GI-GO. Answer B is incorrect because GI-GO will be liable for any deficiency. Answer D is an incorrect statement.

VI. Key Question Checklist Answers to Essay Question:

A. *Is this property covered by Article 9 of the UCC?*

The property in question is covered by Article 9 of the UCC. The autos in question were used as an inventory by Mr. Dweek.

243

B. *What is the nature of the UCC agreement here?*

The nature of the agreement between Mr. Dweek and Bailout Bank is a three party contract where Mr. Dweek made purchases of autos directly from sellers without credit from the seller. Instead, the purchases were financed by a purchase money arrangement with Bailout Bank, i.e., the credit extended by Bailout was used to facilitate the purchases.

C. *Does the agreement provide for the basic elements of a security agreement as called for under Article 9?*

It appears that the elements called for under Article 9 of the UCC were in place in this case. There is a writing between parties. Each has given value and the autos were properly described in the agreement. After acquired inventory can be covered by such an agreement even though it is not yet in place at the time the agreement is entered into.

D. *Has perfection of the security interest taken place per Article 9 of the UCC?*

Bailout Bank perfected its security interest in the inventory by properly complying with the filing requirements of Article 9. Its use of a filing statement acted as constructive notice to subsequent creditors of an existing security interest in the autos as collateral for Bailout's loan to Mr. Dweek.

E. *Assuming attachment and perfection have taken place, what are the priority of claims of the various parties claiming rights to the collateral?*

As for Wholesale Motors, there does not appear to be any security interest in relation to its purchase of the autos from Mr. Dweek. It

is therefore an unsecured creditor and as such would be behind Bailout Bank in terms of priority claims vis-à-vis the autos. Had it extended credit to Mr. Dweek in the form of a purchase money security interest and had that interest been made known to Bailout Bank before the auto went into Mr. Dweek's inventory, the results would have been different. But here, Bailout wins vis-à-vis Wholesale Motors.

Bailout would not win, however, vis-à-vis the ten retail customers who bought the cars directly from Mr. Dweek. They are buyers in the ordinary course of business who bought from a merchant. As such, they take free of any perfected or unperfected security interest in the merchant's inventory. The UCC policy of protecting the retail buyer's reliance in the marketplace is the underlying public policy for this result.

As for Arnold Dweek, his tan should quickly pale if Bailout Bank and Wholesale Motors can get their hands on him. He will be running on no cylinders in the local constabulary.

CHAPTER 28

BANKRUPTCY AND REORGANIZATION

Bankruptcy: life after debt.

D. Robert White

I. Overview:

One of the most nonsensical notions to ever come down the law pike is the idea of putting someone in jail until such time as his debts were paid. Debtor's prisons were holding cells for economic hostages whose ability to get out was directly proportional to the debtor's ability to get others to pay his debt for him. Many of those dungeons became so crowded that the New World became a dumping ground for the detainees. As fate would have it, that migration was most fortuitous for our nation. Very often the same people who were in prison for debt were also the innovators, risk takers, and entrepreneurs who helped build a new economic system less encumbered by class mentalities.

The basic underlying premise of bankruptcy law is founded on a simple reality: bad things happen to good people. How many of us can really provide ourselves with a safe haven from financial disasters brought on by bad health, economic downturns, financial institution failures, and the like? The early bankruptcy laws of England first recognized that businesses can and do fail in spite of the best good faith efforts of their proprietors. That failure should not, in effect, act as a life sentence in keeping that business or its proprietor from reentering the marketplace. Bankruptcy is really one of the earliest forms of recycling, a recycling of economic opportunity for good faith debtors who deserve a second chance.

As with any legal favor, there are people and business entities who get too greedy in asking for the benefit of the law. Bankruptcy is built on a cornerstone of good faith. Where debtors' actions are motivated by bad faith attempts to avoid legitimate obligations, both the law and the larger societal public policy is subverted. The history of the law of bankruptcy is riddled with cases of clear abuse and creditor victimization which have created a dilemma for legislators who must draft our bankruptcy statutes.

The recent history of federal bankruptcy reforms in the U.S. illustrates Congress's attempts to deal with this dilemma of trying to make the law more humane while trying to curb abuses. The Bankruptcy Act of 1978 provided for sweeping reforms which sought to destigmatize bankruptcy in an economy which had grown too dependent on the manna of credit. Unfortunately, with this liberalization came a horde of abuses of the law. Graduates of long and expensive professional studies began their lucrative careers with a bankruptcy discharge of school loans. Many consumers loaded up on all sorts of trinkets on credit and kept them debt free under bankruptcy. Corporations began to use the reorganization provisions of the law as a management wedge to get out from under otherwise binding executory contracts, or even worse, tort judgments. Congress responded with the Bankruptcy Amendments and Federal Judgeship Act of 1984 and other subsequent revisions. This legislation sought to pull in the reins on many of these abuses as outlined in the text.

There is still a great need to further balance the basic dichotomy between relief and prevention of abuse. On one side, the mechanics of bankruptcy law must be made more cost efficient. The law should provide a larger slice of the economic pie for creditors than is presently available while retaining the fresh start opportunities presently provided for good faith debtors. At the same time, present loopholes in the law must be closed. There are still far too many opportunities for charlatans, deadbeats, and unscrupulous managers to abuse the system. The losses generated by these people add a colossal weight to the cost of credit borne by all of us. Witness the mockery of law made by the key protagonists of the junk bond or savings and loan scandals.

A famous commentator on American history, Allistair Cooke, ended his TV series "Allistair Cooke's America" on PBS with a quote from an immigrant from Italy who had lived in the U.S. for four decades. He said: "There is no free lunch." These words are as prophetic as ever. The key question checklist illustrates the mechanics of the federal bankruptcy laws.

II. Hypothetical Multi-issue Essay Question:

Mr. Pinky Flash is not a modest fellow. His personal credo has always been:

> "If you've got it, flaunt it; and if you flaunt it, be sure to telemarket it!"

Pinky invented and patented the original computer-voice telemarketing machine. This is the very same machine which seems to instinctively know exactly when you are about to have dinner or take a shower. It is favored by evangelists, phone companies, and penny stock promoters because it allows them to disturb you in spite of having an unlisted phone number.

As Pinky's business prospered, he proceeded to indulge in his favorite pastime-- buying expensive jewelry on credit. On every one of his fingers he wore a precious pink gem of at least five carats. His supplier, Rocks R Us, extended a $1 million line of unsecured credit to Pinky, and he used it fully. In addition, he owed $5 million each to two other unsecured creditors, Phakky Peripherals Inc. and Magnetic Voices, Inc. Both of them supplied parts for his telemarketing machines. In addition, he owed $1 million to Bailout Bank for his home mortgage. His home's value has gone down to $500,000 since he had it plastered in a shade of luminescent pink to match his rings.

Last week Pinky's world fell in on him when Congress passed a constitutional amendment which banned the manufacture, use, or sale of Pinky's telemarketing machines. The amendment was ratified in record time through the use of Email. Pinky has no other assets other than his house, jewelry, and half-finished machines. In addition, he still owes $100,000 from last year's income taxes to the IRS. What are Pinky's prospects in Bankruptcy Court?

III. Key Question Checklist:

A. Does the bankruptcy law generally apply to the issue at hand?
   1. Does the debtor have standing as a qualified party who may seek protection under the law?
      (a) An individual person?
      (b) Partnership?
      (c) Corporation?
   2. Does the debtor not qualify under the bankruptcy law because he is covered by other statutes?
      (a) Banks?
      (b) Savings and loans?
      (c) Credit unions?
      (d) Insurance companies?
      (e) Railroads?

B. Once you have resolved the issue of standing to seek the protections of the law, which provision of the Bankruptcy Code is to be used in this case?
1. Chapter 7 liquidation?
2. Chapter 11 reorganization?
3. Chapter 12 family farm reorganization?
4. Chapter 13 consumer debt adjustment?
5. Any other miscellaneous sections of the code such as those provisions relating to government subdivisions?

C. Assuming Chapter 7 liquidation is sought, you must then review the appropriate procedural steps to be used in utilizing the statute. They are:
1. Filing the petition?
    (a) Voluntary?
        (1) Statement of debts?
        (2) Insolvency not required to be declared?
        (3) Debtor informed of all options under the code?
        (4) Petition lists all required material schedules?
    (b) Involuntary?
        (1) Person bringing the petition is qualified to do so?
        (2) Must allege material facts with regard to nonpayment of debts or liens?
        (3) Signed by the appropriate number of creditors if more than twelve?
        (4) Aggregate dollar threshold amount met ($5000)?
2. Order for relief?
    (a) If voluntary or unchallenged, granted automatically?
    (b) If involuntary and challenged, may be contested in trial on its merits?
    (c) If order is granted, case is accepted for further proceedings?

3. Stay or suspension?
    (a) Automatic suspension of:
        (1) Legal actions to collect prepetition debts of debtor?
        (2) Enforcing judgments obtained against debtor?
        (3) Obtaining, perfecting, or enforcing liens against property of debtor?
        (4) Attempting set offs of debts owed by the debtor?
        (5) Nonjudicial self-help remedies such as repossession of debtor's assets?
        (6) Some action exempt from the story or suspension order?
            (aa) Alimony?
            (bb) Child support payments?
            (cc) Actions against codebtors?
        (7) Secured creditors may be entitled to alternative forms of protection?
            (aa) Cash payments to cover depreciation costs?
            (bb) Liens?
            (cc) Indubitable equivalents, guarantees from a solvent party?
4. Meeting of the creditors?
    (a) Held in a timely manner?
    (b) With the debtor and his or her creditors?
    (c) Without judge present?
    (d) Full disclosure of material financial facts by the debtor?
5. Appointment of the trustee?
    (a) Becomes legal representative of the bankrupt?
    (b) Reports to the court on all his or her activities?

6. Duties of the trustee?
   (a) Garner the assets of the estate?
      (1) Take possession of the debtor's property?
      (2) Bring in any postpetition property?
         (aa) Gifts, inheritances, life insurance, and divorce settlements inuring within 180 days after the petition is filed?
         (bb) Does not include purchases in the ordinary course of business?
         (cc) Bring back any preferential liens given within 90 days prior to the filing of the petition?
         (dd) Bring back any preferential transfers made to insiders within a year prior to filing of the petition?
         (ee) Bring back any transfers classified by federal or state law as being fraudulent?
   (b) Examine proof of claims made by creditor?
      (1) Timely filed?
      (2) Allowed by the court?
   (c) Allocate and distribute the proceeds of the estate according to the priorities set out in the statute?
      (1) Exemptions to be retained by the debtor as allowed by either federal or state law?
      (2) Distribution of property to secured creditors?
      (3) Distribution of property to unsecured creditors?
   (d) Reports on their activities to:
      (1) Bankruptcy court?
      (2) Debtor?
      (3) Creditor?

7. Discharge of debts?
   (a) Available only to individuals?
   (b) Not available to partnerships or corporations?
8. Exceptions to discharge of debts?
   (a) Taxes accrued within three years of filing the petition?
   (b) Certain fines and penalties owed to governmental entities?
   (c) Claims owed based on fraud, larceny, or embezzlement by the debtor?
   (d) Tort liabilities based on willful or malicious actions of the debtor?
   (e) Alimony, maintenance, and child support owed by debtor?
   (f) Unscheduled claims?
   (g) "Load up" purchases of luxury goods made within 40 days of filing the petition?
   (h) "Load up" credit line advances made within 20 days of the petition?
   (i) D.U.I. liabilities of the debtor?
9. Reaffirmations of debt?
   (a) Must be made before debtor is granted discharge?
   (b) With filing to and consent by the court?

D. Assuming Chapter 11 reorganization?
   1. Same basic procedural steps as used in Chapter 7 filing?
   2. Basic objective is to reorganize and continue to operate the business rather than to liquidate?
   3. Steps which distinguish this proceeding from Chapter 7?
      (a) Debtor-in-possession gets to continue operation of the business?
      (b) Trustee can be appointed by the court if it deems it appropriate?
      (c) Creditors committee formed in order to represent the interests of creditors?

(d) A plan of reorganization is filed:
    (1) Done in a timely manner?
    (2) Disclosure statement provided by debtor?
    (3) Plan is confirmed by the court by:
        (aa) Acceptance method?
        (bb) Cram down method?

E. Assuming Chapter 12 reorganization?
   1. Same procedural steps as used in Chapter 11?
   2. Applies to family farms?

F. Assuming Chapter 13 consumer debt adjustment?
   1. Voluntary petition only allowed?
   2. Must qualify under financial thresholds set out in the law?
   3. If qualified, automatic stay is issued and creditors meeting held with debtor?
   4. Plan of payment is filed with the court?
   5. Plan is confirmed by the court?
   6. If payments not made per plan, creditors may seek conversion to Chapter 7?
   7. If the plan is conformed to, discharge of debts can be ordered by the court?
   8. Court can also order discharge based on proven hardship by the debtor?

IV. Objective Questions:

Terms:

1. By discharging burdensome debts of the debtor, the federal bankruptcy law gives the debtor a _____ _____.

2. A stay which results from the filing of a bankruptcy petition, whether voluntary or involuntary, and suspends certain actions by creditors against the debtor or the debtor's property is called _____ _____.

3. An unsecured creditor is required to timely file a _____ _____ _____ before he will be entitled to share in the distribution of the bankruptcy estate.

4. Those unusual transfers or payments made by the debtor on the eve of bankruptcy that can be avoided by the trustee because they benefit some creditors at the expense of others are called _____.

5. A situation in which a debtor transfers her property with the actual intent to hinder, delay, or defraud her creditors is known as a _____ transfer.

6. If all of the property in the bankruptcy estate is exhausted in satisfaction of allowed claims, remaining unpaid claims will be _____.

7. An arrangement by which the debtor voluntarily agrees to pay an unsatisfied debt that is dischargeable in bankruptcy is called a _____ _____.

8. In a Chapter 11 case, the debtor who is authorized to continue to operate her business is known as a _____ _____ _____.

9. The document by which a bankruptcy proceeding is commenced is known as a _____.

10. The legal representative of the bankrupt debtor's estate is the _____.

True/False:

1. ____ Only partnerships and corporations are entitled to have their debts discharged in bankruptcy proceedings.

2. ____ Alimony, but not child support, is dischargeable in a bankruptcy proceeding.

3. ____ In a Chapter 7 proceeding, the debtors assets (except for exempt property) are sold for cash and the cash is distributed to the creditors.

4. ____ A voluntary petition must state that the debtor is unable to pay his debts as they become due.

5. ____ In a bankruptcy proceeding, secured and unsecured creditors are given the same priority with respect to the distribution of the assets in the bankruptcy estate.

6. ____ If the value of collateral securing the debt of a particular creditor is less than the claim of that creditor, that person becomes an unsecured creditor to the extent of the difference.

7. ____ The bankruptcy trustee is never permitted to liquidate exempt property of the debtor.

8. ____ A debtor who was granted a discharge in bankruptcy five years ago will be denied a discharge of debts.

9. ____ The transfer of assets by an insolvent debtor to her parents within one year of filing a bankruptcy petition may be avoided by the trustee as a preferential transfer.

10. ____ Voluntary bankruptcy proceedings are commenced by the creditor.

Multiple Choice:

1. A downturn in the economy caused Charlie, a construction contractor, to suffer many financial losses. As a result, he was forced to declare bankruptcy. Charlie owns a home that he built valued at $85,000 on which he still owes $77,000, tools and other minor construction equipment worth $700, and a gold watch that he inherited valued at $600. Which of Charlie's assets will not be fully exempted under the Bankruptcy Act?
   A. The house.
   B. The tools.
   C. The watch.
   D. All of his assets will be fully exempted.

2. Paul Playboy was forced into bankruptcy involuntarily. The value of all his nonexempt assets amounted to $75,000. After paying priority claims, $30,000 remained. There are $100,000 of provable unsecured claims. These unsecured creditors will each receive:
   A. Nothing.
   B. One dollar for each dollar of debt owed them.
   C. Thirty cents for each dollar of debt owed them.
   D. None of the above.

3. On March 1, Jack loaned Janet $3,000 to purchase a sailboat. However, Jack insisted that he have possession of Janet's $4,000 diamond ring until she repaid the $3,000. On May 15, Janet filed a voluntary petition in bankruptcy. Fearing he may not be repaid, Jack sold the ring to Hillary Honest on May 20. Which of the following is correct?
   A. The transfer from Jack to Hillary constitutes a voidable preference.
   B. Jack is protected because he sold the ring to a bona fide purchaser for value.
   C. Hillary is entitled to keep the ring unless she knew that Janet had filed a petition in bankruptcy.
   D. None of the above.

4. Which of the following actions is not stayed in a bankruptcy proceeding?
   A. The enforcement of judgments obtained against the debtor.
   B. The institution of legal actions to collect debts against the debtor.
   C. An action to recover alimony from the debtor.
   D. All of the above.

5. Which of the following is not considered an asset of the bankruptcy estate?
   A. A software program created by the debtor.
   B. A time-share apartment in Mexico in which the debtor has an interest.
   C. $11 million the debtor won from a lottery ticket purchased with a dollar bill found on the street four months after filing the voluntary petition in bankruptcy.
   D. $40,000 the debtor inherited from a distant relative three months after filing the voluntary petition in bankruptcy.

6. Sally Slowpay operates a printing business. Her business has been declining slowly for several years. Sally has been unable to pay any of her ten creditors for several months. George Greedy, to whom Sally owes $4,000, is frustrated and has lost his patience with Sally. He signs and files an involuntary bankruptcy petition against Sally. Which of the following is correct?
   A. The petition is invalid because at least three creditors must sign an involuntary petition.
   B. The petition is invalid because unsecured creditors with claims aggregating at least $5,000 must sign the petition.
   C. The petition is invalid if it fails to list Sally's current income and expenses.
   D. None of the above.

7. Which of the following is not a responsibility of the trustee in a Chapter 7 proceeding?
   A. Employ disinterested accountants, attorneys, and appraisers to serve as legal representatives of the estate.
   B. Take immediate possession of the debtor's property.
   C. Make reports to the court, creditors, and the debtor regarding the administration of the estate.
   D. Investigate the debtor's financial affairs.

8. Which of the following is not a primary purpose of the federal bankruptcy laws?
   A. To protect creditors from actions of the debtor that would diminish the value of the bankruptcy estate.
   B. To protect debtors from abusive activities by creditors in collecting debts.
   C. To give the debtor a fresh start by freeing her from legal responsibility for future debts.
   D. To preserve existing business relations of the debtor.

9. CompuTech, a manufacturer of computer components, was beginning to feel the pinch of the slow economy. Several months ago, Bully's Supply, the only supplier of certain components used in CompuTech's manufacturing process, began requiring CompuTech to pay for components upon delivery. In addition, Bully's required CompuTech to give it a note secured by a mortgage on certain properties owned by CompuTech to evidence outstanding balances due Bully's for components delivered in the past. The note and mortgage were executed on June 2, 1994 at which time the mortgage was filed. On August 8, 1994, CompuTech filed a voluntary petition in bankruptcy. Which of the following is correct?

   A. Any payments made to CompuTech for components delivered in June, July, or August are voidable preferences.

   B. The mortgage given to Bully's was a voidable preference.

   C. The mortgage was not a voidable preference because it was executed and filed on the same day.

   D. None of the above.

10. Which of the following acts by a debtor would not bar discharge of the debts of the debtor in a bankruptcy proceeding?

    A. An unusual payment or transfer of property on the eve of bankruptcy that would unfairly benefit some creditors at the expense of others.

    B. Failure to appear at a hearing on an objection to discharge.

    C. Falsifying, destroying, or concealing records of his financial condition.

    D. The transfer, concealment, or removal of property from the estate with the intent to hinder, delay, or defraud creditors.

V. Answers to Objective Questions:

Terms:

1. *Fresh start*. This element represents the recycling aspect of bankruptcy law.

2. *Automatic stay*. This is a procedural "time out."

3. *Proof of claim*. Most proofs are relatively straightforward if they are based on a contract debt.

4. *Preferences*. Note that some of these transfers are presumed to have been made in bad faith.

5. *Fraudulent*. Many of these transfers subvert the intent of the law.

6. *Discharged*. The debt has now been legally ended.

7. *Reaffirmation agreement*. The code is concerned with the possible abuse of marketplace leverage by these creditors and wants to be sure that the debt is reinstated as a matter of free will.

8. *Debtor-in-possession*. Most cases will allow this unless there is a showing of some sort of bad faith on the part of management.

9. *Petition*. This is the opening procedural step.

10. *Trustee*. The trustee is not considered the sole agent of the creditors nor the debtor but is, in fact, responsible to the court.

True/False:

1. False. Only individuals may have their debts discharged in bankruptcy. Partnerships and corporations are required to liquidate.

2. False. Neither alimony nor child support is dischargeable in a bankruptcy proceeding.

3. True. This is why it is called liquidation.

4. False. A voluntary petition is only required to state that the debtor has debts.

5. False. A secured creditor's claim to the debtor's property has priority over the claims of unsecured creditors.

6. True. Many creditors find themselves in this two track position.

7. False. If the debtor's equity in certain exempt property exceeds the exemption limit, the trustee may liquidate the property.

8. True. A debtor will be denied discharge if discharge was granted within six years of the commencement of the present case.

9. True. Relatives are considered insiders, thus making the one year avoidance period applicable.

10. False. Voluntary proceedings are commenced by the debtor.

Multiple Choice:

1. C. An interest in jewelry up to $500 that is held for personal use is exempt under the Bankruptcy Act.

2. D. The Bankruptcy Code provides that unsecured claims are to be satisfied out of the bankruptcy estate in the order of their statutory priority. In this situation, there is not enough information to determine the priority in which the unsecured claims will be paid.

3. C. A creditor who has received a preferential transfer may convey good title to an innocent third party purchaser.

4. C. Congress did not want these sorts of obligations delayed.

5. C. Property acquired after the petition is not property of the bankruptcy estate. However, inheritance is an exception to this rule, and therefore answer D is incorrect. Intangible property, and any

other property in which the debtor has a legal or equitable interest, wherever located, is considered property of the estate, and therefore answers A and B are incorrect.

6. B. If a debtor has fewer than twelve creditors, an involuntary petition may only be filed by a creditor, or creditors, with claims aggregating $5,000.

7. A. The trustee has the responsibility to hire disinterested persons to assist in the administration of the estate. However, the trustee is the legal representative of the estate.

8. C. The purpose is to give a fresh start by freeing the debtor from existing debts.

9. B. CompuTech gave Bully's a preferential lien within 90 days of filing the bankruptcy petition; the lien was given for amounts past due (antecedent debt); and it is presumed that Bully's would receive more because of the lien than as an unsecured creditor in liquidation. Answer A is incorrect because Bully's required payment simultaneously with delivery, and therefore such payments are not made in respect of antecedent debts.

10. A. A preferential transfer can be avoided in bankruptcy. It does not, however, bar discharge of debts. B, C, and D are all items that would bar discharge of debts.

VI. Key Question Checklist Answers to Essay Question:

A. *Does the bankruptcy law generally apply to the issue at hand?*

Things look blue for Pinky. Assuming he has not incorporated his business, he may be able to eventually have most of his debts

253

discharged if he follows the steps outlined under the Bankruptcy Code. His business does not fall into any of the specific activities covered by separate statutes such as banks, railroads, or savings and loan associations, so he does have standing to petition the court as an individual.

B. *Which of the provisions of the Bankruptcy Code should be used here?*

It appears from the case as presented, Pinky's best strategy would lie in a Chapter 7 liquidation of his assets. Chapter 11 reorganization appears unlikely given Congress's decisive (and rare) action in getting rid of these truly obnoxious devices. There is very little likelihood that Pinky's business could be reorganized unless the machines could be reconfigured for some more socially productive use.

C. *What are the procedural steps to be taken?*

Assuming that a Chapter 7 liquidation is in order, the first issue which needs to be resolved is the filing of the petition for bankruptcy. Pinky may chose to file voluntarily, but if he does not, he appears to have little control over this issue. His creditors can force an involuntary filing upon him once he has stopped paying his credit bills on time and is in a position of liquid insolvency, i.e., not being able to pay his bills as they become due. Once the petition is filed, an order for relief will be issued. This order will suspend more creditor's actions against Pinky for the moment. The key exception to this stay would involve Bailout Bank's claims against Pinky's house. The bank is a secured creditor to the extent of the reduced value of the home and an unsecured creditor as to amounts owed above the collateral value.

Bailout may therefore seek to get cash payments to cover depreciation costs or indubitable equivalents, but both remedies seem unlikely in this case.

Once the stay has been ordered, Pinky must meet with all his creditors and fully disclose his financial affairs to them. Soon thereafter, the Bankruptcy Court will appoint a trustee who will take control of Pinky's property. The trustee will seek to garner any assets properly included in Pinky's estate. This would include any accounts receivable for sales of his machines and the like. In addition, the trustee would look to see if there have been any voidable preferences, preferential transfers, or possible fraudulent transactions. The trustee will also examine the claims filed by the creditors.

When all the assets have been brought into the estate, the trustee will proceed, with court approval, to allocate those assets according to priorities set out the Bankruptcy Code. Pinky will be able to keep some exempted property. He will be able to claim a homestead based on either federal or state law. In addition, he will be able to keep one very small pinky ring valued at no more than $500. He may also keep any other property qualified under the listed exemptions set out in the code.

Assuming the home is sold to pay off the secured creditor, Bailout Bank (net of Pinky's homestead claim amount), Bailout Bank's remaining deficiency amount owed will then be classified as a general unsecured debt. As such those creditors will be paid in the priority of payment allowed by the code. The general unsecured creditors will be paid only after the fees and expenses of the administration of the estate are paid along with numerous other preferred creditors. In all likelihood, the computer suppliers and Rocks R Us are not going to fare well in bankruptcy.

When the remaining assets are sold off and the proceeds distributed, the trustee will file his or her report with all parties concerned. The Bankruptcy Court will then discharge Pinky from any further obligations on all his debts except the $100,000 owed to the IRS. Because that debt occurred within three years prior to the filing of the petition, it is not discharged. In addition, if Pinky for some reason chooses to reaffirm any of these debts, he must do so with the consent of the Bankruptcy Court.

All in all, Pinky might consider some other line of work once he gets his fresh start. He should get into a line of work which will not foster invasive intrusions into peoples homes in the middle of the dinner hour.

CHAPTER 29

CREATION AND TERMINATION OF AGENCY RELATIONSHIPS

Those who consent to the act and those who do it shall be equally punished.

Sir Edward Coke

I. Overview:

Qui facit per alium facit per se. He who acts through another acts himself. This simple Latin phrase provides the keystone upon which the mutual obligations of agency law rest. Agency is defined by Section 1 of the *Second Restatement of Agency* as

"the fiduciary relation which results from the manifestation of consent by one person to another that the other shall act on his behalf and subject to his control, and consent by the other so to act."

Agency is a legally recognized relationship which allows an attribution of one person's behavior to another. This carryover process is two-sided in that both benefit and burden inure to the parties involved in the agency relationship.

Under the basic doctrine of agency, the principal is allowed to reap the beneficial harvest of the agent's actions made in his or her behalf. For example, assume an agent has agreed to be paid a set salary of $100 for selling certain kinds of goods. The principal gets to keep the net profits from that agent's selling activities, be they $100 or $1,000,000. This net gain is what allows the use of agency theory to maximize one's profits through the actions of another. Exponential growth of most any sort of enterprise is almost always directly tied to effective use of the talent of others through agency law. There are some limits on this ability to designate others to act on one's behalf based on uniqueness of personal services or on public policy grounds which forbid use of agents, such as voting or serving a criminal sentence. As a practical matter, business as we know it today simply could not be conducted on any scale beyond sole proprietorship without extensive use of agency relationships.

The benefits of agency are not without counterbalancing detriment. The Latin maxim *respondeat superior* may be familiar to you. It means that, in certain instances, a principal is liable to third parties for the acts of his or her agent. Just as the benefits of agency can be great, so can the burdens. One of the fastest growing areas of management specialization in today's business environment is risk management. This area generally concerns business financial responsibility for exposure to specified contingencies or perils. Included in these perils are the acts of the agents for which the principal may be liable. The ironic aspect of all this is that the very same people who help a business grow can lead that same enterprise to financial ruin.

II. Hypothetical Multi-Issue Essay Question:

Jacko Frinton is the quintessence of opportunistic entrepreneurship. No silly rules on employment taxes and social security were going to stop him from creating the largest door to door sales force in used toothbrushes ever assembled. He specifically hired all his salespeople as independent contractors. Under the terms of his agreement with them, he controlled the time, routes, and all working conditions on their sales routes. They, in turn, were to be paid only on commission. In addition, because they were designated as independent contractors, Jacko saved millions on FICA and other employment taxes. The Internal Revenue Service got wind of Jacko's operation from a disgruntled brush salesman who turned him in for an informant's fee. Does Jacko owe any employment taxes to the IRS?

III. Key Question Checklist:

This checklist is designed to help students first identify the nature of the relationships between the various parties listed in the essay question. Based on those relationships, you will then be asked to determine the respective rights, duties, and liabilities of the parties towards each other.

A. How was the agency relationship created?
1. Express agreement?
   (a) Was it oral?
   (b) Was it written?
      (1) Was there a Statute of Frauds requirement in this agreement?
   (c) Was it a specialized form of express agency agreement?
      (1) General power of attorney?
      (2) Special power of attorney?
2. Implied agency?
   (a) No expressed creation of an agency relationship?
      (1) What facts and circumstances would be used to infer an agency relationship?
   (b) Have expressed agency but no clearly defined duties of agent?
      (1) What facts and circumstances would be used to define implied authority to act?
      (aa) Operate a business?
      (bb) Emergency power?

3. Apparent authority?
   (a) No actual, express, or implied authority given to the agent?
   (b) Actions or omissions of principal allow a third party to reasonably believe that an agency relationship does exist between principal and agent?
   (c) If the actions of the principal allow apparent authority to exist in the eyes of a third party, does the principal now become liable to that third party for the acts of the agent?
4. Agency by ratification?
   (a) No authority in existence at the time of the purported agent's act?
   (b) Have actual misrepresentation of agency when in fact there is none?
   (c) The purported principal subsequently ratifies or accepts the unauthorized act as his or her own?
      (1) Ratification expressly stated by the principal?
      (2) Ratification implied from the facts and circumstances at issue?

B. Once the agency relationship has been created, what definition fits that relationship best?
1. Employer/employee?
   (a) What powers are granted to the agent?
   (b) What limitations are agreed upon by the parties regarding those powers?
   (c) Any contractual authority granted to the agent to act on behalf of the principal?

(d) Any tort liability possible to the principal vis-à-vis third parties for the acts of the agent?

2. Exclusive agency?
3. Multiple agency?
4. Foreign agency?

C. If you have decided that there is not an agency relationship created, determine whether a principal/independent contractor relationship exists.

1. Is the purported independent contractor controlled or subject to the control of the principal?
   (a) What is the degree of control?
2. What powers has the principal authorized the independent contractor to use on his or her behalf?
3. What tort liability, if any, can be attributed to the principal for the acts of the independent contractor?

D. Termination of the agency?

1. Express agreement?
   (a) Limitations?
   (b) Security?
2. Implied?
   (a) Acts of parties?
   (b) Passage of time?
3. Operation of law?
   (a) Death?
   (b) Insanity?
   (c) Bankruptcy?
   (d) Impossibility?
   (e) Changed circumstances?
   (f) War?
4. Wrongful termination?

IV. Objective Questions:

Terms:

1. An agency that occurs when a principal and agent agree to enter into an agency agreement with each other is called an _____ agency.

2. An agency that occurs when a principal and agent do not expressly create an agency, but it is inferred from the conduct of the parties is called an _____ agency.

3. An agency that arises when a principal creates the appearance of an agency that in actuality does not exist is known as an _____ agency.

4. An agency that occurs when (1) a person misrepresents herself as another's agent when in fact she is not and (2) the purported principal ratifies the unauthorized act is called an _____ _____ _____.

5. The party who employs another person to act on her behalf is the _____.

6. The party who agrees to act on behalf of another is the _____.

7. Where an employer hires an employee and gives that employee authority to act and enter into contracts on her behalf, there is a _____ _____ _____.

8. A power of attorney that confers broad powers on the agent to act in many matters on the principal's behalf is a _____ _____ _____ _____.

9. The authority beyond an agent's express or implied authority that is created because of something a principal has said or done is _____ _____ _____ _____ _____.

10. A special type of agency relationship that is created for the agent's benefit which is irrevocable by the principal is an

_____ _____

_____ _____

_____.

True/False:

1. _____An agency relationship must be based on consideration. That is, no agency relationship is created if the agent is not paid for his services.

2. _____A power of attorney, which is an express agency agreement, may be established by either an oral or written agreement.

3. _____A principal's ratification of an unauthorized contract must be by express approval. Implied consent is not sufficient to bind a principal under ratification principles.

4. _____Constructive notice is sufficient to inform parties who dealt with an agent that the agency has been terminated.

5. _____An employee in an employer/employee relationship is not an agent since she cannot enter into contracts for her principal.

6. _____An agent in an express agency agreement may have implied authority as well as express authority.

7. _____Under apparent authority, a principal is bound to contracts entered into by an apparent agent even though an agency does not actually exist.

8. _____An agency coupled with an interest, unlike a regular agency relationship, is not terminated by the death or incapacity of either the principal or the agent.

9. _____Generally, where an agent has acted for a person who lacked contractual capacity, any contract entered into is voidable by the principal (who does not have contractual capacity) or the third party.

10. _____A principal has contractual, but not tort liability, for its employee-agents.

Multiple Choice:

1. Roman, an agent for Tom, has the express authority to sell Christine's goods. Roman also has the express authority to grant discounts of up to five percent of list price. Roman sold Sidney goods with a list price of $1,000 and granted Sidney a ten percent discount. Sidney had not previously dealt with either Roman or Tom. Which of the following courses of action may Christine properly take?
   A. Seek to void the sale to Sidney.
   B. Seek recovery of $50 from Sidney only.
   C. Seek recovery of $50 from Roman only.
   D. Seek recovery of $50 from either Sidney or Roman.

2. Mean Master wanted to hire Billy Butler as his personal "man." Generally, under the laws of agency, which of the following acts may Mean Master not hire Billy Butler to do?
   A. Wash, clean, and hand press his dirty jogging clothes.
   B. Clean out his backed up sewer line with a toothbrush.
   C. Brush Mean Master's teeth bare handed.
   D. Have Billy serve Mean Master's time in federal prison for employment tax evasion.

3. Kathleen Company dismissed Sabrina, its purchasing agent. It published a notice in the appropriate trade journals which stated that Sabrina was no longer employed by the Kathleen Company. Sabrina called on several of Kathleen's suppliers with whom she had previously dealt, and when she found one who was unaware of her dismissal, she would place a substantial order for merchandise to be delivered to a warehouse in which she had rental space. Sabrina also called on several suppliers with whom Kathleen had never dealt; she would present one of her old business cards to the secretary and then make purchases on open account in the name of Kathleen. Sabrina then sold all the merchandise and absconded with the money. In this situation:
   A. Sabrina had continuing express authority to make contracts on Kathleen's behalf with suppliers with whom she had previously dealt as Kathleen's agent if they were unaware of her dismissal.

B. The suppliers who previously had no dealing with Kathleen cannot enforce the contracts against Kathleen even if the suppliers were unaware of Sabrina's lack of authority.
C. Kathleen is liable on Sabrina's contracts to all suppliers who had dealt with Sabrina in the past as Kathleen's agent.
D. Constructive notice via publication in the appropriate trade journals is an effective notice to all third parties regardless of whether they had dealt with Sabrina or read the notice.

4. Worker Wendy is an employee in an employer/employee relationship with her employer, Car Parts Company (CPC). In her job, Wendy loads various car parts on a truck for delivery. CPC comes to you, its attorney, and asks about its liability with respect to Wendy. Please advise them.
   A. CPC is liable for any torts committed by Wendy and any contracts she enters into.
   B. CPC is liable for any contracts Wendy enters into, but never for any torts she commits.
   C. CPC is liable for any torts committed by Wendy while acting on the company's behalf.
   D. CPC is not liable for any torts committed by Wendy or any contracts she enters into since she is only an employee.

5. Principal Peter hires Agent Anne to act as a sales agent for his company, Complete Computers. Anne and Peter have a written agreement which states that Anne may negotiate sales contracts and receive customer payments. Although the agreement is silent on the issue, Anne also delivers the computers to her customers. Which of the following is correct regarding Anne's authority?
   A. Anne is an expressly appointed agent with some implied authority.
   B. Anne is an implied agent.
   C. Anne is an agent by ratification.
   D. None of the above.

6. Agent Angie works for Principal Paula. Angie talks to Paula every Wednesday, but for the most part, Angie carries on her responsibility with little day to day contact with Paula. Paula is getting quite old. Unfortunately, one Monday morning, while drinking her coffee, Paula dies. Angie, who is unaware of this fact until Wednesday, continues acting as Paula's agent. Which of the following is correct?
   A. Angie's agency has been terminated by operation of law.
   B. Angie's agency is terminated on Wednesday, when she discovers Paula's death.
   C. Angie's agency has been terminated by operation of the parties.
   D. None of the above.

7. Bob is the principal and Sharlene is the agent in an agency coupled with an interest. In the absence of a contractual provision relating to the duration of the agency, who has the right to terminate the agency before the interest has expired?
   A. Both Bob and Sharlene?
   B. Sharlene, but not Bob?

C. Neither Bob or Sharlene?
D. Bob, but not Sharlene?

8. Insane Ivan was judged insane several years ago. Ivan became very frustrated with the fact that he could no longer conduct the business affairs of his multi-million dollar company since he had no contractual capacity. However, Ivan hired Unknowing Edgar to act as his agent. Edgar's first assignment was to buy a large piece of property. Edgar contracted on behalf of Ivan to buy the property from Landowner Lori for $500,000. Which of the following is correct?
   A. The contract is voidable by Ivan, but not Lori?
   B. The contract is voidable by Lori, but not Ivan?
   C. The contract is voidable by either Ivan or Lori?
   D. The contract is void?

9. Gofer Grant works for HiTech Communications (HTC), a very prosperous telecommunications company, as an errand-runner and message carrier. However, Grant takes his job very seriously; he wears a suit to work everyday and convinces his boss to have his own cards printed up that read as follows: G. Grant, Communication Coordinator for HiTech Communications. One day, a potential customer, Big Bucks, is sitting in the waiting room of HTC. Grant approaches Big and presents his card. Big understandably believes Grant has the authority to contract for HTC. Which of the following is correct?
   A. Grant has express authority?
   B. Grant has implied authority?
   C. Grant has apparent authority?
   D. Grant is an agent by ratification?

10. Assume the same facts as in question 9 except that HTC was completely unaware of Grant's behavior and that Grant had his own cards printed up. Assume that under these circumstances Grant has no authority, apparent, implied, express, or otherwise. Also, assume Grant does enter into a contract with Big Bucks on behalf of HTC. When HTC discovers this, the president is irate. However, as the HTC president reads the contract, he discovers it is really quite good for the company. The president ratifies the contract. Which of the following is correct?

    A. HTC can void the contract after ratification since Grant did not have express authority to bind the company?

    B. HTC is bound by the contract after ratification if all contract elements are met?

    C. Big Bucks is liable to HTC for contracting with a nonagent?

    D. None of the above?

V. Answers to Objective Questions:

Terms:

1. *Express.* This is the most common form of agency. They can be either oral or written unless the Statute of Frauds stipulates that they must be written.

2. *Implied.* The extent of the agent's authority is determined from the facts and circumstances. These can include industry custom, prior dealings between the parties, or any other factors the court may deem relevant.

3. *Apparent.* This agency is also sometimes called an agency by estoppel. If the agency is established, the principal is estopped from denying the relationship. It is the principal's actions (or lack thereof) which can create an apparent agency.

4. *Agency by ratification.* Note, at the time of the purported agency, there was, in fact, no agency in existence. It is the act of ratification (acceptance) by the principal which renders him or her now liable for the acts of the agent.

5. *Principal.* Most principals are known as employers although that has its own set of special characteristics.

6. *Agent.* Most agents are known as employees, and just like employers, the term employee has its own special set of legal characteristics.

7. *Principal-agent relationship.* Look at the powers given by the principal to the agent to help define the relationship and distinguish from other relationships such as principal/independent contractor.

8. *General power of attorney.* A person should be very careful when allowing another to act for him or her with this power. Perhaps, it should be called "power given with the *advice* of an attorney!"

9. *Apparent authority of an actual agent.* These situations can be quite costly to the principal if there has been some sort of failure to control the agent by the principal. Remember, the law tends to look at these situations through the eyes of a third party who may well not be aware of the limitations on the actual agent's powers.

10. *Agency coupled with an interest.* This arrangement is commonly used in security agreements to help secure loans.

True/False:

1. False. An agency relationship may be created even without consideration. Such an agency is known as a gratuitous agency.
2. False. A power of attorney, which is an express agency agreement, must be established by a written agreement. An oral agreement is not sufficient to establish a power of attorney.
3. False. Implied consent may be shown by the principal's conduct and is sufficient to show the principal's intent to ratify an unauthorized contract.
4. False. Parties who have dealt with an agent must be given direct notice of termination of the agency. Constructive notice is sufficient for parties who have no knowledge of the agency.
5. True. An agent is empowered to enter into contracts for her principal. An employee in an employer/employee relationship does not have this power.
6. True. The implied authority may be incidental to the agent's job.
7. True. This is also sometimes known as ostensible authority.
8. True. However, the principal can expressly agree that this sort of agency can be terminated by the agent.
9. False. Generally, where an agent has acted for a person lacking contractual capacity, the contract entered into is voidable by the principal, but not the third party.
10. False. A principal has contractual and tort liability for its employee/agent's acting within the scope of the employee/agent's employment.

Multiple Choice:

1. C. Roman exceeded his express authority when he granted the ten percent price discount to Sidney; therefore, Roman would be liable to Christine for the amount of damage caused by Roman's breach, $50. A, B and D are incorrect because Sidney had not previously dealt with Roman or Tom; therefore, Roman was acting with apparent authority when he granted the ten percent price discount to Sidney. Consequently, Christine would not be able to void the sale or recover from Sidney.
2. D. Public policy prevents Mean Master from trying to have Billy Serve his sentence. He can ask Billy to do A, B, and C, assuming no labor or minimum wage laws are broken. Billy might want to consider another line of work.
3. B. When the agency is terminated, the principal must notify customers of the agent's termination. Publication of the notice in the trade journal (constructive notice) precluded Sabrina's apparent authority to those suppliers who previously had no dealings with Kathleen. A is incorrect because Sabrina did not have continuing express authority. However Sabrina did have continuing apparent authority on behalf of suppliers with whom she had previously dealt if they did not know of her dismissal. C is incorrect because Kathleen is not liable on the contracts with those suppliers who read the published notice and had actual knowledge of the discharge which terminated Sabrina's apparent authority. D is incorrect because constructive notice by publication is sufficient notice only for the third parties who had not previously dealt with Sabrina.

4. C. An employer in an employee/employer relationship is liable for the torts of its employees if the tort was committed by an employee acting on the principal's behalf. A is incorrect because CPC is not liable for any contracts Wendy enters into since she has no authority to do so. B is incorrect because CPC is not liable for contracts Wendy enters into for the reason stated above. In addition, CPC is liable for torts Wendy commits while acting on its behalf. D is incorrect because CPC is liable for some torts even though she is only an employee in an employer/employee relationship.

5. A. Since Anne and Peter have an express agreement regarding Anne's agency for Peter, Anne is an expressly appointed agent. In addition, expressly appointed agents may also have implied or apparent authority to carry out certain activities which are not expressly stated. Here, Anne's authority to deliver computers is implied, not expressed. B is incorrect because the agreement between Anne and Peter is express, not implied. C is incorrect because there is no indication of ratification here. Also, Anne clearly has an express agency agreement.

6. A. An agency is terminated by operation of law where either the principal or agent dies. B is incorrect because Angie's agency is terminated on the day of Paula's death--Monday, not on the day Angie discovers Paula's death--Wednesday. C is incorrect because termination of an agency by death is an operation of law, not the parties.

7. B. CPA question. An agency coupled with an interest arises when an agent acquires from the principal an interest in the subject matter of the agency. In the absence of a contractual provision relating to the term of the agency, the authority of the agent (Sharlene) is irrevocable by the principal (Bob). If there is no time period specified for the agency, then the agency may terminate at any time without liability, regardless of the type of agency.

8. D. Contracts made by the agents of principals who have been adjudged insane are void. A, B and C are incorrect because such contracts are void, not merely voidable.

9. C. Grant's suit, cards, and apparently convincing knowledge of HTC convinced Big Bucks that Grant was, in fact, an authorized agent of HTC. HTC permitted Grant to conduct himself in a manner not typical of a regular errand-runner. Under these circumstances, Grant had apparent authority. However, Grant did not have express authority from the company to act in this capacity. In addition, the company did not do anything to lead Grant to believe he had this authority, thereby granting implied authority. A and B are incorrect for the reasons discussed above. D is incorrect because there has been no ratification here.

10. B. Once HTC ratifies the contract, it is bound by the agreement presuming it meets all contract elements. A is incorrect because although Grant did not have express authority, once the contract is ratified, HTC cannot void it. C is incorrect because Big Bucks understandably misunderstood Grant to be an agent. While he may not be able to enforce the contract against HTC, Big Bucks is not liable for his misunderstanding.

VI. Key Question Checklist Answers to Essay Question:

A. *How was this agency relationship created?*

In this case, it appears that there is an express agreement entered into between Jacko and his salespeople. Under this agreement, the salespeople are given specific authority to act on behalf of Jacko with regard to entering into sales contracts for his products. Implied in this actual authority would be reasonably related activities involved in the sale of the product.

B, C, &D: *What is the best definition of this agency relationship? What will happen to this relationship?*

This question revolves around a very common scenario currently being played out in many of the U.S. District and Tax Courts throughout the U.S. A number of business enterprises have sought to avoid responsibility for increasingly higher employment taxes by seeking to create independent contractor status for their employees. The IRS and local taxing authorities are, in turn, challenging these arrangements as being specious and in contravention to the intended coverage of the tax code. What is particularly unfortunate about these cases is that the "employee" winds up footing the bill one way or the other. If employees are real independent contractors, they must pay all of their own social security taxes. If they are not, often employers' failure to pay into those funds leads to no credit for the time worked in the employee's ultimate computation of retirement or disability benefits. Either way the worker pays.

Because of the large amount of control which Jacko has chosen to exercise over his salespeople, it would appear that the IRS may want to argue that they are, in fact, employees rather than independent contractors. The tax rules on this issue are extensive and go beyond the intended scope of this answer. Assuming that the IRS did challenge Jacko's arrangement, his best rebuttal would be the fact that the salespeople's compensation was based entirely on commissions. That fact alone, however, would not likely shield Jacko from liability for employment taxes. It looks as if Jacko will have to find a better way to do business. Perhaps refilling used toothpaste tubes would be more fulfilling to him?

CHAPTER 30

LIABILITY OF PRINCIPALS AND AGENTS

When written in Chinese the word "crisis" is composed of two characters. One represents danger and the other represents opportunity.
                                    John F. Kennedy

I. Overview:

Every agency liability question having an involvement with third parties has three subquestions which must be answered in order to come to a final resolution of the issues at hand. They are:

1. What are the responsibilities of the principal and agent vis-à-vis each other?
2. What are the responsibilities of the agent vis-à-vis the third party?
3. What are the responsibilities of the principal vis-à-vis the third party?

Invariably a certain pattern of facts emerges. First there is some sort of principal/agent relationship established. This relationship may be based on actual, implied, apparent, or ratified authority. In all events, once that authority line has been drawn, the question of the legal consequences to the principal and agent vis-à-vis each other must be answered. These consequences would include their respective rights and duties to each other as outlined in the key question checklist.

Once the first subquestion is resolved, the rights, duties, and obligations of the agent and principal respectively must be examined vis-à-vis the third party. Often there will be some sort of wrongful and unauthorized act committed by the agent. That act will result in probable liability for both the agent and the principal to the third party who was harmed by the act. Think of the three subquestions as a loop which must be closed in order for the whole case to be resolved. The loop is similar to a legal description used to outline the surveyed ownership of real property. A proper legal description always closes at the point where it began. So must an agency issue. It starts with the establishment of the agency relationship. It goes through the rights and duties of third parties. It terminates back where it began, with a determination of the ultimate responsibilities of the principal and agent vis-à-vis each other.

II. Hypothetical Multi-Issue Essay Question:

The Guerrilla Warfare Messenger Service motto was "Come Hell or High Water, We'll Get Your Message There First!" Gudrun Sigurd was the fastest of the fast. He used an all-terrain bike to dash and spin between pedestrians, cars, trucks, and cabs at break neck speeds to get his messages delivered. He usually left a wake of near misses, rolled-over pedestrians, and angry motorists in his trail on the streets and sidewalks of San Francisco. His favorite area in the financial center was at the corner of California and Montgomery Streets. There he could run the light, stop a cable car, and cause two auto accidents in one fell swoop while racing downhill in the rain. His employer honored his ultrafast delivery with a strong letter of recommendation and a raise in pay.

Last week, poor Gudrun's career as a messenger came to an abrupt end when he collided with and killed a pedestrian named

Herb. Gudrun is being charged with bicycle homicide, and Herb's estate wants both civil and criminal actions brought against Gudrun and Guerrilla Warfare Messenger Service. What result?

III. Key Question Checklist:

A. Assuming an agency relationship is established, the first question is what are the principal and agent's initial respective duties to each other?
   1. Agent's duties to the principal?
      (a) Duty of performance?
      (b) Duty of notification?
      (c) Duty of loyalty?
      (d) Duty of obedience?
      (e) Duty of accountability?
   2. Principal's duties to the agent?
      (a) Duty of compensation?
      (b) Duty of reimbursement and indemnification?
      (c) Duty of cooperation?
      (d) Duty to provide safe working conditions?

B. Once the initial duties and responsibilities are established between principal and agent, determine how the third party was brought into the problem at hand.
   1. By contract?
      (a) Fully disclosed principal?
      (b) Partially disclosed principal?
      (c) Undisclosed principal?
      (d) Nonexistent principal?
   2. By tort?
      (a) Misrepresentation?
         (1) Intentional?
         (2) Innocent?
      (b) Negligence?
         (1) Elements of negligence?
         (2) Within scope of employment?
         (3) Any defenses?
            (aa) Frolic and detour?
            (bb) "Coming and going" rule?
      (c) Intentional tort?
         (1) Elements of intentional tort?
         (2) Motivation test?
         (3) Work-related test?
   3. By criminal behavior?

C. Once the involvement of third party is established, how will the liabilities attach vis-à-vis the respective parties?
   1. Responsibilities of the principal and agent vis-à-vis each other?
   2. Responsibilities of the agent vis-à-vis the third party?
   3. Responsibilities of the principal vis-à-vis the third party?

IV. Objective Questions:

Terms:

1. The information given to a principal by the agent that is attributed to the principal is called _____ _____.

2. When an agent enters into a contract on behalf of another party and impliedly warrants that she has the authority to do so, this is called a(n) _____ _____ _____.

3. The legal theory based on liability without fault is _____ _____.

4. When an agent does something during the course of his employment to further his own interests rather than the principal's, it is called _____ _____ _____.

5. When an agent uses her own possessions or assets in a dealing with the principal without letting the principal know about it, this breach of the duty of loyalty is known as _____ _____.

6. An agency results if the third party entering into the contract knows (1) that the agent is acting as an agent for a principal and (2) the actual identity of the principal. This is called a _____ _____ agency.

7. A rule that says an employer is liable for the tortious conduct of its employees or agents while they are acting within the scope of its authority is called _____ _____.

8. The rule that says a principal is generally not liable for injuries caused by its agents and employees while they are on their way to or from work is called the _____ _____ _____ _____.

9. The test to determine the liability of the principal: if the agent's motivation in committing the intentional tort is to promote the principal's business, then the principal is liable for any injury caused by the tort is known as the _____ test.

10. The test to determine the liability of a principal: if an agent commits an intentional tort within a work-related time or space, the principal is liable for any injury caused by the agent's intentional tort. This test is called the _____ _____ test.

True/False:

1. _____ A gratuitous agent must perform at the same level of care, skill, and diligence as an agent for hire. However, gratuitous agents cannot usually be held liable for breach of contract.

2. _____ Under contingency fee arrangements, the principal must only pay the agent the amount agreed upon if the agency is completed.

3. _____ While a principal's liability for her agent's tortious acts varies depending on the circumstances, the agent is always liable for his own torts.

4. _____ In emergency situations, an agent is allowed to deviate from a principal's specific instructions in order to protect the principal's property.

5. _____ Knowledge of an agent is imputed to the principal if the agent tells the principal the information.

6. _____ In a partially disclosed agency, both the agent and the principal are liable on any contract that the agent makes.

7. _____ An agent of a fully disclosed principal is liable on a contract if he does not specify the principal's name in signing the contract.

8. _____ Both agents and principals are liable for an agent's breach of the implied warranty of authority.

9. _____ A principal is not liable for the criminal conduct of his agent since the principal did not have the criminal intent to commit a crime.

10. _____ An agent is prohibited from using his agency for personal benefit even if the principal is aware of and consents to such actions.

Multiple Choice:

1. A principal will not be liable to a third party for a tort committed by an agent:
   A. Unless the principal instructed the agent to commit the tort?
   B. Unless the tort was committed within the scope of the agency relationship?
   C. If the agency agreement limits the principal's liability for the agent's tort?
   D. If the tort is also regarded as a criminal act?

2. Toulouse, an employee of Bordeaux, was delivering merchandise to a customer. On the way, Toulouse's negligence caused a traffic accident that resulted in damages to a third party's automobile. Who is liable to the third party?
   A. Neither Toulouse nor Bordeaux?
   B. Toulouse and Bordeaux?
   C. Toulouse, but not Bordeaux?
   D. Bordeaux, but not Toulouse?

3. Geri contracted with Burton Paper Corp. to buy paper on behalf of Books Corp., a motel chain. Books instructed Geri to use Geri's own name and not to disclose to Burton that Geri was acting on Books' behalf. Who is liable to Burton on this contract?
   A. Geri, but not Books?
   B. Books, but not Geri?
   C. Geri and Books?
   D. Neither Geri nor Books?

4. Agent Alex works for Leon's Lumber, delivering lumber supplies to construction sites. One day, Alex negligently secures the lumber in his delivery truck. A 2x4 flies out of the truck, causing the driver behind Alex, Dazed Delwood, to swerve and hit a telephone pole. Which of the following is correct?
   A. Leon, but not Alex is liable?
   B. Alex, but not Leon is liable?
   C. Both Alex and Leon are liable?
   D. Delwood can seek contract damages?

5. Assume the same facts as in question 4 except that Alex has no lumber in his truck at all. Instead, on his way to pick up some lumber, Alex sees his neighbor, Obnoxious Ollie, standing on a street corner. Alex and Ollie have been feuding for years. Alex sees a way to end their disputes forever. As Ollie begins to cross the street, Alex speeds up to hit him. Ollie survives the crash, but incurs damages. Which of the following is correct?
   A. Leon, but not Alex is liable?
   B. Alex, but not Leon is liable?
   C. Both Alex and Leon are liable?
   D. Ollie can seek contract damages?

6. Which of the following is not a duty of an agent towards the principal?
   A. Duty of performance.
   B. Duty to provide safe working conditions.
   C. Duty of loyalty.
   D. Duty of obedience.

7. Agent Amy has negotiated a contract for the sale of computer equipment to Merchant Mike. Amy's principal, Principal Pat believes that the equipment is not to be shipped until October 10. However, Mike told Amy he needed the equipment shipped on October 2. Amy does not notify Pat of this change. Consequently, the equipment is not shipped until October 10 and Mike incurs damages. Which of the following is correct?
   A. Amy is liable to Pat for any damages her failure to notify may have caused.
   B. Pat is not liable to Mike since he never knew of the changed date.
   C. If Amy is a gratuitous agent, she does not have a duty to notify Pat.
   D. All of the above.

269

8. Scientist Sam works for Medical Miracles (MM). During his work for MM, Sam acquires knowledge of the company's greatest technological innovation, a single dose pill which immediately replaces hair loss. The pill is known as Single Sensation. Sam leaves MM soon after acquiring this knowledge to start his own medical supplies company. Which of the following is correct?
   A. Sam can use his knowledge of Single Sensation for personal benefit after he leaves MM.
   B. Sam's use of his knowledge of Single Sensation would be a violation of Sam's duty of notification.
   C. Sam cannot use his knowledge of Single Sensation even after he leaves MM.
   D. None of the above.

9. Assume the same facts as in question 8. Also, assume Sam does use the information after leaving MM. What are MM's remedies?
   A. Obtain an injunction against Sam?
   B. Sue Sam for damages?
   C. Both of the above?
   D. None of the above? MM has no recourse once Sam is no longer its employee.

10. Agent Arnold negotiates a contract with Theo on behalf of Principal Peter. Theo is aware that Arnold is working for a principal. However, Theo does not know that Peter is Arnold's principal. Theo and Arnold reach agreement on the contract and sign it. Arnold signs as follows: Agent Arnold, agent. Regarding liability on the contract, which of the following is correct?
   A. Arnold is liable on the contract.
   B. Peter is liable on the contract.

   C. Both of the above.
   D. None of the above. Arnold is not liable since Theo knew he was only an agent, and Peter is not liable since his name is not on the contract.

V. Answers to Objective Questions:

Terms:

1. *Imputed knowledge.* This concept centers around the doctrine that the principal and agent are one in many ways. "What the agent knows, the principal knows."
2. *Implied warranty of authority.* Whenever you examine situations involving terms like "implied" or "imputed," think of these terms as warning signals or red flags which indicate that the law may be looking below the surface in ascertaining rights, duties, and responsibilities.
3. *Vicarious liability.* This doctrine arises out of the principal/agent relationship as opposed to the actual fault of the wrongdoers. As such, liability comes without fault of the principal necessarily being shown. The initial negligence of the agent does still need to be shown, however, before going after the principal.
4. *Frolic and detour.* In these cases, the agent is not really working "for" the principal at the time of the frolic and detour, and as such, the principal should not be held liable for the agent's "own" act.
5. *Self-dealing.* The duty of loyalty is the most important of all the duties of an agent towards the principal and covers a number of breaches of trust, including self-dealing.

6. *Fully disclosed.* In a fully disclosed agency, the contract is between the principal and the third party and the agent is not generally liable.
7. *Respondent superior.* This term is derived from the Latin term meaning: "Let the master answer." The doctrine represents the burden that comes to the principal where he or she can also reap the benefits of the agent's act.
8. *Coming and going rule.* As the labor market adjusts to more off-site work situations through the use of electronic networking, the definition of this employer's defense theory will become more difficult.
9. *Motivation.* If the agent's motivation in committing the intentional tort was personal, than the principal is not liable.
10. *Work-related.* This doctrine rejects the motivation test and will hold the principal liable, regardless of motivation, if the act was committed within a work-related time or space.

True/False:

1. True. Contract consideration is not a traditional element in the formation of principal/agent relationships. Agency relationships are consensual and fiduciary in nature, even if gratuitously entered into.
2. True. The principal owes a duty to compensate the agent for services provided. The debate over the efficacy of contingent fees has hone on for many years. Proponents argue that this arrangement provides access to legal services, while opponents argue that the fiduciary's ethics are compromised by such arrangements.

3. True. It is against public policy to allow an agent to pass off his or her tort liability onto others. The question goes more to the issue of whether the principal should be vicariously liable in addition to the liability of the agent.
4. True. These situations are considered to be in violation of the general duty of obedience and akin to the protections accorded under so-called "good samaritan" laws.
5. False. Most information learned by an agent is imputed to the principal whether the agent actually tells the principal or not.
6. True. Since the actual identity of the principal is not known to the third party in a partially disclosed agency, both the agent and the principal are liable on such a contract.
7. True. Even though agents of fully disclosed principals are not usually liable on contracts for the principals, if the agent does not specify the principal's name in signing the contract, he may be held liable on it.
8. False. Only an agent is liable for an agent's breach of the implied warranty of authority.
9. True. The principal cannot have the requisite *mens rea* to be convicted of a crime which the agent committed and the principal was not involved in.
10. False. An agent may personally benefit from his agency if the principal is aware of such conduct and consents to it.

Multiple Choice:

1. B. Generally, a principal is not liable to a third party for torts committed by an agent. The major exception is if the agent is acting within the authority of the principal; i.e., within the scope of the agency relationship. If the agent is acting

within the scope of the agency relationship, the principal is liable. A is incorrect because the tort must be committed within the scope of the agency relationship for the principal to be liable. An agent's instructions from the principal to commit the tort is not within the scope of the agency relationship. C is incorrect because the principal cannot limit her liability in the agency agreement for torts committed by the agent. D is incorrect because the fact that the tort may also be a criminal act does not protect the principal.

2. B. An employer is generally liable for an employee's torts if the tort was committed within the course and scope of the employment relationship. Since Toulouse was acting within the course and scope of his duties, Bordeaux would be liable for damages caused by Toulouse's negligence. Toulouse, as an individual, is liable for his own torts; therefore, he would also be liable for damages caused by the traffic accident.

3. C. Geri, the agent in this relationship, is liable to Burton on this contract. An agent is liable on a contract when the principal is undisclosed and is only released from liability when the principal performs the contract or when the third party elects to hold the principal liable. Books, the undisclosed principal in this relationship, is also liable to Burton on this contract. An undisclosed principal is liable on a contract where the agent had actual authority to contract with Burton, thereby making Books liable. An undisclosed principal remains liable unless the third party holds the agent responsible, the agent fully performs the contract, the undisclosed principal is expressly excluded by the contract, or the contract is a negotiable instrument.

4. C. Under the circumstances of this case, Alex was almost certainly acting within the scope of employment when he negligently secured the lumber in the truck. Therefore, Leon, Alex's principal will be liable for any resulting damage. In addition, Alex, as an individual, is liable for his own negligent torts. A and B are incorrect because both Leon and Alex are liable. D is incorrect because Delwood can seek tort remedies, not contract remedies.

5. B. Alex's actions were beyond the scope of his employment in this situation. Here, Alex's actions were not motivated in an effort to serve Leon or in any way work-related. Therefore, Leon is not liable for Alex's conduct. However, Alex is liable for his own misconduct whether this is classified as an intentional tort or a crime. A and C are incorrect for the reasons discussed above. D is incorrect because Ollie can seek tort remedies, not contract remedies.

6. B. The duty to provide safe working conditions is owed by the principal to his or her agent(s). A, C, and D are duties owed by the agent to his or her principal.

7. A. Amy has breached her duty to notify Pat. Therefore, she is liable for any damages resulting from this breach. B is incorrect because Pat is liable to Mike since Amy's knowledge of the changed date is imputed to Pat. C is incorrect because even a gratuitous agent must perform the necessary duties owed by an agent to a principal.

8. C. Sam owes a duty of loyalty to MM not to use its trade secrets or technological innovations even after Sam leaves the company. Such a use would be a misuse of confidential information. A is incorrect because this is a breach of the duty of loyalty. B is incorrect because

use of the knowledge is a breach of the duty of loyalty, not the duty of notification.

9. C. MM can seek either of these remedies.

10. C. Both A and B are correct because both an agent and a principal are liable on a contract in a partially disclosed agency situation. D is incorrect because an agent may be held liable in spite of his agency capacity, and a principal is always liable for the authorized contracts of his agents.

VI. Key Question Checklist Answers to Essay Question:

A. *Assuming an agency relationship is established, what are the initial respective duties of the principal and agent towards each other?*

Because there is an agency relationship firmly established between Gudrun and his employer, Guerrilla Warfare Messenger Service (G.W.M.S.). Gudrun was obviously trying to be the best employee he could for good old G.W.M.S. He was loyal, obedient, and ultrafast. Unfortunately, he misplaced his loyalty and obedience to his employer rather than to society as a whole. The duties of an agent do not extend into the realm of illegal acts. An agent is not required to engage in illegal acts at the behest of his or her employer. If he does so, he is at personal risk of being held liable for those acts.

Conversely, it appears that G.W.M.S. was trying to live up to its duties to its employee by paying him for services rendered. It does appear, however, that by fostering and encouraging Gudrun to engage in violations of the law, G.W.M.S. created an unsafe working condition.

B. *Once the initial duties and responsibilities of the principal and agent are established, how did the third party come into the picture?*

The third party was drawn into this situation in an involuntary manner. There was no contact between Herb and G.W.M.S. or its agent at any time prior to this incident. The actual accident appears to be a result of gross and criminally culpable negligence on the part of Gudrun. His basic duty was to operate his vehicle in a safe and legal manner so as to not endanger himself or others. His behavior was clearly below that standard of care, and it was the legally proximate cause of Herb's demise. As such Herb's claim against G.W.M.S. would be based on having had this incident occur in the course of Gudrun's employment.

G.W.M.S. may seek to claim that it never actually authorized or allowed its employees to break the law and could not do so legally even it wanted to. In addition G.W.M.S. can argue that Gudrun was on a frolic and not was advancing his employer's principal purpose at the time of the incident. Given its prior rewarding of Gudrun's behavior, these defenses would likely fail to gain any sympathy from the courts.

C. *Now that all three parties are in the picture, what are the liabilities vis-à-vis each other?*

The three subquestions of agency liability are now to be resolved. Gudrun may be able to hold G.W.M.S. liable for having created an unsafe work environment where an incident of this sort was likely to occur. Gudrun has much bigger problems to worry about. He already has been criminally charged with bicycle homicide. In addition, he can now be sued in civil courts individually for the tortious harm he imposed on Herb.

In addition G.W.M.S. may also have both criminal and civil liabilities to contend with. Even though normally a principal is not held criminally liable for the criminal acts of its agents, there are several growing exceptions to this rule. If G.W.M.S. directed, participated, or somehow encouraged the commission of criminal acts, it too may be criminally liable. That liability appears probable here.

Also, vis-à-vis Herb's estate, G.W.M.S. is clearly in for some liability here. It actively fostered and encouraged Gudrun to operate his bike in a negligent manner in the course of his employment. Under the doctrine of *respondeat superior*, G.W.M.S. will be liable to Herb's estate for the acts of its agent.

As for collecting from Gudrun for reimbursement for the damages, G.W.M.S. may have to pay Herb's estate. It appears that Gudrun will be judgement proof as he sits in San Quentin. The agency relationship itself will have been terminated by operation of law due to the impossibility of Gudrun continuing his duties. In addition, it would also be terminated on the grounds of illegality due to the criminal charges brought against either (or both) of the parties to the agency relationship. Maybe G.W.M.S. should consider converting its operation to E mail. It's a lot safer.

CHAPTER 31

FORMS OF CONDUCTING DOMESTIC AND INTERNATIONAL BUSINESS

In all companies, there are more fools than wise men.

Francois Rabelais

I. Overview:

This chapter has two main objectives. The first is to introduce students to the law of business entity choices. One of the key roles of attorneys engaged in the practice of modern business law is advising their clients on the selection of the best venue for doing business. What seems like a relatively limited set of options is, in fact, quite extensive. These choices can run the gamut from the simplest lemonade stand set up for a youngster to a multinational publicly-traded corporation.

With each choice, the law provides a list of pros and cons. For example, if a person seeks maximum privacy in his or her financial affairs, a private form of sole proprietorship may be best. Compare, however, the business person who wants to leverage the maximum utilization of other people's money while limiting her personal financial exposure. That person may find the corporate form best suited for her needs.

The law literally has something for everyone. The real issue is first finding out what options are legally available and then choosing the best fit. That fit should be tailored by sound advice from a number of quarters including law, accounting, finance, and business management strategy. It is this constant interdependent equation which makes the practice of business law so difficult yet so interesting. The vast majority of the users of this book will never go to law school. Yet that same majority will be influenced every working day by the business entity law choices made in whatever business pursuits they chose.

Take, for example, sole proprietorships. It remains the most widely used form of business entity even though it may no longer be the most important in sheer economic terms. With the advent of the so called "information highway" and more emphasis on entrepreneurial niche marketing of goods and services, this form of business may enjoy a renaissance in the 21st century. The most recent U.S. census report indicates that the self employed individual represents one of the fastest growing forms of business entity choice. This trend is confirmed by statistics reported by the IRS which show a dramatic increase in the use of Schedule C (for self-employed) on Form 1040 reported by U.S. taxpayers.

The second main objective of this chapter is to introduce students to several of the many forms of conducting international business. In many respects, these methods are really variations on the themes established in the first part of this chapter. Yet, the governing rules of business entities will be derived from a combination of two or more sovereign entities. International business law planning is one of the fastest growing areas of law practice today.

II. Hypothetical Multi-Issue Essay Question:

Mr. Dorgis Dimmie was a student at IOU trying to figure out a way to pay for his school expenses. His major was in Artificially Intelligent Gamma Rays, and the cost of his lab equipment and supplies was out of sight.

He noticed that people really ate and drank a lot at the weekend IOU football games in spite of the high concessionaire fees. He decided he could offer them cheaper food if it could be pre-sold before the fans came into the stadium.

He contacted a local eatery, the Et Yet? Cafe and made a deal with them. He could take orders for, sell, and deliver sandwiches prepared by Et Yet? and they would split the proceeds down the middle. During the first five games of the home season, Dorgis was doing well and sold over 5,000 Et Yet Mystery Meat sandwiches to his fellow students and assorted football fans. Last week, things turned ugly, however, when numerous fans who ate these sandwiches became ill due to meat poisoning. Many of them are now suing Dorgis and Et Yet?

Dorgis claims he was only acting as Et Yet's? disclosed agent. Et Yet?, in turn, is saying that it sold the sandwiches to Dorgis, and that he resold them directly to the fans as an independent sole proprietor. What is the result?

III. Key Question Checklist:

A. When initiating any inquiry into selecting a particular form of doing business, the objectives sought in creating a format should be listed in order to help make the proper choice. A sample listing of questions might include:

1. Do you want sole control over management, or are you willing to work with others in operating the business?

2. Do you want sole ownership, or are you willing to share equity ownership in the business?

3. Does your tax status dictate how best to invest your resources in business?

4. Does the nature of the business lend itself to greater efficiencies of scale with more participants or not?

5. How much governmental regulation are you ready to submit to as part of your business entity choice?

6. How much public inquiry into your personal finances are you ready to submit to as part of your business entity choice?

7. Can your business plan be adequately funded out of your own personal resources, or must you bring others into the picture financially?

8. Are you willing to risk the loss of personal assets for the business, or do you seek to shelter them from business risk whenever possible?

9. Are there any other overriding personal or family factors which must be taken into account in making this decision?

B. Once you have listed your personal parameters or key objectives in making your business entity choice, look at the main forms of doing business allowed in your locale. Assuming that your choices are limited to a domestic location, as opposed to international trade, your most likely choices will be:

1. Sole proprietorship?
   a. Owned by one person?
   b. Little or no formalities required in formation?
   c. Taxed to individual not as a separate entity?
   d. Management control retained by owner?
   e. Easily transferred?
   f. Personal liability for business debts, losses, and torts?
   g. Name law complied with?

2. General partnership?
   a. Elements of partnership in place?
      (1) Voluntary associations?
      (2) Of two or more persons (persons can include people, partnerships, corporations, and other associations)?
      (3) Carrying on a business?
      (4) As coowners of the business?
      (5) For profit?
   b. Ease of creation with few formalities (agreement)?
   c. Taxes flow through to individual owners?
   d. Personal liability for business debts, losses, and torts?
   e. Share management decision?
   f. Name law applicable?
   g. Termination by agreement or operation of law?
   h. Partnership by estoppel?
3. Limited partnership?
   a. Elements of limited partnership in place (per Uniform Limited Partnership Act)?
      (1) Most of the same elements as general partnership with following exceptions:
         (a) Limited partners usually liable only to extent of capital contributions.
         (b) Must have at least one general partner.
   b. Taxes flow through?
   c. Management participation by limited partners is restricted?
   d. Termination by agreement or operation of law?
4. Corporation?
   a. Elements of a corporation in place per local statutory requirement?
   b. Taxed as a separate entity?
   c. Limited liability of shareholders for debts, losses, and torts of the corporation?
   d. More regulation and government control in the transfer of ownership in the corporation?
   e. Can have indefinite duration?
   f. Management not directly in the hands of shareholders?
   g. Can be used for special needs such as:
      (1) Nonprofit?
      (2) Professional corporation?
      (3) Chapter Sub-S of the Internal Revenue Code?
5. Other possible forms of doing business:
   a. Joint venture?
   b. Joint venture corporation?
   c. Syndicate or investment group?
   d. Joint stock company?
   e. Joint stock association?
   f. Business (Massachusetts) trust?
   f. Cooperative?
   h. Unincorporated association?
   i. Franchise?

C. What are the possible options open to you if you choose to expand this business on an international scale?
   a. Import-export sales?
   b. Use of overseas sales agents, distributors, and/or representatives?
   c. Joint venture?
   d. Opening a branch or subsidiary office?
   e. Use of possible licensing or franchising arrangements?

IV. Objective Questions:

Terms:

1. A business entity that is noncorporate in nature, and that is not considered a separate taxpaying entity for income tax purposes is known as a _____ _____.

2. Most states require all businesses that operate under a trade name to file a _____ _____ _____.

3. If a sole proprietorship fails in business, the owner is subject to _____ _____ liability for claims against the business.

4. A corporation that has a small number of shareholders and is treated like a partnership for tax purposes is called a _____ corporation.

5. An arrangement whereby an owner of a patent, trademark, trade secret, or product grants a license to another to sell products or services using the name of such owner is generally known as a _____.

6. An arrangement by which two or more persons join together for a limited period of time to achieve a specific purpose is known as a _____ _____.

7. When businesses voluntarily join together to provide services to their membership, this arrangement is sometimes known as a _____.

8. A form of business which allows for legal ownership in one person, with beneficial ownership in another is often known as a _____ _____.

9. A relatively new form of doing business which allows for the best advantages of partnerships and corporations is called the _____ _____ _____.

10. Owners of L.L.C.'s are called _____.

True/False:

1. _____ The general partners of a limited partnership have limited personal liability for the debts and obligations of the limited partnership.

2. _____ The personal liability of a sole proprietor is limited to the extent of her capital contribution to the business.

3. _____ Sole proprietorships are prohibited by law from operating under a fictitious name.

4. _____ A corporation is not a separate taxpaying entity for federal income tax purposes.

5. _____ The death of a joint adventurer does not generally terminate a joint venture.

6. _____ Shareholders in a corporation have limited liability for the debts and obligations of the corporation.

7. _____ A partnership is an association of two or more persons, carrying on a business as coowners for profit.

278

8. ____Under the law of franchising, the franchisor and franchisee must both be held in common ownership.

9. ____Must states require all businesses that operate under a trade name to file a fictitious business name statement with the appropriate governmental agency.

10. ____Joint ventures are generally governed by corporation law.

Multiple Choice:

1. There are several advantages to the sole proprietorship form of operating a business. Which of the following is not one of its advantages?
   A. Formation is simple and low in cost.
   B. The sole proprietor retains the right to make all management decisions concerning the business.
   C. The sole proprietor is legally responsible for the debts and obligations of the business only to the extent of his capital contribution.
   D. A sole proprietorship can be transferred or sold quite easily.

2. Which of the following organizations is a separate taxpaying entity for federal income tax purposes?
   A. Corporation.
   B. General partnership.
   C. Limited partnership.
   D. Sole proprietorship.

3. Which of the following statements about the liability of general partners for the debts and obligations of a partnership is most accurate?
   A. The liability of a general partner is like that of a corporate shareholder.

B. The liability of a general partner is like that of a sole proprietor.
C. The liability of a general partner is like that of a beneficiary of a business trust.
D. None of the above.

4. Which of the following statements about limited partnerships is correct?
   A. Limited partnerships are separate taxpaying entities for federal income tax purposes.
   B. Every limited partnership must have at least one general partner.
   C. Limited partners contribute capital to the business in exchange for a stated rate of return on their capital contribution.
   D. None of the above.

5. Tom Taxbreak is hoping to create a general partnership. Which of the following persons or organizations could not be partners with Tom?
   A. A limited partnership in which Tom is a partner.
   B. Tom's wife.
   C. Tom's best friend who has been adjudicated insane.
   D. Tom's 12-year-old son.

6. In a joint venture, which of the following is true?
   A. A joint venture contemplates a single transaction or a limited activity.
   B. A joint venture requires the formation of a general partnership.
   C. Joint adventurers, like partners, are not permitted to sue other joint adventurers at law.
   D. All of the above.

7. Which of the following statements about a business trust is incorrect?
   A. The beneficiaries are not personally liable for the debts and obligations of the trust.
   B. The death or bankruptcy of a beneficiary of the trust will terminate the trust.
   C. The trustee is personally liable for contracts of the trust.
   D. The trustee is personally liable for torts committed while acting on behalf of the trust.

8. Which of the following is generally *not* an advantage of using a foreign distributor in international sales?
   A. More risk is shared with the distributor.
   B. More tort and contract liability insulation because the distribution is an independent contractor.
   C. Total control of the business plan by the nondistributor.
   D. Saves investment costs of having to establish a branch or subsidiary in the foreign country.

9. Which of the following is *not* an advantage of using franchising to expand international business?
   A. Local franchisees know the local culture.
   B. Generally, there are fewer problems with expropriation of locally owned franchises.
   C. No royalties need to be paid to the franchisor in international contracts.
   D. Less capital is needed to establish the franchisee foothold overseas.

10. Limited liability companies have characteristics of all the following forms of business except:
    A. Partnerships.
    B. Trusts.
    C. Sole proprietorships.
    D. Corporations.

V. Answers to Objective Questions:

Terms:

1. *Sole proprietorship.* Under the tax laws, business income and losses are reported on the individual tax returns of the sole proprietor. Although this has many disadvantages, one major benefit is that the problem of corporate double taxation is avoided.

2. *Business name statement (or certificate of trade name).* These statements are designed to give the authorities information about the principals of the business such as names, addresses, etc. In addition, most of these statutes required publication of this information in a newspaper of general publication.

3. *Unlimited personal.* Because there is no legal distinction between the sole proprietor and his or her business, the liabilities of the business and the proprietor are considered one and the same.

4. *"S."* This form of favorable corporate tax treatment is limited to those entities which qualify under the "S" subchapter of the corporate tax provisions of the Internal Revenue Code, beginning at Section 1361. These rules were substantially overhauled in 1982, but have been part of the tax code since 1958.

5. *Franchise*. This method of doing business has become one of the most important of all. Consider its worldwide implications in such key service industries as food, tourism, and the sale of essential commodities. A growing component of international law involves the interpretation and application of long-term multinational franchise contract agreements.

6. *Joint venture*. This form of business is most commonly used in the real estate industry. Although similar to partnerships, joint ventures have legal doctrines vis-a-vis termination and authority distinct from those used in partnership law.

7. *Cooperative*. Cooperatives may be formed for any number of purposes. The most commonly used versions of this format are found in agriculturally based industries. They can be incorporated or not.

8. *Business trust*. This form of business originated in Massachusetts as an alternative to the corporate form of doing business. Business trusts are not commonly used today, but the trust format remains important for purposes of taxation and estate planning.

9. *Limited liability company (LLC)* This form of business has gained recent popularity because of favorable IRS rulings (Tres. Reg. § 301.7701-2(a)) and acceptance by a number of state legislatures. Professional legal advice is strongly encouraged before embarking on any of the choices listed here because of the wide degrees of variance among the state laws with regard to business entity format.

10. *Members*. Members are not personally liable for the obligations of the LLC and they are taxed as a partnership instead of a corporation.

True/False:

1. False. A corporation is a separate taxpaying entity for federal income tax purposes. Thus, corporations are said to be subject to double taxation.

2. False. A sole proprietor bears the entire risk of loss of such a business and has unlimited personal liability.

3. False. A sole proprietorship can operate under the name of the sole proprietor or a trade name. If a trade name is used, a fictitious business name statement will probably have to be filed.

4. False. A corporation is a separate tax paying entity for federal income tax purposes. Thus, corporations are said to be subject to double taxation.

5. True. Although similar in many ways to partnerships, joint ventures are not partnerships and, as such, are not generally dissolved at the death of joint adventurer.

6. True. The liability of shareholders in a corporation for debts and obligations of the corporation is limited to the extent of their contribution.

7. True. These elements are all required to form a partnership under the provisions of the Uniform Partnership Act.

8. False. The franchisor and franchisee are two separate and independent businesses.

9. True. In addition, these statutes often require that the trade name be published in a newspaper of general circulation in the area in which the business operates.

10. False. In most respects, such as taxation, personal liability, and accounting, joint ventures are governed by partnership laws.

Multiple Choice:

1. C. A sole proprietor has unlimited personal liability with respect to the debts and obligations of the business.

2. A. All of the others are considered conduits for tax purposes, and the taxes are attributable to the partner or proprietor.

3. B. Both general partners and sole proprietors have unlimited personal liability with respect to the debts and obligations of their respective business enterprises.

4. B. Although limited partnerships are required to file an informational return, they are not considered separate taxpaying entities, therefore A is incorrect. C is incorrect because limited partners are only entitled to a share of the profits, not a stated rate of return on their capital contributions.

5. C. One who has been adjudicated insane lacks the capacity to form a contract. A is incorrect because a limited partnership may be a partner, even if Tom is a partner in that organization. There is nothing prohibiting husband and wife from being partners, therefore answer B is incorrect. Finally, minors may be partners, but they have the ability to disaffirm such contracts prior to reaching majority.

6. A. B is incorrect because although they are very similar to a partnership, joint venturers need not form a partnership. Joint adventurers are permitted to sue one another at law, therefore C is incorrect.

7. B. Death or bankruptcy of a beneficiary will not terminate the trust. The other statements are true.

8. C. Less control can be generally exercised over a distributor than a subsidiary or branch office in foreign country.

9. C. This statement is false. Royalty payments and license fees for overseas contracts are very similar to domestic contract arrangements.

10. C. By definition, statutes which allow for the creation of limited liability companies call for participation of two or more persons. Otherwise attributes of partnership, corporate and trust law are all generally found in these statutes.

VI. Key Question Checklist Answers to Essay Question:

A. *What are the business objectives sought? This will help you to make a proper business entity choice.*

Dorgis had a number of objectives when he set out on his entrepreneurial journey. He wanted to set up a business with as little formality as possible. He wanted to retain as much control over the management of his business as possible. He did not want to provide extensive capital contributions to the venture, and in fact, sought to have his key contribution be his 'middleman" or "facilitator" services between Et Yet. and the football fans. Because he did not actively seek to create a separate business entity, such as a corporation, his personal assets will in all likelihood be exposed to possible business loss and tort liabilities.

Et Yet. appears to be motivated by many of the same factors as Dorgis. It wanted to form business relationship which would expand the market for its unique Mystery Meat Sandwiches. It appears that neither party contemplated the use of an actual agreement beyond simply sharing the proceeds.

B. *Once you have decided on the personal parameters and key objectives of your business decision, which entity would be the most likely choice?*

There are elements of a number of possible business entities in place which follow for several interpretations. One view might argue that both Dorgis and Et Yet. are independent sole proprietors. As such, neither could be directly held liable for each other's acts as an agent. Under this theory, the injured fans would have to sue Dorgis and Et Yet. as individual business entities operating as sole proprietorships. This may allow for possible defenses in that each of the defendants might try to point to each other's acts as the source of the negligence which led to the food contamination.

Another viewpoint may argue that the elements of partnership between Dorgis and Et Yet. are in place. They are associated in carrying out a business as coowners for a profit motive. This is evidenced by the sharing of the proceeds from the sale of Mystery Meat Sandwiches. In the alternative, the plaintiffs may want to argue that even if they were not actually partners, partnership by estoppel may be applicable by reason of the appearance of partnership made to them as third parties.

A third theory might involve calling the arrangement a joint venture between Dorgis and Et Yet.. Here there is an association carried on to conduct a limited purpose business--to sell Mystery Meat Sandwiches at IOU football games. The participants would be called adventurers (in more ways than one). As a joint venture which was not incorporated, most states following the Uniform Partnership Act mode would apply partnership law and hold Dorgis and Et Yet. liable as agents of each other's negligent acts.

Of the three scenarios proffered, the latter seems most likely. Both defendants would likely be held responsible for the harm done. It is yet another lesson learned in short-term gain, long-term loss. Had Dorgis and Et Yet. spent a little more time and money setting up a proper business entity, they might not be eating crow now.

C. *Are there any possible overseas options here?*

Based on his track record so far, it does not appear that Dorgis or Et Yet have to worry about overseas expansion. Had they been more successful at the outset of their domestic operations, most any overseas options would have been possible depending on the combined applicability of both domestic laws and the laws of countries into which they chose to extend their operations. Many food purveyors elect to go with franchising. Witness the expansion of American fast food operations to all corners of the globe.

CHAPTER 32

FORMATION AND DISSOLUTION OF GENERAL PARTNERSHIPS

The richer your friends, the more they will cost you.

Elizabeth Marbury

I. Overview:

One of the key distinctions between the partnership form of doing business and the corporate format is the corporation's ability to have an indefinite or perpetual existence. Under state laws of incorporation, a corporation is allowed to continue its juristic existence in spite of the death of its key players. This is not true with partnerships. Partnerships are literally much more personal. A partnership is intrinsically tied to the continuing existence of the partners. When the partner is gone, so too is the partnership.

One of the questions students frequently ask is: how is it that multi-national business organizations, such as large accounting or law firms, stay in business as partnerships when they frequently lose partners through death or changes in partnership associations? The technical answer is that with each of these changes, the partnership is theoretically ended and a new one is created. In fact, a well-crafted partnership agreement should have, as one of its key components, an orderly process of succession in case of death or termination. Where these circumstances are properly planned for, the transition is seamless, and the life of the partnership goes on.

Most partnerships are not, however, large and multi-national in scale. Most are created and operated by individuals who have sought to capitalize on their respective economic or talent contributions by acting together in the legal sense. These business ventures could be set for a short term, specific goal, such as erecting a building, or extend to a full professional career such as a licensed practitioner of law, medicine, or accounting. Just like a marriage, the best intentions at the legal altar of partnership do not always work, and the rules of partnership should provide a means of graceful dissolution.

II. Hypothetical Multi-Issue Essay Question:

Bragg, Bluster, and Big was one of the oldest and most famous law firms in Backwater. Their specialty was personal injury litigation. They really went big time when they started advertising on late night television. They managed to convince hundreds of clients that they really were hurt by their employers looking at them the wrong way. This provided their clients with a chance to hit the courthouse tort lottery!

A practitioner of exceptional loquaciousness was the founder of the firm, Mr. Boskop Borzoi Bragg Esquire, affectionately known as the "Big B" to his partners and clients alike. The Big B could officiously obviate the occasional opposition with opprobrium and obfuscation into oblivion. He loved the battleground of the courts and hated to retire last year.

Big B still enjoyed hanging around the courthouse even in retirement. One day he started up a conversation and talked Ms. Felicity Pembrokershire into suing her employer for looking at her the wrong way. She had heard of the Big B's famous exploits in the courts. Felicity paid Big B a $10,000 retainer to help his former firm prepare the case. In the meantime, Ms. Penbrokeshire realized she may have made a mistake and decided to drop the lawsuit. Big B is insulted and refuses to give back the retainer. Felicity sues Bragg, Bluster, and Big for the money. What result?

III. Key Question Checklist:

A. The dissolution of a partnership can come about in a one of three basic ways: acts of the parties, operation of law, or by court ordered dissolution. Assuming the parties want to voluntarily end the partnership arrangement, what are their options?
   1. Termination of a stated time or purpose?
   2. Voluntary withdrawal of a partner?
   3. Admission of a new partner?
   4. Involuntary withdrawal or expulsion of a partner?
   5. Mutual agreement of dissolution?

B. Assuming an operation of law dissolution is at issue, what scenarios may lead to the termination of a partnership?
   1. Death of a partner?
   2. Bankruptcy of any partner or the partnership itself?
   3. Illegality in the continued carrying on of the partnership business?
   4. Loss or waste in continued operation of the partnership?
   5. Any other equitable reason seen fit by the court?

C. Once the dissolution of the partnership has been initiated, what are the rights and duties of both the partners and third parties vis-a-vis this former business entity?
   1. Notice of dissolution given to:
      (a) Partners?

      (b) Third parties?
         (1) Who dealt with the partnership?
         (2) Who have had no prior dealings with the partnership but have knowledge of it?
         (3) Who have no prior dealings with and no knowledge of the partnership?
   2. Effects on contracts entered into prior to the dissolution?
      (a) Executory agreements not discharged?
      (b) Novations possible?
   3. What if the dissolution was wrongful?
      (a) Rights of other partners?
      (b) Rights of third parties?

D. Assuming the dissolution issues have been resolved, the next step involves the winding up (liquidation) of the partnership. Has the proper priority of distribution been followed?
   1. Creditors outside the partnership paid first?
   2. Partners as creditors paid next?
   3. Return of capital contributions to the partners?
   4. Distribution of any left-over profits to partners?
   5. If there are left-over losses, partners personally liable for partnership debts and obligations?
      (a) Marshaling of assets?
      (b) Federal bankruptcy law applicable?

E. Once the partnership has been dissolved and the liquidation has taken place, any other issues in place with regard to an attempted continuation of the partnership after dissolution?
   1. Rights and duties of new partners?
   2. Rights and duties of old partners?
   3. Rights and duties of third parties?

IV. Objective Questions:

Terms:

1. When the relation of the partners changes because a partner ceases to be associated in the carrying on of the business of the partnership, a _____ occurs.

2. In some circumstances a retiring partner may wish to be relieved of liability for certain obligations of the partnership. This can be accomplished through a _____ agreement which in effect substitutes a third party for the retiring partner with respect to such obligations.

3. An outgoing partner may seek a release of liability for existing partnership obligations from his former partners. This can be accomplished through a(n) _____ _____ agreement between the outgoing partner and one or more of the continuing partners.

4. A doctrine dictating that partnership creditors may not seek satisfaction from the separate assets of individual partners until such time as the debts owed to individual creditors of such individual partners have been satisfied is called _____ _____ _____.

5. Following certain dissolutions of a partnership, the remaining partners may wish to continue the operation and business of the partnership. In these situations, the remaining partners may enter into a(n) _____ _____ setting forth the details of how the partnership will be operated at that point.

6. An agreement among the partners that expressly sets forth the amounts to be paid outgoing partners upon the dissolution and continuation of the partnership is known as a(n) _____ _____.

7. The phase of bringing the operation and existence of the partnership to a close in which the assets of the partnership are liquidated and distributed is known as _____ _____.

8. When information concerning dissolution of the partnership is published in a newspaper of general circulation serving the area where the business of the partnership was regularly conducted, _____ _____ is given.

9. When the existence of a partnership ends following completion of the process of liquidating and distributing the assets of the partnership, _____ occurs.

10. In those circumstances where dissolution would be equitable, a partnership may be dissolved by a(n) _____ _____ _____ obtained by filing an application or petition with the appropriate state court.

True/False:

1. _____ A partnership that is formed for a specific time or purpose dissolves upon the affirmative vote of a majority of the existing partners following the expiration of the time or accomplishment of the objective.

2. _____ A partnership dissolves automatically by operation of law upon the death of a partner.

286

3. ____ A partnership will be dissolved by judicial decree of dissolution following an event that makes it unlawful for the business of the partnership to be carried on or for the partners to carry it on.

4. ____ Assignment of one's partnership interest will cause the dissolution of a partnership.

5. ____ Generally, the dissolution of the partnership terminates the partners' actual authority to enter into contracts or otherwise act on behalf of the partnership.

6. ____ A partner who has not received notice of dissolution of the partnership binds all the partners on contracts entered into on behalf of the partnership prior to receiving notice of dissolution.

7. ____ Constructive notice of dissolution of a partnership must be given to third parties who have actually dealt with the partnership.

8. ____ A partner has the right, but not necessarily the power, to withdraw from the partnership and thereby dissolve the partnership at any time.

9. ____ Because of the finality of such decisions, any actions regarding the winding up of the partnership require the unanimous consent of the winding up partners.

10. ____ New partners are liable for liabilities of the partnership existing at the time of their admission to the partnership only to the extent of their capital contributions.

Multiple Choice:

1. Ted and Fred entered into a written partnership agreement to operate a retail clothing store. Their agreement was silent as to the duration of the partnership. Ted wishes to dissolve the partnership. Which of the following statements is correct?
   A. Ted may dissolve the partnership at any time.
   B. Ted may dissolve the partnership only after notice of the proposed dissolution is given to all partnership creditors.
   C. Ted may not dissolve the partnership unless Fred consents.
   D. Ted must apply to a court and obtain a decree unless Fred consents.

2. Abe, George, and Thomas are partners in a book store specializing in books relating to history. George has loaned the partnership a significant amount of money, and the partnership has since begun the process of termination. If partnership funds are insufficient to repay the amounts owed to George, which of the following statements is correct?
   A. George will not be repaid.
   B. Abe and Thomas must contribute their proportionate share towards repayment of the loan from George.
   C. George will receive only the interest accrued on the unpaid amount.
   D. None of the above.

3. Assume the same facts as in question 2. Which of the following statements is correct?
   A. The partners will be paid their capital contributions after creditors of the partnership have been repaid.
   B. The loan made by George will be repaid before other creditors of the partnership are paid.
   C. George is not entitled to receive interest on the money advanced if not repaid when due.
   D. None of the above.

4. The partnership agreement of one of your clients provides that upon death or withdrawal, a partner shall be entitled to the book value of his or her partnership interest as of the close of the year preceding such death or withdrawal and nothing more. It also provides that the partnership shall continue. Regarding this partnership provision, which of the following is a correct statement?
   A. It is unconscionable on its face.
   B. It has the legal effect of preventing a dissolution upon the death or withdrawal of a partner.
   C. It effectively eliminates the legal necessity of a winding up of the partnership upon the death or withdrawal of a partner.
   D. It is not binding upon the spouse of a deceased partner if the book value figure is less than the fair market value figure.

5. Sandy Shorterm, who has been a partner of Shorterm, Attention, & Span for years, decides to withdraw from the partnership despite the fact that the partnership agreement prohibits such withdrawal. Which of the following is correct?

   A. Sandy's withdrawal will cause the dissolution of the partnership by operation of law.
   B. Because the withdrawal is wrongful, it will have no impact upon the partnership or the continuing partners.
   C. Sandy's withdrawal will cause the dissolution of the partnership if a court decree is sought.
   D. None of the above.

6. Assume the same facts as in question 5. Which of the following statements is correct with respect to the rights of the other partners following the wrongful withdrawal of Sandy?
   A. The other partners can agree to carry on the business but they will have no rights against Sandy for breach of the partnership agreement.
   B. The other partners can agree to carry on the business and sue Sandy for breach of the partnership agreement.
   C. The other partners can liquidate the partnership but will have no rights against Sandy for breach of the partnership agreement.
   D. None of the above.

7. Huey, Dewey and Louie were long time partners in the syndication of foul cartoons. Louie decided to retire, but Huey and Dewey wanted to carry on the business. By agreement with Louie, Huey and Dewey assumed Louie's partnership liabilities. Which of the following is correct?
   A. Louie's withdrawal has no effect on the partnership debt structure.
   B. Louie remains liable for partnership debts incurred prior to his withdrawal.
   C. If Louie had sold his interest to a third party, the partnership is not dissolved.
   D. In any event, Louie will remain liable for all future debts incurred by the new partnership.

8. Charlie Cocker recently became a partner in the partnership of Fido, Rover, and Tip, an organization concerned with dog obedience. A month later, a suit is brought against the partnership for negligent training resulting in severe injuries to a mail carrier. The negligent training occurred before Charlie became a partner. Which of the following is correct?
   A. Charlie is liable for a portion of the judgment, but only to the extent of his contribution to capital.
   B. Charlie will not be liable for any of the judgment because the negligence occurred before he became a partner.
   C. Charlie will be held jointly and severally liable for the full amount of the judgment unless he immediately disclaims his interest in the partnership.
   D. Charlie will be jointly and severally liable for the full amount of the judgment along with the other partners.

9. Fred and Barney operated an excavation partnership. Fred died and left his interest in the partnership to his wife, Wilma. Which of the following statements is correct?
   A. The partnership is dissolved.
   B. Barney and Wilma become partners.
   C. Barney acquires the partnership through his right of survivorship.
   D. Barney inherits the partnership.

10. Flowers, Rose, and Nelson operate a flower business as partners. Which of the following events will not cause the partnership to dissolve?
   A. The death of Flowers if Rose and Nelson continue the business.
   B. Violation of the partnership agreement by Flowers.
   C. An arbitrary decision of any partner to dissolve the partnership.
   D. The bankruptcy of Rose.

V. Answers to Objective Questions:

Terms:

1. *Dissolution.* Per section 29 of the Uniform Partnership Act, a dissolution is defined as "the change in the relationship of the partners caused by any partner ceasing to be associated in the carrying on as distinguished from the winding up of the business."

2. *Novation.* Novation is derived from the Latin term "novus" meaning new. In contract terms, a novation substitutes a new party and discharges one of the original parties to a contract by agreement of all the parties. In the partnership setting, novation is very often used to relieve retiring partners from certain obligations of the partnership.

3. *Indemnification to hold harmless.* This is a reimbursement arrangement between the old and new partners in case the old partner is somehow held liable for existing partnership obligations.

4. *Marshaling of assets.* This is an equitable doctrine requiring an arrangement or ranking of assets in a certain order towards the payment of debt.

5. *Continuation agreement.* These agreements will often be used in tandem with the creation of the new partnership agreement. These agreements are also sometimes referred to as so-called "bridge" agreements because they help facilitate the transition from the old to the new partnership entity.

6. *Settlement agreement.* These agreements often use preset financial formulas in order to help resolve difficulties over disputed dollar amounts between partners.

7. *Winding up.* Once this process has begun, the partners may not create new obligations on behalf of the partnership. They can only complete transactions begun but not finished at the time of the dissolution and winding up of the business of the partnership.

8. *Constructive notice.* This doctrine is used in many areas of the law and is based on a practical realization that actual physical notice may not always be possible and that a legally sufficient alternative may be used.

9. *Termination.* This marks the end of the partnership and a cessation of business.

10. *Judicial decree of dissolution.* Because a partnership is considered a creature made by law, the law can end its existence where circumstances are appropriate for such a decree. Most such decrees are issued where there are irreconcilable differences between the partners or where a violation of law or public policy has been found by a court.

True/False:

1. False. Such a partnership dissolves automatically upon the expiration of the time or accomplishment of the objective.

2. True. Death of a partner acts as an operation of law dissolution of the partnership.

3. False. A partnership will be dissolved by operation of law following an event that makes it unlawful for the business of the partnership to be carried on or for the partners to carry it on.

4. False. Under the UPA, a partner may assign her interest without causing the dissolution of the partnership.

5. True. The partnership has technically ended.

6. True. This rule is designed to protect third parties who deal with the partnership.

7. False. Third parties who have actually dealt with the partnership must be given actual notice of the dissolution or have acquired knowledge from some other source.

8. False. A partner has the power, but not necessarily the right, to withdraw and dissolve the partnership. The wrongfully withdrawing partner will be liable for damages caused by the wrongful dissolution.

9. False. Most actions regarding the winding up of the partnership require only majority consent of the winding up partners.

10. True. This rule is designed to protect the incoming partner from possible fraud by the existing partners. The new partner may, however, waive this protection by contractually assuming the prior debts beyond his or her capital contribution.

Multiple Choice:

1. A. Because the partnership agreement does not state a duration, Ted may dissolve the partnership at any time without liability.

2. B. A partner who makes a loan to the partnership becomes a creditor of the partnership. Partners are personally liable for the partnership's debts and obligations.

3. A. Capital contributions are repaid only after creditors have been paid, but before profits are paid out.

4. C.   Such an agreement does not prevent dissolution, it merely eliminates the necessity of the next step of winding up.

5. D.   Sandy's actions will cause an automatic dissolution of the partnership, not a dissolution by operation of law or by court decree.

6. B.   A partner who wrongfully causes the dissolution of the partnership is liable for damages caused by such dissolution.

7. B.   Louie will remain liable for the debts incurred prior to his withdrawal unless a new contract agreement is reached.

8. A.   Incoming partners are only liable for existing obligations to the extent of their capital contributions.

9. A.   The death of a partnership causes dissolution by operation of law.

10. B.   A partner's violation of the partnership agreement does not cause automatic dissolution of the partnership.

VI. Key Question Checklist Answers to the Essay Question:

A. *What is the basis for partnership dissolution?*

The voluntary withdrawal of partner from a partnership is recognized as an act of party basis for dissolution of a partnership. Here, when Big B left the firm, the existence of the old partnership ended.

B. *What scenarios can lead to the termination of a partnership?*

The law firm should have exercised due care to provide as much notice as is legally required and prudent to both partners within the firm and third parties outside the firm. As for third parties who have had actual dealings with the partnership, they should be given actual verbal or written notice that Big B was no longer authorized to act for the firm. As for persons who knew of his association but did not deal with the firm, they should have been given some sort of media-based constructive notice. Parties who have not dealt with the partnership and do not have knowledge of it do not have to be given notice. There is a real factual issue in this case as to how much Ms. Pembrokeshire had actually known about Big B and his firm prior to her dealings with him. If the firm failed to give any general media-based notice of Big B's retirement from the firm, it may be in some difficulty here. Perhaps the firm chose to trade the "halo" effect of retaining Big B's name.

E. *What are the rights and duties of the firm to Ms. Pempbrokeshire?*

If the partnership had been technically dissolved at the time of Big B's retirement, and he is now allowed to represent himself to third parties as having apparent authority to act on their behalf, the partnership may in fact be liable under Mr. Big B's contract with Ms. Pembrokeshire. As such, if she is entitled to a refund of the retainer fee as a matter of contract law, the firm will be liable for it. The partners can, in turn, seek reimbursement from Big B if they can talk him into it. Better yet, they should talk him into moving to real retirement out of state.

CHAPTER 33

OPERATION OF GENERAL PARTNERSHIPS

In almost every marriage, there is a selfish and an unselfish partner. A pattern is set up and soon becomes inflexible, of one person always making the demands and one person always giving way.

Iris Murdoch

I. Overview:

"For better or worse." These words are used in most major religious ceremonies involving the rite of marriage. The bonds of marriage are expected to run long and deep as evidenced by the absolute terms used in the ceremony. Partnership is, in many ways, akin to marriage. Persons entering into a partnership arrangement must do so voluntarily and with their legal eyes open to the ramifications of their bonding. Just as in marriage, the law attaches great significance to the act of casting one's fate with another person in the formation of a partnership.

The operation of a partnership is one of the oldest recognized methods of cooperative business conduct. Many of its antecedents go back to the age of chivalry where the duties of loyalty were paramount. "All for one and one for all" was more than just a rallying cry before battle. The phrase connoted an expectation which made your acts the acts of your colleague and vise versa. A legal oneness came to be recognized between partners and the third parties with whom they dealt. Subsequent evolution of partnership law has carried forth this unity.

Modern contract law, tort law, and especially agency law all reflect this commonality when it comes to partnerships. Partners are expected to be responsible for eachother's acts in the eyes of the law. These responsibilities may not always seem fair to the layperson. Remember, however, the benefit/burden dichotomy illustrated in the law of the agency. The principal stands to gain much from the efforts of his or her agent. That gain may be offset by the costs incurred for the agent's acts. We also see that the pendulum can swing both ways in partnership law. A partner is an agent of the partnership and yet is also a principal. Agency law dominates as the foundation of partnership law.

Given our nation's divorce rate of nearly fifty percent, many social reformers have argued for making marriage a more difficult institution to enter into. Perhaps the same argument can be raised vis-à-vis partnership. Given the long and sometimes tortuous entanglements that people can find themselves in, maybe they should think long and hard (and get the best legal advice they can) before getting in bed with someone legally by way of partnership. Remember, both partners have a lot of latitude in contracting rights and duties between themselves, but less so vis-à-vis third parties under the Uniform Partnership Act.

II. Hypothetical Multi-Issue Essay Question:

Fabrizio Nasca and his twin brother, Giorgetto, were born into a wealthy and aristocratic family. They never wanted for any of the necessities of life and could have lived at any number of jet-set spots all over the world. Fabrizio preferred Mecanous and Giorgetto liked Yourcanous for their getaways. Unfortunately, they both also suffer from angst of self-doubt and self-worth. They decided they needed to get involved in a socially worthwhile business venture.

They encountered Brimbo Mireval, one of the fastest talking promoters in all of the Gold Coast. Brimbo had a great idea. Why not set up a business to sell health insurance at discount prices to small companies who could otherwise not afford it? The Nasca twins like the idea and entered into a written partnership agreement wherein they formed the "We Make You Feel Good" insurance company. Under the terms of the agreement, Fabrizio and Giorgetto would provide the funding while Brimbo would see to regulatory compliance and provide sales talent as his capital contribution in this equal partnership.

As it turned out, the company failed when a number of policy holder's claims were not paid. They turned the company over to the Massazona State Insurance Commission. Brimbo is now long gone with the money, and the Nasca twins are looking at claims adding up to $30 million. What result?

III. Key Question Checklist:

A. Assuming that a legally recognized form of partnership has been entered into, you must then examine the respective rights and duties between the partners themselves. Did they:
1. Set out the respective management rights among themselves?
2. Provide for a division of profits and/or losses?
3. Accounting among each other for:
   (a) Return of capital?
   (b) Return of advances?
   (c) Indemnification for expenses?
   (d) Compensation?
   (e) An accounting at death or termination?
4. Inspection of books and records of the partnership?

5. Orderly entry to and/or exit of associates in the partnership?

B. Assuming the above arrangements have been made, there are several basic public policy based duties imposed on partners. In looking at the issue before you, determine whether there was any breach of:
1. The fiduciary duty of loyalty?
   (a) Self-dealing?
   (b) Usurping a partnership opportunity?
   (c) Competing with the partnership?
   (d) Secret profits?
   (e) Service to the partnership?
   (f) Confidentiality?
   (g) Personal use of partnership property?
2. Duty of obedience?
3. Duty of care?
4. Duty to inform the partnership?
5. The duty of accountability? (This duty is a fallout of the breach of any one or more of the loyalty duties listed above). It includes reimbursement claims by partners against each other for tort and other claims paid to third parties.

C. The property rights of the partners are normally set out in the partnership agreement entered into at the outset of the formation of the partnership. If the partners failed to do this:
1. Did they properly identify partnership property?
2. Are methods for conveyance or transfer of partnership property in place (including assignment to third parties and death of a partner)?
3. What are the rights of third party creditors to partnership property?

D. After you have defined the basic rights and duties among the partners, you must then examine the situation vis-à-vis third parties who have contact with the partnership.
1. Is this contact by way of a contract?
    (a) With actual express authority?
    (b) Actual implied authority?
    (c) Apparent authority?
    (d) Ratification of an unauthorized act?
2. Was the contact based on a tortious act by a person acting within the ordinary course of partnership or within the authority of copartners?
    (a) Negligent tort?
    (b) Breach of trust or fiduciary duty?
    (c) Intentional tort?
3. Liability to third party is:
    (a) Joint?
    (b) Joint and several?
4. Criminal liability applicable?

IV: Objective Questions:

Terms:

1. In the absence of an agreement to the contrary, all partners have equal rights in the _____ and conduct of the partnership business.

2. When a person joins a partnership, she typically contributes money and property referred to as _____ _____.

3. In a partnership setting, if a person makes a representation that she is a partner, or consents to a representation that she is a partner, she is considered an

    _____ _____

    and is liable to any person who reasonably relied on such representations.

4. The formal judicial proceeding in which a court is authorized to review the partnership and the partner's transactions and award each partner his share of partnership assets is called an _____.

5. Partners owe certain duties to the partnership and other partners. Among these duties is a duty of _____ which requires the partners to adhere to the provisions of the partnership agreement and the decisions of the partnership.

6. A doctrine requiring that upon the death of a partner, the deceased partner's rights in specific partnership property vest in the remaining partners is known as the right of _____.

7. A partner who incurs expenditures in the ordinary and proper conduct of the business and for the preservation of partnership property is entitled to _____ for such expenses.

8. A partner who deals personally with the partnership in transactions such as buying and selling goods and property from or to the partnership has engaged in _____.

9. A partner who is offered an opportunity on behalf of the partnership and takes the opportunity for himself has _____ a partnership opportunity.

10. A partner who is vested with authority in writing or orally to perform a certain function is said to have _____ _____ authority.

True/False:

1. _____The general partners of a limited partnership have limited personal liability for the debts and obligations of the limited partnership.

2. _____To be considered a valid partnership, all partnership property must be owned proportionally by each partner.

3. _____Unless otherwise stated in the partnership agreement, the partners share partnership profits in proportion to their capital contributions.

4. _____Partners may delegate management responsibilities to a committee of partners or to the managing partner, and thereby relieve the delegating partners from liability to creditors for management decisions made on behalf of the partnership.

5. _____Unless otherwise provided, a partner is entitled to remuneration at a reasonable rate for his or her performance in the partnership's business.

6. _____Where a partnership agreement provides for the sharing of profits but is silent as to how losses are to be shared, losses are shared in the same proportion as profits.

7. _____ The liability of a partner who breaches the duty of loyalty is limited to disgorgement of profits made from the breach.

8. _____ The duty of care owed by partners when transacting partnership business is that degree of skill and care that a reasonable business manager in the same position would use in those circumstances.

9. _____ Unless stated otherwise, each partner has an equal right to possess specific partnership property for personal use.

10. _____ With respect to the liability of one partner for the contracts of the partnership, any partner who is made to pay more than his or her proportionate share may seek indemnification from the partnership and from those partners who have not paid their share of the loss.

Multiple Choice:

1. Tom Taxbreak is successful in establishing a new partnership. He and his partners are looking to admit several new partners but are unsure about the capital contributions of these new partners. Which of the following would be considered a contribution of capital to the partnership?
   A. A loan of $5,000 to the partnership.
   B. Legal services valued at $2,300 contributed to the partnership.
   C. Property valued at $4,500 contributed to the partnership.
   D. None of the above.

2. Which of the following statements about the liability of general partners for the debts and obligations of a partnership is most accurate?
   A. The liability of a general partner is like that of a corporate shareholder.
   B. The liability of a general partner is like that of a sole proprietor.
   C. The liability of a general partner is like that of a beneficiary of a business trust.
   D. None of the above.

3. Page Curry, a partner in the Herbs and Spices Partnership, wishes to withdraw from the partnership and sell her interest to Bill Sage. All of the other partners in Herbs and Spices have agreed to admit Sage as a partner and to hold Curry harmless for past, present, and future liabilities of Herbs and Spices.. A provision in the original partnership agreement states that the partnership will continue upon the death or withdrawal of one or more of the partners. As a result of Curry's withdrawal and Sage's admission to the partnership, which of the following statements is correct?

A. Sage is personally liable for partnership liabilities arising before and after his admission as a partner.

B. Sage has the right to participate in the management of Herbs and Spices.

C. Sage acquired only the right to receive Curry's share of the profits of Herbs and Spices.

D. Sage must contribute cash or other property to Herbs and Spices in order to be admitted with the same rights as the other partners.

4. Buff, Chip, and Ralphie operate a mountain bike shop as a partnership on the Hill in Boulder, Colorado. All three partners work full time in the shop. According to the partnership agreement, only Chip is authorized to order bicycle repairs. Ralphie ordered repairs totaling $3,000 from a supplier who knew that Ralphie was a partner, but who did not know that Ralphie was not authorized to order repairs for the partnership. Which of the following statements is correct?

A. Buff, Chip and Ralphie are jointly and severally liable for the repairs ordered by Ralphie.

B. Only Ralphie is liable for the repairs.

C. Ralphie had apparent authority to order the repairs.

D. Ralphie had actual and apparent authority to order the repairs.

5. Assume the same facts as in question 4. One snowy afternoon, Buff was repairing a bicycle on the display floor and did not realize that ice and snow had melted off the bicycle onto the floor. Charlie Clumsy slipped on the puddle and broke his hip. Charlie incurred $10,000 in medical bills. Which of the following statements is correct?

A. Charlie may sue Buff, Chip, and Ralphie in separate actions and recover $10,000 from each of them.

B. Charlie will have to sue the partnership in order to recover for his medical bills.

C. Charlie may sue each of the partners in separate actions for tort.

D. Charlie may sue and recover only from Buff.

6. Zelma Wolf acquired Folsom's partnership interest in FBC Partnership. All partners agreed to admit Wolf as a partner. Unless otherwise agreed, White's admission to the partnership will automatically:

A. Release Folsom from personal liability on partnership debts arising prior to the sale of her partnership interest.

B. Release Folsom from any liability on partnership debts arising subsequent to the sale of her partnership interest.

C. Subject Wolf to unlimited personal liability on partnership debts arising prior to her admission as a partner.

D. Limit Wolf's liability on partnership debts arising prior to her admission as a partner to her interest in partnership property.

7. Abe, George, and Thomas are partners in a book store specializing in books relating to history. George has loaned the partnership a significant amount of money, and the partnership has since begun the process of termination. If partnership funds are insufficient to repay the amounts owed to George, which of the following statements is correct?
   A. George will not be repaid.
   B. Abe and Thomas must contribute their proportionate share towards repayment of the loan from George.
   C. George will receive only the interest accrued on the unpaid amount.
   D. None of the above.

8. Harpo assigns his interest in the ABC Partnership to Dexter. Which of the following statements is most correct?
   A. Harpo would be prohibited by law in most states from assigning his partnership interest.
   B. Dexter is entitled to participate in management.
   C. Dexter is entitled to receive the profits to which Harpo would otherwise have been entitled.
   D. None of the above.

9. Assume the same facts as question 8 except Harpo dies. With respect to Harpo's interest in specific partnership property, which of the following is correct?
   A. Harpo's interest in specific partnership property passes to the surviving partners.
   B. Harpo's interest in specific partnership property passes to his wife.
   C. Harpo's interest in specific partnership property passes to his estate.
   D. Harpo's interest in specific partnership property passes to his wife and his estate in equal shares.

10. Smith and Jones operated a computer consulting as partners. The assets of the business consisted of real property, equipment, inventory, liquid assets, and goodwill. The partnership interest of either Smith and Jones includes which of the following rights?
    A. A right to half of all the partnership tangible assets on demand, but not goodwill.
    B. A right to half of all the partnership assets upon the death of a partner.
    C. A right to share profits and surplus (after payment of creditors).
    D. A right to assign half of the partnership interest to another who will then become a partner.

V. Answers to Objective Questions:

Terms:

1. *Management.* This is one of the cornerstone provisions of UPA, Sec. 18(e).
2. *Partnership capital.* Once this property is contributed by the partners for permanent use of the partnership, it cannot be withdrawn prior to dissolution unless all the partners consent to the withdrawal.
3. *Ostensible partner (or partnership by estoppel).* If these elements are in place, the courts may choose to treat the nonpartner as an actual partner for purposes of personal liability. In addition, if all the partners in a partnership consent to the representatives of the nonpartner, the contract becomes an obligation of the partnership.

4. *Accounting.* This is a formal judicial proceeding in which a court reviews the financial affairs of the partnership and determines the respective financial interests of the partners.
5. *Obedience.* A partner is considered to have elements of both a principal and an agent of the partnership. In this duty, the element of agency is stressed in that he or she must adhere to the provisions of the partnership agreement. If a partner breaches this duty, he or she is liable to the partnership for any damages caused by the breach.
6. *Survivorship.* Under the doctrine of tenant in partnership, a partner is a coowner with other partners of specific partnership property. Under the right of survivorship, upon the death of a partner, the deceased partner's right in that specific partnership property vests in the remaining partners. Note, however, that the value of the deceased partner's interest in the partnership does pass to his or her beneficiaries or heirs upon death.
7. *Indemnification.* This concept is designed to hold the partners harmless for costs incurred on behalf of the partnership.
8. *Self-dealing.* This practice is in direct violation of the fiduciary duty of loyalty owed by a partner to the partnership.
9. *Usurped.* This practice is in violation of the duty of loyalty. Any gains arising from the usurped opportunity must be handed over to the partnership.
10. *Actual express.* Often this authority will be defined per the terms of the basic partnership agreement.

True/False:

1. False. General partners have unlimited liability for the debts and obligations of the limited partnership.
2. False. Partners must share in profits and the management responsibilities of a partnership. They need not share in the ownership of all partnership property.
3. False. The UPA mandates that each partner has the right to an equal share of the partnership profits unless otherwise stated in the partnership agreement.
4. False. A partner may not relieve him or herself from liability to creditors through the use of such delegations.
5. False. A partner is not entitled to remuneration for his or her performance in the partnership's business unless otherwise provided.
6. True. This is called for under the UPA unless otherwise agreed upon by the partners.
7. False. In addition to the duty to disgorge profits, the breaching partner is liable for any damages caused by the breach.
8. True. This rule is sometimes referred to as the "prudent person" rule.
9. False. Each partner has an equal right to possess specific partnership property for partnership use. A partner may possess partnership property for personal use only with the consent of the other partners.
10. True. This secondary action for reimbursement or indemnification does not affect the original obligation paid by the partner to the third party. It is, rather, a matter of accounting among the partners themselves.

Multiple Choice:

1. C. Money and property contributed to the partnership constitute partnership capital. Loans of money or property and the donation of services are not considered partnership capital, therefore answers A and B are incorrect.

2. B. Both general partners and sole proprietors have unlimited personal liability with respect to the debts and obligations of their respective business enterprises.

3. B. An incoming partner has the same rights as all other partners. An incoming partner therefore has the right to participate in the management of the partnership. Thus Sage has the right to participate in the management of the Herbs and Spices Partnership.

4. C. In this situation, the implied authority of the partners has been restricted by the partnership agreement. The supplier was not informed of this restriction, however, and therefore Ralphie had the apparent authority to enter into the contract.

5. C. Partners are jointly and severally liable for torts. Thus, Charlie may sue one or more of the partners separately. However, the partner who is sued may seek indemnification from the partner who committed the wrongful act.

6. D. A new partner who is admitted to the partnership is liable for the existing debts of the partnership only to the extent of her capital contribution. The new partner is personally liable for debts and obligations incurred by the partnership after she becomes a partner. Answer B is incorrect because a withdrawing partner is released from liability on partnership debts only if notice of withdrawal is given to third parties who have previously dealt with the partnership and constructive notice is given to other creditors.

7. B. A partner who makes a loan to the partnership becomes a creditor of the partnership. Partners are personally liable for the partnership's debts and obligations.

8. B. A partner who makes a loan to the partnership becomes a creditor of the partnership. Partners are jointly liable on partnership contracts and may seek indemnification from other partners and the partnership.

9. C. A partner who advances money to the partnership is entitled to interest from the date of the advance.

10. C. Under the Uniform Partnership Act, a partner has a right to receive a distribution of profits unless there is an agreement otherwise under their management powers.

VI. Key Question Checklist Answers to Essay Question:

A,B&C. *What are the respective rights and duties between the partners in this case?*

The partners did attempt to provide a written agreement which sought to delineate some of the respective rights and duties among themselves. Under the terms as presented, there appeared to be an equal partnership between Fabrizo, Giorgetto, and Brimbo. They had not specifically provided for any exact formula of how profits and losses were to be divided, therefore the Uniform Partnership Act (UPA) must be looked at for guidance. Under the UPA, unless otherwise agreed, a partner has the right to an equal share in the partnership's profits and losses. In addition, the partners each have the right to inspect books and accounting rights to return of capital, advances, and expenses.

Unfortunately for the well-motivated Nasca twins, their trust was poorly placed. Brimbo has violated almost every fiduciary duty of loyalty to the partnership. He has engaged in self-dealing, secret profits, embezzlement, and personal use of partnership funds. One of the hallmarks of scam artists is that they prey on the need gaps created by socially important problems. The U.S. is the last major power without a national health insurance plan. Over 39 million Americans are without any private or government health coverage. This is an especially acute problem for small companies who cannot afford to spread the cost among many employees to get favorable rates. Into this coverage gap, all sorts of con artists have jumped offering all sorts of "discount" and "low end" coverage. This usually is found to be non-coverage when investigated by state insurance regulatory agencies.

D. *What is the situation of third parties who have contact with the partnership?*

The contract made by third parties with "We Make You Feel Good" is a true contract. Brimbo had the actual express authority to act for the Nasca twins even though his actions were not authorized by the state. The role of agency law becomes critical at this point because the Nasca twins can now be held jointly and severally liable to the third parties for the wrongful acts of their partner, Brimbo. They may even be subject to criminal penalties imposed by the state for the insurance fraud committed by their partner in the name of the partnership. It is a sad state of affairs for everyone touched by Brimbo, and it illustrated the real damage which can be inflicted on well meaning partners and third parties by white collar criminals. Unfortunately, such situations are not uncommon in the area of insurance fraud.

300

CHAPTER 34

LIMITED PARTNERSHIPS AND CORPORATIONS

I fear nothing so much as a man who is witty all day long.

Mme. de Sévigné

I. Overview:

Compare the first three issues in partnership (creation, operation, and dissolution) with the rules of limited partnership. The law of limited partnership enjoys a rather unique niche in our system of jurisprudence in that its origins are French rather than English. Under the original *partnerships in commendam* as used in France, a partner could enter into a contract with another person or partnership. Under that contract, the partner would be supplied with a certain amount of goods or services in exchange for a share of the profits of the partnership. If there was a loss, the investor would be liable for no more than his investment.

Investment is the key to the original notion of limited partnership. The idea was to create a middle ground between pure partnership and an entity with a totally autonomous existence. In the Middle Ages when limited partnerships were used, the corporate form of business was simply not in existence as we know it today. In many ways, history shows us that limited partnerships were the precursors of more modern methods of capital fund raising used in corporation law.

Today's modern laws of limited partnerships are found in two key statutes: the original 1916 Uniform Limited Partnership Act and its heir apparent, the Revised Uniform Limited Partnership Act first promulgated in 1976. Even though there are substantial differences between the two versions, they remain the same with regard to several key provisions:

1. Both call for statutory creation (as opposed to just contract creation) of limited partnerships, including the use of a certificate of limited partnership.
2. Both call for two key classes of partners to be in place: at least one general partner with unlimited traditional partner's liability and a class of limited partner who normally can be held liable only to the extent of his or her capital contribution.
3. Both statutes generally limit the amount of activity a limited partner may engage in regarding the business as a price of having limited liability protections.
4. Both use the general partnership principles of the Uniform Partnership Act as a fall back position if their respective statutory requirements are not complied with.

In both scenarios, the basic intent of the statutory scheme is the same as was found in the early French versions of *partnerships in commendam*. That intent was to raise capital investment contributions while providing the investors with some assurance of immunity from claims. In spite of many more regulatory compliance rules, it is still easier to float a limited partnership than to go public in the corporate world. In addition, limited partnerships generally provide more opportunities for a small investor (remember these are relative terms) to acquire higher percentages of equity growth than in stocks.

One other undeniably important factor in this equation has been the Internal Revenue Code. Up until 1986, the tax code strongly favored the use of limited partnerships as a means to tax shelter income through what came to be known as PILs (passive investment losses). With the advent of the Tax Reform Act of 1986 and its attendant passive income rule requirements, the most sought after tax shelters are now called PIGs (passive income gainers) because they are needed to offset losses. In spite of the complex rules, most commentators feel that the reforms were needed. Economic reality, not tax supported fictional losses, should be the underlying motive of any good investment, be it partnership, limited partnership, corporation, or any other form of business.

There are three basic sets of issues in the law of limited partnerships: formation, rights and duties of partners vis-à-vis each other, and rights and duties of partners vis-à-vis third parties. These issues are detailed in the key question checklist.

II. Hypothetical Multi-Issue Essay Question:

China has long provided the world with one of the greatest cuisines extant. Few dishes can compare with a *lop cheong* served with *foon tiu meen* spiced with *soon geung* or *hak chih mah*. Top it off with a beautifully prepared *lien ngow* and some proper chrysanthemum tea. Such is the kind of meal Chef T. Bear had in mind when he decided to open his new restaurant, the Woo Woo Cafe. He needed investors to help finance the business, so he asked his old friend, Annie Wise to become a limited partner. Annie would invest $50,000 in return for a 50 percent ownership share in the Woo Woo Cafe.

When T. Bear opened the cafe, it got off to a slow start. He insisted on one hundred percent authenticity and refused to compromise his food or his menu in any way.

Unfortunately his patrons, albeit very sophisticated, could not read all of his menu because it was written in Chinese. Most people don't know the difference between *boak coy, siu choy, and gai choy* without some translation on the menu.

Annie began to fear for her investment and started to run certain aspects of the business. In order to spice up the entrees, she added obscene quotations into the fortune cookies and made numerous changes to the menu offerings, including Korean and Japanese dishes which T. Bear never really mastered.

The business failed and is now in debt for $100,000 to various food and restaurant equipment suppliers. These suppliers are seeking to hold Annie personally liable as a general partner. Annie defends based on her limited partnership agreement with T. Bear. What result?

III. Key Question Checklist:

A. The first issue involves the proper formation of a limited partnership. Our system calls for the formation of a limited partnership to be in compliance with a regulatory statute which allows its creation. Were the elements of the statute complied with?
1. Which statute applies?
   (a) Uniform Limited Partnership Act?
   (b) Revised Uniform Limited Partnership Act?
   (c) The laws of the state of Louisiana (based on French civil law)?
2. Who may be a partner?
   (a) General partner?
   (b) Limited partner?
3. What constitutes a capital contribution?
4. What businesses may a limited partnership be engaged in?

5. Has a certificate of limited partnership been properly prepared and complied with?
6. Any other laws applicable to the limited partnership?
7. Result in case of defective formation of the limited partnership?
8. Any other form of limited partnership possible?

B. Once the limited partnership formation compliance issues have been resolved, you must then establish the respective rights and duties of the partners vis-à-vis each other. Was there:
1. A limited partnership agreement entered into between the partners?
2. Activities permitted to the general partners?
   (a) Under the Uniform Limited Partnership Act?
   (b) Under the Revised Uniform Limited Partnership Act (less restricted)?
3. Activities permitted to the limited partners?
   (a) Under the Uniform Limited Partnership Act?
   (b) Under the Revised Uniform Limited Partnership Act (less restrictive)?
4. General limitations on the individual liability of a limited partner?
   (a) Exceptions to the general rule:
      (1) Defective formation?
      (2) Participation in management?
      (3) Personal guarantees?
5. Partners rights to profits and losses?
   (a) General partners?
   (b) Limited partners?

6. Partners rights to capital contributions?
   (a) General partners?
   (b) Limited partners?
7. Any other rights and duties?
   (a) Right to information?
   (b) Right to vote?
   (c) New partner admissions rules?
   (d) Withdrawal of partner rules?
   (e) Rights of assignment of partnership interest?
   (f) Priorities vis-à-vis each other upon liquidation of the partnership?

C. Assuming the respective rights and duties of the partners have been resolved, third parties rights and duties must be reviewed. Do the third parties have priority rights as creditors?
1. Rights against general partners?
2. Claims (if any) against limited partners?
3. Claims (if any) against new partners?

IV. Objective Questions:

Terms:

1. A person who invests capital in a limited partnership, but does not participate in the management of the corporation and who is not responsible for debts and obligations of the organization beyond his or her capital investment is called a

   _____ _____.

2. When forming a limited partnership, a(n)

   _____ _____

   _____ _____

   must be signed and executed by at least two people before the limited partnership can become legal and binding.

303

3. In order to provide creditors and others with current information concerning the limited partnership and its partners, a _____ _____ _____ must be filed within thirty days of any significant changes in, among other things, the partners and their contributions.

4. Frequently, limited partnerships draft and execute a _____ _____ _____ to set forth the rights and duties of partners and the terms and conditions regarding the operation, termination, and dissolution of the partnership.

5. In those situations where there has been substantial compliance in good faith with the statutory requirements concerning formation of a limited partnership, a _____ _____ will be deemed to have occurred.

6. A limited partnership is considered a(n) _____ _____ _____ in all states other than the state in which it was organized.

7. A limited partnership will generally be permitted to transact business in a foreign state upon the filing of a _____ _____ _____ in that foreign state.

8. A limited or general partners' share of profits, distributions, and capital is his or her _____ _____ _____.

9. In some circumstances it may be necessary to liquidate the assets of the limited partnership and distribute the proceeds thereof. This process is known as _____ _____ the limited partnership.

10. The person who invests capital in the limited partnership, manages the business of the limited partnership, and is personally liable for partnership debts is a _____ _____.

True/False:

1. _____ The formation of a limited partnership is complete when the notification of formation is published in a newspaper of general circulation in the area that the limited partnership is located.

2. _____ Pursuant to the RULPA, a limited partnership may only have thirty five limited partners.

3. _____ A person may be both a limited and a general partner in a limited partnership.

4. _____ A limited partnership cannot engage in banking or insurance but can engage in oil and gas drilling.

5. _____ The surname of a limited partner may be used in the name of the limited partnership so long as it is not also the surname of a general partner.

6. _____ A limited partner who knowingly allows her name to be used in violation of the law concerning the name of a limited partnership is liable as a general partner with respect to any creditor who extends credit to the partnership without actual knowledge of her true status as a limited partner.

7. _____ In a circumstance where there has been a substantial defect in the creation of a limited partnership, a person who erroneously, but in good faith, believed himself to be a limited partner may avoid liability as a general partner by causing the appropriate certificate of limited partnership to be filed.

8. ____ Failure to register as a foreign limited partnership impairs the validity of any act or contract of the unregistered foreign limited partnership in the foreign state but does not prevent it from defending itself in any proceedings in the courts of the foreign state.

9. ____ In a limited partnership, limited partners, but not general partners, owe a fiduciary duty to the limited partnership and to the other partners.

10. ____ Limited partners may participate in the management and control of the partnership without impairing their limited liability status, but they have no right to bind the partnership to contracts or other obligations.

Multiple Choice:

1. Leona Loud is a partner in a limited partnership created for the purpose of distributing stereo equipment. She invested $5,000 in the organization and has agreed to sell stereo equipment on a part-time basis in exchange for commissions on each sale. Which of the following statements is correct?
   A. Leona can be held liable as a general partner if she participates in the management and control of the partnership.
   B. Leona is not a general partner.
   C. Leona can be held liable as a general partner if her name is included in the name of the partnership.
   D. All of the above.

2. John, Ringo, and Paul are partners in a limited partnership for which a certificate of limited partnership has been properly filed. John, Ringo, and Paul, the only three partners, share profits equally according to the certificate of limited partnership but have not stated how losses are to be shared. John loaned the partnership $5,000 interest free and contributed $10,000 in capital; Ringo made a capital contribution of $5,000; Paul made no capital contribution but has devoted all his time to the partnership. John, a general partner, and Ringo, a limited partner, have devoted no time to the management of the partnership. Which of the following statements is false?
   A. Ringo will be liable as a general partner if the name of the partnership is John, Ringo, and Paul, Ltd.
   B. Ringo will be liable as a general partner for willful, intentional torts committed by Paul while acting within the scope of authority.
   C. The partnership will not be dissolved upon Ringo's death.
   D. The partnership will be dissolved upon the bankruptcy of Paul.

3. Assume the same facts as in question 2 except the partners have agreed to dissolve the partnership. Outside creditors are owed $25,000. The partnership and each of the partners are solvent. Pursuant to the Uniform Limited Partnership Act, the order of distribution is as follows:
   A. Outside creditors ($25,000); Ringo for his share of the profits and capital contribution of $5,000; John $5,000 for his loan to the partnership; John and Paul for their share of profits; John $10,000 for his capital contribution.
   B. Outside creditors ($25,000); John $5,000 for his loan; Ringo $5,000 for his capital contribution; John $5,000 for his capital contribution; John, Ringo and Paul then share profits.
   C. The same as that of a general partnership.
   D. The same as the distribution under the Revised Uniform Limited Partnership Act.

4. Which of the following will cause the dissolution of a limited partnership?
   A. The death of a limited partner whose estate is insolvent.
   B. The withdrawal of a general partner.
   C. The discovery of a limited partner's capital contribution to a competing limited partnership.
   D. Sale of a limited partnership interest.

5. Annette, Jeannette, and Lynnette are limited partners in a legal brothel. Due to lack of personal funds, the general partners cannot satisfy the partnership debts. The creditors are demanding payment from the limited partners. Which of the following would *not* cause one or more of the limited partners to be personally liable to the creditors?
   A. The certificate of limited partnership contained an error in listing Annette's address.
   B. Jeannette provided management services as part of her capital contribution.
   C. Lynnette holds herself out as a general partner.
   D. None of the above events will cause any of the limited partners to be personally liable to the creditors.

6. Dick and Jane formed Downhill Racers Ltd., a limited partnership which prepares sites for downhill ski races. When it bid on an Olympic contract, the Olympic Sanctioning Committee had to verify that the limited partnership had been properly created. Which of the following is required in creating the limited partnership?
   A. There must be at least one limited partner, but no general partners are required.

B. The limited partners must contribute property or cash, but not services.
C. The partnership agreement must be filed in the public records.
D. A certificate of partnership must contain the limited partners' names, addresses, and capital contributions.

7. Which of the following events would *not* require the filing of an amendment to the certificate of limited partnership?
   A. The admission of a new partner.
   B. The withdrawal of a partner.
   C. A change in the right of remaining partners to continue the business after the withdrawal of a general partner.
   D. A change in a partner's capital contribution.

8. Widgets R Us, Ltd. is a limited partnership that invests in widget futures on the widget commodities market. To obtain additional capital, the general partners want to admit additional limited partners. Some of the existing limited partners are unhappy with the investments and want to sell their interests. The certificate and agreement of limited partnership provide no guidelines. Which of the following statements is correct?
   A. All partners must unanimously consent to admitting additional limited partners.
   B. If the limited partners may assign their interests, the general partners may admit additional limited partners.
   C. An assignee of a limited partnership interest becomes a limited partner.
   D. A limited partner must give the general partners ten days' notice prior to assigning his/her interest.

9. Which of the following will *not* cause the dissolution of a limited partnership?
   A. The withdrawal of a general partner followed by the written agreement of the remaining partners to continue the business.
   B. The withdrawal of a limited partner.
   C. The entry of a decree of judicial dissolution.
   D. A and B above.

10. Gone to the Dogs, Ltd. is a limited partnership suffering from lack of public interest in their dog biscuit products. The partnership has not had sufficient profits to make any distributions to the limited partners. T. Bear, a limited partner, is upset. He has a right to do which of the following?
   A. Replace the general partners by unanimous vote of the limited partners.
   B. Require the return of his capital contribution.
   C. Have a formal accounting of partnership affairs.
   D. Require interest be paid on his capital contribution.

V. Answers to Objective Questions:

Terms:

1. *Limited partner.* A limited partnership must have at least one general partner who is personally liable for partnership debts. Ordinarily, there are no restrictions on the number of limited partners allowed in a limited partnership.

2. *Certificate of limited partnership.* These requirements are found in the provisions of both the original Uniform Limited Partnership 'act and the Revised Uniform Limited Partnership Act.

3. *Certificate of amendment.* These provisions are designed to protect interested third parties who have financial stakes in the welfare of the limited partnership.

4. *Limited partnership agreement.* Many of the same issues covered in general partnership agreements need to be addressed with regard to limited partnerships. The biggest difference is that these agreements cannot violate public policy or specific limitations outlined in the Uniform Partnership Acts.

5. *Defective formation.* If an error is made in the formation of a limited partnership, it could be deemed to be a general partnership. The RULPA does provide, however, for correction of the problem and/or withdrawal by the limited partners if the problem is not resolved.

6. *Foreign limited partnership.* In the law of business entities in general, "foreign" usually refers to an out-of-state based entity. "Alien" usually refers to entities which are based outside of the country.

7. *Certificate of registration.* This process is generally incorporated into a series of statutes generically known as long-arm statutes. These statutes are designed to assure service of process, if necessary, as against the out-of-state entity in case of a lawsuit being filed against it in a foreign jurisdiction.

8. *Partnership interest.* This interest represents the total financial involvement of the partner in the partnership.

9. *Winding up.* The rules of winding up the financial affairs of a limited partnership under the RULPA are very similar to those of the UPA.

10. *General partner.* This person is subject to the possibility of personal liability for the debts of the limited partnership. He or she, in turn, is responsible for the operation of the limited partnership.

True/False:

1. False. The limited partnership is formed when the certificate of limited partnership is filed in the appropriate government offices.
2. False. There are no restrictions on the number of general or limited partners in a limited partnership.
3. True. This dual status is allowed under the RULPA.
4. True. This limitation provides a good example of preemption by federal law vis-a-vis banking and insurance over state laws which are controlling in the formation of limited partnerships.
5. False. The surname of a limited partner may be used in the name of the limited partnership only if it is also the surname of a general partner or if the business was carried on in that name before the admission of the limited partner.
6. True. The use of a limited partner's name in the management of the limited partnership is expressly forbidden by the RULPA.
7. True. This is allowed under the provisions of the RULPA.
8. False. The sanction for failing to register as a foreign limited partnership is a prohibition on initiating litigation in the courts of the foreign jurisdiction.
9. False. Limited partners generally do not owe a fiduciary duty to the limited partnership and its partners because of the limited nature of their interest in the business. General partners owe the fiduciary duties of care and loyalty to the limited partnership and its partners.

10. False. A limited partner who participates in management or control of the partnership will impair his limited liability status. Management or control includes binding the partnership to contracts or other obligations.

Multiple Choice:

1. D. A, B, and C are all true per the provisions of the RULPA.
2. B. If Ringo's name is not included in the name of the partnership, and if he does not participate in the management or control of the partnership or do anything else to impair his limited partner status, he is a limited partner whose liability is limited to the extent of his capital contribution.
3. A. This is the order of priority payment set out in the RULPA.
4. B. The withdrawal of a general partner will cause the dissolution of a limited partnership.
5. A. Minor errors in the certificate of limited partnership that primarily affect the operation of the partnership or the limited partners are not so substantial as to invalidate the limited partnership.
6. D. Because a limited partnership is created by statute, statutory formalities must be complied with. Under the ULPA, a certificate of limited partnership must be filed containing the names, addresses, and capital contributions of all limited partners in accordance with the state law under which Downhill Racers, Ltd. was formed.
7. C. A, B, and D require the filing of an amendment to the certificate of limited partnership under the RULPA.

8. A. Unless expressly provided otherwise in the partnership agreement, admission of additional limited partners requires the unanimous consent of all existing partners. Most limited partnership agreements provide guidelines on this issue.

9. D. A judicial decree can be used to dissolve a limited partnership.

10. C. Upon reasonable demand, each limited partner has the right to obtain from the general partners true and full information regarding the state of the business, the financial condition of the limited partnership and so on. T. Bear should also assert these rights in a timely manner before all the biscuits are gone.

VI. Key Question Checklist Answers to Essay Question:

A. *Were the statutory requirements for proper formation of a limited partnership met?*

It appears from the facts as presented that T. Bear and Annie Wise properly sought to establish a limited partnership. Under either of the modern Uniform Limited Partnership Acts, a limited partner is allowed to use cash as his or her capital contribution to the limited partnership. In addition, both versions of the statute allow some limited participation in the management of the business by a limited partner. These limitations are more strict under the more traditional Uniform Limited Partnership Act (ULPA) than under the newer Revised Uniform Partnership Act (RULPA).

Assuming the RULPA is in place, Annie may still have some problems. This act allows a number of activities but does have one overall limitation: a limited partner may not participate in the *control* of a business to the same substantial extent at a general partner.

B. *What are the rights and duties of the partners vis-à-vis eachother?*

The respective rights and duties of T. Bear and Annie Wise are not really in question here except to the extent that the activities of Annie are deemed to have been in violation of the applicable statute. If so, the fall back position of the Uniform Partnership Act will be used. Under that position, their profits and losses will be shared equally if their agreement had not spoken to the issue otherwise. Here it looks like Annie's agreement will protect her from paying any overage to T. Bear beyond her capital investment. The same nay not be true vis-a-vis third parties.

C. *Are third party creditors rights involved?*

Under either version of modern limited partnership statutes, third parties may seek to hold limited partners liable as general partners if they violate the management participation prohibitions of the statute. Even under the more liberal RULPA, if a third party reasonably believed that Annie was a general partner, Annie could be liable as a general partner. In this case, the nature and scope of the management decisions made by Annie could have led a reasonable third party to believe that he was now in charge of running the restaurant. In any event, both Annie and T. Bear have learned their lesson. Next week they are opening a new taco stand.

CHAPTER 35

THE FORMATION, AND FINANCING OF CORPORATIONS

There is nothing new in the world, so history is the greatest lesson you can learn about what's happening now.

Garel Rhys

I.   Overview:

Corporations can provide many advantages for business including perpetual existence, limited liability, and numerous tax and other legal opportunities to massage the system. These advantages are not free, nor are they always easily obtained. Corporate law has always been more technically intricate and demanding of legal practitioners. It can also be more unforgiving to its users than sole proprietorships or partnerships if mistakes are made in its formation and financing. The stakes are simply greater because over eighty-five percent of business done in the U.S. uses the corporate format. This chapter has several objectives: to illustrate how the corporate form is established legally and how it is infused with its financial lifeblood, i.e., money. In addition, the process of establishing the basic ground rules for the key players will be examined.

The formation of a corporation starts with a contracting process initiated by a person called a promoter. The word promoter has a unsavory connotation to many people. In the modern vernacular, many people think of a promoter as a person seeking to get rich by doubtful means or chicanery rather than legitimate work. Borderline sporting *cum* entertainment events have not done much to lessen this impression. In point of fact, the law of corporations has a much different expectation of the role of promoter.

A promoter of a new corporation is really the catalyst who brings together the diverse elements of law, finance, entrepreneurial talent, and technical competence which will eventually drive the fortunes of the new business entity. The role of promoter is also tied to the laws of contract, fiduciaries, and agency. He or she is expected to act for the benefit of the eventual corporation and can be expected to be personally liable for contracts entered into on its behalf in the interim.

The promoter's main duties are bifurcated towards two main audiences--the state and potential investors. He or she will be involved in contracts with both of these constituencies. With regard to the state, the actual creation of the new corporate entity is the outgrowth of a document called the charter. This document is the foundation contract between the promoter and the state. The charter takes the form of a certificate of incorporation. This certificate provides the official state-sanctioned ground rules under which the new corporate entity will be allowed to do business. Violation of these ground rules can lead to an eventual corporate death penalty, the revocation of the charter. The second critical task of the promoter is to find legal methods so that the start up of the corporation may be infused with financial lifeblood. The corporate form is unparalleled in its ability to be a fund-raiser. These funds are generated by two basic methods--debt and equity financing.

Once the proper procedures for the establishment of the corporation have been complied with and adequate financing has been secured, the next step is to see what the basic ground rules will be for key players in this arena. The leading protagonists will be the board of directors, shareholders, and managers of the corporation. The distinctions between these roles are sometimes blurred when it comes to the formation and management of corporations. Yet failure to honor these distinctions can lead to disastrous consequences.

II. Hypothetical Multi-Issue Essay Question:

Harvey Wheat and Harry Oats have come upon an entirely new way of growing and promoting natural grain food products. By having as many farm animals as possible use their fields as a place to relieve themselves naturally, they have found their grains to be supercharged with nature's essences. They named their product Relievo Brand Inc. and decided to incorporate their new venture. They hired a recent law school graduate named Fossagium Fossa. All the common stock in the corporation was issued in the names of Harvey Wheat and Harry Oats equally. In addition, the board of directors for the corporation were Harvey Wheat, Harry Oats, John Barley, Peter Hay, and Fossagium Fossa. All of them met at the Tofu Natural Eating and Drinking Club for their board meetings.

The Secretary of State informed Harvey and Harry that their product must first meet certain health inspection requirements before for they could do business in the state of Kannabras. Harvey and Harry took extreme umbrage at this insult to their farming expertise and choose simply to ignore this request. They ignored the inspection requirement and proceeded instead to grow and market their supercharged products at farmer's markets all over the country. In addition, Relievo Brand Inc. entered into numerous contracts with farm equipment suppliers, seed companies, and animal rental agencies in order to get a timely start on the growing season. The contracts totaled $1 million.

Last week Relievo Brand Inc. lost a big lawsuit to Calvin Calumny. It seems the Relievo Brand products were just too much for poor Calvin who lost his continence due to Harvey and Harry's products' unique ingredients. Relievo Brand Inc. now seeks to liquidate, and its creditors are seeking to collect against Harvey and Harry personally. Harvey, Harry, and the Board of Directors are claiming that they are not personally liable for the corporate debts of Relievo Brand Inc. What result?

III. Key Question Checklist:

This checklist is designed to help students with the three distinct stages of the corporate formation process:

1. How is a corporation established?
2. How is a corporation financed?
3. What are the basic ground rules for the key personnel involved in the formation of a corporation?

A. Have the proper procedures for incorporating been complied with?
  1. Which state law of incorporation is to be used?
  2. Which parties are qualified to act as incorporators?
  3. Have the articles of incorporation been properly drafted and filed with the state?
    (a) All required material information set out in the articles (names, addresses, etc.)?
    (b) Corporate name proper?
    (c) Duration of the corporation existence established?
    (d) Lawful purpose properly stated?
    (e) Capital structure statement requirements complied with?
    (f) Registered agent listed?

4. Charter or certificate of incorporation issued by the state?
5. First meeting of board of directors held?
   (a) By-laws adopted?
   (b) Officers elected?
   (c) Initial necessary business conducted?
6. If all the above are properly done, do we have a *de jure* corporation?

B. Assuming there has been an effort to incorporate, but not all the requirements of incorporation have been complied with?
   1. *De facto* corporation?
      (a) Valid statute in place?
      (b) Good faith effort to comply with that statute?
      (c) Conducted business as a corporation?
   2. Corporation by estoppel?
      (a) Defective corporation does not qualify as either a *de jure* or *de facto* corporation?
      (b) Equity in favor of the defective corporation?
      (c) Third party is estopped from raising the issue of defective incorporation?
   3. Results if the incorporation fails?

C. What if the jurisdiction in question has adopted the Revised Model Business Corporation Act provisions with regard to formation of a corporation?
   1. The conclusive proof rule?

D. How will this new corporation be classified?
   1. By way of situs?
      (a) Domestic?
      (b) Foreign?
      (c) Alien?

2. By way of profit motive?
   (a) For profit?
   (b) Nonprofit?
3. By way of ownership?
   (a) Public corporation?
   (b) Private?
      (1) Publicly held?
      (2) Closely held?
4. Special forms of corporate or quasi-corporate formats?
   (a) Professional corporation?
   (b) Sub-S corporation?
   (c) Limited liability company?

E. Once the corporation has been formed, which of the promoter's activities must now be ended or continued?
   1. Original contracts entered into by the promoter with third parties will hold the promoter personally liable?
   2. These contracts shifted to corporation?
      (a) By ratification?
         (1) Promoter relieved of further liability?
         (2) Corporation becomes solely liable?
      (b) By adoption?
         (1) Promoter remains personally liable?
         (2) Corporation now becomes jointly liable on the promoters contract?
         (3) Third party can choose to release the promoter?
      (c) By novation?
         (1) A new contract is entered into between the original third party and the new corporation?
         (2) Promoter released from liability after the new contract is entered into?
         (3) Corporation is now solely liable on the contract?

F. Once the corporation has been established, and the rights and duties of the promoter have been established legally, and the rights and duties of the promoter have been identified, determine what mechanisms will be used to fund the corporation. Two main methods are possible--equity funding and debt funding. Assuming equity funding is to be used, what methods are available to the new corporation?
1. Common stock?
    (a) Generally have the right to vote?
    (b) Generally receive dividends declared by the board of directors?
    (c) Can be stated at either par or no par value?
2. Preferred stock?
    (a) Usually do not vote?
    (b) Usually given certain preferences to dividends and liquidation proceeds?
    (c) Can be cumulative or noncumulative?
    (d) Can be convertible or not to common stock?
    (e) Can be redeemable or nonredeemable?
3. Consideration paid for any stock legally allowable?
    (a) Model Business Corporation Act limits consideration to:
        (1) Money?
        (2) Tangible property?
        (3) Some intangibles?
        (4) Past services already performed for the corporation?
    (b) Revised Model Business Corporation Act is more permissive and allows consideration to be anything of benefit to the corporation?
        (1) Includes all of the items allowed under MBCA?
        (2) Plus promissory notes and promises of future services?
4. Once shares are issued, they must be classified as:
    (a) Authorized?
    (b) Issued?
    (c) Outstanding?
    (d) Treasury?
5. In addition, certain contracts with regard to shares may be entered into. They are classified as:
    (a) Stock options?
    (b) Stock warrants?

G. Assuming debt financing is used by the corporation, what are the main options available?
    1. Debenture?
        (a) Long term note?
        (b) Unsecured?
    2. Bonds?
        (a) Long term notes?
        (b) Secured?
    3. Note?
        (a) Shorter term?
        (b) Can be either secured or unsecured?

H. What are the basic rights and duties of shareholders as set out in the formation of the corporation?
    1. Election of board of directors?
        (a) Regular meetings?
            (1) Per articles of incorporation or by-laws?
            (2) Per minimum statutory requirements?
            (3) Proper notice?
        (b) Proxies?
            (1) Per model acts?
            (2) Per articles of incorporation or by-laws?
            (3) Per Securities Exchange Act of 1934?

(c) Voting rights?
    (1) Per model acts?
    (2) Noncumulative?
    (3) Cumulative?
    (4) Voting agreements applicable?
        (aa) Shareholder agreement?
        (bb) Voting trust?

2. Supramajority issue?
   (a) Per articles of incorporation or bylaws?
   (b) Examples of supramajority issues?
    (1) Mergers?
    (2) Acquisitions?
    (3) Sales of business?
    (4) Consolidation?
   (c) Procedures for changes to supramajority voting rules?
    (1) Per model acts?
    (2) Per articles of incorporation or by-laws?

3. Shareholder's right to transfer shares?
   (a) Per model acts?
   (b) Per articles of incorporation or by-laws?
   (c) Any transfer restrictions?
    (1) Right of first refusal?
    (2) Buy/sell agreement?
    (3) Preemptive purchase rights?
   (d) Procedures to replace lost or stolen shares?

4. Other rights of shareholders (assuming proper motive shown)?
   (a) Inspect books?
   (b) Obtain financial statements?

5. Consequences to shareholders, directors, management, and third parties for wrongful denial or use of shareholders limited management powers?

I. What are the basic rights and duties of the board of directors in the formation of a corporation?

1. To formulate basic policy decisions?
   (a) Appointing, paying, and removing management?
   (b) Which businesses should the corporation be engaged in?
   (c) Declaring dividends?
    (1) Proper?
    (2) Liability for improper declaration?
   (d) Any other basic major policy decisions?

2. Meetings of the board of directors?
   (a) Time and place?
   (b) Quorum?
   (c) Votes taken?

3. Delegation of duties?
   (a) To subcommittees of directors?
   (b) To management officers?

4. Results of wrongful acts of directors?

J. What are the basic rights and duties of officers of the corporation?

1. Agency law controls?
   (a) Actual express authority?
   (b) Actual implied authority?
   (c) Apparent authority?

2. Responsible for day to day operation of the corporation?

3. Results of wrongful acts of officers of the corporation?

IV. Objective Questions:

Terms:

1. The articles of incorporation must identify the _____ _____ of the corporation, which is the person empowered to accept service of process on behalf of the corporation.

2. Very strict procedures must be followed when incorporating. If these procedures are not followed exactly, but there is substantial compliance with them, the resulting organization is known as a(n) _____ _____ _____ under the common law.

3. Promoters frequently enter contracts on behalf of the corporation prior to incorporation. Through the process of _____, the corporation becomes solely liable on such contracts, and the promoter is completely relieved of liability with respect to such contracts.

4. When a corporation sells equity securities, it can choose to establish a _____ _____ for those securities which represents the lowest price at which the shares may be issued by the corporation.

5. In some situations, stockholders have the right to be paid a missed dividend before common stockholders can receive any dividends. Stock possessing such rights is known as _____ _____ _____.

6. Shares repurchased by the corporation are known as _____ _____ while held by the corporation. Such shares cannot be voted by the corporation and are not entitled to dividends.

7. A security that does not represent an ownership interest in a corporation but instead represents money borrowed from the investor is known as a(n) _____ _____.

8. Corporations typically maintain a list of the names and addresses of shareholders with detail indicating the number of shares owned by each. Such a list is referred to as a(n) _____ _____.

9. When a significant event is being approved by the shareholders such as a merger, consolidation, or sale of substantially all of the corporate assets, the articles of incorporation or by-laws frequently require a _____ which means that a greater number of shares is required to constitute a quorum than in other common voting situations.

10. Under the Internal Revenue Code, a certain type of corporation is allowed to act as a conduit for tax purposes and allow its owners to report the income of the corporation on their individual returns. This corporation is known as _____ _____.

True/False:

1. ____A corporation must be incorporated in each state in which it chooses to do business.

2. ____The purpose for which a corporation is formed must be specific and must be stated in the articles of incorporation.

3. ____Following incorporation, a corporation automatically becomes liable for contracts entered into by the promoter on behalf of the corporation.

4. ____Preferred stock is like common stock in that its owners are entitled to dividend distributions. However, unlike common stockholders, preferred stockholders are personally liable for debts and obligations of the corporation.

5. ____If a corporation adopts the contracts of the promoter, the promoter is released from liability with respect to that contract.

6. ____Special shareholders meetings are held to elect directors, choose an independent auditor, or to take similar actions.

7. ____The shares of a deceased, incompetent, or otherwise legally disabled person may not be voted unless such shareholder had previously granted a valid proxy authorizing another to vote his or her shares in the event of such disabilities.

8. ____If an election of directors is not held, current members of the board will serve until they are replaced.

9. ____In most situations, two-thirds of the shares entitled to vote must be represented before there is a quorum to hold a meeting of shareholders.

10. ____The board of directors is responsible for the day to day operations of the corporation, including such tasks as hiring and firing employees, negotiating contracts on behalf of the corporation, and the like.

Multiple Choice:

1. The Hellen-Julie Corporation filed its articles of incorporation with the state, but forgot to include one significant item of information required by the statute. Nevertheless, the state overlooked the omission and issued Hellen-Julie a corporate charter. Under common law, Hellen-Julie will be operating as a:
   A. Nonincorporated association.
   B. Partnership.
   C. *De facto* corporation.
   D. *De jure* corporation.

2. Ms. Margaux was the principal promoter of the New Wine Corporation. Prior to its incorporation, Margaux contracted to purchase $10,000 of inventory in the name of New Wine Corporation. The seller was not aware that New Wine did not yet exist. Who is liable on the contract?
   A. New Wine unless it rescinds the contract.
   B. Margaux unless New Wine adopts the contract.
   C. Margaux because she had no authority to contract for New Wine.
   D. New Wine because a promoter has authority to enter into preincorporation contracts.

3. Lord Byron entered into a contract in his own name to purchase, for $750,000, land zoned for industrial purposes. Immediately thereafter, Lord Byron formed the Tort Mining Corporation, retaining 50 percent of the stock and a seat on the board. At the first board of directors meeting, Lord Byron influenced the members to purchase the land for $1 million, its appraised fair market value, without disclosing his gain. With respect to the $250,000 of profit:
   A. Tort Mining Corporation may return title to the land and receive its money back.
   B. Lord Byron is liable to Tort Mining Corporation for the amount of profit.
   C. Lord Byron is not liable since he did not own more than 50 percent of the stock and the board voted on the purchase.
   D. Tort Mining Corporation has no recourse because the judgment of the board of directors was conclusive under the circumstances.

316

4. In general, which of the following must be contained in articles of incorporation?
   A. The names of states in which the corporation will be doing business.
   B. The name of the state in which the corporation will maintain its principal place of business.
   C. The names of the initial officers and their term of office.
   D. The classes of stock authorized for issuance.

5. Jack and Jill have been conducting business as the J & J Corporation for years despite the fact that they never made any attempt to incorporate. They have never filed documents with the state concerning their corporate status. Humpty entered a contract with J & J Corporation to supply water pails. Humpty did not know that the corporation had not been formally incorporated. Jack and Jill breached the contract by failing to pay for the pails. Which of the following statements is correct?
   A. Jack and Jill are liable to Humpty because they are principals with relation to each other.
   B. Jack and Jill are liable to Humpty because J & J Corporation is a *de jure* corporation.
   C. J & J Corporation is a *de facto* corporation and, therefore, Humpty cannot dispute the existence.
   D. Jack and Jill are liable to Humpty as partners, unless they are estopped from denying the existence of J & J Corporation.

6. Assume the same facts as in question 5, except that Jack and Jill persuade Humpty to purchase stock in the corporation. Humpty does not participate in the management of the business. Which of the following is correct?

   A. An outsider contracting with the corporation will be estopped to deny the existence of the corporation because his expectation was that only the corporation would be liable on such contracts.
   B. Jack and Jill will be required to file articles of incorporation if a third party reports their failure to file to the appropriate state office.
   C. Humpty will not be liable to a third party on a contract entered into by Jack or Jill in the name of the corporation.
   D. Both A and C above.

7. ABC Corporation has been very successful. However, it did not pay any dividends in the past year. Hank is a holder of ABC stock with a cumulative dividend preference. If a dividend is declared this year, Hank will receive a dividend:
   A. For last year in preference to common stockholders but participate with common stockholders for this year's dividends.
   B. For this year only, but before any common stockholder is entitled to be paid a dividend.
   C. For last year before the common stockholders receive anything.
   D. For two years before the common stockholders receive anything.

8. The articles of incorporation of the Barton Corporation provide for 1,000 shares of preferred stock and 10,000 shares of common stock. If nothing is stated in the articles with respect to voting rights, the number of shares entitled to vote at a shareholders' meeting is:
   A. 1,000.
   B. 10,000.
   C. 0.
   D. 11,000.

317

9. Earl Eager recently made an aggressive investment in Barton Corporation by purchasing 9,000 shares of common stock. In an attempt to protect his investment and assure the profitability of the corporation, Earl has been negotiating what he considers to be favorable contracts for the corporation. With respect to Earl's authority to enter into contracts on behalf of the corporation, which of the following is correct?

A. Earl has actual express authority to contract on behalf of the corporation.

B. Earl has actual implied authority to contract on behalf of the corporation.

C. Earl has apparent authority to contract on behalf of the corporation.

D. None of the above.

10. Earl believes that Barton Corporation should declare a dividend. Which of the following statements is correct in this situation?

A. Dividends are paid at the discretion of the board of directors.

B. Shareholders may approve a dividend by a two-thirds vote of all issued and outstanding shares.

C. A committee of the board of directors may be appointed to determine when, where, and how much should be paid in dividends.

D. None of the above.

V. Answers to Objective Questions

Terms:

1. *Registered agent.* This person is usually an individual attorney or law firm who has an established relationship with the company. When businesses seek to establish themselves out of the jurisdiction in which they are incorporated, most states will request the business to designate a registered agent under its jurisdiction.

2. *De jure corporation.* The term *de jure* denotes a condition in which there has been a total compliance with all the requirements of the law. In corporate law, this means the corporation has been created as a result of compliance with all of the constitutional and statutory requirements of the state of incorporation. The RMBCA has eliminated many of the former distinctions between a *de jure* and a *de facto* corporation.

3. *Ratification.* Ratification is but one of several methods by which contracts originally entered into by promoters with third parties are shifted over to the corporation once it comes into existence legally. Other methods include novation and adoption.

4. *Par value.* The face or stated value of a share of stock. This value has little significance vis-a-vis the real market value of the stock. The RMBCA has eliminated the requirement of a par value.

5. *Cumulative preferred stock.* Under this arrangement, dividends accumulate until paid. They must be totally paid before the common stockholders receive their dividends. These provisions are written in so as to provide greater incentives and assurances to potential investors in the company.

6. *Treasury shares.* These shares are originally issued by a company but then reacquired. They may be held in the company's treasury indefinitely,

reissued to the public, or retired. The RMBCA and a number of state statutes have eliminated the concept of treasury shares.

7. *Debt security.* These securities establish a debtor/creditor relationship in which the corporation borrows money from the investor to whom the debt security is issued. The most commonly used forms of debt security are unsecured debentures and collateralized bonds.

8. *Stock register.* Many statutes require formal notification to the corporation of any changes in ownership so that they could be recorded on this list.

9. *Supramajority.* This number may be set out in the article of incorporation and falls typically somewhere between two-thirds and three-quarters of the voting shares. In addition, some state statute require these percentages for certain votes on organic changes to the corporation.

10. *S Corporation.* These companies must comply with the provisions of Section 1361 *et seq.* of the Internal Revenue Code. These sections specifically limit the number of shareholders allowed to take advantage of the double taxation avoidance provided.

True/False:

1. False. A corporation can only be incorporated in one state even though it can do business in all other states in which it qualifies.

2. False. Although the purpose must be stated in the articles of incorporation, a corporation can be formed for any lawful purpose, and no specific purpose need be stated.

3. False. A corporation becomes liable on a promoter's contract only if it agrees to

become bound to the contract by either ratification, adoption, or novation.

4. False. Like common shareholders, preferred shareholders have limited liability.

5. False. A promoter is only relieved of liability on promoter's contracts following adoption by the corporation if the third party agrees to release him.

6. False. Special meetings are held to consider important or emergency issues such as merger or consolidation, removal of directors, or the like. The election of directors and similar actions occur at annual shareholders meetings.

7. False. The shares of a deceased, incompetent, or otherwise legally disabled person may be voted by the legal representative of such an individual.

8. True. Usually, directors serve a one year term. However, if no election is held, the directors serve until a successor is appointed.

9. False. Unless otherwise provided, only a majority of shares entitled to vote need be represented to have a quorum.

10. False. The board of directors is responsible for formulating the policy decisions affecting the management, supervision, and control of the operation of the corporation.

Multiple Choice:

1. C. A *de facto* corporation occurs where there has been a good faith attempt to organize the corporation pursuant to statute. A *de jure* corporation occurs where there has been complete or substantial compliance with the statute. These common law rules have been changed by those states which have adopted the RMBCA.

319

2. C. A promoter must contract in her own name because the corporation is a nonexistent entity. Therefore, unless the corporation adopts, ratifies, or enters a novation with respect to such contract, Margaux remains liable.

3. B. A promoter owes a fiduciary duty to disclose all relevant information. Promoters are liable for any secret profits made by or damages caused by a breach of this duty. Lord Byron is liable to Tort Mining Corporation for the amount of the profit.

4. D. The articles of incorporation should contain the corporation's name, purpose, powers, and other important information in addition to the amount and types of stock authorized. These rules vary in specificity from state to state.

5. D. Promoters are jointly liable on their contracts in those situations where the corporation never comes into existence.

6. D. A third party who deals with the enterprise as if it were a corporation is estopped from challenging its validity.

7. D. Cumulative preferred stock entitles the holders to be paid in the future before any dividends can be paid to common stockholders.

8. D. Unless provided otherwise, each common and preferred share is entitled to one vote.

9. D. Although shareholders are the owners of a corporation, they are not agents of the corporation and have no authority to bind the corporation to contracts.

10. A. The directors as a whole, not as a committee, are responsible for determining when, where, how, and how much will be paid in dividends.

VI. Key Question Checklist Answers to Essay Question:

A. *Have the proper procedures for incorporating been complied with?*

It appears that Mr. Fossa did at least initially prepare the proper documentation for the incorporation of Relievo Brand Incorporated. The state of Kannabras has an incorporation statute which can be used to incorporate a new business in that state. As with all such statues, certain substantive and procedural measures must be taken in order to properly comply with the statute before articles or a certificate of incorporation will be issued. These requirements include a number of items of information which must be supplied to the state such as names and addresses of the key parties as well as agents for service of process. In addition, the purpose for which the business is incorporated must be a lawful one. In this case, the underlying purpose of the business, to engage in organic farming, is not unlawful. But, because it is an activity which can affect the health and welfare of its citizens, the state of Kannabras can regulate the activity under its general police power.

B. *Assume there has been an effort to incorporate, but not all the requirements of incorporation have been complied with under common law.*

Had Harvey and Harry complied with the state's request to submit their products to health inspection, they most likely would have had *de jure* corporation. With the creation of a *de jure* corporation, they would have been entitled to one of the biggest benefits of using the corporate form--limited personal liability. A *de jure* corporation was not formed here.

Because they did not form a *de jure* corporation under the common law, Harvey,

Harry, and the directors might be personally liable for the debts of the corporation unless they can show some other public policy based excuse from that liability. Several possibilities exist under the common law.

They can first argue that they sought to get incorporated in good faith and should now be treated as a *de facto* corporation. Or in the alternative, they can argue that it would be an unjust enrichment to third party creditors to allow such creditors to go after them personally when they thought they were dealing with a corporation. On both accounts, the ultimate answer will rest on how the court defines the good faith efforts of Harvey, Harry, and the board to incorporate. Given the fact that they intentionally refused to submit their products to health inspectors in direct violation of a regulatory requirement of the state, it appears unlikely that they will be able to avoid personal liability.

C. *What if Kannabras had adopted the Revised Model Business Corporation Act (RMBCA)?*

The RMBCA provides that corporate existence begins when the articles of incorporation are filed. The Secretary of State's filing of the articles of incorporation is conclusive proof that the incorporators satisfied all the conditions of incorporation. After that, only the state can bring a proceeding to cancel or revoke the incorporation or involuntarily dissolve the corporation. Third parties cannot thereafter challenge the existence of the corporation or raise it as a defense against the corporation.

The corollary of this rule is: failure to file articles of incorporation is conclusive proof of the nonexistence of the corporation. If a failure to file has taken place, the purported shareholders of the corporation are exposed to personal liability for the debts and obligations of the purported corporation. In this case, if the Kannabras Secretary of State preconditioned the filing to compliance with the health regulations, the filing may be deemed not to have ever taken place. Under the RMBCA, this would then result in personal liability for Harvey and Harry. If, in turn, the filing was allowed to go through by the Secretary of Sate in spite of the problems with the health code, then the RMBCA would deem the filing to be conclusive proof of incorporation. With that proof, Harvey, Harry, and the members of the board of directors could claim limited personal liability from the debts and obligations of the corporation.

D. *How will this corporation be classified?*

It would be classified as a domestic, for profit, closely held corporation.

E. *Which of the promoter's activities are now ended or continued?*

Assuming the corporation is formal, the contracts with the various suppliers would be assumed by the corporation. Whether or not the promoters would continue to remain personally liable would depend on the format used. If the contracts are ratified or renegotiated by way of a novation, then the promoters would be relieved of any further liability. Under an adoption, they would continue to be liable unless released by the suppliers.

F-J. *How will the corporation be funded, and what will be the basic rights and duties of the shareholders, directors, and management upon formation?*

Assuming that Harvey and Harry will be the only owners of common stock in this closely held corporation, they will have to provide legally acceptable consideration for the shares. As owners of common shares, they will be entitled to vote for board members and receive dividends declared by the board. Under this case scenario, no debt financing was used by Relievo Brand Incorporated.

The basic rights of the shareholders, directors, and managers upon formation of the corporation will be based on the articles of incorporation and the applicable laws of Kannabras as illustrated with regard to the common law versus RMBCA rules on filing.

CHAPTER 36

POWERS AND MANAGEMENT OF CORPORATIONS

To know is neither to prove, nor to explain. It is to accede to vision.

Antoine de Saint-Exupéry

I. Overview:

When most people are asked about the associations they have with the word "corporations," they think of the large companies mentioned in the financial news of the day. Usually this group of companies will encompass those entities listed in the Fortune 500, the Dow Jones Industrial, or those companies publicly traded on the New York or American Stock Exchanges. In terms of financial importance, those companies certainly do dominate the corporate landscape.

The world of corporations has, however, a much less public face-the face of the closely held corporation. A close corporation is defined by *Blacks Law Dictionary* as "one wherein the shares are held by a single or closely-knit group of shareholders. Generally there are no public investors and its shareholders are active in the conduct of the business." The vast majority of for profit business entities using the corporate form are, in fact, closely held. Only five percent or fewer of all corporations are publicly traded. In the world of closely held corporations, stock ownership is not widely dispersed, and control is held in virtual perpetuity through proxies and other mechanisms.

What is interesting about this two-sided (public vs. closed) corporate landscape is that, except for some special rules set out in individual state close corporation statutes, the rules of the corporate game are virtually the same for both. The basic rights, duties, and expectations of shareholders, directors, and corporate officers are the same "on paper" of both large and small corporations. The reality is far different. The hows, whys, and wherefores of control over, say G.M., is a whole world different from how a small family business is controlled. The rules of the game must, however, be complied with by both entities. Keeping that "real world" perspective in mind, the key question checklist is designed to set out the basic rights, duties, and obligations of the shareholders, directors, and officers of the corporation. Remember, however, where most people get in trouble in corporate law is in not in being good directors or managers when they have several legal hats to wear and fail to keep their multiple roles distinct from one another.

II. Hypothetical Multi-Issue Essay Question:

Mr. Brian Keyboard was born with the right name. He simply loved sitting at the controls of his Super-duper Model XYZ, ten mega-bite personal computer all day. His passion was to create new and convoluted games wherein little tiny electronic characters would maim and mutilate other little tiny characters on his screen. This battle to the electronic death would mesmerize Brian for hours at a time until he just dropped from fatigue. As fate would have it, one of Brian's programs was quite a hit on the video-game market. "Getsu et Fama" was a runaway hit because it could hypnotize most young players for up to four hours at a time. Brian's attorney, Homagio Respectuando, has arranged for Brian to incorporate his business as "Getsu et Fama Be Me," and has made Brian's family majority shareholders in the new business. They were also made members of the board of directors. Brian is content with his role as Chief Researcher and Minor Vice-President in charge of testing. He really didn't want to pay any attention to trifling business matters when he could be concentrating on his videogames. He did, however, retain the patent on him games in his own name.

Last year, the corporation made $10 million. Brian's family and his attorney ran off to Rio with most of it. Now Brian is being sued in a class action lawsuit for millions by parents who can't get their children out of the hypnotic trance induced by the Gestu et Fama video game. What result?

III. Key Question Checklist:

A. What are the basic rights and duties of a shareholder in the management of a corporation?
   1. Election of board of directors?
      (a) Regular meeting?
         (1) Per articles of incorporation or by-laws?
         (2) Per minimum statutory requirements?
         (3) Proper notice?
      (b) Proxies?
         (1) Per model acts?
         (2) Per articles of incorporation or by-laws?
         (3) Per Securities Exchange Act of 1934?
      (c) Voting rights?
         (1) Per model acts?
         (2) Noncumulative?
         (3) Cumulative?
         (4) Voting agreements applicable?
            (aa) Shareholder agreement?
            (bb) Voting trust?
   2. Supramajority issue?
      (a) Per articles of incorporation or by-laws?

      (b) Examples of supramajority issues?
         (1) Mergers?
         (2) Acquisitions?
         (3) Sales of business?
         (4) Consolidation?
      (c) Procedures for changes to supramajority voting rules?
         (1) Per model acts?
         (2) Per articles of incorporation or by-laws?
   3. Shareholder's right to transfer shares?
      (a) Per model acts?
      (b) Per articles of incorporation or by-laws?
      (c) Any transfer restrictions?
         (1) Right of first refusal?
         (2) Buy/sell agreement?
         (3) Preemptive purchase rights?
      (d) Procedures to replace lost or stolen shares?
   4. Other rights of shareholders (assuming proper motive shown)?
      (a) Inspect books?
      (b) Obtain financial statements?
   5. Consequences to shareholders, directors, management, and third parties for wrongful denial or use of shareholders limited management powers?

B. What are the basic rights and duties of the board of directors in the management of a corporation?
   1. To formulate basic policy decisions?
      (a) Appointing, paying, and removing management?
      (b) Which businesses the cor-poration should be engaged in?
      (c) Declaring dividends?
         (1) Proper?
         (2) Liability for improper declaration?
      (d) Any other basic major policy decisions?

324

2. Meetings of the board of directors?
   (a) Time and place?
   (b) Quorum?
   (c) Votes taken?
3. Delegation of duties?
   (a) To subcommittees of directors?
   (b) To management officers?
4. Results of wrongful acts of directors?

C. What are the basic rights and duties of officers of the corporation?
   1. Agency law controls?
      (a) Actual express authority?
      (b) Actual implied authority?
      (c) Apparent authority?
   2. Responsible for day to day operation of the corporation?
   3. Results of wrongful acts of officers of the corporation?

IV. Objective Questions:

Terms:

1. Corporations typically maintain a list of the names and addresses of shareholders with detail indicating the number of shares owned by each. Such a list is referred to as a(n) _____ _____.

2. A written document by which one shareholder authorizes another to vote her shares in her absence is referred to as a(n) _____.

3. In any given year, the directors of a corporation may choose not to distribute profits of the corporation, but rather to invest such profits for specific corporate purposes. In such situations, these profits are called _____ _____.

4. When determining which shareholders are entitled to receive a dividend, or which shareholders are entitled to vote at a given meeting, the directors look to who owned the shares on the _____ _____.

5. When a significant event is being approved by the shareholders such as a merger, consolidation, or a sale of substantially all of the corporate assets, the articles of incorporation or by-laws frequently require a _____ which means that a greater number of shares is required to constitute a quorum than in other common voting situations.

6. There are several voting methods used when electing directors of a corporation. The method by which each shareholder is entitled to vote the number of shares she owns for each position is called the _____ _____.

7. An arrangement by which shareholders relinquish the right to vote their shares to another who is empowered pursuant to this arrangement to vote such shares is called a _____ _____. The shareholders in such situations retain all incidents of ownership other than the right to vote.

8. If a stock certificate has been lost, stolen, or destroyed, the corporation is required to issue a _____ _____.

9. Often, a shareholder with a minority ownership percentage is very concerned with maintaining that percentage. Some state statutes provide such shareholders with _____ _____ entitling them to purchase a proportional number of new shares issued by the corporation.

10. Frequently, certain individuals serve as both officers and directors of a corporation. Such individuals are referred to as _____ _____.

True/False:

1. ____ Special shareholders meetings are held to elect directors, choose an independent auditor, or to take similar actions.

2. ____ The shares of a deceased, incompetent, or otherwise legally disabled person may not be voted unless such shareholder had previously granted a valid proxy authorizing another to vote his or her shares in the event of such disabilities.

3. ____ Shareholders may take action without a shareholders meeting if all of the corporate shareholders sign a written consent approving such action.

4. ____ If an election of directors is not held, current members of the board will serve until they are replaced.

5. ____ In most situations, two-thirds of the shares entitled to vote must be represented before there is a quorum to hold a meeting of shareholders.

6. ____ If a legal quorum is present, the affirmative vote of a majority of the shares comprising the quorum is sufficient to constitute an act of the shareholders.

7. ____ The board of directors is responsible for the day to day operations of the corporation, including such tasks as hiring and firing employees, negotiating contracts on behalf of the corporation, and the like.

8. ____ A vacant position on the board of directors can be filled by a majority vote of the remaining directors.

9. ____ The board of directors may remove any officer of the corporation with or without cause, but only if the board determines that such removal will be in the best interest of the corporation.

10. ____ If a corporate officer has actual express authority to enter into contracts on behalf of the corporation, such officer will not be personally liable for such contracts.

Multiple Choice:

1. Some of the shareholders of Sonia, Inc. want to be more involved with the corporation. Which of the following issues do shareholders vote on?
   A. Loan to a major shareholder.
   B. Government contracts.
   C. Election of board of directors.
   D. Appointment of corporate officers.

2. Sabrina and Aspen are two corporations, the shares of which are publicly traded. Aspen plans to merge with Sabrina. Which of the following is a requirement of the merger?
   A. The IRS must approve the merger.
   B. The common stockholders of Aspen must receive common stock of Sabrina.
   C. The creditors of Aspen must approve the merger.
   D. The boards of directors of both Sabrina and Aspen must approve the merger.

3. Polly Particular owns 800 shares of common stock of Fly By Night Corporation. Polly has always taken her rights as a shareholder very seriously. If the articles of incorporation authorize cumulative voting and four directors are to be elected at the next shareholders' meeting, how many votes is Polly entitled to?
   A. 800.
   B. 3,200.
   C. 8,000.
   D. 32,000.

4. Assume the same facts as in question 3. Assume in addition that Polly sold her shares to Carl Careless. Three weeks later, the corporation declared a cash dividend. Polly was listed as the record owner of the shares on the date the dividend was declared. Who is entitled to the dividend?
   A. Polly.
   B. Carl.
   C. Polly and Carl in equal amounts.
   D. Fly By Night Corporation.

5. Assume the same facts as in question 4. Upon the sale of her shares to Carl Careless, which of the following actions will be necessary to record the transfer on the books of the corporation?
   A. Polly must merely deliver the share certificates to Carl.
   B. Polly will only be required to indorse the share certificates to Carl.
   C. Polly must not indorse and deliver the share certificates to Carl.
   D. Polly must surrender the share certificates to the corporation and new certificates will be issued in Carl's name.

6. The articles of incorporation of the Barton Corporation provide for 1,000 shares of preferred stock and 10,000 shares of common stock. If nothing is stated in the articles with respect to voting rights, the number of shares entitled to vote at a shareholders' meeting is:
   A. 1,000.
   B. 10,000.
   C. 0.
   D. 11,000.

7. Earl Eager recently made an aggressive investment in Barton Corporation by purchasing 9,000 shares of common stock. In an attempt to protect his investment and assure the profitability of the corporation, Earl has been negotiating what he considers to be favorable contracts for the corporation. With respect to Earl's authority to enter into contracts on behalf of the corporation, which of the following is correct?
   A. Earl has actual express authority to contract on behalf of the corporation.
   B. Earl has actual implied authority to contract on behalf of the corporation.
   C. Earl has apparent authority to contract on behalf of the corporation.
   D. None of the above.

8. Earl is unable to attend the upcoming shareholders' meeting of Barton Corporation. Because of his concern for protecting his investment, he gives written direction and authorization to his sister, Earline, to vote his shares. Which of the following statements is correct?
   A. If Earl changes his mind, he cannot revoke the proxy because it is in writing.
   B. The arrangement between Earl and Earline is invalid because it violates public policy.
   C. Earline cannot vote the shares if she is not also a shareholder of Barton Corporation.
   D. The federal securities laws prohibit the use of proxies.
   E. All of the above.
   F. None of the above.

9. Earl believes that Barton Corporation should declare a dividend. Which of the following statements is correct in this situation?
   A. Dividends are paid at the discretion of the board of directors.
   B. Shareholders may approve a dividend by a two-thirds vote of all issued and outstanding shares.
   C. A committee of the board of directors may be appointed to determine when, where and how much should be paid in dividends.
   D. None of the above.

10. If the board of directors of Barton declares a dividend, which of the following statements is correct?
   A. Once declared, a dividend cannot be revoked.
   B. Dividends can be paid in either cash or property.

   C. If the directors declare a stock dividend, such a dividend will not be considered a distribution of corporate assets.
   D. All of the above.

V. Answers to Objective Questions:

Terms:

1. *Stock register.* This list is not only required for purposes of record keeping, but is also used to establish cut off dates for dividends and the like.
2. *Proxy.* The proxy is an agency appointment for purposes of voting at the shareholder's meeting. If you see the term "proxy fight," it refers to a contest over undecided shareholders votes by competing factions.
3. *Retained earnings.* The determination of how large this fund may be is affected not only by business judgment, but also compliance with tax laws.
4. *Record date.* See notes vis-a-vis stock register in the answer to question 1.
5. *Supramajority.* Depending on the individual provisions of state corporation statutes, a supramajority can range anywhere from two-thirds to as high as ninety percent of voting shareholders.
6. *Noncumulative method.* This method provides less protection for the numerical minority shareholders than is afforded by the cumulative method of voting. It is also referred to as the straight voting method.
7. *Voting trust.* Per section 7.30 of the RMBCA, the voting trust agreement must be in writing and cannot exceed ten years.

8. *Replacement certificate.* In order to get this certificate, the shareholder must post an indemnity bond to protect the corporation from loss in case the original certificate finds its way into the hands of a bona fide purchaser.

9. *Cumulative voting.* This method gives a minority shareholder a better opportunity to elect someone to the board of directors and is provided for by section 7.28 of the RMBCA.

10. *Inside directors.* This member of the board is also an officer of the corporation. Most members of closely-held corporation boards are classified as inside directors.

True/False:

1. False. Special meetings are held to consider important or emergency issues such as merger or consolidation, removal of directors or the like. The election of directors and similar actions occur at annual shareholders meetings.

2. False. The shares of a deceased, incompetent or otherwise legally disabled person may be voted by the legal representative of such individuals.

3. True. Most state corporation statutes allow for this exigency.

4. True. Usually, directors serve a one year term. However, if no election is held, the directors serve until a successor is appointed.

5. False. Unless otherwise provided, only a majority of shares entitled to vote need be represented to have a quorum.

6. True. Most normal business can be done by a simple majority vote. Certain "organic" changes require a supramajority vote.

7. False. The board of directors is responsible for formulating the policy decisions affecting the management, supervision and control of the operation of the corporation.

8. True. Most state corporate statutes allow for this only to the extent of the unexpired term of the vacant position.

9. True. This is allowed under the employment at will doctrine and is subject to contract and/or public policy limitations.

10. False. A corporate officer can be held personally liable for contracts entered into on behalf of the corporation if such officer fails to sign the contract in an agency capacity or fails to disclose the identity of the corporation.

Multiple Choice:

1. C. Shareholders elect the board of directors unless a director position becomes vacant mid-term, in which case a majority of the remaining directors may select a replacement.

2. D. The merger of two corporations requires the approval from the boards of directors of both corporations. In addition, the shareholders of each corporation must normally approve the merger. Also, government approval may be necessary if there are antitrust issues raised by the merger.

3. B. Where cumulative voting is authorized, a shareholder is entitled to the number of votes resulting from multiplying the number of shares held by the number of positions to be filled.

4. A. When a corporation declares a dividend, it sets a date usually a few weeks prior to the actual payment that is called the record date. Persons who are shareholders on that date are entitled to receive the dividend even if they sell their shares before the payment date.

5. D. Usually, shares are transferred by endorsing and delivering them to the purchaser. However, where the shares are not issued in a street name, it may be necessary to reissue new shares in Carl's name.

6. D. Unless provided otherwise, each common and preferred share is entitled to one vote.

7. D. Although shareholders are the owners of a corporation, they are not agents of the corporation and have no authority to bind the corporation to contracts.

8. F. Generally proxies are revocable, unless coupled with an interest. Neither public policy nor the federal securities laws prohibit the use of proxies, although the securities laws regulate the solicitation of proxies. And finally, one need not be a shareholder to vote shares as a proxy.

9. A. The directors as a whole, not as a committee, are responsible for determining when, where, how and how much will be paid in dividends.

10. D. A, B, and C are correct.

VI. Key Question Checklist Answers to Essay Question:

A. *What are the basic rights and duties of a shareholder in the management of a corporation?*

Brian is both lucky and unlucky in this scenario. He is lucky because he obviously has many talents and will probably go on to invent better and safer video games long after this unpleasant episode is closed. He is unlucky in that he may have failed to properly distinguish his personal activities form his corporate activities. As a shareholder in his corporation, Brian is considered a part owner in the eyes of

the law. But unlike a proprietor or partner, a shareholder cannot normally act as an agent for the corporation vis-a-vis third parties. A shareholder's management abilities are limited to election to the board of directors and voting on fundamental changes in the corporation. Here Brian seems to have allowed family members to appropriate those roles for themselves by allowing them to own a majority of the shares. By letting himself become so preoccupied with his videogame development activities, he has inadvertently given up control of his own company.

B. *What are the basic rights and duties of the board of directors in the management of a corporation?*

The board of directors is charged with the basic fiduciary duties to make policy decisions in the best interests of the corporation. They must meet regularly to exercise those duties. They can be held liable for wrongful acts which are in breach of these duties. The family members here clearly violated their duty to the corporation by running off with corporate assets to Rio. If they can be located, they can be both civilly and criminally responsible for their actions. In the meantime, Brian still has problems.

C. *What are the basic rights and duties of officers in the management of a corporation?*

Brian is an officer of the company as Minor Vice President in charge of research and testing of videogames. He has express authority to act for the corporation with regard to the safety and suitability of the games sold in the corporate name. As an agent in charge of research and testing, he has express authority to act for the corporation with regard to the safety and suitability of the games sold in the corporate name. As an agent of the corporation, he may be exposed to personal liability in tort law as well as having the company liable as his principal. In addition, as owner of the patent, the plaintiffs may seek to hold Brian personally liable by seeking to pierce the corporate veil. This is the judicial process whereby the court may choose to disregard the corporate form. In the meantime, Brian might consider changing careers and chose to work as a star war games consultant for the Defense Department.

CHAPTER 37

LIABILITY OF CORPORATE DIRECTORS, OFFICERS, AND SHAREHOLDERS

One of the secrets of life is that all that is really worth the doing is what we do for others.

Lewis Carroll

I. Overview:

Erosion is defined as a gradual wearing away or disintegration. The wall of limited liability for corporations and their main protagonists has suffered from a steady erosion over the past several decades. The flood wall is still holding, but the holes in the dike seem to get bigger every year. What is interesting about these reductions in limited liability is that they are often initiated at the behest of other members of the same corporate family rather than outside parties. Disadvantaged shareholders, disgruntled corporate officers, and quixotic directors have all done their share of diminishing the liability immunities once held so sacred in the corporate scheme of things.

There are two basic theories under which most of the limitations to corporate entity and/or corporate participants' liability are restricted or eliminated. First, public policy never has allowed the corporate form to act as a total shield from liability to third parties. From the very inception of corporate law, courts and legislators have clung to the back door option of holding someone personally liable where circumstances deemed it appropriate. A creature of the law should not be allowed to become a tool of circumvention of the law. Thus in the areas of crimes, torts, and generally undesirable behavior, a number of corporate shield-bursting mechanisms have always been in place. These have ranged from piercing the corporate veil to outright revocation of the continued existence of the corporation. In all these cases, the underlying premise is that the corporate form should not allow a person to do something which would otherwise be prohibited by public policy.

The second theory is found in the intracorporate workings of the organization itself. Just as the corporate form should not be allowed to defraud creditors and the like, so too should it not be allowed to be used by various members of corporate organizations to harm each other. The cornerstone of relationships between shareholders, directors, and officers is founded in the law of fiduciaries, loyalty, and mutual support. Even though not all aspects of these interdependent relationships could ever realistically be expected to be harmonious, some common good is expected to be interwoven into their behavior towards each other. As illustrated by the cases in this chapter, some of the most vociferous battles of all are fought in the confines of the corporate boardrooms around the country.

In both external relationships and intracorporate disagreements, the willingness of the contesting parties to go public with their grievances with more frequency than ever has led to more exceptions to the rule of limited corporate liability. Time will tell whether or not this erosion bodes well for the economy. If it means a crippling of the economic engine of corporate vitality relative to comparable overseas entities, it does provide cause for alarm. If, however, it holds real wrongdoers responsible for harm, who would otherwise be shielded by the false front of a legal stage set, then it is time for the house of cards to come down.

II. Hypothetical Multi-issue Essay Question:

Mr. Clyde Catorski worked as a business manager for the famous rock group Cha Cha and the Potato Heads. The group successfully combined the best elements of Latin Disco sounds with the laid back qualities of Couch Potatoism. Clyde organized the business as a corporation under the laws of California in order to assure the group the benefits of limited liability against lawsuits. Several parents have sued the group alleging that their music turned their children into "potato heads," and that the music fostered potato cults. Under the articles of incorporation, Clyde was a minority shareholder (10 percent), an officer of the corporation, and a member of the board of directors.

Last week the band played in Erfurt and the warm-up band, named Oral Hygiene, really stole the show. Their unique blend of flashy gold teeth and ear-piercing rock sent young fans into an eczematous itching frenzy. Clyde saw the writing on the wall and immediately solicited a business management deal with the lead singer, Harry Cycloid. Their conversation resulted in a secret deal between Clyde and Harry wherein Clyde would book Oral Hygiene into concerts rather than Cha Cha and the Potato Heads. Over the next several months Cha Cha and the Potato Heads lost concert dates and tee-shirt sales worth over $1 million. Clyde, however, is doing better than ever with Oral Hygiene. Last week they played in the Root Canaldome. Cha Cha wants to sue. What result?

III. Key Question Checklist:

This key question checklist itemizes how liability can attach to corporations, directors, officers, and shareholders.

A. The first set of issues in this chapter deals with methods under which the corporate form itself may be dishonored by a court. Generally speaking, a corporation may not act beyond the scope of either its actual or implied powers. If it does so, its actions may be deemed void and liability may result. First look to see what are its:
1. Express powers?
   (a) Based on statutes?
   (b) Based on articles of incorporation?
   (c) Based only on by-laws?
   (d) Based on resolution of the board of directors?
2. Implied powers?
   (a) Power needed to accomplish corporate purposes?
   (b) Examples?
      (1) Legitimate business purposes?
      (2) Protection of corporate assets?
3. Are there express limitations on corporate power applicable?
   (a) Imposed by corporation law?
   (b) Imposed by statutes generally?
   (c) Imposed by articles of incorporation or by-laws?
   (d) Imposed by board of directors resolutions?
4. Are there implied limitations on corporate powers applicable?

B. Assuming the corporation engages in an action which is not expressly or impliedly allowed (*ultra vires*), what are the possible consequences?
1. Liability to internal members of the corporation, (shareholders, officers, and directors)?
2. Liability to external third parties including the state?

C. Assuming the corporation itself did not act improperly, but there was some sort of improper action taken by a director or officer of the company, what was the breach of fiduciary duty?

   1. Duty of obedience?

   2. Duty of care?

   3. Duty of loyalty?

     (a) Self-dealing?

     (b) Loans from the corporation?

     (c) Usurping corporate opportunity?

     (d) Competing with corporation?

     (e) Insider trading?

     (f) Disgorement of secret profits?

     (g) Actions detrimental to minority shareholders?

     (h) Other closely scrutinized actions?

D. Assuming the issue revolves around the possibilities of holding shareholders personally liable, for what actions or omissions will a shareholder be liable to third parties or the corporation?

   1. Under contract?

     (a) Subscription contract liability to the corporation?

     (b) Subscription contract liability to the third parties for "watered" stock (overvalued due to inadequate consideration)?

     (c) Failure to regard the corporate entity (may lead to personal liability to third parties)?

       (1) Examples would include:

         (aa) Not following necessary formalities of the corporate form?

         (bb) Commingling personal and corporate funds and assets?

   2. Under tort or criminal law?

     (a) Sales of stock with intent to defraud creditors?

     (b) Conversion of corporate assets to personal use?

     (c) Formed the corporation with intent to circumvent the law?

   3. Controlling shareholder's breach of fiduciary duty to minority shareholders?

     (a) Create unusual losses for minority shareholders?

     (b) Selling corporate assets to themselves at less than fair market value?

     (c) Selling interests which allow a "loot" of corporate assets?

     (d) Oppressive actions against minority shareholders?

E. Assuming the shareholder has not acted in a wrongful manner, when can he or she act against wrongful actions taken by the corporation?

   1. Direct lawsuit?

     (a) Enforce rights?

     (b) Enjoin *ultra vires* acts?

     (c) Compel dissolution?

   2. Derivative lawsuit?

     (a) Brought on behalf of the corporation by the shareholder?

     (b) Where demand has been made and refused by corporation to bring the action first?

   3. Class action lawsuit?

     (a) Brought on behalf of all members of the class?

     (b) Fairly represents the class?

     (c) Practical method of suit in this case?

IV. Objective Questions:

Terms:

1. A corporation has _____ _____ to conduct those activities necessary to operate as a business whether or not expressly provided elsewhere.

2. When a corporation performs an act that is outside its limited purpose clause or beyond the applicable statutory limitations, the corporation is said to have committed a(n) _____ _____ act.

3. The officers and directors of a corporation owe fiduciary duties to the corporation and its shareholders. The _____ _____ _____ imposes upon the officers and directors an obligation to exercise care and diligence when acting on behalf of the corporation.

4. The rule which relieves corporate officers and directors from personal liability to the corporation and the shareholders for honest mistakes of judgment is known as the _____ _____ rule.

5. Directors of a corporation subject themselves to personal liability for certain decisions made when operating in their capacity as a director. To avoid personal liability for actions of the board, an individual director must either _____ or _____ _____ _____.

6. An officer or director who is personally involved in transactions with the corporation is said to have engaged in _____ _____.

7. When a director or officer trades shares of the corporation because of personal knowledge of a nonpublic nature about the corporation, that person is said to have engaged in _____ _____.

8. The resulting suit when a shareholder brings a lawsuit that belongs to the corporation is known as a(n) _____ lawsuit.

9. The right of a director or officer to be repaid for personal litigation expenses incurred in successfully defending himself is known as _____ _____.

10. The lawsuits of many shareholders against the corporation for the same wrong can be joined into one action known as a _____ _____ lawsuit.

True/False:

1. ___ A corporation typically has express power to borrow money, incur liabilities, and issue notes and other obligations, but not to lend money to assist its employees.

2. ___ If a corporation attempts to engage in an *ultra vires* act, a shareholder can sue for an injunction to prevent the corporation from engaging in such act.

3. ___ The standard used when determining whether a director or officer has acted within the duty of care owed the corporation is whether that person used that level of care that a reasonable director would have used in the conduct of the business of another.

4. ___ A director who relied in good faith upon false or misleading information presented by a reliable employee cannot be held liable for her actions taken in reliance upon such information.

5. ___ A dissenting director may register her dissent only by entering it in the minutes of the meeting at which the action in question was taken.

6. ____ An officer may enter into a transaction with the corporation only if the transaction is fair and reasonable to the corporation.

7. ____ A director who usurps a corporate opportunity has breached her duty of loyalty owed to the corporation.

8. ____ If a corporation chooses not to sue a director for the return of secret profits made by the director, a shareholder may bring the suit and retain the secret profit recovered.

9. ____ A corporation can be held liable for the torts, but not the crimes, of its agents and employees.

10. ____ Before a shareholder is entitled to bring a derivative suit, he is generally required to show that he owned shares of the corporation at the time the wrong occurred.

Multiple Choice:

1. Ms. Nancie Jenner, a shareholder of The Rusty Corp., has properly commenced a derivative action against The Rusty Corp board of directors. Ms. Jenner alleges that the board breached its fiduciary duty and was negligent by failing to independently verify the financial statements prepared by management upon which Michael & Co., CPAs issued an unqualified opinion. The financial statements contained inaccurate information which the board relied upon in committing large sums of money to capital expansion. This resulted in The Rusty Corp. having to borrow money at extremely high interest rates to meet current cash needs. Within a short period of time, the price of The Rusty Corp. stock declined drastically. Which of the following statements is correct?

A. The board is strictly liable, regardless of fault, because it owes a fiduciary duty to both the corporation and the shareholders.

B. The board is liable because any negligence of Michael & Co., CPAs is automatically imputed to the board.

C. The board may avoid liability if it acted in good faith and in a reasonable manner.

D. The board may avoid liability in all cases where it can show that it lacked *scienter*.

2. Assume the same facts as in question 1. If the court determines that the board was negligent and the board seeks indemnification from the corporation, which of the following statements is correct?

A. The board may not be indemnified since a presumption that the board failed to act in good faith arises from the judgment.

B. The board may not be indemnified unless The Rusty Corp.'s shareholders approve such indemnification.

C. The board may be indemnified only if The Rusty Corp. provides liability insurance for its officers and directors.

D. The board may be indemnified by The Rusty Corp. if the court deems it proper.

3. The Elizabeth Corporation decided to acquire certain assets belonging to The Ernie Corporation. As consideration for the assets acquired, the Elizabeth Corporation issued 20,000 shares of its no-par common stock with a stated value of $10 per share. The value of the assets acquired subsequently turned out to be much less than the $200,000 in stock issued. Under the circumstances, which of the following is correct?

A. It is improper for the board of directors to acquire assets other than cash with no-par stock.

B. Only the shareholders can have the right to fix the value of the shares of no-par stock exchanged for assets.

C. In the absence of fraud in the transaction, the judgment of the board of directors as to the value of the consideration received for the shares shall be conclusive.

D. Unless the board obtained an independent appraisal of the acquired assets' value, it is liable to the extent of the overvaluation.

4. Ms. Kathleen Beacon is a director of both Court, Inc. and Pearl Street Corporation. Which fact requires Ms. Kathleen Beacon to make a disclosure to Court's other directors?

A. Ms. Beacon is on Pearl Street Corporation' board of directors even if Court and Pearl Street Corporation are not in competition and do no business together.

B. Pearl Street Corporation is contemplating a major purchase from Court at Court's preset prices.

C. Ms. Beacon is a limited partner in a partnership that owns a cruise ship that Court is contemplating purchasing.

D. Court is purchasing a nominal amount of supplies from Pearl Street Corporation.

5. Johnny Mephisto travels the country looking for shareholder derivative actions which can and should be brought for the betterment of mankind. Which of the following statements is correct with respect to Johnny's right to bring a derivative action?

A. Johnny must persuade at least one other shareholder to participate before he can bring a derivative action.

B. Johnny can acquire stock of a corporation in order to file a derivative action.

C. Johnny can bring a derivative action without trying to persuade the officers and directors to take action to correct the matter.

D. Johnny must have been the owner of stock of the corporation at the time of the alleged offensive action.

6. Assume the same facts as in question 5. Johnny acquires a small amount of stock in Dawgdoo Corporation and comes to you for advice concerning his rights and duties as a shareholder. Which of the following is not a right or duty of Johnny as a shareholder of Dawgdoo?

A. Johnny owes fiduciary duties to the corporation and the other shareholders when exercising his rights as a shareholder.

B. Johnny may be liable to creditors of the corporation if a court disregards the corporate entity.

C. Johnny has the right to vote in elections of directors and other elections involving essential corporate changes.

D. Johnny has the right to bring a derivative suit.

7. Mike Moore, an employee of Billy's Brewing Corporation, was involved in an automobile accident while on his way to an alcoholic's cure meeting one evening after work. Vicki Victim has brought suit against Mike and Billy's Brewing Corporation. Which of the following statements is correct?
   A. Mike is liable for his own negligence whether or not the corporation is also liable.
   B. The corporation is liable for Mike's negligence because it was a foreseeable consequence of Mike's employment.
   C. The corporation is not liable for Mike's negligence because the accident occurred after business hours.
   D. Both A and C.

8. Phil Playboy was elected to the board of directors of HiTech Corporation several years ago. Phil is much more concerned about the prestige of being a corporate director than he was about the duties involved. He has not attended a board meeting in two years. During that time, the president made some very bad loans resulting in serious financial loss to the corporation. Which of the following statements is correct?
   A. Phil has no liability because he merely exercised poor business judgment by missing the meetings.
   B. Phil has no liability because missing the meetings was an honest mistake.
   C. Phil can be held liable if it can be proven that he was negligent in performing his duties.
   D. Phil has no liability.

9. In which of the following situations will a shareholder be deemed to owe a fiduciary duty to minority shareholders?

A. When the shareholder owns at least two-thirds of the shares of the corporation.
B. When the shareholder owns more than 50 percent of the shares of the corporation.
C. When the shareholder owns a sufficient number of shares to effectively control the corporation.
D. None of the above.

10. In which of the following situations would a court be least likely to pierce the corporate veil?
   A. A shareholder employed by the corporation maintains the same checking account for his personal use and for the corporate checking account.
   B. A corporation involved in asbestos removal is capitalized with 3,000 shares of stock which it sold for $.50 per share.
   C. A corporation sells corporate assets to shareholders for fair market value.
   D. None of the above.

VI. Answers to Objective Questions:

Terms:

1. *Implied powers*. These are sometimes referred to as "common sense" powers.
2. *Ultra vires*. Under case law, this definition has been expanded to cover situations where the corporation had the power to act, but the exercise of the power was improper or irregular.
3. *Duty of care*. As this is a rather open ended term, this duty is interpreted on a case by case basis.
4. *Business judgment*. There must still be a showing that the transaction was made with due care and good faith.

5. *Resign; register his/her dissent.* They must take themselves out of the decision-making loop.
6. *Self-dealing.* This may exist any time a person in a fiduciary relationship uses the property of another for his or her own personal benefit.
7. *Insider trading.* Such transactions must be reported to the Securities and Exchange Commission.
8. *Derivative.* This action is called derivative because it is based on the primary rights of the corporation but is being asserted by the shareholder on its behalf.
9. *Mandatory indemnification.* These statutes require that the director be made whole or held harmless for these costs.
10. *Class action.* Where a class is properly recognized as having a common legal action vis-à-vis an opposing party, efficiency is served by combining the multiple proceedings into one action.

True/False:

1. False. A corporation generally has express authority to borrow and to lend.

2. True. In addition, the corporation can sue for damages or the state attorney general can seek a dissolution of the corporation.
3. False. The appropriate standard of care is that level of care that an ordinary person in a comparable position would use under similar circumstances.
4. True. Only if the director had knowledge that would cause reliance to be unwarranted can she be held liable.
5. False. A dissenting director may register his or her dissent either by entering it in the minutes, by filing a written dissent prior to adjournment, or by forwarding a written dissent immediately following adjournment of the meeting.

6. False. Such transactions may be entered into if fair and reasonable to the corporation. In addition, such transactions may be entered if fully disclosed and validly approved by the directors or the shareholders.
7. True. If usurping is proven, the director must return the opportunity to the corporation and return any profits made as a result of the usurpation.
8. False. A shareholder is entitled to bring a derivative suit in this instance, but any profit recovered must be returned to the corporation.
9. False. A corporation can be held liable for both the torts and the crimes of its agents and employees. The normal criminal sanction imposed on a corporation is the assessment of monetary fines or loss of legal privileges.
10. True. The shareholder must have either owned the shares or acquired them by operation of law.

Multiple Choice:

1. C. The board of directors owes a duty of care to the corporation and the shareholders. In exercising this duty, the directors may rely in good faith upon the reports of reliable and competent officers and employees and upon professionals such as public accountants as to matters within their expertise.
2. D. A court may order indemnification if it finds that the director or officer is reasonably and fairly entitled to such indemnification. B is the second best answer, but to be the correct answer, it must also have shown that the director or officer acted in good faith and believed his or her actions to be in the best interest of the corporation.

3. C. In the exercise of its discretion, the business judgment rule provides that the board is protected from liability to the corporation and the shareholders for honest mistakes in judgment. As a practical matter, the rule is necessary to avoid second guessing the fluctuations of the marketplace.

4. C. Directors and officers cannot engage in activities that compete with the corporation unless full disclosure is made and a majority of the disinterested shareholders approve the activity. Ms. Beacon's part ownership of the cruise ship should be disclosed to Court, Inc.

5. D. The requirement is generally imposed by state corporation statutes in order to make sure that these sorts of lawsuits are not abused.

6. A. Only a controlling shareholder is saddled with fiduciary duties and the corresponding liabilities for a breach thereof.

7. D. A corporate employee is personally liable for his own torts. In addition, a corporation is liable for the torts of its agents and employees, but only if such torts occurred while such person was acting within the scope of employment for the corporation.

8. C. A director breaches the duty of care if his negligent in the performance of his duties.

9. C. Majority ownership is not required to effectively control a corporation. A shareholder who effectively controls the corporation owes a fiduciary duty to minority shareholders.

10. C. However, if the corporation sold the assets for less than fair market value, the court would likely pierce the corporate veil.

VI. Key Question Answers to Essay Question:

A. *Which powers of Potato Head Corporation are at issue?*

It appears that the Cha Cha and the Potato Heads' Corporation was duly organized and granted a corporate charter under the laws of California. Under its articles of incorporation, it could pursue most any sort of legal entertainment activity. Assuming its music was not obscene, did not cause persons to riot, and did not create any other clear and present danger to society, the band could play on. If any of the parents had been able to prove that music was creating a potato head cult, the state many have considered revoking their corporate charter. That outcome does not appear likely here.

B. *Assuming the corporation engages in an action which is not expressly or impliedly allowed, what are the possible consequences?*

Here we have a situation where a key person in the corporation has acted in breach of his fiduciary duty. Clyde is an officer of the company as well as a member of the board of directors. In both capacities Clyde is held to a fiduciary duty of loyalty to the corporation and the other shareholders to act in the best interests of the corporation. In undertaking a secret contractual relationship with a direct competitor, he has committed several corporate sins. He has engaged in self-dealing, usurping corporate opportunities for himself, directly competing with the corporation, and generally acting against the corporation's best interests. Based on all these violations of his basic duty of loyalty, he can be liable to the corporation for damages based on the above listed actions.

D. *For what actions or omissions may a shareholder be liable to third parties or to the corporation?*

The other shareholders can look to the Cha Cha and the Potato Heads corporate board of directors to seek these remedies in the name of the corporation. If the board of directors fails to act, the shareholders may seek to bring a derivative lawsuit on behalf of the corporation. In any event, Clyde should have left Cha Cha first before getting involved with Oral Hygiene. A key element of corporation law has always been loyalty to one master at a time. Any good cocker spaniel could have taught Clyde that lesson.

CHAPTER 38

MERGERS AND HOSTILE TAKEOVERS OF CORPORATIONS

In economics, the majority is always wrong.

John Kenneth Galbraith

I. Overview:

The world of corporate combinations through mergers and the like has been turned upside down in recent history. Several factors have contributed to the frenzy of activity on the street, not all of it well motivated. As with so many of these sorts of fundamental changes to how society orders its affairs, there is no one real underlying motive or rhyme or reason to it. As with any major shift in economic alignment, arguments pro and con can be heard through the halls of academia, government agencies and Wall Street.

The proponents for these changes first argue mergers, takeovers, and consolidation are simply marketplace adjustments which reflect attempts to correct inefficiencies in the marketplace. Where a company is poorly managed, running on "cruise control," and is not sufficiently lean and mean, it should be swallowed up by more efficient competitors. This view literally adopts the law of the jungle where only the strong survive. A really open marketplace rewards the most efficient in economic terms, and drags on that efficiency are doomed to failure and absorption in the end. The law and economics or "Chicago School" movement proponents argue that mechanisms of law should not only allow this natural business evolution to take place, but

that to stifle it would do harm to society in the end.

On the other side of the coin, a number of commentators have argued that runaway activity in the areas of mergers, acquisitions, buyouts, and the like breed a whole new generation of unethical, short term thinking, financial charlatans whose only real interest is their personal bank accounts. Critics of the merger phenomenon point to the endless game playing going on in this arena. They argue that what has been created is a big time casino where the chips are bigger than ever. Out of the that gaming mentality, the larger society has had to pay for numerous financial scandals because the original players were not really motivated by the long term good of society. In addition, long term growth, research, and development of essential business fundamentals has been cast aside in the name of greenmail, corporate spin-offs, tax manipulation, and golden parachutes. The net result of this sort of short term thinking is that while the financial market manipulators are playing high stakes poker, our industrial, financial, and transportation infrastructure has sunk into a quagmire of noncompetitiveness in the world marketplace.

The truth probably lies somewhere in between these poles when it comes to these business combinations. Time will ultimately tell if this recent history has reflected a transition cost to stay competitive as a nation, or if we are frittering away our industrial base at the gaming table. However it all turns out, each and every one of us will ultimately share in the processes' ultimate benefit or burden.

II. Hypothetical Multi-issue Essay Questions:

Truly Useless Corporation has been the envy of the widget manufacturing trade for years. Their crystal widgets have been both the price and quality leader in widget markets all over the world even since their invention by the corporate founder, Mr. Lyaeus Lycisca. Lyaeus married Lotis Lovely, and they had three children, Libitina, Lycaon, and Lelaps. Lyaeus and Lotis wanted to see the children go into the family business, so they went to their attorney Linus Lethe, and he drew up a corporate business plan wherein the parents retained 25 percent of the shares in the company and the children each got 25 percent.

Things were cooperative between all the family members for a number of years until Libitina could no longer stand Lelap's coprophagous habits. Libitina convinced her parents and her siblings to sell the company to No Redeeming Value Incorporated for $10 a share (book value). Lelaps objects and wants to stop the pending sale. He contends that crystal widgets are doing better than ever and that the acquiring corporation is really just a shell entity owned by the other family members who want to freeze him out because of his questionable personal habits. What results?

III. Key Question Checklist:

A. As an incident of ownership, shareholders have a right to vote on organic changes to the structure of the corporation owned by them. Organic changes include mergers, acquisitions, consolidations, buys, dissolutions, and liquidations. The first question you must ask yourself is how is this right established and exercised?
   1. Is the right to vote established by:
     (a) Statute?
     (b) Articles of incorporation?
     (c) By-laws?
     (d) Resolution of board of directors?
     (e) A combination of any or all of the above?

2. How can this right to vote be exercised?
     (a) By direct participation at the shareholder's meeting?
     (b) Proxy?
        (1) Federal proxy rules apply?
        (2) State proxy rules applicable?
        (3) Proxy rules set out in articles of incorporation?
        (4) Proxy rules set out in by-laws?
        (5) Proxy rules set out in resolutions of the board of directors?
        (6) Combination of two or more of te above apply?
     (c) What are the consequences of wrongful use of proxy procedures?
        (1) SEC sanctions?
        (2) Private cause of action?
     (d) Who pays for proxy expenses?
        (1) If issue of policy is involved?
        (2) If personal matter is involved?
     (e) Direct shareholder proposals allowable per SEC rules?
        (1) If not in violation of law?
        (2) Relates to corporate business?
        (3) Policy issue? Example: Proposals by shareholders for corporation not to do business in South Africa due to its *apartheid* policies.
        (4) Nonpayment of dividend issue?
        (5) No prior presentment and defeat of same issue within past three years?

B. Assuming the proper procedures have been identified for stockholder participation in the organic changes to the corporate structure, you must then look at the possible options available to the corporation and ask yourself how those elective steps may be taken. The most common combination of two corporate entities takes place either by merger or consolidation. Look to see:

1. Is this a merger or consolidation?
    (a) Did one corporation absorb the other, with the absorbed entity now ceasing to exist (merger)?
    (b) Did two or more corporations combine to form a new entity (consolidation)?
2. Did the board of directors vote to approve the change?
3. Did the shareholders vote to approve the plan?
    (a) Rights of dissenting shareholders?
        (1) Appraisal value?
        (2) Statutory rights of dissent?
4. State and federal statutes complied with?
5. Legal consequences to third parties?

C. Are any forms of combination other than merger or consolidation in play here?
1. Purchase of assets?
    (a) Agreed upon by all required parties?
    (b) Not a disguised merger or consolidation?
    (c) Not designed to commit fraud or avoid liability?
    (d) Effect on third party rights and duties?
2. Share exchange?
    (a) Agreed upon by all required parties?
        (1) Dissenting rights of non-agreeing parties?
    (b) Retain separate legal existence?
    (c) Effect on third party rights and duties?

D. Assuming the form of corporate organic change has been identified, the next question involves the methods by which that change may be initiated, agreed to, or

resisted. The most common method of change, which is not initiated at the behest of the board of directors, is called a tender offer. In a tender offer, the shareholders of the target corporation are solicited directly by the acquiring corporation. In examining the tender offer process, look to see if the following questions have been addressed?

1. Was the Williams Act complied with?
    (a) Timing rules followed?
    (b) Fair price rule followed?
    (c) *Pro rata* rule followed?
2. If the tender offer is being resisted, was a proper method of resistance used, i.e., allowed by state or federal law?
    (a) Persuasion of shareholders?
    (b) Delaying lawsuit?
    (c) Selling "crown jewel"?
    (d) Adopting a "poison pill"?
    (e) "Pac-man" or reverse tender offer?
    (f) Issuing additional stock?
    (g) Employee stock ownership plan?
    (h) Flip-over or flip-in plan?
    (i) Greenmail premium payment with standstill agreement?
3. Rights of minority shareholders if tender offer accepted?

E. Assuming for whatever reason that corporate existence is coming to an end, how can it be ended?
1. Voluntary methods?
    (a) Dissolution by vote of majority of incorporators?
    (b) Expiration of term set in articles of incorporation?
    (c) Voluntary unanimous vote of corporate shareholders?
    (d) Vote by board of directors with majority vote by shareholders?
    (e) Statutory methods otherwise prescribed?

2. Involuntary methods (by judicial proceeding)?
   (a) Management deadlock?
   (b) Illegal, oppressive, or fraudulent acts?
   (c) Shareholder vote deadlock?
   (d) Corporate assets being wasted or misapplied?
   (e) Creditors suit for dissolution?
   (f) Any other statutory basis for dissolution?
       (1) State *quo warranto* proceeding?
3. Once the dissolution has been enacted, what is the order of preference in liquidation?
   (a) Expenses of liquidation and creditor?
   (b) Preferred shareholder?
   (c) Common shareholders?

IV. Objective Questions:

Terms:

1. Where shareholders challenge the incumbent management and both sides solicit proxies from shareholders, this process is generally referred to as a _____ _____.

2. Business combinations can occur in several different forms. A _____ occurs when one corporation absorbs another and the existence of the absorbed corporation ceases.

3. A part owner of a corporation who objects to a proposed merger even though it has been properly approved is called a _____ _____.

4. A shareholder who properly objects to a merger is entitled to a cash payment equivalent to the _____ _____ of his shares.

5. The procedure which may be used to combine a parent corporation with a subsidiary corporation is called a(n) _____ _____ _____.

6. The procedure involving the combination of two or more corporations to form an entirely new corporation is known as _____.

7. The organization whose shares a purchaser seeks to buy in a tender offer is known as the _____ corporation.

8. The payment by a target corporation of a premium over the fair market value of its shares to buy back a block of its stock previously acquired by the tendering corporation is known as _____.

9. These documents must be filed with the secretary of state of the state of incorporation to effectuate a voluntary dissolution; they are known as the _____ _____ _____.

10. In an attempt to fight off hostile takeover attempts, many corporations build provisions known as _____ _____ into their articles of incorporation and other relevant documents which provide for adverse consequences if corporate ownership changes hands.

True/False:

1. ____ One who violates the antifraud provisions of the federal securities laws with respect to the solicitation of proxies is subject to civil and criminal actions by the federal government, and to civil actions brought by private individuals wronged by such violation.

2. ____ In all situations in which the incumbent management becomes involved in a proxy contest, the corporation must reimburse such persons for expenses incurred in that contest whether they win or lose.

3. ____ Following a merger, the surviving corporation gains all the rights, privileges, powers, duties, obligations, and liabilities of the merged corporation.

4. ____ An ordinary merger requires approval of the board of directors of each corporation and of a supramajority of the shareholders of the merged corporation.

5. ____ Approval of a short form merger requires only the consent of the board of directors of the parent corporation.

6. ____ In a short form merger, shareholders of both the parent corporation and the subsidiary corporation have dissenting shareholder's appraisal rights.

7. ____ A consolidation requires the approval of the board of directors of both corporations and the affirmative approval of a majority of the shareholders of each corporation.

8. ____ In a tender offer, the target corporation is absorbed into the tendering corporation.

9. ____ Directors are shielded from liability for breach of their fiduciary duties if the breach occurs in an effort to defend against a tender offer.

10. ____ Under the Williams Act, a tender offer must remain open for fifteen days after commencement of the offer, and must be extended for ten days if the number of shares or the price offered changes.

Multiple Choice:

1. In a short form merger:
   A. The approval of the shareholders of both corporations is needed.
   B. The approval of the board of directors of both corporations is needed.
   C. A short form merger is not allowed under the RMBCA.
   D. All of the above are false.

2. Under which of the following circumstances would a corporation's existence terminate?
   A. The death of its sole owner shareholder.
   B. Its becoming insolvent.
   C. Its legal consolidation with another corporation.
   D. Its reorganization under the federal bankruptcy laws.

3. Which of the following would be grounds for the judicial dissolution of a corporation on the petition of a shareholder?
   A. Refusal of the board of directors to declare a dividend.
   B. Waste of corporate assets by the board of directors.
   C. Loss operations of the corporation for three years.
   D. Failure by the corporation to file its federal income tax returns.

4. Little Dog, Inc. and Big Dog, Inc. are considering a merger. Little Dog is a small, closely held corporation, and Big Dog is publicly traded on a national exchange. A merger would require:
   A. Approval of the SEC.
   B. Creditors of the corporation which does not survive to file claims within thirty days or lose their rights.
   C. That dissenting shareholders have their stock purchased at its fair value.
   D. Approval by at least a two-thirds majority of the board of directors of each corporation, without shareholder approval.

5. Boulder Bikes, Inc. united with Backpacks and Bikes, Inc. to form the Outdoor Shop, Inc. This particular transaction would be classified as which of the following?
   A. A merger.
   B. A subsidiary.
   C. A consolidation.
   D. A reorganization.

6. In question 5, if Boulder Bikes, Inc. united with Backpacks and Bikes, Inc. retaining the name Boulder Bikes, Inc., this particular transaction would be classified as which of the following?
   A. A merger.
   B. A subsidiary.
   C. A consolidation.
   D. A reorganization.

7. In question 5, if Boulder Bikes, Inc. acquires 75 percent of the shares of Backpacks and Bikes, Inc. and both continue to operate, Backpacks and Bikes would be classified as which of the following?
   A. A merger.
   B. A subsidiary.
   C. A split-off.
   D. A reorganization.

8. Grumpy, Dumpy, and Sneezy form the HIHO Corporation. A few months later, Sneezy's ailment gets the best of him and he dies of pneumonia. Which of the following statements is correct?
   A. Ownership of Sneezy's shares of the corporation will vest in Snow White upon his death.
   B. Sneezy's death does not affect the existence of the corporation.
   C. Grumpy and Dumpy will become the sole shareholders of the corporation.
   D. The secretary of state of the state of incorporation is required by law to withdraw the charter of the corporation within six months of Sneezy's death.

9. The shareholders of Cautious Corporation have been approached by Aggressive Corporation who made a tender offer for their shares. With respect to a tender offer, which of the following statements is incorrect?
   A. The tender offer must remain open for fifteen business days following the making of the offer.
   B. If an increased price is offered after certain shares have been purchased, shareholders who previously tendered their shares are entitled to additional consideration.
   C. If the tender offer is not for all of the shares outstanding, the offeror must purchase shares on a first in basis.
   D. The offer must be extended for ten days if the number of shares or the price offered is changed following the initial offer.

10. Which of the following is not a method used to fight a tender offer?
    A. Adopting a poison pill.
    B. Selling a crown jewel.
    C. Issuing additional stock.
    D. None of the above.

V. Answers to Objective Questions:

Terms:

1. *Proxy contest.* The term proxy is derived from the Latin word "procuracy" meaning the writing which authorizes an agent to act for another.
2. *Merger.* This is the amalgamation of two corporations pursuant to statutory requirements.
3. *Dissenting shareholder.* Many corporation statutes provide for appraisal remedies for dissenting shareholders.
4. *Fair value.* This is the term used to define the appraisal remedy.
5. *Short form merger.* It is called short form because of the relatively brief amount of paper work involved.
6. *Consolidation.* Both of the original entities no longer legally exist, and they are replaced by a new entity.
7. *Target.* This entity is the object of the tender offer.
8. *Greenmail.* Because of the widespread use of this payment, it is now subject to a special tax as specified in the Internal Revenue Code, Sec. 5881.
9. *Articles of dissolution.* Because the corporate form is created by law, the law allows its existence to come to a voluntary end.
10. *Poison pills.* This is another example of the increasing colorful, yet hostile, language that has come to be identified with this area of law.

True/False:

1. True. A shareholder who is injured by a material misrepresentation or omission in proxy solicitation materials can recover damages.
2. False. The corporation is only required to reimburse the incumbent management for expenses incurred in a proxy contest if the issue is one of corporate policy.
3. True. It literally steps into the legal shoes of the nonsurviving corporation.
4. False. Unless stated otherwise in the articles or bylaws, a simple majority of the shareholders of each corporation is all that is required. The approval of the shareholders of the surviving corporation is only required if the merger increases the number of voting shares by more than 20 percent.
5. True. This is specified by statute.

6. **False.** Shareholders of the parent corporation do not have dissenting shareholder's appraisal rights because their rights are not significantly affected.

7. **True.** These approvals are required because this is considered an organic change.

8. **False.** Both the tendering corporation and the target corporation retain their legal status.

9. **False.** In attempting to defend against takeovers, the directors and officers must adhere to their fiduciary duties.

10. **True.** These terms are specified by the Williams Act.

Multiple Choice:

1. **D.** Under Section 11.04 of the RMBCA, all that is required is the approval of the parent board of directors if the ownership percentage of 90 percent is met.

2. **B.** A consolidation occurs when two or more corporations combine to form an entirely new entity, and the original corporation's existence will terminate.

3. **B.** A shareholder can institute an action for judicial dissolution where the corporate assets are being misapplied or wasted.

4. **C.** Shareholders are provided a statutory right to dissent. A shareholder who properly registers her dissent is entitled to have her shares purchased at their fair value, as provided in the RMBCA.

5. **C.** A consolidation occurs when two or more corporations combine to form an entirely new corporation.

6. **A.** A merger occurs when one corporation is absorbed into another corporation and ceases to exist.

7. **B.** When one corporation owns a substantial number of the shares of another corporation, the acquiring corporation is known as the parent corporation and the acquired corporation is known as the subsidiary corporation.

8. **B.** Unlike the death of a partner in a partnership setting, the death of a shareholder does not affect the existence of the corporation.

9. **C.** If the tender offer is not for all of the shares outstanding, the offeror must purchase shares on a *pro rata* basis.

10. **D.** All of the methods listed are commonly used to avoid tender offers.

VI. Key Question Checklist Answers to the Essay Question:

A. *How are the rights of the shareholders established vis-à-vis organic changes to the corporation?*

From the facts as given, there appears to be no question that the shareholders in this case each have a *pro rata* right to vote their shares with regard to normal functions such as election of the board of directors. What is unclear is if a supramajority vote would be required for an organic change to the corporate structure like a merger or acquisition. The likelihood is that such a supramajority would be required by most articles of incorporation. If not, then a simple majority of shareholders entitled to vote is all that would be needed to approve a board of directors resolution to merge or be acquired.

B. *What are the remedies available to the dissenting shareholder if the merger is approved?*

If the merger were approved by the requisite majority, or supramajority if

349

applicable, then Lelaps can have his dissent registered and seek to get an appraisal of value for his shares. This appraisal would be conducted according to court procedures pursuant to the state corporation statute and on the articles of incorporation on the bylaws of the corporation. Most corporate valuations are higher than "book" value in the marketplace, and it appears likely that the $10 per share value may be raised by the court.

E. *What other alternatives are available to the dissenting shareholder?*

In the alternative, Lelaps may want to argue for an involuntary dissolution and liquidation of the corporation. To succeed he would have to prove to the court that there has been some sort of improper behavior on the part of the board of directors and/or the majority shareholders which would be deemed oppressive as to him. Dissenting shareholders ordinarily do not have the right to recover the fair market value of their shares upon dissolution of a corporation unless such evidence of wrongful acts is proven. In any event, it looks like Lelaps is out of the new No Redeeming Value corporate scheme of things. Perhaps he should work on improving his personal habits.

CHAPTER 39

SECURITIES REGULATION AND INVESTOR PROTECTION

SEC. Securities and Exchange Commission, a federal agency devoted to providing young lawyers with the experience necessary to secure jobsadvising corporations on how to circumvent the regulations of the SEC.

D. Robert White

I. Overview:

Assume a sporting event were to be contested under the following conditions:

1. All the players were well trained.
2. The rules of the game were fully explained to the players.
3. Those rules are fairly and even-handedly applied to all participants.
4. An even playing field is used as a site for the contest.

With all these suppositions in place, can you rest assured your team will win? Or can you, at best, hope that, win or lose, your team was engaged in a fair contest?

In the broadest sense, the buying and selling of securities is indeed similar to an athletic event. Each participant goes into the game with his or her own self-interest in mind. And all the fair rules in world will not change one essential truth of these or any other contests--there will be winners and there will be losers. That reality must always be kept in mind from the outset by anyone seeking to make his or her fortune through the sale or purchase of securities. Risk is inherent to the nature of this activity, and anyone who fails to appreciate that simple fact should not be there in the first place.

It is most difficult for professionals to master the ins and outs of the financial markets, let alone the casual investor. Yet the lure of playing this game is so strong that every year millions of people invest hard earned money with nothing more than high hopes and a prayer. Securities law was designed to at least give some substance to those hopes and prayers. That substance is public information upon which investment choices can be rationally made. These laws are not designed to assure a win in this high risk game, but rather to provide a more even playing field.

The great financial stock market crash of 1929 and the ensuing Depression brought on by that calamity brought to the fore the need to create a greater governmental role in securities markets. Prior to that period, the sale of stocks in corporations remained essentially unregulated except for the common law doctrines of fraud and the like. Manipulative and unscrupulous trading practices coupled with a lot of hopes and unrequited prayers all pointed to a need for a better set of ground rules by which this game could be played.

The basic rules of the game go back sixty years to the Securities Act of 1933 and the Securities Exchange Act of 1934 which created the Securities and Exchange Commission. Over the years, the Commission's role has greatly increased with the advent of new technologies like programmed trading and the need to expand its regulatory framework into the financial services arena. Because of recent scandals in this sector of the economy, a number of new white collar crimes have been added to the government's arsenal for dealing with abuses in this area. All in all, it has made the specialized practice of securities law or SEC accounting more difficult, yet more challenging, than ever. As future business leaders, you have more than just a self-survival need to stay abreast of these changing rules of the game. As a nation we cannot afford the loses created by the manipulative abuses recently seen in these critical markets. If we do not watch out, 1929 can be revisited upon us, this time only worse. The key question checklist will itemize the applicable statutory provisions.

II. Hypothetical Multi-issue Essay Question:

Mr. Bouteilles Gerbeuses was suffering from a common 20th century malaise, working at a good paying job which provided him only with material but not spiritual satisfaction. He wanted to break away from his golden ball and chain and indulge in his real fantasy of spirits-- wine making. He has not had any formal wine training, but he knew what he liked when he tasted it. He decided to start his own winery called *Cuvees de Prestige* specializing in sparkling wines produced in the Noir Valley of Massazona.

He could not afford to capitalize the entire operation himself, so he came up with a novel idea. Why not sell the individual rows of vines to "partners?" They would each get his expertise in producing the wine, and individually marked barrels with their own labels. These barrels could be consumed by the investors or sold for a tidy profit.

Mr. Gerbeuses convinced several hundred partners to buy one row each for $10,000 and proceeded to start up production of *Cuvees de Prestige* wines. Unfortunately what he didn't tell his partners was that he didn't know how to tell the difference between a *blanc de blancs*, a *blanc de noir*, and a *pinot noir*. Having failed to master the art of malolactic fermentation, the wine tasted more like vinegar

than the nectar of gods Mr. Gerbeuses had hoped for. His partners are also fermenting and look to see if they can get out of this tannic sedimentation of a deal. What results?

III. Key Question Checklist:

This checklist is designed to introduce students to the prominent laws affecting the issuing, buying, and selling of securities and the rights and duties arising under those laws.

A. Congressional response to the 1929 crash was premised on two main securities laws passed in 1933 and 1934. Both assumed that even though the buyer cannot be assured of success in the financial marketplace, he or she should be going into that market as fully informed as possible and that information should be as widely dispersed as possible. The first of these two acts was the Securities Act of 1933. What are the key elements of that Act?
   1. Is a security in existence to which this law may apply?
      (a) Is it an instrument commonly known as a security?
         (1) Stock?
         (2) Bond?
         (3) Debenture?
         (4) Warrant?
      (b) Is it specifically nominated as a security by statute?
         (1) Subscription agreement?
         (2) Oil, gas, and other mineral interest?
         (3) Foreign securities deposit receipts?
      (c) Is it an investment contract?
         (1) Limited partnership interest?
         (2) Investment schemes classified as securities under the *Howey* case test (invest with

expectation of income from effects of promoter or third parties)? Examples: Corporation cultivation contracts, marketing programs, animal care contracts, condominium rental agreements?

2. Is the security being offered?
   (a) Through the use of the mails?
   (b) Through any other facility of interstate commerce?
3. During prefiling period, issuer cannot sell or offer the securities?
4. Basic registration statement required?
   (a) Applies to all securities unless specifically exempted?
   (b) Must contain key material descriptions including financial statements prepared by CPA?
   (c) Become effective 20 days after being filed with the SEC?
   (d) During this waiting period, issuer can condition the market?
5. After the registration becomes effective, the issuer may sell until sold out or withdrawn from the market?
6. Prospectus?
   (a) Submitted along with registration statement to the SEC?
   (b) Used as selling tool with much of the same information as registration statement?
7. Exemptions?
   (a) Exempt securities?
      (1) Government securities?
      (2) Short term (under nine months) commercial paper?
      (3) Securities issued by nonprofit entities?
      (4) Separately regulated securities?
         (aa) Banks and savings and loans?
         (bb) Insurance companies?

   (cc) Transportation companies?
      (5) Securities arising out of stock reorganizations, stock dividends, or stock splits?
   (b) Exempt transactions?
      (1) Transactions covered otherwise by antifraud provisions?
      (2) Intrastate offerings?
         (aa) Issuer resident of the state?
         (bb) 80 percent business rule met?
         (cc) Purchases by residents of the state?
      (3) Private placements?
         (aa) Unlimited number of accredited investors allowed?
         (bb) Up to 35 unaccredited investors?
         (cc) Resale restrictions apply?
      (4) Small offering exemptions?
         (aa) Rule 504--($1 million in 12 months, with no limit on investors)?
         (bb) Rule 505--($5 million in 12 months, with unlimited accredited and 35 unaccredited investors)?
      (5) Nonissuer exemption?
8. Integration rules applicable?
   (a) If more than one transaction, are they really part of one large offering?
   (b) Safe harbor rule applicable (sales more than six months before or after current offering)?
9. Liabilities for violation of the 1933 Act?
   (a) Civil enforcement by SEC?

(b) Criminal actions against issuer by U.S. government?

(c) Civil private actions by parties harmed by the violations?

(d) Defenses possible for persons other than the issuer?

    (1) Due diligence?

        (aa) By nonexpert, shows reasonable inquiry?

        (bb) By nonexpert as to "expertised" portions, lack of reasonable grounds for questioning the expert?

        (cc) By expert, reasonable grounds existed for statements made after reasonable investigation made?

B. The second major legislation in this area is the Securities Act of 1934. While the 1933 act was designed to regulate the original issuance of securities, this act primarily regulates subsequent trading. What are the requirements under this act?

1. Reporting requirements?

    (a) Annual (Form 10-K) report for:

        (1) Issuers with assets of more than $5 million and at least 500 shareholders?

        (2) Whose equities are traded on a national securities exchange?

        (3) Who have made a registered offering under the 1933 Securities Act?

    (b) Quarterly (Form 10-Q) report?

    (c) Material event (Form 8-K) report?

2. Rules under Section 10(b) and Rule 10(b)-5?

    (a) Applies to all transfers of securities?

    (b) Antifraud provisions?

        (1) Cannot use mails, interstate commerce facilities, or national security exchanges to:

           (aa) Defraud?

           (bb) Misrepresent?

           (cc) Engage in deceit?

    (c) Have reliance by injured party?

    (d) Can have both civil and criminal liabilities imposed for violation of the Act?

3. Examples of key violations of the 1934 Securities Exchange Act?

    (a) Insider trading?

        (1) Any person classified as an insider:

           (aa) Officers?

           (bb) Directors?

           (cc) Agents of the company?

        (2) May not use material nonpublic information to make a profit by trading in the securities of the company?

4. Tipper-tippee?

    (a) An improper disclosure of nonpublic material information from a tipper?

    (b) Made to a tippee who receives the information?

    (c) Both may be liable for profits if the information was acted upon?

    (d) May also have criminal liability under Section 34 of the 1934 Act?

5. Section 16(b)--Short-swing profits?

    (a) Trades made by insiders?

    (b) Made within six months of each other?

    (c) Profits go the corporation?

    (d) Strict liability, no defenses allowed?

C. Other related statutes?

1. Racketeer Influenced and Corrupt Organizations Act (RICO)?

2. Securities Enforcement Remedies and Penny Stock Reform Act of 1990?
3. Market Reform Act of 1990?
4. International Securities Enforcement Cooperation Act?
5. State (Blue Sky) security laws?

IV. Objective Questions:

Terms:

1. Two federal statutes designed to require disclosure of information to investors and prevent fraud are known as the _____ _____ _____ _____ and the _____ _____ _____ _____ _____.

2. Generally, a _____ is present when an investor invests money in a common enterprise with the expectation of making a profit from the significant efforts of others.

3. The federal administrative agency empowered to administer federal securities laws is called the _____ _____ _____ _____.

4. A written document used as a selling tool by the issuer which enables prospective purchasers of securities to evaluate certain risks of a particular investment is known as the _____.

5. When an issuer engages in public relations campaigns that tout the prospects of the company and an upcoming securities offering, this is called _____ _____ _____.

6. The time between when a registration statement is filed with the SEC and when the registration statement becomes effective is called the _____ period.

7. The document which must be delivered to investors at the time of confirming a sale or when sending a security to a purchaser is known as the _____ prospectus.

8. Each state is entitled to enact its own laws, known as _____ _____ laws, regulating the offer and sale of securities within its borders.

9. In certain situations, employees and advisors of an issuer of securities use material, nonpublic information to make a profit by buying or selling securities of the issuer. This practice is known as _____ _____.

10. When certain insiders buy and sell securities within a six month period of time, any gains realized are called _____ _____ profits.

True/False:

1. _____ During the prefiling period, the issuer is permitted to offer, but not to sell, securities of the proposed offering.

2. _____ During the waiting period, the issuer may distribute a preliminary prospectus and publish tombstone ads which, in effect, condition the market for the upcoming issuance of securities.

3. ____ Certain transactions in securities are exempt from the registration requirements of the federal securities laws as are certain types of securities.

4. ____ During the posteffective period, the issuer may close the transactions solicited previously, but may not solicit any new transactions.

5. ____ Securities issued by colleges and universities are typically exempt from the registration requirements of the federal securities laws.

6. ____ Securities issued using a private placement exemption may only be sold to 35 investors.

7. ____ Violation of the federal securities laws can result in civil and criminal actions by the SEC as well as private civil actions by individual investors.

8. ____ Certain individuals associated with a securities offering can avoid liability by proving that, after reasonable investigation, they had reasonable grounds to believe, and did believe that at the time the registration statement became effective, the statements therein were true and that there was no omission of a material fact.

9. ____ An insider who trades on public information is subject to prosecution for violating the federal securities laws.

10. ____ If an insider provides nonpublic information to another who knows the information is not public information and who trades the related securities in reliance on that information, both the insider and the trading party have committed violations of the federal securities laws.

Multiple Choice:

1. In general, which of the following is least likely to be considered a security under the Securities Act of 1933?
   A. General partnership interests.
   B. Warrants.
   C. Limited partnership interests.
   D. Treasury stock.

2. Under the Securities Act of 1933, the registration of securities which are offered to the public in interstate commerce is:
   A. Directed toward preventing the marketing of securities which pose serious financial risks to the prospective investor.
   B. Not required unless the issuer is a corporation.
   C. Mandatory unless the cost to the issuer is prohibitive as defined in the SEC regulation.
   D. Required unless there is an applicable exemption.

3. Which of the following is subject to the registration requirements of the Securities Act of 1933?
   A. Public sale of its bonds by a municipality.
   B. Public sale by a corporation of its negotiable five year notes.
   C. Public sale of stock issued by a common carrier regulated by the Interstate Commerce Commission.
   D. Issuance of stock by a corporation to its existing stockholders pursuant to a stock split.

4. The principle purpose of the registration requirements of the Securities Act of 1933 is to:
   A. Prevent public offerings of securities in which management fraud or unethical conduct is suspected.
   B. Provide the SEC with the information necessary to determine the accuracy of facts presented in the financial statements.
   C. Assure that investors have adequate information upon which to base investment decisions.
   D. Provide the SEC with the information necessary to evaluate the financial merits of the securities being offered.

5. Shadee Corporation wishes to sell securities to raise $850,000 for the purpose of financing several corporate expansion projects. The securities will be offered under Rule 504. Which of the following statements is correct with respect to the transaction?
   A. The transaction cannot be completed without registration because Rule 504 only allows the issuance of $750,000 of securities.
   B. The securities can be sold to accredited investors only.
   C. The securities can be sold to an unlimited number of accredited investors and to 35 unaccredited investors.
   D. The securities can be sold to an unlimited number of accredited unaccredited investors.

6. Ricky Risktaker was of the theory that to make it big, he had to take big risks in his investments. He took a huge risk in buying stock in Worthless Corporation. He is now suing the CPA firm that audited the financial statements including in the registration statement in an attempt to recover his investment. Which of the following statements is correct?
   A. The CPA firm is not liable if it can prove that it acted with due diligence in conducting its audit.
   B. The CPA firm is strictly liable for any material defects in the registration statement.
   C. Ricky must prove that he relied on the registration statement before he will be entitled to recover.
   D. None of the above.

7. Diet-Rite Corporation, a corporation whose shares are publicly traded, was having a phenomenal year. Profits were rolling in because rolls were coming off of its customers. However, the fun is about to end. The Food and Drug Administration has notified the president of Diet-Rite that the corporation will be forced to stop selling its product because of a recent discovery of significant health risks created by the product. The president immediately sells his shares and calls his father who also sells his shares. In addition, the president's father calls a friend who also sells his shares. Who has made an illegal sale in this situation?
   A. The president.
   B. The president's father.
   C. The friend of the president's father.
   D. A and B.
   E. All of the above.

8. Hometown Corporation, a Colorado corporation, hopes to raise capital by issuing new securities. Which of the following facts would prevent the issuance of securities pursuant to an intrastate offering exemption?
   A. The principal office of Hometown is located in Omaha, Nebraska.
   B. The securities are offered to several residents of New Mexico, but ultimately purchased by only Colorado residents.
   C. Hometown earns 30 percent of its gross revenues in Wyoming.
   D. A and C.
   E. All of the above.

9. Assume the same facts as in question 8, except that Hometown hopes to issue the securities using a Rule 505 Small Offering Exemption. Which of the following facts would prevent the issuance of securities pursuant to a Rule 505 Small Offering Exemption?
   A. Securities totaling $4,500,000 are sold in the transaction.
   B. The securities are sold to 37 accredited investors.
   C. The securities are offered in newspapers and magazines throughout the region.
   D. The securities are sold to investors whom the issuer knows will transfer the securities within three years of purchase.
   E. C and D.

10. Which of the following statements about a private placement not involving a public offering of securities is incorrect?
   A. Resale of such securities is restricted.
   B. General solicitations of purchasers is prohibited.

C. Securities may only be offered to corporations and partnerships.
D. None of the above.

V. Answers to Objective Questions:

Terms:

1. *Securities Act of 1933; Securities Exchange Act of 1934.* These laws are the two keystones of today's securities law system.
2. *Security.* The definition of securities has expanded to cover more and more sorts of ventures, including some limited partnership offerings.
3. *Securities and Exchange Commission or SEC.* This is the securities equivalent of the IRS.
4. *Prospectus.* Note that this is not a contract *per se*.
5. *Conditioning the market.* There are limitations on this practice.
6. *Waiting.* This period is designed to give time to act if someone may want to object.
7. *Final prospectus.* There is time to act based on this information.
8. *Blue-sky laws.* This is nicknamed after fraudulent sales of securities which had no underlying value beneath the "Blue Sky."
9. *Insider trading.* Much needed reforms have come based on recent scandals.
10. *Short-swing.* These transactions are now targeted by reforms to securities laws.

True/False:

1. False. During the prefiling period, the issuer is not permitted to offer or sell securities.

2. True. Although actual sales are prohibited during the waiting period, the issuer may engage in certain offering activities.
3. True. Cost considerations were taken into account by Congress when these exemptions were allowed.
4. False. During the posteffective period, the issuer may close the transactions arranged previously and solicit new offers and sales.
5. True. Securities issued by nonprofit institutions, such a colleges and universities, are exempt from registration.
6. False. Securities sold using a private placement exemption may be sold to an unlimited number of accredited investors, but may only be sold to 35 nonaccredited investors.
7. True. Depending on the violation, a particular action could result in all of the mentioned actions.
8. True. Such a due diligence defense is available to a nonexpert with respect to that portion of a registration statement prepared by nonexperts.
9. False. If the information is truly "public" in nature, then an insider is free to trade without committing any violations.
10. True. Unfortunately, much of this still goes on.

Multiple Choice:

1. A. Under the *Howey* test, a security exists where the investor invests money in a common enterprise with the expectation of making a profit from the significant efforts of *others*. A general partnership interest would result in profits from the efforts of each general partner including the partner's own efforts as coowner of the enterprise..

2. D. Unless a security or transaction qualifies for an exemption, Section 5 of the Securities Act of 1933 requires securities offered to the public through the use of the mails or any facility of interstate commerce to be registered with the SEC by means of a registration statement and an accompanying prospectus. This rule is designed to afford maximum coverage of the 1933 Act.

3. B. Unless a security or the transaction is exempt, the issuance and sale must be registered. Answer B is not an exempt security because commercial paper of a corporation must have a maturity of nine months or less to qualify as an exempt security. A and C are examples of exempt securities. In answer D, there is no offer or sale of a security because the securities are received in a stock split and not for value given in exchange.

4. C. The primary purpose of the Securities Act of 1933 is to assure that securities issuers provide potential investors with full and fair disclosure of all material information needed to make a prudent investment decision. The Act does not assure that the investor will make a profit on his or her investment.

5. D. Rule 504 exempts the sale of up to $1 million of securities during a 12 month period from registration. The securities may be sold to an unlimited number of accredited and unaccredited investors, but general selling efforts to the public are not permitted.

6. A. To be shielded from liability, the CPA firm only needs to prove that it acted with due diligence with respect to the portions of the registration statement it prepared, i.e., only the financial statements.

7. E. All three parties have made illegal sales in this situation because all knew that they were trading on material nonpublic information.
8. E. To qualify for the intrastate offering exemption, the issuer must be a resident of the state in which the exemption is sought. In addition, the issuer must be doing business in that state, i.e., earn 80 percent of its gross revenues in that state. Finally, the shares may not be offered or sold to a resident of another state.
9. D. To qualify for a Rule 505 Small Offering Exemption, general selling efforts, such as advertising in a newspaper or magazine are forbidden.
10. C. Securities may be sold to an unlimited number of accredited investors and to 35 unaccredited investors.

VI. Key Question Answers to Essay Question:

A. *What key elements of the Securities Act of 1933 apply here?*

Mr. Gerbeuses may have a barrel full of real problems on his hands. The production of alcoholic products has always been a highly regulated industry even before the enactment of the securities laws of the 1930s. Assuming he got through the regulatory maze of the Treasury Department's Alcohol, Tobacco and Firearms Division, he must now worry about possibly having run afoul of the Securities and Exchange Commission. Under the 1933 Act, newly issued securities must comply with the registration requirements of the Act unless they fall into specific exemptions outlined in the 1937 Act. The first issue revolves around the definition of security for purposes of the 1933 Act. Under the court decision of *S.E.C. v. Howey,* any contract which calls for an investment with the expectation of income

from the efforts of a promoter or third person may be deemed to be a security. Here the most likely interpretation is that the sales contracts for rows of vines would be declared a security. Calling it a partnership would not make any difference.

Next, look to see how this security was sold. If there is use of any facility of interstate commerce or the mail, it may be covered under the 1933 Act. Here with sales to several hundred people, lawyers would indicate a very likely use of the mail for purposes of selling the securities.

Then decide if any of the exemptions from registration apply. The securities themselves do not fall into any of the exempt categories. It is not a nonprofit organization, nor is this a sale by a governmental entity. Nor is this only a reorganization or stock split. In addition, it does not appear that any of the transaction exemptions apply. It is not stated as only an intrastate offering. Nor does it appear that Mr. Gerbeuses tried to qualify the sales as a private placement or a small offering under either Section 504 or 505. Because he failed to comply with the 1933 Act, he may now be subject to both civil and criminal sanctions by the government. In addition, he may be sued by the private parties hurt by these violations.

B. *What elements of the Securities Act of 1934 apply?*

In addition to the problems raised by the 1933 Act, there are additional problems possible under the 1934 Act if he engaged in subsequent trading of his partnership interests after they had first been issued. This is particularly a problem for him under Rules 10(b) and 10(b)-5 which are designed to go after fraudulent transfers of securities. These violations could lead to both civil and criminal sanctions against him by both the government and private parties.

C. *What other related statutes may apply?*

In addition to the securities laws violations reviewed above, he may be liable under the RICO statute or one or more of the newer federal securities laws recently passed as a result of scandals in the securities markets. He also may have violated California's Blue Sky Securities Law to boot. All in all, Mr. Gerbeuses probably should have stayed in his office and fantasized about his wine-making abilities over a glass of *Dom Perignon*. It would have cost him far less.

CHAPTER 40

PRIVATE FRANCHISES AND LICENSING

When the going gets weird, the weird turn pro.

Hunter S. Thompson

I. Overview:

The world of franchising combines concepts of marketing, management, finance, and many other diverse skills into a special kind of cooperative venture which is facilitated through the law. Like any business marriage, it can lead to the best of all worlds or the worst. Careful planning, skilled research, and, most of all, a good faith willingness to let each participant do what he does best appears to be the key to today's most successful franchise operations. Under the franchise system, there is ample evidence of the positive effects of good franchise planning. The original basic technology, patent, process, or other trademarked service or product is allowed to reach far more users or consumers through the franchise system. With intelligent planning and quality control, the original franchisor of the product or service can see phenomenal growth through the use of equity-sharing participants in that growth. Witness the fast food industry, convenience stores, food product production, all sorts of consumer good retailing systems, or even professional sports teams. All of these industries rely heavily on the franchise concept to further their businesses.

Another interesting aspect of franchising is its tie in to basic capitalism for the little guy. With sufficient start up capital and a willingness to provide a lot of personal effort, the franchising concept allows the small business person to ride the coattails of the good will, advertising, and technology development of large multi-national enterprises.

There are some down sides to franchising as well. The "get rich quick" mentality of franchising has led to a number of abuses on the part of would be franchisors. Many people have lost substantial sums of money trying to invest in pie-in-the-sky sales of bogus franchises. In addition, the franchise industry has seen more than its share of pyramid schemes, shallow capitalizations, adhesion contracts, and behavior in violation of the antitrust laws. It is interesting to note that many of the rules promulgated by the Federal Trade Commission are designed to protect persons about to enter into franchise agreements rather than the ultimate consumer of the franchise's goods or services.

In addition, the franchise device has not always served the third party well. Because a franchisee is an independent contractor, the franchisor is not normally responsible to third parties for torts or contracts that the franchisee has been involved with. That may all sound well and good in legal terms, but does it always make equitable sense? If the consumer of the goods or services thought he or she was dealing with a megacorporation, why not hold a megacorporation responsible rather than just its franchise? Law works best when the benefit/burden balance is fairly struck. Where large business entities grow through the utilization of its franchise efforts, they should also be willing to take responsibility for their harm.

II. Hypothetical Multi-Issue Essay Question:

Mr. Dawson Curiae and his friend Mr. George Pactum were both tired of their dead-end jobs with the Thingamajig Corporation. They decided to go off on their own and seek their fortunes as franchisees for the Whatyamacallit Corporation. The products sold by Whatyamacallit were highly desirable, standardized, and used every which way. Even though Dawson and George did not have any practical business experience, they felt confident in the growing need for Whatyamacallits in their geographic area, Backwater.

They contacted the Whatyamacallit franchise sales representative through the confidential want ad section of the Backwater Daily News and met with him at the Backwater Bar and Grille. They cut a deal right there and then. For $98,000 each in initial license fees, they were given a written contract which allowed them to exclusively sell Whatyamacallits in Backwater and its surrounding environs. The franchisor was to retain strict quality control and operational controls over the entire course of the ten year contract. In addition, a royalty fee of 8 percent was to be paid for every Whatyamacallit sold by the franchisees. Over the third and fourth beers, Dawson and George were told they could expect to make back their up front costs in the first six months of the contract.

Nine months later, they have yet to sell their first Whatyamacallits. It seems that they have been eclipsed in the marketplace by newer and better designs from the Doohickee Corporation. Dawson and George are depressed and broke. Can they find relief in Backwater?

III. Key Question Checklist:

A. What are the basic elements of a franchise agreement?
    1. Have a contract or agreement between two or more persons?
      (a) Express?
      (b) Implied?
      (c) Oral or written?

    2. One party, the franchisor, allows the other party, the franchisee, to use the franchisor's recognized property right with certain controls retained by the franchisor?
    3. This property right is?
      (a) Trade name or trademark?
      (b) Patent?
      (c) Copyright?
      (d) Process?
      (e) Any other recognized property right?
    4. The intended use of these property rights by the franchisee is to engage in business related to the property right?
      (a) Distributing?
      (b) Processing or manufacture?
      (c) Selling?
      (d) Negotiate additional franchise contracts in a specific geographical area?
    5. In return for the consideration provided by the franchisor, the franchisee is to provide?
      (a) Fees?
      (b) Royalties?
      (c) Assessment fees?
      (d) Rents?
      (e) Any other form of legal agreed upon consideration?

B. Once you have established the basic elements of the franchise agreement, look at some of the key terms within the agreement.
    1. Quality control standards?
    2. Covenants not to compete?
    3. Fee payment arrangements?
    4. Use of trademarks, logos, or trade names?
    5. Operations standards?
    6. Terms for arbitration of disputes?

7. Terms for termination of the franchise?
   (a) Statutory restrictions apply?
      (1) Petroleum marketing practices?
      (2) Automobile Dealers Day in Court Act?

C. Next determine if all statutory requirements have been met with regard to the franchise agreement?
   1. Federal Trade Commission disclosure rules?
      (a) Presale disclosures made?
      (b) Any additional earnings or sales projections made which may call for additional disclosures?
   2. State franchise laws applicable?
   3. Any other state or federal statutory requirements possible?
      (a) Securities laws?
      (b) Trademark, patent, and copyright laws?
      (c) Antitrust laws?
      (d) Tax laws?
      (e) Corporations statutes?

D. Once you have established the essential contract relationships between the franchisor and the franchisee, has there been any breach of that agreement?
   1. Whose breach was it?
   2. Rights and duties of the franchisor based on the breach?
   3. Rights and duties of the franchisee based on the breach?
   4. Any governmental involvement?
      (a) Civil law consequences?
      (b) Criminal law consequences?

E. Look next at third party involvement in the situation and the legal consequences to all the parties involved?
   1. Third party contact based on:
      (a) Contract?
      (b) Tort?

   2. Who was in breach of either a contract or tort duty?
   3. Legal consequences to:
      (a) Third party?
      (b) Franchisor?
      (c) Franchisee?

IV. Objective Questions:

Terms:

1. A person authorized by a franchisor to negotiate and sell franchises on behalf of the franchisor is known as a _____ _____ or _____.

2. Where a seller refuses to sell one product to the customer unless the customer also agrees to purchase a second product from the seller, this is a _____ _____.

3. The practice by which a franchisor or a franchisee charges a different price to different customers for the same product without justification is known as _____ _____.

4. Where a franchisor manufactures a product and licenses a retail dealer to distribute that product to the public, this is called a _____ _____.

5. One who uses the service mark or trademark of another without authorization may be sued for _____ _____ which can result in the assessment of monetary damages or the issuance of an injunction.

6. In a franchise arrangement, the franchisee may be allowed to use the trademarks and service marks of the franchisor. In addition, the franchisee may be allowed to use _____ _____, which are certain ideas that make a franchise successful but which do not qualify for a trademark, copyright, or patent.

7. Several franchisees may enter into an informal agreement whereby they establish a price at which they will sell the franchisor's products or services. Such an arrangement is known as _____ _____ and constitutes a violation of the Sherman Antitrust Act.

8. Many franchise agreements permit the franchisor to terminate the relationship for cause. _____ _____ occurs if the franchise is terminated without cause.

9. In a franchise setting, one party, known as the _____ licenses another, known as the _____ to use a trade name, trademark, commercial symbol, or the like in the distribution and selling of goods and services.

10. One who misappropriates a trade secret may be sued for _____ _____ and be responsible for damages or have an injunction issued against him to prevent further unauthorized use.

True/False:

1. _____ One advantage of franchising is that a franchisee can operate her own business with the benefit of having access to the franchisor's knowledge and resources.

2. _____ A successful plaintiff in a suit against a defendant for restraint of trade violations resulting from an unlawful tying arrangement can recover treble damages.

3. _____ Generally, a franchise agreement can be terminated by either party for any reason.

4. _____ In a chain-style franchise, the franchisor provides a secret formula or the like to the franchisee who manufactures the product at its own location and distributes it to retail dealers in the area.

5. _____ A franchise agreement is not generally required to be in writing under the Statute of Frauds.

6. _____ The remedies for breach of a lawful franchise agreement are based on contract theories for breach of contract.

7. _____ In a franchise arrangement where the franchisee uses the same name as the franchisor, the franchisee will be deemed to be the agent of the franchisor.

8. _____ A franchise agreement cannot limit the geographical territory in which the franchisee can operate.

9. _____ The license fee in a franchise arrangement generally does not cover the cost of buildings and equipment.

10. _____ Generally, a license fee is the only compensation that a franchisor can legally collect.

Multiple Choice:

1. Ms. Rhonda Mae owned and managed a successful dog grooming business. For health reasons, she sold it to the Wet Hydrant chain. Their contract contained a covenant that Ms. Mae would not compete in the dog grooming business in that part of town for two years. After one year, Ms. Mae's health cleared up. She now wants to open another dog grooming business within one mile from the one she sold.
    A. A covenant not to compete is *per se* illegal as restricting competition.
    B. A covenant not to compete for more than one year is unenforceable.
    C. The covenant not to compete is enforceable.
    D. Wet Hydrant cannot stop Ms. Mae from operating a new dog grooming business, but it can recover damages.

2. Brian's Computer Software Company is a well-established firm with many existing retailers selling its fine products. Brian recently patented a popular new spread sheet program. In an effort to expand its retailers, Brian sells its new product to new retailers at a lower price than to its exiting retailers. Which of the following is true about the price discrepancy?
    A. Brian is guilty of illegal price discrimination.
    B. Price discrimination is a *per se* offense.
    C. If Brian's sales are under $100,000 per year, it cannot be charged with price discrimination.
    D. Since this is the only way to obtain new customers, Brian's pricing policy is legal.

3. Four competing gas stations in the town of Gasoline Alley have agreed to keep their rates at a certain low rate in an attempt to attract tourists visiting the town and to buy their gasoline products while visiting Gasoline Alley. Which of the following statements is correct?
    A. Because the agreement is aimed at eliminating cutthroat competition, it is not illegal.
    B. The gas stations have engaged in price fixing, which is illegal *per se*.
    C. Because the prices benefit the customers, the agreement is not illegal.
    D. Only agreements to charge higher prices for gasoline products are illegal.

4. Green Foods, Inc. sells various interrelated products which it processes and distributes. Recently, Green Foods received a patent on a new artificial spinach leaf that is manufactured almost exclusively by Green Foods. Realizing the desirability of the new product, it decided to take advantage of the situation by requiring its purchasers to take its fine artificial croutons if they wished to obtain the new item over which it had complete control. Which of the following best describes the situation?
    A. Since Green Foods has a patent on the new item, it can establish any sales policy it desires.
    B. The plan is legal and the only profitable way to sell slow-moving inventory.
    C. The arrangement is probably an illegal tying agreement.
    D. As long as the other products which must be taken are sold at a fair price to the buyers, the arrangement is legal.

366

5. Cool Corporation manufactures mountain bikes. Cool Corporation has granted Boulder Bikes the exclusive right to sell its products in Boulder, Colorado. The arrangement between Cool Corporation and Boulder Bikes is best described as which of the following?
   A. A chain-style franchise.
   B. An area franchise.
   C. A processing plant franchise.
   D. A distributorship franchise.

6. Magic Burger Corporation has discovered a new special sauce that has sent its sales off the top of the charts. For a modest fee, Magic Burger Corporation grants franchisees the right to use the special sauce and to use the Magic Burger trade name for marketing purposes. The arrangement between Magic Burger Corporation and its franchisees is best described as which of the following?
   A. A chain-style franchise.
   B. An area franchise.
   C. A processing plant franchise.
   D. A distributorship franchise.

7. Assume the same facts as in question 6. In addition, assume that a franchisee served a burger with special sauce that had spoiled causing serious injuries to the customer. If the customer sues Magic Burger Corporation, which of the following is correct?
   A. A franchisee is an independent contractor, and therefore Magic Burger Corporation is not liable.
   B. A franchisor and franchisee relationship constitutes a principal and agent relationship, and therefore the franchisor is liable.
   C. By serving spoiled sauce, the franchisee acted outside the scope of agency and therefore Magic Burger Corporation is not liable.
   D. None of the above.

8. Assume the same facts as in question 7. With respect to termination of the relationship, which of the following is correct?
   A. Unless stated otherwise in the agreement, the franchise will automatically terminate after one year.
   B. Unless stated otherwise in the agreement, the grant of a franchise is irrevocable.
   C. Serving tainted burgers would probably be enough to constitute "cause" to terminate the relationship.
   D. None of the above.

9. Which of the following is not an advantage of franchising?
   A. Franchising allows the franchisor to reach new markets with its product or services.
   B. Both the franchisee and the franchisor are protected from competition in the marketplace.
   C. Consumers are generally assured of uniform product quality.
   D. The franchisee benefits from the knowledge and resources of the franchisor.

10. Which of the following best describes the legal relation of a franchisor and franchisee where there is a high degree of independence between the two?
    A. Principal/agent.
    B. Limited partners.
    C. Employer/independent contractor.
    D. Partners.

Terms:

1. *Area franchisee; subfranchisor.* This person's role is similar to that of a promoter in the law of corporations in that both help start up new businesses.
2. *Tying arrangement.* These sorts of arrangements are classified as an illegal restraint of trade under Section 3 of the Clayton Antitrust Act.
3. *Price discrimination.* This practice is also in violation of the Clayton Act.
4. *Distributorship franchise.* A common example of this sort of franchise arrangement is found in the sale and distribution of new automobiles from the manufacturer through the use of authorized dealers.
5. *Trademark infringement.* The value of the trademark can be inestimable. Consider for example the fair market value of the soft drinks like Coke, Pepsi, or 7-Up. Because these are so valuable, their owners vigorously defend their exclusive use by only authorized franchisees.
6. *Trade secrets.* The interesting aspect of trade secrets is that they are not registered in the same way as certain kinds of other intellectual property, such as patents. Thus they are not as easy to reverse engineer and the like. But they are still considered to be a property and enjoy the protection of the law.
7. *Price fixing.* In spite of all the benefits which inure from the franchisor/ franchisee relationship, the antitrust laws will not allow it to be used as a subterfuge to get around laws designed to protect competition in the marketplace.
8. *Wrongful termination.* Good faith and fair dealing are elements of franchise contracts which more and more courts are reading into franchise contracts even if the parties do not specifically list them as covenants of the agreement.
9. *Franchisor, franchisee.* These are the basic terms used in this body of law.
10. *Unfair competition.* Because the trade secret is a protected property right, wrongful use of another's such property has many legal consequences.

True/False:

1. True. It can be, in effect, the best of both worlds if done properly.
2. True. Before treble damages are allowed, however, the plaintiff must prove that the wrongdoer tied the sales of two separate products, that more than a de minimus amount of commerce was affected, that sufficient market power existed to enforce the arrangement and that the arrangement caused an unreasonable restraint of trade or a substantial lessening of commerce.
3. False. Termination at will clauses in franchise agreements are generally held to be void on the grounds that they are unconscionable.
4. False. The franchise described is a processing plant franchise. A chain-style franchise exists when the franchisor licenses the franchisee to make and sell its products or services to the public from a retail outlet serving an exclusive geographic territory.
5. False. Most states require a franchise agreement to be in writing. However, most will enforce an oral franchise agreement if necessary to prevent unjust enrichment.

6. True. If the franchise agreement is reached, the injured party may sue for rescission of the agreement, restitution, and damages.
7. False. Mere use of the same name does not automatically make the franchisee the agent of the franchisor. If, however, there is no effort to inform the public of the separate legal status, the franchisee may be deemed the agent of the franchisor.
8. False. The franchise agreement is a contractual agreement. Therefore, the agreement can contain any reasonable restrictions to which parties agree.
9. True. The license fee is generally a lump sum payment for the privilege of being granted a franchise.
10. False. There are many types of franchise fees that can be collected by a franchisor including royalty fees, assessment fees, lease fees, and the like.

Multiple Choice:

1. C. A covenant not to compete in a franchise setting is enforceable unless unreasonable, overextensive, or against public policy.
2. A. Price discrimination occurs when a franchisor or franchisee charges different prices to different customers for the same product without any justification. Brian's Computer Software Company is guilty of illegal price discrimination.
3. B. Any agreement as to the price to be charged for a product or service is price fixing and is thus a per se violation of the Sherman Antitrust Act. This would be true in spite of the lower prices charged for the gasoline products.
4. C. This would probably be an illegal tying arrangement which constitutes a restraint of trade and is therefore illegal pursuant to the Sherman Antitrust Act.

5. D. A distributorship franchise exists when a manufacturer licenses a retail dealer to distribute its products to the public.
6. A. A chain-style franchise exists when the franchisor licenses the franchisee to make and sell its products or services to the public using its name.
7. D. Although a franchisee is typically an independent contractor, there are some situations in which the franchisor and the franchisee use the same name and make no attempt to distinguish their existence. Then a principal and agent relationship will be found. However, the mere existence of a franchise setting does not automatically create a principal and agent relationship.
8. C. Failure to meet quality control standards is "just cause" to terminate for cause.
9. B. Franchises are obligated to abide by the antitrust laws the same as any other form of business organization.
10. C. If properly organized, the franchisor and franchisee are independent legal entities.

VI. Key Question Checklist Answers to Essay Question:

A. *What are the key elements of the franchise agreement?*

The parties have entered into a basic franchise agreement. It is an express agreement which has been reduced to writing. Because the contract could not be performed in less than a year, the Statute of Frauds would require a writing in this case. The basic property rights being offered by the franchisor are the exclusive selling rights of its Whatyamacallits products in an agreed upon area. Assuming the product is patented, this product does constitute a recognized property right in the eyes of the law. In return for this exclusive right to sell the products of franchisor, the franchisees have agreed to pay both up front license fees and royalties.

B. *What are some of the key terms within this agreement?*

Under the terms of the agreement, the franchisor retained typical controls over the sales of its products. These controls will be upheld by the courts as long as they do not involve illegal tying agreements or violate any other provisions of the law. These issues are particularly important for purposes of antitrust law.

C. *Have all the statutory requirements vis-à-vis franchising been met?*

The parties to this contract may have a real problem with the disclosures or lack of disclosures made by the franchisor before entering into the agreement. The Federal Trade Commission requires franchisors to make full disclosure nationwide to prospective franchisees. Where the franchise makes hypothetical or actual sales projections, specific additional disclosures must be made. They include:

1. The assumptions underlying the estimates.
2. The number and percentages of actual franchises that have obtained such results.
3. A cautionary statement in at least 12 point boldface print.

D&E. *Have there been any breaches of the contract agreement, and what is the involvement of any third parties?*

The Whatyamacallit Corporation failed to do any of the above on the fateful day in Backwater. Because it did violate the FTC rules, it may now be subject to a number of sanctions and remedies. As for Dawson and George, they are busy trying to negotiate a new deal with the Doohickee Corporation.

CHAPTER 41

EMPLOYMENT CONTRACTS AND WORKER PROTECTION LAWS

Adam ate the apple, and our teeth still ache.
Hungarian Proverb

I. Overview:

A phase commonly used in the area of pension and employee benefits law is "golden ball and chain." This description is meant to illustrate the two sided nature of many of the prerequisites associated with the employment relationship. On one side, the gold comes from the financial security afforded by a steady income and the various employment-related insurance protections designed to buffet one from the vicissitudes of life. The ball and chain aspect comes from the price paid for those perks. This cost not only includes the obvious time and energy commitments involved in doing one's job, but also the lost opportunity costs associated with having chosen one employer over others. For many the employment relationship becomes one of love-hate or at least a standoff based on economic necessity. As one demoralized employee recently stated: "My pension is simply a form of compensatory damages for having endured terminal boredom."

In the past, the dominant contractual form this relationship has taken has been found in the *employment at will* doctrine. This doctrine assumes that given equal bargaining power, and absent express or implied agreement to the contrary, either the employee or employer may

end the relationship. This termination can come about at any time, for any reason, bilaterally or unilaterally. The doctrine has long been under fire because of being myopic on two main scores: it presumes equality of bargaining power between the employer and employee and that the employment relationship is a totally private contractual matter between the contracting parties.

Recent cases and legislative enactments have greatly eroded the doctrine. On the legislative front, a number of states have decided that public policy interests in favor of certain kinds of activities must take precedent over the employer/employee relationship. Examples would include voting rights, antidiscrimination measures, whistleblower protections, and employee health and safety protections. In addition, a number of courts have seen fit to interpret employer handbooks, written and oral job policies, and other acts as indicia of an implied contract between the employer and employee. So what may have appeared originally to be the employee's economic ball and chain has also become the employer's.

The simple truth is that there is a growing involvement of government at every step of the employer/employee relationship. It sets the ground rules for hiring, working conditions, paying for harm, termination, and ultimate payment of pensions and or death benefits. It all has come a long way from the simplistic and archaic notion that the employment contract is only the business of the immediate parties involved.

II. Hypothetical Multi-Issue Essay Question:

Mr. Quincy Harpie has a problem. As a matter of fact, he has a lot of problems. He is chronically complaining about all sort of illnesses, both actual and perceived. His mother was never proud of him and kicked him out of the house at age thirty-two. Finally Mr. Harpie had to face reality and get a job.

He found his first job with Mega Widgets Corporation in Backwater as a crystal widget assembler. Two weeks into the job, he complained of severe backaches and sought worker compensation for his back problems. He was awarded his claim of partial disability and proceeded to stay at home while seeking other employment.

He did find other employment at Mini Widgets Corporation in the adjoining state of Massazona. He did not tell Mini Widgets about his employment history with Mega Widgets. Two weeks on the job as an assembler, guess what happened? His back flared up again. He successfully filed a worker compensation claim against Mini Widgets. He continued to also collect from Mega Widgets claiming that he was still disabled.

Mr. Harpie decided to try once more and moved to East Moncalla where he found employment with Micro Widgets Corporation. Micro had a strict employment at will policy and informed Mr. Harpie of that policy in writing. After two weeks of work on Micro's assembly line, Mr. Harpie again claimed a back injury. He filed yet a third claim under workers compensation. As in the prior incidents, he did not inform Micro of any of his prior job history.

Micro fought Mr. Harpie's claim and also fired him under the employment at will doctrine. Mr. Harpie claims that the doctrine is being wrongfully used against him. He is arguing that he was being fired only because he asserted his rights under the workers compensation law. At the time Micro did not know about Mr. Harpie's history with Mega and Mini Widgets Corporations. Should Mr. Harpie be reinstated at Micro Corporation?

III. Key Question Checklist:

A. In examining the employer/employee relationship, first define the relationship. Is it:
1. Based on contract?
    (a) Express terms?
        (1) Written?
        (2) Oral?
        (3) Both of the above?
    (b) Implied?
        (1) From collateral written or oral statements?
        (2) From the conduct of the parties?
        (3) From any other facts or circumstances?
2. Based on employment at will?
    (a) Either party can terminate the relationship?
    (b) At any time?
    (c) For any reason?

B. Once you have identified the basis for the employer/employee relationship, what restrictions are imposed upon that relationship?
1. By contract between the parties?
    (a) Express limitations?
    (b) Implied limitations?
2. Limitations imposed on the employment at will doctrine?
    (a) Based on statute?
        (1) Civil rights?
        (2) Health and safety?
        (3) Whistleblower protection?
        (4) Labor law?
        (5) Voting rights?
    (b) Based on public policy?
        (1) Protection of substantive law enforcement?
        (2) Protection of procedural law enforcement?

(c) Based on tort law?
  (1) Fraud by employer?
  (2) Intentional infliction of emotional distress?
  (3) Slander or defamation of character?
  (4) Breach of implied covenant of good faith and fair dealing?
  (5) Any other tort-based cause of action?

C. Once you have established the relationship and the restrictions applicable to it vis-à-vis the immediate parties, next look at the role of government. What governmental rules of the road apply to this relationship? (Expect many of these policies to be applicable concurrently)?
  1. Fair Labor Standards Act?
    (a) Child labor law?
    (b) Minimum wage law?
    (c) Hours overtime pay laws?
  2. Worker's Compensation Law?
    (a) Contractual strict liability substitute for tort actions arising out of on the job injuries?
    (b) Funded by insurance program?
    (c) Federal compensation laws apply to certain industries?
    (d) New areas of coverage?
      (1) Occupational disease?
      (2) Job related stress?
  3. Occupational Safety and Health Act?
    (a) Covers virtually all employers?
      (1) Exceptions by statute?
    (b) Designed to promote safety in the workplace?
    (c) Administered by Department of Labor's Occupational Safety and Health Administration?
      (1) Promulgates safety standards?
      (2) Enforcement of the safety standards?

4. Employee Retirement Income Security Act?
  (a) Does the company have a pension plan in place?
  (b) Is this plan in compliance with the rules and regulations set forth by the Department of Labor and the Internal Revenue Service?
  (c) Is the plan insured by the Pension Benefit Guaranty Corporation?
5. Immigration Reform and Control Act?
  (a) Did the employer comply with the provisions of this act?
    (1) Complete INS form I-9?
    (2) Inspect required documents of qualification for work in U.S.?
    (3) Post required notices?
6. Social security laws?
  (a) Proper payments made to the fund by:
    (1) Employer?
    (2) Employee?
    (3) Self-employed persons?
  (b) Consequences for failure to comply?
7. Unemployment compensation laws?
  (a) Federal unemployment tax applicable?
  (b) State unemployment statutes applicable?
  (c) Taxes paid by the employer?
  (d) Employee eligible?
    (1) Available to work?
    (2) Seeking employment?
  (e) Employee ineligible?
    (1) Dismissed for cause?
    (2) Voluntarily quit?

IV. Objective Questions:

Terms:

1. The administrative procedure created so that workers receive compensation for injuries that occur on the job is called _____ _____.

2. The 1970 Occupational Safety and Health Act created the _____ _____ _____ _____, a federal administrative agency empowered to administer the Act and adopt rules and regulations to interpret and enforce the Act.

3. In 1986, the Immigration Reform and Control Act granted _____ to illegal immigrants who were living in the U.S.

4. Since 1935, most workers who are temporarily unemployed are entitled to _____ _____.

5. Under the Fair Labor Standards Act, employers are required to pay a _____ wage to employees.

6. Persons aged _____ and over may work at any job, whether it is hazardous or not, under the Fair Labor Standards Act.

7. The employment relationship in the United States prior to the Industrial Revolution was governed by the _____ _____ doctrine.

8. Under workers' compensation, workers cannot sue their employers in court for damages; thus workers' compensation is an _____ remedy.

9. The Immigration Reform and Control Act made it unlawful to hire _____ _____ except those protected by the Act.

10. The federal administrative agency that administers and enforces the rules on safety in the workplace is called the

_____ _____ _____ _____ _____.

True/False:

1. ____An at-will employee could be discharged by an employer at any time and for any reason under common law.

2. ____The Employee Polygraph Protection Act is administered by the Department of Justice.

3. ____Under the Fair Labor Standards Act, an employer cannot require nonexempt employees to work more than 40 hours per week unless they receive overtime pay.

4. ____Payments under workers' compensation programs include hospital and medical benefits, disability benefits, and death benefits to dependents, but not recovery for certain body parts.

5. ____Employers are required to establish pension plans for their employees.

6. ____Today employment law is a mixture of contract law, agency law, and government regulation.

7. ____Under the Statute of Frauds, employment contracts that cannot be performed within one year need not be in writing.

8. ____The public policy exception is the most used common law exception to the employment at-will doctrine.

9. ____Occupational diseases are covered by workers' compensation legislation.

10. ____A general duty is imposed on employers by the Occupational Safety and Health Act to provide a work environment "free from recognized hazards that are causing or are likely to cause death or serious physical harm to his employees."

Multiple Choice:

1. Under the Fair Labor Standards Act, which of the following does not define lawful child labor?
   A. Children aged 14 and 15 may work limited hours in nonhazardous jobs approved by the Department of Labor.
   B. Children aged 16 and 17 may work unlimited hours in nonhazardous jobs approved by the Department of Labor.
   C. Child actors and performers are exempt from child labor law restrictions.
   D. Children under the age of 14 cannot work as newspaper deliverers.

2. Edwin Employee worked for ABC Creditcard, an employer legally permitted to use polygraph testing. Which of the following statements is not true with regard to Edwin?
   A. ABC must give notice to Edwin.
   B. ABC must use licensed examiners.
   C. The polygraph examiner may ask Edwin any questions he wants to ask.
   D. The polygraph examiner may not ask questions relating to Edwin's religion or sexual behavior.

3. Edna Employee is employed as a secretary by Megacorp. Since this is a slow week for dictation, Megacorp asked Edna to work only 30 hours this week and 50 hours next week. When Edna received her check, she received no overtime pay for the extra 10 hours during the 50 hour week. Edna feels she is entitled to the overtime pay. What result?
   A. Under the Fair Labor Standards Act, an employer can require nonexempt employees to work more than 40 hours per week without overtime compensation.
   B. For purposes of determining overtime compensation, weeks are not treated separately. Therefore, Edna is not entitled to overtime pay for 10 hours of the 50 hour week.
   C. For purposes of determining overtime compensation, each week is treated separately. Therefore Edna is entitled to overtime pay for 10 hours of the 50 hour week.
   D. None of the above.

4. Lunching Linda was on her personal lunch hour at the Et Yet Cafe. Distracted Doris spilled boiling hot split pea soup on Linda. Because Linda does not think Doris has any money, she decides to seek recovery from her employer under workers' compensation. Which of the following must Linda prove?
   A. That she is an employee and not an independent contractor.
   B. That the injury arose out of and in the course of her employment.
   C. That she was at Et Yet on an errand for her employer.
   D. All of the above.

5. Which of the following statements about Social Security is untrue?
   A. Self-employed persons do not have to pay Social Security taxes.
   B. Social Security includes retirement benefits.
   C. Survivors' benefits to family members of deceased workers are included in Social Security.
   D. Social Security is not like a savings account.

6. Which of the following tort theories is not appropriate in a wrongful discharge action?
   A. Fraud?
   B. Strict liability for personal injury?
   C. Intentional infliction of emotional distress?
   D. Defamation of character?

7. Under the public policy exception to the employment at-will doctrine, for which of the following acts may an employee not be discharged?
   A. Serving as a juror?
   B. Refusing to engage in illegal animal research?
   C. Calling his boss a "dumb brain-dead nerd"?
   D. Refusing to distribute defective products?

8. At common law, which of the following is not a defense an employer could raise against recovery by an employee?
   A. *Respondeat superior?*
   B. Contributory negligence of the employee?
   C. Assumption of the risk by the employee?
   D. The fellow servant rule?

9. Under workers' compensation programs, which of the following are employers not required to do to fund the program?
   A. Making payments into a state insurance fund?
   B. Purchasing private insurance?
   C. Self-insuring by making payments into a contingency fund?
   D. Make voluntary contributions to the program?

10. Which of the following statements is not true concerning the Employee Retirement Income Security Act (ERISA)?
    A. Pension plans must be in writing?
    B. There must be a pension plan manager who owes a fiduciary duty to act as a "prudent person" in managing the fund?
    C. The pension plan can loan money to the sponsoring employer?
    D. A pension plan cannot invest more than 10 percent of its assets in the securities of the sponsoring employer?

V. Answers to Objective Questions:

Terms:

1. *Worker's compensation.* The basic statutory scheme is designed to avoid the waste and expense of seeking compensation for work-related injuries through the courts. It is one of the earliest forms of contract-based strict liability.

2. *Occupational Safety and Health Administration.* This agency has power to promote and regulate safety in virtually all workplaces except federal, state, and local government workplaces. It is part of the Department of Labor, and it imposes a number of record-keeping and reporting requirements on employers.

3. *Amnesty*. This act continues to be controversial in that members of certain ethnic groups allege that it is being enforced against them in a discriminatory manner. People on the opposite side of the political fence are saying that the act is not being enforced enough to be effective. You decide.

4. *Unemployment compensation*. The guidelines for these benefits are set by the federal government, but the actual administration of these employer-contributed taxes is handled by the individual states.

5. *Minimum*. This is one of the provisions of the Fair Labor Standards Act of 1938 and it is occasionally amended to reflect the higher costs of living due to inflation. Much political debate revolves around this provision due to its effects on the job market at the lowest end of the employment spectrum.

6. *Eighteen*. This age is now generally considered legal adulthood for most (but not all) purposes. For example, the federal government recently qualified its disbursement of highway funds only on the condition that the states raise the legal drinking age back to 21.

7. *Laissez-faire*. This French term has come to express a political-economic philosophy of government hands off in the machinations of the marketplace.

8. *Exclusive*. The exclusive remedy is considered the contractual trade off for the certainty of being able to collect for work-related harm regardless of fault.

9. *Illegal aliens*. It has been estimated that illegal immigration into the U.S. runs as high as 3,000 people per day. Theis Act is one attempt to try and stem this tide.

10. *Occupational Safety and Health Administration*. Virtually all private employers are within the scope of the Act which this agency is charged with administering.

True/False:

1. True. This common law doctrine is still very important in the study of employment law in spite of all the statutory and public policy based case law exceptions written into it in today's legal environment.

2. False. The Employee Polygraph Protection Act is administered by the Department of Labor. As new detection technologies emerge, we can expect to see more legislation of this sort to help protect employees from abuses of that technology.

3. True. This provision of the act was designed to combat some of the sweat shop abuses commonly used in the early shift of our society from an agricultural base to the industrial era.

4. False. Worker's compensation legislation includes recovery for certain body parts. These schedules are either listed by statute or agreed upon between the contracting parties.

5. False. Private pension plans are not required *per se*. But if they are established, they must conform to all applicable federal and state laws.

6. True. Modern employment law reflects many of the socio-political and legal changes that have come with the diversification of the workplace.

7. False. Such employment contracts must be in writing per the Statute of Frauds.

8. True. The law of employment is interwoven with many other aspects of law, especially the enforcement of civil rights.
9. True. The burden of proof rests on the employee to show that the disease did result from an employment activity.
10. True. This language is found in the Occupational Safety and Health Act of 1970.

Multiple Choice:

1. D.   Newspaper delivery work has always been allowed as an exception to the general rules of child labor. It is interesting to note, however, that hard times are forcing more and more adults into these jobs.
2. C.   There were a number of abuses by employers, coupled with the scientific shortcomings of polygraph inaccuracies, which led Congress to pass the Employee Polygraph Protection Act in 1988.
3. C.   This is one of the requirements of the Fair Labor Standards Act of 1938, as amended.
4. D.   All three are elements required in order to show that Linda is qualified for coverage and payment under typical worker's compensation acts.
5. A.   Under the Self-Employment Contributions Act, self-employed individuals must also pay into Social Security. The amount of taxes self-employed individuals must pay is equal to the combined employer/employee amount.
6. B.   A, C, and D are all tort theory exceptions to the employment at will doctrine. Strict liability is more likely to be used in a products liability case.
7. C.   A, B, and D have all been held by case law or statute to be public policy

bases for an exception to the employment at will doctrine.
8. A.   This common law doctrine holds the master liable in certain cases for the wrongful acts of his or her servant. The terms "master" and "servant" are now dated and have generally been replaced by "employer" and "employee."
9. D.   Voluntary contributions are just that—voluntary and not required by workers' compensation statutes.
10. C.   This practice is expressly prohibited by the Employee Retirement Income Security Act.

VI. Key Question Checklist Answers to Essay Question:

A.   *How would you define the basic employer-employee relationship in this case?*

The employer/employee relationship between Mr. Harpie and Micro Widgets Corporation is clearly one of employment at will. The parties have agreed to this in writing. Under that doctrine, either party may terminate the relationship at any time for any reason, subject to limitations imposed as a matter of public policy, by statute or by court precedent.

B.   *What are the basic restrictions imposed on this relationship, and which of the major employment laws apply to this case?*

There may be limitations imposed by the State of East Moncalla on the employment at will doctrine. Examples might include protection of whistleblowers or protection of persons who refuse to break the law at the behest of their employers. But none of these limitations are designed to protect the employee to the extent of shielding his or her own wrongdoing.

Worker's compensation fraud is one of the fastest growing and costliest crimes that today's employers face. States have not acted in concert to prevent this fraud as well as they should have. That failure to enforce against this sort of fraudulent behavior has made cases like Mr Harpie's very common and very costly. Under the employment at will doctrine, unless Mr. Harpie can show that one of the exceptions applies based or public policy, case law, or statute, Micro Widgets can fire him. If they know how bad an apple he really is, they should seek to have criminal charges filed also. Then maybe he can develop a bad back while punching out license plates.

CHAPTER 42

EQUAL OPPORTUNITY IN EMPLOYMENT

I am free of prejudice. I hate everybody equally.

W. C. Fields

I. Overview:

No single American legal issue is inflamed with more controversy than discrimination in the workplace. The genesis of our nation's heritage is rooted in a diversity of peoples who immigrated to the New World in order to flee the royalist, class, or caste systems which so often predestined their opportunities for social and economic advancement. The U.S. Declaration of Independence, and the government founded on it, was the first major system of self-governance premised on the assumption that all persons are born equal and should be treated equally in the eyes of the law. As we all know, that equality has often been a hope rather than a reality for many.

The same diversity which has been a source of national pride has also been the basis of disparate treatment of persons in the workplace for many years. The term *discriminate* has within it two distinct and opposite meanings. On the positive side, discrimination is simply a fact of life. We are not all equal in all ways. We have different talents, strengths, levels of training, and abilities. Employers, in turn, should be allowed and expected to seek utilization of these divergent talents and strengths in their own best interests. To discriminate in the positive sense is to reward ability and merit on its face. The positive aspect of discrimination really says that uniqueness should be discerned, differentiated, distinguished, and rewarded in the workplace. In the end, economic marketplace factors are blind to any other factors but job performance. Like it or not, positive discrimination is a simple economic necessity which is no different than the laws of nature and cannot be ignored. For example, you can not expect the average man on the street to play football as well as John Elway. He, in turn, is duly rewarded for these talents.

The negative side of discrimination is found in a wrongful process of selection. For a society founded on a premise of equality, we have certainly had more than our share of unequal treatment in the workplace. The negative side of discrimination is inequality of treatment based on wrongful motive, justifications, or rationalizations. Each choice not based on talent, ability, and merit is a step away from the inherent basis of equality before the law. Wrongful discrimination is like cancer. Sooner or later, once it is allowed to grow unchecked, it will kill. None of us can afford to look the other way and say: "It's not my problem." Wrongful discrimination against any group is a wrong upon the society at large. Most everyone appreciates that fact intuitively, if not intellectually.

The issue is not in appreciating that wrongful discrimination is a social cancer that must be cured. The real concern is how to go about the cure? Law is an end product of many larger movements in our society. It is a combination of morality, religious doctrines, social sciences, social engineering, and philosophy. In the end, law reflects, rather than dictates, choices made by society as to how it will help or hurt its members. The evolution of justice has never been painless. With each growing awareness of the pain incurred by wrongful discrimination, the cure will become even more difficult. Law is more readily administered when we have drawn a clear moral line. It is easy to justify the jailing of a rapist in order to protect society. But when there are competing, socially justifiable "goods" on both sides of the issue, the job of judgment is far more difficult.

Consider the dilemma posed by affirmative action. Past history provides vivid proof that patterns of discrimination have deep roots and will continue unless some sort of corrective social engineering takes hold in the workplace. Yet is the cure worse than the disease? Can reverse discrimination really be justified? Is it any wonder that every day this quandary seems to get deeper? It is like kicking in quicksand--the more you try to move, the faster you sink.

One element which provides hope for positive change is goodwill. Where people of goodwill cling to the basic rightness of equity before the law, that equity will eventually result in a changed culture. Until then, law and our courts will continue to be the testing grounds for this monumental change in the social order. It may sound corny, but we all must do our part to live and let live.

II. Hypothetical Multi-issue Essay Question:

An item recently appeared on the news wires:

"Major department store says no to Santa!"

As it turns out, the rest of the story was most interesting. A person who had been working for a major New York City department store was seeking to be reinstated into his seasonal job assignment as a Santa for the holidays. He had performed this job satisfactorily for a number of years.

He was denied reinstatement because he tested positive for HIV since the last holiday season. The department store was concerned that the health and safety of children sitting on Santa's lap would be placed in jeopardy. Even if the risk to health was minimal, the department store argued that the fear of parents to bring their children to a person known to have been tested positive for HIV would cost the store much lost business and damage its goodwill.

"Santa" decides to file a complaint with the EEOC. What will result?

III. Key Question Checklist:

A. In examining issues of discrimination in employment, you must first examine the alleged discrimination itself. Discrimination has a number of definitions found within the Constitution, statutes, and case law. They are far too many to list here, but some main categories of wrongful discrimination are based on:
1. Race?
2. Color?
3. Sex?
4. Age?
5. National origin?
6. Creed or religion?
7. Physical characteristics or condition?
8. Sexual preference?

B. Once you have identified what form of alleged wrongful discrimination is at issue, look to see what specific legal remedies may be available to the person alleging the discrimination. Our Constitution calls for equal treatment before the law generally. More specific statutory remedies relating to employment issues are found in a number of enactments.
1. Civil Rights Act of 1866?
   (a) Prohibits racial discrimination?

(b) In contractual relationships?

(c) Allows recovery for back pay without a statute of limitations?

2. Equal Pay Act of 1963?

  (a) Prohibits pay discrimination based on sex?

  (b) Covers all sectors of employment except federal workers?

  (c) Requires equal pay based on:

    (1) Equal skill?

    (2) Equal effort?

    (3) Equal responsibilities?

    (4) Similar working conditions?

  (d) Allows differential pay based on:

    (1) Seniority?

    (2) Merit?

    (3) Quantity or quality of product?

    (4) Any other factor other than sex?

  (e) Private cause of actions allowed?

3. Title VII of the Civil Rights Act of 1964?

  (a) Targeted at job discrimination based on:

    (1) Race?

    (2) Color?

    (3) Religion?

    (4) Sex?

    (5) National origin?

  (b) Forms of prohibited discrimination covered by the statute?

    (1) Disparate treatment of individuals?

    (2) Patterns or practices against an entire class?

    (3) Policies which have a disparate impact on a protected class?

  (c) Scope of coverage of the statute?

    (1) Most private employees and all employment agencies?

    (2) Most governmental entities?

    (3) Most labor unions?

  (d) Administration of the statute?

    (1) Equal Employment Opportunity Commission is the law's enforcer (EEOC)?

    (2) EEOC may sue in its own name?

    (3) EEOC may allow suit to be brought individually with a "Right to Sue Letter?"

  (e) Remedies under Title VII limited by the statute?

    (1) Damages limited?

    (2) Equity-based remedies?

    (3) Subject to treaty provisions with other countries?

  (f) Defenses to a Title VII claim?

    (1) Merit?

    (2) Seniority?

    (3) Bona fide occupational qualification?

      (aa) Race not included?

      (bb) Color not included?

4. Age Discrimination in Employment Act of 1967?

  (a) Covers most nonfederal employees?

  (b) Certain sectors of federal workers covered?

  (c) Current provisions call for phasing out all age ceilings for persons covered over the age of 40?

  (d) Administered by EEOC?

    (1) EEOC may bring an action?

    (2) Private action allowed under certain conditions?

  (e) Remedies include:

    (1) Money damages?

    (2) Equity relief?

  (f) Defenses?

    (1) Good cause dismissal?

    (2) Bona fide occupational qualifications?

    (3) Bona fide employee benefit plan?

5. Rehabilitation Act of 1973?
   (a) Forbids discrimination based on handicaps?
   (b) Covers employers who have contracts or assistance from the federal government?
   (c) Covers people who:
       (1) Have mental or physical impairments which substantially limit activities?
       (2) Have a record of such impairments?
       (3) Are thought to have such impairments?
   (d) Remedies included?
       (1) EEOC action?
       (2) Damages under private causes of action?
6. Americans with Disabilities Act of 1990?
   (a) Prohibits discrimination based on disability?
   (b) Covers most employers, private and governmental, except for federal government?
   (c) Disabled persons include:
       (1) Same classifications as listed under Rehabilitation Act of 1973?
       (2) Numerous new classifications including persons with human immunodeficiency virus (HIV).
   (d) Employers required to provide reasonable accommodations that would not impose undue burdens?
   (e) Defenses allowed:
       (1) Undue hardship?
       (2) Test criterions not met?
       (3) Threat to health or safety of others in the workplace?
       (4) Infection or communication of disease through food handling (HIV specifically excluded)?
       (5) Religious entities may favor their own members?
   (f) Remedies?
       (1) Administered by EEOC?
       (2) Private actions allowed?
       (3) Damages and equitable remedies both allowable?
7. Bankruptcy Code?
   (a) Protects debtors in bankruptcy from discrimination in employment?
   (b) Applies to both public and private employers?
8. State and local antidiscrimination laws?
   (a) May cover areas not covered by federal law. Example: sexual preference statutes?

C. Once you have decided which form of discrimination is at issue and which statute or group of statutes may be applicable, you must then decide which path is best suited for a remedy to the problem?
   1. Statute enforcement?
   2. Affirmative action?
   3. Any other method?
       (a) New legislation? Example: ERA.
       (b) New administrative regulations? Example: Anti-sexual harassment guidelines?

IV. Objective Questions:

Terms:

1. The right of all employees and job applicants (1) to be treated without discrimination and (2) to be able to prosecute employers if they are discriminated against is generally known as _____ _____.

2. The five-member federal agency responsible for enforcing most federal antidiscrimination laws is called the _____ _____ _____ _____.

383

3. A document given to an employee by the EEOC in the event that the EEOC does not want to act on behalf of an employee in a civil rights suit which gives the employee the right to sue her employer in the appropriate federal district court is called the _____ _____ _____ letter.

4. The treaty which allows "nationals and companies of Japan" to hire specified employees of their choice and creates an exemption from Title VII coverage is called the Treaty of _____ _____ _____ with Japan.

5. The practice of refusing to hire or promote someone unless she has sex with the manager or supervisor is illegal and is called _____ _____ _____ discrimination.

6. The duty that employers owe employees to accommodate (1) the occurrence of religious practices, observances, or beliefs if it does not cause undue hardship to the employer or (2) a handicapped person's special requirements in the workplace is known as the duty of _____ _____.

7. The selection or promotion qualification that is based on work, educational experience, and professionally developed ability tests is called _____ selection or promotion.

8. Discrimination based on sex, religion, and national origin is permitted if there is a legitimate reason for such discrimination and if it can be shown to be based on _____ _____.

9. A hiring policy that provides that certain job preferences will be given to minority or other protected class applicants when an employer makes an employment decision is called _____ _____.

10. Discrimination against a group which is usually thought of as a majority by a group which is usually thought of as a minority is generally referred to as _____ _____.

True/False:

1. ____ Federal workers are the only class which is exempt from the Equal Pay Act of 1963.

2. ____ Under the Equal Pay Act, employers can either increase the wages of the discriminated-against employee, or decrease the wages of the other employees.

3. ____ Back pay, liquidated damages, and overtime pay are all remedies available under the Equal Pay Act.

4. ____ Under Title VII, a private complainant must first file a complaint with the EEOC before bringing suit against the employer.

5. ____ When the EEOC decides to bring suit on behalf of a complainant, it issues a right to sue letter.

6. ____ Both monetary damages and extensive equitable remedies are available to prevailing complainants in Title VII cases.

7. _____ Only women are protected from sex discrimination under Title VII.

8. _____ Title VII, like many local ordinances, prohibits discrimination based on a person's sexual preference.

9. _____ Because of the Age Discrimination In Employment Act of 1967, most nonfederal employers cannot establish mandatory retirement ages for their employees.

10. _____ If the EEOC brings a suit under the Age Discrimination In Employment Act, a private suit arising from the same violation cannot be brought.

Multiple Choice:

1. Employee Edward has been with Super Sales Company (SSC) for ten years. Employee Ellen was hired by SSC two years ago. Edward and Ellen are both managers, perform many of the same tasks, and have similar responsibilities. However, Edward is paid more than Ellen. Is this permissible under the Equal Pay Act?
   A. No, because two people in essentially the same job can never have different pay levels.
   B. Yes, because the Equal Pay Act does not cover managers.
   C. Yes, because Edward can be rewarded for seniority.
   D. Yes, because SSC can set whatever pay level it chooses.

2. Disadvantaged David wants to bring a suit under the Equal Pay Act against his employer, Discriminating Daniel, for pay discrimination. Daniel hired Successful Sarah at the same time David was hired for essentially the same position.

However, Sarah is paid almost twice what David is paid. Which of the following is correct?
   A. David cannot sue Daniel since the Equal Pay Act only protects women.
   B. David must submit a complaint with the EEOC before filing suit.
   C. Both of the above.
   D. None of the above.

3. Prevailing Pam has won a judgment against her employer under the Equal Pay Act. Which of the following is correct?
   A. Pam can receive back pay as damages.
   B. The other employees' wages may be lowered to eliminate disparity.
   C. Pam can receive overtime pay as damages.
   D. All of the above.

4. Infuriated Irene, a well-qualified computer programmer, applied for a position with Computer Corp. (CC). However, CC denied her the position and sought other applicants with Irene's qualifications to fill the position. Irene wants to bring a suit against CC under Title VII. What type of discrimination should Irene base her case on?
   A. Disparate impact discrimination.
   B. Pattern or practice discrimination.
   C. Disparate treatment discrimination.
   D. Any of the above.

5. Assume the same facts as in question 4. Also assume Irene prevails in her suit against CC. What remedies may Irene receive?
   A. Reasonable attorney fees.
   B. An injunction to compel hiring.
   C. Both of the above.
   D. None of the above. Irene can only receive punitive damages.

385

6. Discouraged Doug believes he has been fired from his job with Narrow-Minded Manufacturers (NMM) because of his homosexuality. Doug wants to sue NMM. Under what authority should Doug bring his case?
   A. Title VII of the Civil Rights Act.
   B. The Equal Pay Act.
   C. A local ordinance forbidding such discrimination.
   D. None of the above.

7. Employee Edgar believes he has been discriminatorily fired by Youthful Ventures, Inc. (YVI) because of his age. If Edgar wants to bring suit against YVI under the Age Discrimination in Employment Act, which of the following requirements must be met?
   A. YVI must have at least 20 nonseasonal employees.
   B. Edgar must be at least 40 years old.
   C. YVI must be a nonfederal employer.
   D. All of the above.

8. Assume the same facts as in question 7. Also, assume Edgar prevails in his suit against YVI. What remedies may Edgar receive?
   A. Unpaid back wages.
   B. Attorney's fees.
   C. Reinstatement.
   D. All of the above.

9. Regarding the Rehabilitation Act of 1973, which of the following is incorrect?
   A. People with a history of alcoholism have been held to be handicapped under the Act.
   B. The Labor Department administers the nonfederal aspects of the Act.
   C. Private plaintiffs cannot recover damages.
   D. People with diabetes are considered handicapped under the Act.

10. Regarding the Americans with Disabilities Act of 1990, which of the following is correct?
    A. Employers must make reasonable accommodations to accommodate people with disabilities.
    B. Preemployment medical examinations are forbidden before a job offer.
    C. Title I of the ADA is administered by the EEOC.
    D. All of the above.

V. Answers to Objective Questions:

Terms:

1. *Equal opportunity*. This simple sounding phrase raises some of the most vexing legal issues of our day.
2. *Equal Employment Opportunity Commission*. Justice Thomas was once the head of this agency.
3. *Right to sue*. Most of the cases are farmed out through the use of these letters.
4. *Treaty of Friendship, Commerce and Navigation*. This treaty illustrates the bargaining power that comes with being a major economic trading partner.
5. *Quid pro quo*. In Hollywood parlance, this is known as the casting couch.
6. *Reasonable accommodation*. There are limits on how much the employer can be expected to do based on undue hardship.
7. *Merit*. This is the best qualification of all.
8. *Bona fide occupation qualification*. The burden of proof is on the employer.
9. *Affirmative action*. Debate on this issue will not end in the foreseeable future.
10. *Reverse discrimination*. Two wrongs do not make a right.

True/False:

1. True. They are covered under their own federal work rules.
2. False. Under the EPA, employers may increase the wages of the discriminated-against employee, but may not lower the wages of the other employees.
3. False. While back pay and liquidated damages are available remedies under the EPA, overtime pay is not.
4. True. Under Title VII, a private complainant must first file a complaint with the EEOC. If the EEOC decides not to bring suit on behalf of the complainant, it will issue a right to sue letter.
5. False. A right to sue letter is issued by the EEOC when it decides not to bring suit on behalf of the complainant.
6. True. The remedies granted can be one or both.
7. False. Both men and women are protected from sex discrimination under Title VII. However, the vast majority of the cases are brought by women.
8. False. Though many local ordinances do prohibit discrimination based on sexual preference, Title VII does not.
9. True. There are still some exceptions such as airline pilots.
10. True. This is outlined in the Age Discrimination in Employment Act.

Multiple Choice:

1. C. Under the EPA, employees can receive different wages if the payment system is based on seniority, merit, quantity or quality of product, or any factor other than sex. Here, Edward has been employed for eight years longer than Ellen. Therefore, the wage differential is probably justified. A is incorrect because two people in essentially the same job can have different pay scales if it is based on

a system described above. B is incorrect because the EPA does cover managers. D is incorrect because SSC must follow the guidelines of the EPA and cannot arbitrarily or discriminatorily set pay scales.
2. D. A is incorrect because the EPA protects both men and women. B is incorrect because a private complainant does not have to submit a complaint to the EEOC before filing suit. C is incorrect because both A and B are incorrect.
3. A. Under the EPA, a prevailing employee may be awarded back pay and liquidated damages. B is incorrect because the employer must raise Pam's wages; he cannot lower the other employees' wages. C is incorrect because overtime pay is not awarded as damages under the EPA.
4. C. Disparate treatment discrimination occurs when an employer treats a person less favorably than another because of that person's race, color, national origin, sex, or religion. A and B are incorrect because they are types of discrimination that affect a whole class, not just one specific person.
5. C. Under Title VII, a successful plaintiff can recover up to two years' back pay, reasonable attorney's fees and, where appropriate, compensatory damages. In addition, several equitable remedies are available including an injunction to compel hiring. D is incorrect because punitive damages are seldom awarded and are certainly not the only remedy available.
6. C. At present, none of the acts discussed in this chapter protect employees from discrimination because of sexual preference. An employee's only option is to sue under a local ordinance, if there is one. A and B are incorrect

because these acts do not protect employees from discrimination based on sexual preference.

7. D. These are all threshold tests for bringing a lawsuit under the ADEA.

8. D. All three remedies are provided under the ADEA.

9. C. Private plaintiffs may recover damages in a suit under the Rehabilitation Act. However, the EEOC and the Labor Department administer provisions of the act. A, B, and D are all correct statements.

10. D. Answers A, B, and C are found in the provisions of the ADA.

VI. Key Question Checklist Answers to Essay Question:

A. *Which category of wrongful discrimination is at issue?*

As was mentioned in the overview, the passions involved in many of these antidiscrimination issues run deep. They are often founded on claims by both sides of being morally, economically, or politically correct. Here the alleged wrongful discrimination is based on a physical characteristic or condition, i.e., being tested positive for HIV. The outbreak of AIDS has raised a raucous debate in this country about what body of law is applicable to persons afflicted with this physical condition.

On one side, many argue that it should be treated solely as a health problem. As such, laws with regard to communicable diseases should control. These measures would be based on the theory that certain prophylactic measures are necessary where there is a real and present danger to oneself and others from the disease.

On the other side, a number of commentators have argued that fear of HIV and AIDS-related afflictions have generated the worst sort of civil rights abuses against persons afflicted with those conditions. Discrimination in housing, jobs, education, health care, and insurance have all surfaced as a result of the fears raised by the disease. Where there is no provable risk of communication of the virus, civil rights, including job rights, should not be compromised.

The real answer probably lies somewhere in between. Society does have the right and responsibility to take reasonable measures to protect itself from deadly threats to public health. But, when measures are taken, society should also meet the burden of proof that the measures are reasonable and proper. It cannot and should not trample on civil rights based on panic and ill-founded fear.

B. *Which particular civil rights enactment is at issue?*

In this case, Congress has sought to balance the needs of both society and persons afflicted with HIV through the Americans with Disabilities Act of 1990. Under that Act persons who have tested positive for HIV are classified as disabled persons. As such they are entitled to seek protection under the Act from discriminatory practices in the workplace.

Conversely, the employer is allowed to use the defenses listed in the statute. One of those defenses is the health and safety of others. Another is undue hardship to the employer. In both cases, the burden of proof is on the employer to show that the defenses are applicable. If the department store can show that a real health and safety hazard exists for the persons with whom "Santa" will have contact, it will prevail. In addition, if the department store can show that using this person in this setting would create an undue hardship, it again would prevail. In either case, it must meet the burden of proof. Failure to do so will allow "Santa" to prevail under the Act. "Santa's" best strategy is to seek protection under the Americans with Disabilities Act of 1990. Further legislative on regulatory reforms may eventually be forthcoming, but by then it may be too late to help resolve this situation. In the meantime, this debate goes on in the halls of Congress and in the courts.

CHAPTER 43

LABOR RELATIONS LAW

What wisdom can you find that is greater than kindness?

Jean-Jacques Rousseau

I. Overview:

Organized labor has suffered from a long and steady decline in membership, power, and influence over the past forty years. Much of this slide has been of its own doing, traceable to poor union management, a fat cat image, and sometimes silly work rules which have no economic justification in the face of changed technology. In spite of all this bad news for unions, consider the working conditions that existed before them. It is a hallmark of advanced industrialized economies that the work force is highly organized and has a strong bargaining power over its affairs. The immediate post-Civil War era of industrialization saw the possibilities for abuse of the work force not only become reality, but also a tragedy, when it came to workers' safety. Most modern social legislation, ranging from the minimum wage, to child labor laws, to workplace and antidiscrimination statutes are traceable not to the largess of employers but rather to hard fought collective bargaining agreements. It is no accident that union representation is low in areas of the world still noted for the exploitation of their labor force. Corollaries of low wages are low levels of worker protection, environmental callousness, and an overall diminished standard of living.

The basic employer/employee relationship is a contractual one. As with any contract, both parties are expected to enter into the relationship with their own best interests at heart. The quaint notion of a paternalistic employer who cares for his workers over and above his own interests is simply unrealistic in today's age of cut-throat economic competition. What is realistic is enlightened self-interest. Each side of the labor management relationship still looks out for itself. But in looking out for number one, both must realize their mutual interdependence on each other. Labor must realize that it cannot sustain its own survival on the backs of failed companies brought down by union imposed inefficiencies. Labor must adjust to "Real World 101" and make concessions to both the technological and economic realities of trying to compete in a global economy. Management, in turn, cannot forever continue to erode our economic consumer base at home by running overseas at every opportunity for lower wages and less restrictive hospitalities for doing business.

What good will all that do in the long run if we have allowed our home economy to become depleted of workers who earn real living wages? We can not let our economy degenerate into one of only two classes: the very rich and minimum wage service workers. Our industrial base was built on a working partnership between management and labor. Like any marriage this partnership was not always easy to live with. But it did thrive on a mutual respect for the other's role in the larger scheme of things. What we have had instead for the past forty years is a willingness on the part of both sides to forgo the long term societal benefits which can inure from good faith bargaining. The end result is that our economy is in danger of not only being nonunion, but also more noncompetitive, nonproductive, and nongrowth than ever. Unions and management both need to wake up and smell the coffee before we become a fallen third-rate economic power.

II. Hypothetical Multi-Issue Essay Question:

For years Patty's Patio Palace, Inc. has led the industry in the manufacture of high quality outdoor furniture. The business was successful in no small part because of the contributions provided by its highly skilled labor force. The ironworkers used by Patty's were loyal, highly paid, and unionized. Long ago, they formed the P.P.P. Local 123 Ironworkers and Furniture Workers Union. Under the current contract, they have exclusive bargaining rights with Patty's Patio Palace Inc. for the next ten years.

Unfortunately for Patty's, competition from overseas patio furniture manufacturers has become fierce. Robot-made knock-offs of Patty's creations are selling for about half of the price asked by Patty's for its products. She decides the only way to stay competitive in this business is to seek lower labor costs. The state of Idawaska sits next door to Patty's present location and has a "right to work" statute. Under this statute, individual employees cannot be forced to join a union nor pay union dues even if a union is in place. In addition, the average rate of pay in Idawaska is fifty percent lower than what Patty's is now paying its workers.

Should Patty's decide to relocate to Idawaska, what would be the consequences to it and its unionized employees under our labor laws? Also, which key employment laws should Patty's take into consideration as part of the proposed move?

III. Key Question Checklist:

A. In examining the law of labor relationships, begin by listing the key rules of the game, i.e., what are the main labor law statutes in effect today (listed in chronological order)?

1. Railway Labor Act of 1926?
   (a) Covers employees of railroad and airline carriers?
   (b) Allows self-organization by these employees?
   (c) Administered by National Railway Adjustment Board?
   (d) Decisions of the Board enforceable in court?
2. Norris-LaGuardia Act (1932)?
   (a) Made unionization activity legal?
   (b) Exceptions in Act for violent unionization?
3. Wagner Act or Labor Management Relations Act (1935)?
   (a) Created the National Labor Relations Board?
   (b) Established rights of employees to:
       (1) Form a union?
       (2) Join a union?
       (3) Assist labor organizations?
       (4) Bargain collectively?
       (5) Engage in concerted activities (strikes) to promote these rights?
       (6) Created an affirmative duty on part of employers to bargain in good faith with unions?
4. Labor Management Relations Act, aka Taft-Hartley Act (1947)?
   (a) Expanded activities unions could engage in?
   (b) Gave more power to employers to resist unionization?
   (c) Allowed President to seek injunction actions in case of national emergencies?
5. Labor Management Reporting and Disclosure Act, aka Landrum-Griffin Act (1959)?
   (a) Regulates internal union affairs?
   (b) Established union member rights?
   (c) Provided additional remedies against union officers for defalcations?

B. Once you have reviewed the main labor law statutes, have those statutes been complied with vis-à-vis the formation of a union?
1. Appropriate bargaining unit identified?
2. Petition for election presented to NLRB?
3. Proper election held?
   (a) Any issue of interference?
   (b) Any issue of any other unfair labor practice?

C. Once the union is established, are there any issues with regard to the collective bargaining process?
1. Subject matter proper?
2. Agreement allowable?
   (a) Closed shop?
   (b) Union shop?
   (c) Agency shop?
   (d) Effect of state right to work law?

D. Assuming there is a dispute between labor and management, what actions may each side take?
1. Strike by labor?
   (a) Antistrike agreement?
   (b) Unlawful strike?
      (1) Violent strike?
      (2) Sit down strike?
      (3) Partial strike?
      (4) Wildcat strike?
      (5) Strike during cooling-off period?
2. Picketing by labor?
3. Lock out by management?
4. Poststrike reemployment rights?

E. Any internal union affair issues?
1. Right to vote?
2. Nominate candidates?
3. Participate in meetings?
4. Membership discipline?

IV. Objective Questions:

Terms:

1. Before a union can petition for an election as a bargaining agent, the group that is seeking to represent, called the _____ _____ _____, must be defined.

2. An establishment where union membership is a condition of employment is called a _____ _____.

3. When an employer reasonably anticipates a strike by some of its employees, it may prevent those employees from entering the premises; this is called an _____ _____.

4. When unions try to bring pressure against an employer by picketing his suppliers or customers, this is called _____ _____ _____.

5. The NLRB can be petitioned to investigate and set an election date if it can be shown that at least _____ percent of the employees in the bargaining unit are interested in joining or forming a union.

6. The act of negotiating is called _____ _____.

7. A union may operate a _____ _____ which acts as a job referral service and clearinghouse between employees seeking work and employers seeking workers.

8. In a _____ shop, an employee must join the union within a certain number of days after being hired.

9. When striking employees walk in front of an employer's premises carrying signs announcing their strike, this is called _____.

10. A contract where an employer agrees with a union not to use, handle, transport, deal in, or purchase the products made by nonunion workers of other employers is a _____ _____ contract.

True/False:

1. ____Managers and professional employees may not belong to unions formed by employees whom they manage.

2. ____The NLRB is required to supervise all contested elections.

3. ____When an employer threatens loss of benefits if an employee joins the union, he is guilty of unfair labor practices.

4. ____In a state with a right to work law, individual employees cannot be forced to join a union or pay union dues or fees even though a union has been elected by other employees.

5. ____In a strike situation, an employer may continue operations by using management personnel and hiring replacement workers to take the place of striking employees.

6. ____The American Federation of Labor was formed in 1886 under the leadership of John L. Lewis.

7. ____Once a union is elected and certified, covered employees may negotiate individually with the employer regarding employment benefits.

8. ____Employees with a bona fide religious objection to joining or financially supporting a union do not have to join.

9. ____If a collective bargaining agreement cannot be reached, the union may call a strike.

10. ____Unions cannot spend union dues on political activities.

Multiple Choice:

1. Under which circumstances will the NLRB not permit an election to be held?
   A. A union election was held within the past 12 months by any union, even if the union was not elected.
   B. The employees of the appropriate bargaining unit are represented by a union and already have a valid collective bargaining agreement.
   C. The union has engaged in an unreasonable unfair labor practice.
   D. All of the above.

2. Which of the following is not a compulsory subject of collective bargaining?
   A. Location of plants.
   B. Fringe benefits.
   C. Retirement plans.
   D. Safety rules.

3. Which of the following kinds of strikes is illegal?
   A. Wildcat strike that is quickly ratified by the union.
   B. Strikes during the 60-day cooling off period.
   C. Strikes in violation of a no-strike clause.
   D. B and C, but not A.

4. Idaho potato pickers are angry with their employer. They decide to picket all stores in the area which sell Idaho potatoes and urge potential customers not to shop at the stores. Their boycott is lawful if:
   A. Signs ask the customers not to shop at the grocery stores at all.
   B. Signs ask the customers not to buy Idaho potatoes.
   C. Strikers are picketing a neutral employer instead of the struck employer.
   D. A and C, but not B.

5. Which of the following may a union not discipline members for doing?
   A. Spying for an employer.
   B. Working for wages below union scale.
   C. Testifying in court against the union.
   D. Walking off the job in a nonsanctioned wildcat strike.

6. Which act created the National Labor Relations Board?
   A. Labor-Management Reporting and Disclosure Act.
   B. Norris-LaGuardia Act.
   C. National Labor Relations Act.
   D. Labor-Management Relations Act.

7. Where a union solicitation is being conducted by fellow employees, which of the following may an employer not do?
   A. Restrict solicitation to the employees' free time.
   B. Limit solicitation to nonworking areas such as the cafeteria, etc..
   C. Dismiss employees who do not violate solicitation rules.
   D. Bar off-duty employees from union solicitation on company premises.

8. Which of the following is not a permissive subject of collective bargaining?
   A. Size and composition of supervisory force.
   B. Corporate reorganization.
   C. Work discrimination.
   D. Location of plants.

9. Sally Striker was on strike with her union protesting unsafe working conditions. Her employer hired a replacement worker to replace her during the strike. Now the strike is over and Sally wants her job back, but her employer says she is discharged. What result?
   A. Economic strikers who reapply for their jobs are entitled to a nondiscriminatory review of their job applications prior to new applicants.
   B. Employees who are striking against an unfair labor practice are entitled to reinstatement even if the employer has to discharge replacements hired during the strike.
   C. Illegal strikers may be discharged by the employer and have no right to reinstatement.
   D. Strikers do not have to be paid while they are on strike.

10. Picketing is lawful when it:
    A. Is accompanied by violence.
    B. Prevents nonstriking employees from entering the employer's premises.
    C. Does not obstruct customers from entering the employer's place of business.
    D. Prevents pickups and deliveries at the employer's place of business.

V. Answers to Objective Questions:

Terms:

1. *Appropriate bargaining unit.* This term is defined by Section 7 of the National Labor Relations Act of 1935. This group can be made up of the employees of a single plant or company or even an entire industry. It may not be made up of managers or professional employees who manage members of the same union group.
2. *Closed shop.* This type of agreement required the applicant to belong to the union before the employer could consider hiring him or her. The Taft-Hartley Act made closed shops illegal because they put conditions on the employer's right to select its employees.
3. *Employer lockout.* This practice has become more prevalent in recent years due to fears of possible sabotage and even violence between the striking union members and replacement workers. A well publicized lockout recently took place by professional baseball franchise owners against the players.
4. *Secondary boycott picketing.* This practice is legal only if it is product picketing, i.e., against the primary employer's product. It is not legal if it is directed against a neutral employer instead of the struck employer's product.
5. *Thirty.* This percentage is required under Section 7 of the National Labor Relations Act of 1935.
6. *Collective bargaining.* Once a union has been elected, the employer and union will engage in this process in an attempt to negotiate a contract.
7. *Hiring hall.* Most job assignments made through these halls are made on the basis of seniority.
8. *Union.* Union shops are lawful. Closed shops are not lawful.
9. *Picketing.* This practice is lawful unless it is accompanied by violence or some other improper interference with the employer's business.
10. *Cross-over workers.* These are individual members of a union who chose not to honor a strike.

True/False:

1. True. This prohibition is written into Section 7 of the National Labor Relations Act of 1935. These people can be members of a union whose members they do not manage.
2. True. The National Labor Relations Board is an administrative body comprised of five members appointed by the president and approved by the Senate. One of its numerous functions is to oversee contested elections.
3. True. Section 8(a) of the NLRA makes this an unfair labor practice. The employer is prohibited from interfering with, coercing, or restraining employees from exercising their statutory right to form and join unions.
4. True. These local provisions are allowed under the 1947 amendment to the Taft-Hartley Act Section 14(b) which allow the states to outlaw union and agency shops. Over twenty states have adopted such provisions.
5. True. This practice has long been allowed under the NLRA. A more recent development has been the Supreme Court's approval of retaining replacement workers on a permanent basis after the strike has ended as illustrated in the 1989

case of *TWA v. Federation of Flight Attendants.*

6. False. The A.F.L. was formed by Samuel Gompers.

7. False. The union has now assumed that role.

8. False. Such employees must contribute an amount of money equal to union dues to an approved charity.

9. True. The strike must still be conducted legally in order to be protected by federal law.

10. False. Unions are very active in the political process although their influence has decreased dramatically in recent years.

Multiple Choice:

1. D. A, B, and C are all found in the rules and regulations promulgated by the NLRB pursuant to the National Labor Relations Act.

2. A. This is considered a permissive rather than a compulsory subject. Permissive subjects such as plant location, corporate reorganization, and the like may be bargained for if the company and union agree to do so.

3. D. Not all strike activities are legal. Where the courts have interpreted such actions to be illegal, it is usually because they feel the balance of power may have swung too far in favor of the union if it were allowed.

4. B. This is an example of secondary boycott picketing. Such practices are legal only if they are directed at the struck employer's product. It would be illegal if it were directed against only a neutral employer.

5. C. Unions may adopt internal rules to regulate the operation of their affairs. These rules must, however, be in

compliance with public policy. A union may not punish a member for participating in a civil duty such as testifying in court.

6. C. This Act remains the cornerstone of U.S. labor relations law.

7. C. If the employees comply with the solicitation rules, the employer may not dismiss them for such activities.

8. C. Civil rights laws cannot be violated in the process of collective bargaining.

9. B. If the employer has engaged in an illegal labor practice, he or she must reinstate wrongfully discharged workers who struck against the illegal practice.

10. C. A, B, and D are all examples of illegal picketing practices.

VI. Key Question Checklist Answers to Essay Question:

A&B.   *What rules of the road from the body of labor laws would apply to the proposed move by Patty's Patio Palace Inc.?*

There are a number of labor law statutes, both federal and state in play in this scenario. The problem already listed the Idawaska state "right to work" statute. Those sort of statutes are designed to attract new businesses by offering a nonunion and low wage environment to prospective businesses. They are allowed under the provisions of the Taft Hartley Act.

In addition, because Patty's Patio Palace Inc. is already unionized and involved in a collective bargaining agreement, the provisions of the Wagner Act would also be applicable. Under these provisions, the National Labor Relations Board (NLRB) would have the authority to investigate the possibility of any unfair labor practices which may arise out of the proposed plant move to Idawaska.

Under the provisions of the NLRB Unfair Labor Practices Section 8(a)(3), if an employer specifically seeks to relocate only to escape or discourage unions, an unfair labor practice may be contemplated. If, however, the employer seeks to relocate solely for economic reasons, such as lowering overhead to stay competitive in the world market place, then the move may not be deemed to be an unfair labor practice. Even if the NLRB finds that the move was improperly motivated as an unfair labor practice of setting up a runaway shop, it still could not order Patty's to move back to its home state. At best it could only grant Patty's present employees hiring preferences and award relocation expenses if they choose to move.

C,D&E. *If the move could not be avoided by the union, what are the collective bargaining options available to it and the company in the new location?*

Once they were in Idawaska, they could seek certification as a new bargaining unit by following the proper steps for election of a new union. Given the antiunion climate of the new state location, that may be easier said than done. This scenario is relatively common and illustrates the many dilemmas facing unions today. They must change with the times, yet do we as a society really want this little bargaining power for workers? You decide.

CHAPTER 44

LIABILITY OF ACCOUNTANTS AND OTHER PROFESSIONALS

Men may be born free; they cannot be born wise, and it is the duty of the university to make the free wise.

Adlai E. Stevenson

I. Overview:

The origins of the accounting profession go all the way back to a Franciscan Monk Fra Luca Pacioli (1445-1509 A.D.), who is credited with first having devised the double entry method of record keeping of financial information in his work entitled *Summa de Arithmetica, Geometria Proportion et Propotionality*. Since that time, it has evolved into a critical and highly respected profession. One of the old clichés still often heard in the halls of business schools is that accounting *is* the language of business. There is no question that in today's legal environment of business, the accounting profession has also become one of the prime targets of change. Although the profession is very highly respected, it has not been "business as usual" for accountants in recent history. The profession's future has become more uncertain than ever because of the increased scope of accountant's legal liabilities.

What have been some of the factors which have led to these convulsive *contretemps* within this profession? First and foremost must be the shift of scope of reliance from a two party scenario (accountant/client) to a three party situation. The new order involves not only the two original parties but also third parties who for whatever reason have found standing in the courts to sue based on their reliance on the accountant's work product. The traditional privity and privity-like protections accorded to the profession by doctrines such as *Ultramares* are falling more and more to the wayside. The work product of accountants is simply too important to be expected to be kept in the four walls of the client's office. Today's "glass jar" world of information technology transfer makes it not only foreseeable but probable that information used to establish financial credibility will in fact be used by many of third parties ranging from governmental entities to investors and financial institutions all over the world. It is interesting to note that the word "public" has always been associated with the accounting profession. In today's scheme of things, the public is more involved than ever with the workings of the accounting profession and is holding accountants more accountable than ever.

Another factor that has led to so many suits being filed against accountants today is that the profession has not really decided how it will ultimately react to these drastic changes. It continues to seek the public's confidence in its work and reliance on its work products. In many ways certain elements of its work are not even optional but rather held to a captive audience. Can you imagine the IRS or the SEC waiving its record keeping and financial reporting requirements? Yet when things have gone awry for the profession, it has constantly sought to limit its intended scope of service or reliance on that service. This has led to a sort of schizophrenia within the profession in not knowing what is really expected and losing contact with the changing legal environment.

A number of commentators have said that real equilibrium will return to the profession when it decides that its role has evolved into a real-world insurance function. Under this thinking, ultimate reliance on the work product of the accounting profession will be restored on the basis that what users really wanted all along is comfort in knowing that they can "bank" on what financial statements are really saying. This sort of change will probably happen only when the government is willing to step in to provide financial assurances to the accounting profession the way it has in the financial institution arena. Until that happens, the private sector-funded accounting profession will remain under siege for all sorts of faults which are not of its own making. All too often, today's changing legal environment has allowed accountants to become the last deep pocket in a chain of sequential liability traced back to them through a series of bankrupt stock issuers, tax dodgers, and other miscreants. In a very real sense, the accounting profession is a profession in crisis today, and only time will tell if future generations of the profession will be transmogrified from the practice of this profession as we know it today.

Liability of accountants falls into three main categories: contract, tort, and statutory liabilities. The details of how these liabilities are arrived at are set out in the key question checklist.

II. Hypothetical Multi-issue Essay Question:

Mr. Donny Debit worked long and hard for his client Mr. Charley Credit, and Charley's company, Fleet of Foot, Inc. Fleet of Foot created and patented the first polyurethane based athletic shoes, and it has been a legend in the financial world ever since. Charley was inspired for the technology used in his shoes one day while running through a bed of hot coals for his guru. He just couldn't do it barefoot, and he wound up heating his rubber soled tennis shoes into super-bouncing athletic shoes. Charley's fortunes began to turn when

a number of competitors entered the market with superior products. He decided to go public in order to raise money for diversification into rubberized bodysuits and related products.

He asked Donny to prepare the appropriate financial statements for the SEC, the IRS, and the local shoe police. He specifically asked Donny to put his company in the best light possible including over-valuing assets and understating liabilities whenever possible. Donny was reluctant to "cook the books" but decided to go along with Charley when Charley promised him ten percent of the newly issued stock in the company as his fee. Donny bragged to all his friends at the accounting motorcycle club (The CPAs from Hell) that he was about to make a killing as an insider.

Several months later Fleet of Foot went bankrupt and Charley has run off with the company's money to Rio and is now meditating on the beach where he cannot be extradited. Donny's firm is being looked into by both the government and disgruntled investors who lost their rubber shirts when Fleet of Foot folded. What results?

III. Key Question Checklist:

A. The first step in examining the possible liabilities of an accountant is to examine what functions are included in the practice of the profession. The profession itself is sub-divided into public accountants and certified public accountants (CPAs). Although both groups do perform some common duties, only CPAs are allowed to "sign off" on a number of key financial statements and the like. What are the key categories of within the practice of accounting?
   1. Bookkeeping?
   2. Tax preparation services?

399

3. Preparing financial statements?
4. Auditing financial statements?
5. Rendering opinions about those audits?
   (a) Unqualified?
   (b) Qualified?
   (c) Adverse?
   (d) Disclaimer of opinion?
6. Other consulting services?

B. Assuming a service has been contracted for between an accountant and his or her client, what are the contract theories of liability?
1. Breach of contract by the accountant?
   (a) Were the services contracted for improperly provided or omitted so as to constitute a breach of contract?
2. Breach of contract by the client?
   (a) Failure to pay?
   (b) Does not perform under the terms of the contract?
   (c) Any defenses available to the client?

C. Assuming contract liability theory is not at issue, what are the common law tort theories of liability?
1. Intentional tort?
   (a) Intentional torts committed by the accountant?
      (1) Fraud?
         (aa) Material misrepresentation or omission?
         (bb) Relied on by the client?
         (cc) Harm to client based on first two elements?
   (b) Intentional torts committed by the client?
      (1) Intentional misrepresentation?
      (2) Harm done to accountant as a result?
      (3) Any defenses available to the client?

2. Negligence tort law?
   (a) Basic elements of tort?
      (1) Duty?
      (2) Breach of duty?
      (3) Breach was the proximate cause of harm?
      (4) Any defenses or immunities?
   (b) Negligence on the part of the accountant?
      (1) Duty to perform up to the standards of the profession? (GAAP or GAAS)
      (2) Acting below that standard?
      (3) Proximate cause of harm?
         (aa) Vis-à-vis client?
         (bb) Vis-à-vis third party?
            (i) *Ultramares* doctrine (Privity or privity-like relationship between accountant and third party)?
            (ii) Section 552 of the Restatement (Second) of Torts standard (Limits class of intended user harmed by the accountant's negligence)?
            (iii) Foreseeability standard (Was the third party a foreseeable user o f the accountant's work product)?
      (4) Any defenses or immunities applicable for the accountant?
      (5) Any negligence on part of client towards the accountant?

D. Assuming contract and tort law are not at issue, are there any statutory provisions applicable where liability may be imposed on the accountant?

1. Securities Act of 1933?
   (a) Section 11(a)?
       (1) Material misstatement omission of fact in registration statement?
       (2) Failure to find material misstatements or omissions?
   (b) Section 24?
       (1) Criminal sanctions?
       (2) False statements or omissions?
       (3) Violate any other Rule of 1933 Act?
2. Securities Act of 1934?
   (a) Section 10(b) and Rule 10(b)-5?
       (1) Manipulative or deceptive practice?
       (2) In connection with the purchase or sale of any security?
       (3) With use of mails or interstate commerce facility?
   (b) Section 18(a)?
       (1) Civil liability for false or misleading statements?
       (2) Statements filed with SEC?
   (c) Section 32(a)?
       (1) Criminal sanctions?
       (2) Violate any rules of 1934 Act?
3. Racketeer Influenced and Corrupt Organizations Act (RICO)?
       (1) Civil penalties?
       (2) Criminal liabilities?
4. Tax statutes?
       (1) Civil penalties?
       (2) Criminal liabilities?
5. State securities laws?

E. Accountant/client privilege?
   1. Not traditionally recognized in common law?
   2. Some states have adopted it?
   3. Federal rules to not follow state adoptions for federal law (tax) purposes?

IV. Objective Questions:

Terms:

1. After an auditor has conducted an audit, she generally issues an opinion of her findings. A(n) _____ _____ is issued when the auditor finds that the company's financial statements present fairly the company's financial position, the results of its operations, and the changes in its financial position for the period under audit.

2. One basis upon which an accountant can be held legally liable for damages to a client is _____ _____ which occurs when the accountant acts with reckless disregard for the truth or consequences of his actions.

3. Under the Ultramares Doctrine, unless third parties are in _____ _____ _____ with an accountant, they are considered incidental beneficiaries of the contract between the accountant and her client and therefore cannot sue the accountant on a breach of contract theory.

4. The standard of liability created by Section 552 of the *Restatement (Second) of Torts* is much broader than the Ultramares Doctrine. Under the Restatement, an accountant is liable for his negligence to any member of a _____ _____ _____ _____ _____ for whose benefit the accountant has been employed to prepare the client's financial statements.

401

5. Under the _____ _____, the liability of an accountant for negligence does not depend on his knowledge of the identity of either the user or the intended class of users of the client's financial statements.

6. When one has rendered support, assistance, or encouragement to the commission of a crime, such as securities fraud, one can be held criminally liable for

_____

_____ a criminal violation.

7. Many states have created an _____ _____ _____ which protects an accountant from testifying against a client in actions in the courts of such states.

8. In the performance of their services, accountants often generate _____ which serve to document the services performed.

9. Some states recognize _____ _____ _____ protecting against the discovery of certain documents prepared by accountants.

10. Often, an independent CPA is engaged to conduct a(n) _____ which involves the verification of a company's books and records pursuant to certain laws and guidelines.

True/False:

1. ____ Generally Accepted Auditing Standards define the minimum level of conduct that is required when performing an audit, and failure to perform an audit in compliance with these standards constitutes negligence.

2. ____ An auditor's adverse opinion states that the auditor is unable to draw a conclusion as to the accuracy of the company's financial records.

3. ____ The standard of care by which the conduct of an accountant is judged is that degree of care that a reasonable person would use when working in the business of another.

4. ____ An accountant's showing of compliance with the requirements of GAAP and GAAS constitutes an absolute defense to negligence.

5. ____ Under the *Ultramares* doctrine, an accountant cannot be held liable to a third party unless that third party was in a privity-like relationship with the accountant.

6. ____ In an action under the Securities Act of 1933 against an accountant for negligence, the accountant can be held liable if the financial statements heprepares contain errors and are included in a registration statement or prospectus, whether or not the plaintiff was in privity of contract with the accountant.

7. ____ Only plaintiffs who have purchased or sold securities can sue under Section 10(b) or under Rule 10b-5 of the Securities Exchange Act of 1934.

8. ____ The Racketeer Influenced and Corrupt Organizations Act provides criminal, but not civil, sanctions for violations thereof.

9. ____ The 1976 Tax Reform Act imposes criminal sanctions on accountants for certain wrongful acts committed in the preparation of federal income tax returns.

10. ____ Although an accountant owns all workpapers prepared in conducting services for her clients, she owes the client a duty not to transfer those workpapers without the consent of the client.

Multiple Choice:

1. Ms. Elizabeth Kyushu owns and operated her own CPA firm. Macaw Company engaged Ms. Kyushu to perform the annual examination of its financial statements. The examination failed to discover an embezzlement scheme by one of the employees, Mr. Jay Bluebird. Which of the following is a correct statement?
   A. Ms. Kyushu's adherence to generally accepted auditing standards may prevent liability.
   B. Ms. Kyushu will not be liable if she can show that she exercised the care and skill of an ordinary reasonable person.
   C. Ms. Kyushu may be liable for punitive damages.
   D. Ms. Kyushu will be liable for any embezzlement losses occurring prior to the time the scheme should have been detected.

2. Facts & Figures, CPAs, audited the financial statements used in a registration statement filed with the SEC under the Securities Act of 1933. If sued by a purchaser of these securities, Facts & Figures can defend on the basis that:

A. The purchaser did not buy the securities from Facts & Figure's client.
B. There was only an omission of a material fact, not a misstatement.
C. Facts & Figures used due diligence in its work.
D. Facts & Figures was not grossly negligent or fraudulent.

3. Facts & Figures, CPAs, also audited the financial statements of a client used in an annual report filed with the SEC under the Securities Exchange Act of 1934. The financial statements contained a material misstatement of fact. To hold Facts & Figures liable, a purchaser of these securities need not prove:
   A. Reliance on the financial statements.
   B. The misstatement caused his/her loss.
   C. Negligence on the part of Facts & Figures.
   D. The price of the securities was affected by the misstatement.

4. Ms. Ima Looking is a CPA who has been hired by Marcus Macy, Inc. to audit its year-end financial statements. Which is the best statement of the standard of care owed by Ms. Looking?
   A. To discover and report any fraud or defalcations.
   B. To perform the job using the skill and care of an ordinarily prudent accountant in the same circumstances.
   C. To use reasonable care and judgment based on Ms. Looking's education and experience.
   D. To act without *scienter*.

5. Bradley Bogus, CPA, was hired to perform audit services for the Shiftless & Shady Corporation. In a state which uses the foreseeability standard of liability, which of the following statements regarding Bradley's liability to a third party is correct?
   A. The foreseeability standard is not applicable with respect to Bradley's liability to a primary contract beneficiary.
   B. Bradley must have known that he was hired so that his work product could be relied upon by a particular third party.
   C. Bradley must have known that third parties would be relying upon his work product.
   D. None of the above.

6. Assume the same facts as in question 5 except that the state in which Bradley practices uses the common law theory of liability. Which of the following statements is correct?
   A. Under the common law theory, CPAs are liable to anyone who relies on their work.
   B. Under the common law theory, CPAs have greater liability to third parties than to their clients because there is no contract to determine their relationship and the breach thereof.
   C. Under the common law theory, CPAs are only liable to one who is in privity of contract.
   D. All of the above.

7. Assume the same facts as in question 5. With respect to the workpapers prepared by Bradley in performing audit services, which of the following is correct?

A. Once the audit has been performed, the workpapers become the property of Shiftless & Shady.
B. The workpapers belong to Bradley.
C. The workpapers belong to Bradley and are protected from discovery pursuant to the accountant-client privilege.
D. None of the above.

8. Assume the same facts as in question 5. If, after completing the audit of Shiftless & Shady Corporation, Bradley believes that the financial statements are in conformity with generally accepted accounting principles, he should issue which of the following opinions?
   A. An adverse opinion.
   B. A going concern opinion.
   C. A qualified opinion.
   D. An unqualified opinion.

9. Assume the same facts as in question 5. Shiftless & Shady made negligent misrepresentations in the financial statements, which an investor relied upon when purchasing shares of the corporation. Bradley was not aware of the misrepresentations nor was he negligent in performing the audit. The investor sued Bradley under Rule 10b-5 of the Securities Exchange Act of 1934. Which of the following statements is correct?
   A. Bradley will lose because the statements contained negligent misrepresentations.
   B. Bradley will win because the investor was not in privity of contract.
   C. Bradley will win because the investor failed to prove *scienter*.
   D. Bradley will lose because the investor relied on the false financial statements in making his investment decision.

10. Which of the following is not a principle to which a CPA must adhere?
    A. CPAs must carry out their responsibilities through the exercise of sensitive professional and moral judgment.
    B. CPAs should perform all professional responsibilities with the highest sense of integrity.
    C. CPAs should maintain objectivity and be free of conflicts of interest in discharging their professional responsibilities.
    D. None of the above.

V. Answers to Objective Questions:

Terms:

1. *Unqualified opinion.* This is the most favorable opinion an accountant can give and states that the company's statements fairly present the financial positions by using generally accepted accounting principles.
2. *Constructive fraud.* This type of fraud is also referred to as gross negligence and exists where conduct, although not actually fraudulent, has the same consequences as actual fraud.
3. *Privity of contract.* This doctrine has come under much criticism by many commentators who take the position that the Ultramares Doctrine unduly favors accountants as compared to other fiduciaries.
4. *Limited class of intended users.* Many states have adopted this standard.
5. *Foreseeability standard.* This is the broadest standard for holding accountants liable to third parities for negligence and has been adopted by only a minority of states.

6. *Aiding and abetting.* If the SEC finds evidence of fraud or other willful violation of federal securities laws, the matter may be referred to the U.S. Department of Justice.
7. *Accountant/client privilege.* The U.S. Supreme Court determined in *Couch v. U.S.*, 409 U.S. 322 (1973) that this privilege is not provided for by federal law.
8. *Workpapers.* These can include audit plans, data collection notes, notes on internal controls, memorabilia, and the like.
9. *Work product immunity.* Only a minority of state legislatures have enacted these sorts of accountant work product immunity statutes.
10. *Audit.* This remains one of the accounting profession's key functions.

True/False:

1. True. These standards are constantly reexamined and updated by the accounting profession.
2. False. An auditor's adverse opinion states that the financial statements do not present fairly the company's financial position, the results of its operations, or the changes in its financial position in conformity with generally accepted accounting principles.
3. False. An accountant is required to exercise the same degree of care as a reasonable accountant in similar circumstances.
4. False. Although violations of GAAP and GAAS constitute prima facie evidence of negligence, compliance does not constitute an absolute defense to negligence.

5. True. Such a privity-like relationship can exist, for example, where the client employed the accountant to prepare financial statements to be used by a third party for specific purposes of which the accountant was made aware.

6. True. The accountant can, however, assert a due diligence defense in such circumstances.

7. True. Although privity of contract is not required, the plaintiff must have either purchased or sold securities.

8. False. The Racketeer Influenced and Corrupt Organizations Act provides both criminal and civil sanctions. Civil sanctions include the award of treble damages in certain situations.

9. True. In addition, numerous civil penalties may be imposed on accountants and others who prepare federal tax returns.

10. True. Although generally provided fewer confidentially protections than the attorney/client, these workpapers are considered confidential vis-a-vis the accountant and his or her client.

Multiple Choice:

1. A. Ms. Kyushu must adhere to professional standards of care in the performance of her work. Although not an absolute protection from liability, adherence to GAAS may help to establish that the CPA exercised the requisite standard of care. Her adherence to generally accepted accounting standards may prevent liability.

2. C. The Securities Act of 1933 imposes liability of CPAs for false statements or omissions of material facts. Due diligence is, however, a defense in this regard. Facts & Figures must show that it used due diligence in the performance of its audit.

3. C. A private individual bringing a claim under the 1934 Act need not prove negligence. However, the defendant can raise the defense of lack of *scienter* to shield himself from liability under these provisions. Under the provisions of the 1934 Act, *scienter* means a mental state embracing an intent to deceive, manipulate, or defraud.

4. B. An accountant's actions are measured against those of a "reasonable accountant" in similar circumstances. She is held to the overall standard imposed on the profession.

5. C. Under the foreseeability standard, Bradley would be liable to any foreseeable user of Shiftless & Shady's financial statements.

6. C. Although others may sue CPAs for fraud and negligence under common law theories, CPAs are only liable on a contract basis to those in privity of contract.

7. B or C, depending on state law. The workpapers of an accountant are property of the accountant, subject to certain inspection and other rights of the client. Several states recognize the accountant/client privilege with respect to workpapers of the accountant.

8. D. An unqualified opinion would represent Bradley's opinion that the financial statements fairly present the financial position, results of operations, and changes in financial position.

9. C. To recover under a 10b-5 cause of action, pursuant to *Ernst & Ernst v. Hockfelder*, a plaintiff must establish more than mere negligence, i.e., *scienter*.

10. D. A, B, and C are all required according to the Code of Professional Conduct of the AICPA.

VI. Key Question Checklist Answers to Essay Question:

A. *What are the key categories within the practice of accounting?*

Clearly Donny provided the kind of financial advising and statement preparation services that are normally associated with the accounting profession. Even though he may have been virtually in Charley's employ, Donny was still under an obligation as an accounting professional to live up to the standards and code of ethics of the profession.

B. *Is there a contract theory of liability?*

In terms of contract law, if what Charley asked Donny to do was illegal (and it appears that it was), the common law of contracts would render the contract void. As such, the parties would be declared *in pari delicto* and the courts would leave them where they were without any remedy for enforcement of any of the contract provisions.

C. *Is there a common law tort theory of liability?*

In tort and statutory law, you will find Donny in "deep doo." He has committed both and intentional and negligent torts vis-a-vis both the government entities by submitting these statements to third parties who relied on them. As for the government agencies, he can be made civilly liable for any penalties which may be asserted against him under the various securities, tax, antifraud, and other statutes. In addition, if his transgressions were severe enough, he may also be held criminally liable under these provisions.

Regarding third party civil liabilities, Donny's fate will rest in large part on which standard is being used by the state in which his acts were committed. If the state still uses the Ultramares Doctrine, he may be able to defend himself by saying that third parties had no privity or privity-like relationship with him, and that he should not be liable to them. If the state uses the Restatement (Second) of Torts standard, third parties would have to show that they are in a limited class of intended users of the financial statements. If they were deemed to be members of that class and could show the harm to them was proximately caused by Donny's negligence preparation of the statements, they would win.

D. *Are there any statutory provisions applicable here?*

The most likely scenario will probably unfold under the third standard of foreseeability. Financial statements prepared for submission to the SEC with the purpose of being used in a prospectus are forseeably to be used by potential investors in the new issue. It is only reasonable that, based on that sort of foreseeable chain of events, an accountant who actively participated in material misstatements or omissions should be held liable for those actions. The criminal sanctions imposed by the federal securities acts would come into play and the case would likely be prosecuted by the U.S. Justice Department.

E. *Is accountant/client privilege applicable?*

This privilege is not recognized by federal law and can only be used regarding any state charges of the individual state in which the crimes were committed has such a statute. Poor Donny is now both broke and in jail while Charley is working on his tan in Rio. Justice would be better served if they were roommates in Club Fed.

CHAPTER 45

ADMINISTRATIVE LAW AND GOVERNMENT REGULATION

An expert is one who knows more and more about less and less.

Nicholas Murray Butler

I. Overview:

A labyrinth is identified as a structure or garden characterized by an extremely complex maze with tortuous dead ends and blind alleys. Anyone who has dealt with a large governmental bureaucracy can readily appreciate the frustrations of trying to get through that maze with sanity intact. Government's burgeoning growth of administrative agencies at every level is indeed cause for concern for its constituents. According to statistics published by the U.S. Congress, the federal government alone has over three million civilian employees. In spite of constant calls to reduce the size of government's role in the average person's affairs, that role has grown tremendously. The media headlines may be focused on the goings on in the capitol, but the real functions of government are carried out in the trenches by this "fourth branch of government" (as distinguished from the role of the press popularly known as the "fourth estate") every day. This chapter seeks to outline the basic ground rules about how the agencies are created, how they are authorized to act, and what controls have been put in place so as to protect the rights of both the citizenry and the government.

The basic function undertaken by these administrative agencies is to carry out the ministerial functions necessary to the operation of the government. These functions are first authorized by what are called organic statutes, which create the agency, and enabling statutes, which delegate certain powers to the agency to act for the executive, legislative, or judicial branches of government. It is interesting to note at the outset that the "clean functional lines" of executive, legislative, and judicial can and do often become blurred when examining the breath and scope of administrative agency activities.

Once the existence of the agency is settled upon and its scope of authority is established, you must then decide whether it is acting within that scope vis-à-vis the particular issue at hand. Remember the basic assumption here is that the executive branch, legislative branch, or judicial branch has chosen to designate and delegate a certain portion of its authority to act. This delegation is based on the presumption that the agency can be expected to have certain levels of expertise, scales of economy, and attention to detail which could not be readily expected of the policy makers. The next step is to see if the power in question was in fact truly delegated, and if so, is it being properly exercised by the agency?

The mechanisms for control of agency powers are relatively sparse given the scope of agency activity. The key provisions for control of agency powers are found in the executive branch chain of command and in the overview powers vested in the judiciary. In addition, there have been a number of specific information access statutes, such as the Freedom of Information Act, Government in the Sunshine Act, and the Administrative Procedure Act to help persons dealing with these agencies to get through the labyrinth. Like it or not, what it all points to is that we live in an age of specialization. The days of dealing directly with your elected representative are simply long gone, if in fact, they ever were there in the first place. We need this specialization in many ways in order for the functions of government to be truly effective. Yet one cannot help but wonder if there might be a better way? The key question checklist will itemize the steps of creation, authority and overview control of administrative agencies in more detail.

II.   Hypothetical   Multi-Issue   Essay Question:

Mr. Joe Nebish was the proud owner of a new litter of cocker spaniel puppies. The parents, T. Bear, and Margaux, are AKC Champion show dogs. They have also garnered additional accolades by being temperament tested and certified as tracking companion dogs for field trials. The puppies names are: Enzo, Bordeaux, Harry, Felicity, Patience, Toulouse, Byron, Sonia and Tort. Margaux is one tired mama!

Joe decides that the expenses related to the breeding and raising of these dogs are much the same as caring for any dependent and goes down to the Backwater District Office of the Internal Revenue Service to get some advice from the IRS. Taxpayer Service Representative, Mr. Oliver Officious. Oliver told Joe he also raised cocker spaniels and felt that they made wonderful dependents. As dependents, Oliver saw no reason why they shouldn't be listed as such on Joe's 1040. Joe proceeded to file his tax return on April 15th and listed eleven dependents, all of them having long ears and names like Tort and Enzo. He even got social security numbers for them, hoping that they would eventually work for their keep.

Alas, poor Joe was audited by the IRS on April 16th and was told he could not claim his dogs as dependents in spite of their long-eared

needs to be fed by him. Joe points to Oliver's advice as his defense. What result?

III. Key Question Checklist:

A.   The first question you must resolve when examining the law of governmental regulation is to look for the source of authority given to the agency.

1. Which one of the three branches of federal government did it come from (Remember, in spite of the colloquialism, they are not an autonomous fourth branch of government.)?

(a) The executive branch?

(1) Cabinet level departments and their sub-branches? Example: Department of the Treasury with its sub-branch, the Internal Revenue Service.

(b) The legislative branch?

(1) Independent agencies created by Congress in order to service a particular functional area? Example: Federal Home Loan Bank Board.

(c) The judicial branch?

(1) Certain specialized courts organized within the judiciary? These are not administrative agencies per se, but rather courts having specialized judicial functions. Example: U.S. Tax Court or the U.S. Bankruptcy Court.

2. State or local governmental agencies?

B.   Once you have established which branch of government you are dealing with, look at how the agency was given its authority to act?

1. Organic act?
   (a) Which law of Congress created the agency? Examples: Wagner Act created the National Labor Relations Board.
   (b) Which executive branch order empowered this agency to act? Example: the Defense Department ordered to deploy troops into an area of conflict.
   (c) Which court related functions are assigned to which persons? Example: a law clerk does legal research for his or her judge.
2. Enabling act?
   (a) Which powers were delegated to the agency?
      (1) Make laws (substantive or legislative function)?
         (aa) Rules?
         (bb) Regulations?
      (2) Interpret its rule (interpretive or executive function)?
         (aa) Set out procedures?
         (bb) Set out practice rules before the agency?
      (3) Quasi-judicial (judicial function)?
         (aa) Hold hearings?
         (bb) Decide cases and controversies brought before the agency?
3. Were the proper procedures used per the enabling act?
   (a) Administrative Procedures Act complied with?
      (1) Notice and hearing requirements met?
      (2) Procedures for rule-making complied with?
      (3) Rules for agency adjudicative actions complied with?
4. Any other key administrative law statutes need to be complied with?

(a) Freedom of Information Act?
   (1) What is accessible?
   (2) What is not as an exemption? Example: Information relating to national security and defense.
(b) Federal Privacy Act of 1974?
(c) Government in the Sunshine Act?
(d) Equal Access to Justice Act?

C. If there is a conflict between a person and the administrative agency, what powers of overview or control may be exerted over the agency?
   1. Executive branch chain of command?
   2. Judicial overview of agency actions (bases for review)?
      (a) Constitutional issue?
      (b) Agency acted beyond its scope of authority?
      (c) Agency abused its discretion or was arbitrary or capricious?
      (d) Agency acted illegally in some other manner?
   3. Private claims against government agencies and governmental officers?
      (a) Normally agency immunity will inure to government officials acting in capacity of agent for the government?
         (1) Exception for international torts?
      (b) Federal Tort Claims Act applies?
      (c) Sovereign immunity applicable?

IV. Objective Questions:

Terms:

1. Administrative agencies use _____ _____ _____ to interpret the statutes that the agency is authorized to enforce.

2. An act that establishes certain administrative procedures that federal administrative agencies must follow in conducting their affairs is the _____ _____ _____.

3. A doctrine that says when an administrative agency is created, it is delegated certain powers and the agency can only use those legislative, judicial, and executive powers that are delegated to it is the _____ _____.

4. A rule or regulation issued by an administrative agency that has much the same power as a statute: it has the force of law and must be adhered to by covered persons and businesses is a _____ _____.

5. The adoption of a substantive rule that must be carried out by a trial-like hearing is called _____ rule making.

6. A statement issued by administrative agencies that announces a proposed course of action that an agency intends to follow in the future is a _____ _____.

7. The tangible evidence of an ALJ's decision is an _____. It must state the reasons for the ALJ's decision and becomes final if it is not appealed.

8. A rule that says the decision of an administrative agency must be final before judicial review can be sought is a _____ _____ _____.

9. A test for a standard of judicial review that is used to review formal decision making is the _____ _____ _____.

10. A test for a standard of judicial review that requires the reviewing court to try the case as if it had not been previously heard is the _____ _____ _____ _____ _____.

True/False:

1. ____Administrative agencies can only be created by the federal government.

2. ____Most federal administrative agencies are part of the legislative branch of government.

3. ____The statutes enacted by administrative agencies are the substantive law enforced by the agencies.

4. ____Violators of administrative agency statutes may be subject to civil, but not criminal liability.

5. ____Neither public notice nor participation is required when an agency decides to issue an interpretive rule.

6. ____Statements of policy have the force of law, and any deviation from the policy is a punishable violation.

7. ____Usually, administrative agencies are authorized to perform executive powers.

8. ____Administrative agencies are not restricted by the Fourth Amendment of the Constitution when conducting searches since they are not an official branch of the government.

9. ____Since there are no juries in administrative proceedings, an administrative law judge decides both questions of law and fact.

411

10. ____When an administrative agency's decision is reviewed by a court, questions of law are more easily overturned than questions of fact.

Multiple Choice:

1. Very Important Agency (VIA), an agency recently set up by the federal government, has some questions about how it would conduct its affairs? Where should VIA look for guidance?
   A. The Government in the Sunshine Act.
   B. The Administrative Procedure Act.
   C. The Equal Access to Justice Act.
   D. None of the above. VIA can conduct itself in any reasonable manner.

2. Assume VIA is set up and running properly. Which of the following powers may it have if properly delegated?
   A. Executive powers.
   B. Legislative powers.
   C. Judicial powers.
   D. All of the above.

3. VIA decides there are several important issues which must be examined and developed into rules. Assume VIA can establish these rules by notice and comment rule-making. Which of the following must VIA do?
   A. Publish a notice and invite and consider interested comment.
   B. Have the interested parties present evidence and conduct cross-examination.
   C. Both of the above.
   D. None of the above.

4. VIA decides it is necessary to search the business premises of one of its licensees, a company called On The Edge (OTE). Under what circumstances will a search be considered reasonable?
   A. A warrantless search is conducted in an emergency situation.
   B. OTE is in a business where warrantless searches are automatically considered valid.
   C. OTE voluntarily agrees to the search.
   D. All of the above.

5. VIA has been delegated power to adjudicate cases through an administrative proceeding. Nonconforming Niel has allegedly violated several agency rules. Which of the following is correct?
   A. Niel must receive notice of the charges against him.
   B. Niel must be allowed to present evidence on his own behalf.
   C. Both of the above.
   D. None of the above.

6. Assume the same facts as in question 5. Who will hear Niel's case?
   A. A judge in an ordinary court.
   B. An administrative law judge who is an employee of the administrative agency.
   C. An administrative agency director or official.
   D. A jury.

7. Assume in question 5 that Niel loses his argument before the agency. What may Niel do?
   A. Appeal to a state court.
   B. Appeal to the legislature.
   C. Appeal to a federal court.
   D. Nothing, only the agency can appeal an adverse ruling.

8. Assume now that Niel's case in question 5 has been appealed by an appropriate party to an appropriate authority. What standard of review will most likely be applied to the case?
   A. The arbitrary, capricious, or abuse of process test.
   B. The substantial evidence test.
   C. The unwarranted by the facts test.
   D. None of the above.

9. Which of the following acts requires that certain documents of federal administrative agencies must be open to the public?
   A. The Privacy Act.
   B. The Equal Access to Justice Act.
   C. The Government in the Sunshine Act.
   D. The Freedom of Information Act.

10. Which of the following acts gives a private party who was subject to an unjustified federal administrative agency action the right to sue and recover attorney's fees and costs?
    A. The Privacy Act.
    B. The Equal Access to Justice Act.
    C. The Government in the Sunshine Act.
    D. The Freedom of Information Act.

V. Answers to Objective Questions:

Terms:

1. *Rules and regulations.* Like it or not, ours is a highly regulated society and government agencies have been delegated as the agents of law enforcement in the broadest sense of the term.

2. *Administrative Procedure Act.* This Act was passed in 1946 and is intended to provide a basic set of guidelines by which federal administrative agencies must conduct their affairs.

3. *Delegation doctrine.* An agency cannot be imbued with more power than the original delatator had to give. If an agency exceeds the limits of its delegated powers, it is an unconstitutional act.

4. *Substantive rule.* Before a federal administrative agency proposes to adopt a substantive rule, it must follow the procedures set forth in the Administrative Procedures Act.

5. *Formal.* This procedure may sometimes be required under 5 U.S.C. §556 and usually involves contentious issues in highly regulated activities.

6. *Statement of policy.* Although these pronouncements do not have the force of law, they are very closely monitored by the industries and individuals which may be adversely affected by them.

7. *Order.* These orders may be appealed first to the agency and to the appropriate court if necessary.

8. *Final order rule.* This rule is designed to prevent the judicial branch from having a premature involvement in disputes involving agency proceedings.

9. *Substantial evidence test.* This test requires the reviewing court to examine the entire record to see whether the agency's decision was supported by substantial evidence.

10. *Unwarranted by the facts test.* This test is also known as the *de novo* standard of review and is rarely used.

1. False. Administrative agencies can be created by federal, state or local governments.
2. False. Most federal administrative agencies are part of the executive branch of government.
3. True. The statutes enacted by administrative agencies are the substantive law, as opposed to the procedural law, enforced by the agencies.
4. False. Violators of administrative agency statutes may be subject to either civil or criminal liability depending on the violations.
5. True. Generally, this is true, although many agencies will hold hearings in order to elicit the opinions of interested parties.
6. False. Statements of policy do not have the force of law.
7. True. This function varies widely in definition, and as such, is a source of constant litigation.
8. False. Generally, administrative agencies are restricted by the Fourth Amendment of the Constitution just as any other branch of the government would be.
9. True. These actions are ultimately reviewable by the judicial branch of government.
10. True. Though questions of law are considered the expertise of the court, questions of fact are generally better decided by the original fact-finding entity—the administrative agency.

Multiple Choice:

1. B. The Administrative Procedure Act sets out certain administrative procedures that federal administrative agencies must follow in conducting their affairs. A is incorrect because the Government in the Sunshine Act is an act that was enacted to open certain federal administrative agency meetings to the public. C is incorrect because the Equal Access to Justice Act is an act that was enacted to protect persons from harassment by federal administrative agencies.
2. D. If properly delegated, an administrative agency can have executive, legislative, and judicial powers.
3. A. Notice and comment rule-making, or informal rule-making, involves publishing a general notice of the proposed rule making, giving interested people the opportunity to comment, and reviewing input. B is incorrect because a trial-like procedure is used in formal rule making. C is incorrect because B is incorrect. D is incorrect because A is correct.
4. D. Administrative agency searches are proper under all the circumstances of A, B and C.
5. C. VIA must both give Niel notice of the charges against him and allow him to present evidence on his own behalf. These requirements must be satisfied in order to afford Niel procedural due process.
6. B. When an administrative agency has the power to adjudicate cases itself, such cases are heard by an administrative law judge who is an employee of the agency. A is incorrect because a regular judge does not hear the case unless it is appealed. C is incorrect because only an administrative law judge is qualified to hear the case. D is incorrect because juries are not used in administrative agency cases.
7. C. Since VIA is a federal agency, any case heard by the agency and then appealed, will be heard by a federal court. A is incorrect because since VIA is a federal agency, the case will be appealed

to a federal, not state court. B is incorrect because the case will be appealed within the judiciary system, not the legislative system. D is incorrect because either party can appeal the decision.

8. B. The substantial evidence test is used to review formal decision making and requires the court to examine the entire record to see whether the agency's decision was supported by substantial evidence. A is incorrect because the arbitrary, capricious or abuse of process test is generally applied to informal decisions such as rule making or licensing. This standard is not usually used to reverse a discretionary fact-finding decision. C is incorrect because the unwarranted by the facts test is rarely used and requires the reviewing court to try the case as if it had not been previously heard.

9. D. The Freedom of Information Act requires federal administrative agencies to be open to the public.

10. B. The Equal Access to Justice Act give a private party these rights.

VI. Key Question Checklist Answers to Essay Question:

A. *What is the source of the IRS's authority?*

This issue is being examined by an administrative agency within the executive branch of the federal government. The general power to tax is in the control of Congress, but the actual administrative of tax laws is vested in the powers of the executive branch. Within that branch, the Treasury Department is the cabinet level agency delegated to oversee tax administration for the federal government. That agency has within it the Internal Revenue Service which is the designated administrative arm of the executive branch empowered with the duty to collect taxes.

B. *How was the IRS given authority to act?*

The basic legislation which allows the IRS to act as our country's tax collector is the Internal Revenue Code. it is obviously a very technical act, subject to constant revision and debate. Under that code, the IRS is allowed to issue numerous rules and regulations relating to both substantive and procedural aspects of the tax laws. The IRS must comply with the Administrative Procedures Act and all other statutes relating to providing adequate notice to the public of its proposed rules and the like. In addition, unless it is information specifically exempted such as law enforcement information, it must also comply with the Freedom of Information Act and similar administrative statutes.

Assuming these rules have been complied with, it most likely that the IRS would take the position that its revenue rules do not allow dogs to be taken as personal dependents on the return, no matter how cute they are. This may seem cruel and cold hearted, but that is the way the old dog biscuit crumbles.

C. *What powers of overview or control may be exerted over the IRS?*

What can poor Joe do? He was advised by an IRS agent to do what he did. Shouldn't he be able to rely on that advice? Unfortunately, he cannot use that reliance as a defense in this case. As the Supreme Court said in a case dealing with administrative agencies: "Whatever the form in which the government functions, anyone entering into an arrangement with the government taking the risk of having accurately ascertained that he purports to act for the government stays within the bounds of his authority." (*Federal*

Crop Inc. Corp. v. Merrill, 332 U.S. 380 (1947)). Here Oliver gave Joe bad advice, but that fact does not excuse Joe's duty to find out for himself what the Internal Revenue Code really said on the issue of who qualifies as a dependent.

To make matters worse, Joe probably cannot hold Oliver liable for negligence because it would not be deemed to be an intentional tort by Oliver. The advice was given in the course of his employment as a government agent. Agency law and governmental immunity would protect Oliver from personal liability.

Is it any wonder that so many people have an overriding sense of frustration when dealing with their Uncle Sam?

CHAPTER 46

CONSUMER PROTECTION

The laws assist those who are vigilant, not those who sleep over their rights.

Legal Maxim

I. Overview:

This chapter covers the fourth major set of venues within a quadripartite of remedies available to a wronged or injured consumer. First, there is criminal law. Victims of consumer fraud and similar offenses have always been able to seek state-supported sanctions against wrongdoers. This venue may provide some ephemeral satisfaction for the victim and may even, at least temporarily, protect society from further harm. But criminal law does not truly make the victim whole. As a matter of fact, most of the miscreants convicted of consumer fraud are also judgment proof, i.e., they have no assets from which civil judgments can be satisfied.

The second area of consumer protection is found in tort law and its permutations of intentional tort, negligence tort, and strict liability. These remedies can and do provide meaningful substance to civil correction of wrongdoing where the defendant is found to have some financial means. As seen in the prior discussions of these areas, tort law generally and products liability specifically are ripe with controversy and a great deal of uncertainty in today's legal environment. The major drawback to both the criminal law and tort law methods of consumer protection is that they represent *after-the-fact* remedies to harm already done. They are reactive remedies as opposed to proactive forms of prevention of harm. It has been argued that large civil judgments act as societal signals which are designed to discourage repetition of undesirable behavior.

The third side to our quadrilateral picture is found in contract. Contract law has the advantage of providing the consumer with the opportunity to anticipate any problems before they befall him or her. This notion is traditionally found in the doctrine of *caveat emptor* which courts of another age used with cavalier abandon. Both the common law of contracts and its progeny, the Uniform Commercial Code, have come a long way from the bad old days of "Let the buyer beware."

In spite of all this progress in the areas of crime, torts, and contract, the gap between consumer harm and consumer protection continues to remain unfilled. Legislators at all levels of government have sought to help fill this void with a number of consumer protection measures. These measures often incorporate elements from both civil and criminal areas of enforcement. In addition, these measures can and often do have a prophylactic effect on many potential harms to the consumer. Unfortunately, another hallmark of many of these measures is that they are the end product of a trail of harm which had reached a crisis or disastrous level. Consider how long it took to take certain dangerous prescription drugs or unsafe toys off the market. Where these laws do provide a measure of safety, some consumer comfort may be found in "at least better late than never." On some public safety issues, the damage remains at disaster levels year in and year out. The American Bar Association recently studied the number of homicides attributable to guns in the U.S. at over 24,000 annually. The death toll from all gun-related incidents is expected to surpass that of automobile-related fatalities before the year

2000. Can we continue to suffer such monumental losses of life year after year? Yet the realistic chances of ever finding protection for the average person in this area are zero to nil as long as government is immobilized by special interest groups. Protection from harm has come a long way, but there is still no light at the end of the tunnel.

II. Hypothetical Multi-issue Essay Question:

Springtime Lord Byron was the original canine movie star of the TV series "My Pal Byron." His fan mail numbered hundreds of letters a week from children of all ages who faithfully watched his show. Byron was at the peak of his form in 1994 when his owner decided to spray him with a product called "Air Bomber Lyme Killer," manufactured by Extremely Dangerous Products, Inc. (E.D.P.I.).

E.D.P.I. advertised its products as being effective in preventing Lyme Disease from being transmitted from animals to humans. What they didn't advertise was that a large number of animals, especially the very young and the very old, died after being sprayed with their product. These deaths were due to the extremely strong toxic chemicals used in the product.

Following the instructions on the can, Byron was sprayed with Air Bomber Lyme Killer for twenty seconds at a distance of three feet. Byron went into an anaphylactic shock within one minute after being sprayed. His owner rushed him to his veterinarian who treated him with corticosteroid antipesticide drugs. Byron is lucky to be alive in that the veterinarian said he was saved only by being in his prime and having quick rescue action taken. Byron's owner wants to know what consumer protection laws, if any, would have prevented this near-tragedy?

III. Key Question Checklist:

A. The first question that needs to be examined is which consumer concern is at issue?
   1. Public health?
   2. Product safety?
   3. Trade practices?
   4. Credit?
   5. A combination of two or more of the above areas?

B. Assuming the issue involves public health, what are the main consumer protection laws?
   1. The Federal Food, Drug, and Cosmetic Act?
      (a) First enacted to regulate wholesomeness of food, drugs, cosmetics, and medical products or devices?
      (b) Regulations cover:
         (1) Manufacture?
         (2) Testing?
         (3) Distribution?
         (4) Sales of regulated items?
      (c) Has powers to:
         (1) Inspect?
         (2) Seize?
         (3) Recall?
         (4) Seek remedies in court?
            (aa) Injunctive relief?
            (bb) Criminal penalties brought by the Justice Department?
      (d) Acts administered by the Food and Drug Administration?
         (1) Pesticide Amendment Act of 1954?
         (2) Food Additives Amendment Act of 1985?
         (3) Color Additives of 1960?
         (4) Animal Drug Amendment of 1968?

418

(5) Biologies Act of 1902?

(6) Public Health Services Act, Sections 361 and 354?

C. Assuming the issue involves product safety, what are the main consumer protection laws?
1. Consumer Product Safety Act of 1972?
   (a) Created the consumer product?
   (b) Commission can:
      (1) Adopt rules to enforce the law?
      (2) Do research on product safety?
      (3) Collect data on consumer injuries?
   (c) Certain products regulated by other agencies (Example: autos)?
   (d) Remedies?
      (1) Seek injunctions?
      (2) Can seek seizure?
      (3) Can seek both civil and criminal penalties?
2. Fair Packaging and Labeling Act?
   (a) Requires certain information on product labels?
   (b) Administered by both the Federal Trade Commission and the Department of Health and Human Services?
3. Magnuson-Moss Warranty Act of 1975?
   (a) Requires clear and simple warranty language on products over $15?
   (b) Administered by Federal Trade Commission?
4. Flammable Fabrics Act?
5. Child Protection and Toy Safety Act?
6. Refrigerator Safety Act?

D. Assuming the issue involves trade practice issues, what are the main consumer protection laws?
1. Federal Trade Commission Act of 1914?
   (a) Created the Federal Trade Commission (FTC)?

(b) Section 5 of the Act prohibits:
   (1) Unfair and deceptive practices?
   (2) FTC has powers under this section to:
      (aa) Hold investigative hearings?
      (bb) Issue cease and desist orders?
      (cc) Order corrective advertising?
2. Postal Reorganization Act?
3. State "lemon" laws?

E. Assuming the issue involves a credit issue, what are the main consumer protection laws?
1. Consumer Credit Protection Act and Truth-in-Lending Act of 1968?
   (a) Requires creditor disclosure of all key terms?
   (b) Administered by Federal Reserve Board?
   (c) Provides certain rights of recision for consumers in limited number of transactions, known as the 3-day rule?
   (d) Civil and criminal sanctions allowed under the Act?
   (e) Consumer Leasing Act extended coverage of truth-in-lending provisions to certain leases?
   (f) Fair Credit and Change and Disclosure Act of 1988 extended provisions of truth-in-lending to certain credit card solicitations and applications?
   (g) Other related credit card rules?
      (1) Unsolicited credit cards?
      (2) Lost or stolen credit cards?
      (3) Disputes over faulty products purchased with credit cards?
2. Equal Credit Opportunity Act of 1975?
   (a) Prohibits discrimination based on sex in extension of credit?

419

(b) Amended in 1976 to apply also to discrimination based on:
  (1) Race?
  (2) Color?
  (3) National origin?
  (4) Religion?
  (5) Age?
  (6) Welfare recipients?
(c) Applies to most credit issuing entities?
(d) Enforced by various agencies, including the FTC?

3. Fair Credit Billing Act of 1974?
  (a) Regulates billing practices?
  (b) Allows legal actions by consumers against creditors who violated the Act?

4. Fair Credit Reporting Act of 1970?
  (a) Regulates credit reporting agencies?
  (b) Allows both civil and criminal remedies for violation of the Act?

5. Fair Debt Collection Practices Act 1977?
  (a) Regulates debt collection practices?
  (b) Administered by the FTC?
  (c) Can also work in conjunction with state laws regarding debt collection?

6. Uniform Consumer Credit Code?
  (a) Promulgated by the National Conference of Commissioners on Uniform State Laws?
  (b) Seeks to unify state regulations on credit?
  (c) Allows both civil and criminal remedies for violation of the act?

IV. Objective Questions:

Terms:

1. The statute enacted in 1938 that provides the basis for regulation of much of the testing, manufacture, distribution, and sale of foods, drugs, cosmetics, and medicinal products is known as the _____ _____ _____ _____ _____ _____.

2. Labeling on a food package that does not disclose the name of the food, the name and place of the manufacturer, and the list of ingredients is considered _____ _____ _____ labeling.

3. The independent regulatory agency composed of five commissioners and empowered to (1) adopt rules and regulations to interpret and enforce the Consumer Product Safety Act, (2) conduct research on safety, and (3) collect data regarding injuries is called the _____ _____ _____ _____.

4. The act that requires the labels on consumer goods to identify the product, the manufacturer, processor, or packager of the product and its address, the net quantity of the contents of the package, and the quantity of each serving is known as the _____ _____ _____ _____.

5. The act intended to avoid injury or death from ingestion of a poisonous material by requiring manufacturers to provide childproof containers and packages for poisonous items is known as the _____ _____ _____ Act.

6. A type of deceptive advertising that occurs when a seller advertises the availability of a low-cost discounted item but then pressures the buyer into purchasing more expensive merchandise is known as _____ _____ _____.

7. The act that requires creditors to make certain disclosures to debtors in consumer transactions that do not exceed $25,000 is called the _____ _____ _____ Act.

8. An amendment to the TILA that requires disclosure of certain credit terms on credit and charge card solicitations and applications is known as the _____ _____ _____ _____ Act of 1988.

9. A credit card sent to a person without the person having requested it is called a _____ credit card.

10. Information about a subject's character, reputation, personal traits, and mode of living compiled from personal or telephone interviews with neighbors, friends, and business associates is found in an _____ _____ _____.

True/False:

1. ____ The Federal Food, Drug, and Cosmetic Act has many powers including the ability to seek search warrants, conduct inspections, and seize products.

2. ____ Under the Federal Food, Drug and Cosmetic Act, food with any impurities is considered to be adulterated.

3. ____ Once a drug has been licensed by the Food and Drug Administration, the FDA cannot withdraw approval of the drug.

4. ____ The Food and Drug Administration has the authority to regulate medical devices as well as drugs.

5. ____ The Consumer Product Safety Commission is an independent regulatory agency composed of five commissioners.

6. ____ Under Section 5 of the Federal Trade Commission Act, actual deception must be proven to show deceptive or unfair advertising.

7. ____ Under the Postal Reorganization Act, a person who receives unsolicited merchandise through the mail may use the merchandise without incurring an obligation to pay for it or return it.

8. ____ The Truth In Lending Act covers all creditors, including those who do not impose a finance charge.

9. ____ Creditors must notify their customer/debtors of the debtor's right of recision on credit transactions where the customer's house was used as security for an extension of credit.

10. ____ A cardholder whose credit card is stolen is liable for all unauthorized charges made on the card before the issuer is notified that the card has been stolen.

Multiple Choice:

1. Miracle Workers, Inc. (MWI) is a pharmaceutical company. MWI recently developed a new drug for stomach cancer. MWI wants to get the drug on the market as soon as possible. Which of the following is correct?
   A. MWI should look to the Fair Packaging and Labeling Act for guidance in getting the drug on the market.
   B. The FDA may require extensive testing of the drug before it goes on the market.
   C. The FDA must grant or deny approval of the drug within thirty days after the application is submitted for approval.
   D. All of the above.

2. Questionable Designs, Inc. (QDI) manufactures consumer products. QDI uses low quality materials and poor designs in its products. The CPAC has found several of QDI's products to be hazardous. What may CPSC do?
   A. Require QDI to recall all those products.
   B. Seek civil penalties for violations of the CPSA.
   C. Require QDI to replace all those products.
   D. All of the above.

3. Several Cereals Manufacturer (SCM) makes and packages many different kinds of breakfast cereal. SCM neglects to put its name on the boxes. By not revealing who the manufacturer is, SCM has violated the:
   A. Fair Packaging and Labeling Act.
   B. Consumer Product Safety Act.
   C. Magnuson-Moss Warranty Act.
   D. Food, Drug and Cosmetic Act.

4. Several Cereals Manufacturer has another problem. On its box of corn flakes, SCM has printed the following: PREFERRED 2 TO 1 IN NATIONAL TASTE TESTS! However, no such taste test was ever conducted. Here, SCM has violated:
   A. The Magnuson-Moss Warranty Act.
   B. The Consumer Product Safety Act.
   C. Section 5 of the Federal Trade Commission Act.
   D. None of the above.

5. High-Pressure Harry is a door-to-door vacuum salesman for Vanity Vacuums. Harry uses his aggressive sales tactics to convince Push-Over Paul that he absolutely-positively-without-a-doubt must have a Vanity Vacuum. Which of the following is correct?
   A. Paul may rescind the sales contract if he sends a notice of cancellation to Vanity Vacuums within a certain number of days.
   B. Paul is not bound by the sales contract unless Harry contacts Paul within three days to finalize the contract.
   C. Paul is bound by the sales contract when he signs it and cannot later rescind it.
   D. None of the above.

6. Collector Carrie buys a bronze sculpture from Exquisite Exclusives Gallery (EEG). The sculpture costs $5,000, and Carrie cannot purchase it outright. Therefore, EEG allows Carries to buy the sculpture by paying for the sculpture in two equal payments without a finance charge. Under the Truth-in-Lending Act, which of the following is correct?
   A. EEG must disclose its annual percentage rate.
   B. EEG must disclose any prepayment penalties.
   C. Both of the above.
   D. None of the above. EEG is not subject to TILA.

422

7. Driver Daisy decides to lease a car from Linda's Leasing. The lease is for five years and a total cost of $10,000. Under the Consumer Leasing Act, what must Linda's Leasing include in the lease agreement?
   A. Any express warranties on the car.
   B. Daisy's liability at the end of the five-year term.
   C. An itemization of all lease and finance charges.
   D. All of the above.

8. Careless Chris leaves his wallet sitting on a restaurant counter when he leaves to use the telephone. While he is gone, Slimy Sylvester steals Chris' credit card. Chris is unaware of the theft when he returns to his seat. In fact, Chris does not discover his card has been stolen until five days later. By that time, Sylvester has charged $2,000 on the card. Chris reports the stolen card as soon as he discovers it. Which of the following is correct?
   A. Chris is liable for the $2,000 in unauthorized charges.
   B. Chris is not liable for any of the unauthorized charges.
   C. Chris is liable for $50 of the unauthorized charges.
   D. Chris is liable for one half, or $1,000, of the unauthorized charges.

9. Assume the same facts as in question 8 except that Chris discovers the card missing and reports it immediately. However, Sylvester manages to charge $2,000 on the card anyway. Which of the following is correct?
   A. Chris is liable for the $2,000 in unauthorized charges.
   B. Chris is not liable for any of the unauthorized charges.

C. Chris is liable for $50 of the unauthorized charges.
D. Chris is liable for one half, or $1,000, of the unauthorized charges.

10. Ripped-Off Rhonda purchased a new microwave from Ample Appliances with her credit card. However, the microwave is obviously defective, and Rhonda does not want to pay for the microwave until it is repaired or replaced. Which of the following is correct?
   A. Rhonda can withhold payment to her credit card company until the dispute is resolved.
   B. Rhonda must pay the credit card company and seek a refund from Ample Appliances.
   C. Either of the above.
   D. None of the above. A consumer has no recourse if a faulty product is purchased on a credit card.

V. Answers to Objective Questions:

Terms:

1. *Federal Food, Drug, and Cosmetic Act.* In spite of many amendments since 1938, this act remains the cornerstone in this area of consumer protection.
2. *False and misleading labeling.* Recent changes in this area have called for more clarity with regard to the nutritional value of food products.
3. *Consumer Product Safety Commission.* Funding for this agency's mission has been a constant source of debate in Congress.
4. *Fair Packaging and Labeling Act.* Recent reforms to this act have called for standardization of certain claims which may be listed on products.

423

5. *Poison Prevention Packaging.* These warnings are particularly designed to help parents keep these products out of the reach of children.

6. *Bait and switch.* Remedies such as rainchecks are designed to offset some of the harmful effects of t h e s e sorts of practices.

7. *Truth-in-Lending.* As the average price of autos continues to go up, Congress is expected to raise the threshold coverage of this act.

8. *Fair Credit and Charge Card Disclosure.* This act reflects a trend in the law to make legal documents easier to comprehend by lay people.

9. *Unsolicited.* Few financial institutions do this anymore after having been burned by wrongful users of unsolicited cards.

10. *Investigative consumer report.* The debtor is entitled to request and examine these reports.

True/False:

1. True. These powers are outlined in the act.

2. False. Food must consist in whole or in part of any "filthy, putrid, or decomposed substance" to be considered adulterated. However, impurities may not be sufficient to deem food adulterated unless they are at an extreme level.

3. False. The FDA has the authority to withdraw approval of a drug after it has been licensed.

4. True. This power is considered a practical necessity.

5. True. The commissions are appointed by the president.

6. False. Under Section 5 of the FTCA, actual deception need not be proven to show deceptive or unfair advertising.

7. True. The sender puts him or herself at risk of not being paid if he or she engages in this practice.

8. False. TILA covers many creditors. However, certain guidelines set which types of creditors are and are not covered.

9. True. There are time-line limitations on the use of this right.

10. False. A cardholder whose credit card is stolen is liable only for $50 on all unauthorized charges made on the card before the issuer is notified that the card has been stolen. If the cardholder notifies the issuer before the stolen card is used, the cardholder is not liable for any unauthorized charges.

Multiple Choice:

1. B. The FDA may require extensive, additional testing until it is satisfied that the drug is safe and effective. A is incorrect because the FDCA, not the FPLA, governs the development and sale of drugs. C is incorrect because the FDA is not required to grant or deny approval of the drug within a certain time. In fact, testing may take several years.

2. D. All these powers may be exercised by the CPSC.

3. A. The Fair Packaging and Labeling Act requires that a product package identifies the manufacturer, processor, or packager of the product. B, C, and D are incorrect because these acts do not govern the packaging of products.

4. C. Section 5 of the FTCA prohibits deceptive or unfair advertising. A statement referring to a national test which was never even conducted is clearly deceptive advertising. Actual consumer deception need not be shown.

A and B are incorrect because these acts do not regulate advertising.

5. A. Under Section 5 of the FTCA, a consumer may rescind a door-to-door sales contract by contacting the seller within a certain number of days. B is incorrect because Paul must take the initial step to rescind the contract. Harry does not have to recontact Paul. If Paul does not rescind the contract within the stated time, he is bound by it. C is incorrect because he can rescind it within a certain amount of time.

6. D. Since EEG neither charges Carrie a finance charge nor requires payment in more than four installments, it is not subject to TILA. A and B are incorrect because they only apply to creditors covered by TILA.

7. D. All three are required by the Consumer Leasing Act.

8. C. Chris is liable for $50 of the $2,000 in charges since he did not notify the credit card issuer before Sylvester made unauthorized charges on the card. However, Chris is not liable for more than $50. A is incorrect because the credit card holder is liable for a maximum of $50 in this situation. B is incorrect because Chris did not contact the credit card issuer before unauthorized charges were made on the card. D is incorrect for the same reason A is incorrect.

9. B. Since Chris notified the credit card issuer immediately, he is not liable for any of the unauthorized charges.

10. A. B is incorrect because Rhonda does not have to pay the credit card company. She may withhold payment until the dispute is settled. D is incorrect because a consumer does have recourse if a faulty product is purchased on a credit card.

VI. Key Question Checklist Answers to Essay Question:

A. *Which consumer concern is as issue?*

The issues raised by the incident include health safety, product safety, and trade practice problems related to the manufacture, advertising, and sale of Air Bomber Lyme Killer. The jurisdictional lines among the various agencies who may have control over these issues is not always clearly drawn. Wherever possible, specific jurisdiction is best determined by finding which statute or agency has, as a part of its mission, control over the product.

B&C. *What are the main consumer protection issues in that area?*

In this case, the best place to start will be to look at the health issue first. The Federal Food and Drug Administration is broadly charged with the protection of the public's health as related to the testing, manufacture, distribution, and sale of foods, drugs, cosmetics, and medical products, and devices in the U.S. This general jurisdiction was specifically extended to animal foods and drugs under the Animal Drug Amendment of 1968 to the general Federal Food, Drug, and Cosmetic Act of 1906.

Because the FDA has this specific jurisdiction, Bryon's owner can now seek to get assistance from the FDA in the form of filing a complaint with the agency against E.D.P.I. Under the provisions of the Act, the FDA can inspect, test, seize, and order a recall of the product if it finds it to be dangerous to the health and safety of animals. In addition, if it finds that E.D.P.I. acted in an intentionally dangerous manner, it may seek Justice Department criminal prosecution for violations of the law.

Under the terms of Consumer Product Safety Act, the Consumer Product Safety Commission may do research and gather data on harm done to consumers from dangerous products. If it could be shown that this product had harmful effects on humans as well as animals, E.D.P.I. may have yet another agency to contend with.

D. *Are there any trade practices which may be in violation of consumer protection laws?*

If it can be shown that E.D.P.I.'s advertising was in any way false or misleading, the Federal Trade Commission may also seek to investigate this situation. The transmission of Lyme Disease from dogs to humans has been discredited as a myth by the scientific research done on that issue and to advertise to the contrary may constitute false and misleading advertising. Under its powers, the FTC may seek injunctive orders to prevent any further false advertising and even order corrective advertising by E.D.P.I.

All in all, E.D.P.I. may have a handful of problems. But those problems are nowhere near the trauma of Byron's owner having nearly killed his own beloved dog. Consumer protection may seem overly litigious, but the harm done by defective or dangerous products is very real indeed.

CHAPTER 47

ENVIRONMENTAL PROTECTION

We all live under the same sky, but we don't all have the same horizon.

Konrad Adenauer

I. Overview:

Most TV commercials qualify for the mute button. They are inane, insulting, sexist, or some combination of the above. One refreshing exception to this general rule was recently aired by a large chemical company. It announced that it was going to use double-lined tanker ships to transport its products. The news was shown being greeted with jubilation by all sorts of wildlife accompanied to the stirring sounds of Beethoven's Ninth Symphony. Having witnessed one environmental disaster after another, most of us want to cheer on a more enlightened age of environmental awareness. The 1990's do seem to have ushered in a greater concern for environmental issues than ever before. One would hope this is not just the latest politically correct marketing fashion but rather a realization that our natural resources can no longer be taken for granted. Like it or not, our advances in technology have finally given us the power to permanently alter nature. This power has been used to feed millions and save lives. It can and has also been used to destroy endangered species, burn holes in the ozone, and uproot entire ecosystems.

The law of environmental protection seeks to provide some sort of rhyme and reason to all this by seeking to balance the needs and desires for technological advancement with a realistic perspective of what natural limitations our environment places on these capacities. The age of growth *per se* as a good thing is changing to: "Is the growth worth it?" The environmental movement is not new. Conservationists, animal lovers, and the like have a long and proud history of protecting our natural resources. What is new are the threats raised by oil spills, hazardous wastes, nuclear accidents, and unmitigated depletion of irreplaceable resources. The emergence of environmental legislation which has a sense of urgency and response to these issues is only now in its third decade--a mere second on the ecological clock.

Because this legislation is so relatively new, the growing pains of new social engineering continue. Business has had to adjust to not doing business as usual. Many businesses, in fact, are either no longer in business or radically changed due to the environmental concerns raised by their operations. Industries which have traditionally relied heavily on utilization of natural resources such as mining, oil, gas exploration, and timber have been especially impacted by these laws. Consider also the auto industry. For years automakers outside the U.S. have complained about our pollution controls being too costly and cumbersome. It is no small point of pride that the world is catching up with us on this issue by finally adopting our standards for safety and emissions. As another example, members of the European Economic Community have only recently adopted passive restraint rules similar to the air bag rules already in place in the U.S.

If there is any good that comes out of the Exxon Valdez oil spills and the Love Canals, it is that the world is awakening to the fact that what happens over there is really here. Here is where we all of live and breathe. The job of the law is to help make here a safe place to do just that. The key question checklist outlines the major modern environmental protection statutes in place today in the U.S.

II. Hypothetical Multi-issue Essay Question:

Bailout Bank of Metropolis is seeking to extend its operations to every corner of the great state of Louisiark. The state legislature just passed a law allowing branch banking which now allows Bailout to open branches outside of Metropolis for the first time. Bailout's Vice President in charge of real estate is Mr. Mortimer M. Misque. Mortimer's cousin, Ms. Sallie S. Spillaway, is Vice President in charge of real estate for Dryhole Oil Company. Dryhole's business has been terrible ever since it converted all its self-service operations into combination gas stations and mini-refineries. Dryhole thought it could save a lot of money by not having to ship gasoline from its out-of-state refineries to retail outlets.

Mortimer and Sallie hit upon a great idea. Why not sell the Dryhole gasoline refinery outlets to Bailout and convert them to branch banks? The deal went through, and Bailout proceeded to immediately renovate the gas stations. The old refinery and pump facilities were simply capped into mothballs in case the bank ever decided to go into the business.

Unfortunately, several years after these renovations, Bailout's money began to take on a funny odor. In addition, the residents of the neighborhoods adjoining Bailout branches began to have trouble with their drinking water. What can be done?

III. Key Question Checklist:

A. The Environment Protection Agency has overall jurisdiction over federal environmental laws in the U.S. This power is often shared to one degree or another with other federal, state, or local agencies. The first question you need to ask is who has jurisdiction over the issue at hand?
1. Environmental Protection Agency (EPA) has which basic powers?
   (a) Coordinate environmental laws?
      (1) Over water resources?
      (2) Over solid wastes?
      (3) Over air and radiation issues?
      (4) Over pesticides and toxic substance issues?
      (5) Coordinate research and development on environmental issues?
   (b) Implement and enforce environmental laws?
      (1) Civil enforcement?
      (2) Criminal sanctions?
      (3) Environmental impact statement requirements?
2. Is any other federal, state, or local agency involved in the issue at hand?

B. Once you have decided which agency may have total or partial control over the issue, you must then look at the statute itself. Statutes generally are classified per the natural resources they are designed to protect. Assuming the issue involves air or radiation, what are the main statutes?
1. Clean Air Act?
   (a) Allows EPA to set air quality standards?
   (b) Designates state enforcement of the standards?
   (c) Standards designed for stationary sources of air pollution:
      (1) Reasonably available control technology?
      (2) Best available control technology?

428

(d) Standards designed for mobile sources of air pollution:
    (1) Autos, trucks, etc.?
    (2) Airplanes?
    (3) Fuels?
(e) Standard designed for classification of toxic air pollutants?

C. Assuming the issue at hand involves water resources, what are the main statutes?
1. Clean Water Act?
  (a) Allows EPA to set clean water quality standards?
    (1) Best practical control technology standard applicable?
    (2) Best available control technology standard applicable?
  (b) Thermal pollution issue?
  (c) Wetlands protection issue?
    (1) Jurisdiction shared with the Army Corps of Engineers?
  (d) Oil spill issue?
2. Safe Drinking Water Act?
3. Marine Protection, Research, and Sanctuaries Act?
4. Other related acts which affect water table quality control?
    (1) Federal Insecticide, Fungicide, and Rodenticide Act?
    (2) Toxic Substances Control Act?
5. State water laws?

D. Assuming the issue at hand involves hazardous waste, what are the main statutes?
1. Resource Conservation and Recovery Act?
  (a) Regulates the generation, treatment, storage, and disposal of hazardous wastes?
  (b) Includes cradle-to-grave tracking system with regard to identified hazardous substances?

2. Comprehensive Environmental Response, Compensation, and Liability Act?
  (a) Created Superfund system?
  (b) Identify hazardous sites?
  (c) Has a priority system for cleaning up the sites?
  (d) Provide for financing of the cleanup by:
    (1) Public funds?
    (2) Collection from parties involved with the properties?
3. Nuclear Waste Policy Act?
  (a) Jurisdiction shared between EPA and Nuclear Regulatory Commission?
  (b) Regulate the nuclear industry?
4. State hazardous waste laws?

E. Assuming the issue at hand involves preservation of wildlife?
1. Endangered Species Act?
  (a) Jurisdiction shared between the EPA and the Department of Commerce?
  (b) Identify endangered species?
  (c) Allows measures to be taken to preserve the endangered species?
2. Other legislation related to wildlife preservation?
  (a) Migratory Bird Treaty Act?
  (b) Bald Eagle Protection Act?
  (c) National wildlife refuge system?
  (d) State and local wildlife preservation laws?

F. Assuming the issue at hand involves noise pollution?
1. Noise Control Act?
  (a) EPA given power to establish national noise standards jointly with other agencies?
  (b) Includes aircrafts, autos, trucks, plants?

429

2. States given federal assistance on noise problems through the Quiet Communities Act?

3. State and local laws with regard to noise pollution issues?

IV. Objective Questions:

Terms:

1. In 1970, Congress created the _____ _____ _____ which coordinates the implementation and enforcement of federal environmental protection laws.

2. The document which must be prepared for all proposed federal legislation that would significantly affect the quality of the human environment is called an _____ _____ _____.

3. The major source of mobile air pollution is the _____.

4. The agency responsible for enforcing pollution standards for airplanes is known as the _____ _____ _____.

5. Asbestos, mercury, vinyl chloride, and benzene are examples of _____ _____.

6. The EPA can establish water pollution control standards under the _____ _____ _____.

7. Areas that are inundated or saturated by surface or groundwater that support vegetation typically adapted for life in saturated soil conditions are called _____.

8. The act which extended environmental protection to the oceans is known as the _____ _____ _____ _____ _____ Act.

9. The act which provides for the creation of a fund to finance the cleanup of hazardous wastes is popularly known as _____.

10. Licenses for the construction and opening of commercial nuclear power plants are granted by the _____ _____ _____.

True/False:

1. ____ Under common law, individuals could bring a private civil suit based on private nuisance to recover damages from a polluting party.

2. ____ The Environmental Protection Agency has adjudicative powers to hold hearings, make decisions, and order remedies for violations of federal environmental laws.

3. ____ It is not necessary to prepare an environmental impact statement for all proposed legislation that may affect the environment.

4. ____ Once an environmental impact statement is prepared, the public has sixty days in which to submit comments to the EPA.

5. ____ States establish national ambient air quality standards for pollutants.

6. ____ The EPA can require automobile manufacturers to recall and repair or replace pollution control equipment that does not meet air quality control standards.

7. ____ The first regulation to prevent and control water pollution was enacted in 1886.

8. ____ The Clean Water Act authorizes the U.S. government to clean up oil spills and spills of other hazardous substances in ocean waters within six miles of the shore.

9. ____ The Resource Conservation and Recovery Act defines a hazardous waste as one that may cause or significantly contribute to an increase in mortality or serious illness or pose a hazard to human health or the environment if improperly managed.

10. ____ The EPA can order a responsible party to clean up a hazardous waste.

Multiple Choice:

1. Which of the following is contained in an environmental impact statement?
   A. Description of the affected environment.
   B. No description of alternatives to proposed action.
   C. List of resources that will be committed to the action.
   D. A and C, but not B.

2. Regions that do not meet national ambient air quality standards for certain pollutants are described as nonattainment areas. Which is the worst category?
   A. Moderate.
   B. Severe.
   C. Extreme.
   D. Serious.

3. The Clean Air Act requires new automobiles to meet the following air quality control standards?
   A. Leaded fuel is permitted for highway use after 1995.
   B. Cars must meet air quality standards prior to 1995, five years, or 50,000 miles, whichever comes first.
   C. Production of engines that use leaded fuel is prohibited after model year 1990.
   D. The EPA cannot require automobile manufacturers to recall automobiles which do not meet air quality standards.

4. Which of the following is not a point source of water pollution according to the Clean Water Act?
   A. Toilets in homes.
   B. Mines.
   C. Paper mills.
   D. Municipal sewage plants.

5. The Superfund requires the EPA to:
   A. Identify sites in the U.S. where hazardous wastes have been disposed.
   B. Rank sites based of severity of risk.
   C. Put the highest ranking sites on a National Priority List.
   D. All of the above.

6. The EPA cannot recover the cost of a cleanup from:
   A. The generator who deposited the waste.
   B. Workers who deposited the waste under the direction of their employer.
   C. The owner of the site at the time of the disposal.
   D. The current owner and operator of the site.

7. The Superfund imposes liability without fault; the name for this doctrine is:
   A. *Res ipsa loquitur.*
   B. Contributory negligence.
   C. Strict liability.
   D. *Respondeat superior.*

8. Under the Superfund's right-to-know provision, businesses are required to:
   A. Disclose monthly the presence of certain listed chemicals to the community.
   B. Disclose annually the emissions of chemical substances released into the environment.
   C. Immediately notify the government of spills, accidents, and other emergencies involving hazardous substances.
   D. None of the above.

9. Which of the following is not a federal statute that protects wildlife?
   A. Resource Conservation and Recovery Act.
   B. Bald Eagle Protection Act.
   C. Fishery Conservation and Management Act.
   D. Wild Free-Roaming Horses and Burros Act.

10. Which of the following noises is not regulated by the Noise Control Act?
    A. Aircraft.
    B. Railroads.
    C. Barking dogs.
    D. Trucks.

V. Answers to Objective Questions:

Terms:

1. *Environmental Protection Agency.* The EPA is growing in both economic and political importance. President Clinton has recommended that the office of EPA Administrator be raised to cabinet rank.

2. *Environmental impact statement.* Many states have followed suit and now call for local versions of these statements.

3. *Automobile.* An interesting footnote on this issue is that most auto-related pollution is being generated by the minority of autos built prior to the issuance of pollution guidelines.

4. *Federal Aviation Administration.* The FAA has sought to reduce pollution from airplanes by coordinating takeoffs on a national scale in order to cut down on wasteful holding patterns over major airports.

5. *Toxic pollutants.* As thresholds of scientific discovery expand, this list gets longer every year.

6. *Clean Water Act.* This effort is coordinated with state and local water quality control authorities.

7. *Wetlands.* Arriving at a precise definition of land to qualify for this designation continues to be a political powderkeg.

8. *Marine Protection, Research and Sanctuaries.* Much of the work done under this act is coordinated with state and local agencies.

9. *Superfund.* The actual title of this legislation is the Comprehensive Response Compensation and Liability Act.

10. *Nuclear Regulatory Commission.* As compared to other environmentally sensitive activities, this activity is exclusively controlled by the federal government.

True/False:

1. True. These actions are traceable to old common law property rights.

2. True. This pattern of powers is typical under the rights of the executive branch.
3. False. An environmental impact statement must be prepared.
4. False. The time period is thirty days.
5. False. The EPA establishes NAAQS for pollutants.
6. True. Recalls can be very expensive for manufacturers who often fight over the scope and breadth of the recall.
7. True. This process can take years if there is a dispute.
8. False. The distance is twelve miles off shore.
9. True. This definition has been fought over in the courts because of all the possible interpretations which may arise from it.
10. True. If the party refuses, the EPA may clean it up and sue for the cost of the cleanup.

Multiple Choice:

1. D. Alternatives to the proposed actions are also listed in the environmental impact statement.
2. C. Extreme is considered to be at the near emergency state and has a high priority for corrective action.
3. B. These protections supersede any protections given by the manufacturer's warranty.
4. A. These are assumed to be normal activities which are handled by local authorities.
5. D. All of these activities are required under the Act.
6. B. This is an example of the application of agency law to an environmental statute.
7. C. This is an example of the application of a tort law doctrine to an environmental statute.

8. C. Where the wrongdoer is the business itself, expecting total self-regulation appears unrealistic, which is why informants are often the source of this sort of information.
9. A. This Act is focused on natural resources other than wildlife, although it collaterally benefits wildlife living in protected areas.
10. C. It is expected that local authorities will have control over this issue.

VI. Key Question Checklist Answers to Essay Question:

A&B. *Which agency would be called first to look into the problem?*

The overall jurisdiction over environmental issues is generally given to the Environmental Protection Agency (EPA). On a number of issues, the EPA shares this jurisdiction with other federal or state and local agencies. One of the key regulatory aspects of the EPA function is to gather information on key environmental concerns. State and local agencies often have similar information gathering functions. One common method of gathering such information is through the use of environmental impact statements. Normally the EPA will not require such a statement on proposed projects not covered by the National Environmental Policy Act, but most state and local governments do require such disclosures. Here there appears to be no evidence of Bailout or Dryhole having provided such a statement to any government agency. They may be held liable for such a failure.

C. *Assuming the issue at hand involves water resources, what are the main statutes to be examined?*

It appears that there may be some damage to the water table in the areas underneath the former gasoline outlets *cum* refineries. This sort of problem has become relatively common around the country as older gasoline outlet facilities are closed or converted to other uses. The old tanks are often left in the ground and allowed to rust. As they rust out, toxic chemicals are released from them into the ground water table. These emissions are often in violation of the Clean Water Act and various state and local agencies may seek both equitable injunctive relief and money damages for the cost of cleanup and even criminal sanctions, where appropriate, for the violation of these statutes.

D. *Are there any other statutory provisions which may apply?*

In addition to the violation of the Clean Water Act, this situation may involve imposition of the provisions of the Comprehensive Environmental Response Compensation and Liability Act (Superfund). Under this Act, the costs of cleaning up a designated site may be passed on to any owners of the property who had an active part in the management of the property. There is an exception from liability for those parties whose only interest in the property arose out of a security interest. Here the bank may try to argue that defense but would lose on the merits. Bailout Bank became an active owner of the property when it decided to convert the stations to branch banks. As such, it is subject to joint and several liability with Dryhole Oil to pay for the cost of the cleanup. The EPA can order them to clean it up directly. If they fail to do the cleanup, the EPA can clean it up and seek recovery of the cost from either Bailout, Dryhole, or both. Interestingly enough, both Mortimer and Sallie are now in other lines of work. They took jobs at nuclear power plants.

434

CHAPTER 48

ANTITRUST LAW

Things do not change; we do.

Henry David Thoreau

I. Overview:

Most people do not think of the trust device as a business tool. As seen in other chapters, today's use of trusts centers around the need to hold property for the benefit of others. In another era, however, the business trust was notoriously used as a device to eliminate competition. In the late 1800's, it was common to have key commodities and the industries related to those products controlled by large corporate enterprises. These entities would band together into a form of common trust ownership. The trustee, in turn, was able to control the prices, territories of distribution, and the like of the product. For example, prior to the enactment of antitrust laws, industries like oil, cotton, sugar, and whiskey were all dominated by such trusts. Probably the best known of these trusts was Standard Oil. In 1890 the Standard Oil Trust controlled over ninety percent of the market for oil products in the U.S. By the time the trust was "busted" in 1911, over thirty companies were ordered separated from the parent firm. This sort of monopolization of the marketplace led to the landmark antitrust legislation in 1890, the Sherman Antitrust Act. The act has two main objectives:

1. To prevent combinations in trust or otherwise, which act in restraint of trade, i.e., illegal joining together to restrain trade.

2. To control markets thought to have a monopoly, i.e., illegal domination so strong as to *ipso facto* restrain trade.

These objectives are set out in Sections 1 and 2 of the Act and will be described in more detail in the key question checklist. What is interesting about this act is that Congress used very broad language to give the Justice Department maximum latitude in seeking enforcement of its provisions. This latitude has, in turn, not been consistently used. There appears to have been a constant shift in the enforcement strategies used by various administrations over the years. Enforcement has gone up and down like skirt lengths in the fashion world. Those who favor strict enforcement essentially adhere to the notions originally proffered by Senator John Sherman and his cohorts. Under this traditional philosophy, competition is best served by having as many players in the arena of commerce as possible. Conversely, large concentrations of power in commerce are thought to be inherently bad.

On the other side of the enforcement spectrum, the more modern view says that large concentrations of economic power are not evil *per se* as long as they are efficient and are still fighting for a competitive position on a world-based economic playing field. Recent administrative decisions have clearly favored this more lenient view as evidenced by the large number of mergers, acquisitions, leveraged buyouts, and consolidations which have taken place on Wall Street without objection.

The federal courts, in turn, have taken the middle road. Under their rules of interpretation, two main classifications of offenses have evolved. The *Per se Rule* is used to strike down restraints that courts deem to be so inherently anticompetitive that they cannot be allowed as a matter of law, regardless of any claimed justifications. On the other hand, the *Rule of Reason* has given courts latitude to accept restraints of trade on a case by case basis where legitimate concerns are overriding.

As strong and powerful a tool in the fight against monopolization and restraints of trade as the Sherman Act is, it has proven to be only a partial remedy to the problem. The Sherman Act sets the basic goals and objectives of keeping marketplaces open to competition. The Clayton Act and the Federal Trade Commission Act are designed to provide tools of implementation to those basic public policy objectives. As compared to the almost philosophical tenor of Sections 1 and 2 of the Sherman Act, the Clayton Act and more particularly, the Robinson-Patman Amendment to it, speak to much more specific objectives. These objectives arose out of discriminatory practices aimed at getting the little guy.

The biggest problem with the Clayton Act, and to a lesser extent with the FTC, is the government's commitment to enforcement combined with some very problematic aspects of the statutes themselves. On the issue of governmental level of commitment to enforcement, there is no question that things have changed in the geo-global scheme of economic competition. In many ways the market factors which were sought to be protected in the early part of the Twentieth Century are different as we are about to enter the Twenty-First Century. A free and open market is not measured now on regional or even national scales, but rather on world-wide competitive position. These changes have provided the philosophical underpinnings for the much more tolerant view taken by the government towards mergers, acquisitions, combinations, and the like. Yet the basic economic principles of monopolization, restraint of trade, and unfair trade practices have not changed. So government finds itself in a dilemma. It is trying to recognize the need to allow our economy to try and stay competitive on a world-wide playing field, but it must continue to keep the rules fair in that game.

The second factor involves questions which have been raised about the economic sense of the Clayton Act itself. Many critics of the act have argued that while provisions seeking to prevent price discrimination look good on the sheet music, they flop in the concert hall. The reason these particular measures have failed to live up to their billing is that some price volume costs, incentives, and the like are all part of the competitive edge that all players are constantly looking for. To deny the reality of those competitive needs not only frustrates real competition, it may give noncompetitive parties an unwarranted wedge against more efficient competitors by way of officious intermeddling on the part of government.

Where antitrust laws do not work, they actually become part of the problem. No one really wants to go back to the bad old days of robber barons and unmitigated jungle warfare in our economic system. Yet the time has probably come for a wholesale reexamination of our antitrust laws. This examination should focus on two main goals: (1) rewrite the laws so as to really provide a level playing field for all competitors and (2) get the government to act when needed instead of being an immobilized Hamlet who cannot decide what to do.

All in all, antitrust law is in a greater state of flux than ever. Out of this debate, many are now arguing that the time has come for a overhaul of the entire antitrust law structure. Given the sporadic history of enforcement, who will enforce the law as intended no matter how it may be rewritten? These choices are ours to make in the voting booth.

II. Hypothetical Multi-issue Essay Question:

Spookey's Scareys specializes in Halloween costumes in Salem, Mazazona. Spookey's has 11 percent of a declining market. Its competitors are Ghosts and Goblins with 29 percent, Witches and Wanderers with 31 percent, Midnight Costumes with 20 percent and several other Mom and Pop operations with the remaining 9 percent. On an average costume selling for $100, Spookey's has an overall cost of $90, including $75 paid to its main supplier, Bad Taste Haberdashery.

Because the market has been bad, Spookey's is looking for a buyer. It entered into a deal with Ghost and Goblins to sell a 51 percent interest in the store. Ghosts and Goblins would continue to operate both stores under their separate names. In addition, because of its combined buying power, the newly merged company is now able to get costumes from Bad Taste at $50 apiece and pass on the savings with lowered retail prices. Are there any antitrust problems with the above transactions?

III. Key Question Checklist:

This checklist is designed first to introduce the student to the broad underlying public policy reasoning behind the antitrust laws. Second, it provides a more technical listing of the most important provisions found in those laws.

A. The first question you need to examine in antitrust issues is to look at the basic public policy behind the law. What are antitrust laws generally designed to promote and to protect?
1. Competition is protected best in an open and fair marketplace?
2. Monopolization and concentrations of economic controls in any market are inherently anticompetitive?
3. Even though many contracts by their very nature may cause some restraints on trade, reasonable interpretation of antitrust laws allows the government to strike a balance between business needs and the needs of the larger society?
4. History has proven that monopolization can and will take hold without the existence of these sort of statutes?

B. The next question is to look to see which one of the main statutes is available to the government seeking to prevent business behavior which may be in restraint of a free and open marketplace?
1. The Sherman Antitrust Act of 1890?
   (a) Generally seeks to limit concerted anticompetitive activities and monopolistic behavior?
   (b) Enforced by the U.S. Justice department?
2. The Clayton Act of 1914?
   (a) Generally regulates mergers and certain dealing arrangements?
   (b) Enforced by both the U.S. Justice Department and the Federal Trade Commission?
3. The Federal Trade Commission Act of 1914 (FTC)?
   (a) Generally regulates unfair methods of competition?
   (b) FTC has exclusive jurisdiction over the enforcement of this act?
4. Robinson-Patman Act of 1930?
   (a) Generally prohibits discriminatory pricing practices?
   (b) Enforced by both the U.S. Justice Department and the FTC?

5. In addition, where interstate commerce is not involved, many states have similar statutes at the local level?

6. Certain activities or industries are exempted from antitrust laws based on:
   (a) Specific statutory coverage under other legislation?
       (1) Agricultural co-ops?
       (2) Labor unions?
       (3) Insurance?
       (4) Joint export companies?
       (5) Railroads and shipping companies?
   (b) Court case-based implied exemptions?
   (c) State regulated economic regulations?

C. Assuming that the actions at issue involve possible violations of the Sherman Act, what are the key provisions of the act which you must examine?
   1. Section 1?
      (a) General and broad prohibition of all contracts, combinations, conspiracies, or other acts which are in restraint of trade?
      (b) Makes the conduct listed above unlawful when committed by two or more parties?
      (c) Two judicial interpretation tests possible because the law is so broad:
         (1) Rule of Reason?
            (aa) Allows a case by case examination of all relevant factors to see if the restraint of trade is reasonable?
            (bb) Examples of factors include competition in the industry, market share, and effects of the restraint on competition?

      (2) *Per se* Rule?
         (aa) if courts decide the restraint is inherently anticompetitive, it is barred *per se*, regardless of any further evidence of its justification?
         (bb) Examples include price fixing, division of markets, tying agreements, and certain group boycotts?

   2. Actions generally subject to Section 1 scrutiny?
      (a) Horizontal restraints of trade?
         (1) Price fixing?
         (2) Division of markets?
         (3) Group boycotts?
         (4) Trade association actions?
      (b) Vertical restraints of trade?
         (1) Vertical price fixing or resale price maintenance?
         (2) Tying arrangements?
         (3) Exclusive dealing or refusal to deal?

   3. Section 2?
      (a) General and broad prohibition of monopolistic behavior?
      (b) Looks for two elements:
         (1) Possession of monopoly power?
         (2) Willful acquisition or maintenance of that monopoly power?
      (c) Do not need two or more parties to violate this provision; can be only one?
      (d) Defenses?
         (1) Superior business acumen?
         (2) "Natural" monopoly?

D. What are the main provisions of the Clayton Act and Federal Trade Commission Act?

1. Section 7 of the Clayton Act?
   (a) Generally directed towards merger and other sorts of expansionist activities which may have anticompetitive effects on the marketplace?
   (b) Enforced by both the U.S. Justice Department and the FTC?
   (c) Specific actions covered by Section 7?
      (1) Mergers by stock acquisition?
      (2) Mergers by asset acquisition?
      (3) Consolidations?
      (4) Joint ventures?
      (5) Subsidiary operations?
      (6) Any other expansion which may have an anticompetitive effect on the marketplace?
   (d) Specific notice requirement met?
      (1) Notice of proposed action given to U.S. Department of Justice and FTC?
      (2) Thirty day waiting period complied with?
   (e) Specific kinds of mergers covered by Section 7?
      (1) Horizontal merger?
         (aa) Combination of firms engaged same line of business?
         (bb) Competing in same geographical area?
         (cc) Comply with Herfindahl-Hirschman guidelines?
      (2) Vertical merger?
         (aa) Combinations of suppliers with customers?
         (bb) Can be a forward vertical merger wherein the supplier acquires a customer?
         (cc) Can be a backward vertical merger wherein the customer acquires a supplier?
         (dd) Any anticompetitive effects due to foreclosure of competition?
      (3) Market extension merger?
         (aa) Where firms in similar fields combine to extend sales coverage which had not overlapped prior to the merger?
         (bb) Can be a product market extension?
         (cc) Can be a geographic market extension?
         (dd) Any anticompetitive effects?
      (4) Conglomerate merger?
         (aa) A merger of two firms in unrelated lines of business?
         (bb) Any anticompetitive effects?
   (f) Once you have identified what kind of merger you are looking at under Section 7, answer the prior subquestion with regard to anticompetitive effects. Which theory of anticompetitive effect will best fit this situation?
      (1) Unfair advantage theory?
         (aa) Acquiring firm may now have unfair advantage in a number of related business fields of activity?
         (bb) Examples: finance, marketing, expertise?
      (2) Potential competition theory?
         (aa) Would this merger eliminate or reduce potential entrants into the marketplace?

439

(bb) Example: large company acquires a new line of business in order to keep out potential small competitors in that same line?

(3) Potential reciprocity theory?

  (aa) Will this merger create too cozy a relationship between the merged firms and other firms?

  (bb) Example: customer buys raw material supplier so as to get a better deal from manufacturer?

(4) Other theories?

  (aa) Toehold?

  (bb) *De Novo*?

(g) Defenses to a Section 7 action?

  (1) Failing company doctrine?

  (2) Small company doctrine?

  (3) Covered by other statutes?

2. Section 3 of the Clayton Act:

(a) Prohibits certain tying arrangements?

(b) Prohibits certain exclusive dealing arrangements?

3. Section 2 of the Clayton Act: The Robinson-Patman Act?

(a) Generally aimed at price discrimination practices?

(b) Enforced by both the U.S. Justice Department and the FTC?

(c) Specific practices covered by the Act?

  (1) Section 2(a)--prohibits direct or indirect price discrimination between buyers of like goods?

  (aa) Defenses include cost justification, changing conditions and meeting the competition?

  (2) Section 2(c)--prohibits certain incentives by sellers to buyers except for actual services rendered in connection with the sale?

  (3) Section 2(d)--prohibits discrimination in providing advertising or product?

  (aa) Defense allowed for meeting the competition?

  (4) Section 2(e)--prohibits discrimination in providing promotional services to buyers?

  (aa) Defense allowed for meeting the competition?

  (5) Section 2(f)--prohibits buyers from seeking discriminatory pricing from seller?

4. Section 8 of the Clayton Act?

(a) Prohibits certain interlocking directorships?

  (1) Companies worth $10 million?

  (2) Companies are competitors?

  (3) Agreements between companies would violate antitrust law?

(b) Some statutory exceptions?

E. The Federal Trade Commission Act?

1. Created in 1914 with power of enforcement in the Federal Trade Commission?

2. Designed to generally:

(a) Prohibit unfair competition?

(b) Covers certain conduct included under the preview of the Sherman Act and the Clayton Act?

3. Has powers to:

(a) Issue interpretive rules?

(b) Set definitions of unfair or deceptive practices?

(c) Enforce both through its own actions and private actions by injured parties?

F. State antitrust laws.
 1. Patterned after the federal laws?
 2. Generally cover issues in intrastate commerce?

IV. Objective Questions:

Terms:

1. Three times the actual damages ordinarily awarded is called _____ _____.

2. The rule that holds that only unreasonable restraints of trade violate Section 1 of the Sherman Act is called the _____ _____ _____.

3. The standard that is applicable to those restraints of trade that are considered inherently anticompetitive is called the _____ _____ rule.

4. A restraint of trade that occurs when two or more parties on different levels of distribution enter into a contract, combination, or conspiracy to restrain trade is called a _____ _____.

5. The doctrine that states that if two or more firms act the same but no concerted action is shown, there is no violation of Section 1 of the Sherman Act is called _____ _____.

6. A merger between two or more companies that compete in the same business and geographical market is called a _____ merger.

7. The test for determining the lawfulness of horizontal mergers which finds horizontal mergers presumptively illegal under Section 7 if (1) the merged firm would have thirty percent or more market share in the relevant market and (2) the merger would cause an increase in concentration of thirty three percent or more in the relevant market is called the _____ _____ test.

8. A merger that does not fit into any other category or a merger between firms in totally unrelated businesses is a _____ merger.

9. A defense to a Section 7 action that says a competitor may merge with a failing company if (1) there is no other reasonable alternative for the failing company and (2) no other purchaser is available is called the _____ _____ _____.

10. A form of price discrimination that is less readily apparent than direct forms of price discrimination is _____ _____ _____.

True/False:

1. _____ All of the major federal antitrust acts have both civil and criminal sanctions.

2. _____ Under the *per se* standard of determining whether conduct is prohibited by the Sherman Act, there is no balancing of pro- and anticompetitive effects.

3. _____ Whether price fixing is a violation of Section 1 of the Sherman Act is determined by the Rule of Reason.

4. ____ To show a violation of the Sherman Act, two or more firms acting the same way must be acting in concert. That is, if each firm independently reaches the same decision, there is no violation.

5. ____ Under Section 2 of the Sherman Act, a plaintiff must show a defendant's specific intent to monopolize a market; the showing of mere deliberate or purposeful conduct is not sufficient to support a Section 2 action.

6. ____ A natural monopoly is a defense to the charge of monopolizing even if the natural monopoly operates in a predatory way.

7. ____ Under Section 7 of the Clayton Act, there must be proof of an actual decrease in competition for the court to forbid a merger.

8. ____ The merger guidelines of the Herfindahl-Hirschman Index are law, and any increase in the index resulting from a merger will raise a presumption of illegality.

9. ____ Conglomerate mergers are always legal since they involve mergers between firms which conduct totally unrelated business.

10. ____ Under the meeting the competition defense to a Section 2(b) of the Robinsion-Patman Act charge, a seller can lower his selling price below that of his competitor to be competitive in a market.

Multiple Choice:

1. Elvira, Inc. sells various interrelated automotive products which it manufactures. One of the items, an antilock braking system, was manufactured almost exclusively by Elvira, Inc. Elvira, Inc. realized the importance of the product to its purchasers and decided to capitalize on the situation by requiring all purchasers to take at least two of its other automotive brake products if they wished to obtain the antilock braking system over which it has almost complete market control. Which of the following best describes the situation?
A. The plan is both ingenious and legal and should have been resorted to long ago.
B. The arrangement is an illegal tying agreement and is *per se* illegal.
C. Since Elvira, Inc. did not have complete market control over the unique product in question, the arrangement is legal.
D. As long as the other products which must be taken are sold at a fair price to the buyers, the arrangement is legal.

2. The Hilmer Duck Decoy Company entered into an agreement with retail merchants whereby they agreed not to sell beneath Hilmer Duck Decoy's minimum suggested retail price in exchange for Hilmer's agreeing not to sell its duck decoys at retail in their respective territories. The agreement does not preclude the retail merchants from selling competing duck decoys. What is the legal status of the agreement?
A. It is legal if the product is sold under a trade name or is trademarked.
B. It is legal if the power to fix maximum prices is not relinquished.
C. It is illegal unless it can be shown that the parties to the agreement were preventing cutthroat competition.
D. It is illegal even though the price fixed is reasonable.

442

3. Sharlene's Firm and Bob's Firm, who have been competitors for years, contract to restrain trade so as to increase their own profits. Which of the following is correct?
   A. The behavior of these two firms is governed by the National Labor Relations Act.
   B. To be liable under the Sherman Act, the contract must be in writing.
   C. The two firms have engaged in a horizontal restraint of trade.
   D. All of the above.

4. High Tech Sound (HTS) and Super Sonics (SS) are both producers of stereo equipment. HTS conducts a market research study and decides to set the prices of its stereos at $200, $300, and $400 according to the various levels of quality. SS is located in a different state and does its own market research study. SS also decides, without knowledge of HTS' prices, to set its stereo prices at $200, $300, and $400 depending on the quality of the stereo. Which of the following is correct?
   A. This is price fixing and therefore, a *per se* violation of Section 1 of the Sherman Act.
   B. This is price fixing and will be examined under the Rule of Reason.
   C. This is price fixing and therefore, a *per se* violation of Section 2 of the Sherman Act.
   D. Under the doctrine of conscious parallelism, this conduct is permitted and there is no violation of the Sherman Act.

5. Superior Systems (SS) has devoted an enormous amount of resources to research and development of its product, water purification systems. In doing this, SS has clearly developed a superior product and, consequently, a monopoly in the purification market. Which of the following is correct?
   A. SS has violated Section 2 of the Sherman Act.
   B. SS has violated Section 1 of the Sherman Act.
   C. SS has not violated the Sherman Act since its monopoly is a result of a superior product.
   D. SS has not violated the Sherman Act because a single firm cannot be considered a monopoly.

6. Fantastic Feet and Showtime Shoes, both shoe retailers, have proposed a merger. Both companies sell nationwide. What type of merger is this?
   A. A vertical merger.
   B. A conglomerate merger.
   C. A horizontal merger.
   D. A market extension merger.

7. Assume the same facts as in question 6. How is this proposed merger likely to be treated under Section 7 of the Clayton Act?
   A. Nothing will happen until the merger has taken place since there must be actual proof of a lessening of competition under Section 7.
   B. Nothing will happen under Section 7 since mergers between the same types of companies are always permitted if they both conduct business on a national level.
   C. The merger will be subjected to strict review under Section 7 since this will certainly increase the concentration in the relevant market.
   D. None of the above.

8. Assume the same facts as in question 6 except that now that instead of merging with Showtime Shoes, Fantastic Feet wants to merge with National Shoe Manufacturers. This merger would allow the newly formed company to both produce and sell the shoes. What type of merger is this for Fantastic Feet?
   A. A forward vertical merger.
   B. A backward vertical merger.
   C. A conglomerate merger.
   D. None of the above.

9. Assume the same facts as in question 8. How is this proposed merger likely to be treated under Section 7?
   A. Nothing will happen until the merger has taken place since there must be actual proof of a lessening of competition under Section 7.
   B. Nothing will happen under Section 7 since mergers between two companies which are not in the same market are always permitted if they both conduct business on a national level.
   C. The merger will be subjected to strict review under Section 7 since this will certainly increase the concentration in the relevant market.
   D. None of the above.

10. Technophonics, a large manufacturer of car phones, has proposed a merger with Traveling Talkers, another car phone manufacturer. Though Technophonics is successful in this competitive market, Traveling Talkers is on the verge of collapse. In an effort to salvage what it can, Traveling Talkers has sought other companies with which to merge, but Technophonics is the only interested firm. A merger between these two companies would violate Section 7 of the Clayton Act. What is Technophonic's best defense?
    A. The Small Company Doctrine.
    B. The Failing Company Doctrine.
    C. The Potential Reciprocity Theory.
    D. The *De Novo* Theory.

V. Answer to Objective Questions:

Terms:

1. *Treble damages.* Under Section 4 of the Clayton Act, single damages found by a jury are tripled in amount for antitrust violations.
2. *Rule of Reason.* If Section 1 of the Sherman Act were literally applied, it would prohibit many business contracts. In order to mitigate against that literal interpretation, the Rule of Reason is designed to allow the courts to weigh a number of factors when deciding if a contract question is in restraint of trade.
3. *Per se.* No balancing is required if the restraint is considered to be inherently anticompetitive. If so determined, a court will not permit any defenses or justifications to save it.
4. *Vertical restraint.* This restraint can take the form of a contract, combination, or conspiracy between the parties and is subject to the scrutiny of both the Rule of Reason and the *per se* rule interpretations of Section 1 of the Sherman Act.
5. *Conscious parallelism.* It must be shown that the parties acted independently of each other and arrived at their decisions separately.
6. *Horizontal.* This can involve a merger of one company with another company producing a similar product and selling it in the same geographic market.

7. *Presumptive illegality.* This test was adopted by the U.S. Supreme Court in the landmark antitrust case of *United States v. Philadelphia National Bank,* 374 U.S. 321 (1963).

8. *Conglomerate.* Where the merger may not fit into any other category, it may still be a violation of Section 7 of the Clayton Act if it creates an unfair advantage, hurts potential competition, or creates potential reciprocity between competitors.

9. *Failing company doctrine.* Unfortunately, there are far too many examples of this defense on the economic landscape in a period of prolonged recession.

10. *Indirect price discrimination.* Any number of methods have been devised to favor certain customers. They can include favorable credit terms, freight charges, and the like.

True/False:

1. False. The Sherman Act is the only federal antitrust act which has criminal sanctions. The other federal antitrust acts allow only civil sanctions.

2. True. The balancing of pro- and anticompetitive effects is used in the Rule of Reason test, not the *per se* standard of determining whether conduct is prohibited by the Sherman Act.

3. False. Price fixing is a *per se* violation of the Sherman Act.

4. True. Under the doctrine of conscious parallelism, two or more firms must be acting in concert to be in violation of the Sherman Act.

5. False. The showing of deliberate or purposeful conduct is sufficient to support a Section 2 action. Showing a defendant's actual specific intent to monopolize a market is not required.

6. False. Innocent acquisition and natural monopoly are defenses to the charge of monopolizing. These defenses are lost if the firm acts in a predatory or exclusionary way.

7. False. Under Section 7 of the Clayton Act, if a merger is likely to substantially lessen competition, the court may prevent the merger. Actual showing of the lessening of competition is not required.

8. False. The merger guidelines of the HHI are only guidelines, not law. In addition any increase in the index does not raise a presumption of illegality. Depending on the degree of the change in the index, a merger proposition may be challenged by the Justice Department.

9. False. Conglomerate mergers are not always permitted under the Clayton Act. The lawfulness of such mergers are examined under several different factors.

10. False. Under the meeting the competition defense, a seller can lower his selling price to match that of his competitor. However, the seller cannot set his price below that of his competitor.

Multiple Choice:

1. B. The situation described here is a tying arrangement and is *per se* illegal. A is incorrect because the plan is illegal and definitely not ingenious. C is incorrect because tying arrangements are illegal even is the seller does not have complete market control over the unique product. D is incorrect because tying arrangements are *per se* illegal even if the other products are sold at a fair price. Elvira, Inc. cannot use market dominance of antilock braking systems in this illegal manner.

2. D. The situation described here is a price fixing arrangement and is illegal even though the price is reasonable. A is incorrect because price fixing is illegal whether the product is trademarked or sold under a trade name. B is incorrect because price fixing is illegal whether it is for a minimum or maximum price. C is incorrect there is no defense for price fixing. Thus, the Hilmer Duck Decoy Company has to shoot down this bad idea.

3. C. When two or more firms at the same level of distribution contract for such an arrangement, this is horizontal restraint of trade. A is incorrect because the behavior of these two firms is governed by Section 1 of the Sherman Act. B is incorrect because such a contract is illegal whether it is oral, written, or implied from the circumstances.

4. D. Since there was no intentional effort by these firms, nor did they even know of the other's pricing system, there was no intent to fix prices. Therefore, under the doctrine of conscious parallelism, this conduct is not prohibited under the Sherman Act. A, B, and C are incorrect because since neither firm knew of the other, there is no price fixing and this activity is not a violation of the Sherman Act.

5. C. A company which acquires a monopoly because of superior business acumen, skill, and foresight has an innocent acquisition of a monopoly. This is a defense to the charge of monopolizing. Therefore, SS has not violated the Sherman Act. A and B are incorrect for the reason discussed above. D is incorrect because a single firm can be considered a monopoly.

6. C. A merger where both companies are in the same level of distribution is a horizontal merger. Here, both companies are shoe retailers. A is incorrect because a vertical merger involves an integration of the operations of a supplier and a customer. B is incorrect because a conglomerate merger is between two companies in unrelated businesses. D is incorrect because a market extension merger is a merger between two companies in similar fields whose sales do not overlap. Here, both companies sell nationwide. Therefore, their fields do overlap.

7. C. Where two companies that compete in the same geographical market merge in a horizontal merger, the merger is subjected to strict review under Section 7 because it will clearly result in an increase in concentration in the relevant market. A is incorrect because Section 7 actions may be brought based on the probability of a lessening of competition. Actual proof is not necessary. B is incorrect because horizontal mergers of this type are almost always strictly scrutinized under Section 7.

8. B. Where a retailer merges with a producer, this is a backward vertical merger. A is incorrect because a forward merger would involve a company lower on the chain of distribution merging with a company higher on the chain of distribution. C is incorrect because a conglomerate merger is a merger between two companies in unrelated fields.

9. D. A is incorrect because actual proof of a lessening of competition is not required since Section 7 actions are based on the probability of a lessening in competition. B is incorrect because such mergers are not always automatically permitted. C is incorrect because such mergers do not increase the concentration in the relevant market since there are

different markets involved. Vertical mergers will be examined considering such factors as the past history of the firms, the trend toward concentration in the industries involved, the barriers to entry, the economic efficiencies of the merger, and the elimination of potential competition caused by the merger.

10. B. The Failing Company Doctrine is a defense to Section 7 actions if (1) there is no other reasonable alternative for the failing company and (2) no other purchaser is available. Here, both these requirements are met. A is incorrect because the Small Company Doctrine is a defense to Section 7 actions for two or more small companies which wish to merge to compete more effectively with a large company. C and D are incorrect because they are theories for enjoining mergers, not defenses to Section 7 actions.

VI. Key Question Checklist Answer to Essay Question:

A. *What was the basic public policy behind the antitrust laws?*

The basic policy presumes that competition is best protected in an open and fair marketplace. Monopolization and concentrations of economic controls are contrary to an open and fair marketplace and may be anticompetitive.

B. *Which of the main antitrust statutes is available to the government when seeking to prevent behavior which may be in restraint of a free and open marketplace?*

The main statutes which may be used are the Sherman Act of 1890, the Clayton Act or 1914, and the Robinson-Patman Act of 1930. In this case, the second two acts provide the best possibility for putting the actions of Spookeys and Ghost and Goblins to the antitrust law litmus test.

D. *Were there are any problems with this arrangement under the Clayton Act merger provisions? Was the new pricing arrangement in violation of the Robinson-Patman Act?*

The partial acquisition of a competitor in the same geographical area may injure competition. In examining this horizontal merger, the Justice Department will use its Herfindal-Hirshman guidelines to see if the new arrangement will create an illegal concentration of costume sales in Salem in one controlled company. As a defense to this possible challenge, Ghost and Goblins can raise the argument that Spookey's was a failing company. That defense appears weak because there was no evidence of it losing money or that it was about to go bankrupt. Thus the merger could most likely be disallowed under Section 7 of the Clayton Act.

With regard to the new pricing arrangement with Bad Taste. The problems with Robinson-Patman become more apparent. Here the ultimate price charged to the consumer is lower and it would appear on its face (mask?) that competition is actually fostered by the new arrangement. The other costume stores in Salem might argue, however, that they have been discriminated against by predatory pricing. The best defense here would be to show that the new prices reflect efficiencies realized from higher volume purchases, i.e., lower costs. In addition, if Bad Taste can show that any buyer who purchased the higher volume would get that same lower price, price discrimination would be much more difficult to prove.

E&F. *Was Ghosts and Goblins engaged in any unfair trade practices prohibited by the Federal Trade Commission Act or state law?*

From the problem as presented, it appears that no unfair trade practices were used. If for example, faulty products were fraudulently substituted for originals or some sort of false advertising were used by Ghosts and Goblins, then the FTC would have to assume the role of "Ghostbusters!"

CHAPTER 49

AGRICULTURAL, NATURAL RESOURCE, AND COMMODITIES LAWS

All mankind is divided into three classes:
those that are immovable,
those that are movable,
and those that move.

Arab Proverb

I. Overview:

The demographics of the U.S. has always been in a constant state of flux. For many years prior to the post-Civil War age of industrialization, we were a nation of farmers and ranchers. With industrialization, the inexorable shift from country to city began with all its attendant social upheavals. Futurists tell us that the next wave is already here, the age of the service and information society. How all these large social and economic shifts benefit or hurt the larger society is the grist of the intellectual mills of political science, sociology, business studies, and numerous other disciplines.

The basic importance of agriculture continues to hold sway in spite of the radically changing demographics of rural America. Agriculture still provides our nation with its greatest single source of trade exports, lowest per capital cost of food in the world, and most efficient production of food stuffs to be found anywhere. The law of agriculture and the related areas of water and commodities have a long and proud tradition which have essentially served all concerned well over the years. In

many ways, unique regional needs have evolved into these areas of the law. The early state laws of homestead reflected the evolution of settlement of the Great Plains from open ranching into farm use. So too did the development of water laws reflect the unique regional needs of the West as compared to the more traditional riparian rights used in the East.

What makes the study of agricultural-related laws more interesting and challenging than ever is the changes taking place in that sector which are more radical than ever. Take, for example, the growth of the cities. Who would have imagined, even a generation ago, the explosive growth of today's modern urban areas? Metropolitan areas literally cover vast expanses of land formerly used in agriculture. Even "high end" agricultural use does not necessarily forego or stop this expansion. In areas like northern California, the constant press of suburban growth has pushed out many family farm operations formerly engaged in fruit, vegetables, and wine grapes.

Another major factor affecting the agricultural industry in this country is the seemly inexorable shift from family to corporate control. The efficiencies of scale simply make it more and more difficult for the small farmer to stay in business when trying to compete with large agri-business corporate entities. Many of the laws discussed in this chapter seek to address this change in the agricultural landscape by trying to foster and encourage continued small family owned farming and ranching.

Finally, markets for agricultural products have proven themselves no different than any other market mechanism. They have been victimized by assorted charlatans and con artists of every ilk. The passage of the Commodity Futures Trading Commission Act is part of the government's continued response to the problems related to those markets. The key question checklist specifically lists the legal issues raised in this very important segment of the U.S. economy.

II. Hypothetical Multi-Issue Essay Question:

Agnatio Agnatic is the oldest son of a family with a long and proud tradition of raising some of the world's best *petit sirrah* grapes in the Rutherford appellation of Napa Valley California. The wine has an exquisite prunelle quality with the tastes of cassis, plums, and black cherries layered over with licorice flavor. Agnatio's' father, Annates, was a master winemaker.

Unfortunately, the last ten years have not been kind to the Agnatic family farm. California has undergone a prolonged drought, and wine tastes have steadily shifted to assorted pink wine coolers which Agnatio calls *"pipi de chat."* The farm is deeply in debt ($750,000), and Agnatio's dad died last week. The other members of the family want to sell off the land to Wino Acres, a land development company which wants to erect a subdivision with homes starting in the low 700's. This year's crops cannot service the debt, and Agnatio doesn't want to give up his way of life. What can he do?

III. Key Question Checklist:

A. The first area covered by this chapter centers around the major elements of agricultural law and who has jurisdiction over it. Generally speaking agricultural law jurisdiction is shared between the states and the federal government. How are those basic jurisdictional lines drawn?
   1. State police power?
      (a) General common law of contracts?
      (b) General contract law as modified by the UCC?

(c) General common law of torts?
(d) General common law of real property?
(e) Specific state laws regulating local agricultural activities?
   2. Federal jurisdiction?
      (a) Generally given to U.S. Department of Agriculture (USDA)?
      (b) USDA has enforcement powers over a number of specific federal agricultural statutes?
         (1) Examples: Animal quarantine Act, Federal Meat Inspection Act, U.S. Grain Standards Act?
      (c) U.S. has exempted farm co-ops from many antitrust provisions?

B. What are some of the major USDA programs affecting U.S. agriculture?
   1. Price support programs?
      (a) Sets target prices?
      (b) Makes deficiency payments to qualified farmers?
      (c) Establishes loan programs to qualified farmers?
      (d) Uses crop set-aside programs?
      (e) Provides disaster crop insurance?
   2. USDA inspection programs?
      (a) Designed to protect health of consumers of farm products?
      (b) Covers main agricultural products?
         (1) Meat?
         (2) Poultry?
         (3) Egg products?

C. Other federal statutes affecting agriculture?
   1. Farm Credit Administration?
   2. Chapter 12 of the U.S. Bankruptcy Code--Family Farmer Bankruptcy?

D. What are the major water systems used in the U.S.?
   1. Riparian rights water laws?
      (a) Used mainly in the Eastern portion of the U.S.?
      (b) Gives rights of usage to water burdening property?
      (c) Doctrine of reasonable use applies?
      (d) Subject to public's rights of navigation and limited access?
   2. Prior appropriation water laws?
      (a) Used mainly in the Western portion of the U.S.?
      (b) Requires beneficial use of the water?
      (c) Gives rights of usage based on first in time utilization?
      (d) Rights are lost if not used?
      (e) Transfer of water rights allowed separate from land in some states?
      (f) In case of water shortage, senior user has first claims to the water?
   3. Hybrid system water laws?
      (a) adopted by ten states, all in western portion of the U.S.?
      (b) Made up of a combination riparian and prior appropriation elements of water law?
   4. Permit system?
      (a) Regardless of system used, most states have adopted a permit system to allocate water rights?

E. Commodities regulation?
   (a) Types of commodities?
      (1) Agricultural products?
      (2) Metals?
      (3) Minerals?
      (4) Oil?
   (b) Main federal controls?
      (1) Commodities Futures Trading Commission?
         (2) Regulates trading of commodities and contracts relating to commodities?
         (3) Has both civil and criminal sanctions against fraudulent practices commodities marketplace?

IV. Objective Questions:

Terms:

1. A broad scope of federal regulation concerning agriculture is authorized by the _____ _____.

2. For each specific farm product, the USDA establishes a _____ price.

3. Congress has authorized the USDA to make special payments called _____ payments to farmers as a result of natural disasters.

4. The Farm Credit Administration and the Farm Home Administration were created by Congress to extend _____ _____ to farmers.

5. Land owners who own property that borders on waterways have _____ rights.

6. The public has a right of _____ for commercial transportation, pleasure boating, and recreation over navigable waters.

7. States which employ a combination of riparian and prior appropriation doctrines in their water laws are said to have _____ systems.

8. Water found underground in pools or streams is called _____.

9. Waters that have not yet joined a watercourse are called _____ _____ water.

10. An agreement to buy or sell a specific amount and type of commodity at a future date at a price established at the time of contracting is called a _____ _____ _____.

True/False:

1. _____Items such as grains, ores, and oil are called commodities.

2. _____Cooperatives are legal enterprises created by state statute and designed to assist members in achieving mutual benefits.

3. _____Agricultural cooperatives are generally made immune from federal antitrust laws by Chapter 12 of the Bankruptcy Code.

4. _____Water is governed by state law only.

5. _____Riparian land owners do not actually own the body of water that borders their land.

6. _____Riparian rights are property rights that transfer with the sale of property in all cases.

7. _____In the western United States, a custom of prior appropriation is used to allocate water rights.

8. _____Under the prior appropriation doctrine, beneficial water uses include domestic, municipal, agricultural, and industrial uses.

9. _____In states that use the prior appropriation doctrine, appropriated water rights are lost if they are not used within a stated statutory period.

10. _____A put option confers upon the holder the right to buy a contract.

Multiple Choice:

1. Federal antitrust laws do not prohibit:
   A. Mergers which may lessen competition.
   B. Competitive activities.
   C. Acts of monopolization.
   D. Price discrimination.

2. Which of the following statements does not describe a cooperative?
   A. Bargaining cooperatives act as bargaining agents with third parties.
   B. Supply cooperatives make bulk purchases of supplies.
   C. Cooperatives are for-profit enterprises.
   D. Marketing cooperatives market their members' products.

3. Which may the USDA not do with regard to farmers?
   A. Adjudication proceedings.
   B. Rule making.
   C. Reparation proceedings that decide disputes between private parties.
   D. Price fixing.

4. The federal government provides price, income, and loan support programs to farmers in order to:
   A. Keep the farm lobby happy.
   B. Lower farm incomes.
   C. Stabilize prices through production control.
   D. Keep prices at artificially high levels.

5. Cropland production controls are implemented by the USDA in all but one of the following programs. Which one is not part of this set of programs?
   A. Cropland set-aside programs.
   B. Federal Crop Insurance Corporation.
   C. Paid acreage program.
   D. Conservation resource program.

6. Which one of the following is not part of the USDA food and animal inspection process?
   A. Pet Store Inspection Act.
   B. Meat Inspection Act.
   C. Poultry Production Inspection Act.
   D. Egg Products Inspection Act.

7. Which of the following is not a threshold requirement under Chapter 12 of the Federal Bankruptcy Code?
   A. The petitioner must be engaged in farming or ranching.
   B. The land must be best used for farm or ranch purposes.
   C. The petitioner has debts not exceeding $1.5 million.
   D. 80 percent of the debt must be related to farming or ranching operations.

8. Which of the following is not one of the state water law systems used in the U.S.?
   A. Riparian water rights.
   B. Lakes and streams water rights.
   C. Prior appropriation water rights.
   D. Hybrid combinations of riparian and prior appropriations.

9. Who would not be able to use futures contracts to hedge against volatile price shifts?
   A. Farmers.
   B. Milling companies.
   C. Food processors.
   D. Investors in CD's.

10. The Commodities Exchange Act requires the following people to register with the Commodity Futures Trading Commission:
   A. All attorneys.
   B. All farmers.
   C. All commodities advisers.
   D. All ranchers.

V. Answers to Objective Questions:

Terms:

1. *Commerce Clause.* This provision of the U.S. Constitution is found in Article 1, Section 8, Clause 3 and gives Congress considerable power over the regulation of agriculture.
2. *Target.* These prices are set by the USDA in order to provide income support to farmers. If the average market price for a specific product does not meet the target price set by the USDA, deficiency payments are made to the farmer in order to make up the difference.
3. *Disaster.* These payments can be in the form of loans, direct payments, reduced price sales of feed grains, or other appropriate relief.
4. *Farm credit.* These agencies provide both long and short term financing arrangements to farmers and ranchers who may not be able to find credit through more conventional channels.
5. *Riparian.* Although riparians do not own the body of water which borders their land, they may make reasonable use of the water which does not interfere with the reasonable uses of other riparians.
6. *Navigation.* In determining whether water is navigable, a factual inquiry is make as to its capacity for use in commerce and/or transportation.

7. *Hybrid.* Ten states, most notably California, use this system.

8. *Groundwater.* The old rule of unlimited use of groundwater flowing under a landowner's property has given way to the more modern rule known as the "correlative rights doctrine." This doctrine calls for only reasonable use and ratable reductions if all reasonable user's needs cannot be met.

9. *Diffused surface.* Most jurisdictions permit a land owner to made unrestricted use of diffused waters captured on his or her property.

10. *Commodity futures contract.* The standardized terms for these contracts are established by the Commodity Futures Trading commission whose authority is derived from the Commodity Exchange Act, as amended.

True/False:

1. True. All of these items are traded on recognized commodity markets. Commodities can be made up of almost any article of movable or personal property.

2. True. These entities are created by state statutes and are usually nonprofit enterprises whose main purpose is to benefit their members as opposed to investors.

3. False. Chapter 12 of the Bankruptcy Code does cover agricultural enterprises, but the antitrust immunity was granted by Congress in the Capper-Volstead Act, the Cooperative Marketing Act, and other federal statutes.

4. False. Water is also governed by federal law.

5. True. Riparians are land owners who own property that borders on waterways. They have numerous rights vis-a-vis the use of the water, but they do not actually own the body of water that borders their land.

6. False. Riparian rights transfer unless the seller reserves certain riparian rights.

7. True. Under this doctrine, the first user of water had priority over other later users. This system is used in nine states.

8. True. Once an appropriator puts water to a recognized beneficial use such as domestic, municipal, agricultural, or industrial applications, the right is considered perfected.

9. True. These provisions are similar to statutes of limitations which are used throughout the law in order to encourage vigilance over legal rights, i.e., use it or lose it.

10. False. A put option confers the right to sell a contract; a call option confers the right to buy the contract.

Multiple Choice:

1. B. Competitive activities are encouraged by antitrust laws and exempt agricultural cooperatives under the Capper-Volstead Act. The other activities are prohibited by the antitrust laws.

2. C. Most agricultural cooperatives are nonprofit enterprises.

3. D. The USDA does have great influence over the lives of individual farmers, but it may not act as a lobbying agent for individuals. The other acts are allowed.

4. C. Price, income, and support programs are designed through production control. They are not designed for answers A, B, or D.

5. B. Answers A, C, And D are all part of the USDA Cropland program. The FCIC is not part of this program.

6. A. The USDA does have jurisdiction over animal welfare generally, but there is no specific Act entitled the Pet Store Inspection Act. The others are specific inspection acts.

7. B. The land may, in fact, have a "higher and better" use but that is not a requirement for qualification under Chapter 12 of the Bankruptcy Code. The other answers are.

8. B. Lakes and streams are certainly affected by water rights systems, but there is no water rights systems names as such. The others are the three recognized water systems used in the U.S.

9. D. Investors in CD's have fixed returns already agreed upon. The others regularly engage in commodities investments and futures contracts.

10. C. Commodities advisors are required to register as commodities professionals under the CEA.

VI. Key Question Checklist Answers to Essay Question:

A. *Does the federal government or the state have jurisdiction over this issue?*

Jurisdiction over this matter will be divided between the state of California and the federal government. California will have control over how the estate of Annates Agnatic will be probated. In addition, the state will have primary responsibility over the ultimate land use zoning which will control how this land is to be used. It is interesting to note that many states have a number of provisions designed to foster and protect continued family farming where it would not be economically viable to do so otherwise. One example of this type of state law is property valuation based on farm use rather than the "highest and best" alternative development uses.

The federal government will also have jurisdiction over a number of issues in this case. The growth and sale of wine products is heavily regulated by the Treasury Department's Alcohol, Tobacco, and Firearms Division. In addition, the USDA has a number of programs which may involve regulation of agricultural products in interstate commerce. Also, the federal government has its own tax structure with regard to transfers of family wealth in the form of gift, estate, and generation-skipping taxes. These tax laws have provisions designed to help preserve continued family use of farms and ranches. One such example is found in Section 2032(A), which allows an alternative valuation based on income rather than higher development potential values.

B. *What other sources of relief may be available to the Agnatic family?*

The Agnatic family may want to look into the use of Chapter 12 of the U.S. Bankruptcy Code. They may qualify by having debts under $1.5 million, 80 percent of which are related to farming and by asserting that regular income will be forthcoming once the drought ends. With qualification, they may be able to reorganize their operation and eventually emerge from bankruptcy as a reorganized enterprise.

As can be readily seen from problems like this, many farmers find themselves in the dilemma of being cash poor and land rich. Such strains coupled with the vicissitudes of nature make staying on the family farm more difficult than ever. In spite of it all, life in rural America is a tradition which should not be lost.

CHAPTER 50

PERSONAL PROPERTY, BAILMENTS, AND DOCUMENTS OF TITLE

The most common and durable source of faction has been the various and unequal distribution of property.

James Madison

I. Overview:

Courses in business law and the legal environment have consistently been at the top of the charts in popularity among business students. There are numerous explanations for this, not the least of which is the dedication of law professors who have foregone more lucrative options to work in the academy. One of the other big reasons for the high level of interest in law classes is the relevance the subject matter brings to the students' personal lives. It is all well and good to teach how major corporations strategically plan their affairs. But students find it equally important to learn how to plan their own personal affairs through the law. The laws of contracts, property, and torts all have not only significant roles in business but also vital roles in how one arranges his or her personal affairs. Personal property is one such key area.

The study of personal property revolves around being able to answer three key questions:

1. How is this property classified?
2. How is this property acquired or transferred?
3. What are the legal consequences of the answers to questions 1 and 2?

All personal property falls into one classification or another. The type of classification used will have important consequences on how property will be treated in the eyes of the law. For example, consider the basic distinction between real and personal property. Sales of real property transactions generally come under the purview of the common law of contracts. Sales of goods, however, are generally covered by the UCC. If you are selling trees on the land, that property is classified as real, and the common law of contract controls. If the trees have been cut and are being sold to a mill, the UCC will now call the shots. If that lumber becomes part of a house, the common law of contracts again controls because the house is treated as real property.

In addition to classification, the acquisition and transfer of rights and duties to property are of key personal and business importance. Most property is transferred by way of contract with some sort of reciprocal exchange of consideration. You work, get paid, and that money is exchanged for property. You may be lucky, however, and find it, or inherit, or just have it given to you. In all these events, the acquisition or transfer must be made in compliance with the elements required by law. Once you have acquired the property, what are the rights and duties that arise out of that ownership? What if you found it? What if others have claims against it? These issues are of key importance in both business and private lives.

The second teaching objective this chapter focuses on the law of bailments. The term bailment is derived from the French word *baillier* meaning to deliver. In the legal sense, a bailment is a delivery of personal property with a special purpose. That purpose involves some particular use or deposit of that property with the expectation that it be redelivered to the person who originally delivered it or otherwise dealt with at his or her direction. What is not expected to occur in a bailment is any sale, gift, or transfer of title.

One of the aspects of the study of bailments that surprises first-time students of the law is just how common this sort of transaction is. Drop your clothes off at the dry cleaners, it is a bailment. Have your car parked, it is a bailment. Check your bags with an airline, it too is a bailment. Bailments are indeed an everyday occurrence. What is not as common is that things can go wrong in bailments. Just like insurance claims, many people find out about the rules of the bailment game after there has been a loss.

Bailments are essentially a special kind of contract. Normal contract rules would apply except that a number of special circumstances have arisen often enough to have warranted legislative responses to the problems raised by those situations. Consider the example of common carriers. Here the public wants and expects a high level of reliance in being assured that goods entrusted to the common carrier, for a fee, will be protected. The public's expectation has been reflected in the insurance-styled strict liability of carriers for goods in their possession.

In addition, another element which often shows up in bailment cases is the interaction between the law of torts and contracts. Almost invariably what has happened is that there is an attempt to limit, by contract, the liability which may otherwise have inured to one of the parties by reason of tort. Courts are then confronted with the age old problem of choosing between freedom of contract and public policy. On the contract side, good, clear limitations of extent of liability serve everyone well if they are fairly arrived at between the parties. Conversely, contract limitations should not be allowed to become a false front behind which all sorts of negligent behavior may be somehow hidden or excused.

The other materials covered in this chapter are part and parcel of the bailment story. In the commercial setting, warehouses, common carriers, and innkeepers are involved in special bailments. The various rights, duties, and liabilities of these special situations are also reviewed.

II. Hypothetical Multi-Issue Essay Question:

Bloke and Crissy Carrington have been married for the past 50 years (the first 20 in California) and live on the Worthmore Ranch in Aspen, Colorado. Bloke met Ms. Misty Blue (age 21) at the annual "How's your Aspen?" cookout on the ranch. He decides it's now or never for his mid-life crisis and runs off with Misty to Miami, telling Crissy: "My lawyer will call your lawyer about the divorce." Three days later Bloke expires on the beach from overstimulation. He did not leave a will but told Misty just before he died, "I leave you everything! It was worth more."

Crissy comes to you for advice as to the following properties acquired during the marriage (she was always a faithful housewife):

1. The Worthmore Ranch, held as tenancy in the entirety.
2. Bank accounts in California and Colorado. They had been held in joint tenancy, but Bloke tried to wire the money to Miami the day before he died. The money had not yet been wired to Miami.
3. Jewelry worth over $1 million which Bloke had handed to Misty on the plane to Miami.

What result?

III. Key Question Checklist:

A. How is the property at issue classified?
  1. Real property (will be covered in detail in Chapter 51)?
    (a) Includes:
      (1) Land or surface rights?
      (2) Mineral rights below the surface?
      (3) Air rights above the surface?
      (4) Improvements on the land?
    (b) Transfers of rights to real property generally covered by common law principles, contract, and specific state laws on zoning, land use, and the like?
  2. Personal property (property not classified as real property)?
    (a) Tangible?
      (1) Derived from the Latin word *tangere*, meaning to touch?
      (2) Most property classified as tangible has its value within the property itself? Examples: TVs, furniture, appliances.
    (b) Intangibles?
      (1) Value of the property only represented by some sort of representational tangible?
      (2) Examples:
        (aa) Stock certificate: the document represents rights of ownership in a corporation?
        (bb) Bond: the certificate represents money owed to the bond holder?
        (cc) Patent: the certificate represents a government recognized property right in the invention?

  3. Ownership:
    (a) Privately held?
    (b) Government owned?

B. Once you have classified the property at issue, you must then decide how the property may be acquired or transferred legally?
  1. By possession or capture?
    (a) Acquiring unowned property by possession or capture?
    (b) Rarely applicable except for things in natural state?
    (c) Subject to laws of jurisdiction wherein it was captured? Example: hunting license.
  2. By purchase or exchange of consideration?
  3. By production?
    (a) Property either transformed or added to? Example: artist transforms paint and canvas into painting?
  4. By gift (need three elements)?
    (a) Donative intent?
      (1) Inferred from all the circumstances?
      (2) Must have capacity to form the intent?
    (b) Delivery?
      (1) Can be actual physical transfer of the gift itself?
      (2) Can be constructive or symbolic delivery?
      (3) Delivery must be legally effective?
        (aa) Transfer to own agent may not be enough?
        (bb) Transfer may be revocable?
        (cc) Transfer may be conditional (no gift if condition is not met)? Example: gifts *causa mortis*.

(c) Acceptance?
   (1) Usually presumed?
   (2) Inferred from all circumstances?
(d) Other specialized gift situations?
   (1) Uniform Gifts to Minors Act?
      (aa) Adopted by all states (at least in part)?
      (bb) Allows transfers to minors with retained control by donor until minor becomes of age?
   (2) By will or inheritance?
      (aa) All states have probate statutes which establish procedures for transfer of property at death?
      (bb) Transfers generally classified as testate (by will) or intestate (without a will)?
      (cc) Many sorts of nonprobate transfers possible? Examples: joint tenancy, insurance, employee benefits.
5. By accession?
   (a) Accession is an increase in value of the property?
   (b) The increase may come from within itself? Example: breeding of animals.
   (c) The increase can be provided by others? Example: repair of a car.
      (1) If third party added value, that party may now be able to claim certain rights in the property?
      (2) Generally falls under lien law or loan law?
6. By confusion?
   (a) Defined as commingling of fungible goods?

   (b) Owners share ownership in proportion to amounts contributed to the combined property?
7. Mislaid property?
   (a) Defined as property voluntarily placed and inadvertently forgotten?
   (b) Finder becomes involuntary bailee?
   (c) Finder has superior rights to all except original owner?
   (d) Estray statute may apply?
      (1) If terms of statute are complied with, finder may become owner?
8. Lost property?
   (a) Defined as inadvertent loss of control of the property by owner?
   (b) Finder becomes responsible to try and find owner?
   (c) Finder has superior rights to all except true owner?
   (d) Rules of *locus in quo* may apply?
      (1) Private owner can claim property found on that property?
      (2) Employer entitled to claim property found by employees on employer's property?
   (e) Estray statute may apply?
9. Abandoned property?
   (a) Defined as property either voluntarily discarded or mislaid or lost property given up on by owner?
   (b) Finder acquires title?
10. Treasure trove?
   (a) Ancient properties?
   (b) Finder acquires title in U.S.?
   (c) Other countries may claim treasure trove as government owned property?

C. Once you have classified the property and determined how ownership is established, you must decide the general legal

459

consequences of that ownership. What are the basic rights and duties with regard to the property?

1. If it is government owned?
2. If it is privately owned?
   (a) If you are sole owner?
   (b) If you are a coowner?
      (1) Tenant in common?
      (2) Joint tenant?
      (3) Tenancy by the entirety?
      (4) Community property?
      (5) Any other possible forms of shared ownership?

D. If the fact pattern you are examining involves a possible bailment rather than an outright transfer of ownership, the first issue you must resolve is whether a bailment is in place or not. Are the elements of bailment present?

1. Is the property in question classified as personal property?
   (a) Tangible?
   (b) Intangible?
2. Is there a delivery of possession of that personal property?
   (a) Exclusive control handed over to bailee?
   (b) Did the bailee knowingly accept the personal property?
3. Was there a duty established to either return the goods to the bailor or direct them towards a third party at the bailor's direction?
   (a) Express terms?
   (b) Implied terms?

E. Once you have established the elements of a bailment, you must now classify the general type of bailment at issue?

1. Ordinary bailment?
   (a) Mutual benefit?
      (1) Both parties benefit from the bailment?

(2) Reciprocal duties arise out of the mutual benefit?
   (b) Examples of mutual benefit bailments?
      (1) Goods delivered for repairs?
      (2) Goods delivered for storage?
      (3) Conditional sales?
2. Bailment for benefit of the bailor?
   (a) Usually a favor for the bailor without compensation to bailee?
   (b) Bailee owes only a duty of slight care?
   (c) Example: Neighbor watches car while owner is out of town.
3. Bailment for benefit of the bailee?
   (a) Usually a favor for the bailee without compensation to the bailor?
   (b) Bailee owes utmost duty of case? Example: Neighbor borrows car while owner is out of town.

F. Assuming a mutual benefit bailment is in place, what are the ordinary rights and duties of the parties?

1. Bailee has temporary right of possession?
2. Bailee has duty to return goods or deliver to third party at bailor's direction?
3. Bailor has absolute liability for nonreturn of goods?
4. Bailee may limit liability by fairly arrived at disclaimers, liquidated damage clauses, or exculpatory clauses if:
   (a) They are communicated to the bailor?
   (b) They are not against public policy?
5. Bailor has duty to warn the bailee of any defects in the goods?
6. Bailor has duty to live up to any warranties made with regard to the goods?

(a) Express?

(b) Implied?

7. Both have duties to provide any compensation or consideration agreed upon?

G. Is this bailment considered a special situation where the general common law rules of bailment have been modified by statute?

1. Common carriers?

(a) Under the UCC, common carriers are held to a standard of strict liability for bailed goods?

(b) Some limited defenses to that general liability (must show full loss under the defense)?

(1) Act of God?

(2) Act of public enemy?

(3) Order of government?

(4) Act of shipper?

(5) Inherent nature of goods?

(c) Carrier can limit liability under federal law by:

(1) Rate structure?

(2) Declarations of value?

2. Warehouse companies?

(a) General rules of mutual benefit bailment apply?

(b) Some common carriers are also warehouses; which hat were they wearing at the time of loss?

3. Innkeepers?

(a) Formerly held to same strict liability standards as common carriers?

(b) Most states have modified innkeeper's liabilities by imposing limitations for other's negligence?

(c) In case statute not applied, old strict liability rules apply?

IV. Objective Questions:

Terms:

1. Property that consists of tangibles such as automobiles, furniture, and jewelry, and intangibles such as securities, patents, and copyrights are all classified as _____ _____.

2. When property is owned by two or more persons at the same time, there are four types: (1) joint tenancy, (2) tenancy in common, (3) tenancy by the entirety, and (4) community property. All these are forms of _____ _____.

3. All real property and physically defined personal property such as buildings, goods, animals, minerals, and such are deemed to be _____ _____.

4. The effectiveness of the gift can be inferred from the circumstances or language used by the donor. These factors are used by the courts to help determine _____ _____.

5. A gift that is made in contemplation of death is called a _____ _____.

6. When an owner discards property with the intent to relinquish her rights to it or when an owner of mislaid or lost property gives up any further attempts to locate it, it is called _____ _____.

7. A bailment for the sole benefit of the bailor or the bailee is called a _____ _____.

8. The duty of care that goes beyond ordinary care that says common carriers and innkeepers have a responsibility to provide security to their passengers or guests is called the duty of _____ _____.

9. A contractual provision that relieves one or both parties to the contract from tort liability is called an _____ _____.

10. Common carriers can limit their liability for goods that are lost, damaged, destroyed, or stolen. These limitations are set out by _____ _____.

True/False:

1. ____The method of acquiring ownership in property by capture is very important and widely used in today's society.

2. ____A gift is only valid if the donee gives some consideration for the property which the donor gives.

3. ____Under the Uniform Gifts to Minors Act, a gift which complies with the act is revocable until the donor's death.

4. ____A gift *causa mortis* is only effective if consistent with the donor's written will.

5. ____The owner of the premises when mislaid property is left has rights to the property which are superior to the rights of the person who finds the property.

6. ____The finder of lost property need not return the property to the rightful owner if the owner's identity is known, but he has not demanded the return of his property.

7. ____In bailment, like a sale, title to the goods transfers to the bailee.

8. ____In a bailment for the sole benefit of the bailor, the bailee owes a duty of ordinary care.

9. ____A bailor who does not warn the bailee of any defects in the bailed property is liable for damages which result from such defects.

10. ____If one party terminates a bailment at will, the party is liable for any damages resulting from the termination.

Multiple Choice:

1. Farmer Fran owns several acres of farmland in Nebraska. At present, much of the land is planted with corn which is growing. How would Farmer Fran's property be characterized?
   A. Both the land and corn are personal property.
   B. The land is personal property, and the corn is real property.
   C. The corn is personal property, and the land is real property.
   D. Both the land and corn are real property.

2. Aunt Adrian wishes to give her niece Nancy a gift. Adrian is in good health. Adrian gives Nancy a diamond ring which has been in the family for generations. Adrian tells Nancy that since she had no daughters, she wants Nancy to have the ring. Nancy graciously accepts the ring. Which of the following is correct?
   A. Nancy has received a gift *causa mortis*.
   B. Nancy has received an *inter vivos* gift.
   C. Nancy has received an inheritance.
   D. None of the above.

3. Homeowner Helen contracts with Builder Bob to have Bob build a deck on to her house while she is on vacation for two weeks. Helen gives Bob her address and instructions about the deck. Helen then leaves town. However, Bob mistakenly builds the deck on Hank's house. Hank is Helen's neighbor and is also out of town for two weeks. The deck is a permanent structure, firmly secured to one side of the house. Which of the following is correct?
   A. Hank is an owner by production.
   B. Hank is an owner by accession.
   C. Hank is an owner by purchase.
   D. Hank is an owner by gift.

4. Loser Larry loses his gold watch in City Park. Stroller Stella finds the watch while walking in the park one day. Stella discovers Larry's name and address on the back of the watch. Which of the following is correct?
   A. Stella may keep the watch since it is lost property.
   B. Stella may keep the watch since Larry has not demanded its return.
   C. Stella must return the watch to Larry since she knows his identity.
   D. Stella must leave the watch where she finds it.

5. Guest Gary takes off his diamond studded ring to help wash dishes at his friend Sarah's house after a dinner party. Gary places the ring on top of a cabinet so it will not be lost. However, Gary leaves Sarah's house and forgets the ring. Mary, Sarah's housekeeper, discovers the ring one day while cleaning. Which of the following is correct?
   A. Mary has superior rights against everyone but Gary since she found the ring.

B. Sarah has superior rights against everyone but Gary since the ring was misplaced in her house.
   C. Mary is a bailee of the ring.
   D. None of the above.

6. Diner David patronizes his favorite restaurant, Creative Caribbean Cuisine. Tonight, David plans to propose to his girlfriend. When David enters the restaurant, he gives his coat to the coat clerk. The coat clerk gladly accepts the coat. However, the clerk is unaware that David has a diamond ring in the pocket of the coat. Which of the following is correct?
   A. There has been a bailment of David's coat.
   B. There has been a bailment of the diamond ring.
   C. Both of the above.
   D. None of the above.

7. Allen asks his friend Brenda if he can borrow her car. Brenda agrees to allow Allen to use her car for the day. Which of the following is correct?
   A. This is a gratuitous bailment.
   B. Brenda is a bailor here.
   C. Allen owes a duty of utmost care to protect the car.
   D. All of the above.

8. Distinguished Daniel takes his pocket watch to Wilfred's Watch Repair (WWR) to have the watch repaired. When Daniel get his watch back, the crystal has been cracked. Which of the following is correct?
   A. WWR owed a duty of utmost care.
   B. WWR is presumed to have breached its duty of care since the crystal is cracked.
   C. WWR is an involuntary bailee.
   D. WWR is strictly liable.

9. Mel asks Ned if he can borrow Ned's motorcycle for the weekend. Ned agrees but tells Met it will cost $50 for weekend use of the motorcycle. Mel picks up the motorcycle on Friday afternoon. However, Ned forgets to tell Mel that the motorcycle cannot be driven over 40 mph or it will overheat. In addition, although Ned does not know this, the back wheel is loose. This problem could have been easily discovered, but Ned has not really had time to inspect the bike lately. On Saturday, Mel is riding the bike at 55 mph when it overheats and severely burns Mel's leg. Mel is trying to get to a doctor when the back wheel flies off, and Mel falls from the bike and breaks his arm. Which of the following is correct?
   A. Ned is liable for Mel's burns caused by the overheating.
   B. Ned is liable for Mel's broken arm caused by the loose back wheel.
   C. Both of the above.
   D. None of the above.

10. Designer Duds, a clothes manufacturer, delivers an order of clothes to Trans Country Transport (TCT), a common carrier, for delivery to retail outlets around the country. TCT agrees to ship the clothes for $1,000. Which of the following is correct?
    A. This is a mutual benefit bailment.
    B. TCT is strictly liable for damage to the clothes.
    C. TCT can limit its liability to a stated dollar amount.
    D. All of the above.

V. Answers to Objective Questions:

Terms:

1. *Personal property*. Technically, personal property is any property that cannot be classified as real property. Remember, however, that property which may have started as personal may be converted to real (such as a fixture) or vice versa (such as timber which has been severed from the land).

2. *Concurrent ownership*. Coownership can take place over both real and personal property. It can be between only two persons, such as a marital community property, or between thousands of persons, as seen in large publicly traded companies.

3. *Tangible property*. This is property having a physical form, capable of being touched. Sometimes the physical evidence of an intangible property is called a semitangible, such as a stock certificate. This is a tangible paper, but its real value is the share of ownership that it represents in the corporation.

4. *Donative intent*. Intent is one of the three key elements when examining possible gift transfers. The other two are delivery and acceptance on the part of the donee.

5. *Gift causa mortis*. A gift *causa mortis* is established when the donor makes a gift in anticipation of approaching death from some existing condition and then dies without having revoked the gift.

6. *Abandoned property*. When these two elements are in place, the property is considered discarded in the eyes of the law, and it will belong to the first person who claims it after the abandonment.

7. *Gratuitous bailment.* These bailments are for the sole benefit of the bailor and most often arise when the bailee is requested to care for the bailor's property as a favor. The bailee owes only a slight duty of care in these scenarios.

8. *Strict liability.* This means that the law imposes a very high duty of care because of the special nature of the bailment. With common carriers, only a limited set of circumstances will act as defenses. Innkeepers liabilities have been more restricted by state statutes.

9. *Exculpatory clause.* These are contract clauses which seek to release one of the parties from his or her liability for a wrongful act. The scope of the clauses is limited by overriding public policy. For example, such clauses cannot be used to excuse a crime.

10. *Federal law.* These laws require that where common carriers are allowed to limit their liability, they must offer shippers the opportunity to pay a premium and declare a higher value for the goods.

True/False:

1. False. In today's society, there is very little property that is not already owned. Acquiring ownership in property by capture was much more common during the early years of our country's history.

2. False. Lack of consideration is what distinguishes a gift from a purchase. If consideration is required, it is not a gift.

3. False. If a gift complies with the Uniform Gifts to Minors Act, the gift is irrevocable.

4. False. A gift *causa mortis* need not be consistent with a donor's written will, and it takes precedent over a conflicting will.

5. True. The rationale for this rule is that the true owner may return to the premises to find the mislaid property. If this happens, the owner of the premises must return the property.

6. False. If the true owner's identity is known to the finder, the finder must return the lost property. That is, the finder cannot keep the property until the true owner demands its return if the finder knows the true owner's identity.

7. False. A bailment is different from a sale or gift because title to the goods does not transfer to the bailee, but remains with the bailor.

8. False. A bailment for the sole benefit of the bailor is a gratuitous bailment. In such a bailment, the bailee only owes a duty of slight care.

9. True. The specific defects a bailor must warn a bailee about vary depending on the type of bailment. However, the bailor must at least warn the bailee of any known defects in the bailed property.

10. False. A bailment at will is not for any fixed term and may usually be terminated by either party at any time. If a bailment is for a fixed term, a party who terminates the bailment prior to the end of the term will be liable for resulting damages.

Multiple Choice:

1. D. Land and property permanently attached to it are real property. In addition, crops which have not yet been harvested and removed from the land are also real property. Therefore, both the land and corn are real property. A is incorrect because personal property is everything which is not real property. Since both the land and corn are real property, they are not personal property. B is incorrect because the land is real

465

property. C is incorrect because the corn is real property here since it has not been removed from the land.

2. B. Nancy has received an *inter vivos* gift from Adrian. Adrian was alive and well at the time the gift was made. In addition, Adrian had donative intent to give the ring to Nancy, Adrian actually delivered the ring to Nancy, and Nancy accepted the ring. A is incorrect because a gift *causa mortis* is made by a dying donor and is conditional upon the donor's death. C is incorrect because an inheritance is received under a will when the deceased has already died.

3. B. Since Bob mistakenly made improvements on Hank's house and such improvements cannot be easily removed, Hank is an owner by accession. A is incorrect because ownership by production is where a person uses raw materials to produce a finished product and therefore owns the product. C is incorrect because ownership by purchase is where a person buys property. D is incorrect because ownership by gift is where a person voluntarily transfers property to another. Here, Bob did not intend to give Hank a new deck.

4. C. If a finder knows the identity of the true owner, she must return the property. A is incorrect because since Stella knows Larry's identity, she must return the watch. B is incorrect because Stella must return the watch since she knows Larry's identity even if Larry does not demand it be returned. This is because Larry may not know Stella has found the watch. D is incorrect because Stella may take the watch, but must return it under the circumstances discussed above.

5. B. Sarah has superior rights to the ring as to everyone except Gary since it was lost at her house. A is incorrect because

the owner of the premises has rights to the mislaid property, not the finder. C is incorrect because Sarah, not Mary, is the involuntary bailee of the ring.

6. A. There has been a bailment of David's coat because the clerk knowingly accepted the coat. B is incorrect because the clerk was unaware of the diamond ring and did not knowingly accept the ring. C is incorrect because B is incorrect.

7. D. A is correct because Brenda is allowing Allen to use her car as a favor and is not charging him anything. B is correct because Brenda is the owner of the car and is loaning the car to Allen. Therefore, Brenda is the bailor and Allen is the bailee. C is correct because in a bailment which is for the sole benefit of the bailee, the bailee owes a duty of utmost care to protect the bailed property.

8. B. The law presumes that if bailed property is damaged while in the possession of the bailee, it is because of lack of proper care by the bailee. However, this presumption is rebuttable. A is incorrect because WWR owes a duty of ordinary care, not a duty of utmost care. C is incorrect because WWR voluntarily took the pocket watch to repair it and is therefore not an involuntary bailee. D is incorrect because strict liability is imposed on common carriers, but not ordinary bailees.

9. C. Since Mel paid $50 for weekend use of the car, this is a mutual benefit bailment. In such bailments, the bailor must warn the bailee of defects which the bailor actually knows of, as well as those which could have been discovered by reasonable inspection. Therefore, Ned is liable for damages resulting from both the overheating problem as well as the loose back wheel.

10. **D.** A is correct because both parties benefit from this arrangement. B is correct because common carriers are strictly liable for bailed goods. C is correct because although TCT cannot avoid strict liability, it can limit its liability to a stated dollar amount if this is brought to the bailor's attention and it is not against public policy.

VI. Key Question Checklist Answers to Essay Question:

A. *How is the property in question to be classified?*

First, the properties in question must be generally classified. The ranch is clearly classified as real property. This classification would include the surface, mineral, and air rights associated with land. It would also include any permanent improvements on the land, including buildings, fixtures, and the like. The bank accounts would be classified as personal property. Because the accounts may be represented by passbooks or some other indicia of ownership such as a certificate of deposit, these assets would be classified as intangibles in that the real value of the property is found in what these documents represent, i.e., monies deposited with the financial institution. The jewelry is classified as tangible personal property. All the property involved is privately held.

B&C. *How can this property be transferred or otherwise legally acquired? And what are the consequences of any attempts to change the legal ownership of the properties?*

Because all the properties were presumed to be acquired during a fifty year marriage, it must be assumed that in the hands of Bloke and Crissy, the property was either purchased or somehow otherwise legally acquired by them. The more important immediate issue is: was any of the property in question transferred to Misty in the problem as presented? Of overriding concern is the attempt by Bloke to deprive Crissy of her legitimate marital claims to the properties. Here the laws of Colorado, Florida, and California will all come into play to one extent or another.

With regard to the ranch, under the laws of tenancy by the entirety, the property will pass automatically at death to the surviving spouse. This right of survivorship is by operation of law, and the property will not pass by way of probate, with or without a will. Transfer of the property must have been made with the consent of both tenants and must be evidenced by some sort symbolic written document, i.e., a deed. None of those occurred here. Some states sever the tenancy by entirety in case of divorce. Here the divorce had not yet taken place, so Crissy takes the ranch as surviving tenant by the entirety.

As for the bank accounts, many of the same issues apply. Joint tenancy rules are such that a transfer of the property must be made with the consent of both parties. Some states allow a unilateral severance of the joint tenancy but limit the ability to pull out the money to the one half claimed by the severing joint tenant. Because there was no actual or constructive delivery of these monies to Misty under the purported gift *causa mortis*, this attempted transfer also appears to have failed. If the accounts are still deemed to be held in joint tenancy at the time of Bloke's death, Crissy will take these assets as surviving joint tenant. The property will pass outside of probate.

If the accounts are deemed to have been severed out of joint tenancy, Crissy can still claim her half. The other half would become part of Bloke's estate. As part of his estate, it would be subject to the probate laws of the states involved. Because he did not leave a will, the laws of intestacy would apply. Under most of these laws, the surviving spouse would be the first taker of the estate.

As for the jewelry, it appears that a completed gift may have taken place. But even here, Misty's claim to the jewelry may be subject to Crissy's marital property claims. This may have been a fraudulent attempt to deprive Crissy of marital property.

D-G. *Are there any issues of bailment in this problem?*

It appears that there are no intended bailments in the ordinary sense of the word. Most bailments involve some sort of commercial purpose where there is an expected mutual benefit to both parties, such as goods delivered for repairs or a rental of some personal property. The only real possible bailment here is the possession of the jewelry. If Crissy is able to prove that Bloke committed a fraud on her marital property vis-à-vis the transfer of possession to Misty Blue, then she can argue that Misty is a wrongful bailee of her property. As such, Misty would have a duty to return the goods, if not directly to Crissy, at least to the control of the court for its final disposition of the matter.

All in all, let's hope that Misty Blue has other assets to rely on. Crissy looks like a clear winner here, as well it should be.

CHAPTER 51

REAL PROPERTY

The mind covers more ground than the heart but goes less far.

Chinese Proverb

I. Overview:

This chapter is designed to introduce students to the law of real property from two key perspectives: first, ownership and the rights and duties that arise out of the ownership of real property, and second, use of real property and the respective rights and duties can arise out of that use vis-à-vis others.

Real property represents the largest single outlay most people make in the course of their earning years. Even if they choose to rent, the price of keeping a roof over one's head will still probably be their biggest expense. Real estate is not only necessary as a matter of physical survival, it is critically important to our economic system because of this large dollar outlay. One of the most basic terms used in the law of real estate is "fee simple absolute." It connotes the highest form of recognized ownership in real property. The term is originally derived from the words *feud* or *fief* and *fief d'haubert* meaning a fee held by tenure of a knight's service to the lord of the manor. It is infinite, with no limitation on inheritability, and does not end upon the happening of any event. Think of fee simple as the whole pie. That pie, in turn, may be sliced and diced into all sorts of smaller morsels.

Another way to look at real estate as a circular object is in the physical shape of the earth. It is round, and each ownership of land has an unique wedge-shaped slice of that round body. The basic parameters of that ownership start with the surface rights as defined by the surveyed metes and bounds in the legal description. In addition to those rights, real estate extends theoretically to the center of the earth in minerals below the surface and in development of air rights. Both these rights are subject to use limitations and the rights of other owners of adjoining properties.

The other interesting aspect of this chapter goes into more detail on forms of coownership of property. Most of us, sooner or later, will get involved with coownership of property in one way or another. Anyone who is married is a likely coowner. Anyone who shares property interests by gift, inheritance, or earnings is likely to be a coowner. Even if one's property is entirely his or her own, he or she will need to know the rules of the coownership game for purposes of credit, finance, business planning, and the like. How, when, and where coownership rights and duties are created is as important as the basic terms of real property law itself.

II. Hypothetical   Multi-Issue   Essay Question:

This question is designed to help students identify some of the key issues arising out of a break up of a substantial amount of property due to divorce. Unfortunately, with a national divorce rate of over 50 percent, such scenarios are an every day occurrence in our society. As with so many other aspects of the legal environment in the law of real property, it is fine to hope for the best, but best to plan for the worst.

Dufus Duffee and his wife, Loquacia, were married in Boulder, Colorado on April 1, 1970 by the Rev. Tammy Bigbucks. They still live and own a home in Boulder even though they have become very wealthy. Dufus realized that even though most people were not to the manor born, they still wanted to have a family crest other than toothpaste. Dufus devised a great marketing gimmick. Why not emboss luxury goods with a Royal Dog named Lord Throckmorton T. Thurston the Third? The Big T. Brand Holding Company now nets over $15 million annually by selling everything from fashion goods to hardware, all identified by the Big T. status symbol.

Dufus and Loquacia also own, in fee, homes in California, New Mexico, and New York City. All of them are patterned after the Newport Cottage and are valued at $10 million each. In addition, the Big T. Brand Holding Company owns and operates plants in Montana, Louisiana, and Illinois. All the family assets, including 100 percent of the shares in Big T. Brand Holding Company, are held in Dufus' name alone. Loquacia stayed at home to raise their six children, Otter, Bubba, Rollo, Misty, Dufus II, and Dufus III.

Dufus decides to seek a divorce because he falls in love with the young and mysterious Margaux de Mollin while visiting the islands of Myorca and Yourorca. What can he claim as his besides Margaux's affection?

III. Key Question Checklist:

A. What are the basic physical classifications of real property?
    1. Surface rights?
        (a) Land?
        (b) Permanent improvements on the land?
            (1) Fixtures?
                (aa) By attachment?
                (bb) By adaptation?
                (cc) By agreement?
        (c) Plant life growing on surface?
    2. Subsurface rights (mineral rights)?
        (a) Minerals?
            (1) Coal?
            (2) Oil?
            (3) Gas?
            (4) Precious metals?
            (5) Any other extractable minerals?
        (b) Can be transferred separately?
        (c) Mineral rights owner's rights subject to certain limitations?
            (1) Lateral and subjacent support?
            (2) Excavation damage liability?
            (3) Restoration of surface after excavation?
    3. Air rights?
        (a) Right to development above the surface?
        (b) Subject to zoning and air navigation laws?

B. What are the main classifications of legal estates in real property?
    1. Freehold estates?
        (a) Defined as possessor interest in real property of indeterminate duration?
        (b) Fee simple absolute?
            (1) Highest recognized form of ownership in real property?
            (2) Infinite in duration?
            (3) No limitation on inheritability?
            (4) Does not end upon happening of any event?
        (c) Fee simple defeasible?
            (1) Same incidents of ownership in grantee but subject to:
                (aa) A condition which may or may not occur?
                (bb) If the condition does occur, the estate may terminate?

(2) Three types of defeasible fees:
  (aa) Fee simple determinable?
  (bb) Fee simple subject to a condition subsequent?
  (cc) Fee simple subject to executory limitation?
(d) Life estate?
  (1) Life tenant treated as owner during his or her lifetime?
  (2) Life tenancy can be measurable by life of another person *per autre vie*?
  (3) Upon termination of the life tenancy, the property either reverts or goes to the remainderman?
  (4) Life tenant must observe the property rights of the next taker?
  (5) Life estate can be defeasible?
(e) Future interests?
  (1) Use of property in future?
  (2) Two classes of future interests?
    (aa) Reversions, which go back to original grantor or his or her estate?
    (bb) Remainders, which go forward to third parties after present right of possession has ended (can be vested or contingent)?

C. Are there any forms of coownership in place?
  1. What are the main possible forms of coownership of property?
    (a) Joint tenancy?
      (1) Creation requires four unities?
        (aa) Time?
        (bb) Title?
        (cc) Interest?
        (dd) Possession?
      (2) Equal ownership among joint tenants?
      (3) Right of survivorship in surviving joint tenant at death of joint tenant?
      (4) Property passes outside of probate?
      (5) Termination of joint tenancy?
        (aa) Transfer of interest by joint tenant?
        (bb) Voluntary partition by parties?
        (cc) Court ordered partition?
        (dd) Death of joint tenant if there is no more than one surviving joint tenant?
      (6) If terminated, tenancy in common presumed?
    (b) Tenancy by the entirety?
      (1) Same elements as joint tenancy plus one: marriage?
      (2) Consent of spouse required to sell or transfer property?
      (3) Terminated by divorce?
    (c) Tenancy in common?
      (1) Presumed form of coownership?
      (2) Ownership interest is per tenant's interest, not pro-rata?
      (3) No right of survivorship?
      (4) Property passes through probate?
      (5) Termination by partition or other agreement?
      (6) Tenant can sell or convey his or her interest without consent of other tenant(s)?
    (d) Community property?
      (1) U.S. system based on Spanish tradition (*Bienes Gananciales*)?
      (2) Eight traditional states have it?
        (aa) Arizona?
        (bb) California?

(cc) Idaho?

(dd) Louisiana?

(ee) Nevada?

(ff) New Mexico?

(gg) Texas?

(hh) Washington?

(3) Wisconsin recently adopted community styled marital property law.

(4) Also used by the Commonwealth of Puerto Rico?

(5) Recognizes equal coownership, as community, of property earned during the marriage, regardless of who earned it?

(6) Does allow for some separate property?

    (aa) Separate acquired prior to the marriage?

    (bb) Gifts during marriage?

    (cc) Inheritances during marriage?

(7) Separate property commingled with community may be deemed to be community property?

(8) Location of the property determines whether community property law applies?

(9) Under doctrine of community, separate property state may recognize community interests acquired in the community property state?

    (aa) Parties may alter their rights by contract subject to public policy limitations?

    (bb) Federal law does not follow community property?

    (cc) Examples: social security and military benefits.

(e) Condominiums?

    (1) Form of common ownership of multiple-dwelling buildings?

    (2) Each individual unit owned separately?

    (3) Common areas held as tenancy in common?

(f) Cooperatives?

    (1) Form of coownership of multiple dwelling buildings?

    (2) Building owned by a corporation?

    (3) Shares issued to individuals in proportion to size of units?

    (4) Vote taken to approve sales of stock?

D. In addition to coownership, it may be possible for one person to own a nonpossessory interest in another's real estate. What are the main classifications of these interests?

1. Easements which give a limited right to make use of another's property?

    (a) Affirmative easements are premised on use of another's property?

    (b) Negative easements are premised on limiting another's use of their land in a specified manner?

    (c) Easements appurtenant are given over adjacent land?

        (1) Runs with the land?

        (2) Land that benefits from it is dominant estate?

        (3) Land subject to it is servient estate? Example: access easement?

    (d) Easement in gross authorizes another nonadjoining person to use the land?

(1) Personal right which does not run with the land?

(2) No dominant estate? Example: telephone lines?

(e) Easements can be created by:
   (1) Grant?
   (2) Reservation?
   (3) Necessity?
   (4) Prescription?
   (5) Dedication?
   (6) Eminent domain?

(f) Termination of the easement?
   (1) Expiration of a specified period?
   (2) Abandonment by holder?
   (3) Transfer?
   (4) Merger with dominant estate?

2. License is a grant to enter upon another's property for a specified time. Example: parks pass?

3. Profits *a pendre* give the holder the right to remove something from another's property?
   (a) Profits appurtenant?
   (b) Profits in gross?

E. After you have classified all the various possible real estate holdings, next look at the methods of transfer possibly with regard to those holdings:

1. Sale?
   (a) Most common method?
   (b) May involve brokerage?
   (c) Real estate contracts covered by the Statute of Frauds?
   (d) Deeds used to evidence the transfer of title?
      (1) Warranty deed?
      (2) Bargain sale deed?
      (3) Quit claim deed?
   (e) Recording statute complied with?
      (1) Pure race statute?
      (2) Pure notice statute?
      (3) Race-notice statute?

2. By gift?
   (a) Elements of gift required?
      (1) Donative intent?
      (2) Delivery?
      (3) Acceptance?
   (b) Deed usually used as evidence of the transfer?

3. By will or inheritance?
   (a) Testate?
   (b) Intestate statute?
   (c) By outside of probate process?
      (1) Right of survivorship?
         (aa) Joint tenancy?
         (bb) Tenancy by the entirety?
      (2) By contract?

4. Tax sale?
   (a) Government entity obtains property to satisfy tax claims?
   (b) Right of redemption?
   (c) Excess proceeds to taxpayer?

5. Adverse possession?
   (a) Certain qualified wrongful possession may result in change in ownership to possessor?
   (b) Qualifications?
      (1) Statutory period of possession?
      (2) Possession must be open, visible, and notorious?
      (3) Possession must be actual and exclusive?
      (4) Possession must be continuous and peaceful?
      (5) Possession must be hostile and adverse vis-à-vis the original owner?

F. Once title has been transferred, what methods can be used to assure that the title is correct and marketable?
   1. Attorney's opinion letter?
   2. Torrens system?
   3. Title insurance?

IV. Objective Questions:

Terms:

1. Real property includes some items of personal property that are affixed to real property which are called _____.

2. Common law provided that a surface owner had possessory rights above the surface to the _____.

3. Plant life and vegetation growing on the surface of land is considered to be _____ property.

4. The highest form of ownership in real property which grants the owner the fullest bundle of legal rights is called a _____ _____ _____.

5. An interest in real property that lasts for the life of a specified person is called a _____ _____.

6. The two most prominent forms of future interests are called _____ and _____.

7. Property is usually classified as _____ or _____.

8. A person's ownership rights in real property is called an _____.

9. The party who transfers an ownership interest in real property is called a _____.

10. An act which would cause a substantial and unreasonable reduction in the value of a property is called _____.

True/False:

1. ____Owners of land do not possess mineral rights to the earth located beneath the surface of the land.

2. ____When determining whether personal property has become a fixture, courts can look to the intent of the parties.

3. ____Leases are classified as freehold estates.

4. ____A reversion is a right of possession that returns to the grantor after the expiration of a limited or contingent estate.

5. ____Land is the most common form of real property.

6. ____Subsurface rights may be sold separately from surface rights.

7. ____When land is sold, any plant life growing on the land is included unless the parties agree otherwise.

8. ____A fee simple absolute is the type of ownership most people connect with owning real property.

9. ____A person may not be given the right to possess property in the future.

10. ____Tenancy by the entirety is a form of coownership which can be used by anyone.

Multiple Choice:

1. Which of the following is not one of the three types of freehold estates?
   A. Fee simple absolute.
   B. Reversion.
   C. Fee simple defeasible.
   D. Life estate.

2. A owns a life estate to real property so long as B is alive. A owns a:
   A. Fee simple absolute.
   B. Fee simple defeasible.
   C. Simple life estate.
   D. Estate *pour autre vie*.

3. Which of the following is not an example of a fixture?
   A. Furniture.
   B. Wall to wall carpeting.
   C. Dishwasher.
   D. Door knobs.

4. Which of the following is true of a fee simple absolute?
   A. It has no limitation on inheritability.
   B. It is infinite in nature.
   C. It does not end upon the happening of any event.
   D. All of the above.

5. Which of the following is *not* one of the four unities necessary for a joint tenancy?
   A. Interest.
   B. Possession.
   C. Unity of marriage.
   D. Title.

6. Larry Landowner is one of five tenants in common who own Blackacre. Larry dies with a will leaving all of his property to Barry. Which statement is *not* true of Barry?

A. Barry becomes a tenant in common with the other four landowners.
B. Barry's interest is subject to the claim of Larry's creditors.
C. Barry receives Larry's interest in the tenancy in common.
D. Barry may not terminate the tenancy in common by agreement of him and the other parties.

7. Pat and Mary live in California, a state which recognizes community property. Pat is an artist who makes $15,000 per year and Mary is a business owner who makes $75,000 per year. Which of the following statements is *not* true with regard to Pat and Mary?
   A. If Pat or Mary dies, the surviving spouse automatically receives all of the community property.
   B. Each owns one half of the assets acquired during the marriage.
   C. Each spouse has joint authority to manage community property.
   D. Upon a divorce, each spouse has the right to one half of the community property.

8. Which of the following is not a way to create an easement?
   A. Eminent domain.
   B. Grant.
   C. License.
   D. Necessity.

9. Which of the following is a way to transfer real property?
   A. Adverse possession.
   B. Inheritance.
   C. Gift.
   D. All of the above.

10. Which of the following states are classified as community property states?
    A. Colorado.
    B. Illinois.
    C. Idaho.
    D. Montana.

V. Answers to Objective Questions:

Terms:

1. *Fixtures*. Certain personal property is so closely associated with real property that it can become part of the realty. Under the common law, several methods can be used by the courts to decide if personal property has become a fixture. These include the intent of the parties, attachment or annexation, or the use of item in question.
2. *Heavens*. Air rights include the airspace above the property theoretically to the heavens. In reality this right is limited not only in practical terms but even more by zoning laws and airspace navigation rules. Air rights are, however, still very important in congested areas and often are used as bargaining chips in the zoning process such as set-backs for office buildings.
3. *Real*. Plant life and vegetation growing on the surface is considered real property. This includes both natural and cultivated plant life. When the land is sold, these assets are considered part of the land unless agreed otherwise. Once severed, they are, however, considered personal property.
4. *Fee simple absolute*. This is the highest form of ownership in real property because it grants the owner the fullest bundle of rights that a person can hold in real property. The term is traceable to the fee paid by the lord of the manor to his knights for services to the realm.
5. *Life estate*. This interest in real property is measured by the life of a specified person. This method of ownership is very often used in conjunction with a will or trust and is designed to take advantage of certain favorable provisions of wealth transfer tax laws.
6. *Reversions, remainders*. In a future interest, the right to possess the property lies in the future rather than in the present. Ordinarily, there is some sort of precondition to the use. In a reversion, the property may revert to the original transferor or his heirs after the condition has been met. In a remainder, it will pass on after a prior holding period, such as a life estate, has been completed.
7. *Real, personal*. Some jurisdictions refer to this dichotomy as movables vs. immovables.
8. *Estate*. When used in the context of real property, this term helps define the degree, quantity, and extent of interest the person has in the property.
9. *Grantor*. The grantor is the person by whom a grant is made.
10. *Waste*. The term implies neglect or misconduct resulting in damage but does not include ordinary depreciation due to age or normal use.

True/False:

1. False. Mineral rights are part of the bundle of sticks presumed owned unless otherwise agreed upon by the parties.
2. True. This is one of the key considerations taken into account by the courts on this issue. Oftentimes commercial fixtures appear very permanent, yet can be removed based on

476

the contractual agreements between the parties.

3. False. Leases are not classified as freehold estates because they are contract-based use not ownership estates.

4. True. This is one of the categories of interests in property which is classified as a future interest.

5. True. Most people think of real property in the surface sense. In fact, real property rights include mineral rights below the surface and air rights above the surface.

6. True. All of these tiers--air, surface, and subsurface--may be divided and sold separately from eachother.

7. True. Plant life, while growing on the land, is classified as part of the land interest. Once removed, it has been converted from real to personal property.

8. True. This classification is considered the highest and most complete form of ownership of real property.

9. False. Such a right is called a future interest.

10. False. It can only be used by married couples.

Multiple Choice:

1. B. The reversion is a future interest and is thus not considered a freehold estate until such time as it vests. The other estates are all classified as freehold estates.

2. D. An estate *pour autre vie* is a life estate measured in the life of a third party. A's life estate is measured in terms of B's life, and it will end at B's death.

3. A. Furniture is usually, but not always, movable and therefore not classified as part of the real property. Courts can look at intent, use, or annexation to see if an item of personal property has been converted to a fixture.

4. D. A, B, and C are all elements found in the definition of a fee simple absolute.

5. C. marriage is a required element for the creation of a tenancy by the entirety. A joint tenancy does not require marriage as a prerequisite.

6. D. Unless otherwise agreed, Barry can sell, give, devise, or otherwise transfer his interest in Blackacre without the consent of the other four landowners.

7. A. When a spouse dies, the surviving spouse automatically receives one-half of the community property. The other half passes to the heirs of the diseased spouse as directed by will or by a state intestate statute if there is no will.

8. C. A license is a personal privilege that may be revoked at any time by the licensor.

9. D. All of the above are recognized in the law as methods of transferring real property.

10. A. Idaho is a community property state.

VI. Key Question Checklist Answers to Essay Question:

A&B. *What are the physical classifications of the property held by Dufus and Loquacia prior to the initiation of the divorce action?*

It appears from the description of the real properties that they are held in fee simple absolute. When estates in property are described, the presumption is that ownership is of the complete bundle of sticks which make up fee simple absolute ownership. This would include the land, mineral, and air rights. This would also include the full freehold estate not subject to any life estates or defeasible conditions. In other words, the title unites all present and future interests.

C. *Are there any forms of coownership in place which would have an impact on the respective rights, duties, and liabilities of parties to the divorce action?*

From the question as given, it appears that Dufus owns all the property in his name alone. As much as he would like to tell that to the mysterious Margaux, Dufus cannot readily make that sort of claim. A number of the properties in his inventory are situated in community property states: the homes in California, New Mexico, and the plant in Louisiana. At the very minimum, Loquacia would be able to claim a community property interest in those parcels. Under the general rules of community property, equal coownership is attributed to all property earned during the marriage regardless of who earned it. Separate property status is generally allowed for property brought into the marriage and gifts of inheritance acquired during the marriage. Even in those instances, it must be shown that the property was not commingled.

In addition to the community claims that Loquacia may make, most noncommunity property states have effectively adopted community property-like results in divorce proceedings. The basic and equitable premise is that a marriage is more than just a spiritual and sexual union. It is also an economic partnership which provides mutual support and opportunity for eachother's enrichment. Here Dufus did well in business because he had the support system of having his wife care for his personal and family needs. It is only fair to recognize that work in economic terms if the property has to be divided due to divorce.

D. *In addition to coownership, it may be possible for one person to own a nonpossessory interest in another's real estate. Are any such interests at issue in this case?*

It appears from the facts given that there are no claims to the real property owned by Dufus and Loquacia which are based on easement or license.

E&F. *What are the possible methods of transfer between the parties with regard to these holdings?*

Even though it appears that Dufus sought to avoid any transfer of these assets to his wife's name by structuring the Big T. Brand Holding Company in his name, any number of transfer methods would have been available to him had he been more considerate of his wife's interests in the marital property. He could have made gift transfers and the like. Because he has failed to do so, the most likely result will be that all the properties, including the Big T. Brand Holding Company, will be ordered equally divided. Dufus can then go back to Myorca, and Loquacia can get on with her life.

CHAPTER 52

LANDLORD-TENANT RELATIONSHIP AND LAND USE CONTROL

After a good dinner, one can forgive anybody, even one's own relations.

Oscar Wilde

I. Overview:

An interesting comparative measure of the U.S. way of life is the percentage of home ownership versus rental. Our economy has traditionally boasted of a high percentage of home ownership relative to most any other part of the world. In most economically backward countries, the percentage of home ownership is very low. Even in the more highly developed parts of the world like Western Europe, the percentage has been much lower than in the U.S. This achievement has been one of the foundations of the great middle class dream of Americans and certainly a stabilizing influence in our society.

The disturbing aspect of this particular economic and sociological measure is that recent history has witnessed a decline in the number of Americans who can realistically aspire to own their own homes. As the percentage goes down, the laws involving the rights, duties, and obligations of persons involved in nonfreehold estates of all sorts become increasingly important. With over half of our population now living under someone else's roof, the law of leasing needs constant and fair reexamination and updating. As in any such process, the legitimate claims of both sides must be listened to.

The landlord is entitled to a fair return on his or her investment. This includes not only a financial return but also a return on the investment. Income property should be protected from waste and harm just like any other property. Too many people seem to have adopted an attitude which says: "If it's not mine, then the hell with it."

Conversely, the bargaining power between landlord and tenant has never been entirely equal. Between market limitations of supply and the tenant's lesser economic bargaining position, the common law can hardly have been accused of being the tenant's friend in the past. More modern attitudes and statutory enactments have given the tenant a more even playing field, but not real parity. Whether we like it or not, nonownership is still looked upon as second class citizenship.

This chapter also examines some of the main land use statutes used in this country. Here, the law moves away from its first and second tier treatment based on ownership and looks instead more to the common good. The days of wide open spaces are long gone, and along with them the notion that an owner can do whatever he or she wants with his property. Land use is simply too important and too interwoven with the rights of others to adapt a *laissez-faire* attitude. The constant balancing act must be performed by various branches of government. On the owners and user's side of the equation, public policy wants free, quiet, environmentally sensitive use of land. Good zoning controlled growth and other governmental regulations can and do provide enlightened measures towards those goals. Properly executed, good land use law literally translates into good quality of life for users.

Conversely, where government sets up measures that are unreasonable and even confiscatory, the larger society is badly served.

The results are not only higher costs of doing business, but also depreciation of the American Dream. Zoning laws and the like have been pointed to by many commentators on the American scene as an invidious subterfuge to extend governmental control too far into our personal lives. The government does have the duty to assure the health, safety, and welfare of its citizenry through the use of its police power on land use. It should be used to help us live well but not to tell us how to live.

II. Hypothetical Multi-Issue Essay Question:

Because he was heir-apparent to the vast Gutterball Bowling Incorporated fortune, Mr. Pinhead Widebottom started life with a silver spoon in his mouth. Unfortunately this start gave him a very big mouth. He turned out to be the prototypic "yuppie" in the worst meaning of the word. He is loud, obnoxious, overbearing and works as a land developer.

His latest venture is in Boulder, Colorado on Canyon Boulevard. In a mixed commercial and residential zoning area, Pinhead decided to put up an office building that reflected the essence of his personality. It is totally out of character with the low rise, natural materials look of the rest of the neighborhood. Because it is mixed zoning, the back of the building faces a residential area. The building attracted tenants like the American Supercilious Sales Corporation and "Kill for Money" magazine.

Pinhead was worried about security for his monstrosity and decided to put in a high intensity lighting system all around his building. It was attached to the top of his building and shown brightly unto and into the homes behind it. In addition, he put in a loud alarm system that went off at all hours because his non-so-bright tenants could not figure out how to use it.

The neighbors are fed up. What can they do?

III. Key Question Checklist:

A. If you have decided that the issue is not freehold but rather a nonfreehold estate, you must then examine the basic relationship entered into between the parties?
   1. Was it entered into by contract (a lease)?
      (a) Oral?
         (1) Less than a year?
         (2) Actual terms?
         (3) Implied terms?
      (b) Written?
         (1) More than a year?
         (2) Key express terms?
            (aa) Examples: time, consideration, rights on default, etc?
         (3) Implied terms?
      (c) Which laws apply?
         (1) Recording statute?
         (2) Uniform Residential Landlord and Tenant Act?
         (3) Any other laws applicable?
   2. Was the relationship entered into on some other basis (more details in subsequent portions of this outline)?
      (a) Tort law?
      (b) Agency law?
      (c) Governmental action?

B. Assuming the basic relationship is contract based, what are the main forms of nonfreehold estates?
   1. Tenancy for years?
      (a) Agreed upon specific duration of lease?
      (b) Terminates automatically at end of term?
      (c) Can terminate prior to end of term if certain conditions occur?
         (1) Nonpayment of rent?
         (2) Constructive eviction?

480

2. Periodic tenancy?
   (a) Specified intervals set for payment of rent?
   (b) No specific length of duration of lease?
   (c) Can be created by implication?
   (d) Can end at end of any period?
      (1) Notice may be:
         (aa) Expressly required?
         (bb) Impliedly required from circumstances?
         (cc) Required by statute?
      (2) Either party may give notice?
3. Tenancy at will?
   (a) May be terminated at any time by either party?
   (b) Death terminates the tenancy?
   (c) Common law lack of notice amended by statute?
4. Tenancy at sufferance?
   (a) Wrongful possession by tenant after expiration of another tenancy?
   (b) Owner can elect:
      (1) Eviction?
      (2) Treat it as new periodic lease?
   (c) Tenant liable for payment of rent during period of sufferance?

C. What are the basic duties of the parties?
   1. Landlord vis-à-vis tenant?
      (a) Deliver possession?
      (b) Not to interfere with tenants' quiet enjoyment of the premises?
         (1) Unlawful eviction?
         (2) Constructive eviction?
         (3) Retaliatory eviction?
      (c) Maintain the premises?
         (1) Per agreement?
         (2) Per codes?
      (d) Basic tort duties of care?
   2. Tenant vis-à-vis landlord?
      (a) Pay rent?
         (1) Per agreed upon terms?

(2) Implied from circumstances?
      (b) Pay any other agreed upon items?
         (1) Deposits?
         (2) Utilities?
         (3) Insurance?
         (4) Repairs?
         (5) Taxes?
      (c) Legal use of the property?
      (d) Duty not to commit waste?
      (e) Duty not to disturb others?
      (f) Basic tort duties of care?
   3. Landlord vis-à-vis third parties?
      (a) Maintain common areas?
      (b) Disclose any hidden defects?
      (c) Repairs?
      (d) Protect access to public areas?
      (e) Maintain some control over tenants?
      (f) Protect against foreseeable criminal activities?
   4. Tenant vis-à-vis third parties?
      (a) Basic tort law duty of care?
      (b) Protect against foreseeable criminal activities?

D. How can rights to nonfreehold estates be transferred to third parties?
   1. By assignment?
      (a) Per express terms of the contract?
      (b) Implied from the circumstances?
      (c) Original parties may still remain liable?
   2. By sublease?
      (a) Per express terms of the contract?
      (b) Implied from the circumstances?
      (c) Limited rights in sublease?
      (d) Original parties may still be liable?

E. Termination of the nonfreehold estate?
   1. By expiration of the lease?
   2. By actions of the parties?
      (a) Examples: mutual recision, release, and merger?

481

3. By operation of law?
   (a) Examples: destruction of the premises by fire, flood, etc?

F. Land use controls can be exercised by private or government control. What are the main methods of private controls over land use?
   1. Restrictive covenants in contracts and deeds?
      (a) Can be made to run with the land?
         (1) In writing?
         (2) Intended to be binding on subsequent takers?
         (3) It touches and concerns the land?
         (4) Original parties in privity of estate when covenants were created?
   2. Equitable servitude (restrictions)?
      (a) Same first three basic requirements as covenants that run with the land?
      (b) Notice given to purchaser of the restrictions?
   3. Private restrictions must be legal?
      (a) Cannot violate civil rights?
      (b) Illegal covenants may be severable from the remainder of the contract or deed?
   4. Private nuisance actions?
      (a) Test used to determine nuisance?
         (1) Reasonable use?
         (2) Time of use?
         (3) Importance of the use?
      (b) Harm done by improper land use?
      (c) Damages or injunctive relief may be granted by a court?
   5. Governmental controls on land use?
      (a) Extensive study of law in place on every aspect of land use?
      (b) Public nuisance?
         (1) Same issues as in private nuisance?

      (2) Usually regulatory statute being violated? Example: Noise abatement law?
      (3) Sanctions can include:
         (aa) Equitable relief?
         (bb) Fines?
         (cc) Criminal penalties?
   (c) Eminent domain?
      (1) Government can take property for proper governmental use?
      (2) Owner entitled to compensation under the constitution?
   (d) Zoning?
      (1) Types of zoning?
         (aa) Use of zoning?
         (bb) Height, bulk, and area zoning?
         (cc) Architectural limitation zoning?
      (2) Sanctions for zoning law violations?
         (aa) Equitable relief?
         (bb) Fines?
         (cc) Criminal penalties?
         (dd) Private actions?
      (3) Relief from zoning laws?
         (aa) Amendment?
         (bb) Special permits?
         (cc) Spot zoning?
         (dd) Judicial review?

IV. Objective Questions:

Terms:

1. A tenancy created when a lease specifies intervals at which payments are due but does not specify how long the lease is for is called a _____ _____.

2. A covenant that says a landlord may not interfere with the tenant's quiet and peaceful possession, use, and enjoyment of the leased premises is called a covenant of _____ _____.

3. A remedy for nonpayment of rent in which the landlord is entitled to reclaim the leased premises from the tenant is called _____ _____ _____.

4. The legal doctrine used to enforce private restrictions on land use in many modern real estate developments is called _____ _____.

5. An estate situation in which the tenant has a right to possession of the property but not title to the property is a _____ estate.

6. An eviction that occurs when the landlord causes the leased premises to become unfit for their intended use is called _____ _____.

7. Discrimination in the sale and rental of real property based on race, color, national origin, sex, or religion is illegal under the _____ _____ Act and the _____ _____ Act.

8. A warranty that provides that the leased premises must be fit, safe, and suitable for ordinary residential use is a _____ _____ _____.

9. A private agreement between landowners that restricts the use of their land is a _____ _____.

10. The taking of private property by the government for public use, provided just compensation has taken place is called _____ _____.

True/False:

1. _____ In a landlord tenant relationship, the tenant receives a nonfreehold, rather than a freehold, estate in the property.

2. _____ A tenancy for years is a lease which is for more than one year.

3. _____ Generally, a lease is considered the personal property of the lessee and can therefore be transferred to the lessee's heirs upon his death.

4. _____ A landlord always has the right to enter leased premises, whether it is allowed under the lease or not, since the landlord still holds title of ownership to the premises.

5. _____ Zoning laws do not affect uses and buildings which were already in existence when the laws were enacted.

6. _____ Under a lease assignment, once the assignor assigns his rights to an assignee, the assignor is released from all obligations he owes to the landlord.

7. _____ Under a sublease, the landlord can sue either the sublessor (tenant) or the sublessee to recover rent payments.

8. _____ A restrictive covenant, although it is a private agreement between landowners, binds all subsequent landowners as well.

9. ____ Generally, the landlord, not the tenant, must maintain and repair common areas.

10. ____ Generally, a tenant is generally liable for injuries to a third person if the injuries were caused by the tenant's negligence.

Multiple Choice:

1. Which of the following is not one of the four unities necessary for a joint tenancy?
   A. Interest.
   B. Possession.
   C. Unity of marriage.
   D. Title.

2. Landlord Larry and Tenant Tom have a lease agreement whereby Tom is to lease commercial property from Larry for three years. Tom is to pay rent to Larry at the beginning of each month. Which of the following is correct?
   A. This is a tenancy for years.
   B. This lease must be in writing.
   C. Both of the above.
   D. None of the above.

3. Landlord Laura neglects her property even after several calls from Tenant Theresa about the lack of water from clogged pipes. Finally, after days without water, Theresa is fed up and infuriated. Which of the following is correct?
   A. Laura has constructively evicted Theresa.
   B. Theresa may stay on the premises and sue for damages.
   C. Theresa may leave and stop paying rent.
   D. All of the above.

4. Visitor Vicky is coming to visit her friend Tenant Tamara. Vicky is injured as she walks up the stairs of the apartment building because Landlord Lazy has neglected to fix a loose step. Which of the following is correct?
   A. Tamara is liable for Vicky's injuries.
   B. Lazy is liable for Vicky's injuries.
   C. Neither Tamara or Lazy is liable since Vicky is a third party.
   D. Vicky may choose to sue either Tamara or Lazy.

5. Tenant Toy Company (TTC) has a lease agreement with Landlord Commercial Property (LCP). TTC assigns its lease to Assignee Art Gallery (AAG). Which of the following is correct?
   A. TTC is released from all obligations to LCP.
   B. AAG acquires all rights that TTC had under the lease.
   C. AAG may never sublet the premises.
   D. All of the above.

6. Mr. and Mrs. Yuppie are looking for the perfect lot on which to build their new house. One major consideration is the zoning restrictions which they must comply with. The Yuppies find a great lot with a beautiful view. The area requires that only houses, but no businesses, may be built. In addition, all the houses must be no less than 3,000 square feet. Finally, there must be some brick in the exterior architecture of the building. The Yuppies have fallen in love with a lot that has:
   A. Use of property zoning restrictions.
   B. Height, bulk, and area zoning ordinances.
   C. Architectural limit zoning ordinances.
   D. All of the above.

7. Assume the same facts as in question 6. Also assume the Yuppies can only afford to build a house that is 2,200 square feet. What should the Yuppies do if they still want to build on the lot?
A. Apply for a variance.
B. Apply for spot zoning.
C. Either of the above.
D. None of the above. The Yuppies have no choice but to comply if they want to build on the lot.

8. Under the terms of a triple net lease, the tenant is responsible for:
A. Taxes.
B. Insurance.
C. Utilities.
D. All of the above.
E. A and B only.

9. Neighbor Nancy and Neighbor Ned agree that neither one shall ever build a house higher than three stories on his or her land. Nancy and Ned intend to have this covenant run with the land, and they put the covenant in writing. However, Nancy and Ned are not in privity of estate. If Nancy or Ned sells their land to a purchaser who is aware of this agreement, what is the remaining neighbor's best argument for binding the purchaser to the covenant?
A. This is a restrictive covenant.
B. This is an equitable servitude.
C. A house over three stories is a private nuisance.
D. None of the above.

10. Now assume Nancy is Ned's wealthy aunt. Nancy gives Ned the property adjacent to hers as a gift. When Nancy gives the property to Ned, the two agree never to build a house higher than three stories on their land. Nancy and Ned

intent to have this covenant run with the land and they put the covenant in writing. If Nancy or Ned sells their land to a purchaser, what is the remaining neighbor's best argument for binding the purchaser to the covenant?
A. This is a restrictive covenant.
B. This is an equitable servitude.
C. A house over three stories is a private nuisance.
D. None of the above.

V. Answers to Objective Questions:

Terms:

1. *Periodic tenancy.* A periodic tenancy may be terminated by either party at the end of any payment interval, but adequate notice of the termination must be given. At common law, this notice period equaled the payment period. More modern statues have shortened this period.

2. *Quiet enjoyment.* This covenant is implied by the law in all leases. It is designed to assure that the landlord will not interfere with a tenant's legal and proper use of the leased property. Breach of this covenant is called wrongful or unlawful eviction.

3. *Recovery of possession.* In spite of all the protections which have been added to tenants rights by modern statutes, the basic duty to pay rent remains. Failure to comply with that duty allows the landlord to reclaim control over his or her property.

4. *Equitable servitude (or restrictive covenants).* These are private agreements between landowners which restrict the use of their land. They must be lawful and in compliance with public policy. They cannot be used for

illegal purposes such as violation of another person's civil rights.

5. *Nonfreehold.* The tenant's interest in the property is called a leasehold estate, which creates a lease which will determine the type of tenancy.

6. *Constructive eviction.* While not depriving the tenant of actual possession, the premises have been rendered uninhabitable by the landlord's acts or omissions.

7. *Civil Rights; Fair Housing.* These statutes prohibit discrimination in the rental or sale of real property..

8. *Implied warranty of habitability.* This warranty has been imposed by most jurisdictions even if the parties to the lease have failed to expressly mention terms like habitability or fit for ordinary use.

9. *Restrictive covenant.* These covenants must be in compliance with both public policy and not in violation of civil rights statutes.

10. *Eminent domain.* Under the Fifth Amendment to the U.S. Constitution, just compensation must be paid to the owner of the property which has been taken for public use.

True/False:

1. True. In a landlord/tenant relationship, the tenant receives the right to possession of the property, but does not receive ownership rights in the property. Such an estate is a nonfreehold estate.

2. False. A tenancy for years is a lease which is for any specific duration, no matter how long or how short. The lease may be for less than or more than one year.

3. True. Unless the tenancy is a tenancy at will, which is terminated on the death of

either party, the lease is personal property and may be transferred to the lessee's heirs upon his death.

4. False. A landlord may only enter the leased premises if this right is specifically reserved in the lease. This is true even though the landlord still has ownership rights in the premises.

5. True. Zoning laws act prospectively and do not prohibit uses or buildings which were in existence before the law was enacted.

6. False. The assignor is only released from his obligations to the landlord if both parties come to an agreement releasing the assignor. If there is no such agreement, the assignor is still obligated to the landlord.

7. False. Under a sublease, the landlord can only sue the sublessor (who is the original tenant), but not the sublessee.

8. True. It can run with the land, which means that the covenant will follow or accompany the title.

9. True. This is the general rule, which can be modified by the terms of the lease. If the lease is silent on the issue, the general rule will apply.

10. True. The tenant owes a duty of reasonable care to persons who enter upon the leased premises.

Multiple Choice:

1. C. Unity of marriage is not a requirement of joint tenancy. Any person can choose to enter into a joint form of ownership with another as long as the elements of unity are met. Marriage is a requirement for holding property as tenants in the entirety.

2. C. A is correct because since the lease is for a specific period of time, it is a tenancy for years. B is correct because

486

under the Statute of Frauds, a lease for greater than one year must be in writing. D is incorrect because a periodic tenancy does not have a stated period of time and only runs from one payment to the next.

3. D. A is correct because by not fixing the running water in Theresa's residence, Laura has permitted the premises to become unlivable and, therefore, constructively evicted Theresa. B and C are correct because these are tenants' remedies for a landlords' constructive eviction.

4. B. Lazy is liable for the injuries to tenants as well as third parties if the injury results from failure to maintain common areas. A is incorrect because Tamara does not have a duty to maintain common areas and is therefore not liable for injuries resulting from failure to maintain these areas. C is incorrect because Lazy is liable to Vicky even though she is a third party. D is incorrect because Vicky cannot sue Tamara.

5. B. Under a lease assignment, the assignee acquires all the rights that the assignor had. A is incorrect because unless agreed upon, TTC is still obligated to LCP. C is incorrect because AAG may sublet the premises unless there is a lease provision which prevents it.

6. D. A is correct because restricting the land to only residential use is a use of property zoning ordinance. B is correct because the square foot requirements are a height, bulk, and area zoning restriction. C is correct because the brick requirement is an architectural limit zoning restriction.

7. C. The Yuppies may try to make an exception to the zoning requirements by either a variance or spot zoning. However, spot zoning is not likely to be permitted. D is incorrect because the Yuppies have some, although few, options here.

8. D. All of the above are generally included in the terminology used in triple net leases.

9. B. Because Nancy and Ned are not in privity of estate here, there is not a restrictive covenant. However, if the purchaser was aware of this agreement, the remaining neighbor could try to argue this is an equitable servitude. A is incorrect because there is no privity of estate here. C is incorrect because this is an unreasonable assertion.

10. A. Here, there is privity of estate since Nancy is giving the land to Ned. B is incorrect because with privity of estate, restrictive covenant is a stronger argument. C is incorrect because this is an unreasonable assertion.

VI. Key Question Checklist Answers to Essay Question:

A&B. *What relationship was entered into by the parties?*

The basic relationship between Pinhead and his tenants is one of a nonfreehold estate. In commercial building situations, the most likely arrangement to be used is a leasehold entered into by written contract. Most commercial leases are written up as tenancies for years. As such the parties have an agreed upon duration of the lease. The lease will terminate automatically at the end of the term unless there is some prior nonpayment or constructive eviction before the end of the agreed-upon term.

C,D,E,&F. *What are the basic duties of the parties to eachother?*

The basic duties of the landlord are to provide a lawful and safe use of the premises. The landlord is to maintain those premises per the agreement and all relevant building site requirements. Failure to do so may allow the tenant to claim that he or she has been unlawfully or constructively evicted. In addition, the landlord has certain tort-based duties to maintain the property free of danger. Here Pinhead can argue that his lighting and security system are efforts to live up to that duty towards his tenants and third parties who use the premises.

The tenants must live up to their contractual duties to pay rent, use the property legally, not commit waste, and not disturb others. In addition, they have a tort-based duty to maintain the leased premises free of danger, including guarding against any foreseeable criminal behavior.

G. *Are any land use controls applicable here?*

The problem with this case is really not so much the landlord/tenant relationship, but rather how those parties use the property in question vis-a-vis the rights of adjoining landowners. The control of land use can be based either on private arrangements through covenants or by enforcement of private or public nuisance actions against the offending owner or user.

A private nuisance complaint must show an improper land use. The impropriety is shown based on all the circumstances surrounding the issue. Factors such as time and frequency of disturbance will be examined by the courts. In addition, the court will weigh the justification for the original behavior in the first place.

There are a number of government controls on land use which may come into question here. Zoning and land use ordinances are specifically directed at lighting of property. Lighting form one parcel which washes over only another in an unwelcome manner may be illegal. Consider your own bedroom. Would you like to have it floodlit at night? In spite of the need to provide site access lighting, Pinhead probably violated this ordinance by letting that light go past his own property.

As for the alarms, most cities have decided that false alarms are not only costly in the use of police and other city services, but are also dangerous. Many accidents occur both at the site of a false alarm as well as in transit to false alarms. In addition, the noise disturbance is quite annoying to many. This sort of behavior is both a violation of these ordinances and a public nuisance. Courts can give equitable and damage relief.

Perhaps Mr. Widebottom should go into the family Gutterball business instead of making his building a pain for all concerned. Thank goodness the "go go" 1980s are over. The world does not need yet another decade of self-centered yuppie entrepreneurs who have no sense of social responsibility to others.

CHAPTER 53

INSURANCE

Education never ends... It is a series of lessons with the greatest for the last.

Sir Arthur Conan Doyle

I. Overview:

Insurance is defined as a contractual arrangement whereby one undertakes to indemnify another against loss, damage, or liability. Even though the law of insurance is derived from contract, the need for insurance is rooted in reality. Few activities in today's overly litigious world are not in one way or another involved with insurance. Contracts of insurance may concern us from our moment of birth to our moment of death and every time in between. Insurance is more important than ever because it appears that new risks never even fathomed by our forefathers emerge every day. One very real and unfortunate truth of conducting one's personal and business affairs is that financial safety nets are more necessary than ever. How many of us can really afford to be self-insured? What are some of the factors which have led to this state of affairs?

One large element in this picture is found in the results of having a legal system which is willing to attach responsibility for many heretofore unforeseen situations. Modern technology has raised expectations to the point where every product must be perfect, every operation a success, and every accident avoidable. 20/20 hindsight seems to be a particularly costly form of myopia to the insurance industry.

Another element is found in the insurance industries own backyard. State regulations, and policy owner political initiatives, such as those seen in California recently are in many ways an outgrowth of perceived mismanagement and greed in the halls of insurance companies. The legal environment has spawned all sorts of new insurance sales opportunities for insurance companies such as Medicare gap coverage. When these coverages fail to deliver, resentment grows.

Yet another problem is found in the legal departments of many insurance companies. Attempts to obfuscate the real coverage by convoluted technical legal language and words of art has led to much resentment over what insurance companies really can or will do in case of need. This problem is exacerbated by perceived bad faith efforts to avoid coverage for large scale costs arising out of ailments such as AIDS. Expensive experimental treatments have also severely tested insurance companies willingness to pay. Large scale disasters like Hurricane Andrew have led to many examples of insurance company flight from high risk areas.

In spite of all these problems, the role of insurance is more vital than ever. Witness the recent calamitous fire in the hills of Oakland and Berkeley, California costing many lives and over a $1 billion in property damage. Not to have insurance would surely be pouring salt on an already grievous wound. Insurance law is ripe with controversy and litigation. Yet no one really wants or can imagine a legal, political, or social environment without it.

II. Hypothetical Multi-Issue Essay Question:

Autocross is an automobile-related sport wherein the driver tries to navigate his or her car through a set of difficult turns and roadways without going off course or hitting

489

pylon markers. The driver who gets through this obstacle course in the fastest time wins. Because autocrossing does not involve any head-to-head racing, it affords a low cost opportunity for many of the Walter Mittys of the world to try their hand at auto sports and dream of moving up to Formula One someday.

One such dreamer was Enzo Autre Droit. All his life he wanted to race at "Ring," LeMans, Indianapolis, and other such famous venues. Alas, his talents and his pocketbook confined his racing exploits to the local autocross held on weekends at the County Fairgrounds. The events were sponsored by "Boy Racers Autoclub."

Boy Racers obtained event insurance for its autocross events. This insurance required that all participants sign an exculpatory clause releasing Boy Racers from any harm or liability arising out of the event. In addition, Enzo's own auto insurance company, Airbag Insurance, excluded coverage for "motorsports" events.

Last week, Enzo "lost it" on a hard left banking turn and went into a trailing throttle oversteer. His mean green driving machine went into a roll and was badly damaged. Enzo and members of the Boy Racers Autoclub pushed the car into a nearby ditch. Enzo now claims it was all a "normal" accident due to bad road conditions. What results?

III. Key Question Checklist:

A. Before you can examine the insurance contract itself, you must determine whether the parties to the contract have a recognized ability to enter into the contract?
1. Do the parties have legal capacity?
    (a) The insurer?
        (1) Licensed to sell insurance?
        (2) Agent of the company?
        (3) Independent broker?
    (b) The insured?
        (1) Have a legal capacity (see contracts chapters for details)?
2. Have an insurable interest?
    (a) Based on recognized personal relationship. Example: family members insuring other family members?
    (b) Based on economic relationship. Examples: creditors, business relationships, or coownership?

B. Once you have established the capacity of both parties to enter into the insurance relationship you must then examine the contract itself. What are the key elements of the insurance contract?
1. What are the main provisions of the contract?
    (a) What is covered?
    (b) What is excluded from coverage?
2. Any mandatory provisions imposed by government?
3. When will the contract go into effect?
4. Rules of interpretation?
5. Provisions for cancellation?

C. Assuming life insurance is an issue, what are the key elements?
1. Types of life insurance?
    (a) Whole life (aka ordinary life and straight life)?
        (1) Provides coverage during entire life of insured?
        (2) Has a savings element?
    (b) Limited payment life?
        (1) Coverage over whole life of insured?
        (2) Payment period fixed?
        (3) Can have savings element?
    (c) Term life?
        (1) Payments and coverage set for term?
        (2) No savings element?

490

(d) Universal life insurance?
   (1) Combines term and whole life insurance?
   (2) Premium or contribution is apportioned between term and whole life elements?
(e) Endorsement policy?
   (1) Agreed upon lump sum payment?
   (2) Payment upon agreed upon contingency?
(f) Annuity?
   (1) Agreed upon periodic payments?
   (2) Payment on agreed upon age threshold?
2. Who are the parties to life insurance contracts?
  (a) The insurer?
  (b) The owner of the policy?
  (c) The insured?
  (d) The beneficiary?
3. Any basis for exclusion?
  (a) Military action?
  (b) Execution by government?
  (c) Private aircraft accidents?
  (d) Suicide?
  (e) Material misrepresentation?

D. Assuming health and/or disability insurance is at issue?
1. Parties?
2. Key provisions?
3. Exclusions?

E. Assuming fire and/or homeowner's insurance is at issue?
1. Standard fire policy?
  (a) Key provisions?
   (1) Hostile and friendly fire clause?
   (2) Occupying clause?
   (3) Proof of loss clause?
   (4) Coinsurance clause?
  (b) Exclusions?

2. Homeowner's policy?
  (a) Key provisions?
   (1) Property coverage?
   (2) Liability coverage?
   (3) Additional floaters?
  (b) Exclusions?

F. Assuming automobile insurance is at issue?
1. Key provisions?
  (a) Collision?
  (b) Comprehensive?
  (c) Liability?
  (d) Medical payments?
  (e) Uninsured motorists coverage?
  (f) No-fault applicable?
2. Exclusions?

G. Other forms of insurance coverage?
1. Business insurance?
  (a) Business property protection?
  (b) Business liability?
  (c) Business interruption?
  (d) Products liability (see products liability chapter for more details)?
  (e) Directors' and officers liability insurance?
  (f) Workers' compensation insurance?
  (g) Malpractice insurance?
  (h) Fidelity insurance?
  (i) Credit insurance?
  (j) Exclusions?
2. Real estate title insurance?
3. Marine insurance?
4. Combination plans?
  (a) Umbrella policies?
   (1) Combine homeowners' and auto insurance?
   (2) Stipulated maximum coverage?
5. Group plans?

H. Once you have identified the parties and types of policies at issue, you must then examine the basic duties of each of the parties to the contract?

1. Insurer's duties?
   (a) Live up to the covenants of the contract?
   (b) Defend the insured?
   (c) Defenses from performance?
       (1) Misrepresentation by insured?
       (2) Breach of warranty by insured?
       (3) Concealment of material facts by insured?
2. Insured duties?
   (a) Live up to covenants of the contract?
   (b) Pay premiums?
   (c) Notify insurer of insured event?
   (d) Defenses to claimed excuses for nonperformance by insurer?
       (1) Waiver?
       (2) Estoppel?
3. Rights of subrogation after payment?
   (a) Rights of insurer?
   (b) Rights of insured?

IV. Objective Questions:

Terms:

1. Insurance is defined as a contract whereby one undertakes to _____ another against loss, damage, or liability arising from a contingent or unknown event.

2. This act, passed in 1945, gave the regulation of insurance to the states. It is called the _____ _____ Act.

3. Insurance which features both term and whole life insurance is generally called _____ _____.

4. An employer can purchase _____ insurance to protect against dishonesty and defalcation of employees.

5. When an insurance company pays a claim, it succeeds to the right of the insured to recover from a third party. This right is called _____.

6. The insurance contract is called a _____.

7. Many insurance policies contain _____ _____ that provide for payment only after the insured has paid a certain amount.

8. To obtain insurance for specific valuable items, a _____ _____ _____ may be added to a homeowner's policy.

9. A form of property insurance that insures an automobile from loss of damage from causes other than collision is _____ insurance.

10. The insurer has a duty to _____ against any suit brought against the insured that involves a claim within the coverage of the policy.

True/False:

1. ____An insurance broker works exclusively for one insurance company.

2. ____Insurance companies are regulated by the federal antitrust (Sherman and Clayton Acts) laws.

3. ____There are two parties to a life insurance contract.

4. ____A fire insurance policy is assignable without consent of the insurance company.

492

5. _____ When an insurance company reinsures, it sells a portion of the policy's' risk and right to receive premiums to another insurance company.

6. _____ A person must have an insurable interest in anything he or she insures.

7. _____ Insurance sold from a vending machine is not effective until approved by the insurance company's home office.

8. _____ In most states, an insured can cancel the insurance policy at any time, but an insurance company can only cancel an insurance policy for certain reasons.

9. _____ D.O.C. automobile liability coverage protects the insured while driving other automobiles.

10. _____ Title insurance protects against defects in title and liens or encumbrances that are fully disclosed on the title insurance policy.

Multiple Choice:

1. Which of the following does not represent a recognized insurable interest?
   A. Life of a partner.
   B. Life of a friend.
   C. Life of a parent.
   D. Life of a debtor.

2. If Fred pays $100 a month for insurance all his life, and it now has a cash value of $10,000, he most likely has a:
   A. Term life policy.
   B. A comprehensive policy.
   C. An umbrella policy.
   D. Straight life policy.

3. Mr. Big owns Mega-Widgets Corporation. To insure against the financial loss of Mr. Big's death, Mega-Widgets can take out what kind of policy on his life?
   A. Job title insurance.
   B. Job disability insurance.
   C. Key person life insurance.
   D. Standard New York fire policy.

4. Which of the following events would not be covered by a homeowner's comprehensive personal liability insurance policy?
   A. Professional malpractice.
   B. Injuries sustained from a slip and fall on the insured's property.
   C. Property damaged by the insured.
   D. Injuries inflected by members of the insured's family.

5. Which of the following are not defenses of the insurer from having to pay on a covered claim?
   A. Misrepresentation of a material fact by insured.
   B. Breach of warranty by insured.
   C. Commission of suicide after period of incontestability has expired on a life insurance policy.
   D. Concealment of material fact.

6. Which of the following is an example of self-insurance?
   A. Purchasing only catastrophic insurance.
   B. Purchasing an umbrella policy.
   C. Purchasing co-insurance.
   D. Purchasing title insurance.

7. Most insurance contracts allow which of these parties to change the beneficiary under a life insurance policy?
   A. The insurance company.
   B. The beneficiary.
   C. The owner.
   D. The person whose life is insured.

8. Under the New York standard fire insurance form, which of the following natural disasters is normally not covered without a separate policy?
   A. Fire.
   B. Lightning.
   C. Flood.
   D. Water damage other than flood.

9. Comprehensive auto insurance would not cover the following:
   A. Fire.
   B. Theft.
   C. Collision.
   D. Vandalism.

10. Which of the following are not duties of the insured towards the insurer?
   A. Pay premiums.
   B. Pay nondeductible losses.
   C. Notify insurer of covered event.
   D. Cooperation in investigating claims.

V. Answers to Objective Questions

Terms:

1. *Indemnity*. This means to restore the victim for a loss, in whole or in part, by payment, repair, or replacement. It is a means of transferring and distributing risk of loss.

2. *McCarran-Ferguson*. This act was enacted by the federal government with two objectives in mind: to allow the states to take primary control over the regulation of the insurance service industry and to exempt insurance companies from federal antitrust laws.

3. *Universal life*. This type of policy features elements of both term and whole life insurance. Most of these policies provide for a variable interest rate on the savings element of the contract.

4. *Fidelity*. Often these policies will call for certain procedures to be carried out by employers before the insurance is issued. For example, background and credit checks are commonly conducted on potential employees who are expected to be entrusted with the employer's property.

5. *Subrogation*. If an insurance company pays a claim to an insured for liability or property damage caused by a third party, the insurer succeeds to the right of the insured to recover from the third party.

6. *Policy*. The written instrument which sets forth the contract of insurance is the policy.

7. *Deductible clauses*. These clauses have the insured act as a copayer of the loss up to the agreed-upon contractual amount.

8. *Personal articles floater*. These types of clauses are often used to cover difficult to value items such as jewelry or art.

9. *Comprehensive*. These clauses are designed to assure coverage for losses for a whole host of calamities which can befall the automobile owner ranging from acts of nature to acts of miscreants.

10. *Defend*. The insurer is, in effect, the agent of choice for the insured vis-a-vis defending the insured from claims by third parties in matters covered by the policy. This defense smut be a good faith, best efforts protection for the insured.

True/False:

1. False. A broker is an independent contractor who can represent a number of companies.
2. False. This is exempted from federal antitrust laws by the McCarran-Ferguson Act of 1945.
3. False. There are four parties: the insurance company, the owner of the policy, the person whose life is insured, and the beneficiary.
4. False. Because the insurer looks at the character of the insured in making its decision to issue the policy, assignments must be approved by the insurance company.
5. True. This practice is especially prevalent in situations which involve very high dollar loss exposure. Examples would include the insurance for a supertanker or satellite.
6. True. This rule is based on public policy and is designed to discourage fraud, abuse, and criminal activity in insurance contracts.
7. False. This is effective when the applicant receives the receipt from the machine.
8. True. These rules are generally designed to have the insured time to obtain alternative coverage in case of cancellation.
9. True. "Drive-other clauses" cover the insured while he or she is driving automobiles other than his or her own.
10. False. This protects against defects in title and liens or encumbrances which are not disclosed on the title insurance policy.

Multiple Choice:

1. B. Mere friendship does not constitute a recognized monetary or family based insurable interest.
2. D. A straight life policy provides coverage for the entire life of the insured and usually involves an element of savings.
3. C. Key person insurance may be taken out by a company to protect its pecuniary interest in a key executive's life. The other policies listed are not life insurance policies.
4. A. Professional malpractice is not normally covered by homeowners policies.
5. C. A, B, and D are all grounds for defense by the insurance company. The period of incontestability is a period after which certain defenses cannot be raised by the insurance company. Suicide after a certain period is a common example.
6. A. Purchasing only catastrophic insurance is one of the examples given of self-insurance. The others are considered forms of insurance by another.
7. C. The owner has the power to name and change the beneficiaries under a life insurance policy.
8. C. Floods are not normally covered. The federal government provides special flood insurance programs for areas which are especially prone to this sort of hazard.
9. C. Collision coverage is separately provided under collision insurance as distinguished from comprehensive insurance.
10. B. The insured only pays the deductible amounts, not the nondeductible amounts. The others listed are all duties owed to the insurer by the insured.

I. Key Question Checklist Answers to Essay Question:

A, B&C. *What were the legal capacities of Enzo and Boy Racers Autoclub in entering into this insurance contract? What are the key elements of the insurance policies in this case?*

Both Enzo and Boy Racers Autoclub had the legal capacity to enter into insurance contracts. There is no evidence of any age or mental limitation basis for limiting their capacity to contract.

They each had the requisite insurance interest to purchase insurance in their respective contracts. Enzo had an economic property interest in his mean green driving machine (his auto). Boy Racers had an economic interest in insuring against liabilities which could arise out of staging such an event. In both cases, the insurance companies imposed definite key provisions with regard to certain conditions of coverage.

D. *What are the basic duties and liabilities of each of the parties?*

With regard to the auto insurance contract signed by Enzo, his actions were clearly in violation of the provisions of the policy. He is certainly free to engage in such events, but he could not expect to be covered in case of any mishaps traceable to engaging in auto sports. The accident as it occurred was not covered by the policy. To roll the car into a ditch and then claim coverage is even worse. This is insurance fraud and is punishable as a crime in addition to any civil consequences.

With regard to Boy Racers, their liability for aiding and assisting Enzo to commit a fraud on his insurance company would not likely be covered by their event liability policy. Most such policies do not cover illegal acts.

In addition, they would also be criminally liable along with Enzo for insurance fraud.

Maybe they should all stick to simply dreaming about racing in Formula One. They will have plenty of time to dream if convicted.

496

CHAPTER 54

WILLS, TRUSTS, AND ESTATES

The only gift is a portion of thyself.

Ralph Waldo Emerson

I. Overview:

You can't take it with you, but you can control where it goes. The laws of wills and trust are about control. This control is not absolute now and never has been. Yet with intelligent foresight and timely estate planning, the extent and breath of possible control would surprise most people. It is no coincidence that the money of large family fortunes first accumulated in the early industrial age remain essentially intact today with the help of wills, trusts, and proper estate planning.

The origins of the laws of wills, trusts, and estates go back to the *canon* laws of the medieval church. The church had much control not only over the spiritual life of its members, but also over the more temporal affairs such as the disposition of worldly goods. The early church-based patterns of disposition of property based on family relationships are still reflected in more modern day laws such as the Uniform Probate Code. These traditions are strongly evidenced in civil law countries where the notion of forced heirship is still alive and well. England's break from the church under Henry VIII started a more tolerant tradition within the common law. In other parts of the world, such as Muslim countries, religion remains the cornerstone of the laws of devolution.

Transfers of property can be generally categorized into two main classifications; lifetime or *inter vivos* and death or testamentary transfers. With lifetime transfers, the main motivation elements are taxes, control, and present needs. The federal wealth transfer tax structure is extensive and very complicated. The three main components of that tax structure are the gift, estate, and generation skipping taxes. In addition, states have also developed their own property transfer tax structures based on inheritance taxes, estate pick-up taxes, or some combination thereof. All these taxes are premised on the notion that wealth accumulation was done with the blessings of the law structure, and transfers of that wealth afford an opportunity for the government to share in those riches.

The control element also goes to the issue of how much the owner is actually willing to give up before he or she departs this life. Tax laws are specifically designed to tax the substance of control rather than just the appearance of having given up control. Various code provisions with regard to life estates, incomplete transfers, retained powers over trusts, and possibilities of reverter are all patterned on that premise. In addition, simple human nature is such that it can be most difficult to give up control over assets which took the better part of a lifetime to accumulate. This problem is further exacerbated if the intended donee is too young, too immature, or an out and out spendthrift.

Lifetime needs make *inter vivos* transfers ever more difficult. In an age of being exposed to possible catastrophic health care costs late in life, many people simply cannot afford to make lifetime transfers which would otherwise make for good estate planning. The burgeoning growth of living trusts and similar financial planning devices are testaments to efforts to try to resolve this dilemma.

Once the end has come, the next classification of transfers can be subcategorized into testate and intestate death transfers. Testate means that the person has spoken by way of a legally recognized will or will substitute. The law of wills is much like the laws of death taxes--very complicated and formalized. The general public often looks at the cases on admission of wills to the probate process and sees them as being overly harsh or doctrinaire. The basic point which must be remembered is that the decedent is not there to challenge any arguments against his or her purported intent. There is a rhyme and reason to it all in spite of the sometimes arbitrary nature of such proceedings.

If a person has not written a will, or the will is not admitted to probate, he or she is deemed to have died intestate. Every state has stepped into this void and written a will by way of an intestate statute. Under these laws, the devolution follows the pattern originally created by the medieval church. This pattern is basically designed to convey the property on to the person's perceived natural bounty. The problem is that in an age of a 50 percent national divorce rate, the possibility of multiple families claims makes having a will more necessary than ever. In all events, if you want to control the disposition of your property at your death, have an up to date will at the ready.

Once a probate proceeding has begun, the person appointed by the court to administer the estate will be charged with three major duties:

1. To garner the assets of the estate.
2. To net out those assets by paying all proper claims, taxes, and costs of administration.
3. To distribute the net proceeds of the estate per the will or the intestate statute.

It is all very complex and emotionally draining for the parties directly involved, but death has always been the most inescapable fact of life.

II. Hypothetical Multi-Issue Essay Question:

Ms. Mary Margaret Alexander had quite a story. She emigrated to the U.S. after World War II from her home town of Ravenna, Italy. She was orphaned by the war and was adopted at age 10 by Mr. and Mrs. Olivier Alexander of Paris, Texas. Growing up with the best influences of her combined Italian and Texas cultural backgrounds, she came upon an idea for a new line of cosmetics called The Finer Face.

The product was marketed through the use of make-up parties in private homes conducted by sales partners who sold distributorships. The pyramid nature of the marketing made Mary a very rich woman by the age of thirty. She never married and preferred to live the life of a single jet-setter with homes in Myorca, Yourorca, in addition to her Paris, Texas home. In addition, her business was valued in the millions and operated out of the Finer Towers in Paris, Texas. Her favorite pastimes were collecting Ferrari automobiles and raising prize winning show Abyssinian cats. Her two favorite cats were Bijoux and Chaton.

She died accidentally from a skin reaction to using too much make-up at age 55. She left a last will and testament in her office. Under the terms of the will, she left the following bequests and devises:

1. To my dear cats, I hereby set up a trust for their care during their lives and at their death, all my property to the Society for the Prevention of Cruelty to Animals.

2. For my burial, I wish to be dressed in my sexiest negligee behind the wheel of my *1958 Ferrari 250 GT Scaglietti Berlinetta.*

Mary's next of kin were outraged! They could hardly stand the idea of all those millions going to the cats and having that beautiful Ferrari buried six feet in the ground. They seek to have the will overturned and to inherit the estate under the intestate statutes of Texas, Myorca, and Yourorca. What results?

III. Key Question Checklist:

A. What are the possible transfer options available before death?
  1. Outright gift?
      (a) Donative intent?
      (b) Completed delivery?
      (c) Acceptance of the gift?
  2. Creation of an *inter vivos* trust?
      (a) Transfer of assets into a trust during life?
      (b) Elements of a trust in place?
          (1) Settler or transferor?
          (2) Transfer by settler of the property to trustee?
          (3) Legal ownership in trustee?
          (4) Beneficial ownership in third person called a beneficiary?
          (5) Done for a legal reason?
              (aa) Tax savings?
              (bb) Business planning?
              (cc) Personal property planning?
              (dd) Benefit beneficiary?
      (c) Duties of trustee?
          (1) Per trust instrument?
          (2) Per state statute?
      (d) Types of *inter vivos* trusts?
          (1) Express? Examples: private purpose, charitable purpose, spendthrift, and totten?
          (2) Implied or constructive trusts?

  (e) Termination?
      (1) By act of parties if revocable?
      (2) By operation of law?
      (3) Any other form of legal lifetime transfer?

B. Once you have reviewed the possibilities for lifetime transfers, you must then examine the possible methods of transfer of property at death. The first question is: did the person leave a will?
  1. If no will was left, an intestate statute will be used to determine the devolution of probate property?
      (a) Real property will be passed on per the intestate statute of the state where the property is located?
      (b) Personal property will be passed on per the state of the decedent's domicile?
      (c) General pattern of distribution (varies from state to state)?
          (1) Spouse's share?
          (2) Children's' share?
          (3) Grandchildren's' share?
              (aa) *Per stirpes*?
              (bb) Per capita?
          (4) Parents' share?
          (5) Siblings' share?
          (6) Collateral heirs?
          (7) Next of kin?
          (8) State (escheat)?
  2. If a will was left by the decedent, a number of issues need to be examined. First look to the will itself. Was it:
      (a) A formal will (recognized by the state wills statute)?
      (b) A type of will which is not formal, yet recognized by some states?
          (1) Holographic will (handwritten)?
          (2) Nuncupative will (oral or dying declaration)?
          (3) Soldier's and sailor's will (made on active duty)?

3. If a formal will was used, have the formalities of execution of the will been complied with (requirements vary from state to state)?
   (a) Writing?
   (b) Signed by the testator?
   (c) Witnessed?
   (d) Testator had capacity?
   (e) Publication?
   (f) Any special situations apply?
      (1) Joint will?
      (2) Conditional will?
      (3) Mutual or reciprocal wills?
4. Any changes to or revocations of the will based on:
   (a) Destruction?
   (b) Alteration?
   (c) Subsequent will?
   (d) Marriage?
   (e) Divorce?
   (f) Annulment?
   (g) Codicils?
5. Testamentary trust (see outline for *inter vivos* trusts)?

C. After you have examined the property which will pass by probate, next look to see what property will pass outside the probate proceeding?
   1. By contract?
      (a) Insurance?
      (b) Employee death benefits?
      (c) Any other contract based transfer?
   2. By joint tenancy or tenancy in the entirety?
      (a) Automatic right of survivorship in cotenant?
      (b) Any reason for denial of survivorship?
         (1) Murder?
         (2) Undue influence?
D. Once the properties have all been identified and a probate proceeding has been initiated, have the three main functions of the probate proceeding have been completed?
   1. Garnering of the decedent's assets (collection)?
   2. Netting out of the estate?
      (a) Payment of proper claims?
      (b) Payment of taxes?
      (c) Payment of costs of administrators?
   3. Distribution of assets?
      (a) Per will?
      (b) Per intestate statute?

IV. Objective Questions:

Terms:

1. A person who makes a will is called a _____.

2. Wills that are entirely handwritten and signed by the person making the will are called _____ wills.

3. The principle of _____ applies if the property is not sufficient to satisfy all the beneficiaries as planned by the testator.

4. The person to receive the trust corpus upon the termination of the trust is called the _____.

5. A trust which is an equitable trust that is imposed by law to avoid fraud, unjust enrichment, and injustice is called a _____ trust.

6. A person who dies without having a will or whose will is not admitted to probate dies _____.

7. Nieces, nephews, aunts, and uncles are _____ heirs.

8. When a specific devise of property to a beneficiary is no longer in existence when the testator dies, _____ occurs.

9. A trust where creditors of the beneficiary cannot recover the trusts' assets to satisfy personal debts owed them by the beneficiary is a _____ trust.

10. A trust which is created when a person deposits money in a bank account in his or her own name and holds it for the benefit of another person is a _____ trust.

True/False:

1. _____ Wills transfer the property of an intestate person.

2. _____ Residuary gifts identify specific property from which the gift must be made.

3. _____ Mutual or reciprocal wills occur where two or more testators execute the same instrument as their will.

4. _____ Grandchildren who participate in the distribution of the estate by equal rights with children of the deceased take by the rule of *per stirpes*.

5. _____ All property of the decedent must pass through the probate process.

6. _____ The trustee is the beneficial owner of the trust corpus.

7. _____ Nuncupative wills are oral wills made before witnesses.

8. _____ The Uniform Probate Code does not require any attestation of a will by witnesses.

9. _____ A joint will is where two or more testators execute the same instrument as their will.

10. _____ *Inter vivos* trusts are created by will.

Multiple Choice:

1. Which of the following gifts by will are a devise?
   A. A joint tenancy right of survivorship in real property located at 123 Main Street.
   B. A set of gold earrings.
   C. $10,000 cash.
   D. The family farm.

2. Which of the following types of wills has no writing requirements?
   A. A holographic will.
   B. A soldiers and sailors will.
   C. A nuncupative will.
   D. A UPC formal will.

3. Jake and Blake are old buddies (not related) who want to leave their respective properties to each other at death. The best possible method available to them is:
   A. A joint will.
   B. Mutual wills.
   C. Reciprocal wills.
   D. Intestate succession.

4. Which of the following is not a form of wealth transfer taxation imposed by the federal government?
   A. Gift tax.
   B. Inheritance tax.
   C. Estate tax.
   D. Generation skipping tax.

5. Which of the following is not one of the elements necessary for the creation of a trust?
   A. A designated trustee.
   B. A designated name of the trust.
   C. A transfer of title and delivery of the property to the trustee by the settler.
   D. A legal purpose for the trust.

6. To have testamentary capacity, which of the following is not required?
   A. Extreme wealth?
   B. A comprehension of what property is owned?
   C. A comprehension of who is intended to benefit under the will?
   D. Legal age?

7. Assuming Massazona has a per capita statute, if Gramps dies, leaving no spouse, two living sons and two grandchildren of a predeceased daughter, each grandchild will get what percentage of the estate?
   A. 25 percent?
   B. 33 percent?
   C. 16 percent?
   D. 10 percent?

8. Under the Uniform Probate Code, if a decedent leaves a surviving spouse, no children, and one surviving parent, the surviving spouse gets:
   A. All of the estate?
   B. None of the estate?
   C. Half the estate?
   D. Half the estate plus $50,000?

9. Fred dies leaving specific devise of his car to Ethel of his house at 123 Spruce Street. At the time of his death he had already sold his house on Spruce and moved to Main Street. His devise has:
   A. Abated?

B. Adeemed?
C. Been inherited?
D. Been gifted?

10. Which of the following does not act as a revocation of a will?
    A. Accidental destruction of the will?
    B. Intentional burning of the will?
    C. Intention obliteration of the will?
    D. Directing another person to tear up the will?

V. Answers to Objective Questions

Terms:

1. *Testator*. This is derived form the Latin term "to speak," as originally used in civil law. Because this is the last evidence of intent, many formalities have arisen over the years to assure that the last word is truly the last will.

2. *Holographic*. State laws vary widely on the use of these sort of wills. Many categorically refuse to enforce them because of the lack of attestation (witness) while others recognize them only in limited circumstances. The Uniform Probate Code allows them under Section 2-503 if the signature and material provisions are in the handwriting of the testator.

3. *Abatement*. All state probate statutes have an order of abatement in them by which certain bequests to add devises are abated first. Generally speaking, residuary, then general, and finally specific gifts are abated in that order.

4. *Remainderman*. This is the person or entity which takes the property of the trust after the expiration of intervening interests such as a life estate or the like.

5. *Constructive.* This is an equitable remedy where the holder of the actual title to the property, i.e., the trustee, holds the property in trust for its rightful owner.
6. *Intestate.* This term literally means "not spoken." Under such circumstances, the state steps in and prescribes who will receive the decedent's property under the terms of its intestate succession statute.
7. *Collateral.* This is a person who is not of the direct line of the deceased but rather from a collateral line such as a brother or sister.
8. *Ademption.* The original devise may have been withdrawn, given in life, or revoked. In any event, because it is no longer in existence at the time of death, the doctrine of ademption usually applies.
9. *Spendthrift.* These trusts are designed to protect the improvident against their wasteful actions. Most states allow these trusts in spite of the possible harm that may come to creditors who rely on the beneficiary's appearance of attachable wealth. England has curtained the use of these sorts of trusts.
10. *Totten.* It is a tentative trust created by a bank account and is revocable at will until the trustor dies or makes a completed gift during life

True/False:

1. False. By definition a person who dies with a will admitted to probate dies testate.
2. False. Residuary gifts come from any portion of the estate that is left after debts, taxes, specific, and general gifts have already been paid.

3. False. Mutual or reciprocal wills arise where two or more testators execute separate wills and make testamentary dispositions of their property in favor of the other.
4. False. *Per stirpes* means taking by representation of the grandchild's parent.
5. False. Property may pass outside of probate by way of insurance, contract, joint tenancy, and a number of other legally allowable methods.
6. False. The trustee is the legal owner who holds the trust property for the benefit of a third person, the beneficiary.
7. True. Note however, few states recognize these sort of wills and often limit the amounts which can be transferred by them.
8. False. The UPC requires the attestation of two witnesses.
9. True. Most attorneys would strongly advise against using a joint will because of the complications which often arise in these situations.
10. False. *Inter vivos* trusts are created when the settlor is alive.

Multiple Choice:

1. D. B and C are bequests of personal property. A does not pass under the will in probate but rather by operation of law.
2. C. A nuncupative will is oral. Few states recognize it. All the others require a will to be in writing to one degree or another.
3. D. A, B, and C are all possible methods of passing property on to each other reciprocally. The odds are not good that an unrelated person can take under most intestate succession statutes. These statutes favor related family members and the state.

4. B. Inheritance taxes are imposed by the states. The other three taxes are all imposed by the federal government.

5. B. A trust does not require a formal name. The other items listed are all elements necessary for the creation of a trust.

6. A. B, C, and D, are components of testamentary capacity which go to "sound mind" and legal age. Wealth is not a prerequisite for being able to execute a will.

7. A. 25 percent. Per capita gives surviving grandchildren the same standing as children of the deceased. Here the two surviving children and the two surviving grandchildren would all take equally at 25 percent each of the estate.

8. C. The surviving spouse gets half the estate.

9. The house on Spruce street has been adeemed. It is not part of the estate at death, and the specific devise fails.

10. A. The accidental destruction of a will does not revoke it. The other methods listed all constitute a revocation.

VI. Key Question Checklist Answers to Essay Question:

A. *What lifetime options were available for the remainder of Ms. Alexander's property to be transferred?*

Ms. Alexander did not appear to take advantage of many lifetime opportunities for estate planning. By not having been married or having children, she had less natural bounty to worry about. In addition, if she knew she was going to leave most of her estate to charity, tax worries would not be as prominent as they would be for most people in her economic situation. Under the U.S. wealth transfer tax laws, qualified transfers to charities have no dollar limit for deduction purposes.

B. *What are the possible methods of transfer of property at death in this case?*

The next of kin are seeking to have the will disallowed and want to use the intestate statutes of Texas, Myorca, and Yourorca to inherit the property. These statutes would apply if they could show that Ms. Alexander did not have testamentary capacity to make a will. This standard took into account whether or not the person was of sound mind at the time of the making of the will. Sound mind means that the person understands what property she had, who the beneficiaries will be, and what the plan for disposal of the property was. Having been a very successful business person, it appears that Ms. Alexander was of sound mind and had the capacity to write the will. It appears, therefore, that the will will be admitted to probate and that the intestate statutes would not be operative in this case.

C&D. *What will happen to the properties as they pass either through probate or other proceedings?*

Assuming the will is admitted to probate, the court will next examine the validity of its provisions. The clause which establishes the trust for the cats' care will be upheld. Animals may not be direct takers of property under a will, but provisions for their care have been recognized as legitimate transfers to natural bounty. They are called "honorary" trusts. The trust elements will be put in place by the probate court, and the trustee will be held accountable for living up to his or her fiduciary duties to the beneficiaries. Bijoux and Chaton should do nicely, thank you.

As for the burial instructions, it may seem wasteful to bury a perfectly magnificent Ferrari, but it was her property. She could take it with her, at least in this world. Whether or not she could use it in the next world is not for us to know.